THE

California Dog Lover's Companion

by Maria Goodavage

ISBN 0-935701-73-7

BOOKS BUILDING COMMUNITY™

51695 >

9 780935 701739

D1005610

Foghorn Press
555 DeHaro Street #220
San Francisco, CA 94107
415-241-9550

Foghorn Press titles are distributed to the book trade by
Publishers Group West, Emeryville, California. To contact
your local sales representative, call 1-800-788-3123.

To order individual books, please call Foghorn Press at
1-800-FOGHORN (364-4676).

Printed in the United States of America.

THE

California Dog Lover's Companion

by Maria Goodavage

Foghorn Press

BOOKS BUILDING COMMUNITY.

Credits

Managing Editor—*Ann-Marie Brown*

Associate Editor/Research—*Howard Rabinowitz*

Research Editor—*Jessica Whitney*

Assistant Editors—*Samantha Trautman, Douglas Lloyd*

Book Layout/Maps—*Michele Thomas*

Graphics—*Kirk McInroy*

Cover Illustration/Inside Illustrations—*Phil Frank*

Special thanks to Lyle York, who graciously
contributed material to Bay Area chapters.

*For Mom, Dad and Muttley, who made growing up
as much fun as walking in a lush redwood forest
with a dog who heeds every word you utter.*

--- ❧ ---

Note to all dogs and dog lovers:

While our information is as current as possible,
changes to fees, regulations, parks, roads and trails
sometimes are made after we go to press. Businesses can
close, change their ownership or change their rules.
Earthquakes, fires, rainstorms and other natural phenomena can radically change the condition of parks, hiking
trails and wilderness areas. Before you and your dog
begin your travels, please be certain to call the phone
numbers for each listing for updated information.

Attention dogs of California: If we've missed your
favorite park, beach, outdoor restaurant, hotel or dog-
friendly activity, please let us know. You'll be helping
countless other dogs get more enjoyment out of life in the
Golden State. We welcome all your comments and
suggestions about *The California Dog Lover's Companion*.
Please mail in the enclosed postcard or write to us at:
Foghorn Press, 555 DeHaro Street #220, San Francisco,
CA 94107.

ABOUT THE AUTHOR

Maria Goodavage and her canine corps research assistants. From left to right, Bill, Nisha, Maria (the human in the hat) and Joe.

Joe Dog, Bill Dog and Nisha Dog have traveled throughout the state to check out some of the most dog-friendly parks, beaches, lodgings and restaurants in the world. As part of their research, they've ridden on ferries, horse-drawn carriages and steam trains. They've also visited drive-in movies, marched in numerous dog parades and inspected their share of kitschy tourist attractions.

Since none of the dogs has a driver's license, Maria Goodavage, co-author of *The Dog Lover's Companion* (a guide to the San Francisco Bay Area) and news correspondent for *USA Today*, went along as chauffeur. "Maria was of invaluable assistance in interpreting our reactions for human consumption," says Joe. "She did a four-paw job."

Nisha and Joe live with Maria and Craig Hanson in a house two blocks from a leash-free beach in San Francisco. Bill, a stray dog who Maria found during her travels for this book, lived with them for a few months and is now thriving in another loving San Francisco home.

ACKNOWLEDGMENTS

Thanks and arf....

To all the parks department and chamber of commerce folks who gave their time, their maps and their patience with questions like "Are you *sure* you don't have any off-leash parks?"

To the following dog-loving people and organizations who went out of their way to tell me about their favorite dog-friendly places: Michael Allen, of *The American Cocker Magazine;* Betty Denny Smith, American Humane Association, Los Angeles County; Animal Press, Los Angeles; *Animal's Voice Magazine;* Pennie Eisen, Antioch Animal Services Department; Avalon Humane Society; Cheryl Pannell, Benicia/Vallejo Humane Society; Burbank Animal Shelter; Contra Costa SPCA; Davis Dog Training Club, Inc.; Cindy Szerlip, of Friends of Redondo Beach Dog Park; Guide Dogs of the Desert, Palm Springs; Carla Jackson, Haven Humane Society, Redding; Jeanne Hurney, Helen Woodward Animal Center; Johanna Lack, Santa Monica.

Doggone it, there's more: Rachel H. Moffett, Humane Society of Calaveras County; Dawn Armstrong, Lake Tahoe Humane Society; Daphne Stark, Lassen Humane Society; Jan McClellan, Last Chance for Animals; Rose Marie Channer, Los Angeles SPCA; Rick Johnson, Marin Humane Society; Mono County Animal Control Division; Napa County Animal Control; Lt. Marie Hulett-Curtner, Orange County Animal Control; Palm Springs Animal Shelter; Pets in Need, Inc., Redwood City; San Francisco SPCA; Pamela D. Christian, Santa Barbara Animal Control; Mike, of the Sonoma Humane Society; Vicky Fletcher, Yolo County Sheriff's Department Animal Services; and Lyle York, my much-missed former co-author.

To Motel 6, who left the light on for me after many a dog-day afternoon.

And finally, to Craig Hanson, for being a sweetie pie extraordinaire.

CONTENTS

INTRODUCTION...page 11

NORTHERN AREA COUNTIES

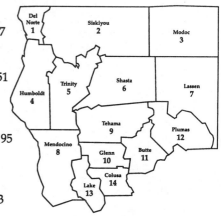

SIERRA AREA COUNTIES

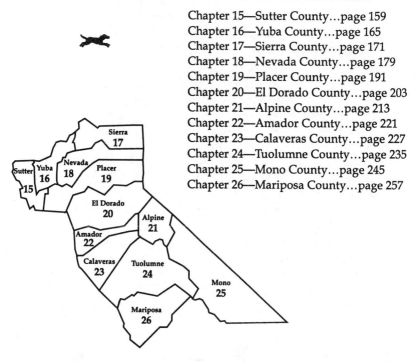

BAY AREA/DELTA COUNTIES

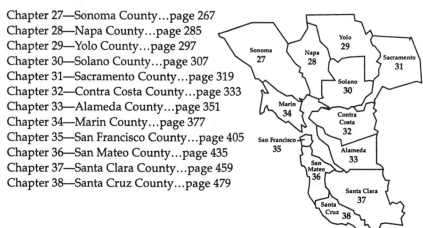

CENTRAL AREA COUNTIES

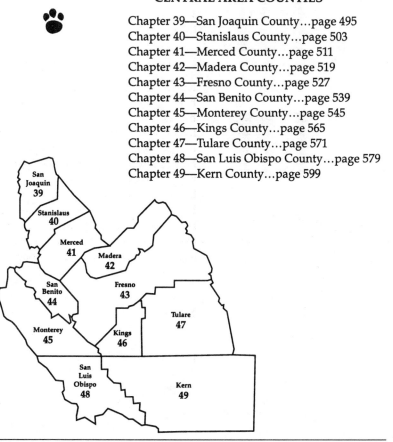

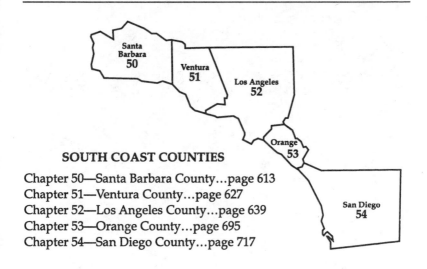

SOUTH COAST COUNTIES

SOUTH INLAND COUNTIES

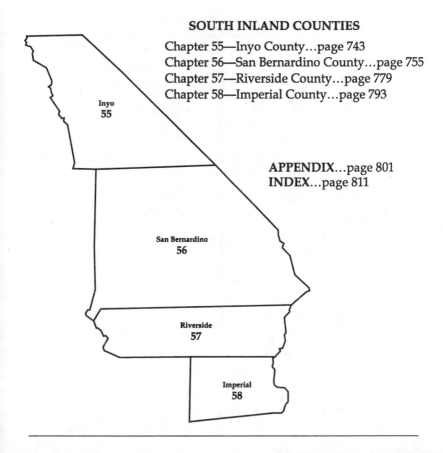

INTRODUCTION

INTRODUCTION

"Now, Charley is a mind-reading dog. There have been many trips in his lifetime, and often he has to be left at home. He knows we are going long before the suitcases come out, and he paces and worries and whines and goes into a state of mild hysteria, old as he is."
From *Travels with Charley*, by John Steinbeck.

There was a time when dogs could go just about anywhere they pleased. Well-dressed dogs with embarrassing names attended afternoon teas, while their less-kempt counterparts sauntered into saloons without anyone blinking a blood-shot eye.

No one thought it strange to see a pug-nosed little snoochum-woochums of a dog snuggled on his mistress' lap on a long train journey. Equally accepted were dogs prancing through fine hotels, dogs at dining establishments and dogs in almost any park they cared to visit.

But as the world gets more crowded and patience grows thinner, fewer and fewer places permit dogs. As deep as the human-dog bond goes, people seem to feel increasing pressure to leave their dogs behind when they take to the open road.

The guilt that stabs at you as you push your dog's struggling body back inside the house and tug the door shut can be so painful that sometimes you just can't look back. Even a trip to the grocery store can become a heart-wrenching tale of woe.

Joe, my Airedale terrier, was born with an unparalleled gift for knowing how to make people feel guilty. And not your ordinary, run-of-the-mill guilt where you smart for a couple of hours after seeing your dog's moping eyes follow your car as you speed away. It's that deep-in-the-gut-for-days guilt, where the sight of that pouting snout, those drooping ears and that tail lowered to half-mast hangs with you until you return home.

John Steinbeck's blue poodle, Charley, was a master of powerful pleas that were carefully designed to allow him to accompany his people on trips. Eventually, his hard work paid off and he won himself a seat in Steinbeck's brand-new truck/house on their epic journey across America. They sought and found the heart of this country in their adventures across 34 states.

Joe's guilt-inducing expertise won him a spot in my rusty, beat-up, hiccuping pickup truck in our sporadic little journeys throughout California. We sought and found hundreds of dog-friendly places in our misadventures through California's 58 counties.

Joe and I were frequently joined by two other experts in the field of rating parks and sniffing out good dog attractions. Nisha, our old lady springer spaniel, insisted on standing in the back of the truck, under the camper top, and madly wagging her tail for hours on end as we drove and drove and drove. She was a real asset to have around when it came to checking out beaches, lakes, rivers and ponds, any area with water. (Joe hates to get his paws wet, so he couldn't be impartial in his rating of watery attractions.)

Bill, a big, loveable galoot of a dog, was my other canine researcher. I found him partway through my travels. He was trembling in the middle of a Northern California road, with a big chain tight around his neck. He'd evidently broken loose, because the last link of the thick chain was mauled. I came to find out that his owner beat him regularly. Bill went back to San Francisco with me that afternoon.

During the months when I was looking for the perfect home for him, he became one of the friendliest, most outgoing dogs I've ever had the pleasure to meet. His presence during my journeys was invaluable. He lifted my spirits when I was tired, and his 85 pounds of muscle kept away bad spirits when we visited questionable areas.

You'll be meeting up with the three dogs throughout this book. I think you'll find them fine representatives of the 5.7 million dogs who live in California. (The dog population was derived by the American Veterinary Medical Association from the group's recent survey of 80,000 California households.)

Many of the areas we visited together had higher elevations than populations. Those were often our favorite places. "The remoter, the better" seems to be the creed of dogs everywhere. People in relaxed, out-of-the-way communities would sometimes call a leash a "leach." Or a "lease." No wonder dogs love the countryside.

These were some of the most polite folks I came across. Sometimes people I met in urban areas would immediately ask me why I was traveling alone with dogs—was I running away from something, or just trying to find myself? The more rural folks would smile at me, nod at the dogs and ask no pointed questions. They'd feel around in an indirect manner ("You don't see that brand of dog much anymore. Did you travel far with him?"), but they'd rarely come right out with a heat-seeking missile of a question.

I spent a good deal of time in these less-populated areas, because during my research, I discovered an amazing statistic: That far from the reaches of most cities, 40 percent of California is open to dogs who are obedient enough to be off leash. Wowza—40 percent! I normally jump for joy to find two acres that permit off-leash pooches, but 40 million acres? The thought is enough to make a grown dog swoon.

This amazing acreage is part of two federal entities—the Bureau of Land Management and the U.S. Department of Agriculture's Forest Service. I've described many of these parcels throughout the book. The national forests also have their own appendix here (see page 801). If you have a dog who longs to be a real off-leash explorer, take advantage of California's wealth of leash-free lands.

I've tried to find the very best of everything you can do with your dog in California, so you'll never again have to face the prospect of shutting the door on your dog's nose. This book is packed with descriptions of hundreds of dog-friendly parks, restaurants with outdoor tables, and lodgings.

The book also describes dozens of unusual adventures you and your dog can share in this crazy Golden State. You can ride on steam trains, ferries and surries. You can gaze at the stars with an astronomy club or sip sauvignons together at a winery. You can pan for gold, march in pet parades, visit small museums, go to drive-in movies and shop at high-fashion stores. You can even get married, with your dog serving as flower girl or best man.

After reading even a few pages of this book, I think you'll come to find that California is a magical place to be a dog or just to hang out with one.

THE PAWS SCALE

At some point, we've got to face the facts: Humans and dogs have different tastes. We like eating oranges and smelling lilacs and covering our bodies with soft clothes. They like eating road kill and smelling each other's unmentionables and covering their bodies with horse manure.

The parks, beaches and recreation areas in this book are rated with a dog in mind. Maybe your favorite park has lush gardens, a duck pond, a few acres of perfectly manicured lawns and sweeping views of a nearby skyline. But unless your dog can run leash-free, swim in the pond and roll in the grass, that park doesn't deserve a very high rating.

The very lowest rating you'll come across in this book is the fire hydrant symbol (🐾). When you see it, that means the park is merely "worth a squat." Visit one of these parks only if your dog just can't hold it any longer. These parks have virtually no other redeeming qualities for canines.

Beyond that, the paws scale starts at one paw (🐾) and goes up to four paws (🐾 🐾 🐾 🐾), with increments of half a paw in between (such as 🐾 🐾 1/2). A one-paw park isn't a dog's idea of a great time. Maybe it's a tiny park with few trees and too many kids running around. Or perhaps it's a magnificent-for-people national park that bans dogs from every inch of land except paved roads and a few campsites.

Four-paw parks, on the other hand, are places your dog will drag you to visit. Some of these areas come as close to Dog Heaven as you can get on this planet. Many have water for swimming or zillions of acres for hiking. Some are small, fenced-in areas where leash-free dogs can tear around without danger of running into the road. Many four-paw parks give you the option of letting your dog off leash (although most have restrictions, which I detail in the descriptions).

You will also notice a foot symbol (👣) every so often. The foot means that the park offers something extra special for the humans in the crowd. You deserve something for being such a good chauffeur.

This book is not a comprehensive guide to all of the parks in California. If a book included all the parks, it would be larger than a multi-volume set of *Encyclopedia Brittanica*. I tried to find the best, largest and most convenient parks. Some counties have so many wonderful parks that I had to make some tough choices in deciding which to include and which to leave out. Other counties had such a limited supply of parks that, for the sake of dogs living and visiting there, I ended up listing parks that wouldn't otherwise be worth mentioning.

I've given detailed street directions to the major parks and to parks near highways. Other parks are listed by their cross streets. I highly recommend picking up detailed street maps from the California Automobile Association (they're free to members) before you and your dog set out on your adventures.

TO LEASH OR NOT TO LEASH

That is not a question that plagues dogs' minds. Ask just about any normal, red-blooded American dog if she'd prefer to visit a park and be on leash or off, and she'll say "Arf!" No question about it, most dogs would give their canine teeth to be able to frolic about without a cumbersome leash.

When you see the running dog symbol in this book (🐕), you'll know that under certain circumstances, your dog can run around in leash-free bliss. The rest of the parks demand leashes. I wish I could write about the parks where dogs get away with being scofflaws. Unfortunately, those would be the first parks the animal control patrols would hit. I don't advocate breaking the law, but if you're going to, please follow your conscience and use common sense.

And just because dogs are permitted off leash in certain areas doesn't necessarily mean you should let your dog run free. In national forests and large tracts of wild land, unless you're sure your dog will come back to you when you call, or will never stray more than a few yards from your side, you should probably keep her leashed. An otherwise docile homebody can turn into a savage hunter if the right prey is near. Or your curious dog could peturb a rattlesnake or dig up a rodent whose fleas carry bubonic plague. In pursuit of a strange scent, your dog could easily get lost in an unfamiliar area. (Some forest rangers recommend having your dog wear a bright orange collar, vest or backpack when you're out in the wilderness.) And there are many places where certain animals would love to have your dog for dinner—and not in a way Miss Manners would condone.

Be careful out there. If your dog really needs leash-free exercise but can't be trusted off leash in remote areas, she'll be happy to know that several beaches permit well-behaved, leashless pooches, as do a growing number of beautiful, fenced-in dog exercise areas. The San Francisco Bay Area is the best place to find such freedom, but many other parts of California are starting to follow suit.

THERE'S NO BUSINESS LIKE DOG BUSINESS
There's nothing appealing about bending down with a plastic bag or a piece of newspaper on a chilly morning and grabbing the steaming remnants of what your dog ate for dinner the night before. It's disgusting. Worse yet, you have to hang onto it until you can find a trash can. And how about when the newspaper doesn't endure before you can dispose of it? Yuk! It's enough to make you wish your dog could wear diapers.

But as gross as it can be to scoop the poop, it's worse to step in it. It's really bad if a child falls in it, or—gasp!—starts eating it. And have you ever walked into a park where few people clean up after their dog? The stench could make a hog want to hibernate.

Unscooped poop is one of a dog's worst enemies. Public policies banning dogs from parks are enacted because of it. At present, a few really good California parks and beaches that permit dogs are in danger of closing their gates to all canines because of the negligent behavior of a few owners. A worst-case scenario is already in place in several California communities—dogs are banned from all parks. Their only exercise is a leashed sidewalk stroll. That's no way to live.

Just be responsible and clean up after your dog everywhere you go. Stuff plastic bags in your jackets, your purse, your car, your pants pockets—anywhere you might be able to pull one out when needed. Or if plastic isn't your bag, newspapers do the trick. If it makes it more palatable, bring along a paper bag, too, and put the used newspaper or plastic bag in it. That way you don't have to walk around with dripping paper or a plastic bag whose contents are visible to the world.

If you don't enjoy the squishy sensation, try one of those cardboard or plastic bag pooper scoopers sold at pet stores. If you don't feel like bending down, buy a long-handled scooper. There's a scooper for every taste.

This is the only lecture you'll get on scooping in this entire book. To help keep parks alive, I should harp on it in every park description, but that would take another 100 pages, and you'd start to ignore it anyway. And if I mentioned it in some parks and not others, it might convey that you don't have to clean up after your dog in the descriptions where it's not mentioned.

A final note: Don't pretend not to see your dog while he's doing his bit. And don't pretend to look for it without success. And don't fake scooping it up when you're really just covering it with sand. I know these tricks because I've been guilty of them myself—but no more. I've seen the light. I've been saved. I've been delivered from the depths of dog-doo depravity.

ETIQUETTE REX—THE WELL-MANNERED MUTT

While cleaning up after your dog is your responsibility, a dog in a public place has his own responsibilities. Of course, it really boils down to your responsibility again, but the burden of action is on your dog.

Etiquette for restaurants and hotels is covered in other sections of the introduction. What follows is some very basic dog etiquette. I'll go through it quickly, but if your dog's a slow reader, he can go over it again:

No vicious dogs; no jumping on people; no incessant barking; dogs should come when they're called; dogs should stay on command; no leg-lifts on surf boards, backpacks, human legs or any other personal objects you'll find hanging around beaches and parks.

Joe, Nisha and Bill have managed to violate all but the first of these rules. Do your best to remedy any problems. It takes patience and it's not always easy. For instance, there was a time during Joe's youth when he seemed to think that human legs were tree trunks. Rather than pretending I didn't know the beast, I strongly reprimanded him, and apologized to the victim from the depths of my heart and offered money for dry cleaning. Joe learned his lesson—$25 later.

SAFETY FIRST

A few essentials will keep your traveling dog happy and healthy. For further reading on the subject, I recommend the book *The Portable Pet*, by Barbara Nicholas (1983, The Harvard Common Press, Boston). It's soon to be out of print, and some of the information about state regulations is out of date, but the basics about car and air travel safety is valuable and still pertinent.

•*Heat:* If you must leave your dog alone in the car for a few minutes, do so only if it's cool out, and if you can park in the shade. Never, ever, ever leave a dog in a car with the windows rolled up all the way. Even if it seems cool, the sun's heat passing through the window can kill a dog in a matter of minutes. Roll down the window enough so your dog gets air, but so that there's no danger of your dog getting out or someone breaking in. Make sure your dog has plenty of water.

You also have to watch out for heat exposure when your car is in motion. Certain cars, like hatchbacks, can make a dog in the back seat extra hot, even while you feel okay in the driver's seat.

Try to take your vacation so you don't visit a place when it's extremely warm. Dogs and heat don't get along, especially if the dog isn't used to heat. The opposite is also true. If a dog lives in a hot climate and you take him to a freezing place, it may not be a healthy shift. Check with your vet if you have any doubts. Spring and fall are usually the best times to travel.

•*Water:* Water your dog frequently. Dogs on the road may drink even more than they do at home. Take regular water breaks, or bring a heavy bowl (the thick clay ones do nicely) and set it on the floor so your dog always has access to water. When hiking, be sure to carry enough for you and a thirsty dog.

•*Rest stops:* Stop and unwater your dog. There's nothing more miserable than being stuck in a car when you can't find a rest stop. No matter how tightly you cross your legs and try to think of the desert, you're certain you'll burst within the next minute. But think of how a dog feels when the urge strikes and he can't tell you the problem. There are plenty of rest stops along the major California freeways. I've delineated many parks close to freeways as well, for dogs who need a good stretch with their bathroom break.

How frequently you stop depends on your dog's bladder. If your dog is constantly running out the doggy door at home to relieve himself, you may want to stop every hour. Others can go for significantly longer without being uncomfortable. Watch for any signs of restlessness and gauge it for yourself.

• *Car safety:* Even the experts differ about how a dog should travel in a car. Some suggest doggy safety belts, available at pet food stores. Others firmly believe in keeping a dog kenneled. They say it's safer for the dog if there's an accident, and it's safer for the driver because there's no dog underfoot. Others say you should just let your dog hang out without straps and boxes. They believe that if there's an accident, at least the dog isn't trapped in a cage. They say that dogs enjoy this more anyway.

I'm a follower of the last school of thought. Joe, Nisha and Bill love sticking their snouts out of the windows to smell the world go by. The danger is that if the car kicks up a pebble or ires a bee, their noses and eyes could be injured. So far they're okay, but I have seen dogs who needed to be treated for bee stings to the nose because of this practice. If in doubt, try opening the window just enough so your dog can't stick out much snout.

Whatever way you choose, your pet will be more comfortable if he has his own blanket with him for the endurance. A veterinarian acquaintance uses a faux-sheepskin blanket for his dogs. At night in the hotel, the sheepskin doubles as the dog's bed.

• *Planes:* Air travel is even more controversial. Personally, unless my dogs could fly with me in the passenger section (which very tiny dogs are sometimes allowed to do), I'd rather find a way to drive the distance or leave them at home with a friend. I've heard too many horror stories of dogs suffocating in what was supposed to be a pressurized cargo section, and of dogs dying of heat exposure, and of dogs going to Miami while their people end up in Seattle. There's just something unappealing about the idea of a dog flying in the cargo hold, like he's nothing more than a piece of luggage. Of course, many dogs survive just fine, but I'm not willing to take the chance.

But if you need to transport your dog by plane, make sure you schedule take-off and arrival times when the temperature is below 80 degrees (or not bitterly cold in winter). You'll want to consult the airline about their regulations and required certificates. And check with your vet to make sure your pooch is healthy enough for the trip.

The question of tranquilizing a dog for a plane journey is very controversial. Some vets think it's insane to give a dog a sedative before flying. They say a dog will be calmer and less fearful without taking a disorienting tranquilizer. Others think it's crazy not to afford your dog the little relaxation he might not otherwise get without a tranquilizer. Discuss the issue with your vet, who will take the trip's length and your dog's personality into account.

THE ULTIMATE DOGGY BAG

Your dog can't pack his own bags, and even if he could, he'd probably fill them with dog biscuits and chew toys. It's important to stash some of those in your dog's vacation kit, but here are some other items to bring along: Bowls, bedding, a brush, towels (for those muddy days), a first-aid kit, pooper scoopers, water, food, prescription drugs, tags (see below), treats, toys and, of course, this book.

Be sure your dog wears his license, identification tag and rabies tag. On a long trip, you may even want to bring along your dog's rabies certificate. Some parks and campgrounds require rabies and licensing information. You never know how picky they'll be.

It's a good idea to snap one of those barrel-type IDs on your dog's collar, too, showing the name, address and phone number of where you'll be vacationing. That way, if she should get lost, at least the finder won't be calling your empty house.

Some people think dogs should drink only water brought from home, so their bodies don't have to get used to too many new things. I've never had a problem feeding my dogs tap water from other parts of the state, nor has anyone else I know. Most vets think your dog will be fine drinking tap water in most other U.S. cities.

"Think of it this way," says Pete Beeman, a long-time San Francisco veterinarian. "Your dog's probably going to eat poop if he can get hold of some, and even that's probably not going to harm him. I really don't think that water that's okay for people is going to be bad for dogs."

DINING WITH DOG

In Europe, dogs enter restaurants and dine alongside their folks as if they were people, too. (Or at least they sit and watch and drool while their people dine.) Not so in America. Rightly or wrongly, dogs are considered a health threat. But health inspectors I've spoken with say they see no reason why clean, well-behaved dogs shouldn't be permitted inside a restaurant. "Aesthetically, it may not appeal to Americans," an environmental specialist with the State Department of Health told me. "But the truth is, there's no harm in this practice."

Ernest Hemingway made an expatriate of his dog, Black Dog (a.k.a. Blackie), partly because of America's restrictive views on dogs in dining establishments. In *The Christmas Gift*, a story published in *Look* magazine in 1954, he describes how he made the decision to take Black Dog to Cuba, rather than leave him behind in Ketchum, Idaho.

"This was a town where a man was once not regarded as respectable unless he was accompanied by his dog. But a reform movement had set in, led by several local religionists, and gambling had been abolished and there was even a movement on foot to forbid a dog from entering a public eating place with his master. Blackie had always tugged me by the trouser leg as we passed a combination gambling and eating place called the Alpine where they served the finest sizzling steak in the West. Blackie wanted me to order the giant sizzling steak and it was difficult to pass the Alpine...We decided to make a command decision and take Blackie to Cuba."

Fortunately, you don't have to take your dog to a foreign county in order to eat together at a restaurant. California is full of restaurants with outdoor tables, and hundreds of them welcome dogs to join their people for an *alfresco* experience.

The law on patio-dining dogs is somewhat vague, and each county has differing versions of it. But in general, as long as your dog doesn't go inside a restaurant (even to get to outdoor tables in the back) and isn't near the food preparation areas, it's probably legal. The decision is then up to the restaurant proprietor.

The restaurants listed in this book have given us permission to tout them as dog-friendly eateries. But keep in mind that rules can change and restaurants can close, so I highly recommend phoning before you get your stomach set on a particular kind of cuisine.

Since some of the restaurants close during colder months, phoning ahead is a doubly wise thing to do. (Of course, just assume that where there's snow or ultra-cold temperatures, the outdoor tables are indoors for a while.) If you can't call first, be sure to ask the manager of the restaurant for permission before you sit down with your sidekick. Remember, it's the restaurant owner, not you, who will be in trouble if someone complains.

Some basic restaurant etiquette: Dogs shouldn't beg other diners, no matter how delicious their steak looks. They should not attempt to get their snouts (or their entire bodies) up on the table. They should be clean, quiet and as unobtrusive as possible. If your dog leaves a good impression with the management and other customers, it will help pave the way for all the other dogs who want to dine alongside their best friends in the future.

A ROOM AT THE INN

Good dogs make great hotel guests. They don't steal towels, and they don't get drunk and keep the neighbors up all night.

California is full of lodgings whose owners welcome dogs. This book lists dog-friendly accommodations of all types, from motels to bed-and-breakfast inns to elegant hotels. But the basic dog etiquette rules are the same.

Dogs should never be left alone in your room. Leaving a dog alone in a strange place is inviting serious trouble. Scared, nervous dogs can tear apart drapes, carpeting and furniture. They can even injure themselves. They can also bark non-stop and scare the daylights out of the housekeeper. Just don't do it.

Only bring a house-trained dog to a lodging. How would you like a house guest to go to the bathroom in the middle of your bedroom?

It helps if you bring your dog's bed or his blanket. Your dog will feel more at home, and won't be tempted to jump on the bed. If your dog sleeps on the bed with you at home, bring a sheet and put it on top of the bed so the hotel's bedspread won't get furry or dirty.

After a few days in a hotel, some dogs come to think of it as home. They get territorial. When another hotel guest walks by, it's "Bark! Bark!" When the housekeeper knocks, it's "Bark! Snarl! Bark! Gnash!" Keep your dog quiet or you'll both find yourselves looking for a new home away from home.

For some strange reason, many lodgings prefer small dogs as guests. All I can say is yip! Yap! It's really ridiculous. Large dogs are often much calmer and quieter than their tiny, high-energy cousins.

If you're in a location where you can't find a hotel that will accept you and your big brute, it's time to try a sell job. Let the manager know how good and quiet your dog is (if he is). Promise he won't eat the bathtub or run around and shake the hotel. Offer a deposit or sign a waiver, even if they're not required for small dogs. It helps if your sweet, soppy-eyed dog is at your side to convince the decision-maker.

I've sneaked dogs into hotels, but I don't recommend doing it. The lodging might have a good reason for its rules. Besides, you always feel as if you're going to be caught and thrown out on your petard. You race in and out of your room with your dog as if ducking sniper fire. It's better to avoid feeling like a criminal and move on to a more dog-friendly location. For a sure bet, try a Motel 6. Every single Motel 6 in the nation permits one small pooch per room. Some have more lenient rules than others. Their nationwide reservation and information line is (505) 891-6161.

The lodgings described in this book are for dogs who obey all the rules. Rates listed are for double rooms, unless otherwise noted.

RUFFING IT TOGETHER

Whenever we go camping, Joe insists on sleeping in the tent. He sprawls out and won't budge. At the first hint of dawn, he tiptoes outside (sometimes right through the bug screen) as if he'd been standing vigil all night. He tries not to look shame-faced, but under all that curly hair lurks an embarrassed grin.

Actually, Joe might have the right idea. Some outdoor experts say it's dangerous to leave even a tethered dog outside your tent at night. The dog can escape or can become bait for some creature hungry for a late dinner.

All state parks require dogs to be in a tent or vehicle at night. Some county parks follow suit. Others policies are more lenient. Use good judgment.

If you're camping with your dog, chances are that you're also hiking with him. Even if you're not hiking for long, you have to watch out for your dog's paws, especially the paws of those who are fair of foot. Rough terrain can cause a dog's pads to become raw and painful, making it almost impossible to walk. Several types of dog boots are available for such feet. It's easier to carry the booties than to carry your dog home.

Be sure to bring plenty of water for you and your pooch. Stop frequently to wet your whistles. Some veterinarians recommend against letting your dog drink out of a stream, because of the chance of ingesting giardia and other internal parasites, but it's not always easy to stop a thirsty dog.

On any but the most strenuous hikes, most dogs can muscle a little of the load themselves, if given the right attire. Dog backpacks enable a pooch to carry dog food, maps, bowls or just about any other essentials that aren't too heavy. They're also convenient if you bring your dog fishing. What dog wouldn't want to help you carry a bunch of worms?

There are many good brands of dog backpacks out there. Joe's favorite is his bright orange backpack from Dog Togs, Inc. Most of this husband-and-wife team's packs come in more subtle colors, but orange is great for hiking in the wilderness. The packs are attached to a comfortable harness (which comes with the packs) and can readily convert into buoyancy vests when you insert ethylene foam or some other very buoyant material. Joe, who can't swim, appreciates this. If you can't find Dog Togs products at your outdoor store, call (800) DOG-TOGS.

NATURAL TROUBLES

Chances are that your adventuring will go without a hitch, but you should always be prepared to deal with trouble. Make sure you know the basics of animal first-aid before you embark on a long journey with your dog.

The more common woes—ticks, foxtails, poison oak and skunks—can make life with a traveling dog a somewhat trying experience.

Ticks are hard to avoid in Northern California. They can carry Lyme disease, so you should always check yourself and your dog all over after a day in tick country. Don't forget to check ears and between the toes. If you see one, just pull it straight out with tweezers, not your bare hands.

The tiny ticks that carry Lyme disease are difficult to find. Consult your veterinarian if your dog is lethargic for a few days, has a fever, loses her appetite or becomes lame. These symptoms could indicate Lyme disease. Some vets recommend a new vaccine that is supposed to prevent the onset of the disease.

Foxtails—those arrow-shaped pieces of dry grass (see illustration) that attach to your socks, your sweater and your dog—are an everyday annoyance. But in certain cases, they can be lethal. They

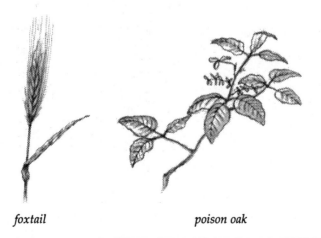

foxtail   *poison oak*

can stick in your dog's eyes, nose, ears or mouth and work their way in. Check every nook and cranny of your dog after a walk if you've been anywhere near dry grass. Despite my constant effort to find these things in Joe's curly fur, I've missed a few and they've beaten a path through his foot and into his leg. Be vigilant.

Poison oak (see illustration) is also a common California menace. Get familiar with it through a friend who knows nature or through a guided nature walk. Dogs don't generally have reactions to poison oak, but they can easily pass its oils on to people. If you think your dog has made contact with poison oak, avoid petting her until you can get home and wash her (preferably with rubber gloves). If you do pet her before you can wash her, don't touch your eyes and wash your hands immediately.

If your dog loses a contest with a skunk (and she always will), rinse her eyes first with plain warm water, then bathe her with dog shampoo. Towel her off, then apply tomato juice. We once went through four gallons of the stuff before Joe started smelling less offensive. (And walking into the store to buy it was a real hoot. I had obviously absorbed some of the stench myself. Everyone was turning around and saying, "Whew! Do you smell a skunk?" as I wafted by.) If you can't get tomato juice, you can also use a solution of one pint of vinegar per gallon of water to decrease the stink.

HE, SHE, IT

In this book, whether neutered, spayed or *au naturel*, dogs are never refered to as "it." They are either "he" or "she." I alternate pronouns so no dog reading this book will feel left out.

A DOG IN NEED

If you don't currently have a dog, but could provide a good home, I'd like to make a plea on behalf of all the unwanted dogs who will be euthanized tomorrow and the day after that and the day after that. Animal shelters and humane organizations are overflowing with dogs who would devote their lives to being your best buddy, your faithful traveling companion and a dedicated listener to all your tales of bliss and woe.

Need a nudge? Remember the oft-quoted words of Samuel Butler: "The great pleasure of a dog is that you may make a fool of yourself with him and not only will he not scold you, but he will make a fool of himself, too."

NORTHERN AREA COUNTIES

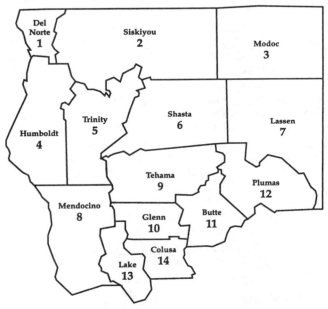

DEL NORTE COUNTY

SNIFF!
SNIFF!

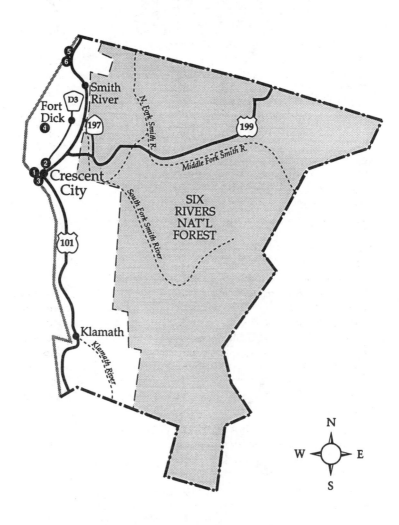

1
DEL NORTE COUNTY

Don't call this beautiful coastal redwood empire "Del Nort-*ay*" County, as many Californians do because of all the Spanish influence in this state. It's as much of a giveaway that you're from out of town as pronouncing the next state north "Or-ih-*gohn*" instead of "Or-ih-*ghin*." Pronounce this county "Del Nort," even if it does remind you of something Ralph Kramden would say.

If you want a real coastal getaway, you couldn't ask for a more beautiful, remote area. Part of the reason so few Californians know the local pronunciation of this county is because it's so out of the way that we don't often hear about it.

As one of the state's best-kept secrets, it's a gem for people vacationing with a dog. While there are plenty of leash laws, there are also many places where civilization hasn't yet encroached sufficiently to make leashes a mandatory part of a dog's attire. The 305,000-acre Smith River National Recreation Area (see Six Rivers National Forest below), which makes up the majority of this county, allows dogs off leash everywhere except in campgrounds!

The climate in Del Norte County is very mild, with coastal temperatures generally ranging from 65 to 75 degrees Fahrenheit. That's good news for dogs who don't like temperature extremes. But this region is also known for its rain. One hundred inches a year here is common, making outdoor cafes almost nonexistent. The forests are actually rainforests. They're lush and verdant. They're also often wet. Some dogs and people prefer this to the drought scenarios in other parts of the state. With a slicker, a dog towel and a love of the outdoors, you and your dog could be very happy here.

NATIONAL FORESTS

See the National Forests/Wilderness Areas chapter starting on page 801 for important information and safety tips for visiting national forests with your dog.

• **Six Rivers National Forest** 😊 😊 😊 😊 😊 🐾 🐕

This county is green thanks in great part to the lush 305,000-acre Smith River National Recreation Area, which is part of Six Rivers National Forest. The U.S. Forest Service has been designated as the steward of this fairly new national recreation area, and that's fantastic for dogs. The Wild and Scenic River, the 65 miles of trails and the seven distinct plant communities can all be enjoyed by off-leash dogs, as long as they're obedient. See page 809 for a more complete description of the forest.

CRESCENT CITY

This 1.25-square-mile coastal city was devastated by a giant tsunami in 1964. A series of waves about 12 feet high rushed inland as far as 1,600 feet, destroying 29 downtown blocks, and killing 11 people. The city has since rebuilt, and the beach that the tsunami washed over is now the best doggy place for miles (see Beachfront Park below).

PARKS, BEACHES & RECREATION AREAS

• **Beachfront Park** 🐾 🐾 🐾 🐾 🐾 🐕

Pooches are free to be their doggy selves at this 177-acre beach/grassy park. They can run and roll and watch you play bocci ball and volleyball here. They can stretch out in the gazebo as you read and relax. They can help you beachcomb. All this without a leash!

The only place dogs have to be leashed here is at the children's playground. It's also a good idea to restrain them at the 850-foot public fishing pier. No sense getting the anglers and their fish all upset about a nosy dog. And watch out for Elk Creek, which empties into the harbor here. Occasionally it can be too swift for even the strongest dog paddler.

From US 101, go west on Front Street. The park is at Front Street between B and F streets. (707) 464-9507. → *See #1 on map p. 28.*

• **Florence Keller Regional Park** 🐾 🐾 🐾

This 30-acre county park is one big redwood grove with space carved out for trails, playing fields and playgrounds. It's a good balance of wild and civilized, if you need that kind of balance. Dogs have to be leashed. Camping at any of the 25 sites here costs $10 a night. It can fill up in the summer, so reservations are recommended.

Exit US 101 at Cunningham Lane and follow the signs to the park. (707) 464-7230. → *See #2 on map p. 28.*

• **Redwood National Park (north section)** 🐾 🐾 1/2

For a national park, this is a fairly unrestrictive place, both here and in its south half in Humboldt County. In national parks, dogs are usually permitted only on paved roads, in parking lots and in the occasional campground. But here, leashed dogs are actually allowed on a trail and a beach.

The Enderts Beach Trail is a 1.2-mile walk on the bluffs behind

Enderts Beach. Crescent Beach, just off Enderts Beach Road, is a good place for beachcombing dogs. Both are fine if you don't mind leashing your dog. But if you're not bent on being near the coast, the Smith River National Recreation Area can make a dog much happier. (See Six Rivers National Forest, page 29.)

Start your visit to the Redwood National Park at the park's headquarters in Crescent City, at Second and K streets. You can get maps, brochures and trail updates that will make your visit a more enjoyable one. (707) 464-6101. ➡ *See #3 on map p. 28.*

PLACES TO STAY

Days Inn: No big dogs allowed. Rates are $39 to $55. 220 M Street, Crescent City, CA 95531; (707) 464-9553.

Del Norte Coast Redwoods State Park: Dogs aren't allowed on the trails here, but they can sleep in one of the 107 campsites under a grove of redwoods. Rates are $12 to $14. Dogs are $1 extra. The campground is about 10 miles southeast of Crescent City, just off US 101. For reservations, call MISTIX at (800) 444-PARK. For information on the park, phone (707) 464-9533.

Econo Lodge: Dogs are allowed at the manager's discretion. Rates are $32 to $55. 119 L Street, Crescent City, CA 95531; (707) 464-2181.

Florence Keller Regional Park camping: See page 30.

Pacific Motor Hotel: Rates are $39 to $65. Dogs are $10 extra. Smallish dogs only, please. 440 US 101 North, Crescent City, CA 95531; (707) 464-4141.

Royal Inn: Rates are $33 to $70. There's a $5 fee for dogs. 102 L Street, Crescent City, CA 95531; (707) 464-4113.

Town House Motel: Rates are $26 to $50. There's a $20 dog deposit, and smaller dogs are preferred. 444 US 101 South, Crescent City, CA 95531; (707) 464-4176.

FESTIVALS

Crescent City Crab Race: Take your dog to the races at this crustacean celebration! Leashed dogs are allowed to watch Dungeness, hermit and rock crabs compete for the title of Crab of the Year. Maybe one of the reasons they run so fast is that they can smell the carnage of the crab feed going on just down the road from the race course. The race is held each February at the Del Norte County Fairgrounds. There's a modest fee. (707) 464-3174.

FORT DICK
PARKS, BEACHES & RECREATION AREAS
• **Lake Earl Wildlife Area** 🐾🐾 🐕

Dogs can come to this 5,000-acre state wildlife area only if they're here to help when you shoot waterfowl (and we're not talking cameras here).

Off leash is okay because of the feats the dogs are performing. During hunting season, working dogs and their gun-toting buddies can hunt the lake itself and 100 feet from the edge of the water.

From Crescent City, take Lake Earl Drive north. Turn left at Old Mill Road. Proceed 1.5 miles to the wildlife area headquarters on the right. (707) 464-2523. → *See #4 on map p. 28.*

KLAMATH
DIVERSIONS
He's tall, he speaks, he mystifies dogs: A visit to the campy-but-fascinating Trees of Mystery will be a visit you and your canine buddy will never forget. First, a 50-foot-tall Paul Bunyan greets patrons in the parking lot. His ox doesn't speak, but Bunyan utters enough sentences to make even the most savvy dog stand in open-mouthed awe. Then the nature trail takes you through some of the world's oldest and largest trees. But these are no ordinary trees: These are Trees of Mystery! We won't ruin the many surprises that await you, but let's just say you'll definitely want a camera with a wide-angle lens. Entry fee is $6 for adults and $3 for children ages 6 to 12. Dogs get in free. 15500 US 101. (707) 482-5613 or (800) 638-3389.

SMITH RIVER
PARKS, BEACHES & RECREATION AREAS
• **Pelican State Beach** 🐾🐾🐾

It's only five acres, but that's plenty of running room for a dog who's been cooped up in the car all day. Pelican State Beach is actually a few miles northwest of Smith River, the closest California city to the Oregon border. It seems to be a popular stop for folks who have just gone over or are about to go over to visit our northern neighbor. Dogs are supposed to be leashed, but they love sniffing around the beach for the driftwood that's so plentiful here.

The beach is just west of US 101, five miles south of the Oregon border. (707) 445-6547. → *See #5 on map p. 28.*

• Smith River County Park 🐾 🐾 🐾

This is a beautiful park, right on the mouth of the Smith River, which is part of the state's Wild and Scenic River system. It's a great place to relax on the pebbly beach and take in the sights, or walk to Pyramid Point and do a little birdwatching with your leashed dog. It's also a popular backdrop for photographs. If your dog wants to be in pictures, this might be the place to snap away.

The park is at the end of Smith River Road. (707) 464-7230.

➡ See #6 on map p. 28.

PLACES TO STAY

Casa Rubio: This beach house is dog heaven—at least female dog heaven. Boy dogs are banned here. Owner Tony Rubio says too much of his exquisite landscaping has been ruined by male dogs exploring and marking the territory here.

Joe is still trying to cheer up after hearing the news. This is his kind of place. Of the three units in this 1940s beach house, one allows girl dogs (Joe now wants to call them by their true name). It's roomy, with a private yard and a kitchen. And when you open the door, you're right on the sands of a wide beach!

Here's a real bonus: When you stay here, you can have two meals for the price of one at Rubio's, a yummy restaurant in Brookings, Oregon, just up the road. And your dog can accompany you if you eat at the patio tables. The restaurant is at 1136 Chetco Avenue (US 101). Ask the staff at Casa Rubio for directions.

Room rates are $78 to $88. 17285 Crissey Road, Smith River, CA 95567; (707) 487-4313 or (800) 357-6199.

Ship Ashore Best Western: If yours is a teeny-weeny dog, she can stay here with you. The weight limit for pets is 10 pounds. Fortunately, there is no weight limit for human guests. But in case you need the exercise, there's a pooch path on the premises. Rates are $50 to $75. 12370 US 101 North, Smith River, CA 95567; (707) 487-3141 or (800) 528-1234.

SISKIYOU COUNTY

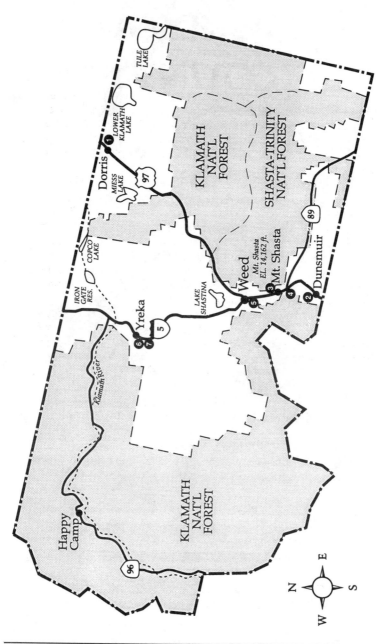

2
SISKIYOU COUNTY

Siskiyou County is home to some of the least creative names for parks that we've ever seen. Even Joe was yawning when we checked out four cities which had parks called "City Park." But fortunately, two of the four City Parks are really outstanding—as are many of the parks and recreation areas in this huge and wild county.

The visual highlight of Siskiyou County is towering Mount Shasta, but there's so much beauty here that almost anywhere you go, something's bound to impress your senses. Two national forests make up a big part of the county. As you travel on Highway 96, you'll find dozens of places to pull off and explore the Klamath River in the Klamath National Forest. If you stop at a wide river access point that's far from the road, your dog can trot around off leash while you fish or soak your weary legs. Be careful, though. The current can really whip in some spots.

Lava Beds National Monument on the eastern edge of the county is off-limits to dogs, unless they like walking on paved roads. It's a sore disappointment to many dogs and their drivers. You can drive through here with a dog, but this park is more of a stop-and-check-it-out place, where you should walk through gigantic lava tubes and experience other unusual adventures. Rangers say they've been getting more strict about dogs recently because they've noticed that dogs have been doing their doggy business in the caves, so if you think you're going to get away with sneaking your dog around here, you're probably wrong. There are plenty of other places to visit that welcome dogs, although they don't have lava tubes.

NATIONAL FORESTS

See the National Forests/Wilderness Areas chapter starting on page 801 for important information and safety tips for visiting national forests with your dog.

- **Klamath National Forest** 🐾🐾🐾🐾 🦴 🐕
  See page 805.
- **Shasta-Trinity National Forest** 🐾🐾🐾🐾 🦴 🐕
  See page 808.

DORRIS

PARKS, BEACHES & RECREATION AREAS

• **Lower Klamath National Wildlife Refuge** 🐾 🐾 🐾 1/2 🐕

This 54,000-acre waterfowl haven may be home to the largest wintering concentration of bald eagles in the lower 48 states. Dogs are allowed off leash only if they're helping you during waterfowl and pheasant hunting seasons. Otherwise, they have to be leashed at all times to protect this important nesting and migration area.

The Lower Klamath Lake, and surrounding marshy area and uplands, are a birdwatcher's paradise. During summer you'll see avocets, grebes, herons, white pelicans, black-necked stilts and killdeer. Nearly one million waterfowl use this and nearby Tule Lake during fall migration. Keep those binoculars peeled.

The refuge has many entrances. From US 97 at the Oregon border, head east on Highway 161. The refuge's entrances will be on your right in a few miles. Call (916) 667-2231 for information and directions to other areas of the refuge. → *See #1 on map p. 36.*

DUNSMUIR

When I first visited this old town on the Sacramento River, it was July of 1991 and I was covering the toxic metam sodium spill that wiped out river life and made residents ill. The sign at the town's entrance boasting "Dunsmuir—home of the best water on earth" was nothing but a sad irony and a good line for an article.

But these days, the river is clean and burgeoning with life again. The sign at the town's entrance is no longer incongruous. Check out the crystal-clear water from City Park (see below) while you and your leashed dog picnic along the river. It's so nice not to have bright green clouds of toxic pesticides floating by while you're trying to eat.

• **City Park** 🐾 🐾 🐾 1/2

This is not your typical, well-groomed city park. It's wild and woodsy, and full of trails winding up and down hills surrounding the Sacramento River. It's almost completely shaded here, so it's cool during all but the hottest days of summer.

If you're feeling adventurous, you can cross the river and the railroad tracks and find yourself in a small part of the Shasta-Trinity National Forest. If you're feeling mellow, just hang out and have lunch at one of the riverside picnic tables.

Take the Central Dunsmuir exit off Interstate 5 and go north on Dunsmuir Avenue. The park will be on your left. (916) 235-4822. → *See #2 on map p. 36.*

RESTAURANTS
Burger Barn: Dogs like to drool while you dine on a burger at this eatery's picnic tables. 5942 Dunsmuir Avenue; (916) 235-2140.

PLACES TO STAY
Caboose Motel/Railroad Park Resort: These restored caboose cars are intriguing places to stay with a dog, but only dogs who are cocker spaniel-sized and smaller are allowed. The owners prefer dogs to bring their own beds. The grounds of the resort are like a park. Dogs just have to stay off landscaped areas. Rates are $60 to $80. Dogs are $2.50 extra. 100 Railroad Park Road, Dunsmuir, CA 96025; (916) 235-4440.

Dunsmuir Travelodge: Your dog is a mere quarter mile away from the city park here. Rates are $40 to $70. Dogs are $5 extra. 5400 Dunsmuir Avenue, Dunsmuir, CA 96025; (916) 235-4395 or (800) 235-3050.

HAPPY CAMP

PLACES TO STAY
Forest Lodge Motel: This is the only motel in town with phones in the rooms. The managers stress that dogs have to be housebroken to stay here (as they must always be when you're taking them to a hotel). They've had some bad experiences here with pets who weren't housebroken. Rates are $42 to $58. 63712 Highway 96, Happy Camp, CA 96039; (916) 493-5424.

MOUNT SHASTA

This small town sits under the watchful eye of the mighty mountain that goes by the same name. Mount Shasta can provide a quick highway rest stop for the weary, or an enchanting place to unwind for days. Some who have come here for days end up spending the rest of their lives here. It's got the best of all worlds—it's remote and wildly natural, yet civilized to the point of being the area's cultural hub. Even dogs like the combination.

PARKS, BEACHES & RECREATION AREAS
• City Park 🐾 🐾 🐾 👣

We have to stop here every time we pass Mount Shasta. We bring a couple of empty water bottles and a big thirst: This fairly small city park is actually home to the headwaters of the Sacramento River. The crystal-clear, cold water comes bubbling down the rocks of a couple of small streams that become the Sacramento. It's the best water we've ever tasted, and it's free! There are no

---

rules yet on how much water people can take, but there may be in the future if people abuse the privilege. Don't be a glutton and you'll be able to dip your cup into eternity.

Dogs have to be leashed at this shady park, but they don't seem to mind. This is a relaxing place, where you have the chance to sit under a tree in a green meadow or under the gazebo and tune out the world for a while. Bring a picnic and toast your favorite dog with your favorite water at one of the riverside picnic tables. If your dog needs to stretch his legs more, there's a wide trail that starts in the area behind the stream. But do keep him out of the water. Dog hair doesn't go well with bottled water.

From Interstate 5, take the Mount Shasta Boulevard exit and head southeast. Turn right within a half mile at Nixon Road and bear right into the park. (916) 926-3464. *See #3 on map p. 36.*

• **Lake Siskiyou** 🐾 🐾 🐾 1/2 🐾

This man-made reservoir, created solely for recreational use, sits in the morning shadow of awesome Mount Shasta. Trout fishing is one of the big draws—the lake is stocked with 20,000 trout each year! But you can also have a great vacation just camping and hiking in the area surrounding this 437-acre lake. Leashed dogs may go pretty much everywhere except the swimming beach.

Several trails wind through the ponderosa pines and cedars that encircle much of the lake. You can actually leave the campground and walk around the entire lake with your dog, as long as you don't mind hoofing it across a small section of the Sacramento River. Soon this segment of trail will be improved so you and your dog won't have to get your paws wet, but for now, consider it an adventure.

The day-use fee is $1 per human. Dogs don't pay anything during the day, but it costs $1 a night if your dog camps with you. There are 360 sites with fees ranging from $13 to $17. From Interstate 5, take the Central Mount Shasta exit, turn left at the stop sign, and follow the signs west on W.A. Barr Road to the lake. (916) 926-2610. *See #4 on map p. 36.*

RESTAURANTS

Avalon Square Deli: Dogs love to watch you dine on salads and sandwiches at the many outdoor, umbrella-covered tables here. 401 North Mount Shasta Boulevard; (916) 926-4998.

PLACES TO STAY

Alpine Lodge: Rates are $30 to $50. There's a $20 deposit for dogs. 908 South Mount Shasta Boulevard, Mount Shasta, CA 96067; (916) 926-3145.

Mountain Air Lodge: If your dog likes a little grass around his lodgings, he'll like a night or two here. Rates are $32 to $56. Dogs are $5 extra. 1121 South Mount Shasta Boulevard, Mount Shasta, CA 96067; (916) 926-3411.

Swiss Holiday Lodge: Sleep here and watch the sun rise on Mount Shasta right from your window. Rates are $33 to $57. 2400 South Mount Shasta Boulevard, Mount Shasta, CA 96067; (916) 926-3448.

The Tree House Best Western: There's no tree house here, but the place is made of cedar, so dogs are still in a woody surrounding. Some of the rooms have views of Mount Shasta. Rates are $56 to $130. 111 Morgan Way, Mount Shasta, CA 96067; (916) 926-3101.

WEED

At times, the name Weed has been a stumbling block in public relations, but it doesn't stop people from visiting this old town nestled in the western slopes of Mount Shasta. Today it's a sleepy place with breathtaking views of the mountain. But between the 1900s and the 1940s, it was considered to be the Sodom and Gomorrah of Siskiyou County. Because of its remote location, the law was barely enforced. Things sometimes would get so out of hand that train conductors would warn people not to disembark here.

PARKS, BEACHES & RECREATION AREAS

We were disappointed in Lake Shastina, the beautiful lake that's recently been turned into a golf resort just outside town. It used to be much wilder, but now about the wildest areas the public can access are the sand traps. And since dogs aren't permitted on the courses, it's not much fun.

Fortunately, just to the east of Weed is the Shasta-Trinity National Forest's Shasta Wilderness Area, complete with the magnificent 14,162-foot Mount Shasta and even a few fairly non-strenuous trails (see page 808 for a description of the Shasta-Trinity National Forest).

•City Park 🐾 1/2

Much of this park is taken up by ball fields, but there's still some room for leashed dogs to roam and a few trees for them to mark. It's a convenient stop if your dog is crossing his legs while you're driving on Interstate 5. Exit at the College of Siskiyou turnoff and take South Weed Boulevard south one block. Go right on College Avenue. The park is on your left after three blocks. (916) 938-5020.

➡ *See #5 on map p. 36.*

RESTAURANTS

Pizza Factory: Joe's favorite food here are the juicy calzones, which he enjoys smelling at a table under the awning. 132 North Weed Boulevard; (916) 938-3088.

PLACES TO STAY

Motel 6: Rates are $32 for the first adult, $6 for the second. All Motel 6s allow one small dog per room. 466 North Weed Boulevard, Weed, CA 96094; (916) 938-4101.

Sis-Q-Inn Motel: Macho dogs may not like the name, but they're bound to appreciate the views of Mount Shasta that most rooms here offer. Rates are $30 to $48. Dogs are $5 extra. 1825 Shastina Drive, Weed, CA 96094; (916) 938-4194.

YREKA

Yreka, Eureka, Ukiah, Arcata. Traveling in Northern California can be confusing, with cities whose names sound like bad Scrabble hands. But here's an easy way to have Yreka (pronounced "why-reek-uh") stick out in your mind: When you're here, just look south. See spectacular, snowy Mount Shasta in the distance? *Yreka* is an Indian word for "white mountain." The "Y" in Yreka sounds sort of like the "white" in white mountain. Got it?

This is the county seat of Siskiyou County, and it's an attractive, historic place on the eastern edge of a huge portion of the Klamath National Forest. (See page 805 for a description of the forest.) Dogs prefer to run around unleashed in the forest, but there's a city park in town where they can enjoy a more civilized walk. And if your dog is small, he can have a roaring good time aboard the Blue Goose Steam Train (see Diversions, page 43).

PARKS, BEACHES & RECREATION AREAS

•City Park 🐾 🐾

This small city park is conveniently located near the historic district of Yreka. Dogs like it just fine, as long as they don't mind a leash. The grass is green and the shade trees are big. There's also a playground and a ball field so the kids can work off their energy while the dog explores.

From Highway 3, drive west about six blocks on West Miner Street. The park is on your left, at Gold and West Miner streets. (916) 842-4386. ➡ *See #6 on map p. 36.*

•Greenhorn Park 🐾 🐾 1/2

The park is indeed green. The only problem is that dogs aren't allowed on the vast, lush lawn areas here. They're relegated to the trails, which aren't bad. You can walk next to Greenhorn Creek, which leads to Greenhorn Reservoir on the eastern end of the park. But no swimming is allowed for dogs or their people.

From Highway 3, drive west for one block on Payne Lane, then south on Oregon Street until the road comes to a T. Then drive right on Greenhorn Road about a half mile. The park entrance is on your left, just past the reservoir. (916) 842-4386. → *See #7 on map p. 36.*

PLACES TO STAY

Best Western Miner's Inn: Small and medium-sized dogs are invited to sleep here. Rates are $44 to $85. 122 East Miner Street, Yreka, CA 96097; (916) 842-4355.

Thunderbird Lodge: There's plenty of land around here for a little romping with your pooch. Rates are $32 to $40. 526 South Main Street, Yreka, CA 96097; (916) 842-4404.

Wayside Inn: This bright inn has interesting knotty pine furniture. Rates are $32 to $48. Dogs are $3 extra. 1235 South Main Street, Yreka, CA 96097; (916) 842-4412.

DIVERSIONS

Choo choo with your poochoo: Put on your engineer caps and get ready to steam along a short-line railroad that's been in continuous operation since 1889. Dogs who fit on your lap are allowed to accompany you on the Blue Goose Steam Train for this magical three-hour tour from Yreka east through Shasta Valley. You'll pass lumber mills, cross the Shasta River and chug along through beautiful cattle country—all with majestic Mount Shasta in the background.

The 1915 Baldwin steam engine stops at the old cattle town of Montague, where you can picnic in the park while listening to the entertainment that's been rustled up for you. You can visit the old-fashioned soda fountain in town or take a wagon ride set up for the train's guests.

Dogs who are small adore this ride. Dogs who are larger would love it, too, but unfortunately railway manager Larry Bacon says too many people gripe about anything larger than a lap dog. "These complainers are a bunch of old poops, young poops, too, who'd moan about anything," says dog-loving Bacon. To partially remedy the problem, Bacon may soon offer free kenneling to dogs who are too big to ride with their owners. The kennels would be in the shade, and he'd supply water and the occasional dog biscuit.

Meanwhile, back on the train, teacup poodles, beagles and their ilk will get to choose from an open car, two 1920s cars and a couple of vintage 1948 passenger cars. Unless your dog doesn't like the wind in his face or the sound of steam bursting forth in Wizard of

Oz fashion, the open cars are the best ones for canines. Just keep hold of that leash, in case Toto or some other interesting creature comes charging by.

The train runs from Memorial Day weekend through the end of October. Rates are $9 for adults, $4.50 for kids. Dogs who qualify size-wise go for free. Exit Interstate 5 at the Central Yreka exit. The depot is just east of the freeway. (916) 842-4146.

MODOC COUNTY

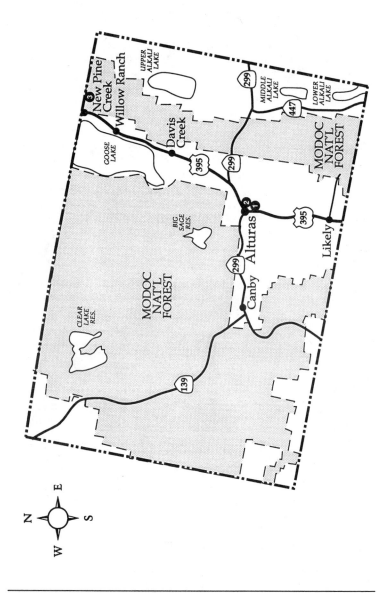

3
MODOC COUNTY

Not too many people or dogs venture to the far northeast reaches of the state, but those who do find dog heaven. About 90 percent of this county is made up of Modoc National Forest and other public lands. That means years of off-leash walks for you and your pooch.

Many folks travel through here on Highway 395 on the way from the Pacific Northwest to Reno. Alturas is a popular stopping point. But check out the numerous entrances to the eastern chunk of Modoc National Forest. Just north of Alturas you can follow Highway 299 east into the Cedar Mountain area, where there are a couple of primitive campgrounds. Closer to the town of Likely, you can head east and enter the South Warner Wilderness for access to numerous lakes, streams and trails.

Alturas, the county seat and only town of notable size, has a population of 3,000. That should tell you all you need to know about this get-away-from-it-all county.

NATIONAL FORESTS

See the National Forests/Wilderness Areas chapter starting on page 801 for important information and safety tips for visiting national forests with your dog.

• **Modoc National Forest** 🐾 🐾 🐾 🐾 🐾 🥩 🐕

The South Warner Wilderness, located about 14 miles east of the town of Likely, is a serene place to visit. Clear little lakes abound, as do the creeks that feed them. See page 807 for more information on Modoc National Forest.

ALTURAS

Even though there's not much going on here for the dog in your life, if you visit Veteran's Memorial Park (see below), you can be entertained by the stories of 88-year-old Virgie Meyer, who works at the neighboring Alturas Chamber of Commerce. Meyer, a native of Alturas, makes the history of this area come alive through her colorful narratives.

PARKS, BEACHES & RECREATION AREAS

• **Veteran's Memorial Park** 🐾 🐾

The park is about the size of a city block. It's chock full of trees on one side and covered with grass on the other. Picnic tables dot the park. Since there are no restaurants with outdoor tables for dogs and their people in Alturas, this is a good place to bring your lunch so you can break bread with your pooch.

Dogs must be leashed. The park is on County Road 56 and Highway 395. (916) 233-2512. ➤ *See #1 on map p. 46.*

• **Modoc National Wildlife Refuge** 🐾🐾🐾 🖐 🐕

The only dogs who are allowed off leash here are bird hunters, and only during the appropriate seasons. Otherwise, dogs have to wear leashes in the Dorris Reservoir area of the refuge.

Sections of the reservoir are closed during nesting season, but you can usually take your leashed dog on a hike on the horse trail that goes across the top of the dam and down to the surrounding land. The birdwatching is excellent at the right time of year. Bring your binoculars and get up close and personal with tundra swans, Canada geese and cinnamon teal. Earth-bound residents include coyotes, antelope and rabbits. It's hard to hold binoculars while your dog is tugging at the leash, but make sure your pooch doesn't get away.

From Alturas, drive about three miles east on Parker Creek Road. Call (916) 233-3572 for dates and restrictions. ➤ *See #2 on map p. 46.*

PLACES TO STAY

It may seem as though Alturas has an incongruously high number of motels per capita, but when you consider how many people pass through here, it makes sense. The dogs sure appreciate their small-town hospitality.

Best Western Trailside Inn: Rates are $42 to $50. Dogs are $5 extra and the management prefers smaller dogs who don't shed. 343 North Main Street, Alturas, CA 96101; (916) 233-4111.

Drifters Inn: This one's on lots of property. Rates are $28 to $46. Dogs are $2 extra. 395 Lake View Road, Alturas, CA 96101; (916) 233-2428.

Essex Motel: Rates are $35 to $48. Small dogs only, please. 1216 North Main Street, Alturas, CA 96101; (916) 233-2821.

Frontier Motel: There's a big backyard behind the motel, and good dogs are allowed to check it out. Rates are $28 to $43. 1033 North Main Street, Alturas, CA 96101; (916) 233-3383.

Hacienda Motel: Rates are $27 to $45. 201 East 12th Street, Alturas, CA 96101; (916) 233-3459.

Wagon Wheel Motel: Rates are $27 to $39. 308 West 12th Street, Alturas, CA 96101; (916) 233-5866.

NEW PINE CREEK

PARKS, BEACHES & RECREATION AREAS

• **Cave Lake/Lily Lake** 🐾 🐾 🐾 🐾 🐕

You can't get much more remote than this in California. These small, trout-filled lakes are on the Oregon border, and it takes a six-mile drive up a fairly steep gravel road to get there. You probably won't find any people here, but you'll find all the peace you need. The world is truly hushed at this 6,600-foot elevation.

Dogs love it because they're allowed to hike leash-free. The campground at Cave Lake has six sites, each available on a first-come, first-served basis. Leash your dog if anyone else is camping here. The campground is free, and is open from July to October.

From US 395 in New Pine Creek, take the unpaved Forest Service Road 2 east about six long, uphill miles. The campsites are just after the Lily Lake picnic area. (916) 233-4611. *→ See #3 on map p. 46.*

HUMBOLDT COUNTY

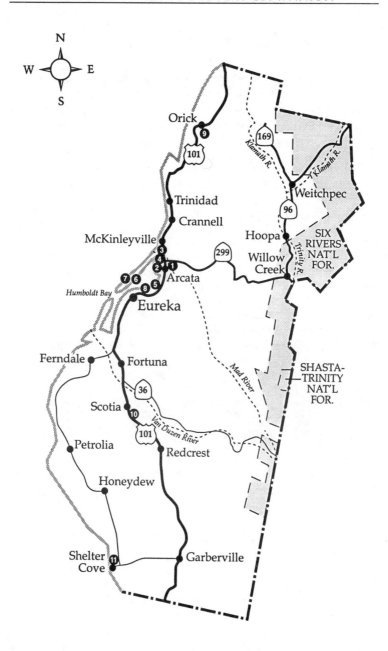

4
HUMBOLDT COUNTY

Bigfoot. Giant redwoods. Fog. Off-leash beaches. Humboldt County is home to the magical, mythical wonders of Northern California. Dogs love them all, with the possible exception of Bigfoot (see Willow Creek, page 64).

The coast here is one of the best in the state, as far as dogs are concerned. Several beaches and one 62,000-acre coastal park allow your dog to strip and go leashless.

Sun worshippers won't share a dog's excitement about the coast. If fog is a four-letter word to you, try another county, or at least drive inland a bit. The fog can be so thick in Arcata that you'll have a hard time seeing your dog on the beach. But then as you drive east on the mountainous Highway 99, the fog gives way a little at a time. As you reach higher elevations, white mist swirls around the taller trees, and on the way downhill, it's suddenly gone. You're free to frolic in the sun, but your beaches will be far behind.

If you and your dog like fishing, the Eel, Trinity and Klamath rivers offer easy roadside access at hundreds of points throughout the county. Joe always gets excited when there's a fish at the end of the line. He'll sit and watch for hours for the pleasure of witnessing the moment of truth, and if we throw the fish back, he'll sit and stare at the water, awaiting its return.

No visit to Humboldt County is complete without a drive down the Avenue of the Giants. This world-famous 31-mile scenic drive between Redway and Peppermill will take you past some of the biggest and most magnificent redwoods in the world. Just about all the adjectives for "really old" have been used to name the giants in this area. You can visit the Grandfather Tree, the Eternal Tree, and the Immortal Tree, to name a few of the elderly stars appearing on The Strip.

NATIONAL FORESTS

See the National Forests/Wilderness Areas chapter starting on page 801 for important information and safety tips for visiting national forests with your dog.

• **Six Rivers National Forest** 🐾🐾🐾🐾 🐕
See page 809.

• Trinity National Forest 🐾 🐾 🐾 🐾 🐾 ➡️ 🐕
   See page 808.

ARCATA

For a university town, Arcata is a mellow place. But dogs who want to have a wild time have ample opportunity. Although canines are not permitted in the lush green park in the old town square, they're allowed off leash at a couple of really prime areas, and on leash in a few more magical spots. For added dog pleasure, it's usually cool and foggy here, so it's a wonderful place to visit when the rest of the state is broiling.

PARKS, BEACHES & RECREATION AREAS

• Arcata Community Forest/Redwood Park 🐾 🐾 🐾 1/2
   Just a couple of minutes away from the quaint old downtown area of Arcata, this 575-acre park offers 17 trails with 10 miles of hiking for you and your leashed dog. Mornings are enchanting here. Songbirds come to life, and the earth and the redwoods smell fresh in the damp, foggy air.

From US 101, exit at Samoa Boulevard and drive east. At Union Street, go north a few blocks and make a right onto 14th Street. Drive into the forest and park in the large lot. Several trailheads start here. (707) 822-7091. → *See #1 on map p. 52.*

• Arcata Marsh and Wildlife Sanctuary 🐾 🐾 🐾 ➡️
   Formerly a sanitary landfill, this 174-acre model restoration project has three freshwater marshes, a brackish lake and one saltwater marsh. Together, they attract some 200 species of birds, as well as critters like river otters and muskrats. To add to your dog's joy, treated wastewater helps in wetlands restoration here.

Dogs must be leashed, for obvious reasons. Birdwatchers come from all over the state to view a vast array of fine feathered friends, including Iceland gulls, old-squaws, bald eagles and endangered brown pelicans. Despite Joe's exemplary behavior on a recent visit, he got the evil eye from a couple of people who were chirping to some birds hidden in a tree. I found that walking around with binoculars helps these avid folks realize you're just like them, except you have a dog who shares in the wonders of our fine feathered friends. If you've got a yapper dog, take him somewhere else.

Exit US 101 at Samoa Boulevard and drive west, following the coastal access signs. Turn left on I Street and drive about a mile. The parking lot is on your right. Once in the marsh area, bear right at the wood chip trail for the best walk possible. You can get a map and guide to the area by calling (707) 822-7091. →*See #2 on map p. 52.*

• **Clam Beach County Park** 🐾 🐾 🐾 🐾 🐕

Not only can your dog run leash-free at this long ocean beach, you can actually get here very easily from US 101! The combination is almost nonexistent in Northern California.

The beach is a good clamming area, as even your dog might have guessed from the park's name. Some dogs like to help you dig for your bivalve supper, which you can cook at the campground here. There are 12 to 14 tent sites available in sand dunes, available on a first-come, first-served basis. Sites are $8 to $10. Dogs are $1 extra.

From US 101, about 7 miles north of Arcata, take the Clam Beach Park exit west a couple of miles. (707) 445-7652. →*See #3 on map p. 52.*

• **Mad River County Park** 🐾 🐾 🐾 🐾 🐕

As you drive here past old barns and huge green fields full of grazing cows, you'll feel as though you're in the English country-side, especially if it's foggy. Dogs are delirious enough about the rural five-mile drive from Arcata. But when they behold the magnificent beach where they can run leashless, they're dumbstruck. Joe didn't talk the whole time we were there.

The beach is wide, long and desolate. Beachcombing is fun and there's plenty of driftwood to keep your dog intrigued. The only other people we've ever seen here have been old men with metal detectors, hippies who sometimes spend the night, and dedicated dog owners willing to make the labyrinthine drive from town so their pooches can experience heaven on earth.

From US 101, exit west on Giuntoli Lane and go right almost immediately onto Heindon Road. Follow the signs to the park. On the way, you'll pass one end of the Hammond Trail, a 2.2-mile hiking/biking coastal trail between Arcata and McKinleyville. It's an invigorating walk, but you have to keep your dog leashed. Once at the Mad River, you'll see a sign leading you to the right for fishing access. That's where you can launch your boat on the river, but chances are your dog would prefer to run on the beach, so keep going straight until you hit the small parking lot at the end of the road. (707) 445-7651. →*See #4 on map p. 52.*

RESTAURANTS

Hole In the Wall: This is a popular pooch hangout. The sandwiches and vegetarian dishes are very satisfying. 590 G Street; (707) 822-7407.

Michelanjelo's Pizza Parlor: Besides good pizza, pasta and sandwiches, Michelanjelo's features microbrewery beer. Eat, drink and be merry on the three maple benches outside. At 6th and H streets; (707) 822-7602.

PLACES TO STAY

Best Western Arcata Inn: Rates are $52 to $78. Dogs are $5 extra and are allowed only in smoking rooms (hack, woof). 4827 Valley West Boulevard, Arcata, CA 95521; (707) 826-0313.

Clam Beach County Park camping: See page 55.

Hotel Arcata: Dogs seem to sense the history at this refurbished 1915 hotel. When Joe visited, all he could do was stick his snout around the baseboards and snort in the scents. It's not a graceful technique, but apparently it's efficient. Rates are $45 to $120. A $100 deposit is required for dogs. 708 9th Street, Arcata, CA 95521; (707) 826-0217.

Motel 6: Rates are $28 for the first adult, $6 for the second. All Motel 6s allow one small dog per room. This one is right beside US 101, and they'll often put dogs and their human companions in the rooms closest to the highway because there's a little on-leash dog-relief area there. The constant drone of cars can actually be soothing at 3 a.m. when your dog decides to start scratching himself. 4755 Valley West Boulevard, Arcata, CA 95521; (707) 822-7061.

Quality Inn-Mad River: Medium-sized dogs are more than welcome. And there's a beach next door where leashed dogs like to roam. Rates are $38 to $76. 3535 Janes Road, Arcata, CA 95521; (707) 822-0409.

EUREKA

This is the county seat of Humboldt, and it's a bustling small city. Fortunately, it also has some Victorian charm, as well as the ocean and Humboldt Bay, so it's not a typical center of commerce.

PARKS, BEACHES & RECREATION AREAS

Dogs aren't allowed in Eureka's best city park, Sequoia Park, but that's okay. We found a couple of areas that more than make up for the loss.

•**Downtown Mini Park** 🐾

You should visit this tiny park if, and only if, you and your dog are strolling through the Victorian downtown section of Eureka and your leashed dog gives you that "If I don't find a park, we're both going to be embarrassed" look.

There's a tiny bit of grass and a modern gazebo right along Humboldt Bay. It's pretty, but it's not the place to come for exercise.

It's around L Street and Waterfront Drive, just east of the Adorni Recreation Center (which also houses the city Parks and Recreation Department). (707) 444-9792. → *See #5 on map p. 52.*

• **Samoa Boat Ramp County Park** 🐾 🐾 1/2 🐕

If you own a boat and a dog, and you've got them both with you, you'll be glad to know about this small park. Not only is there a launch ramp into the south end of Humboldt Bay, there's a small beach here so your dog can run around and stretch his legs before he becomes your crewmate during a cruise of the bay. Dogs are allowed off leash on this tiny beach, but somehow, the privilege isn't as magnificent as it would be if the Samoa Dunes Recreation Area (see below) weren't just across the street.

From Eureka, turn west on Highway 255, and cross the Samoa Bridge. Once on the Samoa Peninsula, turn left on New Navy Base Road. The park is about five miles south of the bridge, on the left side of the street. (707) 445-7651. → *See #6 on map p. 52.*

• **Samoa Dunes Recreation Area** 🐾 🐾 🐾 🐾 🐕

Does your dog like sand, sand and more sand? How does 300 acres of coastal dunes between the Pacific and Humboldt Bay sound? How about boundless, fairly calm ocean? Cool breezes year-round?

If your dog isn't salivating about this park yet, here's the clincher: Canines can run off leash on this Bureau of Land Management park! While you cast for surf perch, hunt for driftwood, hike on the nature trail or just relax and listen to the foghorns and gulls, your dog is free to run around, as long as he'll come when you call.

We learned about the vital importance of voice control when we spotted an injured duck waddling along the shore. Another dog, a retriever-type, scooped up the bird in her mouth and brought it back to her owner. Fortunately, Joe was well leashed by the time he decided he'd like to look into a duck dinner. And even more luckily, once the bird overcame its fear, it got up and continued waddling down the beach as if nothing had happened.

The retriever's owner was shocked that her dog had taken off. "She's so obedient. She always comes when I call," she explained after severely reprimanding her dog. It just goes to show that even the most obedient dogs can get out of hand in tempting situations, so even if you've got a voice control champ, keep a close eye on him when he's off leash.

This area is actually for off-highway vehicles to peruse, but we didn't see any on either of our visits. The place was deserted, except for a few beachcombers, a couple of dogs and a kayaker. But keep in mind that your peace might be shattered by the roar of engines. The drivers of these noisy vehicles may not always be aware of dogs, so make sure you and your dog are aware of them. Also be aware that cars are allowed on the beach, but they generally tend to drive very slowly. There's ample room for vehicles, people and dogs.

From Eureka, turn west on Highway 255, and cross the Samoa Bridge. Once on the Samoa Peninsula, turn left on New Navy Base Road. The park is about five miles south of the bridge, on the right side of the street. There are also several small access points along the road, but it's best to start from the main lot here. (707) 822-7648. →*See #7 on map p. 52.*

• **South Eureka Coastal Access** 🐾
The signs along US 101 might beckon you to visit, but you'll be disappointed. The beach here is tiny, narrow and very close to the road. What's more, it's right next to the Elk River Sewage Treatment Plant. Dogs might like the odd odors that waft by, but they're not generally appealing to the human olfactory system.

Dogs must be leashed. Here are the directions, in case your dog can't hold it until you get to a decent park: From US 101, go west on Hilfiker Lane, and follow the road as it veers south. A small parking area is on the right. (707) 444-9792. →*See #8 on map p. 52.*

RESTAURANTS
This often foggy city does not exactly abound with outdoor eateries.

Fresh Freeze Drive-In: You like burgers and ice cream? Tell your dog to make sure you visit this decadent place. At Harris and F streets; (707) 442-6967.

PLACES TO STAY
Eureka Inn: Dogs don't often get to stay in a national historic landmark (the Benbow Inn, page 60, is a local exception), so take advantage of the dog-friendly attitude here. From the Tudor architecture to the lobby with high beam ceilings and a fireplace, and the rooms with Queen Anne-style furnishings, the place exemplifies casual elegance. Dogs are asked to stay in the ground floor rooms. It's usually cooler there in the summer, anyway. Rates are $70 to $135. 518 7th Street, Eureka, CA 95501; (707) 442-6441 or (800) 862-4906.

Red Lion Inn: Rates are $100 to $175. There will soon be a small fee for dogs. 1929 4th Street, Eureka, CA 95501; (707) 445-0844.

Travelodge: Rates are $60 to $70. 4 4th Street, Eureka, CA 95501; (707) 443-6345 or (800) 255-3050.

FERNDALE

This sweet Victorian town is so historically and architecturally authentic that the entire village is a state historic landmark. You and your dog can savor a walk down Main Street, where you're sure to pass at least a few other dogs with their people. It's so old and refined that it looks like it could be the model for Disneyland's Main Street. If you're hungry, try one of the eateries where dogs can dine at your side on this historic street.

RESTAURANTS

Ferndale is filled with great places to eat. Most of them didn't want to publicize that they allow dogs at their outdoor tables, but here are two that didn't mind:

No Brand Burger Stand: Their logo is a steer skull. The place is located right behind the Yancey Feed Company. Is there any connection here? Eat big burgers at the picnic table here. 989 Milton Avenue; (707) 786-9474.

Red Front Store: This is a convenience store with a little bench where you and your dog can eat the little hot dogs they make inside. 577 Main Street; (707) 786-9611.

PLACES TO STAY

Ferndale Laundromat and Motel: If you have to wash some clothes while on the road, boy are you in luck! This is the only lodging in all of Ferndale that allows dogs. You can walk right out your front door and do your wash in the commercial laundry located in this long, low building.

The two rooms here are clean and very large. They were designed specifically with families in mind. Each room is actually made of two sections, with at least one bed per section. Management here will be more than happy to supply you with cribs or extra cots if you need them. The rooms are not exactly from the Ritz, but they're a good deal more comfortable than the garage and woodworking shop that used to be here.

Rates are $48 for two people. Each extra person is $5. A deposit is required for dogs. 632 Main Street, P.O. Box 337, Ferndale, CA 95536; (707) 786-9471.

GARBERVILLE

This is a town where many weary travelers with dogs pull off the road for a restful night on their way to magnificent parks in the north, south, east and west.

PLACES TO STAY

Benbow Inn: The comfort of luxurious old England pervades this fabled Tudor inn in the midst of giant redwoods. This is the last of the true English carriage house inns around, and it's designated as a national historic landmark. Some rooms have fireplaces, most have antiques and a few even have access to lush gardens. In fact, dogs are allowed only in the garden-access rooms. Although management is fond of dogs, some guests don't enjoy seeing them wander through the lobby.

You and your dog may never want to leave, especially after you've had the inn's charming afternoon tea. (Bring it to one of the outdoor tables here so you can sip with your dog at your side.) Rates are $88 to $260. The inn is two miles south of Garberville, just off US 101. 445 Lake Benbow Drive, Garberville, CA 95440; (707) 923-2124.

Benbow Lake State Recreation Area: Of the 975 acres here, dogs are relegated to the campground areas. We've seen some people fishing with their dogs down by the South Fork of the Eel River here, but rangers differ about whether or not that's okay. The park is just off US 101, about two miles south of Garberville. Follow the signs. Campsites are $12 to $14. Dogs are $1 extra. To reserve one of the 75 sites, call MISTIX at (800) 444-PARK.

Best Western Humboldt House Inn: Dogs are allowed in a few of the smoking rooms here. This is a decent place to stop if you're on a long road trip, and it's fairly earthquake resistant, if that's the kind of thing that concerns you. I stayed here one night when I was covering a big earthquake. A big old aftershock rattled everyone out of bed, but nothing fell on our heads and the front desk had plenty of flashlights to go around. Fortunately, Joe was back in safe, unshakable San Francisco, but one of the pooches who was a guest here went tearing out of his owner's room and hid until dawn. Rates are $52 to $80. 701 Redwood Drive, Garberville, CA 95542; (707) 923-2771.

ORICK

PARKS, BEACHES & RECREATION AREAS

•**Redwood National Park (south section)** 🐾 🐾 1/2
This is a very dog-friendly place, considering it's part of the very dog-restrictive National Park System. The Humboldt County segment of this 106,000-acre park actually allows dogs on a trail! But you can leave your dog's backpack at home, because she won't be needing it on the one-mile, self-guiding Lady Bird Johnson

Grove Interpretive Trail. The trail leads through a mature redwood forest to the spot where Lady Bird Johnson dedicated the national park in 1968.

In addition, dogs are allowed at the Redwood Information Center parking lot and picnic area, the Lost Man picnic area, and the undeveloped Freshwater Lagoon camping area. Sites are free and available on a first-come, first-served basis.

And of course, dogs are permitted in their usual national park haunts: on or within 100 feet of public roads and parking lots. Leashes are the mandatory attire.

From US 101, follow the signs to the park's information center, where you can pick up literature and maps. (707) 488-3461. ➔ *See #9 on map p. 52.*

PLACES TO STAY
Redwood National Park (south section) camping: See above.

REDCREST

You want redwood gifts? This is your town. The few stores in this tiny community along the Avenue of the Giants carry every redwood gift imaginable, most of no practical value. From redwood burl wall clocks to giant redwood Indians, they've got it all.

RESTAURANTS
Eternal Tree Cafe: Dine on big old redwood tables under the shade of big old redwoods. (Is this like eating a hamburger in front of a cow?) Then visit the Eternal Tree House giant redwood tree, just behind the building (see Diversions, below). 26510 Avenue of the Giants; (707) 722-4247.

LODGINGS
Redcrest Motor Inn Resort: You and your dog can spend the night in a teepee amid the giant redwoods. Dogs are not permitted in the resort's cabins, but you can pitch a tent here for $12 or stay in one of three teepees for $16. Dogs are $1 extra.

And as if staying in a teepee isn't exciting enough for your dog, you can take her to visit the resort's weekend "zoo." Here, she can see deer, sheep and pot-bellied pigs. There's no charge, but it costs 25 cents to feed the critters. Although the animals are fenced in, keep a firm grasp on your pooch's leash. 26459 Avenue of the Giants; (707) 722-4208.

DIVERSIONS
Survive the ultimate temptation: Your boy dog won't believe his eyes when he visits the Eternal Tree House, along the Avenue of the

Giants. When Joe saw this 2,500-year-old giant redwood, he tugged on his leash incessantly so he could get a closer sniff and decide what part of this tree he wanted to claim. It took all my strength to convince him not to desecrate this natural wonder. It's just one of many reasons your dog should be leashed here. The tree (there's no actual "tree house") is at 26510 Avenue of the Giants; (707) 722-4262.

SCOTIA

This small mill town is actually owned by the Pacific Lumber Company. Scotia is home to the world's largest redwood saw mill, and you can tour it for free, but someone else has to wait outside with your dog. Your dog is allowed to visit the Demonstration Forest just four miles south of town. It's much quieter than the sawmill, and the trees here are upright—the position that boy dogs prefer.

PARKS, BEACHES & RECREATION AREAS

•**Pacific Lumber Company Demonstration Forest** 🐾 🐾 🐾 🐾

This 50-acre forest just off the Avenue of the Giants is where you can learn all about native plants and trees. As you walk the two short trails here, signs explain what you see. You'll emerge from the forest enlightened and your dog will emerge refreshed.

Many dogs and people like to bring a snack and eat it at the shaded picnic tables here. Don't forget to bring an empty water bottle: The creek here has some of the best-tasting water in California.

Tempting as it may be, do not let your dog off leash. Darrell Jarman, who runs the place some summers, says an Akita recently bolted away after a deer. The dog's owners searched for hours, but never found him. There are a few roads around the perimeter of the forest, which makes it even more hazardous if your dog runs away.

The forest is open only in the summer. From US 101, take the Jordan Creek exit (about 5 miles south of Scotia) and go left. You'll see a large billboard advertising the forest. Follow the signs. (707) 764-2222. ➡ *See #10 on map p. 52.*

SHELTER COVE

This coastal community is located in the heart of the Lost Coast area of California. It's known for its pristine beauty and prime fishing. But dogs like it because it's surrounded by the King Range National Conservation Area (see page 63). Three areas of this pre-planned, privately-owned community provide ocean access. We like the Little Black Sand Beach, just off Dolphin Drive.

PARKS, BEACHES & RECREATION AREAS

• King Range National Conservation Area 🐾🐾🐾🐾 🐕 🐕

We came upon this magnificent 62,000-acre coastal area by accident, and all Joe can do is thank the Great Dog in the Sky. This primitive region, which constitutes a good chunk of the Lost Coast, has everything a dog desires deep in his heart: ocean, grassy flats, sandy beaches, trees galore and best of all—leash-free living.

In less than a three-mile stretch, the King Range rises from sea level to 4,087 feet. The topography is rugged, but far from impassable. Several trails take you across some of the most unspoiled coastal territory in California.

A few Indiana Jones-like dogs can handle the 35-mile wilderness trek along the Lost Coast Trail. Most of the trail is along the beach, and in the mornings you'll likely come to know one of the reasons this area is called the Lost Coast. The fog sometimes gets so thick that even the gulls are silent. But when it lifts, what spectacular sights you'll see! You and your dog will traverse green meadows, Douglas fir groves and many streams. The terrain is fairly flat, so the real challenge is its length, if you should choose to hike the entire trail. Don't forget, there's always the walk back! Most people prefer to leave a car at one end to make the round-trip easier.

Joe is the kind of dog who prefers trails like the Lightning Trail. It's the shortest and shadiest route to King's Peak. Joe approves of the sparkling mountain streams, the shade from the firs and the brushy meadowland where he can roll like a fool. He especially likes the trail's length—a mere two-and-a-half miles. The view from the top is hard to beat.

You may camp anywhere you please, but you need a permit for campfires. Dogs must be leashed in designated campgrounds. It's a good idea to leash your dog at night anyway. Many dogs feel even safer in your tent.

During your hikes, you may run into deer, cattle, sheep, horses, rattlesnakes and poison oak, so if you let your dog off leash, do so only if she's under excellent voice control. And be sure to keep your pooch very far away from the marine mammals who clamber onto the beaches and rocks. This is a popular rookery, and dogs and sea critters do not mix.

Exit US 101 at Redway and follow Briceland Thorne Road west to this Bureau of Land Management area. For more specific directions to your exact destination in this sprawling conservation area, contact the Bureau of Land Management, Arcata Resource Area, 1125 16th Street, P.O. Box 1112, Arcata, CA 95521; (707) 822-7648.
➡ See #11 on map p. 52.

PLACES TO STAY

King Range National Conservation Area camping: See page 63.

TRINIDAD

PLACES TO STAY

Bishop Pine Lodge: Sleep among the pines and redwoods with all the comforts of home. You can have a kitchenette here so you don't have to worry about dining out with the dog. And if you're feeling a little paunch coming on from your good cooking, you can work it off in the exercise room. Better yet, check out the nearby Trinidad State Beach. Dogs have to be leashed, and it's not exactly a monstrous place, but it's good for a romp. Room rates at the lodge are $50 to $95. Dogs are $5 extra. 1481 Patricks Point Drive, Trinidad, CA 95570; (707) 677-3314.

WILLOW CREEK

Nestled along the banks of the wild and scenic Trinity River, this rustic community boasts that it's the gateway to Bigfoot Country. People in these parts frequently report seeing Bigfoot, a.k.a. Sasquatch—a man-like, 700-pound hairy creature who's seven to nine feet tall and reputedly has body odor.

I'm not sure what Joe would do if he came across Bigfoot, but since he slunk backwards with his tail between his legs when he saw the statue of Bigfoot in the center of town, it probably wouldn't be one of his prouder moments.

Willow Creek is surrounded by Six Rivers National Forest, where dogs can run around off leash. Stop at the Chamber of Commerce here and pick up maps of the forests and explanations of the available trails. The town is at Highways 255 and 96, about an hour west of Arcata.

RESTAURANTS

Lou's Family Restaurant: Dogs like to watch you dine on the big, hot breakfasts the folks here serve you at the outdoor tables. 39116 Highway 299; (916) 629-2404.

Wimpy's Burgers: Munch with your dog at this old-fashioned ice cream parlor and fast-food joint. At the junction of Highways 299 and 96; (916) 629-2092.

FESTIVALS

Bigfoot Days: Bigfoot is guaranteed to make an appearance once a year in Willow Creek and thousands witness the phenomenon at this Labor Day weekend bash in the center of town. So what if the

Bigfoot who leads the parade is just a man in hairy clothing? Dogs still are wowed by the sight. Beware: It can get very hot this time of year. Depending on the day's temperatures, you may want to leave your fuzzy friend at home. Call (916) 629-2693 for more information.

TRINITY COUNTY

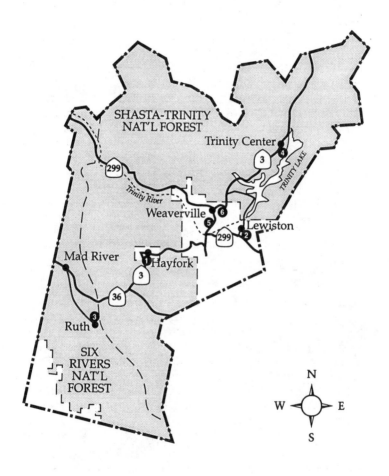

5
TRINITY COUNTY

Think about this place we call Dog Heaven. What are some of the ingredients your dog would desire in his Elysian ideal? Besides having you at his side without a leash, he'd want lots of trees, that's for sure. Rivers. Lakes. The scents of nature and rich earth. And maybe some decaying woodland critter to roll on.

Trinity County has all a dog could ever want in heaven or on earth. Joe even managed to find a decaying woodland critter when we last visited, and he rolled all over it and then came running up to me to spread the good news all over my jeans. When I walked into a store to buy some supplies later that day, the clerk and all the customers started asking each other if they smelled a mighty bad stench. I joined them in wrinkling my nose and nodding my head, praying no one would figure out my guilt until I was long gone.

The county has a couple of charming old towns, but the real charm here for dogs and their people is that more than 90 percent of the land is part of the national forest system. When driving from just about any location to just about any other location in the county (other than the few main towns on the east side), there are countless places where you can pull over your car and take your obedient dog for a leash-free hike. As long as you're in a national forest and away from houses and developed areas, it's generally okay.

While here, you mustn't miss the magnificent Trinity Alps. You'll feel as if you're in Switzerland, only your dog won't have to be quarantined for six months! The only papers you'll need to hike the Trinity Alps Wilderness is a permit from the U.S. Forest Service. See page 808 (Shasta Trinity National Forest appendix) for more information on this spectacular area.

NATIONAL FORESTS

See the National Forests/Wilderness Areas chapter starting on page 801 for important information and safety tips for visiting national forests with your dog.

- **Shasta-Trinity National Forest** 🐾 🐾 🐾 🐾 🍖 🐕
  See page 808.
- **Six Rivers National Forest** 🐾 🐾 🐾 🐾 🍖 🐕
  See page 809.

HAYFORK

PARKS, BEACHES & RECREATION AREAS

•**Hayfork Park** 🐾 🐾 1/2

The spreading oak trees are enough to make a grown dog quiver with joy. Humans adults love to lounge in the shade of the trees' canopies or stroll across the park to visit the historic schoolhouse here. Kids love the pool, the playground and the tennis courts. Dogs like the grass, but they're not fond of the leashes they must wear. The park is at Community Drive and Highway 3. (916) 623-1319. ➡ *See #1 on map p. 68.*

LEWISTON

This is a tiny old mining town that has so few tourists, you'll think you're in a time warp.

What's really great about a visit to Lewiston is that there's plenty of access to the Trinity River. Just look around and it's there. The area off Rush Creek Road at Lewiston Road is a popular access point.

PARKS, BEACHES & RECREATION AREAS

•**Community Park** 🐾

You may as well take your dog on a walking tour of this quaint town, because you'll definitely cover more land, and you'll surely see more grass, trees and bushes than you will in this small park. It's a pretty spot for humans, but only about one of its two acres is accessible right now. Dogs may find it a little restricting, but if your leashed dog just needs to stretch her legs, it's not a bad place to set a spell.

The park is on Lewiston Road at Viola Lane. The park is entirely a volunteer effort by the residents of this small community, so there's no phone number for it. ➡ *See #2 on map p. 68.*

RESTAURANTS

The Hitchin' Post: Buy your nightcrawlers here and have a bite to eat at this charming old house, chock full of outdoor tables. The place doesn't serve food at all in the winter. At the Lewiston Turnpike and Deadwood Road, in historic Lewiston; (916) 778-3486.

RUTH

PARKS, BEACHES & RECREATION AREAS

•**Ruth Lake** 🐾 🐾 🐾

Ruth Lake doesn't need to go on a diet—it's skinny enough. On a map or from the air, it looks like an eight-mile-long caterpillar.

But seen in person, it's an attractive lake surrounded by alpine lands. Dogs have to be leashed here, but they have a good time following you around from the campsites to the lake. Plenty of dogs go fishing in their people's boats. Some anglers say their dogs bring them good luck. There are plenty of trout here and even some black bass.

The lake is actually a reservoir, created by the Mad River being dammed. In good times, it's about 1,200 surface acres. The Six Rivers National Forest has hundreds of thousands of off-leash acreage not far from here. Call the ranger district office at (707) 574-6233. Unfortunately, at the moment there are no trails close to the lake. But Ranger Steve Pollard says he recently discovered a very rundown trail that was used by pioneers back in the late 1800s. If the U.S. Forest Service can clean it up and make it hikeable again, dogs will be allowed, but only on leash.

The trail would be accessible from both campgrounds here. Sites at the Bailey Canyon Campground are $5. That campground is about 13 miles southeast of the town of Mad River on Lower Mad River Road. The Fir Cove Campground is just 12 miles southeast of Mad River. Sites there are $5. The campgrounds are open from May to mid-October. Call the ranger district at (707) 574-6233 for details. →See #3 on map p. 68.

PLACES TO STAY
Bailey Canyon Campground: See above.
Fir Cove Campground: See above.

TRINITY CENTER
This tiny community is the home, in spirit if nothing else, of the giant and breathtaking Trinity Lake. It's also quite close to the breathtaking Trinity Alps Wilderness, where dogs can hoof it off leash (see page 808).

PARKS, BEACHES & RECREATION AREAS
• Trinity Lake 🐾 🐾 🐾 🐾 🍖 🐕
Even the national forest staff here call this place dog heaven. One dog-friendly ranger told me, "You just take your boat, pull up to just about any bank, and say, 'Okay, Fido, let's get a little exercise. No leashes required!'"

And he's right. While its 145 miles of shoreline have no real trails, there are still plenty of places where your dog can stretch his unleashed body. The lake is quite low of late and it's probably going to remain that way. The folks who decide such things have deemed that, for flood purposes, the lake should be 20 feet lower than the past norm. That means that except for some steep banks and developed areas, there's plenty of romping room for dogs.

Your best bet is to take your dog to the more remote parts of the lake. And the best way to get there is by boat. If you don't have one, why not rent one? And what better boat to rent than a houseboat? (See Diversions, page 73 for details on this great adventure.)

Mid-June to mid-July is the best time of year to come here. Snow still covers the peaks of the glorious Trinity Alps (which you can see in all their glory from almost anywhere on the lake), but the weather here is great. So is the fishing. It's not nearly as crowded as Lake Shasta to the west, so you can fish without worrying about too many loud jetskiers or fast boats.

The south end of the lake is 14 miles north of Weaverville on Highway 3. Call the Shasta-Trinity National Forest District Office at (916) 623-2121 for more details and suggestions on which area would best suit your purposes. → *See #4 on map p. 68.*

PLACES TO STAY

There are campgrounds all around Trinity Lake. Most are concentrated on the lake's south side, but a couple of the more secluded ones are toward the north. Below we've listed one on each side of the lake. Call the Shasta-Cascade Wonderland Association at (916) 243-2643 for more information on cabins and other lakeside lodgings.

Cedar Stock Resort: This is a great place to enjoy a vacation at Trinity Lake. The cabins are rented by the week, with costs ranging from $325 to $725. Dogs are $35 a week extra. Just bring your own bedding and you'll be set. The kitchen and utensils are all part of the deal. The resort is 15 miles north of Weaverville on Highway 3. The mailing address is HCR 1, Box 510, Lewiston, CA 96052; (916) 286-2225 or (800) 982-2279.

Clark Springs Campground: There are enough lakeside sites to make everyone happy. An added bonus for boaters: There's a boat ramp that's just a stick's throw away. Sites are $5, first come, first served. Dogs must be leashed. From Weaverville, drive 18 miles north on Highway 3. The campground is at Mule Creek Station. (916) 623-2121.

Jackass Springs Campground: This one's a rustic and fairly secluded campground with 22 sites on the northeast section of the lake. There's no fee, so you can buy your leashed pooch a bone with the money you save. All sites are first come, first served.

This is not the kind of place you want to visit for just one night. The ride itself may make you want to stay for the rest of your life or be airlifted out. From Highway 299, turn north on Trinity Mountain Road (west of Whiskeytown Lake) and drive about 12 miles to the Trinity Mountain Station. Turn right and drive about 12 miles on East Side Road—it's gravel, so be ready for some hopping around. At Delta Road (it's dirt), go left and drive about three more miles to the campground. It's actually worth the drive to get away from the more crowded southeast side. (916) 623-2121.

Ripple Creek Cabins: The Trinity River runs right by these cozy, homey cabins. You'll have no shortage of outdoor adventures to share with your dog here. Rates are $60 to $100. Dogs are charged a $10 one-time fee. Box 3899, Star Route 2, Trinity Center, CA 96091; (916) 266-3505.

DIVERSIONS

Float in a houseboat: Wow! This is one adventure your dog will never forget. Renting a houseboat is the ultimate way of staying with your dog on vacation. As long as you pull up to shore enough for her to get plenty of exercise and do her thing, she's going to be one happy pooch. Remember that the lake is pretty much surrounded by national forest land, where your dog can exercise leash-free. Make sure you keep an eye on her, though, and don't forget about her while you're inside making a soufflé.

Houseboats can be small and simple or large and fairly luxurious. (Okay, okay, they usually do look like mobile homes, but they are comfortable.) Chances are pretty good that you don't already own your own houseboat, but fear not. There are plenty of places to rent them in the area.

One of the largest and most dog-friendly is the Cedar Stock Resort. "Dogs are just as much a part of the family as everyone else. They can't miss a vacation like this," says Steve, one of the resort's managers. Bringing a dog along will cost you $35 extra per week. The houseboats here run from $825 to $2,300 weekly. You may want to invite some friends along to share the costs. The smaller ones fit up to six folks and the larger ones can stash all your relatives.

The Cedar Stock Resort's houseboat headquarters is 15 miles north of Weaverville on Highway 3. The mailing address is HCR 1, Box 510, Lewiston, CA 96052; (916) 286-2225 or (800) 982-2279. For other houseboat rental companies, call the Trinity County Chamber of Commerce at (916) 623-6101. Be sure to reserve early. Sometimes all the houseboats for the summer are booked by April!

WEAVERVILLE

This is the gateway to the Trinity Alps, and what a gateway it is. It's a former boomtown with a Main Street that's almost unchanged from the 1850s, complete with spiral staircases and brick facades.

Some 2,500 Chinese immigrants were among the miners who came here during the Gold Rush. The Joss House State Historic Park contains the oldest active Chinese temple in California. Dogs aren't allowed inside, but as you're driving to the adjacent Lee Fong Park (see below) on Main Street, you can take a gander at it.

Plans are in the works to create an integrated trail around the periphery of Weaverville. When it's done, it will be an excellent way to explore the town with your leashed dog. Call the Trinity County Chamber of Commerce at (916) 623-6101 or the Shasta Trinity National Forest ranger station at (916) 623-2121 for updates.

PARKS, BEACHES & RECREATION AREAS

• **Lee Fong Park** 🐾 🐾 🐾 1/2 🐾

Set on the land once owned and farmed by a prominent local Chinese family, this magnificent park still has the appeal of an old-time farm. It even has several apple and pear trees that still bear fruit—but don't steal from the branches. (We were told that it's okay to pick up a piece of fruit from the ground, though.)

The park is undeveloped and fairly large. It's far from the paved road, but leashes are the law here anyway. A dirt path will take you around the park's perimeter in about 10 minutes if you want a fast walk, but most people who come here like to stop and smell the fresh and fruity air. You can pretend it's your own orchard, and chances are good that no other park user will stop by and ruin your fantasy. For some reason, the place gets very little use.

Dogs seem to love this park. Joe and Bill had a field day sniffing the freshly fallen fruit and checking out what was lurking in the tall grass. Each walked away with a fairly mushy apple in his mouth.

The park is on Main Street/Highway 299 just south of the historic part of town. It will be on your right as you're driving south. Although a small sign points to the park, the bigger farmers market sign is actually a better landmark. Turn right and drive a few hundred feet to the dirt parking lot. When you see the bathroom in front of you and the old ranch house on your left past some trees, you'll know you're in the right place. (916) 623-5925.
➤ *See #5 on map p. 68.*

• **Lowden Park** 🐾 🐾 1/2

Dogs who like big pine trees like Lowden Park. The park has playing fields, playgrounds and an area where you don't have to do anything at all. Its edges are lined by pines and a tall fence. Dogs have to be leashed, but it's good to know that if they pull the leash from your hands, they'll still be pretty safe from traffic.

From Highway 3 in the north part of town, go south on Washington Street. The park will be on your left in about a block. (916) 623-1319. → *See #6 on map p. 68.*

RESTAURANTS

Alan's Oak Pit: Come here and get just about anything that can possibly be barbecued. 1324 Nugget Lane; (916) 623-2182.

Burger Mine: They really like dogs here. 1104 Main Street; (916) 623-5182.

Dockins Drive-In: You can sit at the outdoor area here, or pretend you're living back in the 1950s and be served at your car. Joe likes the latter technique, but I think he's just hoping to see a waitress in a poodle skirt. 796 Main Street; (916) 623-4585.

The Gooseberry Cafe: If your dog isn't a beggar, he can join you at the outdoor tables for some "grass-roots cooking," as the folk here describe it. The menu's never the same from day to day, but you can be sure the food's always delicious. There's usually even something for vegetarians. 233 Center Street; (916) 623-4666.

LaGrange Cafe: If it's crowded, they won't let your dog join you at the outdoor tables here. But otherwise, good dogs are welcome to watch you eat the kind of traditional American food you probably ate as a kid. 315 North Main Street; (916) 623-5325.

The Mustard Seed Cafe: There's one word for this place, and it's—I hate to say it—cute! This small yellow house has a wonderful patio where only the most well-behaved dogs are permitted. The food here is extremely tasty, with omelettes, Belgian waffles and seven-grain cereals topping our list of breakfast favorites. If you're a vegetarian, you'll be in heaven here. 52 Main Street; (916) 623-2922.

PLACES TO STAY

49er Motel: Rates are $30 to $40. 718 Main Street, Weaverville, CA 96093; (916) 623-4937.

SHASTA COUNTY

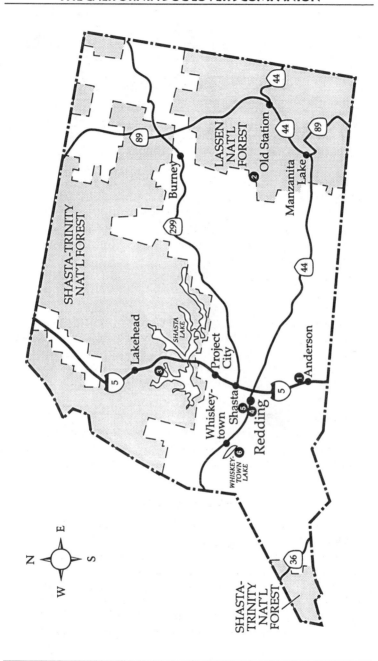

6
SHASTA COUNTY

If you and your dog are aching to get away from city life, have we got a county for you! See that leash draped over your banister? You'll have to bring it, but you won't have to use it much.

Between the national forests here, a state forest and even a small city park, your obedient pooch can get all the leash-free exercise she needs. She'll go home with a wide grin on her snout. Your snout will be smiling, too.

NATIONAL FORESTS

See the National Forests/Wilderness Areas chapter starting on page 801 for important information and safety tips for visiting national forests with your dog.

• **Lassen National Forest**
See page 805.

• **Shasta-Trinity National Forest**
The forest pretty much surrounds beautiful, fish-filled Shasta Lake (see page 82). If it's not too snowy before Christmas, you and your dog can pay $8 and go find yourselves a Christmas tree. Not many people have hundreds of thousands of acres of Christmas tree lots. See page 808 for more information on this forest.

NATIONAL PARKS

• **Lassen Volcanic National Park**
Dogs are barely allowed to set paw in this fascinating park. For more details on what you and your dog are not missing if you stay away from this national park, see the description on page 91 in the Lassen County chapter.

ANDERSON

PARKS, BEACHES & RECREATION AREAS

• **Anderson River Park** 1/2
This 425-acre park has plenty of trees for boy dogs with bottomless bladders. Dogs seem to like the one-mile nature trail better than anything, except for the sweet little pond full of ducks. The ducks would like to remind you that dogs must be leashed here.

For the humans in the crowd, the park has picnic tables and a playground. The park is on Rupert Road at the Sacramento River.

Driving south on Interstate 5, exit at the North Street off-ramp and follow North Street north a few blocks to Stingy Lane. Turn right and drive a few blocks to Rupert Road, where you'll turn left. Drive to the end and you'll be at the park. (916) 378-6656. →*See #1 on map p. 78.*

PLACES TO STAY
Best Western Knights Inn: Only lap dogs are allowed to stay here, and no—your 80-pound snugly mutt won't be exempted, no matter how many times he's tried to squeeze onto your lap. Rates are $40 to $54. A dog deposit is required. 2688 Gateway Drive, Anderson, CA 96007; (916) 365-2753.

BURNEY
This scenic mountain community is an excellent place to get away from urban life without getting carried away with the idea. There's enough civilization here to please even the primmest poodle.

PARKS, BEACHES & RECREATION AREAS
You won't find many community-style parks in these parts. What you will find are forests everywhere—many thousands of acres. Much of the surrounding land is public land, and people and their pooches just have to pull off the road for a fun little hike. But make sure you're not treading on private property first. Just ask around town, and you'll get so much help from the dog-friendly folks here that you'll have a hard time deciding which piece of dog heaven to visit.

For a great hiking experience in a place with well-defined dog rules (off leash!) and boundaries, take your dog to the Latour Demonstration State Forest.

• **Latour Demonstration State Forest** 🐾 🐾 🐾 🐾 🐕
This 9,033-acre forest provides sweeping vistas of the Cascade Range. The 67 miles of logging roads are open to people and their leash-free pooches. But don't take your dog off leash unless she's 101-percent obedient: The park is home to bobcats and mountain lions and bears (oh my!). "Be careful, because dogs are real tasty tidbits to bears," says Dan Higgins, assistant manager of the forest.

Firs, pines, mountain shrubs and delicate wildflowers abound. You don't have to stay on the logging roads to enjoy the forest. Because of the sustainable-yield forestry practiced here, it's not a dense forest. "You can just pick out a creek and follow it all day and have a magnificent time," says Higgins.

And camping is terrific—it's fairly primitive, and the biggest campground has two sites. All told, there are 14 sites for tents, each first come, first served. Better yet, there's no fee. The forest is off-limits through the winter, unless your dog knows how to use a snowmobile. From Highway 299 just west of Burney, drive south on Tamarack Road. In about 10 miles, Tamarack will fork. Take the road that keeps going straight, Jack's Backbone Road/Road 16. In about six more miles, you'll see a sign for the forest. Turn right and drive to the forest headquarters to pick up a map. The park is also accessible from Redding. Call for directions. (916) 225-2435. ➜ *See #2 on map p. 78.*

RESTAURANTS
Alpine Drive-In: The beef is here. Eat a hamburger at the outdoor tables with your pooch. 37148 Main Street; (916) 335-2211.

Web's Drive-In: Share a hamburger at the picnic tables of this family-run business. 36879 Main Street; (916) 335-3221.

PLACES TO STAY
Charm Motel: Rates are $46 to $75. Dogs are $5 extra. 37363 Main Street, Burney, CA 96013; (916) 335-2254.

Latour Demonstration State Forest camping: See above.

McArthur-Burney Falls Memorial State Park: This park is home to the breathtaking 129-foot Burney Falls, which Theodore Roosevelt once dubbed "the eighth wonder of the world." Dogs can get a glimpse of this wonder from a point at the top of the falls, next to the parking lot. But since they can't go on any trails here, this is the only area where you and your dog can *ooh* and *ahh* at the falls.

Fortunately, you can camp at one of the park's 128 sites with your pooch. Rates are $12 to $14. Dogs are $1 extra. From Burney, drive about five miles northeast on Highway 299, and go north on Highway 89 about another six miles to the park. Call MISTIX at (800) 444-PARK for reservations. For park information, call (916) 335-2777.

FESTIVALS
Burney Basin Days: If your dog is so ugly that even Rodney Dangerfield would be speechless, enter him in this festival's Ugly Dog Contest. The contest is part of the weekend-long celebration around July 4. Call (916) 335-2111 for details.

LAKEHEAD

PARKS, BEACHES & RECREATION AREAS

• Shasta Lake 🐾 🐾 🐾 🐾 ⬤➤ ✂

At 29,500 acres, this is California's largest man-made lake. If you and your dog fish, swim or watch waterfowl, you'll be in heaven here. When full, it has 370 miles of shoreline—more than San Francisco Bay.

The lake is surrounded by national forest land. More than 30 miles of trails travel into the nearby forest, and once you're away from civilization and campsites, your dog can throw his leash to the wind. Depending on where you hike, you'll pass all kinds of natural wonders, from wooded flats and secluded creeks to rocky mountains and gushing waterfalls. Keep in mind that even though this is a northern lake location, it can still get mighty toasty in the summer, so try to bring your dog here at some cooler time of year.

The U.S. Forest Service manages 380 sites at 22 campgrounds. Some are very primitive, while others seem like mini-motels. Sites cost from $7 to $12. The lake is one of the few in California where you and your dog can camp along the shore. If your pooch has been extra good, he deserves to "ruff" it at one of these sites. (Note: Starting in the summer of 1994, reservations through a private concessionaire will be required at all campgrounds. As we went to press, this concessionaire had not yet been selected. Call the Forest Service at (916) 275-1587 for information on how to reserve a campsite.)

A first visit to the lake can be a confusing experience. The lake has so many arms and so many trails that it's hard to know where to go. The trails at Jones Valley, Packers Bay, Bailey Cove, Shasta Dam and Hirz Bay not only make for excellent woodland hiking, but provide good access to shoreline fishing. (The lake can get very crowded during the summer, so be prepared to sacrifice solitude for the sounds of waterskiers and jetskiers.)

There's also such a wide variety of campsites that it can make your head ache just thinking about the possibilities. And who needs that just before a four-paw vacation?

Here's a suggestion: Get a map or a brochure of the lake, and a little advice from a ranger. The folks at the visitors center are very helpful, but you may find them insisting that your dog must be leashed everywhere in the forest. As of this printing, that's just not true. To get to the visitors center, take the Mountain Gate-Wonderland Boulevard exit off Interstate 5 about four miles south of the lake. Follow the signs. The number there is (916) 275-1587. The

Forest Service supervisor's phone is (916) 246-5222. The folks there will have the latest on the leash/leashless law. ➜*See #3 on map p. 78.*

PLACES TO STAY

The area has numerous places to park your pooch for the night. Around here, they're called resorts, but please don't start thinking of Beverly Hills spas and lush oceanside luxury suites. The resorts here are usually rustic, wooden lakeside cabins. They make wonderful retreats after a long day at the lake. And many are surrounded by great hiking land. We're listing just a couple here, but the Shasta Cascade Wonderland Association can provide you with more. Call the dog-friendly folks there at (800) 326-6944.

Antlers Resort & Marina: You and your down-to-earth dog will love the modern housekeeping cabins set amid the tall pines. The cabins have porches overlooking the lake and marina, and many have fireplaces. The rates for these completely furnished cabins run from $90 to $170 per day. Dogs are $10 extra. During the peak season, cabins are rented by the week. Rates are $630 to $1,190. The mailing address is P.O. Box 140, Lakehead, CA 96051-0140. There's no street address, but you can find the place by exiting Interstate 5 at the Antlers Road exit and driving east to Antlers Road (just past the Shell station). At Antlers Road, turn right and drive to the end of the street. (916) 238-2553 or (800) 238-3924.

O'Banion's Sugarloaf Cottages Resort: The comfortably furnished cottages here are just a frisbee's-throw from the lake. We've really enjoyed our sojourns to these modern-but-cozy cabins. If you visit at the right time, you'll be stunned at the peace and quiet. We stayed here once in April, and boy was it ever quiet. Of course, it was freezing cold and pouring rain, so maybe that had something to do with it. But the comfy cabins were sure good to come home to after a long day of wet outdoor fun.

Daily rates from Labor Day to Memorial Day are $59 to $122. During the rest of the year, the cabins must be rented by the week, and they cost from $570 to $1,388. 19667 Lakeshore Drive, Lakehead, CA 96051; (916) 238-2448.

Shasta Lake camping: See page 82.

DIVERSIONS

Leave the doggone Dramamine behind: Life on the waters of Shasta Lake is bliss for anyone of the seasick persuasion. The best way to experience this calm, flat body of water is to rent a houseboat for a few days. The only thing that may make you nauseated is having to go home at the end of your floating vacation.

Most houseboats aren't terribly attractive on the outside (unless you have a predilection for the mobile-home look), and they're not fast or exciting, but they're so much fun that you may wish you could stay forever. Imagine waking up in a secluded cove in the morning, taking your dog off the boat for a lakeside hike and a brief swim, and then sitting down to a big breakfast cooked in your boat's well-equipped kitchen before setting off to cruise around the lake. (Joe, the landlubbing Airedale, says pass the bacon but forget about the swim.)

Several local houseboat outfits permit pooches on their boats. Rates start at about $650 a week, but are generally considerably more. Although houseboats are meant to be shared with friends, you won't want to fill the boat to capacity if you're bringing your dog along. Two people and a dog on a boat that sleeps six gives you plenty of paw room.

Three dog-friendly houseboat renters: Antlers Resort, (916) 238-2553 or (800) 238-3924; Holiday Harbor, (800) 776-BOAT; and Jones Valley Resort, (916) 275-7950.

PROJECT CITY

It's a terrible name for a town, but it's a great place for a dam. Visit it with your leashed pooch.

PLACES TO STAY

Shasta Dam El Rancho Motel: Rates are $26 to $36. Dogs cost $5 extra. 1529 Cascade Boulevard, Project City, CA 96079; (916) 275-1065.

REDDING

It may be full of franchise motels and restaurant chains, but this city is the hub of the northern reaches of California. It's an excellent base for exploring the surrounding wildlands.

PARKS, BEACHES & RECREATION AREAS

Dogs have their own park here and they're allowed to hike on the Sacramento River Trail. Other than that, city parks are off-limits to pooches.

•**Benton Airpark Park** 🐾🐾🐾🐾 🐕

Joe's eyes opened wide and he stood utterly still for a few moments when he first saw this park. Somehow, although there were no dogs in it at the time, it seemed he could tell that this was a place of great dog happiness. He sniffed that joyous dog smell in the air, his tail started twitching and he began pawing the gate to get in.

Once inside this large, completely fenced dog park, he rolled for several minutes. He rolled underneath the cold aluminum picnic table. He rolled on the mud around the water fountain. He rolled in the grass on the park's east side, and then in the grass on the west side. He only stopped rolling when another dog came in to share the park with him. They chased each other around like fiends for 30 seconds. Then he started rolling again, this time on the grass in the north side of the park. He was in heaven.

Most dogs who come here find it to be pooch paradise. They can tear around off leash, stop for a drink and tear around again. Or they can just walk around and smell the grass without the tug of a leash. The fact that there are only a couple of small trees here doesn't seem to bother them. If they want shade, they can go under the picnic tables. If they need to lift a leg, there's always a fencepost.

From Interstate 5, exit at Highway 299 and go west for about two miles, following Highway 299 through a couple of turns in central Redding. At Walnut Street, turn left. Drive five blocks, and turn right on Placer Street. You'll see the park in one block, at the corner of Placer Street and Airpark Drive, adjacent to the Benton Airpark airport (whose airplane activity provides amusement for bird dogs here). (916) 225-4095. → *See #4 on map p. 78.*

• **Sacramento River Trail** 🐾 🐾 🐾 1/2 🐾

This 5.7-mile paved trail follows the wide and wonderful Sacramento River, leading you and your leashed dog through riparian riverside terrain and rolling hills. It's best to visit on weekdays or uncrowded weekends, because on some days your dog can get the feeling of being mighty squished with the masses who like to hike and bike through here.

Bill loves to take a dip in the water when we visit. He could lay in the Sacramento all day, but he hates the idea that he's missing out on sniffing the scents left by other dogs. When he's in the river, he's constantly looking to see who passes on the trail. When he's on the trail, he always keeps one eye on the beckoning river. It's a real doggy dilemma, but he manages.

From Market Street/Highway 273, go west on Riverside Drive (just south of the river). Head west to the parking area. There are many other access points. Call (916) 225-4095 for details. See Diversions for a couple of the dog-oriented events that take place here every year. → *See #5 on map p. 78.*

RESTAURANTS

Between the Bun: You and your pooch are welcome on the veranda of this aptly-named burger joint. 1718 Placer Street; (916) 243-2449.

Damburger: You and your favorite dog can sit on the patio and eat their classic burgers. The place has been here since 1938. 1320 Placer Street; (916) 241-0136.

Harpo's Deli and Grill: Build your own sandwich here from a wide variety of cold cuts and cheeses. Stop for a few minutes to dine on the patio on your way to the lake. 1970 Eureka Way; (916) 241-2490.

Hill o' Beans: Eat good croissant sandwiches and wash them down with hot coffee at the outdoor patio here. 1804 Park Marina Drive; (916) 246-8852.

Italian Cottage: They love having dogs as guests on the patio of this funky Italian restaurant. "We'll even sneak him a meatball if we have extras toward the end of the night," one very dog-friendly waitress told me. Although the floor inside the restaurant is covered with sawdust, dogs must remain outside. The restaurant is located next to hotel row. 1630 Hilltop Drive; (916) 221-6433.

Judy's Espresso: Share a chair and a bite to eat with your dog at the outdoor area of this little cafe. 1100 Hartnell; (916) 223-6500.

Slender Treat: "Dietary but tasty," says Wes, the chef. He takes great pride in creating delicious low-calorie, low-fat and low-or-no-sugar/salt meals. Eat one at the outdoor tables with your healthy pooch at your side. 2633 Park Marina Drive; (916) 243-8830.

PLACES TO STAY

Best Western Hospitality House: Rates are $42 to $49. Dogs require a $25 deposit. 532 North Market Street, Redding, CA 96003; (916) 241-6464.

Best Western Ponderosa Inn: Rates are $40 to $53. Small pooches only, please. 2220 Pine Street, Redding, CA 96001; (916) 241-6300.

La Quinta Inn: Rates are $59 to $79. 2180 Hilltop Drive, Redding, CA 96002; (916) 221-8200.

Motel 6: One small pooch per room is permitted. Rates are $34 for the first adult, $6 for the second. 1640 Hilltop Drive, Redding, CA 96002; (916) 221-1800.

Park Terrace Inn: Rates are $60 to $83. 1900 Hilltop Drive, Redding, CA 96002; (916) 221-7500.

Red Lion Inn: As long as your dog isn't of the Great Dane/Saint Bernard size, she's welcome here. Rates are $80 to $115. 1830 Hilltop Drive, Redding, CA 96002; (916) 221-8700.

DIVERSIONS

Jog your dog: Each April, the city sponsors a canine run along the Sacramento River Trail. Leashed dogs have a choice of running three miles or 5.7 miles. Most prefer the three-mile course. Water and treats are ample rewards for a jog well done. For entry information and exact dates, call (916) 225-4095.

Bless your dog, then take a hike: This terrific doggy day in early October starts with a nondenominational Blessing of the Animals, honoring St. Francis (your dog's patron saint). Then it's off for a one-mile strut or a three-mile stroll along the Sacramento River Trail. Your dog will get plenty of water along the way. Afterward, join the rest of the leashed pooches for a slew of post-walk activities, including flyball, obedience and agility demonstrations. Call the Haven Humane Society at (916) 241-1653 for entry info and dates.

WHISKEYTOWN

PARKS, BEACHES & RECREATION AREAS

• **Whiskeytown Lake** 🐾 🐾 🐾 1/2

Many miles of trails await you and your leashed, four-legged beast at this 42,500-acre segment of the Whiskeytown-Shasta-Trinity National Recreation unit. The lake has 36 miles of shoreline for great fishing and paw dipping, but most dogs seem to like to hang out here with all four feet planted on terra firma.

The short Shasta Divide Nature Trail, the three-mile Davis Gulch Trail and many miles of unimproved backcountry trails beckon dogs who like to wake up and smell the earth. You can get a map and a little advice from a ranger about your hiking options. For pooches who like to sleep in all day, the camping here is divine. Sites range in price from free to $10. There's no day-use fee.

From Redding, drive about eight miles west on Highway 299. The information center and overlook is at Highway 299 and Kennedy Memorial Drive. It's not far from Dog Gulch, in case your dog was asking. (916) 246-1225. ➡ *See #6 on map p. 78.*

PLACES TO STAY

Whiskeytown Lake: See above for camping information.

LASSEN COUNTY

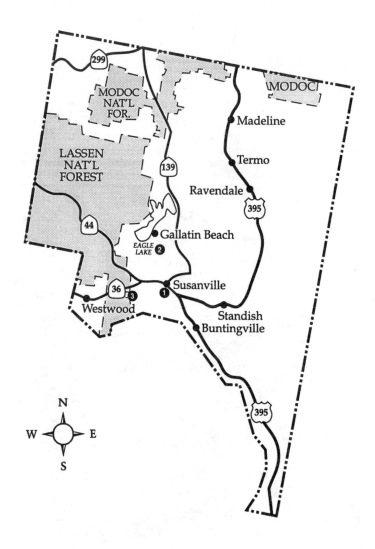

7

LASSEN COUNTY

There's not much civilization around here, so you and your dog will have to be content with hiking, camping or cross-country skiing. Blue skies, crystal lakes, rugged mountains and silent deserts await you, so it's not a bad fate—unless your teacup poodle is absolutely longing to visit a really *nouvelle* sushi joint.

The county is home to six state wildlife areas. The birdwatching is phenomenal. The dog regulations at these large and marshy areas are in flux right now, so if you want to know if and when your dog can walk, birdwatch and hunt with you, call the state Department of Fish and Game at (916) 355-0978.

NATIONAL FORESTS

See the National Forests/Wilderness Areas chapter starting on page 801 for important information and safety tips for visiting national forests with your dog.

• **Lassen National Forest** 🐾🐾🐾🐾 🦴 🐕
They're a little more sticky about off-leash dogs here than at most national forests. Dogs are allowed off leash, but rangers say they're quick to bow to the county leash law if there's any complaint. This could be because the forest surrounds Lassen Volcanic National Park, which has extremely strict dog laws. See page 805 for more information on this forest.

• **Modoc National Forest** 🐾🐾🐾🐾 🦴 🐕
See page 807.

NATIONAL PARKS

• **Lassen Volcanic National Park** 🚹
Don't get your hopes up about enjoying this astounding national park with your dog. Pooches are all but banned from this geological wonderland.

Here's the long and exciting list of places they're allowed to visit: parking lots, paved main roads and campgrounds.

Since walking in a parking lot or along a heavily used road probably isn't your dog's idea of a good time, we'll just describe the camping. Dogs are permitted, on leash, at the four campgrounds that are accessible by car. There are a total of 357 campsites, all first come, first served. Sites are $5 to $7, and are located in both Shasta and Lassen counties. Call (916) 595-4444 for directions to the campground most convenient to you.

SUSANVILLE

Susanville is the second-oldest town in the western Great Basin, and a stroll through the historic uptown area with the city's free "Come Walk With Us" guide will fill you with all the historical knowledge you and your dog could ever need. But quite frankly, your dog will probably enjoy romping outdoors in this area much better than boning up on the local lore.

PARKS, BEACHES & RECREATION AREAS

• Biz Johnson Rail Trail 🐾🐾🐾🐾 🐾 ✕

Whether your dog is a couch poochtato or a super athlete, this trail is bound to become a favorite. The wide trail winds more than 25 miles from Susanville to Mason Station, and then follows existing roads another four-and-a-half miles into Westwood. You'll know you're there when you see the 25-foot carved redwood statue of Paul Bunyan and Babe the Blue Ox. (Boy dogs, have some respect for this folklore hero and fight the temptation to do leg lifts on him and his bovine buddy. This is his "birthplace," and they say his ghost doesn't take kindly to such indiscretions.)

With 11 bridges and two tunnels, the trail follows the Fernley and Lassen Railway line, which was built in 1914 to serve the world's largest pine mill. As you hike, you'll find signs marking the locations of a 300-man logging camp, freight and passenger stations, and logging spur lines. The place is popular in the warmer months. Obedient dogs are allowed off leash, but beware of fast mountain bikes. In winter, it's a cross-country skier's heaven. Leashless dogs love charging through the white powder at your side.

If your dog prefers his hikes or ski jaunts to be short, you can use any of six trailheads and flip around when he's looking bored or bedraggled. If he's a rugged outdoor kind of guy, you'll want to consider hiking longer portions of the trail and camping along the way. Primitive sites are open year-round along the very scenic Susan River, and there's no fee. It's advisable to pack your own water or treat the river water before you drink it.

From Susanville, follow Highway 36 to South Lassen Street at the western end of town. Go left on South Lassen Street for four blocks to the trail. Call the Bureau of Land Management's Eagle Lake Resource Area at (916) 257-0456 for directions to other trailheads, and for pocket-sized trail guides and plant identification

keys. Some of the land here is also under the management of Lassen National Forest. Call their headquarters at (916) 257-2151.
→*See #1 on map p. 90.*

• **Eagle Lake** 🐾 🐾 🐾 1/2

Tired of all those look-alike man-made reservoirs and lakes? Here's a lake that's large and natural. In fact, at 42 square miles, Eagle Lake is the second-largest natural lake in California. Better yet, it's also one of the state's cleanest and least crowded lakes.

If you like trout fishing, you and your dog will enjoy angling for Eagle Lake trout, which are found nowhere else in the world. In the cold fall months, you can fish from the north shore and land some big ones. But don't forget that even though your dog is wearing a coat, he's going to freeze if you don't occasionally get up and walk around with him.

The northern end of this clear blue lake is characteristic of high desert country with sage and juniper, rocky shoreline and reed patches. There's plenty of open land where you and your dog can dillydally the day away. The land leading down to the south shore is a drastic contrast, with lush pine forests and mountains of green.

Dogs should be leashed, because critters ranging from deer and pronghorn antelope to bald eagles are quite common here.

The U.S. Forest Service runs four campgrounds here, with a total of 325 sites. Fees range from $7 to $11. Call (800) 283-CAMP for reservations. The Bureau of Land Management's North Eagle Lake campground has some rugged sites on the north end. Call (916) 257-0456 for BLM camping information. From Susanville, drive 2.5 miles west on Highway 44, then turn north at County Road A1. After about 16 miles, you'll reach the south shore campgrounds. Watch for signs. For more information, call Lassen National Forest at (916) 257-2151. →*See #2 on map p. 90.*

RESTAURANTS

Mamaluka's Bistro: If there aren't outdoor tables at this lovely French restaurant, there will be some soon. The owners plan a French country-style outdoor area for their delicious cooking. 44 North Lassen Street; (916) 251-LADY.

Primo Deli: Eat soups and sandwiches with your hungry pooch at the outdoor tables. 614 Main Street; (916) 257-6694.

PLACES TO STAY

Best Western Trailside Inn: There's a good little spot here for little Spots to get a little exercise. Small dogs only, please, and no cats! Rates are $46 to $74. 2785 Main Street, Susanville, CA 96130; (916) 257-4123.

Biz Johnson Rail Trail campsites: See page 92.
Eagle Lake campsites: See page 93.
River Inn Motel: Rates are $36 to $50. 1710 Main Street, Susanville, CA 96130; (916) 257-6051.
Super Budget Motel: Rates are $34 to $46. 2975 Johnstonville Road, Susanville, CA 96130; (916) 257-2782.

FESTIVALS

Main Street Fair: You and your spendthrift dogs can buy things all day long together at this mid-June sidewalk sale in historic uptown Susanville. The profits from the sales go to worthwhile nonprofit groups. (916) 257-6506.

WESTWOOD

PARKS, BEACHES & RECREATION AREAS

• Biz Johnson Rail Trail 🐾🐾🐾🐾 🌭 🐕

See page 92, under Susanville, for trail information. The Westwood section of the trail starts at Ash Street near Third Street and follows Ash Street and County Road A21 four miles to the Mason Station trailhead. That's where the main part of the trail begins. → *See #3 on map p. 90.*

FESTIVALS

Paul Bunyan Mountain Festival: How's this for a list of things you and your leashed dog can do at this three-day festival in July? Visit giant statues...watch champion lumberjacks throw axes...go to Brimstone Bill's Bullwhacker Bunkshanty Carnival...eat at Sourdough Sam's eateries...try your luck at blue ox bingo...and even dance under the stars. (Dogs like to lead, but they're used to following.) Call (916) 256-2456 for this year's dates and locations.

MENDOCINO COUNTY

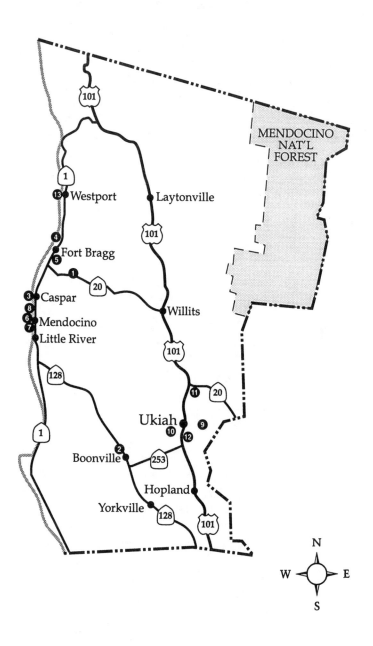

8
MENDOCINO COUNTY

When people from out of town think of Mendocino County, they often think of quaint inns, sweeping seascapes and perfect little coastal villages teeming with artists and tourists. But there's one vital image missing, that of a nosy dog sniffing about, exploring forests and fields, oceans and rivers, and some of the most dog-friendly inns in the state.

While the coast of Mendocino County attracts most visitors, dogs have much more freedom inland, where they're allowed to run off leash in three very large parcels of land. But there's still something magical about the Mendocino coast. Although it offers no leash-free areas, dogs thrive on the ever-cool climate and the salty air. Joe once perched himself on a Mendocino blufftop for a solid hour and sat utterly still, except for his flaring nostrils. For Mr. Mobility to have such patience and fascination, there must be magic in the air (or at least the smell of a few deceased fish).

NATIONAL FORESTS

See the National Forests/Wilderness Areas chapter starting on page 801 for important information and safety tips for visiting national forests with your dog.

•**Mendocino National Forest** 🐾 🐾 🐾 🐾 🐾 ⬤ 🐕

Only a tiny portion of this national forest rests in its namesake county. Some rangers prefer to have dogs off leash only in the two wilderness areas, neither of which is in Mendocino County. Others say it's okay for dogs to be leash-free everywhere but in camping areas. See page 806 for more information.

STATE FORESTS

•**Jackson State Forest** 🐾 🐾 🐾 🐾 ⬤ 🐕

What a treat! Almost all of this 50,000-acre park is available to dogs who don't want to be attached to a leash. This is a demonstration area for forest management practices, featuring self-guided educational nature trails and many miles of hiking available on old logging roads.

One of the more popular trails is the Tree Identification Trail, just off Highway 20, about 11 miles east of Highway 1. It's one of the few areas of the forest that's actually marked from the highway.

And it's a great place for you and your dog to learn the difference between a madrone, oak, redwood and fir and any other varieties that confuse you. Dogs probably already know all about these trees, since the males of the species have made intimate acquaintances with so many in their lives. But they won't mind going along for the walk.

Sadly, the budget for the state forests has been cut so drastically that some trails might become neglected and some campgrounds may have to close. Call the forest before you visit to find out the status and obtain maps. As of press time, the forest had 44 primitive campsites, available at no fee. You'll need a camping permit and a campground map. Call (707) 964-5674 or pick up maps and information in person at the Department of Forestry office at 802 Main Street in Fort Bragg.

The forest stretches along Highway 20 from just east of Mendocino and Fort Bragg to about nine miles west of Willits.
→*See #1 on map p. 96.*

BOONVILLE

PARKS, BEACHES & RECREATION AREAS
• **Faulkner County Park** 🐾 🐾 1/2

Since you and your dog probably each enjoy flowering shrubs for your own reasons, you'll have a pleasant stroll here. Of the two trails that wind through this 40-acre park, the Azalea Discovery Trail is the one nosy dogs like best. This is a 12-stop nature trail through a stand of azalea shrubs and redwoods. Difficult as it may be, try to prevent your dog from doing one-leg salutes to the azaleas.

The park also features a hiking trail to the top of the ridge. It's a short trail, but it gets the blood flowing after a long car trip. Kids enjoy the small playground near the entrance.

The park is on Mountain View Road, two miles west of Boonville. (707) 463-4267. →*See #2 on map p. 96.*

CASPAR

PARKS, BEACHES & RECREATION AREAS
• **Caspar State Beach** 🐾 🐾 🐾

The beach here is small, but it's a good place to walk your dog if you're between Mendocino and Fort Bragg and your dog starts getting that desperate look. You won't find many people here, but dogs still have to be leashed. The beach is at Doyle Creek, off Point Cabrillo Road (Old Highway 1). (707) 937-5804. →*See #3 on map p. 96.*

PLACES TO STAY

Caspar Beach RV Park: A mini-city, this RV park is for people who want to get away from civilization while not getting too far from it. Some tent sites are available, but you can feel lost among the mobile homes. In addition to hiking with your on-leash dog at the adjacent beach, you can also rent a video or play your favorite game in the video arcade. It's not exactly roughing it, but some people and their dogs are in heaven here.

Rates are $15 to $22. Dogs are $1 extra. From Mendocino, drive three miles north and take the Point Cabrillo Drive exit to Russian Gulch State Park. Take Point Cabrillo Drive west to the campground. (707) 964-3306.

FORT BRAGG

While Fort Bragg is now the commercial hub of the Mendocino Coast, it once served as a fort built to maintain order for the Mendocino County Indian Reservation. That was abandoned in 1864, and it wasn't until 20 years later that Fort Bragg found its calling as a lumber town.

You and your dog can visit the Chamber of Commerce and pick up a walking-tour map of historic Fort Bragg. This won't substitute for a visit to the many wonderful beaches in the area, but it's a good way to learn about history while your dog puts his nose to the ground and learns who's been walking on the city's sidewalks.

Joe's favorite part of town is the Noyo fishing village. Fishing fleets come in here with their catches and unload them at restaurants and processing plants. This is the real thing, not a San Francisco Fisherman's Wharf façade where selling T-shirts has come to replace the real business of fishing. And *mmmm,* it smells *so* fishy. Dogs are exhilarated just breathing the air.

PARKS, BEACHES & RECREATION AREAS

•MacKerricher State Park 🐾 🐾 🐾 1/2

This eight-mile beach encompasses a few smaller beaches, including the secluded Pudding Creek Beach at MacKerricher's southern end. Unfortunately, dogs are forbidden at the strip of beach near the main parking lot, but all you have to do is walk north or south a few hundred yards and miles of beach are all yours.

Joe adores this seaweed-strewn beach, although his species is supposed to be leashed. There's a little of everything here, from headlands to forests to a small lake. For dog exercise, it's best to stick to the beach. You'll run into fewer people and horses than you will in other park areas. Near the northern section of the beach, it gets so wide that you feel as though you and your dog are walking with Lawrence of Arabia. It may be tempting to walk on for what seems like eternity, but keep an eye on the time: It's tough walking back when it's dark.

Wildlife is everywhere. More than 100 species of birds inhabit the park. Tidepools are rich with life. And harbor seals bask and breed on secluded rock outcroppings, sometimes even in the beach areas. But don't go anywhere near them, with or without your dog! They're shy creatures, and will balk at the slightest disturbance, sometimes diving for long periods of time to avoid the possible threat.

It's fun to camp with your dog here. The 142 campsites are roomy, and often surrounded by trees. Sites are $12 to $14. Dogs are $1 extra. Phone MISTIX at (800) 444-PARK for reservations.

The best place to have doggy access to the beach is at the Ward Avenue entrance, about a half mile north of the main park entrance. This is also where the beach starts becoming an enormous sandy mass. But if you're camping in the main section, beach access is just a short walk north or south. If you're unsure of where you and the pooch can walk on the beach, ask a ranger. The areas are not clearly marked. The main entrance is on the west side of Highway 1, about three miles north of Fort Bragg. It's marked by a large sign. You'll pass by a ranger kiosk, but there's no fee for day use. (707) 937-5804. ➤ *See #4 on map p. 96.*

•Noyo Beach 🐾 🐾 🐾

A better name would be Solitude Beach. We've never seen anyone here, although we've seen footprints, so someone else must know about this place. This small, sandy beach on the mouth of the Noyo River has a leash law, but dogs enjoy trekking around and watching the boats come in with the catch of the day.

This is also a good place to pick up the Coastal Trail. For great views, follow it northwest to the entrance to Noyo Bay. Heading north on Highway 1, go right on North Harbor Drive and loop around down to the beach. (707) 964-4719. ➤ *See #5 on map p. 96.*

RESTAURANTS

Jenny's Giant Burger: Dogs love to smell the fries frying, the burgers grilling, the milkshakes shaking. It may not be healthy food, but it's good. 940 North Main Street; (707) 964-2235.

Salmon Inn Market: Buy some smoked salmon or albacore and picnic at the bench of this Noyo fishing village store. 32301 North Harbor Drive; (707) 964-0770 or (800) 336-9833.

Thai Cafe: When we dined on the porch here, we were in the company of a big huge black dog who sneaked some of his owner's *pad thai* dish when his back was turned. Tables are shaded by umbrellas. At Chestnut and Main streets; (707) 964-7931.

PLACES TO STAY
Beachcomber Motel: Dogs love this place. It's just a pinecone's throw to the beach and MacKerricher State Park. Rates are $30 to $150. Dogs are $10 extra. 111 North Main Street, Fort Bragg, CA 95437; (707) 964-2402.

Coast Motel: Who needs a dog park with this place around? The owner permits dogs to run leashless on five tree-filled acres of land behind the motel! It's pretty safe from traffic. Rates are $32 to $55. Dogs are $5 extra. 18661 Highway 1, Fort Bragg, CA 95437; (707) 964-2852.

Ebb Tide Lodge: If your dog weighs under 20 pounds, he's allowed to join you here. Rates are $45 to $60. 250 Main Street, Fort Bragg, CA 95437; (707) 964-5321.

MacKerricher State Park campgrounds: See page 99.

FESTIVALS
Paul Bunyan Days: Dogs not only get to witness three days of people showing off their strength and logging skills, they actually get to participate! They can't take part in the ax throwing or the power saw bucking. But if your dog is ugly—so ugly that cats laugh at him and babies scream when he walks by—he can take part in the annual Ugly Dog Contest! It usually takes place on the Saturday of this four-day Labor Day weekend event. There are also contests for the largest dog, the smallest dog, the smartest dog and the frisbee-est dog. The dog part of the festival takes place at the middle school fields, at the corner of Harold and Laurel streets. (707) 964-9446 or (707) 964-4465.

HOPLAND
RESTAURANTS
Hopland Farms General Store: Located across the street from the Fetzer winery, you and your dog can eat tasty deli food at any of three outdoor tables. The employees here are very dog-friendly. 13501 US 101 South; (707) 744-1298.

LAYTONVILLE
PLACES TO STAY
Gentle Valley Ranch and The Ranch Motel: These dog-friendly lodgings are completely separate. Dogs prefer the Gentle Valley

Ranch cottages. The ranch is on 260 acres of prime valley land which, until recently, was a working cattle ranch. The new owners are letting the acreage return to a natural state and the place is becoming a miniature wildlife preserve. A creek cuts through the northern portion of the Gentle Valley and it helps attract plenty of wildlife, so keep your dog leashed!

Guests at the comfortable, homey motel, located in the heart of laid-back Laytonville, also have access to the ranch land. It's a good thing, too, because many a dog owner has come here thinking they could take advantage of the nearby Northern California Coast Range Preserve. This is more than 7,500 acres of old-growth forests and wildlife habitats run by the Nature Conservancy. But alas, dogs are banned, ixnay, verboten and just plain old forbidden.

You may even be able to talk the owners into letting you camp on the ranch land. Motel rates are $26 to $45. Cottages at the ranch and in town are $65 to $150. The mailing address is P.O. Box 1535, Laytonville, CA 95454; (707) 984-8456.

LITTLE RIVER

PLACES TO STAY

S.S. Seafoam Lodge: If your dog is a water dog, she'll take to this place in a snap. Each room has some kind of nautical motif, and some provide views of the shoreline in the distance. You'll even have access to a secluded little beach.

The cottages and small buildings are set in big tree territory, just a few miles south of Mendocino. Rates are $85 to $175. Dogs are $10 extra. 6751 North Highway 1, Little River, CA 95456; the mailing address is P.O. Box 68, Mendocino, CA 95460; (707) 937-1827.

MENDOCINO

Take your dog to New England and never leave the Golden State! Visiting this quaint village, which stands in as Angela Lansbury's home town in *Murder, She Wrote*, is like stepping across the country and back in time.

The wooden towers and carpenter's Gothic houses look more like they belong in Cape Cod than on the California coast. Dogs enjoy it here, but not as much as people: There's nowhere for pooches to officially run off leash.

The art galleries that give this town its flavor generally don't allow dogs. But at least you can window shop with your favorite canine critic. If you see something you like, the artists and gallery owners tend to be very accommodating. One art collector we know ended up having tea and toast in a gallery where she was buying several small prints. Her mutt, Rosy, got her own piece of toast and was offered a pot of tea, which she couldn't drink because it was too warm. The artist obligingly found some ice.

PARKS, BEACHES & RECREATION AREAS

• **Friendship Park** 🐾 🐾

If your dog is bursting at the seams, this is a decent place to pull off Highway 1. Otherwise, the Mendocino Headlands (see below) are a much better deal for dogs.

The park is small, but friendly to leashed dogs. There's green grass, a playing field and even some picnic tables in case your dog doesn't want to visit the local eateries after taking care of essential business here. Friendship Park is at Little Lake Road and School Street. (707) 937-5790. → *See #6 on map p. 96.*

• **Mendocino Headlands State Park/**
  Big River Beach 🐾 🐾 🐾 1/2 🐾

Mendocino's sculpted shoreline is a spectacular place for you and your dog to enjoy the sights, scents and sounds of the Mendocino coast. Unlike most state parks, this one allows leashed dogs on the trails, which wind around the rocky bluffs and provide good views of wave tunnels and arched rocks. Fields extend along the cliff tops, so there's plenty of room for dogs who don't like to hover over the edge of promontories. It's cool year-round, so even malamutes can enjoy an August romp.

A sandy beach at the mouth of the Big River near the southern headlands is a tempting place to let your dog off her leash, but watch out: The place can be heavily patrolled.

It's difficult to explore the tiny town of Mendocino without running into the headlands at every turn. Exit Highway 1 at Lansing Street and drive west. The park actually surrounds the little Mendocino peninsula, so just stop at any part that looks appealing. Parking won't be far away. To get to the sandy beach, exit Highway 1 at the sign for Mendocino Headlands State Park and Big River Beach. Follow the signs east. (707) 937-5804. → *See #7 on map p. 96.*

• **Russian Gulch State Park** 🐾 🐾 🐾

Your dog will enjoy this small, wild park whose streams drain Russian Gulch. You must leash up, though. A rough dirt trail leads in through deciduous forest. Huge groves of willows line the gulch. In wet season, you'll have to wade across the gulch to reach the beach, a small one with cliffs at each end. The surf is ferocious; don't let your dog near it. Swimming in the fresh creeks is much more fun for her, anyway.

About two miles north of Mendocino, watch for a small brown sign marking the turnoff. There's a dirt parking lot at the entrance. (707) 937-5804. ➡️*See #8 on map p. 96.*

RESTAURANTS

With all the wonderful cafes and restaurants here, we could find only one that allows dogs on a routine basis. It's too bad, because dogs and their people make loyal customers, especially in such a tourist haven as Mendocino.

Mendocino Bakery: The food here is scrumptious and often even good for you. The bakery concentrates on vegetarian meals and the pizza is out of this world. Dine with your dog at the many outdoor tables alongside the restaurant. 10483 Lansing Street; (707) 937-0836.

PLACES TO STAY

Sears House Inn: Dogs are welcome to lounge around with you at the small cottages that surround this Victorian inn in the heart of Mendocino. Joe's favorite is atop a water tower, where he can watch tourists and local cats stroll by in three directions. The Sears House Inn is an ideal place to stay, close to the ocean and the eateries. The cottages all come with yards, so if your dog feels the urge to visit the WC at 3 a.m., you don't have to trudge to the parks. As usual, you must clean up after your pup. Rates for cottages are $80 to $90. If the inn starts offering breakfast again, the rates will go up about $10. Dogs cost $5 extra. 44840 Main Street, Mendocino, CA 95460; (707) 937-4076.

The Stanford Inn by the Sea: Do you and your pooch love luxury, love rustic surroundings, and love the ocean? Have we got a place for you!

The Stanford Inn by the Sea has plenty of all three. There's luxury: The beds are antiques, big and comfortable. The rooms all have fireplaces and French doors leading to private decks. There's rustic scenery: The redwood inn is tucked into a grove of pines, surrounded by 11 acres. There's ocean: On one side of the property is the Pacific, on the other is the Big River.

What more could you want? Red-carpet treatment for your dog? How's this: Dogs stay free and are provided with doggy sheets so they can relax anywhere in your room and not leave it covered with their dogginess. Not enough? Okay, we'll tell all: Dogs get the canine equivalent of a pillow chocolate—dog biscuits wrapped with ribbons.

Rates are $145 to $250. The inn is at Comptche-Ukiah Road and Highway 1. The mailing address is P.O. Box 487, Mendocino, CA 95460; (707) 937-5615 or (800) 331-8884.

UKIAH

PARKS, BEACHES & RECREATION AREAS

• **Cow Mountain Recreation Area** 🐾🐾🐾🐾 🐕

How does 27,000 acres of leashless bliss sound? This rugged recreation area, run by the Bureau of Land Management, is heaven for dogs who need real, off-leash exercise. With elevations ranging from 800 to 4,000 feet, a good-sized portion of this land is probably off-limits for couch-potato dogs. But there are plenty of trails that even the most sedentary dog/human pair can enjoy.

Dogs can be off leash everywhere but in developed areas like the two small designated campgrounds. (Pitching a tent at one of the 12 designated, first-come, first-served sites won't cost you a cent.) Make sure that your dog is under voice control when he is off leash: Many mountain lions, deer and bears call Cow Mountain their home, and you don't want your dog tangling with any of them.

If you like nature watching, you'll really enjoy it here. Quail, dove, rabbit and feral pigs are common sights. Hunters also like it here for the same reasons. Anglers have fun at the cold-water streams, which often brim with rainbow trout. Several of the small reservoirs have been stocked with sunfish. The entire area can be fished.

The park is actually 50,000 acres, but 23,000 of those acres in the South Cow Mountain Recreation Area are devoted to off-highway vehicles. If you venture on that acreage with your dog, do keep him on leash. But why go there when you can stay to the north, where the only forms of transportation you have to watch out for are horses and bicycles?

Other than Jackson State Forest and little bits of Mendocino National Forest that sneak into this county, this is the only public land that allows dogs off leash in all of Mendocino County. Use it well, tread lightly and pack out what you pack in.

Exit US 101 at Talmage Road and drive east until you come to the City of 10,000 Buddhas, where the road ends. Make a right onto East Side Road, and in about a half mile, go left on Mill Creek Road. The entrance to Cow Mountain will be on your left. For information and maps, call (707) 462-3873. → *See #9 on map p. 96.*

• **Low Gap Regional County Park** 🐾🐾🐾 1/2

Location isn't everything. This 80-acre park is located just west of the county jail and kitty-corner from the huge Ukiah Cemetery—not exactly ideal neighbors, but that's okay. The park is a great place to go for an afternoon romp with the dog. You won't even know that gravediggers and prisoners are just down the road.

The park's amenities include six-and-a-half miles of hiking trails, an 18-hole disc golf course, an amphitheater and ball fields. Just watch out that your dog doesn't become a bull's-eye for the archery range here! It's about the only possible danger, because since no bikes are allowed, you won't be run over by speed demons. In summer, Joe likes the nature trail the best. It offers the most shade, and it's the most secluded.

Exit US 101 at Perkins Street and drive west to State Street. Go north on State Street, then west on Brush Street/Low Gap Road. The entrance is on your left in about a mile. (707) 463-4267. ➜*See #10 on map p. 96.*

•**Mendocino Lake Recreation Area** 🐾 🐾 🐾 1/2

Next time there's a full moon rising at sunset, this is the place to take your dog. He probably won't become a werewolf, or even a weredog, but there's something magical here when the moon rises over the mountains and lake. It starts its lunar journey as an enormous, orange disk on the horizon, almost as grand as the moon Mrs. Moore saw in *A Passage to India.* As it rises through the fading sky, its face stares into eternity and glows whiter with each degree it ascends. The white cuts a gossamer streak through the lake, and the chorus of serenading crickets becomes almost deafening. You'll want to stay all night, but this is when you should exit, because park gates close shortly after sunset. While the moon provides a wondrous show, it's not worth staying late and having to sleep in your car until the next day. Doggy morning breath can be atrocious.

For all those other days of the year when there's not a full moon rising at sunset, this huge area is still a fun place for a dog who doesn't mind a leash. A couple of trails wind around about half of the lake, and frequently take you right down to the lake's edge. It's very quiet here, barring jetskiers. You can throw a line into the lake and come up with dinner in the form of bass or trout. Or just take time out from your hike to watch the deer and the buffleheads play.

From US 101, take Lake Mendocino Drive and follow it east to the lake. You'll have to make a short jog north on North State Road, but you'll catch up with Lake Mendocino Drive in 30 seconds. Then veer east again. The best place to enter with your dog is at the Joe Riley Area, past the boat launching ramp. This is a grassy picnic area, perfect for lunch before a hike. The trailhead starts just beyond the picnic area. (707) 462-7581. ➜*See #11 on map p. 96.*

• **Mill Creek County Park** 🐾 🐾 🐾 1/2

This 400-acre park directly across from Cow Mountain (see page 105) has everything dogs could want, except off-leash freedom. They can hike, splash in streams, picnic, relax in the shade of bay trees and draw deep dog breaths on ridge tops.

Exit US 101 at Talmage Road and drive east until you come to the City of 10,000 Buddhas, where the road ends. Make a right onto East Side Road, and in about a half mile, go left on Mill Creek Road. After you pass the pond, you'll see signs for the park. Go right almost immediately, into a group picnic/playground area. Your dog can frolic in the meadow or hike with you on the trail that starts on the west end of the group picnic area. That trail branches off into several different trails, including a nature trail that follows the creek and a trail that leads you to the top of the southernmost ridge where the views are unbeatable. Alternate entrances, in case the gate to the picnic area is shut, are available around the creek and pond, near the small, strategically located parking lots. (707) 463-4267. ➜ *See #12 on map p. 96.*

RESTAURANTS

Angel's Mexican Food: Eat good Mexican grub at a couple of umbrella-covered tables. 499 North State Street; (707) 463-3735.

Country Chef: This is a family restaurant, serving breakfast, lunch and dinner at many outdoor tables shaded by umbrellas. 697 South Orchard Avenue; (707) 468-8323.

Foster Freeze: Everyone who works here seems to be a dog lover. Your dog might even get a biscuit just for showing up. 749 South State Street; (707) 462-3883.

House of Pizza: Eat pizza on picnic tables. 545 North State Street; (707) 462-1494.

North State Cafe & Bakery: Yum. This little place has a great variety of food you and your dog can dine on at the outdoor benches here. Just don't tie your big dog to the bench while you order inside, unless you're certain he won't walk away, dragging the bench behind him. 247 North State Street; (707) 462-3726.

PLACES TO STAY

Cow Mountain Recreation Area camping: See page 105.

Motel 6: Rates are $30 for the first adult, $6 for the second. And 35 cents will get you 15 minutes of vibrating bed time. It's always relaxing after traveling with the dog. All Motel 6s allow one small dog per room. 1208 South State Street, Ukiah, CA 95482. (707) 468-5404.

WESTPORT

Here's another New England look-alike. Westport is a tiny coastal town with a couple of inns and restaurants, and a whole lot of charm. It's a wonderful place to visit if you like the appeal of Mendocino but prefer your sidewalks tourist-free and your beaches isolated.

PARKS, BEACHES & RECREATION AREAS

• **Westport-Union Landing State Beach** 🐾 🐾 🐾 1/2

On one of the busiest weekends of the year, not a soul was using this beach. Only one of the 100 campsites was occupied. This is the kind of place you can pretend is your own almost year-round. You and your dog may well find yourself alone in the campgrounds and along the sandy beaches here, but pooches are still supposed to be leashed.

One of the best times to visit is during the grey whale migration. There are several good spots on the blufftops where you can whale watch in comfort. Just set up a lawn chair, sit back with your binoculars and wait. Even if you don't see a leviathan, at least you and your dog will have spent some good outdoor hanging-out time together. To make it even better, have a picnic.

Campsites are $9 and are first come, first served. Dogs are $1 extra. The sites are all on the blufftops, near the park road, and not far from Highway 1. There's no shade, no privacy unless there's no one there (you camp just off the parking lots), but plenty of quiet. At night, it's easy to fall asleep to the gentle churning of the Pacific. The park has three entrances. We hear that the farther north you go, the better your chances of finding people. The beach is about 2.5 miles north of the town of Westport. You can't miss the empty parking lots, but if you do, you'll still see the signs. (707) 937-5804.
➡️ *See #13 on map p. 96.*

PLACES TO STAY

Howard Creek Ranch: This rustic redwood inn offers privacy, quiet and 20 acres of coastal beauty. Each room is unique, with features so special it's hard to decide where to stay. Joe likes the old boat, which is now a miniature cabin, complete with wood-burning stoves and low wooden ceilings. He doesn't have to duck here like his human companions often do, and he seems to get a real kick out of hearing the *thwack* of a Homo sapien's head against a thick beam. Rooms are $50 to $90 a night. 40501 North Highway 1, Westport, CA 95488; (707) 964-6725.

Westport-Union Landing State Beach campgrounds: See above.

WILLITS

Although it's at the junction of US 101 and Highway 20 (a main artery to Fort Bragg), there's precious little for dogs here. We couldn't even find a hotel that allows dogs, although once I did manage to sneak Joe into a motel here. But it got embarrassing when Joe literally ran right into the innkeeper on a midnight walk. In a panic I thought of telling Mr. Motel that I'd just found Joe on the side of the road, but I was honest, and Joe ended up spending the night in the car…at least until Mr. Motel was safely back in his room. This is not a good example of proper dog etiquette.

YORKVILLE

PLACES TO STAY

Sheep Dung Estates: People often ask about staying somewhere really dog-friendly. You won't find many better places than the two cottages on 160 acres in this rustic haven near Boonville. To attest to this, more than half of the visitors here bring dogs!

The place looks much better than its name implies: From the huge windows of the homey, airy cottages, you and your dog can enjoy sweeping vistas of the Anderson Valley and surrounding forests. The cottages each have private roads, wood-burning stoves, down comforters and covered porches. Owners Anne and Aaron Benning ask that you bring a sheet if your dog insists on sleeping on the bed with you, because the luxurious bedding can't take the beating dogs give.

Your pooch need not look farther than his own front door for a place to run around and just be a dog: Voice-controlled dogs are free to run and explore the huge property! There's even a very large pond where water dogs can practice the dog paddle. The property is actually larger and more enticing than the land that used to house Sheep Dung's single cottage down the road.

While exploring, don't be surprised if your dog runs into a 300-pound pig. Her name is Isadora Pork Chop. The Bennings' nephew captured the formerly wild pig in 1993, and she was to be Christmas dinner that year. But then she worked her way out of her cage and into the Bennings' hearts. She now thinks she's a very big dog. She tries to sneak inside to sleep on the dog comforter on the Bennings' Oriental rug. She tags alongside when she likes someone. And she's best buddies with the resident retriever here.

There's a two-night minimum stay. Rates for this chunk of dog heaven are $75 nightly. Sheep Dung Estates is about 40 miles southeast of Mendocino, near Highway 128. The mailing address is P.O. Box 49, Yorkville, CA 95494; (707) 894-5322.

TEHAMA COUNTY

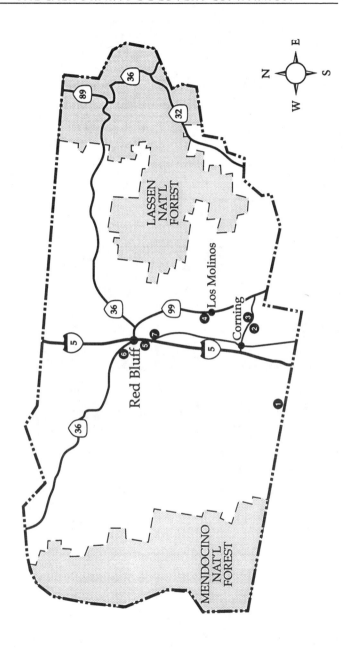

9
TEHAMA COUNTY

The county has a little bit of Lassen National Forest on one side, a touch of Mendocino National Forest on the other, and lots of farmland in between. If you feel like doing your dog a favor, stop in Red Bluff and visit lush and lovely Dog Island (see page 115). If it weren't for the leash thing, dogs would probably never want to go home.

NATIONAL FORESTS

See the National Forests/Wilderness Areas chapter starting on page 801 for important information and safety tips for visiting national forests with your dog.

• **Lassen National Forest** 🐾🐾🐾🐾 🥾 🐕
See page 805.

• **Mendocino National Forest** 🐾🐾🐾🐾 🥾 🐕
The forest is full of campgrounds in the southwest part of the county. See page 806 for information on the forest.

CORNING

PARKS, BEACHES & RECREATION AREAS

• **Black Butte Lake** 🐾🐾🐾🐾 🐕
See page 120 in the Glenn County chapter. →*See #1 on map p. 112.*

• **Tehama County River Park** 🐾🐾🐾 1/2
This park is almost directly across from the Woodson Bridge State Recreation Area (see page 114). While it's not as large as the state park, there's no fee to use it, which makes it a very attractive alternative.

South Avenue bisects the park. The north side is grassy and fairly undeveloped, with great fishing access. When we visited, each of the three people fishing in the Sacramento had at least one dog. All the dogs were in and out of the river constantly, shaking on their masters and chasing each other back in again. You've rarely seen such happy, content pooches. Of course, if the ranger had stopped by, their owners may not have been so happy. They could have gotten slapped with a fine for allowing their dogs off leash here. It's too bad there's a leash law here, because the area is quite safe from the road or other people.

The section to the south of South Avenue is more developed, with playgrounds, a little store and a picnic area. You can go back and forth between the two sections via a very, very short tunnel under the road.

From Interstate 5, take the South Avenue exit and drive about eight miles east to the park. (916) 527-5765. → *See #2 on map p. 112.*

•**Woodson Bridge State Recreation Area** 🐾 🐾 🐾 1/2

You're in the middle of giant oak country here—a fact that sends many dogs into fits of happiness. Between all the oaks (and poison oak—watch it!), walnuts, cottonwoods, elderberries and willows, your boy dog will hardly be able to contain himself.

Wildflowers are abundant in this 428-acre park. With its location, flanking both sides of the Sacramento River, there's plenty of beauty here, especially in spring. Autumn is also a spectacular and colorful sight. Just get on the nature trail and hike your city woes away.

During your visit, some of your neighbors may include Columbian black-tailed deer, bats, muskrats, hares, river otters and skunks. The law requires that you keep your dog on a leash here. If you like to birdwatch, you'll love this place. If you're lucky, you may even spot the rare and endangered yellow-billed cuckoo. You'll know it when you see it.

The day-use fee is $5. There are 46 campsites here, ranging from $10 to $12 each. Dogs are $1 extra during the day or when camping. From Interstate 5, take the South Avenue exit and drive about eight miles east to the park. Call MISTIX at (800) 444-PARK for campsite reservations or (916) 839-2112 for park info. → *See #3 on map p. 112.*

PLACES TO STAY

Days Inn: Rates are $30 to $60. There's a $25 deposit required for dogs. 3475 Highway 99W, Corning, CA 96021; (916) 824-2000.

Shilo Inn: This is a quiet place, with a good continental breakfast and a relaxing steam room. (Sorry, dogs. No steam for you.) Rates are $54 to $65. Dogs are $6 extra. 3350 Sunrise Way, Corning, CA 96021; (916) 824-2940.

Woodson Bridge State Recreation Area camping: See above.

LOS MOLINOS

PARKS, BEACHES & RECREATION AREAS

•**Mill Creek County Park** 🐾 🐾 1/2

There's great access to the Sacramento River here for dogs who like to help you catch dinner or like to screw up your chances of catching it by wading in all the fishy water. Since dogs are supposed to be leashed, you can usually control the situation pretty well.

Landlubbing pooches prefer the shaded meadows and the fenced-in ball fields. All in all, this is a peaceful, relaxing place to come with a dog.

From Highway 99E, go west on Tehama & Vine Road. (If you find that you're in a spot where you can only go east, drive north a bit and you'll come to the right portion of the road.) In about a mile, you'll come to the Hidden Harbor fishing resort. Immediately after it is the gate to Mill Creek Park. (916) 384-1250. → *See #4 on map p. 112.*

RED BLUFF

PARKS, BEACHES & RECREATION AREAS

• **City River Park** 🐾 🐾 1/2

Dogs don't give a hang about the features of this park that humans enjoy most: an Olympic-size swimming pool, a bandshell, playgrounds, and plenty of playing fields and ball courts. But tell them that the park is directly on the Sacramento River and they'll pull you as fast as they can to the nearest entry point (where you must keep their leashes fastened—that's the law here).

From Interstate 5, take the Red Bluff/Highway 36 exit west, cross the river and turn left on Main Street. After two blocks, turn left at Sycamore Street and drive to the end of the street for park access. Or you can keep driving and turn left at any of the next three blocks to enter other sections of the park. (916) 527-2605. → *See #5 on map p. 112.*

• **Dog Island Park/Samuel Ayer Park** 🐾 🐾 🐾 1/2

Wow! A park named for the very creatures who most enjoy being here! Now if only dogs could legally run off leash, someone would have to change the name of this place to Dog Heaven Park.

This is a terrific place to take a dog. The park is lush, wild and alive with riparian vegetation. You almost feel like somehow it's too verdant to be part of California. We hiked through here during a light rain once. It was incredibly relaxing. (All Joe could do was shake those evil raindrops off his coat, but he had a big smile plastered on his snout for the rest of the day once he was in the dry car.)

There are numerous nature trails winding throughout the park. One of them leads to a footbridge which takes you over to Dog Island, a big chunk of land nestled securely in the crook of a Sacramento River bend. The island is just as enchanting as the mainland section of park. It's not super quiet in the island area, though. Interstate 5 crosses over the river a mere two-tenths of a mile to the north.

From Interstate 5, take the Red Bluff/Highway 36 exit west, cross the river and turn right on Main Street. Follow Main Street to the sign for Dog Island Park, which will be on your right in a few blocks. (916) 527-2605. →*See #6 on map p. 112.*

• **Red Bluff Diversion Dam Recreation Area** 🐾 🐾 🐾

Don't be fooled. On a map, this area looks like it must be dog heaven: It's on the water (called Lake Red Bluff here, but it's actually just a wider, dammed section of the Sacramento River), it's fairly big and it's got several campsites perched over the river. But in person, it looks more like something you'd find in Brooklyn. It's almost barren, slightly industrial, and can smell a little funky at times.

A couple of trails take you and your leashed dog short distances, but at least there's plenty of parking. You won't be excited about the fishing, but the fish watching can be interesting. There's a fish-viewing platform set up next to the dam.

Camping at the 30 sites is first come, first served and costs $6 per site. Each campsite has a pretty good tree next to it, so you'll be buffered from the hot summer afternoons a little. You can fish here, but the fishing's not always so good these days, especially from shore.

Exit Interstate 5 at Highway 36 and head east. Take the first right turn, Sale Lane, and follow it to the end. That's where you'll find the camping and the visitor kiosk. Call the Corning Ranger District of Mendocino National Forest for the best times of year to watch the fish. (916) 824-5196. →*See #7 on map p. 112.*

PLACES TO STAY

Cinderella Riverview Motel: You really can see the river from here, and there are plenty of balconies to prove it. Rates are $32 to $48. Small pooches only, please. 600 Rio Street, Red Bluff, CA 96080; (916) 527-5490.

Red Bluff Diversion Dam Recreation Area camping: See above.

GLENN COUNTY

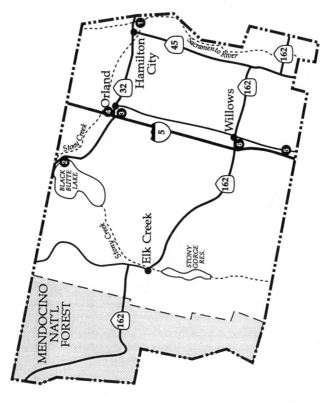

10
GLENN COUNTY

There's not much here that people or dogs would drive hundreds of miles to see. But several big wildlife areas can provide you and your dog with many memorable nature-watching hikes. Don't come here if you're seeking the Bohemian cafe society life.

NATIONAL FORESTS
See the National Forests/Wilderness Areas chapter starting on page 801 for important information and safety tips for visiting national forests with your dog.

• **Mendocino National Forest** 😊 😊 😊 😊 🐾 🐕
You'll find many rugged, attractive camping areas in the northwest corner of the county, where the land is about a mile above sea level. See page 806 for more information on the forest.

HAMILTON CITY

PARKS, BEACHES & RECREATION AREAS
• **Bidwell Sacramento River Park Project** 😊 😊 😊
Sacramento River access here is easy as one, two, wade. Fishing along the four miles of riverfront here is popular, but chances are you won't find too many people on the hiking trail. That's good news if you want to exercise your leashed dog before a day of angling together.

Dogs have limited access to this 180-acre state recreation area. They're not allowed at the Chico Creek Day-Use Area. Your best bet is to stop at the first section of park you come to, the Indian Fishing Day-Use Area, where there's a small picnic setting and an attractive wooded trail leading down to the river. It's usually really quiet here.

From Interstate 32, go south on River Road. It's about 4.5 miles to the Indian Fishing Day Use Area. (916) 323-3047. ➤ *See #1 on map p. 118.*

ORLAND

PARKS, BEACHES & RECREATION AREAS
Great news for dogs in Orland: As with most other cities, there's an ordinance stating that pooches must be under their owner's control. But the similarities to most other cities stop there. That

control can be via leash or via voice. That means freedom for obedient dogs at the city's four parks! The parks are not exactly Golden Gate Park in San Francisco, but you can't be choosy when it comes to leashless lolling.

The Black Butte Lake area isn't part of the city, but it also has its own off-leash potentials (see below).

• **Black Butte Lake** 🐾 🐾 🐾 🐾 🐕

It's mighty secluded out here in the undeveloped parts of this big reservoir area. So secluded, in fact, that you can hunt, if that's what you like to do. And if you hunt for birds, you can bring your dog along leash-free during the appropriate seasons.

Non-hunting pooches are supposed to be leashed, even in the most remote acreage. The deer and rabbits appreciate it. If you're not going to be hunting, you might want to stay away from the very roughest land and enjoy any of three self-guided nature trails. Here's where you'll find nature at its best, without the brambles and burrs that take hours to pull out of your dog's coat. The Buckhorn Trail is an easy one-and-a-half-hour walk. It's at its freshest and most vibrant in the spring. You can pick up trail guides at the park headquarters.

The fishing here is excellent in the spring and early summer. If some folks in your party aren't the angling types, they can hang out on land and picnic, visit the playground or hike the nature trails. There are 40 miles of shoreline here, and while dogs aren't allowed to swim at official beaches, they can practice the dog paddle in most other places.

Camping with your dog is loads of fun, especially when the full moon slips over the lake and turns it a ghostly white. The 100 campsites are $12 a night apiece, and they're on a first-come, first-served basis.

As of press time, a day-use fee ranging from $1 to $3 was being considered.

Exit Interstate 5 at the Highway 32/Black Butte Lake and drive northwest (the road will turn into Road 200) for about six miles. You'll come to a fork in the road. To get to the park headquarters, continue straight another couple of miles. That's also the way to the Buckhorn recreation area, with its nature trail and plenty of camping. To get to the other two nature trails, go left at the fork in the road, onto County Road 206. The trails will be marked.

The most remote area is Grizzly Flat, which is barely accessible by car. Drive around the southernmost point of the lake on County Road 200A (a continuation of County Road 206) and you'll soon come to a rough gravel road, and then no road at all. You'll know you're there when you're still bouncing even though your car has stopped. (916) 865-4781. → *See #2 on map p. 118.*

• **Library Park** 🐾 🐾 🐾 🐾
Library Park may occupy only one city block, but the landscapers have made the very best of that one block. The grass is more perfect than AstroTurf, and there are so many tall trees that the place is shaded during much of the day, making for a refreshing summertime outing for you and your hot dog.

The really good news is that dogs under voice control may be off leash here. Just make sure your dog is truly obedient, because with the small size of the park, there's not much room for error.

From Highway 5, exit at Newville Road/County Road 200 and drive southeast one-third of a mile to County Road 200. The road then becomes Swift Street. Continue on Swift Street for three blocks, then turn right at 4th Street. Drive two blocks south. The park is on the corner of 4th and Mill streets. (916) 865-9053. → *See #3 on map p. 118.*

• **Vinsonhaler Park** 🐾 🐾 1/2 🐾
This isn't a terribly attractive city park, but very obedient dogs are allowed off leash here, as they are at Orland's other parks. At four square blocks, it's the biggest of the city's parks. The only fenced area is the ball field, and it's not foolproof, so be careful if your dog is an escape artist.

There's enough grass for rolling on and enough trees for lots of leg lifts. Unfortunately, there are also enough people hanging out at picnic tables all day that your dog may just be in the way at times.

From Highway 5, exit at Newville Road/County Road 200 and drive southeast one-third of a mile to County Road 200. The road then becomes Swift Street. Continue on Swift Street for seven blocks, then turn left at A Street. Drive three blocks north, and the park will be right in front of you, on Shasta Street. (916) 865-9053. → *See #4 on map p. 118.*

PLACES TO STAY

Amber Light Inn Motel: Small dogs are allowed, but only at the manager's discretion. Rates are $26 to $36. 828 Newville Road, Orland, CA 95963; (916) 865-7655.

Black Butte Lake campgrounds: See page 120.

Orland Inn: Rates are $28 to $40. 1052 South Street, Orland, CA 95963; (916) 865-7632.

WILLOWS

PARKS, BEACHES & RECREATION AREAS

•**Sacramento National Wildlife Refuge** 🐾🐾🐾 1/2 🐟 🐕

Only hunting dogs are allowed off leash here, and only in specified areas during hunting season. But plain old average everyday pooches are allowed to explore along the 10,700 acres of marshy waterfowl territory, as long as they're leashed and stay on the walking trails. Fortunately, the trails aren't muddy and mucky, so tell your dog not to feel too bad about being tethered.

More than 300 species of birds and mammals use the refuge throughout the year. It's a phenomenal place for wildlife observation. Bring your binoculars and a field guidebook, and you and your dog can learn all about the birds and the beasts here.

The refuge is open year-round. The entrance is about eight miles south of Willows. From Willows, take the Road 57 exit and drive south along the frontage road about six miles to the entrance. The refuge is off-limits during certain times of year. Call (916) 934-2801 for the schedule. ➡See #5 on map p. 118.

•**Sycamore Park** 🐾🐾 1/2

This is a pretty big park for Willows. It's green, grassy and groovy for dogs who like to roam around open fields wearing a leash. A paved path runs through the park and passes by medium-sized trees and several picnic tables.

The park is on the corner of Sycamore Street and Culver Avenue, right next to downtown Willows. (916) 934-7041. ➡See #6 on map p. 118.

PLACES TO STAY

Best Western Golden Pheasant: Small dogs are allowed and larger ones may be permitted if you call first. There's plenty of room on the hotel's grounds for your pooch to stretch her legs. Rates are $45 to $60. 249 North Humboldt Avenue, Willows, CA 95988; (916) 934-4603 or (800) 528-1234.

Cross Roads West Inn: All you Saint Bernard owners, rejoice. They have absolutely no compunctions at all about the size of the dogs who stay here. They even had an elephant as a guest once! (Although he didn't stay in a room.) Rates are $30 to $50. 452 North Humboldt Avenue, Willows, CA 95988; (916) 934-7026.

BUTTE COUNTY

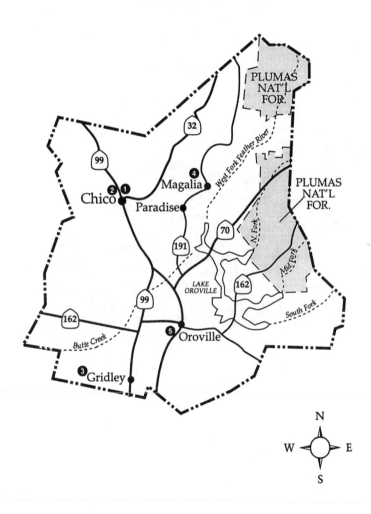

11
BUTTE COUNTY

A couple of large off-leash parks, as well as the off-leash Plumas National Forest, make Butte County a fine place to take the four-footed beast in your life.

NATIONAL FORESTS

See the National Forests/Wilderness Areas chapter starting on page 801 for important information and safety tips for visiting national forests with your dog.

• **Plumas National Forest** 🐾🐾🐾🐾 🦴 🐕

A good-sized chunk of the northeast corner of the county is made up of this magical forest. See page 807 for more information.

CHICO

The laid-back atmosphere of California State University Chico helps make this community a more relaxed, dog-friendly place. The cafes around town generally give pooches a wink and a nod when it comes to sitting at the outdoor tables. And there's even a sweeping section of a park near campus where dogs can run around off leash.

PARKS, BEACHES & RECREATION AREAS

• **Bidwell Park** 🐾🐾🐾🐾 🐕

Some city brochures claim this is the third-largest municipal park in the United States. Others step the claim down a notch and call it the fourth largest. Dogs don't care about such distinctions. They just know this 2,250-acre park is a happening place for dogs to trot around, do leg lifts and get back to nature.

Most dogs Joe knows prefer the rougher, untamed sections of the Upper Park segment. And guess what? That's exactly where they're allowed to run around off leash. The entire huge area north of Upper Park Road is a leash-free swath of dog heaven. You can explore the terrain via miles of trails that run through here or just kick up your heels in a grassy field. Only the lakes are off-limits.

If you want your dog to be leashless in a more developed area, you'll have to get up early. The large section of park west of Manzanita Avenue permits leashless dogs from one-half hour before sunrise to 8:30 a.m. You have to stay away from playgrounds, picnic areas and swimming holes, but your dog can still have a great run here. There are plenty of trails and wooded portions that are well-protected from traffic.

The park stretches 10 miles, from the university area all the way east to the rugged crags of Big Chico Creek Canyon. From Highway 99, exit at Highway 32 and head east to Bruce Road. Turn left on Bruce Road and drive north. The road will curve sharply to the right and become Chico Canyon Drive. Bear left at Manzanita Avenue and drive about a half mile to Upper Park Road. Turn right and you'll be in the park. Watch for signs for the dog area on your left. For the limited leash-free area, a good way to find a place with trails is to make a left turn from Manzanita Avenue onto Vallombrosa Avenue. Park on the road and walk in at any of several open areas in the wood fence. (916) 895-4972. → *See #1 on map p. 124.*

• **Chico City Plaza** 🐾 1/2

This is a sweet little park tucked in between municipal buildings in the center of town. Leashed dogs can hang out at the gazebo, on the lawn area, or under tall shady trees.

The park is in the heart of the old downtown area of Chico, so if you're going cafe hopping or window shopping with your pooch, you'll have a green spot for resting all your weary bones.

Concerts are held here during the summer, and as long as your dog doesn't disturb the peace, she's welcome to accompany you. See Diversions, page 127, for details.

The park is on Main Street between East Fourth and East Fifth streets. (916) 895-4711. → *See #2 on map p. 124.*

RESTAURANTS

Cafe Max: This place rates right up there in coffee-shop land. Sit on the patio with your pooch and sip a white chocolate mocha. Or indulge in any of 45 Italian sodas and dozens of scrumptious pastries. It's enough to make you lick your chops. 101 Salem Street; (916) 345-6655.

Campus Cafe: Dine with your dog under the trees at the charming backyard patio here. 121 Broadway; (916) 342-0578.

Oy Vey Cafe: If you're the type who wakes up at the crack of noon, you'll be happy to know that this hopping cafe serves breakfast until 3 p.m. Eat bagels, omelets, and all that good morning stuff with your dog at the outdoor tables here. And if you get up at 6 a.m. and are ready for lunch, no problem. Order yourself a big sandwich (but please hold off on the onions until at least 11 a.m.). 146 West Second Street; (916) 891-6710.

PLACES TO STAY

Holiday Inn of Chico: As long as your dog is "no bigger than a polar bear or a desk clerk," says the desk clerk, you and he (your dog, not the clerk) can cozy up together and watch satellite TV. Rates are $70 to $85. 685 Manzanita Court, Chico, CA 95926; (916) 345-2491.

Motel Orleans: Small dogs only, please. Rates are $35. A $25 dog deposit is required. 655 Manzanita Court, Chico, CA 95926; (916) 345-2533.

Motel 6: All Motel 6s allow one small pooch per room. Rates are $27 for the first adult, $6 for the second. 665 Manzanita Court, Chico, CA 95926; (916) 345-5500.

Safari Garden Motel: If you and your pooch stay here, you'll be only a mile from wonderful Bidwell Park (see page 125). Rates are $32 to $45. A $10 to $25 deposit is required for dogs (depending on your dog's size). 2352 Esplanade, Chico, CA 95926; (916) 343-3201.

FESTIVALS

Fourth of July Celebration: Good leashed dogs can have a blast at this community celebration of our nation's birth. The daytime activities at Bidwell Park are free. There's a small fee for the fireworks at night. Many dogs prefer to stay as far from the rocket's red glare as possible, so if your dog is at all noise-shy, it's best to leave him at home. For more information, call (916) 891-5556.

DIVERSIONS

Listen to paw-stomping music: Every Friday evening, from May through mid-September, you and your very quiet leashed dog are welcome to attend a free concert in lovely little Chico City Plaza. The music ranges from country to classical to jazz. Dogs think it's a real hoot to hang out with you on a blanket while you listen to Beethoven's greatest hits.

The park is on Main Street, between East Fourth and East Fifth streets. Call the Chico Chamber of Commerce at (916) 345-6500 for schedule information.

GRIDLEY

PARKS, BEACHES & RECREATION AREAS

•**Grey Lodge State Wildlife Area** 🐾🐾🐾🐾 🐕

Hunting dogs are the only ones who can be off leash in this spectacular wetland, and only during certain times of year. But this 8,400-acre wildlife area is a wonderful place to take well-behaved, leashed dogs the rest of the year. Barkers and yappers should be left at home, especially during waterfowl season. Many of the birds here have flown thousands of miles, and if they're disturbed, it could be detrimental to their health.

For most of the year, you can walk around on about 25 miles of hiking trails and levees. During waterfowl and nesting seasons, the hiking is very limited. But you don't have to walk a marathon to see amazing wildlife here. Among some of the critters you may run into: sandhill cranes, hawks, river otters, egrets, waterfowl, deer, beavers, orioles and black-shouldered kites.

From Highway 99, turn west on Sycamore Road and go six miles to Pennington Road. Turn left and continue three miles to the entrance on the right. The main parking lot is two miles to the west. (916) 846-5176. ➡ *See #3 on map p. 124.*

PLACES TO STAY
Pacific Motel: Rates are $32 to $50. 1308 Highway 99, Box L, Gridley, CA 95948; (916) 846-9915.

MAGALIA

Magalia was once known as Dogtown. According to a recent article in a clever historical publication called the *Dogtown Territorial Quarterly*, there were once far more dogs here than people.

That was thanks to a woman named Mrs. Bassett, who had only a tent and three mutts when she arrived during the Gold Rush. She was in dire straits when one of her dogs had a big litter of pups. Realizing that most men who came to California back then came by themselves or with other men, she had the idea that the pups would provide good companionship for the fellows. She began selling dogs to local miners for one pinch of gold dust per pup.

According to the article, "Soon every cabin in the area had a canine companion. There were dogs in the stores, dogs in the saloons, dogs everywhere!" (Read that section out loud to your dog. They love that part.)

Unfortunately, Dogtown lost its name in 1862. It seems the women friends of these miners were starting to come out from the east and call Dogtown home—and there was something about calling Dogtown home that turned their stomachs. An item appeared in the local paper from one of the discontented wives, who wrote, "We should hate to live in a place called Dogtown, particularly if we had a large correspondence and had to write the name frequently."

The female residents of Dogtown subsequently demanded that the community be renamed Magalia. It's the Latin word for "cottages." (If your dog whimpers right about now, please try to understand why.)

You can find out more about Dogtown and the *Dogtown Territorial Quarterly* by writing Bill Anderson at 6848-U Skyway, Paradise, CA 95969. The publication is working on gathering a list of the dozen or so Dogtowns that sprung up in California around the Gold Rush. It should make for interesting reading.

PARKS, BEACHES & RECREATION AREAS

• **Upper Ridge Nature Preserve** 🐾 🐾 🐾 1/2

The soft dirt trails here are covered with pine needles, making this one of the cushiest parks around. Dogs enjoy winding along these nature trails while you stop at the numbered stations and learn all about this piece of pine and oak forest.

When you arrive at the preserve, go to the kiosk near the parking area, pick up a wonderfully detailed nature-trail map and get your bearings. You can follow one of two mile-long trails. Both are lovely and will take you and your leashed pooch past streams, springs and a whopping variety of trees. Joe prefers the trail across the street from the parking area. It's a little more secluded.

The 80-acre park is leased from the Bureau of Land Management by a group of energetic, wilderness-loving retired men and women. They created the trails so people could learn about the natural environment here. They're working on many more projects, including a wheelchair-accessible trail. Says Tom Rodgers, 84, who helped get the group started, "It's such a pleasure knowing that nature is a little better for what we've done, and that so are the people who nature helps educate."

From the Magalia area, follow Skyway to Ponderosa Way and turn left. Drive a little more than a mile, and follow the signs to the preserve, which is just down the road on a gravel drive. The leasees have no phone number, but you can contact them by writing Upper Ridge Wilderness Areas, P.O. Box 154, Magalia, CA 95945. The Bureau of Land Management may be able to help with questions. Call them at (916) 224-2100. ➡ *See #4 on map p. 124.*

FESTIVALS

Dogtown Fair: This festival celebrates the usual July 4 stuff. But more important to pooches, it gives a nod to dogs and their contribution to this community (see page 128). A humorous dog show features pooches competing in categories such as "Best Smile" and "Waggliest Tail." Dogs really seem to enjoy themselves.

The festival is held on the grounds of the Magalia Community Church, at 13700 Old Skyway. Call (916) 877-7963 for information.

OROVILLE

PARKS, BEACHES & RECREATION AREAS

Dogs are not allowed in any Oroville city parks, nor in any Feather River Recreation and Park District parks.

• Oroville State Wildlife Area/
Thermalito Afterbay 🐾🐾🐾🐾 🐕

Unlike at many other wildlife areas, if your dog isn't a hunting companion, she can still be off leash here as long as she's under voice control.

There are some 5,000 acres of grasslands, marshlands and riparian forests for you and your dog to explore. Where it's too wet to walk, take a levee.

Be sure to bring your binoculars if you enjoy birdwatching. More than 140 songbirds have been seen here. As you wander through the forests of cottonwoods, willows and valley oaks, you may also spot other interesting fauna. If you're not certain your dog will stay close by, do the animals a favor and leash her.

From Highway 162, go south on Larkin Road (just east of the Oroville Airport). Follow the road a few miles to Vance Avenue and turn left. In three-quarters of a mile, you'll be at the wildlife area. Maps are usually available at the entry stations. (916) 538-2236.
➡ *See #5 on map p. 124.*

PLACES TO STAY

Best Western Grand Manor Inn: Rates are $53 to $90. Dogs require a $50 deposit. 1470 Feather River Boulevard, Oroville, CA 95965; (916) 533-9673.

Motel 6: Rates are $27 for the first adult, $6 for the second. All Motel 6s allow one small dog per room. 505 Montgomery Street, Oroville, CA 95965; (916) 632-9400.

Lake Oroville State Recreation Area: This is a state park and it's one of the strict ones. Although it's a 30,000-acre park with 22 miles of trails, dogs can't go on the trails or the picnic areas or far off a paved road. In essence, all they can really do here is hang out with you on your boat or go camping with you.

There are 382 sites available. Campsites are $10 to $16. Dogs are $1 extra. If you choose to stay on and around the paved roadways with your leashed pooch, you can enter the park for a $3 day-use fee, plus $1 for the dog. From Montgomery Street in the main part of Oroville, follow the green line down the road to the lake. Call MISTIX at (800) 444-PARK for reservations. For park information, call (916) 538-2200.

PARADISE

As you enter town, a big wooden sign announces "PARADISE. To be all its name implies." Sorry, Paradise. You failed the dog test. The Happy Hunting Grounds you are not. Dogs are banned at all municipal parks here, and that gets their fur standing on end. (Besides, if you're going to have a sign like that, maybe you should put it in a place where the next thing you see is not a sign advertising duplexes, and then a Burger King, and then a tire shop and a wig store. It kind of takes the oomph out of a heavenly idea.)

Fortunately, the beautiful Upper Ridge Nature Preserve (see page 129) just north of town in Magalia, has everything a leashed dog could want. And some of the scenery in the less-populated parts of Paradise really is beautiful. The town is surrounded by mountains, spectacular canyons and tall pines.

RESTAURANTS

Brunch House: Your dog is welcome to join you for brunch until 3 p.m. on the combination patio/porch here. The restaurant even provides a small lot out back if your pooch needs to discreetly relieve herself. 6333 Skyway; (916) 877-7176.

Dolly O Donuts: 591 Pearson Road; (916) 877-4331.

PLACES TO STAY

Palos Verdes Motel: Small dogs only. Rates are $35 to $40. 5423 Skyway, Paradise, CA 95969; (916) 877-2127.

Ponderosa Gardens Motel: Rates are $47 to $57. Dogs are $5 extra. 7010 Skyway, Paradise, CA 95969; (916) 872-9094.

PLUMAS COUNTY

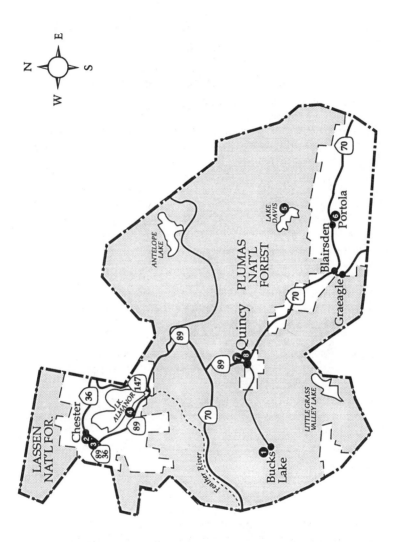

12
PLUMAS COUNTY

Hidden between the ever-popular vacationlands of Shasta and Tahoe, Plumas County lives up to its publicity slogan, "California's Best Kept Secret." Even people in the next county asked, "Where's that?" when I told them where we'd just visited.

This county is 67 percent Plumas National Forest, which means there's natural beauty and off-leash dog heaven at almost every turn. It's Feather River Country here, with dozens of lakes and hundreds of miles of streams and rivers. That translates into endless good times hiking, fishing, swimming, wading and cross-country skiing for you and your pooch.

Plumas is one of those counties so untouched by tourists that you can still find the best of rural life. The towns of Quincy and Portola have some of the most delicious country-style cooking we've ever tasted. And the country-style humor (like how all those yellow roadside deer warning signs have the deer sporting big red noses) isn't bad either.

NATIONAL FORESTS
See the National Forests/Wilderness Areas chapter starting on page 801 for important information and safety tips for visiting national forests with your dog.

• **Lassen National Forest** 🐾 🐾 🐾 🐾 🐕
Only a tiny portion of this national forest falls in Plumas County. See page 805 for more on this magnificent forest.

• **Plumas National Forest** 🐾 🐾 🐾 🐾 🐕
See page 807.

BLAIRSDEN
RESTAURANTS
Cromberg Country Cafe & Store: You can set a spell with your pooch and eat the lunch you bought inside. 59655 Highway 70; (916) 836-1048.

BUCKS LAKE

PARKS, BEACHES & RECREATION AREAS

•**Bucks Lake** 🐾🐾🐾🐾 ⚫ 🐕

During warmer months, you and your dog can hike, swim and fish 'til you drop. Campgrounds here are good places to drop, and the 49 sites in Plumas National Forest are free. Many of these sites are right along the lake's 14-mile shoreline, making for exquisite views. All are first come, first served.

If trout fishing is your fancy, you'll have a hard time finding a much troutier lake. The lake is stocked annually with rainbow trout, so it's a great place to take young anglers and dogs who are entertained by fishing activity.

The lake is almost completely surrounded by Plumas National Forest, where dogs can run free in undeveloped areas. On the northeast side is the beautiful Bucks Lake Wilderness, where your obedient dog may also accompany you without a leash. From some of the peaks in this wilderness, you can see forever—or at least as far as Mount Lassen.

During winter, the Bucks Lake area is a great spot for cross-country skiing. Dogs love going along for a little exercise, as long as the snow isn't too high.

From Highway 70 in Quincy, take Bucks Lake Road west about 12 miles to the lake. For information on campgrounds and the lake, call (916) 283-2050. ➡See #1 on map p. 134.

PLACES TO STAY

Bucks Lake camping: See above.

CHESTER/LAKE ALMANOR

PARKS, BEACHES & RECREATION AREAS

•**Chester Park** 🐾 1/2

The ball field here is fenced in, so it's good for dogs who roam too far (they have to be leashed anyway). The rest of the park is just so-so for dogs, with a grassy area, picnic tables and wood benches. Kids enjoy the little playground here.

From Highway 36, go northwest on Willow Way. The park is on the right in less than a block. (916) 283-0188. ➡See #2 on map p. 134.

•**Collins-Almanor Forest** 🐾🐾🐾🐾 ⚫ 🐕

"Dogs love trees, and we love dogs," says dog-loving forester Dan Howell. That's why the Collins Pine Company rolls out the pine needle carpet for pooches on its 91,000-acre mixed conifer forest. Leashes can be shoved in your backpack, and you and your dog can hike unattached throughout this glorious working forest.

This is one of the most environmentally-correct timber companies in the country, so you won't be seeing clear-cut patches that make the landscape look like a dog with mange. The family-owned company has been logging this forest since 1941, but with such a commitment to long-term sustainable forestry that they even win accolades from environmentalists.

You'll love this place so much that you may want to spend a few days here. That means spending a few nights here. Many camping areas are available, and the ones near streams are the best. There's no fee for any of this.

You'll want to stop in at the Chester office to get additional information about the best access routes for your level of hiking, and to find out what areas of the forest are open. The office is at 500 Main Street. It's the one with the big green lawn (at least in the spring and summer). The phone number is (916) 258-2111. → *See #3 on map p. 134.*

•Lake Almanor 🐾 🐾 🐾 1/2

The azure waters of this idyllic lake make a beautiful centerpiece for an adventurous canine time here. The lake is big (52 square miles), and sections of the surrounding areas are controlled by many different entities, both public and private. It can be confusing, and you can get yourself into trouble if you stumble onto the wrong land parcel with a dog.

Although parts of the lake are surrounded by both the Plumas and Lassen national forests, neither of these areas is set up for hiking around the lake. They're geared more toward camping. Dogs should remain on leash in the portions of forest immediately around the lake. That will also keep them from bounding onto the privately-owned land that weaves throughout the public lands here.

If you stay at the resorts along Lake Almanor, keep in mind that most have their own land which you can explore with a leashed dog. Some even have views of magnificent snow-capped Mount Lassen rising in the distance.

A fun stop with your pooch comes just after the dam at the south end of the lake as you're driving north on Highway 89. You can pull off to the right, near the Canyon Dam Boat Launch, and trot along the flats near the lake. Bring your fishing equipment and make a few casts as you meander along. The lake, actually a reservoir, is known for its salmon, trout and even smallmouth bass.

For general lake and camping information, contact the Almanor

Ranger District of the Lassen National Forest at (916) 258-2141. When in Chester, you can visit the ranger station and pick up maps and advice. It's at 900 East Highway 36. The Chester/Lake Almanor Chamber of Commerce can also provide you with good information. Call them at (916) 258-2426. ➤*See #4 on map p. 134.*

RESTAURANTS
We could find only one restaurant that allows dogs, although several others have outdoor tables in the summer. Bummer.

The Hamburger Tree: 336 Main Street; (916) 258-2072.

PLACES TO STAY
Cedar Lodge Motel: Rates are $29 to $53. Some rooms have kitchens. Highway 36, Box 677, Chester, CA 96020; (916) 258-2904.

Collins-Almanor Forest campsites: See page 136.

Lake Almanor Resort: Cabins and a cozy lodge are available to you and your dog. The lodge is right on the lake and provides good views. The cabins are set among the trees. Open May to mid-October. Rates are $47 to $90. Dogs are $5 extra. 2706 Big Springs Road, Lake Almanor, CA 96137; (916) 596-3337.

Lassen View Resort: The housekeeping cabins here range from $42 to $92. The 94 campsites are $12 to $14. Open May to November. 7457 Eastshore Drive, Lake Almanor, CA 96137; (916) 596-3437.

Little Norway Resort: Dogs enjoy the lakeside housekeeping cabins here almost as much as they dislike the loud jet skis the resort rents out. It usually is quiet here, though. Rates are $50 to $100. Pooches are $5 extra. 432 Peninsula Drive, Lake Almanor, CA 96137; (916) 596-3225.

Timber House: They say they don't want Shetland ponies or Saint Bernards here, but just about any other size pooch is okay. Rates at this motel are $35 to $60. Dogs are $5 extra. Chester Park is nearby. The lodge is at First and Main streets. Box 1010, Chester, CA 96020; (916) 258-2729.

GRAEAGLE

PLACES TO STAY
Plumas-Eureka State Park: Dogs are very limited in their activities in this historic 5,000-acre park surrounding the old mining town of Johnsville. But one thing they can do is camp with you at one of the 67 sites here. Fees are $12 to $14 a night. Dogs are $1 extra. From Highway 89, take County Road A14 west to the park. The campground can get crowded, so call MISTIX at (800) 444-PARK for reservations. For park info, call (916) 836-2380.

PORTOLA

This old town's best features are the Portola Railroad Museum (see page 140) and the Middle Fork Feather River. The river is very accessible from many parts of town. Just bring your rod, reel, hiking shoes and dog, and you can create a canine's dream day.

PARKS, BEACHES & RECREATION AREAS

• Lake Davis 🐾 🐾 🐾 🦴

This is the largest of the three Upper Feather River lakes, with 32 miles of shoreline, most of it in Plumas National Forest (see page 807). The hiking right at the lake is limited, but you can manage to get in some exercise on trails and dirt roads that extend into the national forest from the lake area.

It's the perfect spot if you're vacationing with an avid angler. The hiking is excellent and off leash once you're out of the campgrounds and adjacent state game refuge, and into the undeveloped areas of the Plumas National Forest. And there's plenty of nature to watch: Waterfowl, bald eagles and bats are easy to see at various times of year.

From Highway 70, take Grizzly Road or Lake Davis Road about seven miles north to the lake. They have a total of 186 sites available on a first-come, first-served basis. Tent campsites are $8. Self-contained mobile homes stay for free. For information on Lake Davis or to get maps of the forest near the other two Upper Feather River lakes, call (916) 836-2575. ➡ *See #5 on map p. 134.*

• Portola City Park 🐾 🐾

Much more space is devoted to human activities than dog activities here, but there's still a decent little field, some trees and a gazebo that leashed dogs seem to enjoy. It's a good rest stop before or after a visit to the nearby Portola Railroad Museum (see page 140).

From Highway 70, go south on South Gulling Street. The park will be on your left, across from City Hall, shortly after you cross over the bridge. (916) 832-4216. ➡ *See #6 on map p. 134.*

RESTAURANTS

Good & Plenty Restaurant: This place doesn't have outdoor tables, but it has such delicious down-home cooking that Joe recommended I mention it anyway. You can always get your food to go and eat it beside the nearby Feather River with your dog drooling at your side. When it's cold out, the windows get steamy from the wholesome food cooking in the kitchen, and the railroad workers flock here. It's a little off the beaten path, so you'll be hard pressed to find a tourist. If you're longing for a little Thanksgiving in the middle of March, try the huge, hot turkey dinner with all the fixings for only $5.25! 241 Commercial Street; (916) 832-5795.

Troy's Drive-In: Dogs love to help you eat the fish and chips they serve here. 74384 Highway 70; (916) 832-5555.

Weenie World: Dogs adore the smell of the hot dogs that make this a popular hangout. 73136 Highway 70; (916) 832-5090.

PLACES TO STAY

Lake Davis camping: See page 139 for details.

Sleepy Pines Motel: The owners of this homey motel have their own dog, and they'll often allow dogs as guests, but they want "nothing huge or dangerous." The lodging is very close to the Feather River. The owners can point you to the best fishing spots. Rates are $40 to $70. 74631 Highway 70, Portola, CA 96122; (916) 832-4291.

DIVERSIONS

Locomotivate your dog: The Portola Railroad Museum is one of those rare museums relaxed enough to welcome dogs to sniff out the attractions. Home to one of the largest collections of preserved diesel locomotives in the world, the museum has 25 locomotives and 50 freight, caboose and passenger cars.

Not only can your well-behaved dog accompany you around the grounds, she can also go with you on a train ride around the one-mile track. You'll ride in a five-car train made up of cute old cabooses. The loop is vaguely reminiscent of that *Twilight Zone* episode where the couple wakes up in a strange town and just can't escape, only to find out they're the latest additions to a giant alien girl's new "miniature" dollhouse/railroad station. But have no worries here, unless you see a giant shadow of a hand descending on you.

The ride is $2 per person, $5 per family. There's no fee for dogs. The museum doesn't demand an entry fee, but they do ask for an optional $2 donation. Train rides are given every half hour from 11 a.m. to 4 p.m. on weekends from Memorial Day to Labor Day. (916) 832-4131.

QUINCY

This is a Main Street community with restored and preserved buildings dating back to the town's roots in the mid-1800s. If you whiz through town heading west, you'll barely get a glimpse of the downtown area, which is home to a couple of good, dog-friendly restaurants. Main Street only goes east and it's worth a gander.

PARKS, BEACHES & RECREATION AREAS

• **Gansner Park** 🐾 🐾 🐾

Dogs enjoy bouncing around this long and luscious park. They're supposed to bounce around on leash, but if your dog happens to escape from your grasp, there's little danger: The park is almost entirely fenced. Generally, where there aren't fences, trees and brush are so thick that dogs would have a difficult time getting out. The grass is very green, the pines are very large, and the park generally is very uninhabited. You can picnic, barbecue, play tennis or watch the kids at the park's small playground.

From Highway 70/89 just north of town, turn east on Gansner Park Road (there will be signs for the park). (916) 283-3278. ➛*See #7 on map p. 134.*

• **Pioneer Park** 🐾 1/2

Dogs on long journeys don't mind stretching out at this small park. Since it's just off Highway 70 in town, it's a convenient place to stop. And since it has ample shade from surrounding trees, it's decent on hot summer days.

From Highway 70/89, go north on Plumas Fairgrounds Road. The park is on your right, before the fairgrounds. (916) 283-3278. ➛*See #8 on map p. 134.*

RESTAURANTS

The Bakery & Deli: 411 West Main Street; (916) 283-2253.

Morning Thunder Cafe: Eat hearty food on this really sweet, old wood porch, shaded with lattice work and grapevines. 557 Lawrence Street; (916) 283-1310.

Stoney's Country Burger: Try the Stoney burger here. You'll love it, and if you don't, your dog will. 11 Lindan Avenue; (916) 283-3911.

FESTIVALS

Mountain Harvest Festival: Your dog can howl at the costumes on parade and check out the carved pumpkins with you at this autumn festival on the courthouse lawn. But of all the colorful events swirling around them, dogs seem to prefer the food side of things: The festival features "A Taste of Quincy," where you can pay $5 to sample food at tables representing the city's restaurants. It's a great way to try food at the eateries that don't permit pooches.

The festival is held each October at the courthouse lawn in downtown Quincy (520 West Main Street). Call (916) 283-0188 for this year's dates and schedule of events.

LAKE COUNTY

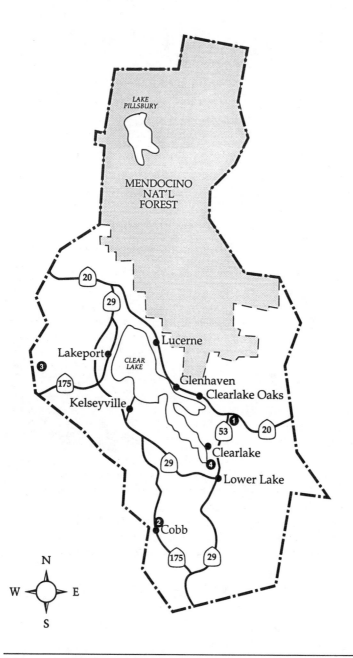

13
LAKE COUNTY

This is a county with an attitude about dogs—a bad attitude. Dogs aren't allowed in any county parks. Since parks in the small towns are county parks, that's a double dose of bad news. The major cities (Clearlake and Lakeport) also ban dogs from their parks. Dogs aren't permitted at public beaches around Clear Lake.

Signs throughout the county shout that dogs must be licensed, leashed and will be shot if they're caught molesting farm critters. Even the trash barrels in county parks are painted with big white "No Dogs" warnings. Looks like you can't even walk your dog in a garbage can around here.

Welcome to Lake County, a major disappointment for our fine four-legged friends. The county slogan that occasionally pops up here is "Lake County: Dare to Explore." But that's a cruel joke for the canines in our midst. If they dare to explore too much, they're going to get socked with a big fine. And guess who has to pay?

What's a dog to do? She could start by thanking the Big Dog in the Sky for the national forests, for the Bureau of Land Management, for the California Department of Forestry, and (I never thought I'd say this) for the state park system. If not for these, dogs would have to sneak around everywhere.

If your dog wants to hang out near the lake, you'll have to stay in one of the private resorts that has lakeside access. It's a fun way to spend a weekend, but it's much cheaper to get her heart set on a hike in one of the few dog-friendly areas of the county.

NATIONAL FORESTS

See the National Forests/Wilderness Areas chapter starting on page 801 for important information and safety tips for visiting national forests with your dog.

•**Mendocino National Forest** 🐾 🐾 🐾 🐾 🐾 ➡ 🐕

A huge portion of this forest is in Lake County. It's a relief to dogs who aren't even permitted to set paw in county parks. See page 806 for more information.

CLEARLAKE

Dogs aren't allowed in any parks here. The woman at the Chamber of Commerce is sorry about that, but it's not her fault.

She wears a doggy charm bracelet, and owns a toy poodle who's the star of the parties she attends. Her solution to the area's strict dog rules? "My dog is just like a person," she says. "She just walks around the neighborhood with me on a leash and we go home and eat."

RESTAURANTS

Burger King: Have it your dog's way at the patio here. 15165 Lakeshore Drive; (707) 994-6209.

PLACES TO STAY

Clearlake Travelodge: This motel is located in downtown Clearlake, one block from the lake. Rates are $34 to $48. Dogs are $10 extra. 4775 Old Highway 53, Box 5166, Clearlake, CA 95422, (707) 994-1499.

CLEARLAKE OAKS

PARKS, BEACHES & RECREATION AREAS

•**Cache Creek Recreation Area** 🐾 🐾 🐾 🐾 🐕

This 50,000-acre Bureau of Land Management area is a very welcome sight for dogs, who are banned from most parks in the county. Not only can they explore this huge and wild area, they can do so off leash, as long as they're obedient sorts. If you can't trust your dog not to wander away and get eaten, or not to wander away and eat another animal, then please keep him leashed.

Bring your binoculars, because you'll need them. You may see bald eagles, blue herons, tule elk or even a black bear. A seven-mile trail (steep at times) provides you and the dog in your life with ample room to start an adventure. We like to visit in the spring, when the wildflowers open their blazing petals to a new year.

You can also camp here, in primitive, fee-free sites. You'll need to get a permit from the California Department of Forestry office. The entrance to this patch of dog heaven is about eight miles east of town, on the south side Highway 20. You'll see the signs. (707) 462-3874. ➡*See #1 on map p. 144.*

PLACES TO STAY

Cache Creek Recreation Area campsites: See above.

Lake Haven Motel: This motel is located on a sheltered canal. The folks here love dogs, and welcome leashed pooches to sniff out the surrounding area. Rates are $36 to $53. 100 Short Street, Clearlake Oaks, CA 95423; (707) 998-3908.

COBB

PARKS, BEACHES & RECREATION AREAS

• **Boggs Mountain Demonstration
State Forest** 🐾 🐾 🐾 🐾 ⬅ 🐕

You and your blissfully leash-free dog can hike for days in a 3,500-acre forestry experiment. The forest is being studied as an example of how a forest that was nearly stripped by someone else can be brought back and managed for continuous forest production, public recreation, wildlife habitat and a watershed.

It's working. You'll hike on miles of trails that wander through mixed conifer forests and grasslands. As long as your dog is obedient, you can let her off leash. But if she can't be trusted around deer and other critters of the woods, keep her leashed.

You may like it here so much that you'll want to stay. You can camp here at one of 14 sites, and so far, it won't cost you a cent. The state is considering asking a small fee, but luckily nothing has happened yet. Dogs must be leashed at the campground.

From Highway 175 about a mile north of Cobb, watch for a blue and white sign for the state fire station. At the first intersection past it, go east for about a quarter-mile to the park's entrance. (707) 928-4378. → *See #2 on map p. 144.*

PLACES TO STAY

Boggs Mountain Demonstration State Forest campsites: See above.

GLENHAVEN

PLACES TO STAY

Indian Beach Resort: Stay at any of nine cottages on the lake. All have kitchenettes. There's plenty of room to walk your leashed pooch here. Rates are $35 to $100. 9945 East Highway 20, Box 648, Glenhaven, CA 95443; (707) 998-3760.

KELSEYVILLE

PLACES TO STAY

Clear Lake State Park: Dogs enjoy spending the night under the oaks at one of the 147 sites at this lakeside park. Since they're not permitted on trails or in the water, they can't do much else here anyway. Rates are $12 to $17. Dogs are $1 extra. From Highway 29, take the Kelseyville exit and turn north on Main Street. The road will turn into State Street, then Gaddy Lane. In about two miles, go right on Soda Bay Road. The park will be on your left in about a half mile. For reservations, phone (800) 444-PARK. For park information, call (707) 279-4293.

Creekside Lodge: Rates are $34 to $50. You have to sign a waiver taking responsibility for dog damage, and you may have to pay a dog deposit. 79901 Highway 29, Kelseyville, CA 95451; (707) 279-9258.

Jim's Soda Bay Resort: Stay in an attractive housekeeping cottage on the lake. There's plenty of room for your leashed dog to walk around and dip her paws. Rates are $45 to $55. 6380 Soda Bay Road, Kelseyville, CA 95451; (707) 279-4837.

LAKEPORT

PARKS, BEACHES & RECREATION AREAS

•**Cow Mountain Recreation Area** 🐾🐾🐾🐾 🐕 🐕

This is a great place to visit with your dog, who can run leash-free in many areas. The main entrance is on the other side of the county border, near Ukiah. From Lake County, enter at Younce Road (Old Toll Road). See page 105 for more details. *→See #3 on map p. 144.*

RESTAURANTS

Cindy's Drive-In: Eat good old burgers at the outdoor tables of this drive-in. 1005 North Main Street; (707) 263-5019.

Park Place: The fresh-made pasta here is delightful. Wash it down with your favorite local wine while you and your dog relax at the outdoor tables here. The restaurant is next to a lakeside park, but since dogs aren't permitted at the park, all they can do is watch the ducks go by. 50 Third Street; (707) 263-0444.

PLACES TO STAY

Chalet Motel: Some kitchenettes are available at this lakefront motel, located north of downtown. There's a little walking room for your dog here. Rates are $35 to $45. 2802 Lakeshore Boulevard, Lakeport, CA 95453; (707) 263-5040.

Rainbow Lodge Motel: Rates are $30 to $36. 2569 Lakeshore Boulevard, Lakeport, CA 95453; (707) 263-4309.

LOWER LAKE

PARKS, BEACHES & RECREATION AREAS

•**Anderson Marsh State Historic Park** 🐾🐾

For humans without dogs, this 870-acre park is a terrific adventure. Several miles of trails lead to remote birdwatching areas far from any roads.

But if you're lucky enough to be traveling with a dog, this park is just a leg-stretching zone. Dogs are not permitted on trails here. They're relegated to the open fields behind the old Anderson barn. Since only the area adjacent to the barn is mowed, there's not much room to roam. The tall grass beyond the lawn can be full of ticks.

At least your leashed dog will get to sniff an old outhouse or sit patiently outside the portable toilet while you explore its inner realms.

The fee is $2 per car and $1 per dog. The ranger is usually in the form of a metal post with a box on it, so if you'll be here only a few minutes, you might not need to pay. But real human rangers can come out of the woodwork (and there's quite a lot of wood around the barn), so be careful.

From Highway 53 just north of Lower Lake, turn west at Anderson Ranch Parkway, and make an immediate right into the park. (707) 994-0688 or (707) 279-4293. ➜ *See #4 on map p. 144.*

LUCERNE

PLACES TO STAY

Lake Sands Resort: There's plenty of land for a leashed pooch to peruse at this lakefront lodging. Rates are $50 year-round. There's a one-time $25 dog fee. 6335 East Highway 20, Box 48, Lucerne, CA 95458; (707) 274-7732.

COLUSA COUNTY

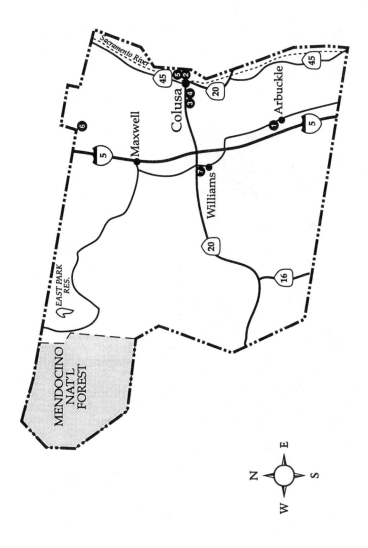

14

COLUSA COUNTY

This is a county of refuge. Actually, it's a county of a few refuges. Birds see the refuges on their little bird maps and flock here by the millions. It's an amazing sight to see with your leashed pooch during the winter months.

ARBUCKLE

PARKS, BEACHES & RECREATION AREAS

• **City Park** 🐾 🐾

We made an emergency rest stop for the dogs here one time and they were most grateful. The park has a big, green field that's fairly far from the road (dogs must be leashed anyway), and a fenced-in ball field, a wooden playground and many picnic tables. In addition, the park is edged with bushes—something boy dogs can appreciate.

From Interstate 5, take the Arbuckle exit and follow it south about a half mile to Hall Street. Turn right. The park will be on your right in a couple of blocks. There's no phone number to contact for information about the park. ➡ *See #1 on map p. 152.*

COLUSA

PARKS, BEACHES & RECREATION AREAS

• **Colusa Levee Scenic Park** 🐾 🐾 🐾

If you have a dog, you've got a great excuse to take a hike through the historic part of town. This park takes you on a wide and wonderful levee above the Sacramento River, on the edge of the sweet old River District. There's a real genteel feel here.

Our favorite entry point is between 6th and 9th streets at Main Street (across from the brick River District Building). A couple of wooden staircases on Main Street take you up to the levee. (916) 458-5622. ➡ *See #2 on map p. 152.*

• **Colusa National Wildlife Refuge** 🐾 🐾 🐾 1/2

Unless your dog is helping you hunt here, he has to follow the dress code and wear a leash. The 4,040-acre refuge has a self-guided auto tour, but better for dogs, there's a really good walking trail. Pick up a pamphlet or check out the interpretive panels at the kiosk. You won't believe all the waterfowl you'll see, especially if you visit in December or January. We're talking flocks bigger than even Alfred Hitchcock could have conjured. (If you're at all spookable, you may not want to rent the movie *The Birds* just before your visit.)

From Colusa, drive a half mile west on Highway 20 to the refuge entrance. The refuge is off-limits during certain times of the year. Call (916) 934-2801 for the schedule. → *See #3 on map p. 152.*

•Jay Park 🐾 🐾 1/2

The park is in a really beautiful old section of town. It fits in well here, with graceful palms, stately trees, ultra-green grass and plenty of places to sit. It's only a square block in area, but leashed dogs get plenty of fulfillment. Humans also enjoy the posh and relaxing surroundings.

It's located between Market and Jay streets and 9th and 10th streets. (916) 458-5622. → *See #4 on map p. 152.*

•Sacramento River State Recreation Area 🐾 🐾 🐾 1/2

Primitive trails and mucky riverbeds are begging to be explored here. Dogs adore this place, but they're supposed to be leashed.

Our favorite trail starts right next to the boat launch area. If you ignore some of the smaller trails that branch off it, the main trail will take you down to the sandy/muddy "beach" area along the Sacramento River. Some folks like to fish here, so if you want to get away, just head left and walk down the riverbed. You'll likely see dozens of beasty footprints from the night's activities. Dogs love to sniff at raccoon, deer and bird prints.

The day-use fee is $5. It costs $10 to camp at one of their 14 sites. Dogs are $1 extra for day-use or camping. Campsite reservations are accepted from the middle of April through September. Highway 20 will take you directly to the park. Coming from Interstate 5, Highway 20 changes its name to 10th Street once you enter Colusa. Follow 10th Street through town and into the park. For camping reservations or park information, call (916) 458-4927. → *See #5 on map p. 152.*

RESTAURANTS

Rick's Burgers & Shakes: They like dogs here and will probably give your pooch some water if she's thirsty. 854 10th Street; (916) 458-2831.

PLACES TO STAY

Sacramento State Recreation Area campgrounds: See above.

MAXWELL

PARKS, BEACHES & RECREATION AREAS

The Delevan National Wildlife Refuge is not currently open to the public, but the Sacramento National Wildlife Refuge is quite a place to visit with a dog.

• **Sacramento National Wildlife Refuge** 🐾 🐾 🐾 1/2 🦴 🐕

The southern end of this magnificent refuge extends into northern Colusa County. See page 122 for a description. *➜See #6 on map p. 152.*

WILLIAMS

Guys who wear cowboy hats for real hang out here. So do oodles of people traveling on Interstate 5. The latter folks don't stop because of any tourist attraction. They stop for gas and food. Fortunately, this town has much more ambience than most pit stops on the interstate.

PARKS, BEACHES & RECREATION AREAS

• **City Park** 🐾 1/2

If you're stopping in Williams for gas, you may as well come here and give your pooch a quick walk. A few trees and a bit of grass will be welcome sights to the dog in your life, and a tiny playground seems to please any tots tagging along.

Exit Interstate 5 at the main Williams exit and drive west to 9th Street. Turn left. The park will be on your left in a couple of blocks. (916) 473-5389. *➜See #7 on map p. 152.*

RESTAURANTS

A&W: Dine on good old-fashioned fast food burgers and famous root beer at the half-dozen outdoor tables here. It's at the corner of 7th and D streets. (916) 473-5616.

La Fortuna Bakery: Eat fattening bakery food at two picnic tables. 669 F Street; (916) 473-2023.

Granzella's: The food here is *mahhvelous.* You can eat at any of the several wood picnic tables on the porch here. Joe drools like a fool when he sees anyone eating the special hot turkey and gravy sandwich. Best of all, the restaurant folks love dogs as much as dogs love the restaurant. "We're real animal lovers," says Linda Granzella. "We'll even go around the restaurant and find people who left their dogs in the cars with the windows rolled up." And of course, they'll be happy to give your dog all the water he needs. 451 6th Street; (916) 473-5583.

PLACES TO STAY

Comfort Inn: Rates are $43 to $50, and that includes a continental breakfast. Dogs are $5 extra. 400 C Street, Williams, CA 95987; (916) 473-2381.

Stage Stop Motel: There's a fridge in every room here. It's not quite like a chicken in every pot, but it's not bad. Rates are $38 to $50. Dogs are $5 extra. 330 7th Street, Williams, CA 95987; (916) 473-2281.

SIERRA AREA COUNTIES

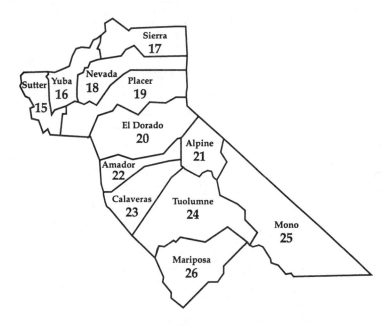

SUTTER COUNTY

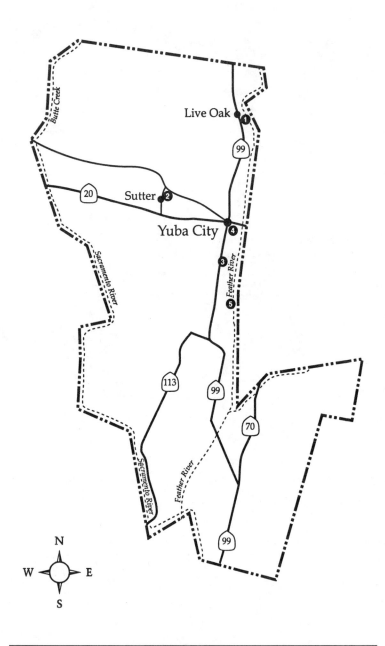

15
SUTTER COUNTY

There's not much to do here with a dog, but where there's a full bladder, there's a way.

LIVE OAK

• **Live Oak Recreation Park** 🐾 🐾 🐾

There aren't any big trails here, but you and your leashed dog can hike around the dirt roads that wind through the park or just walk around the grassy fields. There's a decent boat launch here for Feather River fans. People with pooches like to picnic under the oaks and willows before turning in for the night at the county's only campground. Small trails lead to the river, but it's a little rough at times and swimming is not allowed.

The day-use fee is $3 per car. Camping at one of the 20 sites is $7 a night, first come, first served. Exit Highway 99 at Penington Road and drive east about a mile to the end of the road, where you'll find the park. (916) 741-7407. ➡ *See #1 on map p. 160.*

PLACES TO STAY
Live Oak Recreation Park camping: See above.

SUTTER

PARKS, BEACHES & RECREATION AREAS

• **Vera Carroll Park** 🐾

The huge orchard across the street from this tiny park will be much more tempting to visit with your dog, but alas, if you don't own it or work on it, you can't set foot on it.

The park has a fenced-in playing field, a few shaded picnic tables and a swimming pool. As long as your dog is leashed and stays out of the pool, he'll be welcome here.

From Highway 20, go north on Acacia Avenue for about two miles. The park will be on your right, at College Avenue. It's run by the Sutter Youth Organization. (916) 673-2495. ➡ *See #2 on map p. 160.*

YUBA CITY

PARKS, BEACHES & RECREATION AREAS

"Our parks are for the people, not for the animals. We'd rather not be put in that book," a parks department staffer told me. But since dogs are permitted at all city parks on an eight-foot leash, Joe thought it would be nice for dogs to know their rights.

•Blackburn Talley Park 🐾 🐾 1/2

The South Water Reclamation Plant is right next to this nine-acre park. There's always a high-pitched hum here, like a TV set gone bad, but dogs don't seem to mind. Something much better comes along with the reclamation plant—a slightly foul odor. And the dogs love it. Their noses flutter with joy when the odor hits them broadside.

When we visited, there was an ugly, torn-up field on the Burns Drive side of the park. It's the best place to take a dog in this otherwise well-manicured, recreation-oriented park. We hear that field could soon be re-seeded and just as green as the rest of the park, but for dogs' sakes, we hope it's left as rough as can be.

From Highway 99, turn east on Lincoln Road and drive about a mile to Garden Highway, where you'll turn right. The park will be on your left in just under a half mile. Turn left onto Burns Drive and park in the lot or on the street. (916) 741-4650. ➡*See #3 on map p. 160.*

•Sam Brannan Park 🐾 🐾 1/2

The back area of this park is nicely fenced, so if your leashed dog makes a break for it, she'll be relatively safe. Otherwise, peruse the big grassy area, let your dog sniff the trees or have a relaxing picnic at the many tables here.

From Highway 99, turn east on Bridge Street, drive a few blocks and go left on Gray Avenue. The park is on your left in a few more blocks. (916) 741-4650. ➡*See #4 on map p. 160.*

•Shanghai Bend Park 🐾 🐾 1/2

This is an extremely narrow strip of grass with picnic tables. But it's saved by a stairway that leads you over the levee, where you can walk another 300 yards or so to the edge of the Feather River. The fishing is very good here, as is the paw-dunking, if you find a calm spot for your leashed pooch.

From Highway 99, turn east on Lincoln Road and drive about a mile to Garden Highway, where you'll turn right. Drive nearly 1.5 more miles south and turn left at Shanghai Bend Road, driving past all the suburban-style subdivisions, and past a wild-looking, undeveloped area (which may be another subdivision by the time you read this). When the road curves sharply, you can park in the designated parking areas on the right, near the picnic tables. (916) 741-7407. ➡*See #5 on map p. 160.*

RESTAURANTS

Izzy's Burger Spa: This place serves giant burgers to match its giant outdoor picnic area. 411 Colusa Avenue; (916) 674-9400.

Metcalf's Eat & Run: What a combo—you can pick between fried chicken and donuts to enjoy at the picnic tables here. If you're going to fall off the diet wagon, this is a good place to do it. 716 Colusa Avenue; (916) 674-3847.

Pizza Pizzazz: You and the pooch can share pizza, pasta and sandwiches at this garden cafe. 1190 Bridge Street; (916) 671-2323.

Wienerschnitzel: Share a dog with your dog on a bench. 1245 Bridge Street; (916) 673-7078.

PLACES TO STAY

Garden Court Inn: Rates are $26 to $38. 4228 South Highway 99, Yuba City, CA 95991; (916) 674-0210.

Motel 6: All Motel 6s allow one small dog per room. Rates are $29 for the first adult, $6 for the second. 700 North Palora Avenue, Yuba City, CA 95991; (916) 674-1710.

YUBA COUNTY

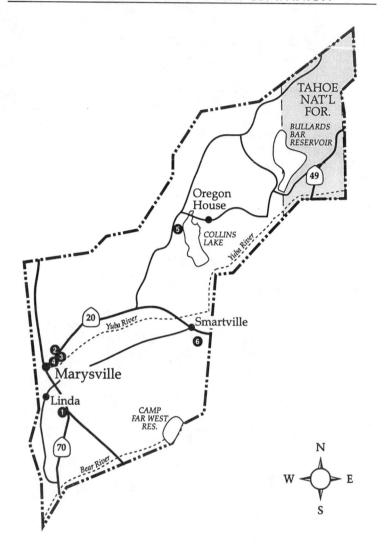

16
YUBA COUNTY

If you're just passing through with a dog, you're doing the right thing. With the exception of a small piece of national forest land, it's not exactly dog heaven here. Besides, if you want to spend the night, you'll have to either camp or knock on a friend's door. Dog-friendly lodgings are nonexistent.

NATIONAL FORESTS

See the National Forests/Wilderness Areas chapter starting on page 801 for important information and safety tips for visiting national forests with your dog.

• **Tahoe National Forest** 🐾 🐾 🐾 🐾 🐾 ✏️ 🐕

A tiny portion of this forest creeps into the eastern edge of Yuba County. See page 810.

LINDA

PARKS, BEACHES & RECREATION AREAS

• **Fernwood Park** 🐾 🐾 1/2

The park is only nine acres, but there's so much interesting stuff here that it seems larger. The jogging trail is a fun place to walk your leashed pooch and get a little exercise yourself. There's a playground, a playing field, a picnic area and a non-producing almond orchard here, too. The park is at Fern and Maywood drives. (916) 741-6421. → *See #1 on map p. 166.*

MARYSVILLE

The historic district here is a real charmer—quite different from anything else you'll find in this sprawling, suburban-style county.

PARKS, BEACHES & RECREATION AREAS

• **Ellis Lake Park** 🐾 🐾 🐾

Swans, ducks and geese enjoy this quaint park at least as much as people and their dogs. Most of the park's 30 acres is taken up by a decent-sized lake, which was once a sprawling swamp. In 1924, John McLaren, designer of San Francisco's Golden Gate Park, presented a local women's civic group with plans for transforming the swamp to its present pleasant state.

An attractive path encircles the lake, but you and your leashed pooch can also spend time at an old stone footbridge, a gazebo and picnic tables. Dogs who like grass and dirt (and what dog doesn't?) enjoy lounging in the shade of the maples that dot the park.

Ellis Lake Park is between 9th and 14th streets and B and D streets. You won't want to hang out at the B Street side, because that's where all the car shops and convenience stores are. (916) 741-6666. ➡ *See #2 on map p. 166.*

•**Plaza Park** 🐾 1/2

This park is very tiny, but it's green, close to the Yuba River, and it's in the historic district next to the Chinese Bok Kai Temple. The temple is the home of Bok Kai, the river god of good fortune.

Joe likes to picnic at the little table here. It's a very peaceful setting and it's usually quite lush, unlike the neighboring Riverfront Park. Dogs must be leashed. The park is at the foot of D Street, at 1st Street. (916) 741-6666. ➡ *See #3 on map p. 166.*

•**Riverfront Park** 🐾 🐾

When you see this park on the map, you'll say "Wow! This place is almost half the size of Marysville itself! We must visit, Rex." (Or something like that.) But when you visit, you're apt to be more than a little disappointed: Two major roads straddle the park and the noise creates anything but a peaceful park-like setting. About a third of the park is devoted to a British Motor Cross course. Much of the park is fenced off and out of commission. And there's a water treatment plant (peeeuw!) that occupies a nice-sized chunk of the southern area of the park.

So what's a dog to do at this 193-acre park? Well, there are some softball and soccer fields that are good for a leashed stroll when there's no one playing. And a few grassy areas where no one plays anything but footsie are always okay for a walk. Other than these sections, dogs don't think too highly of the place.

From the southern end of the historic district, go west on 1st Street, which turns into Bizz Johnson Drive once in the park. The first thing you'll notice may be the odor of the water treatment plant. No matter how much your dog begs you to stop at the stinky treatment plant, keep going until you get to the area that interests you. (916) 741-6666. ➡ *See #4 on map p. 166.*

RESTAURANTS

Four Seasons Deli: Located right beside Ellis Lake (see page 167), this is the place to go after you've become thirsty and tired from playing at the park there. 423 B Street; (916) 743-8221.

Silver Dollar Saloon: This is a wonderful place with a big side patio for you and your dog. It's right next to Plaza Park's Chinese

Bok Kai Temple. Just sit at the edge of the patio, near the gate, to keep your dog out of the bustle of this busy place. The saloon has a pretty substantial menu, including steaks, sandwiches and salads. 330 First Street; (916) 742-9020.

OREGON HOUSE

PARKS, BEACHES & RECREATION AREAS

•Collins Lake 🐾🐾🐾🐾 🐕

Good dogs who won't chase deer, skunks and other critters are welcome to strip off their leashes and trot naked around the 600 acres of oaks and pines here that surround the 1,000-acre lake. Dog paddling is a popular pastime with unleashed pooches, so if you have a water dog, you couldn't ask for a more dog-friendly swimming hole. The fishing here is terrific, too. Make sure your dog is leashed when you go anywhere near anglers or the developed area of the lake.

There's one developed campground here and one undeveloped one. The latter is dog heaven. There are no barbecues or tables, but you won't have any neighbors, either. You'll be surrounded by trees and plenty of land. It's a first-rate way to get away from noise, loud kids, radios and just about everything that reminds you of civilization.

There are 150 sites here, with nightly fees ranging from $13 to $19. Reservations are recommended in spring and summer. Dogs are $1 extra. The park's day-use fee is $5 per vehicle. From Marysville, take Highway 20 east for 12 miles and turn north on Marysville Road. The lake entrance will be on your right in about 10 miles. (916) 692-1600. ➡See #5 on map p. 166.

PLACES TO STAY

Collins Lake camping: See above.

SMARTVILLE

In 1968, the new post office was built here and all the paperwork had gone through when someone realized they'd added an extra "s" to Smartville's name. Since then, its name has gradually shifted to reflect the "Smartsville" error. But because the old-timers here cringe when they hear "Smartsville," we'll refer to it as "Smartville," in their honor.

PARKS, BEACHES & RECREATION AREAS

•Spenceville Wildlife & Recreation Area 🐾🐾🐾🐾 🐕

First the bad news: If your dog isn't a hunting companion, she can't be off leash here. Now the better news: Non-hunting dogs are welcome at this 11,213-acre wildlife area year-round.

More than 20 miles of hiking trails await you, your dog and your binoculars. Among the wildlife you may see are coyotes, mule deer, quail and great blue heron (there's a great blue heron rookery here). If you have a hankering to do some angling, the fishing is fine at pure, cool Dry Creek. Don't miss its waterfall.

From Highway 20 in Smartville, take Smartville Road south. You'll find several entryways in the next several miles. Call about hunting seasons and off-limit areas. (916) 538-2236. ➡ *See #6 on map p. 166.*

SIERRA COUNTY

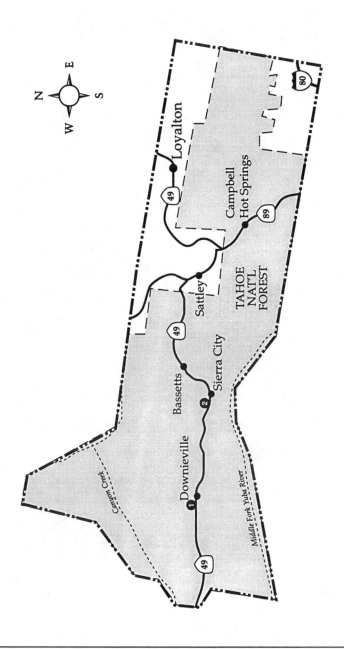

17
SIERRA COUNTY

Tahoe National Forest makes up a huge portion of this mountainous county, causing dogs to give almost the entire county a four-paw rating. Peaks stretch up to 9,000 feet above sea level and plunge down into gigantic, serene meadows carpeted with wildflowers in the spring and snow in the colder months.

The North Fork of the Yuba River cuts through big rocks and mountains of tall pines and oaks. In summer, you and your dog can pull off Highway 49 and swim, fish or pan for gold in the river. The fly-fishing is exceptional here. In autumn, bask in bright colors as the water maples and aspens prepare for winter.

Campgrounds are plentiful along Highway 49. They can be good places to start hikes, but there are actually only a few trailheads that start near the road. A portion of the Pacific Crest Trail passes between Bassetts Station and Sierra City. It's a great place to hike with an off-leash dog, because this section is on dog-friendly national forest land.

NATIONAL FORESTS

See the National Forests/Wilderness Areas chapter starting on page 801 for important information and safety tips for visiting national forests with your dog.

• **Tahoe National Forest** 🐾 🐾 🐾 🐾 🦴 🐕
See page 810.

BASSETTS

Hush Puppy dogs are honored by the name of this tiny community. They're bound to appreciate all the trailheads they can access just a few miles down the road. From Highway 49, turn onto Gold Lake Road and follow the signs to myriad lakes within Tahoe National Forest (see page 810). There's also easy access to the Pacific Crest Trail from around here.

(Don't tell your dog, but the town's namesakes were Mary and Jacob Bassett, not Fred Basset or any other basset hound.)

RESTAURANTS

Bassetts Station: Sit at either of the two tables outside this homey cafe with your dog, and dine on the specialty of the house:

Bassett Burgers! Tell your dog not to worry—the meat is chopped cow, not canine. Highway 49 and Gold Lake Road; (916) 862-1297.

CAMPBELL HOT SPRINGS

PLACES TO STAY

Stampede Reservoir: This is a huge and popular campground on the huge and popular Stampede Reservoir. The reservoir has 25 miles of shoreline. Fishing is great, and hiking is even better. When you get away from people, you can even let your dog off leash, since it's all part of Tahoe National Forest (see page 810).

You'll have your choice of 252 campsites here, on the south side of the reservoir. Sites are $9. From Interstate 80, take the Boca-Hirschdale/Stampede Meadows exit about eight miles north. At the reservoir's dam, turn left and drive a mile to the campground. Call (800) 280-CAMP for campsite reservations. For more information, phone (916) 582-0120.

DOWNIEVILLE

While visiting this Old West gold town, you and your dog may feel as if some old miner might come running up behind you screaming he's hit the Mother Lode. It could happen. A couple of years ago, Joe and I ran into a prospector who was selling a chunk of gold big enough to pay his bills for two years. Granted, his bills were minimal since he lived out of a camper truck, but it was still impressive. He bought a drink for everyone within 100 feet, and treated Joe to a piece of pizza.

Authentic is not the word for Downieville. Authentic implies that something has changed over time and then been restored to be more like the original. But Downieville has barely changed since its heyday in the 1850s. Wood planks still serve as sidewalks and many buildings still have walls made of thick stones. The streets are narrow and jagged, just wide enough for a few stagecoaches (although cars do manage here nowadays). Ghastly green gallows stand next to the County Jail, a grim reminder of the town's rowdy past. And gold miners still gather at the local assay office at dusk to weigh and sell the gold flecks and chunks they find in the North Fork of the Yuba River.

Inspired by this gold, Joe and I bought a $4 gold pan and a little red book that tells you how to pan for the stuff. We drove west of town a few miles on Highway 49, and stopped when we found what looked like a lucky spot on the Yuba River in Tahoe National Forest (see page 810). We could feel our fortune in the air. We knew that after we spent a couple hours sifting gravel and dirt, we'd find something that would let us retire early, or at least buy a bag of dog food. It was one of those things you could just sense.

Two hours later, I was still trying to get Joe to stop digging holes and covering up my freshly shaken gold pan with his freshly dug river dirt. It was bad enough that we had to watch the little red instruction booklet float away, then sink, after Joe crashed into me and knocked me into the river in a fit of canine glee within minutes of getting to our spot.

We left with soggy coats and unfulfilled dreams. That night, we bought a lottery ticket, won $5 and felt much better.

PARKS, BEACHES & RECREATION AREAS

• Lion's Memorial Park 🐾 🐾

If you like looking at old mining equipment, you'll enjoy this park. Several old, rusty gold mining relics are constantly on display here. The park is also a decent place to take a break from exploring town and relax on a bench with your dog.

The best part of this small, on-leash park is that it provides easy access to the Downie River, which runs right through town. Just watch out for the pair of geese who seem to run the place. Both times we visited, they honked us right off the beach. The park is just next to Courthouse Bridge. (916) 386-3122. → *See #1 on map p. 172.*

RESTAURANTS

Indian Valley Outpost: Step inside and order a good, home-cooked meal. While you wait (with someone waiting by the picnic tables outside with your dog), shop the little store here for things like handmade earrings and other local crafts. It's a fun place to spend a few extra dollars. On Highway 49, about 12 miles west of Downieville; (916) 289-3680.

River View Pizzeria: Dine at any of several rugged picnic tables in the front of the restaurant, or take your pizza out back to Lion's Memorial Park (see above) and eat at the picnic tables overlooking the Downie River. At 103 Nevada Street. (916) 289-3540.

PLACES TO STAY

Saundra Dyer's Resort: If you really want the Old West flavor, stay at this homey inn and ask Baron, the resident rottweiler, to sing "Happy Trails." When you start singing it, chances are he'll join in. His repertoire may be limited, but in this town, what better song could he sing? Owner Saundra Dyer loves dog guests, and will even show good dogs a special secret riverfront beach they can visit. Rates are $54 to $125. The inn is at 9 River Street, across the river and just west of the main part of town. The mailing address is P.O. Box 406, Downieville, CA 95936; (916) 289-3308 or (800) 696-3308.

FESTIVALS
Miners Day Weekend: Dogs love to watch the panning contests, but those are nothing compared with the mucking contests! Besides all the gold hoopla, there's street dancing, arts and crafts, musicians and lots of food. The festival is held on Downieville's Main Street the first weekend in August. The town's library is the official info center for this one. Call (916) 289-3544.

SATTLEY

PLACES TO STAY
Yuba Pass Campground: Stay here, and your dog can brag to his buddies that he slept right on Yuba Pass, at an elevation of 6,708 feet. With only 20 campsites, it's fairly private and quiet. Dogs have to be leashed in the camping areas, but if you go on a hike in surrounding Tahoe National Forest, obedient dogs can go off leash.

Sites are $4. The campground is about seven miles west of Sattley, off Highway 49 at Yuba Pass. (916) 265-4531.

SIERRA CITY

PARKS, BEACHES & RECREATION AREAS
• **Sierra County Historical Park** 🐾 🐾 1/2 🐾

A restored hard rock gold mine and stamp mill are the main attractions at this hilly, forested park a mile east of Sierra City. It's fascinating to learn about how gold ore is mined, crushed and has its gold extracted. While dogs are not allowed in the museum, they are sometimes permitted to go on a guided tour of the Kentucky Mine with you. Or you can take your own tour, looking into a restored miner's cabin or down a deep hole into the mine.

Leashed dogs enjoy the paved paths that lead to the attractions and the amphitheater (see Diversions, page 177). But they seem to like the smaller, dirt paths above the amphitheater even more. If you continue on those paths, eventually you'll be in national forest jurisdiction. But it's best to start one of those magical off-leash romps at designated sites within the forest.

The park is just east of the main part of Sierra City, on Highway 49. It's open Memorial Day through October. Hours vary, so contact the park at P.O. Box 260, Sierra City, CA 96125, or call (916) 862-1310.
➡️*See #2 on map p. 172.*

RESTAURANTS

Sierra Country Store: There's no street address, but it's on Highway 49, and you can't miss it. Eat grocery store cuisines with your dog at the outside benches. (916) 862-1181.

DIVERSIONS

Give your canine culture: The Kentucky Mine Concert Series, at Sierra County Historical Park (see page 176), provides a summer of musical entertainment for you and your extraordinarily well-behaved dog. The concerts feature a wide variety of music, from Broadway to Celtic to Old West. Dogs who promise not to bark, howl or thump their foot while scratching are allowed to sit with you in the small, outdoor amphitheater here.

An added requirement: Dogs must be able to remain calm when Willie, the resident cat, streaks across the stage with a mouse in his mouth. He does this during at least a couple of concerts each season. Concerts are $10 at the door, $8 in advance. For schedules and information, write P.O. Box 368, Sierra City, CA 96125, or call (916) 862-1310.

NEVADA COUNTY

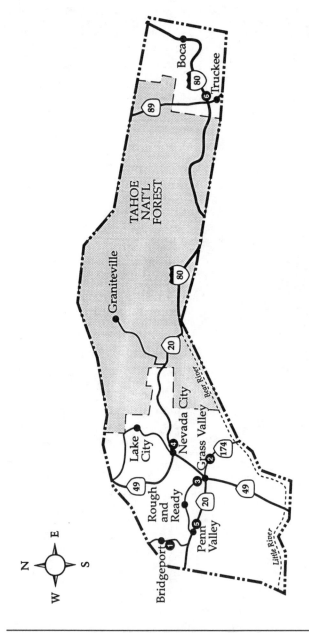

18
NEVADA COUNTY

Do you have a digging dog? Buy yourself a plot of land and start scooping that dirt: Locals boast that more than half the gold that came out of California during the Gold Rush was found in Nevada City, Grass Valley and other foothill areas of this county. Your hot-diggedy dog probably won't come up with much, but it's always fun to dream.

If you want to see where the riches really were, your best bet is to visit the Empire Mine State Historic Park (see page 183), where hole-digging dogs can *ooh* and *ahh* at the mouth of the mine shaft that winds 5,000 feet below the surface.

Autumn in Nevada County is about as beautiful as autumn in New England. Pick up a self-guided tour to Nevada City's fall colors from the city's Chamber of Commerce, at 132 Main Street.

Much of the county, especially Tahoe National Forest (see page 810) in the east, shows its true colors in the winter, when mountains are a crispy white. In Spanish, the very name *nevada* means "snow-covered." If you've always wanted a white Christmas, this is a spectacular place to watch the flurries fly.

NATIONAL FORESTS

See the National Forests/Wilderness Areas chapter starting on page 801 for important information and safety tips for visiting national forests with your dog.

• **Tahoe National Forest** 🐾 🐾 🐾 🐾 👞 🐕
See page 810.

BOCA

PLACES TO STAY

Boca Rest Campground: This is one of a few campgrounds along the striking Boca Reservoir. It's at an elevation of 5,700 feet, surrounded by tall pines, low grassy areas and steep bluffs. The Boca Rest Campground, with 25 sites, is the only one with piped water. Better yet, there's plenty of hiking available, and since it's in Tahoe National Forest (see page 810), it's okay to unleash your dog on the trails outside the campground.

The campground is open May through October. Sites are fee,

first come, first served. Take the Boca-Hirschdale/Stampede Meadows Road exit north from Interstate 80. The campground is on the northeast edge of the lake. (916) 587-3558.

BRIDGEPORT

PARKS, BEACHES & RECREATION AREAS

• **South Yuba River Project** 🐾 🐾 🐾 1/2

This is one of the newest and most interesting units in the state park system. The project is a patchwork of lands spread over a 20-mile length along the South Yuba River Canyon, from the top of Englebright Lake at Bridgeport to Tahoe National Forest above Malakoff Diggins State Historic Park (see page 184).

There are many access points to the project, but our favorites are in the western section. For seclusion and serene beauty, try the westernmost access area. Driving north from Lake Wildwood on Pleasant Valley Road, you'll see a sign for the project, and a small parking/pullout area on your left (there's space for only a few cars).

As soon as you get out of your car, you and your leashed dog will hear the flowing river. Hike down the wide dirt path and when you come to a gravel section, go left. A few yards in, you'll come to one of the most beautiful sections of the South Yuba. The beach around it is sandy and the water in the river is a clear tropical blue. You'll want to stay forever.

If you're going to run into any people in this part of the project, it's going to be here. The maximum number of humans we've seen at one time at this beachy area have been two. If you want real privacy, you can always ford the river. If the river is high, the current is slow and your dog's a swimmer, just do the dog paddle across. You're almost guaranteed that no one will be on the other side. Or if you are looking for exercise, continue along the first dirt trail and you can hike your heart out.

Just a few hundred feet up Pleasant Valley Road is the Bridge-port Recreation Area, a much more widely used part of the project with bigger parking lots. Here's where you and your leashed dog can walk across the longest (243-foot) single-span covered bridge in existence. It's been around since 1862! Back then, it cost a whop-ping $5.50 to get across, but the fee included you, a loaded wagon, and six mules, oxen or horses. These days, it's free.

You can also relax and picnic at a riverside table, swim in the crystal-clear Yuba or hike a number of trails. One of the most rugged and scenic trails starts to the left of the covered bridge as you cross from the parking lot. The narrow trail takes you to Englebright Lake, about a mile away. (916) 273-3884. →*See #1 on map p. 180.*

GRANITEVILLE

PLACES TO STAY

Bowman Lake Campground: If you want to get away from all those city-like campgrounds, try this one. Since there are only seven campsites, you'll never feel the crunch of crowds. And if you're willing to do a little hiking, you can really escape civilization. The campground and surrounding areas are part of Tahoe National Forest (see page 810), so good dogs may go leash-free in forests outside the camping area. There is no fee. All sites are first come, first served.

From Highway 80 just east of Emigrant Gap, you can take Bowman Lake Road north to the lake. It's about 10 miles east of Graniteville. (916) 265-4531.

GRASS VALLEY

Like Nevada City a few miles up the road, Grass Valley is a classic Old West town, only older and wester.

PARKS, BEACHES & RECREATION AREAS

We had a major disappointment when we tried to visit Condon Park, a huge, hilly, wooded city park. A big sign, somewhat hidden behind a rapidly growing tree, announced "NO DOGS ALLOWED." If you find yourself in the park's vicinity just west of the historic downtown, and your dog is getting that desperate look, your only alternative is Minnie Park (see page 184).

• **Empire Mine State Historic Park** 🐾 🐾 🐾 🐾

At one time, miners descended in cage-like trains deep into the earth here, and rumbled the ground searching for gold in 350 miles of tunnels. The place was alive 24 hours a day—dirty, dusty and dancing with gold: Miners extracted more than six million ounces of the precious ore during the mine's century of use.

Now, it's a quiet, calm 800-acre park with lush gardens and green meadows. While the mine and surrounding buildings are inactive, they're still fascinating to inspect. On hot summer days, a dog's favorite place is the shaft viewing area. It's a few dozen feet below ground, and the earthy scents are almost as relaxing as the cool, damp air.

The fee for adults is $2. For kids and (leashed) dogs, it's $1. From Highway 49, drive east on Highway 20/Empire Street about 1.5

miles. The park is on the right. (916) 273-8522. ➡️*See #2 on map p. 180.*
•**Minnie Park** 🐾 **1/2**

Minnie Park, in comparison to the large, canine-banning Condon Park right next to it, seems like it should be called "Mini" Park. It's a relatively tiny, unremarkable park, but it does have shade, decent lawns, picnic tables and a small playground. And it does allow your leashed pooch. It's on Cornwall Avenue and Brighton Street. (916) 273-0941. ➡️*See #3 on map p. 180.*

RESTAURANTS
Cousin Jack's Pasties: British dogs go wild when they smell the Cornish pasties (yummy meat-and-potato pies) you can eat on the porch here. 100 South Auburn Street; (916) 272-9230.

Subway Sandwiches & Salads: 716 Freeman Lane; (916) 273-7789.

PLACES TO STAY
Alta Sierra Resort Motel: Your dog will like the views of the small lake you can see from your roomside deck. The lodging is on four acres, all of which have views of the lake or the golf course. Rates are $45 to $85. Dogs are $10 extra. 11858 Tammy Way, Grass Valley, CA 95949; (916) 273-9102.

Golden Chain Resort Motel: If it's hot, this is a cool place to stay—shady trees abound on the property. Rates are $35 to $70. Dogs are $4 extra; they like small dogs here. 13363 Highway 49, Grass Valley, CA 95949; (916) 273-7279.

Holiday Lodge: You and your leashed dog can go on gold-panning tours run by the hotel! They welcome dogs here, "as long as they're not bigger than a horse," says the manager. Rates are $38 to $60. Dogs require a $25 deposit. 1221 East Main Street, Grass Valley, CA 95949; (916) 273-4406.

Swan-Levine House: This big, airy house was built in 1880 and soon after was transformed into a small hospital. Now it's a magical inn, complete with an art studio (where you can try your hand at printmaking), brightly colored rooms furnished with antiques, and cozy fireplaces. Dogs who stay here should like cats—there are plenty of these critters on the property. Rates are $65 to $95. 328 South Church Street, Grass Valley, CA 95945; (916) 272-1873.

LAKE CITY
PLACES TO STAY
Malakoff Diggins State Historic Park: If only dogs could explore this fascinating park with you, they'd get to see what the world's richest and largest hydraulic gold mine was like in its

heyday. Fortunately, dogs don't care about such things. But they do generally enjoy a good night of camping, and this park lets them stay overnight for $1. And while dogs aren't allowed on the trails or in the Blair Lake area, they are permitted to join you in certain spots in the park. Ask the ranger which ones, because the rules were scheduled to change as of this book's press time.

Sites are $10 to $12. Take Highway 49 from Nevada City, and go right at Tyler Foote Crossing Road. Drive 16 miles to the park on this sometimes paved, sometimes precipitous, gravelly road. For camping reservations, call MISTIX at (800) 444-PARK. For park information, phone (916) 265-2740.

NEVADA CITY

Dogs are everywhere in this colorful Gold Rush town in the Sierra foothills. They dine with their owners, frolic off leash in Pioneer Park and hang out with human friends on historic Broad Street. They sometimes even get to go shopping in some of the cutesy tourist-oriented stores.

The entire Old West/Victorian downtown is registered as a national historic landmark. On winter nights, when snow falls around the gaslit lamps in the narrow streets, it's classic Currier & Ives (see Festivals, page 186). Your dog trotting along will only add to the sweet scene.

PARKS, BEACHES & RECREATION AREAS
• **Pioneer Park** 🐾 🐾 🐾 🐾 🐕

The one exception to this historic city's leash law is at this fine, green park. Dogs who are under extremely good voice control can go leashless. The park has open fields for running. Dogs love the tall pines that edge park. These trees provide both shade and places for dogs to do their thing. Ball fields, a playground, a pool and a shed with old firewagons are the major human interests here.

From northbound Interstate 80, exit at Sacramento Street and go right immediately on Nile Street (at the sign for Pioneer Park). When the road comes to a "T", go right. The park is on your left. You can either drive all the way in and park near the fountain, or park on Nimrod Street and walk down a paved road into the park's largest open field. (916) 265-2521. ➡ *See #4 on map p. 180.*

RESTAURANTS

El Bandito Mexican Restaurant: Dine on traditional and veg-etarian Mexican dishes on the big shaded patio here. They'll be happy to give your pooch water. All that the dog-friendly folks here request is that your dog doesn't bark when the tourist-filled horse carriages trot past. 401 Commercial Street; (916) 265-6138.

Walking Dog: The hot dogs at this stand are quite tasty, but the Walking Dog logo looks more like Mister Peanut on a bad hair day than an ambulatory weiner. Joe thinks it should look more like a walking canine, but the implications of that idea might make you think twice before biting that frankfurter. The stand is at 408 Broad Street. There's no phone number.

FESTIVALS

Victorian Christmas: You, your leashed dog and your family can have your best white Christmas ever if you visit Nevada City during the four or five evenings of this old-fashioned festival. Strolling Christmas carolers, bell ringers and wagon and carriage rides are everywhere in the downtown district, which is closed to cars for the duration of the celebration.

You'll be intoxicated by the scents of hot cider and roasting chestnuts. You'll be mesmerized by turn-of-the-century hawkers, food vendors and entertainers. And there's always the chance that dogs who have been good, for goodness sake, will get to visit with Santa.

The festival is in downtown Nevada City, from Commercial to Spring streets, and Factory to Union streets. It can get crowded, and the Chamber of Commerce tries not to encourage canines, but they are permitted. For dates and times, call (916) 265-2692 or (800) 655-NJOY.

PENN VALLEY

PARKS, BEACHES & RECREATION AREAS

•Western Gateway Regional Park 🐾🐾🐾

One of the favorite summertime activities here is for kids to lie face down on the big water pipes over the creek and watch the water gurgle by. Dogs love to watch the water, too, but it's best if they do it downstream a little. Just walk down the bank to a more secluded spot, where your splashing dog won't frighten or dampen kids.

The park has wide meadows, a mini-forest area with small dirt trails and lots of shrubs for dogs. Leashed dogs love all that. For kids, the place is loaded with playgrounds, ball fields and basketball courts. Dogs are banned from the playing fields, but are free to walk on leash around the rest of the park.

From Highway 20, go south about a half block on Indian Springs Road, then turn left on Penn Valley Drive. The park is on the left. (916) 432-1990. ➤ *See #5 on map p. 180.*

ROUGH AND READY

This tiny community was once a thriving little Gold Rush town that took its name from "Old Rough-and-Ready" Zachary Taylor.

In 1850, about a year after the town was settled, the townfolk concluded that mining taxes were getting to be too much and voted to secede from the Union. But the Great Republic of Rough and Ready was not destined to last long. When the Fourth of July came along just three months after the secession, Old Glory went up the flagpole and the new Republic was down the tubes.

DIVERSIONS

Bring Ruff and get ready to say those vows: Many, many couples get hitched at The Wayside Wedding Chapel in the center of Rough and Ready. It's a rustic wood building that looks like it's half-barn, half-chalet. If you're into pink bows and white plastic floral arrangements, try another chapel. You won't find any froufrou here, but you will find a very dog-friendly atmosphere.

Remember Frank Capra's *It's a Wonderful Life*, where an angel gets his wings every time a bell rings? Here in Rough and Ready, every time a bell rings, you can be pretty sure that the bride and groom are kissing. The sound echoes across the hillsides. Town dogs look up and cock their heads, and little children giggle to think of the smooch.

The chapel is on Rough and Ready Road. For information, contact P.O. Box 845, Rough and Ready, CA 95975; (916) 273-6678.

TRUCKEE

If you want a preview of just what you're going to see when you visit this colorful old city, rent the silent Charlie Chaplin flick *The Gold Rush*. Some of the late-1800s architecture along Truckee's main street, Commercial Row, appears in the film. As rapidly as towns grow in California, you'll see that this enchanting old street hasn't changed much.

Your dog will enjoy the rough, Old West feel of the historic part of town. You'll like the myriad enchanting shops and restaurants. But sadly for people with dogs, Commercial Row is so old-style that it doesn't have room for outdoor tables for human and doggy dining.

Truckee is home to Donner Lake, where many in the ill-fated Donner Party died in the winter of 1846 after running out of provisions during a "short cut" leg of their journey from the Midwest. The tragic tale of their starvation and resulting cannibalism is recounted at Donner Memorial State Park (see page 189).

A more upbeat way to experience Truckee's freshwater wonders is to go hiking or trout fishing at the Truckee River. One of the access points just outside downtown is described below. It's a great location if someone you're traveling with wants to shop while you and the dog get your paws wet.

PARKS, BEACHES & RECREATION AREAS

Truckee has a perfectly manicured regional park, but dogs don't feel welcome here. We prefer to drive another mile down the road and enjoy the wonders of the Martis Creek Lake. The recreation area surrounding the lake straddles two counties, and is described on page 198 in the Placer County chapter.

• **Truckee River, access outside downtown Truckee**

This is a beautiful, trout-filled river that beckons hikers and anglers and their adventurous canines. The really good news is that dogs are allowed off leash along the river here, since it's in Tahoe National Forest! Your pup can frolic while you catch and release all day. Use artificial lures and barbless hooks only.

Once you get past the first couple of hundred feet along the riverbank, the trail can be narrow and rocky. If your dog is a klutz or has thin-skinned paws, you may not want to go any farther. She can still have plenty of fun sniffing around while you cast all day for the big one hiding behind the boulder.

From central Truckee, drive northeast on Highway 267 and go right on Glenshire Drive (it's about halfway between downtown and Interstate 80). After 4.5 miles, you'll come to the Glenshire Bridge. Make a sharp right onto a dirt road after the bridge. Park in the flat, dirt area near the river. When choosing a fishing spot, be sure to head to the left as you face the river. If you walk to the right, you'll be in very private fishing grounds very quickly.

The folks at Mountain Hardware can give you fishing tips and updated regulations. Call them at (916) 587-4844. The Truckee Ranger District of Tahoe National Forest wasn't as knowledgeable about this part of the river when we called, but they can be helpful with other information. (916) 587-3558. ➡*See #6 on map p. 180.*

RESTAURANTS

Gateway Deli: 11012 Donner Pass Road; (916) 587-3106.

Sizzler Restaurant: This is one of few franchises in this chain with outdoor seating. You'll need to tie your dog near the deck if other folks are on it, but otherwise, good dogs are mighty welcome here. 11262 Donner Pass Road; (916) 587-1824.

PLACES TO STAY

Alpine Village: Last time we visited, a big sign in front of the motel advertised "PETS WELCOME." That's the kind of sign we like to see. The motel is conveniently located just off Interstate 80, near Donner Lake. Rates are $50 to $79. 12260 Deerfield Drive, Truckee, CA 96161; (916) 587-3801.

Donner Memorial State Park: Dogs aren't allowed on the trails here, or in the museum that tells the tragic story of the Donner party, trapped here for the winter of 1846. But they can stay with you at any of the park's 154 campsites. And they can also accompany you to pay homage to the dozens of pioneers who perished here. There's a 22-foot-high monument on a stone base that's 16 feet high—22 feet was the depth of the snow during that desperate winter. It's within doggy access.

Sites are $12 to $14. Dogs are $1 extra. The park is about two miles west of the town of Truckee, on Donner Pass Road. Phone MISTIX at (800) 444-PARK for reservations, or call the park at (916) 587-3841 for more information.

PLACER COUNTY

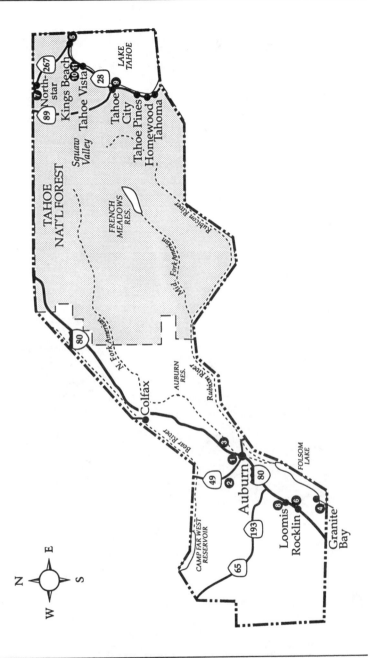

19
PLACER COUNTY

If your dog likes fresh mountain air, world-class ski resorts and rivers rushing over hidden gold, Placer County is her kind of place. The county has a little of everything, and dogs should experience its diversity.

Most dogs think the county gets better as they go from its more populated western end past the Mother Lode and into the magnificent mountains. Unless your dog likes to shop 'til she drops, the western valley region of Placer County probably won't be nearly as appealing as the high country.

Part of the appeal of the eastern half is that much of it is Tahoe National Forest land, where dogs can shed their leashes everywhere except in campgrounds and developed recreation areas. Keep in mind that the northwest corner of the Granite Chief Wilderness bans dogs from May 15 to July 15 because of deer fawning (see page 810).

The western half of the county is far from a suburban slumberland. In fact, a good part of it is heavily agricultural. You and your dog can experience the farming life firsthand by driving the 49er Fruit Trail. The Fruit Trail passes by 100 farms, where you (and often your dog) can stop, look around and buy very fresh farm goods—everything from apples to grapes to walnuts. There are even places to buy trout, sheep and catfish! Before you let your dog out of the car, ask the farmer if it's okay. If it's not, and it's hot, continue on. Don't leave your dog in the car in warm weather even for a few minutes. For a map and list of all the farms, send a note and a stamped, self-addressed legal-sized envelope to 49er Fruit Trail, P.O. Box 317, Newcastle, CA 95658.

Be aware, anyone stopping in Placer County with a female dog in heat: While she may be in the mood, you'll be in a bad mood if she gets caught seducing a guy dog. The fine for her "contact with male dogs" (that's county talk for "messing around") is $47.

NATIONAL FORESTS
See the National Forests/Wilderness Areas chapter starting on page 801 for important information and safety tips for visiting national forests with your dog.

• **Tahoe National Forest** 🐾 🐾 🐾 🐾 🐾 🦴 🐕‍🦺
   See page 810.

AUBURN

While this city has sprawled in so many directions that it looks like a giant mall, there's still a fairly large, very historic downtown that's great for walking through with your dog. This is Joe's favorite Gold Country city. It looks like one big old valuable antique.

PARKS, BEACHES & RECREATION AREAS

• **Ashford Park** 🐾 🐾

   This city park is convenient to Interstate 80 travelers whose leashed dogs like their restroom breaks nice and pretty. While the park is only seven acres, it has a little pond, and is full of trees and picnic tables on well-manicured grass. Kids like the playground here, so it's an ideal rest stop for your whole carload.

   From Interstate 80, exit at Foresthill Road and go west for a couple of blocks. When you cross over railroad tracks, the entrance will be coming up on your left. Park on the street. (916) 885-8461.
   → *See #1 on map p. 192.*

• **Auburn District Regional Park** 🐾 🐾 1/2

   You can roll up your overalls and fish in the willow-shaded pond here and feel remarkably like Tom Sawyer. Except for the sports fields and playground, this 62-acre park is a quiet one. Dogs may feel a little intimidated by the perfect green meadows, but if you look hard, there are a couple of scruffier sections around the edges. Leashes are a must.

   Take the Dry Creek Road exit from Highway 49 and go west a few blocks to Richardson Drive. (415) 885-8461. → *See #2 on map p. 192.*

• **Auburn State Recreation Area** 🐾 🐾 🐾 1/2

   This 30,000-acre park is located along 30 miles of the North and Middle forks of the American River. A few of the activities (and inactivities) available include: fishing, gold panning, rafting, swimming, hiking, biking, horseback riding, sunbathing, picnicking and camping. Since dogs are supposed to stay out of the rivers and don't ride bikes or horses, their selection is more limited.

   On a quiet day, when it's just you, your leashed dog and the river, try to imagine 10,000 miners crowded into this area in hot pursuit of gold. It makes the occasional passerby seem less obtrusive.

   If you and your dog have good hiking feet, 57 miles of trails await you. There are several trailheads. For an easy-to-find, quick hike to break up a long Interstate 80 trip, take the Foresthill Road exit off Interstate 80 and drive east. As soon as you pass over the Foresthill Bridge (it's the one that's 750 feet above the North Fork of the American River and a little more than a mile from the highway), pull over in the tiny off-road parking area to the right. Walk back toward the bridge and bear left when you see a little dirt area with signs that ban motorcycles from the trails.

This is not only a superb area to view the lands around the north fork of the river, it's also the starting point for several trails that wind their way down toward the river. Some are very steep and attract mountain bikers. From the trailhead you can see which trails have a gentler grade—it's better for everyone if you choose one of the less precarious ones.

If you want a longer hike, a very popular starting point is behind the Auburn Fairgrounds, at Pleasant Avenue. Park in the large lot. If you're planning on hiking the whole trail, you'd better bring a few horses to carry your gear: The trail goes to the confluence of the Middle and North forks of the American River, and then continues through national forests all the way to Squaw Valley!

Dogs are allowed at all areas and campsites in the Auburn State Recreation Area except around Lake Clementine and its campsites. Supervising Ranger Mike Van Hook says that area was recently closed to canines because inconsiderate owners didn't clean up after them and let them wreak general havoc. It's rare to find a state park that allows dogs on the trails, so let's be careful out there.

There are 64 sites. They are first come, first served and cost $7 to $9 a night. Dogs are $1 extra. A favorite for people who like to get away from the crowds is the Ruck-A-Chucky Campground. It's a quiet, primitive campground next to the Ruck-A-Chucky rapids on the Middle Fork of the American River. Ruck-A-Chucky has only 10 campsites available. (916) 988-0205. →*See #3 on map p. 192.*

RESTAURANTS
Dairy Queen: 13411 Lincoln Way; (916) 823-6257.
La Bou: Eat yummy baked goods, sip stimulating coffee. Do it all under the shade of La Bou's canopy. 2150 Grass Valley Highway; (916) 823-2303.

PLACES TO STAY
Auburn State Recreation Area camping: See page 194.
Country Squire Inn: Rates are $37 to $55 a night. 13480 Lincoln Way, Auburn, CA 95603; (916) 885-7025.

COLFAX

DIVERSIONS

Give your dog a golden opportunity: Want your dog to help pay for some of those precious dog food bills? Take him along on a Sierra Gold Adventure Tour and have him help you hunt for precious gold nuggets. Co-owner Jerrie Glover brings his dog every time. He says people frequently bring their dogs on his gold-exploring tours.

What's the reason so many dogs go? Are there dogs who can sniff out gold? Do canines have special powers we don't know about? "Naw, they mostly lay around and watch you all day, if they're not swimming around ignoring you," says Glover. (But, Mr. Glover, why is your dog part *golden* retriever?)

Glover shows you the Mother Lode region and the best spots for doing a little recreational prospecting. He explains about the geology and history of the area and gives practical tips so you can pan for gold yourself next time you're near a good river.

Half-day trips are $40 for adults and $20 for kids ages 10 to 15. Full-day trips, including lunch, are $85 for adults and $45 for the kids. There's no fee for dogs, but you have to supply their eats and drinks. For a brochure, contact Sierra Gold Adventure Tours, P.O. Box 569, Colfax, CA 95713; (916) 637-5957. When reserving your trip, make sure there won't be any cats in your group. Glover is an equal-opportunity expedition leader.

GRANITE BAY

PARKS, BEACHES & RECREATION AREAS

• **Folsom Lake State Recreation Area** 🐾 🐾 🐾 1/2

An important entrance to this popular lake is in Granite Bay, just south of Folsom Road. Although most of this large park is in Placer County, we've listed it in Sacramento County, under its namesake, the town of Folsom. See page 324. ➤ *See #4 on map p. 192.*

HOMEWOOD

RESTAURANTS

Obexer's Market: You want old-fashioned fun? This place is a general store with a deli featuring homemade rolls, barbecued chicken and potato salad. If you need a fishing rod or firewood, you can get it here, too. 5300 West Lake Boulevard; (916) 525-1300.

KINGS BEACH

PARKS, BEACHES & RECREATION AREAS

• **Coon Street Beach** 🔥

This beach is one of only two that allow dogs on the north shore of Lake Tahoe. And what a disappointment! It's tiny. It's so rocky it's hard to walk on. It's open to dogs only from 6 a.m. to 10 a.m. and 5 p.m. to dark. And the two times we visited, lecherous, shirtless guys swigging beers were our company at the small picnic area. Joe did not appreciate the cat calls.

But it is a place to take a desperate dog, and we understand that local dog lovers fought hard to win rights to it. Every bit helps when it comes to making the world a more dog-friendly place. To avoid the $4 parking fee at this beach, park along Highway 28 around Coon Street and walk in. (916) 546-7248. *→See #5 on map p. 192.*

RESTAURANTS

Char Pit: Munch on burgers, frosties and ice cream here. 8732 North Lake Boulevard; (916) 546-3171.

LOOMIS

PARKS, BEACHES & RECREATION AREAS

• **Loomis Basin Regional Park** 🐾 🐾

This park is divided into two sections—one for people, one for horses. Dogs can enjoy both, as long as they're leashed, and as long as they stay off the baseball fields and the corral area when they're in use. That doesn't leave much room to romp, but it's a decent place to stop, especially if you have kids. The playground is a popular one.

The park is an easy stop off Interstate 80. Exit at Penryn Road and go south about a half mile and turn right at Kings Road. Within a few blocks, the road bisects the park. (916) 652-1840. *→See #6 on map p. 192.*

FESTIVALS

Loomis Eggplant Festival: You like eggplant? There's so much of it around here that you'll either really love it or wish you'd never seen it by the time you leave this fall festival, usually held one weekend in September. It's eggplant, eggplant, eggplant. Leashed dogs are welcome, but keep in mind that it can get quite busy. The festival is held downtown. Call (916) 652-7252.

NORTHSTAR

PARKS, BEACHES & RECREATION AREAS

•**Martis Creek Lake** 🐾 🐾 🐾 1/2

This is a prime wildlife viewing area, with great catch-and-release trout fishing and more than 1,400 acres of meadows, rolling sagebrush hills and dense conifer forests. What more could a dog want? Free camping? Done! The no-fee campground here is set in a prime wildlife-viewing area. It's a fairly quiet campground, with its 25 sites often filled with early-rising anglers or birdwatchers.

Around the lake itself, there's very little shade, so in hot weather don't plan to paddle around the lake all day while a friend and your dog watch from shore.

You and your leashed dog will have a chance to gawk at all kinds of wildlife, including red-tailed hawks, mule deer and chickadees. In spring, you can lay back in the meadows full of alpine wildflowers and watch life unfold.

The lake is halfway between Truckee and Northstar. From Northstar, travel about two miles northwest on Highway 267 to the park entrance. The campground is open May through September. (916) 639-2342. ➡ *See #7 on map p. 192.*

PLACES TO STAY

Martis Creek Lake camping: See above.

ROCKLIN

PARKS, BEACHES & RECREATION AREAS

•**Johnson-Springview Park** 🐾 🐾 🐾

Dogs like picnicking here after walking on the park's well-maintained trails and working up an appetite. When we visited, a black lab was sitting on his family's picnic table, right beside the fried chicken. This is fairly large for a community park, and there's plenty of shade under the big oaks.

It's an easy drive from Highway 80. Take the Rocklin Road exit west for several blocks and go left on Fifth Street. The park is on your right. (916) 632-4100. ➡ *See #8 on map p. 192.*

SQUAW VALLEY

PLACES TO STAY

Squaw Valley itself doesn't allow dogs in lodgings. But there's a good campground up the road about three miles that welcomes pets.

Silver Creek Campground: This attractive summertime campground is for people and dogs who like to be near water. Deer Creek meets the Truckee River here. The fishing is good, the hiking along Deer Creek is great, and the 27-site campground isn't half bad either. Sites are $8. For reservations, call MISTIX at (800) 283-CAMP. The campground is about three miles north of Squaw Valley on Highway 89. For information, phone (916) 587-3558.

DIVERSIONS

Get high with your dog: During summer and autumn, you and the dog of your choice can be whisked halfway to the stars by cable cars normally used for skiers. You'll dangle high above the mountains on the way up, so if you've ever felt like James Stewart in *Vertigo,* here's some advice: Don't look down! Not even at your dog, who will probably be smiling and sniffing everyone's feet anyway.

Once the cable car drops you off, you can hike down the mountain on any number of trails. Or if you just wanted to visit for the view, you can turn around and go back on the next cable car. Dogs and their people think the hike is the best way to go, especially in early summer when it's still cool and the wildflowers are blooming.

The Squaw Valley ski resort cable car ride costs $11 per adult. After 5 p.m., it's $5. Dogs go for free. Hours can vary, but are usually around 9:30 a.m. to 9:30 p.m. But unless there's a full moon or a guide dog around, nighttime hikes down the mountain trails can be tricky. (916) 583-6985.

TAHOE CITY

Tahoe City is a fun place to go for a bite to eat with your dog. During summer, there are so many eateries with outdoor tables that you and your dog will drool just making the choice. It's an ideal place to bring your appetites after a long day of hiking in nearby Tahoe National Forest.

PARKS, BEACHES & RECREATION AREAS

• **William B. Layton Park** 🐾 🐾

Dogs are banned from all Tahoe City parks and beaches except this one. While they have to stay out of the park's most interesting feature, the Gatekeeper's Cabin Museum, leashed dogs may stroll the three-and-a-half green acres of park on the shores of Lake Tahoe. Because of the park's picturesque gardens and ancient conifers, the place is often rented out for weddings and private parties. If your dog isn't invited, he has to stay away. ➡ *See #9 on map p. 192.*

The park has picnic tables in the shade, but it's so close to many of the city's dog dining joints that you probably won't be hungry by the time you arrive here. The park is at 130 West Lake Boulevard. (916) 583-1762.

RESTAURANTS

Here's a sampling of the dog-friendly restaurants in Tahoe City:

Izzy's Burger Spa: Chicken, fries, onion rings and beer are the staples here. Dine at umbrella-covered tables. 100 West Lake Boulevard; (916) 583-4111.

Naughty Dawg: Attention all dogs! Come here! Eat here! Drink here! Run up and down a doggie run here (on leash)! Bring your picture and put it up on the Dog Wall of Fame here! Dogs, this is *your* place! You're not in Tahoe, you're in heaven. The dog motif goes deep here, thanks to co-owner Laurie-Jean Shaw and her dalmatian, Clyde Naughty Dawg. The bar is even a part of the dog theme, with entertaining beach-dog mosaics. If you still have time after checking out all the cool dog stuff here, you can eat at one of the many patio tables outdoors. Pooches get free water bowls. People can choose from a mouth-watering variety of dishes, including Cajun shrimp tacos and juicy steaks. The restaurant is in the heart of downtown Tahoe City, "a stick's throw from Lucky's," says Shaw. 255 North Lake Boulevard; (916) 581-DAWG.

Rosie's Cafe: Eat steaks, burgers and pasta on the charming porch. 561 North Lake Tahoe Boulevard; (916) 583-8504.

Sunnyside Market: It's not exactly the most elegant dining experience, but you and your pooch may eat on benches outside this little convenience store. 1780 West Lake Boulevard; (916) 583-7626.

TAHOE PINES

PLACES TO STAY

Kaspian Campground: This small summertime campground has room for only 10 tents, so you probably won't be encountering The Camp Party from Hell here. Sites are $10. No reservations needed. The campground is four miles south of Tahoe City, on Highway 89. Follow the signs when you get there. (916) 573-2600.

TAHOE VISTA

PARKS, BEACHES & RECREATION AREAS

•**National Avenue Beach** 🐾 🐾 1/2

This sandy beach is the better of the two North Shore beaches that allow dogs. It's not big, but there's enough room to exercise your leashed dog. There's plenty of shade from the trees adjacent to the beach. That's good news in the summer, when it gets toasty.

The beach is at the end of National Avenue, on Lake Tahoe. (916) 546-7248. →*See #10 on map p. 192.*

• **North Tahoe Regional Park** 🐾 🐾 🐾

This kind of land is very rare in these parts. Leashed dogs are allowed everywhere except on the playing fields and bleachers in this 108-acre park. That means four miles of hiking trails are at their disposal. Better yet, some of those trails lead to the Tahoe National Forest, where your dog can run untethered (see page 810). The regional park is even fun in the winter because of its popular snow play hill.

If you're shopping around for a companion for your dog, stop in at the county animal shelter, just a frisbee's throw away from the park. You can't miss the signs for it. There are many sweet dogs here who would much rather be romping around in parks with you than caged up and worrying about their fate. They're at 875 National Avenue; call (916) 546-4269.

The park is at the corner of Donner Road and National Avenue. From Highway 28, drive inland a few blocks past the scenic cinderblock manufacturer and its neighboring mobile home park. Turn left at the sign for the park. (916) 546-7248. →*See #11 on map p. 192.*

RESTAURANTS

The Mustard Seed: This vegetarian deli is out of this world. 7411 North Lake Tahoe Boulevard; (916) 546-3525.

PLACES TO STAY

Tatami Cottage Resort: They've welcomed pets at this heavenly resort since 1925! The cottages have kitchens, fireplaces and great views of Lake Tahoe. But best for dogs, the place is on two acres, with an enclosed pet lot, a beach in front, and a beaver pond in the back. Your dog can run leash-free here, thanks to Dave, the resort's dog-loving owner. Rates are $69 to $129. 7449 North Lake Boulevard, Tahoe Vista, CA 96148; (916) 546-3523.

TAHOMA

PLACES TO STAY

Alpenhaus: People and their dogs may stay at the rustic, century-old cabins here. Many have fireplaces, and all are renovated for your cozy comfort. Rates are $100 to $150. There's a $50 deposit for pooches. 6941 West Lake Boulevard, Tahoma, CA 96142; (916) 525-5000.

EL DORADO COUNTY

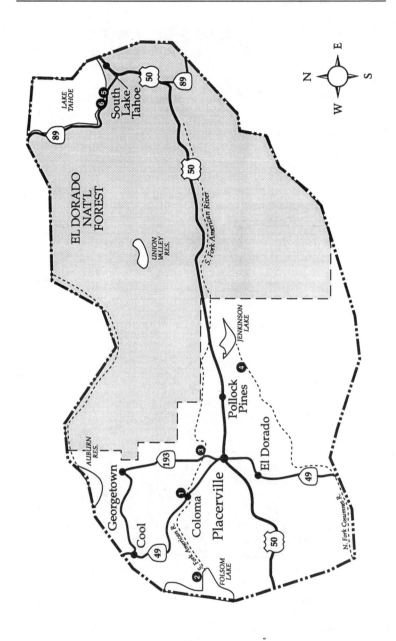

20

EL DORADO COUNTY

From Lake Tahoe to the lands east of the Mother Lode vein, this county is as attractive to people as it is to their dogs. Unfortunately, El Dorado County doesn't exactly roll out the gold carpet for canines. The south edge of Lake Tahoe isn't very hospitable to dogs, and formerly wild and wooly Gold Rush towns like Placerville and Georgetown are doggone deficient in such canine creature comforts as parks.

If it weren't for Eldorado National Forest, which makes up more than half the land here, dogs might ask to visit another county. Dogs can run leashless in most of this mighty Sierra Nevada forest. Keep in mind that a huge stretch of the forest is recuperating from the devastating 1992 blaze that left thousands of acres of charred tree skeletons starting just west of Kyburz. Tread gently.

NATIONAL FORESTS

The major portion of Eldorado National Forest is located in its namesake county. An exception to the off-leash policy of the national forests is in the Desolation Wilderness, where dogs are supposed to be leashed at all times. See the National Forests/ Wilderness Areas chapter starting on page 801 for important information and safety tips for visiting national forests with your dog.

• **Eldorado National Forest** 😺 😺 😺 😺 🐟 🐕
   See page 804.

COLOMA

PARKS, BEACHES & RECREATION AREAS

• **Marshall Gold Discovery State Historic Park** 😺 😺 😺
   James Marshall, whose discovery of gold in John Sutter's mill here started the Gold Rush, died a penniless recluse. But at least he had a dog-friendly state park dedicated to him.

Dogs are allowed in more places here than at most state parks. While they're banned from American River beaches and all trails, they can hang out with you at picnic areas and walk with you in the meadow behind the visitor center. They can stroll along Main Street and peer at historic buildings, including a replica of Sutter's Mill. Dogs are even permitted to accompany you to the Munroe

Orchard, where you can pick a piece of fruit and sit under a tree to while away the afternoon while your friends pan for gold in the river.

Rates are $5 per car, with dogs costing $1 extra. The park is on Highway 49 between Placerville and Auburn. (916) 622-3470. →*See #1 on map p. 204.*

COOL

By virtue of its name alone, this town southeast of Auburn is worth a stop. Cool has a couple of restaurants that allow dogs, but it doesn't have any parks for dogs. For this reason, we think the town should be renamed Kinda Cool. So far, residents aren't buying the idea.

Just a couple of miles up Highway 49 is the Auburn State Recreation Area. Most of it is in Placer County, and it's described more fully in that chapter (see page 194). But there is a section you can hike in with your dog which starts less than a half mile before the first bridge you come to after leaving Cool. The parking area and trailhead are unmarked, so be on the lookout for a dirt road that veers off sharply to the right. If you miss it, just turn around at the bridge and come back almost a half mile and you'll be there.

RESTAURANTS
Country Rose Cafe: Dogs and humans love visiting the outdoor tables here. Not only does the staff serve homey meals and home-made desserts, the owner makes personalized dog collars with the dog's name woven right in. It may not taste good, but it's in good taste, and you can order one here anyway. 1020 Northside Drive, at Highway 49; (916) 885-9639.

Cool Sandwiches & More: 3602 Highway 49; (916) 823-2314.

EL DORADO

Upon entering this tiny town south of Placerville on Highway 49, a sign announces "Population: 26." For such an small place, El Dorado has a great deal of charm, and one dog-friendly eatery.

RESTAURANTS
El Dorado Grocery and Deli: Eat at the shaded table outside this old-fashioned deli. 6203 Main Street; (916) 626-1015.

GEORGETOWN

On the way here on Highway 193, don't be surprised if you run into signs warning strongly against letting dogs run free near a couple of farms. The penalty: Your dog gets shot.

Fortunately, Georgetown is not known for its parks, so there's little danger of your dog escaping and running into an angry farmer.

PLACES TO STAY

American River Inn: If you want to bring a dog here, you'll have to prove to the owners that your dog will behave better than Miss Manners herself. If they say no, please don't hassle them. This bed-and-breakfast is full of antiques and expensive furnishings, and you should give them credit for even considering pooches. It's a huge old place with a beautiful New England-style backyard and sitting area. It's located at Main and Orleans streets. P.O. Box 43, Georgetown, CA 95643; (916) 333-4499.

PILOT HILL

PARKS, BEACHES & RECREATION AREAS

• **Folsom Lake State Recreation Area** 😺 😺 😺 1/2

A big portion of this 12,000-acre lake is in El Dorado County, but it's listed under Folsom in Sacramento County. See page 324. ➔ *See #2 on map p. 204.*

PLACERVILLE

When this city was one of the great camps of Gold Country, it was first known as Dry Diggins. The name lasted about a year. In 1849, after a number of lynchings, the place became known as Hangtown.

People had it tough back then. But dogs may have it even tougher here today. These days, there are very few parks. Open land has been replaced by strip shopping centers and new housing. The name Placerville may have been good for welcoming suburbia, but dogs should be sorely disappointed at the changes the decades have brought to this city on the east side of the famous Mother Lode vein.

Still, the historic downtown is a fun place to stroll with your dog. And you can even learn something about the old Gold Rush days if you visit Hangtown's Gold Bug Park (see below).

PARKS, BEACHES & RECREATION AREAS

• **Hangtown's Gold Bug Park** 😺 😺 1/2

Dogs dig it here. But it's not the gold they dig (lucrative as they may be, such terrier-like habits are discouraged). It's the park itself. This is the city's largest park. While dogs aren't allowed to run around here without a leash, it's a great place to come to stretch their legs while they explore a park that was once home to 250 mines.

If you're traveling with another human, one of you can walk around the park's dirt paths with the dog or picnic in the shade of oaks and pines while the other visits the Gold Bug Mine, which bans dogs. The mine is an educational experience for anyone who ever wondered what it was like inside one of these places. Admission to the mine is $1 for adults. An additional $1 will rent you a fascinating tape-guided tour.

The park is easily accessible from US 50. Take the Bedford Avenue exit north for almost a mile and you're there. (916) 642-5232. ➤*See #3 on map p. 204.*

RESTAURANTS
Sweetie Pie's: The owners describe themselves as "major dog lovers," so your dog will feel right at home at the umbrella-topped tables here. The muffins, fresh fruit, sandwiches, quiche and homemade soups taste extra good knowing you're not getting the evil eye from the management. 577 Main Street; (916) 642-0128.

Togo's Eatery: 1390 Broadway; (916) 621-2050.

PLACES TO STAY
Gold Trail Motor Lodge: There's plenty of shade here on the well-landscaped grounds. That's a real plus in the hot summer months. Rates are $36 to $51. Dogs are $5 extra. 1970 Broadway, Placerville, CA 95667; (916) 622-2906.

Mother Lode Motel: Rates are $43 to $51. 1940 Broadway, Placerville, CA 95667; (916) 622-0895.

POLLOCK PINES
PARKS, BEACHES & RECREATION AREAS
•**Sly Park Recreation Area** 🐾 🐾 🐾
Does your leashed dog like boating, hiking and watching people go by on horses? Does she like camping, but prefer to do it in a somewhat civilized fashion? If so, this Jenkinson Lake camping area is for her. There are 190 sites in this year-round campground, so she'll never feel alone.

All sites are first come, first served. Sites are $10 a night. Dogs are an additional $1.50. From US 50, go south on Sly Park Road for about five miles. (916) 644-2545. ➤*See #4 on map p. 204.*

RESTAURANTS
D's Burgers: The ice cream here tastes really good on warm summer afternoons. 6373 Pony Express Trail; (916) 644-7590.

Pioneer Kitchen: Dogs are welcome to join you on the sweet, awning-covered deck. They don't serve dinner here, but breakfast and lunch are great. 6404 Pony Express Trail; (916) 644-2805.

PLACES TO STAY
Sly Park Recreation Area camping: See page 208.

SOUTH LAKE TAHOE

Most hotels and motels here greet you with big "No Pets" signs. Most beaches and parks do the same. South Lake Tahoe is not doggy paradise.

One of the reasons so many lodgings don't allow dogs is that they don't want them left alone in the room while their owners sneak over the state line to gamble the night away. Do your pooch a favor. If you're going to do the night scene in Nevada, don't bring her unless someone will be with her while you're gone.

If you're among those who come here just to see Lake Tahoe from a park or (gulp) to get married, your dog will be happy here.

PARKS, BEACHES & RECREATION AREAS
There are very few places to walk with your dog in South Lake Tahoe. Dogs are banned from city beaches and even from those federal beaches and federal parks that charge entrance fees. State parks here allow dogs only in camping and picnic areas. But there are a couple of places (both run by the folks who run the national forests) that dogs will be as excited to visit as humans.

• **Kiva Beach** 🐾 🐾 🐾 1/2
The huge swath of scattered pine that greets you as you enter this area is just as enticing for your leashed dog as the beach itself. There's some sage undergrowth, but it's fairly easy to navigate.

If you want to go directly to the beach, just park and take the long dirt trail there. The beach is large and sandy, and provides a great panorama of Lake Tahoe.

If lounging around in the sand is boring your canine, take him on a hike up the Tallac Historic Trail, which starts near the east end of the beach. There, he'll be shaded from the sun and inundated with fascinating tidbits about the area's past.

From the junction of US 50 and Highway 89, take Highway 89 north about 2.5 miles. The entrance is on your right. (916) 573-2600.
➡ *See #5 on map p. 204.*

• **Lake Tahoe Visitors Center** 🐾 🐾 🐾 1/2 🐾
This is among the most fascinating and well-developed wildlife viewing areas in the state. You and your dog can spend the whole

day here agog at Mother Nature while learning about this wet meadow area and the abundant life it supports.

A half-dozen trails with interpretive displays lead you over creeks, through aspen forests and grassy wetlands, and among wildlife you never dreamed you'd see so close to Harrah's and Caesars Tahoe. Among some of the critters you might spot: ospreys, beavers, Canada geese, Kokanee salmon, trout and yes—hairy woodpeckers. There's even the possibility you'll see some deer and coyotes, so keep a tight hold of that leash.

The park may have the only aquarium in the world that welcomes dogs. It's not exactly the Monterey Bay Aquarium, but it is an underwater building where you can see native fish in their native stream.

The beach and undeveloped forest lands around the visitors center provide ample room to get away from the crowds that can get heavy in the summer. If you plan to make a day of it, pack a lunch to eat at the park's comfortable picnic areas.

The park is also the site of the Lake Tahoe Kokanee Salmon Festival (see page 211). From the junctions of highways 50 and 89, the park is north about 3.5 miles. The entrance is on your right. (916) 573-2600. ➔*See #6 on map p. 204.*

RESTAURANTS

Bayer's Bagel Bakery: Oy, the bagels here are great, but your dog will really drool when you slather the bagels with some of the bakery's fancy cream cheeses. 2701 Lake Tahoe Boulevard; (916) 541-7882.

Grass Roots Natural Foods: This is a great place to visit for healthful, wholesome food. It even tastes delicious! Your dog can join you at the picnic tables outside the big old blue house and restaurant. 2040 Dunlap Drive; (916) 541-7788.

Snow Flake Drive-In: Eat burgers and fries at the picnic tables here. 3057 Lake Tahoe Boulevard; (916) 544-6377.

Sprouts: As the name might imply, fresh natural foods, not greasy onion rings and shakes, are their forte here. Eat at the picnic tables with your pooch. 3125 Harrison Avenue; (916) 541-6969.

PLACES TO STAY

Alder Inn and Cottages: If you feel like hitting the slopes, but your dog just doesn't have the urge to don her skis, the inn will supply you with a convenient pet-sitting service. It costs $5 per hour to babysit one dog, $6 for two dogs, and dogs get lots of tender loving care. Rates are $35 to $90. Dogs are $10 extra. 1072 Ski Run Boulevard, South Lake Tahoe, CA 95729; (916) 544-4485.

Emerald Bay State Park: Camping here is available only in the summer months. Although dogs are not allowed on the park's trails, it's worth it to camp here just to be in this park's splendor. Some 100 campsites are located on the south side of the tranquil bay.

Sites are $12 to $14. Dogs are $1 extra. The park is located on Highway 89, about eight miles north of the junction of Highway 89 and US 50. Call park headquarters at (916) 541-3030 for information. For reservations, call MISTIX at (800) 444-PARK.

Fallen Leaf Lake: This is a good place for dogs who enjoy socializing. In summer, chances are good that you'll be in close proximity to dozens of campers in this popular recreational lake area on U.S. Forest Service land. Anglers with dogs like to come here to take advantage of the hot bite the lake has in the summer months.

There are 205 campsites. Fees are $12 a night. From the junction of Highway 89 and US 50, go north about two miles on Highway 89 to the Fallen Leaf Lake turnoff. Go left, and drive 1.5 miles to the camping area. Call (916) 573-2600 for park information. For reservations, call (800) 280-CAMP.

If you prefer to be away from the madding crowd, the Desolation Wilderness is accessible from here. There you can camp in peace, except for the occasional twittering of songbirds. There's no fee for camping in this wilderness area, but you must have a permit. And unlike many other wilderness areas, dogs must be leashed.

Motel 6: Rates are $36 for the first adult, and $4 for the second. All Motel 6s allow one small pooch per room. 2375 Lake Tahoe Boulevard, South Lake Tahoe, CA 95731; (916) 542-1400.

Tahoe Sands Inn: Rates are $48 to $98. Dogs are $6 extra, and there may be a $100 deposit. 3600 Lake Tahoe Boulevard, South Lake Tahoe, CA 95705; (916) 544-3476.

Tahoe Valley Motel: Rates are $85 to $150. Dogs are $10 extra. 2241 Lake Tahoe Boulevard, South Lake Tahoe, CA 96150; (916) 541-0353.

FESTIVALS

Lake Tahoe Kokanee Salmon Festival: You can learn all about Kokanee salmon during this family weekend in early October. You can also cook salmon in a contest, eat salmon, listen to stories about salmon and find out how to fish for the slippery fellas. Children enjoy seeing salmon under water and watching people parading around in fishy costumes. Dogs seem to enjoy it all. The festival is at the Lake Tahoe Visitors Center of the U.S. Forest Service. (See page 209 for a description of this park.) (916) 573-2600.

DIVERSIONS

Here comes the bride... and the groom... and the dog: They've seen it all at the Chapel of the Bells. Dogs have worn tuxedos to weddings. They've been the best man, the maid of honor, the ring bearer. They've given away the bride. "They've even cried," says manager Carolyn Lewis.

The chapel has both an indoor and an outdoor facility, located in the heart of a woodsy but suburban neighborhood. The basic wedding costs $111 including the license, excluding the donation for the minister. For that kind of price, you can afford to bring the dog along on the honeymoon.

If you're in the Tahoe area and want to get married fast but this chapel doesn't ring your bells, just pick up a phone book and look in the Yellow Pages under Weddings. You're sure to find something the bride, groom and pooch will all remember happily ever after.

The Chapel of the Bells is at 2700 Highway 50. Their mailing address is P.O. Box 18410, South Lake Tahoe, CA 96151. Call the chapel at (916) 544-1112 or (800) 247-4333.

ALPINE COUNTY

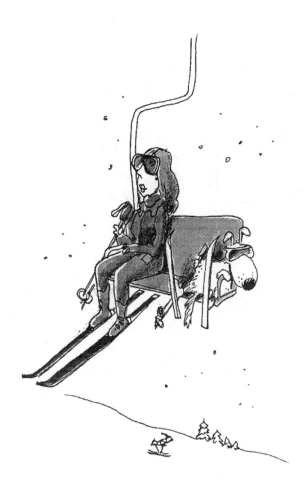

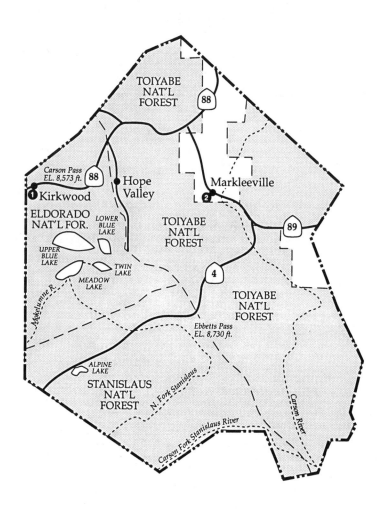

21
ALPINE COUNTY

More people live in one Los Angeles high rise than in this entire county! With a population of only 1,100, this county has plenty of room for a few good dogs. More than 90 percent of the land here is public land, most of it in the form of very dog-friendly national forests.

You'll find trailheads into the Eldorado, Stanislaus and Toiyabe national forests along Highways 88, 89 and 4. You can just pull over into a safe zone and hike with your dog if you know it's national forest land. As soon as you're away from roads and campgrounds, your dog can go leashless in nearly 800 square miles of meadows, alpine forests and rocky mountains. There's one exception to this, just east of the county line in the Mokelumne Wilderness of El Dorado National Forest off Highway 88 (see page 804).

A drive along Highway 4 can be exciting as well as very scenic. The street gets so narrow that eventually the stripes in the middle of the road disappear. It's steep and winding in parts, so tell your dog to look up if he's scared of heights. As you ascend to nearly 9,000 feet, the scenery becomes other-worldly. Huge rock formations are everywhere. They're rounded from the passage of time and some are stacked in impossible configurations.

Since the road is so winding, it's a good idea to make frequent stops, especially if your dog starts turning green. At Ebbetts Pass (elevation 8,730 feet), you can pull over and take the dog out to a large meadow on your left or to the rocky hill on your right. Because it's part of the Stanislaus National Forest, he can go leashless. There are several campgrounds and limitless backcountry camping in the national forests along the way, so there's no shortage of places to pitch a tent.

Dogs also like to visit Mosquito Lake and Lake Alpine. Since there can be many other visitors, dogs should be leashed in these areas. (See Stanislaus National Forest, page 810.)

The four seasons are magical in Alpine County. Springtime brings an incomparable carpet of wildflowers. Summer days rarely get too warm. When we last visited, it was mid-August. During the day, people were wearing sweaters. Dogs, even those sporting thick coats, weren't panting.

In autumn, aspen and cottonwoods burst into magnificent oranges, yellows and reds. Dogs who claim to have black-and-white vision may not appreciate it, but the seasonal change can be a bit of a thrill for their caretakers.

During winter, Alpine County is a wonderland of white, but some of the mountain roads can be impassable. It's a good idea to call your destination to check road conditions before setting paw out of your front door.

NATIONAL FORESTS

Sections of the following three national forests are located in Alpine County. See the National Forests/Wilderness Areas chapter starting on page 801 for important information and safety tips for visiting national forests with your dog.

- **Eldorado National Forest** 🐾🐾🐾🐾 🐕
  See page 804.
- **Stanislaus National Forest** 🐾🐾🐾🐾 🐕
  See page 810.
- **Toiyabe National Forest** 🐾🐾🐾🐾 🦴 🐕
  See page 810.

KIRKWOOD

Kirkwood, one of the best ski and summer recreation areas in California, is also quite accommodating to dogs. Kirkwood is split among three counties, but most people here consider Alpine County home.

PARKS, BEACHES & RECREATION AREAS

- **Kirkwood Ski and Summer Resort** 🐾🐾🐾 1/2
  During summer, you can't help but see dog after dog romping around this serene high Sierra playground. Most of them have smiles on their slobbery faces because they're welcome to explore the resort's 12 miles of trails through meadows and up slopes and back bowl areas. They have to be on leash, but it's a small price for your dog to pay to be able to tell his friends he vacationed here. After a day on the grassy slopes, your whole family (dog included) can share an evening singing around the campfire and eating food someone else barbecues for you. (See Diversions, page 217).

  The resort is about 60 miles northeast of Jackson, on Highway 88. You can't miss the signs for it. Once there, ask for a map of the trails from the general store/reservations desk. (209) 258-8000.
  →See #1 on map p. 214.

RESTAURANTS

Kirkwood Inn: This place has barely changed since it was built in 1864 by early settlers Zachary and Eliza Kirkwood. You'll still find bullet holes in the thick wood ceiling when you walk inside to order your down-home cooking. And the bar is the original one (except for a section a drunk woman crushed while dancing on it in the winter of 1992). Dogs like it here, but despite the place's wild and wooly past, they're relegated to the outdoor tables when they're not covered with snow. If you like burgers and steak, this is an excellent place to visit. The restaurant is at Highway 88, across from the entrance to Kirkwood Ski and Summer Resort (six miles west of Carson Pass); (209) 258-7304.

PLACES TO STAY

While dogs aren't allowed to stay in the lodges or condominiums at Kirkwood Ski and Summer Resort, they can sometimes be your roommate if you rent a house or cabin through Kirkwood Accommodations. Call (209) 258-8575.

Or if you want to "ruff" it, the nearby Eldorado and Toiyabe national forests offer ample camping opportunities.

DIVERSIONS

Howl beside the campfire: Tired of watching your campfire fizzle in the nearby national forest before you and the family can roast a marshmallow? Shame-faced that even your dog won't eat the thing that started out as a hamburger on your Coleman stove? Fear not! If it's Saturday night in the summer, Kirkwood Ski and Summer Resort has the answer: Sierra Saturdays.

Sierra Saturdays provide you, the kids and the dog with good old-fashioned family fun. From singing and storytelling around the campfire to throwing horseshoes and eating a delectable barbecue dinner, this is one of the best "together" times you and your family may ever have.

The price of the entire evening, food included, starts at $6.95 per person (unless your dog insists on a burger and beans, she doesn't have to pay anything). Sierra Saturdays are generally held for two months on Saturday evenings in the summer. Call (800) 967-7500 or (209) 258-7000 for information and reservations.

HOPE VALLEY
PLACES TO STAY

Sorensen's Resort: Several trails that start around the Sorensen property are ideal for hiking or cross-country skiing. The two cabins that allow dogs here are decent places to stay if you want to take the dog on a cross-country ski vacation. One has a wood-burning stove and the other is warmed by conventional modern means.

Unfortunately, of the 28 cabins that make up the resort, the two that allow dogs are closest to the road. Highway 88 isn't exactly a superfreeway, but it's also not what you want to see out your window when you're trying to get away from civilization.

Rates for the dog cabins vary seasonally, from $55 to $135. Since not many places around here take dogs, these cabins are in high demand, so reserve well in advance of your stay. 14255 Highway 88, Hope Valley, CA 96120; (916) 694-2203 or (800) 423-9949.

MARKLEEVILLE

Jacob Marklee founded this Old West town in 1861. He spent the rest of his years—all three of them—here. In 1864, he was dead, the loser in a shootout with a fellow named H. W. Tuttle. Today, Markleeville has the distinction of being the county seat of the least-populous county in California.

PARKS, BEACHES & RECREATION AREAS

•**Grover Hot Springs State Park** 😺 😺 😺 1/2

This is a rare bird for a state park: It actually allows dogs to walk with you on trails. Leashed dogs can hike through ponderosa pine, incense cedars and quaking aspen year-round. They're also al-lowed to camp with you in all four seasons. About the only thing they can't do is bask in the 105-degree Fahrenheit water in the pools here or refresh themselves in the cold plunge area.

But that doesn't mean you have to deprive yourself of the possibly therapeutic effects of the waters. You and a friend can take turns. One can soak in the hot mineral water (it actually comes out of the ground at 148 degrees Fahrenheit!) while the other takes the dog for a walk or on a mini-fishing trip at the creeks and lakes here. Then switch. This way, everyone gets to enjoy the best this park has to offer.

It costs $4 per adult to enter the pool and $2 for children. Use of the picnic area is $2 for under an hour, or $5 for the day. Sleeping at one of the 76 campsites costs $12 to $14 a night. Dogs cost $1 extra, for day use and camping. The park is three miles west of Markleeville, off Highway 88 on Hot Springs Road. Call (916) 694-2248 for information. For reservations, call MISTIX at (800) 444-PARK. ➡ *See #2 on map p. 214.*

RESTAURANTS

After a day at the hot springs, there's nothing like a good meal. And in warmer weather, Markleeville has plenty of restaurants with outdoor tables where dogs are welcome.

Funny thing is, these places are not listed in the phone book or with directory assistance. In fact, they just recently got street addresses, and people there still don't use them. The best advice they have is to just come into town, look for the places with outdoor tables, check with the manager if it's okay to set a spell with your dog, and enjoy. Among the eateries whose employees told us good dogs are generally allowed outside: *The Deli, Markleeville General Store, Tiers of Joy* (excellent cinnamon rolls) and *J. Marklee Toll Station's Restaurant.* They're all along a very short strip of Highway 89, so you won't have any trouble finding them.

PLACES TO STAY

Grover Hot Springs State Park campgrounds: See page 218.

J. Marklee Toll Station: Rates for this old downtown Markleeville hotel are $35. Dogs are $5 extra. It's a homey place to stay if you want to get the feel for old-style Markleeville. The place even has a restaurant with outdoor tables. 14856 Highway 89, Markleeville, CA 96120; (916) 694-2507.

AMADOR COUNTY

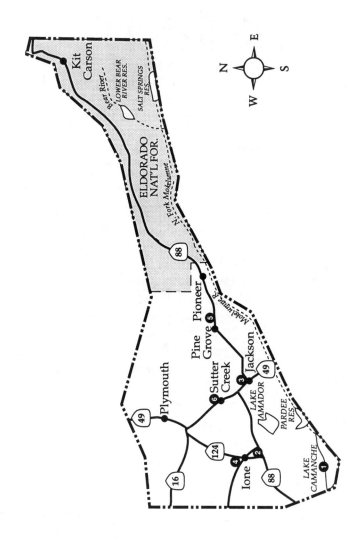

22
AMADOR COUNTY

Amador County is a place too many people drive through without stopping to take a look around. Highway 88 makes it easy to cruise through this narrow county on the way to another destination. But if you drive past here with blinders on, not only are you missing some quaint old Gold Rush towns, you're also bypassing some of the most unusual vista points in California.

Among the sights you should try to take in is the Devil's Garden vista point, along the eastern part of the county along Highway 88 in Eldorado National Forest. If a devil ever did have a garden, it would be here in this rocky terrain. Nearby are several trailheads leading into portions of this vast forest where dogs can usually prance about leashless. (See page 804.) Eldorado National Forest is the only swath of public land in Amador County where dogs can experience this blissful freedom.

NATIONAL FORESTS

See the National Forests/Wilderness Areas chapter starting on page 801 for important information and safety tips for visiting national forests with your dog.

• **Eldorado National Forest** 😊 😊 😊 😊 🐾 🐕
   See page 804.

CAMANCHE VILLAGE

PARKS, BEACHES & RECREATION AREAS

• **Lake Camanche** 😊 😊 😊
   See the Calaveras County listing for Lake Camanche on page 234 for details. Camanche Village is just north of the lake's north shore.
→ *See #1 on map p. 222.*

IONE

PARKS, BEACHES & RECREATION AREAS

• **Charles Howard Park** 😊 😊 1/2
   This is your basic community park. Nice trees, nice grass, nice cemetery. Keep in shape together by jogging on the track that goes around the park. It's at Brickyard Road and Church Street. (209) 274-2412. → *See #2 on map p. 222.*

JACKSON

Jackson is one Old West town where there's still plenty of evidence of a rich and colorful heritage. The streets of downtown look like they were pulled from a Hollywood back lot. You can even hear lively piano music pouring out of the classic old National Hotel (no dogs allowed).

Dogs are welcome to stroll through the historic downtown district with you. A couple of stores that sell goods reminiscent of the Gold Rush era might allow you in with your dog. These shop owners asked Joe not to tell anyone he shopped there, so we can't divulge the names.

The city has only a couple of parks, but there's no shortage of restaurants that will let your dog dine outside with you during good weather.

PARKS, BEACHES & RECREATION AREAS

• **Detert Park** 🐾 🐾 1/2

Does your pup like square dancing? Then dog-se-do on over to this pleasant community park's bandstand. Two local square dancing clubs practice here some enchanted evenings, and if you're lucky, you might get to watch (or take part in) some of the finest square dancing around.

If your dog prefers to stroll (on leash), the park has lush lawns and many shady trees. For the kids, there's a swimming pool and a very unique playground. The park is an ideal stop if you're visiting the historic part of town. It's just east of Highway 49/88, north of Hoffman Street. (209) 223-1646. ➔ See #3 on map p. 222.

• **Kennedy Tailing Wheels Park** 🐾 🐾

This is the less lovely of the two larger city parks. Instead of grass, there's usually dirt underfoot. But there's plenty of shade from large oak trees, so your leashed dog will be comfortable as you walk around learning about the history of the gold mines from the kiosks and placards here. The park is famous for its huge tailing wheels, built to carry non-gold waste away to nearby ponds. (Boy dogs: Keep your legs down. These are antiques!)

Follow North Main Street to the northern part of the city, where the name of the street changes to Jackson Gate Road. Big signs mark the park on the east side of the street. (209) 223-1646. ➔ See #4 on map p. 222.

RESTAURANTS

Caffe Tazza: This congenial, European-style cafe features great pasta and vegetarian dishes. Dine under the cool shade of umbrella-topped tables. 214 Main Street; (209) 223-3547.

Mel & Faye's Diner: Dine on burgers, steak and chicken while sitting out on the patio. 205 North State Highway 49; (209) 223-0853.

PLACES TO STAY

Amador Motel: Rates are $37 to $42. 12408 Kennedy Flat Road, Jackson, CA 95642; (209) 223-0970.

Best Western Amador Inn: Rates are $50 to $65. Dogs are $6 extra. 200 South Highway 49, Jackson, CA 95642; (209) 223-0211.

Jackson Holiday Lodge: Rates are $37 to $60 a night. There's a $10 doggy deposit. 850 North State Highway 49, Jackson, CA 95642; (209) 223-0486.

KIT CARSON

PLACES TO STAY

Kit Carson Campground: If you and your dog like trout fishing or peace and quiet, this high Sierra camp on the West Fork of the Carson River is a great spot to pitch a tent. Since there are only a dozen campsites, you won't have typical Tent City woes.

Campsites are $7 a night and are available only from spring to late summer. The campground is about six miles southeast of Kirkwood on Highway 88. (702) 882-2766.

PINE GROVE

PARKS, BEACHES & RECREATION AREAS

• **Indian Grinding Rock State Historic Park** 🐾 🐾

Dogs aren't permitted on trails here, but they are allowed to visit bits of the reconstructed Miwok village and sniff at the old grinding rock. Leashed dogs can even read some of the petroglyphs around the park if they're of the erudite ilk.

It costs $5 per carload for day-use visits. There are 23 campsites. Rates are $14 per night. Dogs are $1 extra, for day use and camping. The park is about halfway between Pine Grove and Volcano, on Pine Grove Volcano Road. Call (209) 296-7488 for park information. For reservations, call MISTIX at (800) 444-PARK. ➡ *See #5 on map p. 222.*

RESTAURANTS

Pine Grove Village Florist & Sweet Shop: While you eat your deli sandwich and sip on your malted milkshake, your dog will be served a bowl of water. 20200 Highway 88; (209) 296-1699.

PLACES TO STAY

Indian Grinding Rock State Historic Park camping: See above.

PIONEER

RESTAURANTS

Sutter Trading Post: Dogs like to dine at the picnic table outside this old-style convenience store on Highway 88. (209) 295-3725.

SUTTER CREEK

John Sutter, who owned the mill where gold was first discovered in the Mother Lode, also had his Midas-touch hand in a nearby creek. The creek was named after him and the town came next.

PARKS, BEACHES & RECREATION AREAS

•Minnie Provis Park 🐾 🐾

How often does a dog get to visit a park named after a city clerk? Minnie Provis Park, set in the heart of historical Sutter Creek, may be the only one with such a namesake. Minnie was the first city clerk here. She must have been a good one.

This small, green park is ideally located if you and your leashed dog happen to be exploring the old downtown section of Sutter Creek. The park is located just behind City Hall. Exit Highway 49 at Church Street and go east a half block. Park on the street. (209) 267-5647. ➡ *See #6 on map p. 222.*

FESTIVALS

Great Sutter Creek Duck Race: More than 8,000 rubber ducks bob along the creek here every April, giving all their energy to this unique race. It's a real quack up watching their adoptive parents (rubber duckies cost $5 each for the race) scream and coax their protégés to the finish line.

Water dogs really love the event, but they have to stay leashed and on dry land. Any intervention, be it human, doggy or divine, can disqualify ducks.

The event benefits different charities. It's held at Minnie Provis Park. (209) 267-0252.

CALAVERAS COUNTY

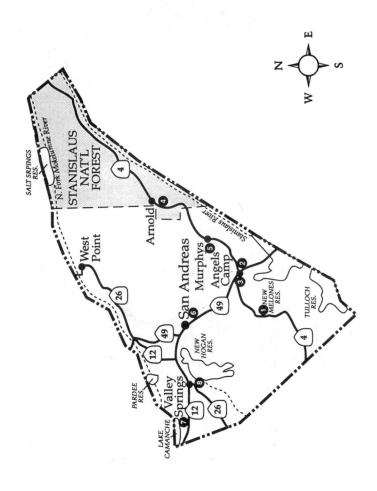

23
CALAVERAS COUNTY

There's not one traffic light in this entire Mother Lode county. Only one town is incorporated. If you want to mall-hop, you have to drive at least 70 miles. And just about every pickup truck has a dog.

"This is where dogs are still dogs, and there may be more of them than of us people," says Pat Mulgrew, the resident caretaker of a park in the "town" of Murphy. "It's very old California. There's a leash law and it should be obeyed. But local dogs often choose to walk on their own, visit the park and hang out with their friends. It's just that kind of place."

At least it's that way until the rest of their world moves in with all its ugly baggage. The folks at the Calaveras Lodging and Visitors Association boast that this is the fastest-growing county in California. They're trying to attract more and more companies so they can bring in more residents. The real estate business is booming.

Get here while you can, before this historic land succumbs to suburban sprawl.

NATIONAL FORESTS

See the National Forests/Wilderness Areas chapter starting on page 801 for important information and safety tips for visiting national forests with your dog.

• **Stanislaus National Forest** 🐾 🐾 🐾 🐾 🐜 🐕

About one-third of Calaveras County has the privilege of being part of Stanislaus National Forest. See page 810.

ANGELS CAMP

You can still check out the saloon in the Angels Hotel, on Main Street, where a barkeep told 29-year-old Mark Twain the tale that inspired his first published short story, *The Notorious Jumping Frog of Calaveras County*.

Since the story was set in this dog-friendly land, it wouldn't have been complete without an interlude about a dog. The one in Twain's story was named Andrew Jackson, and he was apparently a bulldog. Twain's narrative could easily have been called *The Notorious Fighting Dog of Calaveras County*, but publishers may not have jumped at it.

Fighting dogs aren't welcome here, but jumping frogs have never been forgotten. Each year, the town hosts the world-famous Jumping Frog Jubilee. As you may have guessed, dogs are not particularly welcome.

PARKS, BEACHES & RECREATION AREAS

•New Melones Reservoir 🐾 🐾 🐾 1/2

When the lake is full, the trail that meanders around part of it may actually come close to the shore. But usually, you and your leashed dog will have to be content wandering around the rolling foothills, among small scrub oaks that provide little shade. In the summer, it's probably not worth the visit. But the rest of the year, the hiking is pleasant—and the scenery is quite breathtaking in the spring.

The lake's five-mile trail will become much longer if the U.S. Bureau of Reclamation can secure prison labor to continue to build it. That's about the only way it's going to happen, according to the folks who run the reservoir.

Fishing isn't the best in the area, but in the spring the bass bite isn't bad, especially at the lake's northern arms. Your dog is welcome to wet his paws while you fish from shore or to join you on your fishing boat.

There are 239 campsites. They cost $10 a night and are available on a first-come, first-served basis. There's no day-use fee. From Angels Camp, head south on Highway 49 and follow the signs to the lake's north end. (209) 536-9094. → *See #1 on map p. 228.*

•Tryon Park 🐾 🐾

You and your gold-digging canine can pan for gold at Angels Creek, which runs right through this small park. It's a good place to take a rest if you're traveling on Highway 4. The park is located on Highway 4 at Booster Way. (209) 736-2181. → *See #2 on map p. 228.*

•Utica Park 🐾 🐾

Mark Twain's statue is here, and your leashed dog is welcome if he promises not to do leg lifts on it. (Twain may have been amused, but it's just not a respectful way to treat the memory of someone who wrote so much good stuff about dog beasts.)

The park is only 2.63 acres. (When you get this small, you can afford to measure land by the hundredth of an acre.) It seems a good deal bigger. There's plenty of grass for rolling on and plenty of trees for shading you on warmer days. During the summer, you and your dog can attend a few free concerts here (see Diversions, page 231). The park is conveniently located on Highway 49/Main Street at Sam's Way. (209) 736-2181. → *See #3 on map p. 228.*

RESTAURANTS

Mother Lode Frosty: Share a shake with your pooch on the patio of this fast-food eatery. 22 North Main Street; (209) 736-4312.

The Pickle Barrel: You and your hungry pooch can dine on prime rib or pasta in the courtyard out back. You can have deli food here every day, but the restaurant is only open for dinner on Friday and Saturday nights. 1225 South Main Street; (209) 736-4707.

PLACES TO STAY

Angels Inn Motel: Rates are $60 to $70. Dogs require a $10 deposit. 600 North Main Street, Angels Camp, CA 95221; (209) 736-4242.

Gold Country Inn: Rates are $46 to $76. Dogs require a $25 deposit. 720 South Main Street, Angels Camp, CA 95222; (209) 736-4611.

New Melones Reservoir campsites: See page 230.

FESTIVALS

Zucchini Festival: If you and your dog love (or even remotely like) zucchini, this is the party for you. There's a competition for local zucchini growers, along with arts and crafts, music, games and tons of food. There's even a zucchini catapult. It's a really corny celebration. This one-day festival is usually held in September at Utica Park. Call (800) 225-3764 for more information.

DIVERSIONS

Lend a pointy ear: Floppy ears, hairy ears and ears that drag all the way down to the ground are welcome to enjoy the series of free summertime concerts at Utica Park. These Wednesday evening affairs feature a variety of musicians, from Gypsy violinists to bluegrass bands. "People are encouraged to bring a picnic and a well-behaved dog," says Rachel Martin, of the Calaveras Lodging and Visitors Association. See page 230 for info on the park. Call (800) 225-3764 for a schedule of this year's concerts.

ARNOLD

PARKS, BEACHES & RECREATION AREAS

• **Calaveras Big Trees State Park** 🐾 🐾 🐾

Dogs aren't permitted on the trails here, but nothing's stopping them from hiking along the fire roads. "You and your dog might see more wilderness on these fire roads than you would on the regular trails," says interpretive ranger Joe Von Herrman.

The giant sequoias aren't accessible from the fire roads, but you'll probably pass by some of the largest sugar pines in existence. Depending on which roads you take, you could hike close to the Stanislaus River, pass by a historic logging railroad or walk through chaparral-covered slopes and fir-filled forests.

For $1, you can buy a map of the fire roads and trails at the entry kiosk. The day-use fee is $5. There are 129 campsites, with nightly rates ranging from $12 to $14. Dogs are $1 extra. The park is four miles northeast of Arnold, on Highway 4. Follow the signs. For camping reservations, call MISTIX at (800) 444-PARK. For park information, phone (209) 795-2334. → *See #4 on map p. 228.*

RESTAURANTS

The Hungry Prospector: You have to tie your dog up here, but she'll still be close to you. The place serves typical fast-food fare, from burgers and fried chicken to deli sandwiches and fish. You can also get breakfast. 961 Highway 4; (209) 795-2128.

Just Delicious: Most of the food is as advertised. Dogs like to join you on the patio. 140 Highway 4; (209) 795-2805.

Tallahan's Cafe: Your dog can't be at your feet here, but he'll be grateful for that if you've just come back from a hard and sweaty hike. Dogs seem content to be tied within a few feet of your table at the outer edge of the deck. The food is an eclectic mix. 2224 Oak Circle; (209) 795-4005.

PLACES TO STAY

Calaveras Big Trees State Park campsites: See page 231.

Ebbett's Pass Lodge: Small to medium dogs only, please. Rates are $40 to $74. 1173 Highway 4, Arnold, CA 95223; (209) 795-1563.

Meadowmont Lodge: Huge dogs can't stay here, but all others are welcome. Rates are $54 to $75. The location is Country Club Drive and Highway 4, and the mailing address is P.O. Box E, Arnold, CA 95223; (209) 795-1394.

Sierra Vacation Rentals: Rent a cabin or mountain chalet to take your favorite canine companion and a few friends for an extra-special vacation getaway. All of the rentals have fireplaces or wood-burning stoves for those cold winter nights. Rates for up to six people and a dog are $130 to $170 for the first night and $70 to $90 for each additional night. Each extra person costs $10 per night. Dogs require a $150 deposit. P.O. Box 1080, Arnold, CA 95223; (209) 795-2422 or (800) 995-2422.

MURPHYS

PARKS, BEACHES & RECREATION AREAS

• Murphys Park 🐾 🐾 1/2

This is where the local dogs hang out. They like the shade, they enjoy the creek that flows through here year-round, and they appreciate each other's company. Many of them don't even wait for their owners to leash them up and walk them here. They head over by themselves. "It's breaking the rules, but they don't get themselves in trouble and they have real street smarts," says Pat Mulgrew, a park caretaker.

They also have good taste. The creek here is large, with a wood footbridge you can cross to walk on the shadier, more secluded side of the park. It's located at Main and South Algiers streets. (209) 728-8726. → *See #5 on map p. 228.*

RESTAURANTS

If you and your dog are hungry, beware of being lured to *Murphys Dog House.* It may have a dog-oriented name, but my researchers and I were treated so rudely here that we tremble to think that any kindly dog owner might make the same mistake we did. Try Celeste's instead.

Celeste's: Eat homemade soup and rolls at the many outdoor tables here. Dogs don't mind if you order Celeste's tasty pizza with extra pepperoni. (Joe made me write that.) 409 Main Street; (209) 728-2875.

SAN ANDREAS

PARKS, BEACHES & RECREATION AREAS

• Nielsen Park 🐾 🐾 1/2

If you've just come from visiting the haunting Mokelumne Hill area (eight miles north), this park is an excellent place for a pit stop. It's not only grassy, shady and set along the refreshing San Andreas Creek, it's also right along the way. It's on Main Street, just east of Highway 49, close to the local visitors center. There's no official phone number for the park. → *See #6 on map p. 228.*

PLACES TO STAY

Black Bart Inn and Motel: You and your dog won't have to sniff out a park if you stay here—the Black Bart Inn comes complete with its own park. It even has a gazebo and a huge barbecue area. Rates are $20 to $47. 55 North Saint Charles Street, Box 216, San Andreas, CA 95249; (209) 754-3808.

The Courtyard Bed and Breakfast: This is a truly enchanting inn. Dogs, don't tell a soul about it. It's our little secret.

One of the two rooms here is so romantic it could make a grown dog blush. It's the honeymoon suite, complete with a baby grand piano, a hot tub, private access, a private deck and a fireplace. There's even a stained glass window over the bath, for those who like to watch Mr. Bubble in living color. The rate for that magical suite is a mere $75. The other room is also enchanting and it's only

$55. The folks here don't have doggy visitors here very often, so they get a kick out of the occasional canine companion. 334 West Saint Charles Street, San Andreas, CA 95249; (209) 754-1518.

VALLEY SPRINGS

PARKS, BEACHES & RECREATION AREAS

•**Lake Camanche** 🐾 🐾 🐾

Come here during the off-season, when it's not too hot or too inundated by waterskiers, and your dog will have a delightful visit. Pooches aren't allowed on trails here, but the land is very open, with scattered oaks on rolling hills and lakeside flats. Dogs can walk anywhere you do, as long as you stay off the trails.

Your dog can dip her paws in the water, but since she's supposed to be leashed, she can't pull an Esther Williams. The fishing is fantastic in the spring and early summer. If thoughts of catching bass, bluegill or trout keep you awake at night, come here, fulfill your dreams, and rest easy.

There are 250 campsites, with rates of $13 a night. Dogs are $1 extra. Sites are open year-round, available on a first-come, first-served basis. The day-use fee is $5.50, with that extra $1 charge for hairy beasts. The lake is north of Highway 12 in the easternmost part of the county. Follow the signs seven miles to the entrance. (209) 763-5178. ➡See #7 on map p. 228.

•**New Hogan Reservoir** 🐾 🐾 🐾

It's cheaper to visit here than Lake Camanche, and leashed dogs actually get to romp around on the trails. The terrain is about the same, with open land, rolling hills, rocks, dirt and some oaks. Dogs can dip their paws in the lake, and they can even join you in your boat as the two of you pursue supper.

Waterskiers can make it noisy in the summer, but there are still plenty of places to escape most of the madness. The lake has 50 miles of shoreline, and partiers can't overtake every inch of it.

The day-use fee here is $3. There are 182 campsites, all available on a first-come, first-served basis. Nightly rates range from $10 to $12. From Highway 26 in the Valley Springs area, you can't miss the signs for the lake. It's about three miles to the entrance. (209) 722-1343. ➡See #8 on map p. 228.

PLACES TO STAY

Lake Camanche camping: See above.
New Hogan Reservoir camping: See above.

TUOLUMNE COUNTY

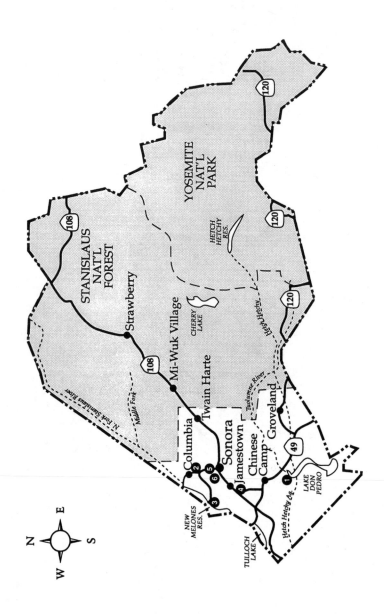

24
TUOLUMNE COUNTY

For any dogs who don't know how to pronounce the name of this county, think of what you'd say if someone asked you, "To whom should I give this huge, rare steak?" You'd probably pipe up and shout, "To all o' me!" or something like that. And that's close enough.

Tuolumne is a colorful Mother Lode county, with many exciting adventures awaiting dogs and their people. Be sure not to miss Jamestown or the Columbia State Historic Park. Dogs adore these places (during off-season when they're not so crowded).

NATIONAL FORESTS

See the National Forests/Wilderness Areas chapter starting on page 801 for important information and safety tips for visiting national forests with your dog.

• **Stanislaus National Forest** 🐾 🐾 🐾 🐾 👣 🐕

There are plenty of places in this stunning forest where you can pull off along the northeast section of Highway 108 to hike or camp. See page 810 for more information on this forest.

NATIONAL PARKS

• **Yosemite National Park** 🐾 👣

Since a dog can barely even set paw inside this park, we can give it only a "worth a squat" rating. It's too bad because the park is so great for people. See page 259 for more information.

CHINESE CAMP

PARKS, BEACHES & RECREATION AREAS

• **Lake Don Pedro** 🐾

Dogs can't go camping here and they aren't permitted to walk on land anywhere near people. These rules are thanks to a recent biting incident. I wanted to sink my teeth into this and find out just who bit what, but no one knew.

The only way your leashed dog can really be with you here is if you let her out of your car and immediately walk her to your waiting boat. She can fish with you (you can actually catch salmon here!), or you can drive the boat to a shore far from the developed areas and let her walk on land. Since there are 160 miles of shoreline, you'll probably be able to find something that's not too steep or too inaccessible.

The day-use fee is $5. From Chinese Camp, drive east on Highway 49/120 for five miles, turn left at Moccasin Point and follow the signs to the launch ramp. This will get you into the lake at its northern end. For directions to boat ramps at the lower part of the lake, call (209) 852-2369. → *See #1 on map p. 236.*

COLUMBIA

PARKS, BEACHES & RECREATION AREAS

• **Columbia State Historic Park** 🐾 🐾 🐾 1/2 🐾

This park is actually a ghost town from the Gold Rush. But it's preserved in such a manner that it still has a pulse. It's alive. You can get a haircut at the state's oldest barbershop, sip sarsaparilla at a saloon and buy old-style dry goods at one of the 1850s stores here.

Be sure to bring a friend if you want to enter these establishments, because dogs have to stay outside (and be leashed), and you shouldn't leave them tied up, even for a few minutes. Just take turns dogsitting.

But you don't have to go into the buildings to enjoy this town. The dogs and I like to saunter down the streets (no cars allowed!), kicking up dust as we amble along. We can stop and look inside these wonderful old buildings, but we get along fine without having to actually go inside. No shopping means no cash outflow. Since there's no admission fee at this "living museum," it's a very cheap date.

To give a dog a break from all the history here, go to the old schoolhouse and find the adjacent Karen Bakersville Smith Memorial Trail (named after a local teacher who died in a car crash). It's only six-tenths of a mile long, but it's a wonderful way to spy on nature as you hike through meadows and oak woodlands. So far, dogs are permitted, but if there are any problems, the rangers are ready to nail up the "No Dogs" signs.

Please don't bring a dog here during the summer, unless it's raining, or at least threatening to. It gets torturously crowded. We last visited in October, and it was perfect weather and almost empty.

Stop by the park headquarters and pick up a brochure outlining a one-and-a-half-hour tour. From Highway 49, drive north on Parrott's Ferry Road/County Road E18. The entrance is in just over 1.5 miles, and it's on your right. (209) 532-4301 or (209) 532-0150. → *See #2 on map p. 236.*

RESTAURANTS

Columbia Frosty: This place only serves breakfast and lunch. Eat it in the company of your canine on the patio at the side of the restaurant. 22652 Parrotts Ferry Road; (209) 532-6773.

PLACES TO STAY

Columbia Inn Motel: Rates are $32 to $76. 22646 Broadway Street, Columbia, CA 95310; (209) 533-0446.

GROVELAND

PLACES TO STAY

Buck Meadows Lodge and Yosemite Westgate Motel: This lodging assumes that young dogs are not as well-trained as adults, and charges a $20 puppy deposit. Rates are $50 to $80. 7647 Highway 120, Groveland, CA 95321; (209) 962-5281 or (800) 253-9673.

Groveland Hotel: The suites at this Gold Rush-era inn come with a fireplace and a Jacuzzi so that you can have an evening of romantic relaxation. Rates are $75 to $155. A dog deposit is required. 18767 Main Street, Groveland, CA 95321; (209) 962-4000 or (800) 273-3314.

Sugar Pine Ranch: When you ring the bell here, don't be surprised to find Boo Boo, a little poodle-terrier guy, running to the door to greet you. But don't worry, says Mary, the manager here and Boo Boo's owner. "He wouldn't bite a flea." Watch out if you don't give him enough attention, though. "He sits up and starts doing patty-cake at you," she says. "He'll win your heart. He's the toast of the inn."

Dogs are only allowed in the cabins, which run from $69 to $95 per night. Dogs cost $5 extra per night plus a deposit. The lodging is on Highway 120, about four miles past Groveland on the way to Yosemite. The mailing address is P.O. Box 784, Groveland, CA 95321; (209) 962-7823 or (800) 222-7823.

Yosemite Inn: This inn is open Thursday through Sunday in the winter and all week in the summer. It's set up like a hostel, with showers and bathrooms in the hall. Rates are $28 to $55. 31191 Hardin Flat Road, Groveland, CA 95321; (209) 962-0103.

JAMESTOWN

Jamestown is one of Bill's favorite places to visit. During off-season, it's so uncrowded that he feels like one of the locals in this small Mother Lode town. That's when the town stops being quaint and becomes a real Old West hangout. Bill likes to sit on a bench outside one of the dusty buildings and listen to a couple of old natives tell their stories. But more than anything else, he enjoys wearing his rust-colored bandana around his shiny black neck. He knows he looks devastating.

Dogs can really have fun here. Between panning for gold, riding in a horse-drawn carriage and checking out some famous old locomotives, they'll have enough entertainment to last them until their next vacation.

PARKS, BEACHES & RECREATION AREAS

• **New Melones Reservoir** 🐾🐾🐾 1/2

Since the bulk of the lake (and the best fishing) is on the Calaveras County side, you'll find its description on page 230.
➡ *See #3 on map p. 236.*

• **Railtown 1897 State Historic Park** 🐾🐾🐾 🐾

If you and your dog are train fans and movie buffs, prepare to be impressed. Remember the train in the movie *Back to the Future III*? How about the train in *Unforgiven, High Noon* or the return of *Bonanza*? Get out your autograph book, because the vintage steamers at this park have acted in these and hundreds of other films, TV shows and commercials.

Dogs can't go on rail excursions, but leashed pooches are allowed to walk around the grounds with you and check out the locomotives. They're also permitted to go on an intriguing 30-minute roundhouse tour offered during the warmer months. The fare is $2.50 for adult humans and dogs ride free.

Be sure to bring a picnic lunch if you're with friends who are taking the train ride (given only during summer; $8 for adults, $4 for kids ages 3 to 12). You and your dog can share a lunch in the shaded picnic area while the rest of your party steams around Jamestown for an hour. When they're done, you'll have eaten all the good stuff and those fun-loving, wind-blown buddies of yours will have to settle for the squished sandwiches and generic sodas.

There's no entry fee. From Highway 49 traveling east, turn right on 5th Avenue. Drive a few blocks and you're there. (209) 984-3125.
➡ *See #4 on map p. 236.*

RESTAURANTS

Jimtown Frostie: Joan, the manager here, will be glad to give your pooch a drink of water, and maybe even a meat patty or a dab of Frostie ice cream. And humans can eat here, too. Pooches and their people get to eat at the patio seating. The restaurant is located at the corner of Main Street and Highway 108; (209) 984-3444.

PLACES TO STAY

Mountain River Motel: Lots of fishermen and fisherdogs stay here. Rates are $35 to $39. 12655 Jacksonville Road, Jamestown, CA 95327; (209) 984-5071.

National Hotel: Want some luxury with your history? Try this enchanting place. Built in 1859, it's one of the oldest hotels in California which has run continuously since it opened. Your dog can't wet his whistle at the old-fashioned saloon downstairs, but he'll probably be too busy admiring the simple antique decor in your room to notice. Rates are $75 to $85. 77 Main Street, Jamestown, CA 95327; (209) 984-3446 or (800) 894-3446.

DIVERSIONS

Get hot to trot: Tom Fraser's Carriage Tours provides a terrific way to experience Jamestown with your well-behaved pooch. You and your dog will sit side-by-side in an antique carriage while a beautiful horse pulls you along the historic streets. But when you talk with your dog after your trip, you'll realize that the two of you had completely different experiences.

What humans see: antique shops, wooden sidewalks, great Old West buildings, turn-of-the-century trains and tourists taking pictures.

What dogs see: a horse's butt, a horse's butt, a horse's butt, a passing cat and a horse's butt.

Co-owner Jan Fraser says she and her husband, Tom, love having quiet dogs as riders. "We've had Chihuahuas, poodles, collies, you name it. For most travelers, their pets are like their kids. How can we say no?"

The price is right. A 20-minute ride is $5 per adult, $3 per child. Dogs who can fit on the floor are free. Otherwise, they have to buy a seat and sit next to you. The carriages load at the lower end of town, across the street from Boomer's, on Main Street. They run on weekends throughout the year, with additional hours during the summer. Special rides are available. Call (209) 984-3125.

Hit the Mother Lode: Cowabunga! No, er...Eureka! Aroooo! You and your dog will be hopping around like Yosemite Sam if you find a few specks of gold around here.

The folks at Gold Prospecting Expeditions say they've never met a dog who didn't like helping his owner pan for gold in the cool creeks and rivers here. You and your dog can take a walking tour guided by a prospector, then get down to the business of panning. You keep what you find—and the folks here say you'll always find something in their special section of the Mother Lode.

If your dog can pan like Twinkles, the company's resident poodle, you'll be rich. Twinkles sticks her head under water in a panning trough and comes up with a gold nugget every time. Of course, she's been trained, and the nugget is always there, so don't be too disappointed if your dog doesn't scoop up the down payment for your new house.

For a real outback prospecting experience, you and your dog (as long as he's of calm disposition) can fly in a helicopter to some of the most remote areas of California's Gold Country. You can stay for just a day or camp for two weeks, panning and digging the whole time. The adventure isn't cheap, but if you're feeling lucky, it might be worth a try.

Prices range from $25 for an hour to hundreds of dollars per week for the helicopter excursion. Gold Prospecting Expeditions is at 18170 Main Street, Jamestown, CA 95327; (209) 984-GOLD.

MI-WUK VILLAGE
PLACES TO STAY
Mi-Wuk Motor Lodge: There are VCRs in the country-style rooms, so if all the nature around here is just too natural for you, you can snuggle up with your dog in front of a campy old flick. Rates are $50 to $85. The street address is 24680 Highway 108, and the mailing address is P.O. Box 70, Mi-Wuk Village, CA 95346; (209) 586-3031.

SONORA
This is the county seat of Tuolumne County and it's a real charmer. A stroll through the colorful downtown area with your leashed dog is a fun way to feel out the town's history.

The early Gold Rush days here were times of bull fights, bear fights and gold camp justice. The rough edges have changed form a little, but they've never completely disappeared. Witness the case of Ellie Nessler, recently convicted of killing the man accused of molesting her son. She shot him while he stood in court on trial. Locals were divided on the issue, but vigilante justice is a deep-rooted tradition here and she had many supporters.

If you like an Old West town with an attitude, you'll enjoy Sonora.

PARKS, BEACHES & RECREATION AREAS
•Coffill Park 🐾 1/2
Dogs like the scenery here, but not the carpeting. This tiny park runs along an attractive creek, but there's no grass—just concrete.

It's a convenient place to stop and smell the trees and sit for a bit while you're out on the town. It's between Washington and Green streets, just north of Stockton Street on Sonora Creek. (209) 532-4541. ➡ *See #5 on map p. 236.*

•**Woods Creek Rotary Park** 😊 😊 1/2

Woods Creek runs through this pretty, shaded park. Dogs love to wet their paws in it on warm summer afternoons. Joe, the consummate landlubber, prefers to picnic at the tables set under shade trees. It's a great place to come to sample the tasty gourmet items you just bought downtown.

The park is just southwest of town, on Stockton Street and Woods Creek Drive (almost directly across from the Mother Lode Fairgrounds). (209) 532-4541. ➡ *See #6 on map p. 236.*

RESTAURANTS

Caffeine Mary's: This sweet little joint is a combination bakery/cafe/bookstore/coffee shop. The little tables outside, recessed slightly from the sidewalk, are perfect for you and your dog. 52 South Washington Street; (209) 532-6261.

J.C. Deli: You and your pooch can picnic at the tables on the lawn here. The sandwiches are hefty. You may even have enough to give a bite to your pleading pooch. 21770 Parrotts Ferry Road; (209) 532-8373.

PLACES TO STAY

Kennedy Meadows Resort: These cabins surround a scenic meadow, and the Stanislaus River flows by. It's a great escape from civilization. Rates are $52 to $105. As of press time, there was no deposit for canine customers, but the managers are considering changing that policy. The folks here say there's no actual street name or address here. Call for directions. P.O. Box 4010, Sonora, CA 95370; (209) 965-3900.

Miner's Motel: Small pooches only, please. Rates are $35 to $50. It's located at 18740 Highway 108, and the mailing address is P.O. Box 1, Sonora, CA 95370; (209) 532-7850 or (800) 451-4176.

Sonora Inn Hotel: Dogs can only stay in the motel section of this hotel. (Dogs aren't allowed in the hotel lobby, so they can't get to the hotel rooms beyond it.) Rates for the motel are $49 to $59. There's a $25 deposit for dogs. 160 South Washington Street, Sonora, CA 95370; (209) 532-2400.

Rail Fence Motel: This hotel will give your dog a special blanket. Awww. We like that. Just don't let your dog eat it, because you do have to give it back. Rates are $35 to $47. Dogs are $8 extra. 19950 Highway 108, Sonora, 95370; (209) 532-9191.

STRAWBERRY

RESTAURANTS

Strawberry Store: This is a cute old building painted a bright red/strawberry color. It's actually more of a store than a restaurant, but since there aren't too many places to eat around here with your dog (none, to be exact), we thought it just might do the trick when you have a hankering for a pre-made deli sandwich. There's a bench outside where you and your pooch can split your lunch. The place is located on Highway 108. There's no street address, but you won't miss it because it's one of only two businesses in these parts. (209) 965-3597.

PLACES TO STAY

Sparrows Resort: If you and your dog want to stay in cabins right on the Stanislaus River, try the cabins here. Rates are $115 to $185, and there's a $50 deposit for dogs. There's no street address, but the resort is one of the two businesses on Highway 108 in Strawberry. P.O. Box 1, Strawberry, CA 95375; (209) 965-3278.

TWAIN HARTE

Dogs enjoy strolling along the sidewalks of this charming little town, especially if they're of the literary persuasion. The town was named for writers Mark Twain and Bret Harte. It's a good thing Aleksandr Solzhenitsyn and Michel Eyquem de Montaigne weren't big in the area when the place was named.

RESTAURANTS

C'est Cheese: Richard, the restaurant's dog-loving, pun-loving owner, is considering putting an arbor outside with more tables than are already out there. That way he can cater even more to doggy customers and their human companions. The food here hits the spot. 22966 Joaquin Gulley Road; (209) 586-1407.

Mary's Diner: Dine with your dog on the fairly large patio here. You can get ribs, chicken, burgers and thick shakes. 23079 Fuller Road; (209) 586-3118.

PLACES TO STAY

El Dorado Motel: Rates are $39 to $65. 22678 Black Hawk Drive, Twain Harte, CA 95383; (209) 586-4479.

MONO COUNTY

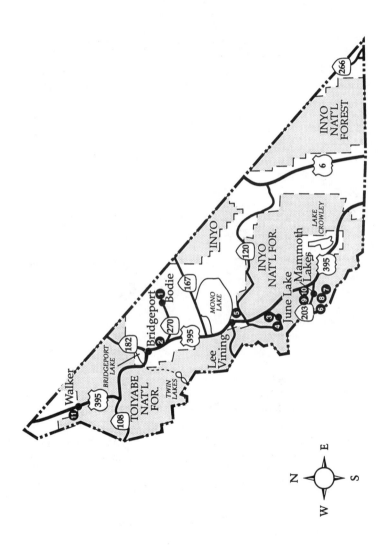

25
MONO COUNTY

This is raw and rugged eastern Sierra country, where the cows graze amid such spectacular scenery that it's hard to believe they don't moo and ahh whenever we turn our backs.

When you contemplate the origins of the word "mono," you'll probably think of words like "alone," "one" or "single." Certainly these words capture the feel of this unique land. But in this case, the meaning of the word isn't so romantic. *Mono* is the Yokut Indian word meaning "flies."

Brine flies, abundant on the shores of salty Mono Lake, were an important source of protein for the Yokut. The brine flies are still the most visible insect at Mono Lake. Fortunately, the flies don't bite, eat your picnic or otherwise act tempestuously toward humans and their dogs.

In "Fly County," often you can just pull off the road into open public land and hike your heart out, especially in the county's northern reaches. As you drive along US 395, you'll see so many signs for camping, fishing and other outdoor recreation that you won't know where to turn first. This chapter describes a few of the more dog-friendly areas, but know that when you see signs for places like Convict Lake, Crowley Lake and Bridgeport Lake, generally you and your leashed dog will be welcome.

A note to dogs: Don't get too excited when you see signs for the Dogtown State Historic Landmark, on US 395 just south of Willow Springs. It's interesting, but it's not what you think.

NATIONAL FORESTS

See the National Forests/Wilderness Areas chapter starting on page 801 for important information and safety tips for visiting national forests with your dog.

• **Inyo National Forest** 🐾🐾🐾🐾 🦴 🐕
   See page 804.

• **Toiyabe National Forest** 🐾🐾🐾🐾 🦴 🐕
   See page 810.

BODIE

PARKS, BEACHES & RECREATION AREAS

• **Bodie State Historic Park** 🐾 🐾 🐾 👞

This ghost town looks so much like *Gunsmoke*-land on a really bad day that it's hard to picture it as a thriving, raunchy, pulsating boomtown. But that's exactly what it was back in the 1870s during this area's gold rush. Dozens of saloons, a burgeoning red-light district and murders nearly every day kept this lawless mining camp hopping.

These days, dogs can enjoy the 486 acres of this town-turned-historic park as long as they're law-abiding citizens on a leash. They're allowed to walk down the dusty streets with you and sniff at the 170 dilapidated buildings that remain. Or they can kick up their heels in the more open areas of the park. Dogs seem to appreciate the wild and wooly luster that still shines through the educational veneer here.

From US 395 just south of Willow Springs, take Highway 270/Bodie Road east about 13 miles. The last three miles are unpaved and can be impassable in winter. Fees are $5 per vehicle and $1 extra per dog. (619) 647-6445. → *See #1 on map p. 246.*

BRIDGEPORT

If you and your dog are *film noir* fans, you'll want to stop at this quiet little village and see if it looks familiar. Remember the movie *Out of the Past*, starring Robert Mitchum? Much of it was set right here in Bridgeport.

• **Bridgeport Park** 🐾

This tiny county park is just a bunch of picnic tables on grass in the midst of a few pieces of old mining equipment. It's right next to the Mono County Museum, in case you're with someone who wants a little culture.

From US 395, go east on School Street and left on Middle Street. (619) 932-5248. → *See #2 on map p. 246.*

PLACES TO STAY

Best Western Ruby Inn: Stay here and you get a small area to walk your leashless pooch! Rates are $75 to $125. 33 Main Street, Bridgeport, CA 93517; (619) 932-7241.

Silver Maple Inn: Rates are $40 to $80. 310 Main Street, Bridgeport, CA 93517; (619) 932-7383.

Walker River Lodge: Rates are $45 to $110. 1 Main Street, Bridgeport, CA 93517; (619) 932-7021.

JUNE LAKE

PARKS, BEACHES & RECREATION AREAS

The June Lake Loop consists of four lakes west of US 395. Dogs are permitted at all of them. Here we'll discuss only the two smaller lakes.

• Gull Lake 🐾 🐾 🐾

As the smallest lake of the June Lake Loop chain, Gull Lake also tends to be the quietest. People are apt to miss this stunning 64-acre lake while on the prowl for its three bigger sisters. That's what dogs like about this place: Very few people get underfoot.

Nonetheless, pooches should be leashed here. And they're not supposed to swim, so watch those slippery water dogs. But they do have a good time watching you fish from shore for all those planted trout. They even seem to enjoy the scenery, or at least the smellery. The lake is set in what could be called "the Sierra Bowl," a dramatic, rocky expanse with all kinds of critters running around.

Camping is good here during the warmer months. There are 11 sites that go for $8 a night, first come, first served. From US 395 about 13 miles north of Mammoth Lakes, exit at the June Lake Junction and drive southwest about three miles to the lake. (619) 647-3000. ➡ *See #3 on map p. 246.*

• Silver Lake 🐾 🐾 🐾 🐾 🦮

Leashed dogs may wag a tail or two when you catch trout after trout here. This 80-acre lake is stocked with many thousands of rainbows each year. But what really sets dogs off is when you take them for a long hike up the magnificent trail that takes you far, far away from the bait store, the full-service resort and the boat rental facility that make this lake seem a little less secluded than it is.

The trailhead is near the camping area ($8 per site, dogs must be leashed). Once you start hiking, you and your leash-free dog may never want to return. The trail actually can loop you into Yosemite National Park, so you have to watch how long you tread, because dogs are banned from Yosemite's trails. But an exciting and not-too-strenuous hike will take you along the Rush Creek drainage, past Gem Lake and Agnew Lake and into the pristine Ansel Adams Wilderness. Bring a big lunch and lots of water for your pooch pal, and you'll have a vacation your dog will remember into her old age.

The lake is about halfway on the June Lake Loop, so you can exit US 395 at the north or south end of the loop (Highway 158), depending on the direction you're traveling. The campground, which has about 63 sites, is open May through September. All sites are first come, first served. (619) 647-3000. ➡ *See #4 on map p. 246.*

PLACES TO STAY

Gull Lake camping: See page 249.

Gull Lake Lodge: You're surrounded by forest here. Rates are $60 to $165, and that includes fish cleaning facilities! The higher-end lodgings are cottages with fireplaces and kitchens. Dogs are $6 extra. The lodge is between June and Gull lakes. 132 Leonard Street, June Lake, CA 93529; (619) 648-7516.

June Lake Motel and Cabins: Rates are $48 to $54. Dogs are $5 extra. Besides a sauna and indoor whirlpool, you'll find fish cleaning facilities. The motel is three miles west of US 395 on the south June Lake Loop turnoff. 300 Boulder Avenue, June Lake, CA 93529; (619) 648-7547.

Silver Lake camping: See page 249.

LEE VINING

PARKS, BEACHES & RECREATION AREAS

• Mono Lake 🐾 🐾 🐾 1/2 🐾

Spending the day at this strange and ancient lake is about the closest you and your dog will come to visiting another planet. You'll want to check your map and make sure you're still on Earth when you see the eerie volcanic formations, the old lake and the tufa spires that look like giant oozy sand castles.

This 700,000-year-old lake covers 60 square miles, but it's just a shadow of its former self. Since Los Angeles started using the fresh streams that fill Mono Lake, the lake has dropped 40 feet, and its salinity has doubled. These days, the lake is nearly three times as salty and 80 times as alkaline as sea water. The salinity increase in this already salty lake seems to be creating some problems for the local environment, and studies on its effects are ongoing. But on the up side, it does make for buoyant swimming.

The alkaline water isn't a new phenomenon. Mark Twain wrote of Mono: "Its sluggish waters are so strong with alkali that if you only dip the most hopelessly soiled garment into them once or twice, and wring it out, it will be found as clean as if it had been through the ablest of washerwoman's hands." You may be tempted to toss your dirty dog in for a little cleansing splash, but the water can be irritating to the eyes.

The land surrounding the lake is run by different agencies. Fortunately, these agencies all have the same rules, which makes it easy to traipse from one part of the lake to the other without getting busted for a dog violation. Dogs are permitted, but they have to be on a leash, even in the Mono Basin National Forest

Scenic Area. It's that simple.

Drive on US 395 to the Mono Lake Visitors Center in Lee Vining and pick up some brochures about the geology of this fascinating area. Then look for signs for areas like the Mono Lake Tufa State Reserve (there are areas on either side of the lake and the one on the south side is best) or the Mono Basin National Forest Scenic Area. Drive east until you're either in the middle of a dormant, pumice-covered volcano, or standing on the shores of one of the oldest lakes in North America. It's ideal dog territory, with few souls venturing on the longer hikes.

The state reserve charges $2 per person or $5 per vehicle for day-use. The national forest is free. Call the reserve at (619) 647-6331, or the national forest at (619) 647-6572. → *See #5 on map p. 246.*

RESTAURANTS
Lee Vining Market: Eat grocery-store cuisine with your dog at the benches outside this little market. 395 Main Street; (619) 647-6301.

PLACES TO STAY
Lundy Canyon: This county-run campground is set at 8,000 feet near Lundy Lake, just across the highway from Mono Lake. It's a barren, otherworldly dreamscape. Leashed dogs love it. They also seem to enjoy the county park where the campsites are located. But if you want to take your dog for a long and fascinating hike, just take a quick ride to nearby Mono Lake.

There are 53 sites, all first come, first served. Sites are $5. From US 395 about five miles north of Lee Vining, look for the signs for the campground, which is on the west side of the highway. (619) 934-6876.

Murphey's Motel: Rates are $32 to $68. The motel is directly on US 395 in Lee Vining. You can't miss it. 51493 Highway 395, Lee Vining, CA 93541; (619) 647-6316.

MAMMOTH LAKES
PARKS, BEACHES & RECREATION AREAS
This charming resort town is a magical ski haven in the winter and an angler's dream in the summer. It's an excellent base for exploring the 200,000 surrounding acres known as Mammoth Lakes Recreational Area.

The lakes in this region are numerous and abound with great fishing and camping opportunities. The mountains and forests are rife with hiking and cross-country skiing areas for you and the pooch of your dreams. You can ski just about anywhere in the national forest, as long as you keep your dog off the groomed cross-country trails. And once you get away from people, you can unleash your obedient dog and bound through nature together.

•Devil's Postpile National Monument 🐾 🐾 🐾 1/2 🐾

Although Devil's Postpile is actually just over the border in Madera County, it is accessible only via its neighbor, Mammoth Lakes. If you're in the area with your dog, take advantage of this great exception to the national park system—dogs are allowed just about everywhere people can go, as long as they're leashed.

And what a place it is. If the devil ever did have a pile of posts, this would be it. The 60-foot wall of columnar basalt "posts" is truly awe-inspiring. Pick up a brochure and find out the fascinating geology behind these geometric (and geologic!) wonders.

In addition to the postpile, this 800-acre park is also home to Rainbow Falls, where the Middle Fork of the San Joaquin River drops 101 feet over a cliff of volcanic lava. It's a remarkable sight.

Exit US 395 at Mammoth Junction and drive west along Highway 203/Main Street through the town of Mammoth Lakes. Turn right at Minaret Summit/Minaret Road. Drive about seven miles to the park. There's a small entry fee. The road is impassible in the winter, so the park is closed during snowy months. During summer, you and your leashed dog can ride the shuttle bus from town to Devil's Postpile. The cost is $6 round-trip for adults. Dogs go free. Call the U.S. Forest Service at (619) 934-2505 for bus schedules and pickup locations. Phone (619) 934-2289 for Devil's Postpile information. ➡ *See #6 on map p. 246.*

•Horseshoe Lake 🐾 🐾 🐾 🐾 🐕

Most of the lakes in this part of the eastern Sierra are developed and popular among humankind. But although Horseshoe Lake is just a stick's throw from civilization, it's a refreshing exception. Not only is it breathtaking, it's quiet.

You really can get away from folks here. In summer, it's not as heavily fished as other local lakes, partly because it's not stocked with trout. But if you visit with a dog, chances are you'll have more on your mind than fishing anyway. And that's where this lake is a little piece of dog heaven: While your dog has to be leashed around the lake, he's allowed to romp leash-free once he hits the connecting trails.

At the north end of the lake, you'll find a trailhead that leads you through magnificent landscapes, all set around 9,000 feet. The air is so clean you can almost feel yourself getting healthier with each step. Joe thinks it's the cat's pajamas. Eventually, the trail runs into the Pacific Crest Trail, where you can choose to venture off on longer or shorter treks. Consult an Inyo National Forest ranger at (619) 934-2505 for maps and guidance.

To reach the lake, exit US 395 at Mammoth Junction and drive west along Highway 203/Main Street, through the town of Mammoth Lakes. The road curves to the left and becomes Lake Mary Road. Follow it about seven miles. It loops by Lake Mary, and eventually ends at Horseshoe Lake. (619) 934-2505. ➛*See #7 on map p. 246.*

•**Lake Mary** 🐾 🐾 🐾 🐾 🦮

Dogs have to be leashed around the developed and heavily used Lake Mary, but they can trot around leash-free when they accompany you on the scenic trail that starts on the east side of the lake.

Lots of folks like to take their dog on an early morning walk on the trail, then turn around and fish for dinner. The trout are planted, and it's hard not to catch one while trolling, or even fishing from shore. Most dogs seem to enjoy watching people fish, even if nothing is being caught. Some people don't even mind just walking around the lake with a leashed dog. There's a real gold mine there with an interesting interpretive trail.

Other folks come here just for the off-leash hiking. The trail takes you many miles away. If your dog is a water dog, she'll love it: You pass by several quiet little lakes, and one big one, on the way to the Pacific Crest Trail. Consult an Inyo National Forest ranger at (619) 934-2505 for maps and guidance.

From June to November, about 50 campsites are available here for $8 a night, first come, first served. Dogs must be leashed, but with the great views of the lake they get, they just don't seem to mind.

To reach the lake, exit US 395 at Mammoth Junction and drive west along Highway 203/Main Street, through the town of Mammoth Lakes. The road curves to the left and becomes Lake Mary Road. Follow it about three miles to the lake. (619) 934-2505. ➛*See #8 on map p. 246.*

•**Mammoth Mountain** 🐾 🐾 🐾 1/2 🐾

See Diversions, page 255, for information on the exciting gondola ride you and your dog can take to get to some great hiking trails during the summer months. To get here, exit US 395 at the Mammoth Junction exit and drive west along Highway 203/Main Street, through the town of Mammoth Lakes. Once past town, follow the signs to the mountain. (619) 934-2571. ➛*See #9 on map p. 246.*

•**Shady Rest Trail** 🐾 🐾 🐾 🐾 🦮

This off-leash trail is on the edge of the town of Mammoth Lakes, making it as convenient as it is splendid. During the summer, you can walk or run on the six-mile forested trail that loops around Shady Rest Park (a Mammoth Lakes recreation park where leashes are a must).

In winter, it's a stunning place to take your dog on a little cross-country ski trip. Although well-behaved dogs are allowed to run leashless, we've seen some people attach their dog to their belt with a leash. When there's a little uphill slope, guess who's the engine? Most dogs wouldn't appreciate this, and are more than happy to gambol through the woods leash-free.

From US 395, exit at Mammoth Junction and drive west along Highway 203 until the U.S. Forest Service Visitors Center, which will be before town on your right. You can stop in here and ask for additional trail information, or proceed west on Highway 203 another quarter of a mile to Old Sawmill Road. Turn right and follow the road to Shady Rest Park. You'll see parts of the trail weaving around the park's perimeter, and even along the entry road. Call (619) 934-2505 for more information. → *See #10 on map p. 246.*

RESTAURANTS

Gourmet Grocer & Company: Dogs are welcome to join you on the covered patio and watch you eat gourmet deli food; 3399 Main Street; (619) 934-2997.

Schat's Bakery: This is a great place to grab a coffee and warm pastry before a morning hike. 3305 Main Street; (619) 934-6055.

Swiss Cafe: Your dog can be just on the other side of the rail on this cute patio here when you eat the all-American food they serve. (So what's in a name?) 343 Old Mammoth Road; (619) 934-6196.

PLACES TO STAY

Austria Hof: This one's on a mountain. Rates are $33 to $105. 924 Canyon Boulevard, Mammoth Lakes, CA 93546; (619) 934-2764.

Crystal Crag Lodge: Stay at this beautiful mountain resort and wander around the beautiful land with your leashed dog. Rates are $49 to $175. Dogs are $6 extra. 307 Crystal Crag Drive, Mammoth Lakes, CA 93546; (619) 934-2436.

Econolodge Wildwood Inn: Rates are $50 to $90. There's a fish cleaning station here, in case you have the hankering to clean a fish. They've also got a decent little continental breakfast. Traveling west on Highway 203, you'll find the inn three blocks into the main part of town. 3626 Main Street, Mammoth Lakes, CA 93546; (619) 934-6855.

Lake Mary camping: See page 253.

Mammoth High Country Inns/Englehof Lodge: Englehof Lodge is one of six Mammoth High Country Inn locations, all of which allow dogs! They've got motel rooms, cabins, condos, suites, and the works at these inns. Rates at this one are $35 to $80. 6156 Minaret Road, Mammoth Lakes, CA 93546; (619) 934-2416.

Motel 6: Rates are $38 for the first adult, $4 for the second. This one looks more like a giant ski lodge than a roadside motel. All Motel 6s allow one small dog per room. 3372 Main Street, Mammoth Lakes, CA 93546; (619) 934-6660.

North Village Inn: All dogs at this small, friendly motel must be older than one year. Rates are $70 to $100. A $100 pooch deposit is required. 103 Lake Mary Road, Mammoth Lakes, CA 93546; (619) 934-2925.

Old Shady Rest Campground: Believe it or not, you're pretty much in town when you camp here. You'll never know it, though, by the scenery. You're in the woods, without a trace of civilization. Dogs are permitted on leash. There are 51 sites. Fees are $8 a night, first come, first served.

From US 395, drive west on Highway 203 for three miles to the Mammoth Visitor Center. Turn right and follow the signs to the campground. Sites are open year-round. (619) 934-2505.

Royal Pines Resort: Rates are $70 to $102. Dogs are $5 extra, and they're allowed only in the housekeeping units. The resort is on Viewpoint Road, about one-half mile into town as you're traveling west on Highway 203. 3814 Viewpoint Road, Mammoth Lakes, CA 93546; (619) 934-2306.

Shilo Inn: Don't worry about your large dog being allowed to stay here—the manager prefers big dogs! All the rooms are mini-suites, and they're air-conditioned, which is a rare feature up here. Rates are $69 to $131. Dogs are $6 extra. The motel is a half block east of Old Mammoth Road, on Highway 203. 2963 Main Street, Mammoth Lakes, CA 93546; (619) 934-4500.

Tamarack Lodge: This is one of the most beautiful and rustic Sierra inns that welcomes dogs. Unfortunately, they're only welcome in May and October, but those are mighty beautiful months in these parts. Another limitation: Dogs are allowed in only two cabins. Rates are $55 to $195. It's on Tamarack Lodge Road, west of town near Twin Lakes. The mailing address is P.O. Box 69, Mammoth Lakes, CA 93546; (619) 934-2442.

Zwart House: Rates at these one- and two-bedroom units are $36 to $100. Dogs are $3 extra. 76 Lupine Street, Mammoth Lake, CA 93546; (619) 934-2217.

DIVERSIONS
Up, up and away: If your dog gets white knuckles just looking

out of your second-story window, it might be wise to forget about this lofty adventure. But if the idea of dangling 11,000 feet above sea level doesn't make you or your pooch break out in a sweat, you're bound to have an exciting time aboard the Mammoth Mountain Ski Area gondolas.

Actually, during your ascent from 9,000 feet to 11,000 feet, you'll glide only a few dozen feet above the ground. The spectacular views of the rugged surroundings just make it seem as though you're higher. While the ascent is a stimulating experience, it lasts only about 10 minutes. Your dog is almost certain to appreciate the descent more—you get to hike down the mountainside together. It can take several hours, if you're not in a rush.

We like to hike in early summer, when new life is abloom in this otherwise fairly barren land. As long as there's no skiing on the slopes, you can bring your dog. Some people even tote their dogs up during ski season and ski down the back of the mountain, but the practice can be dangerous and is highly discouraged by the people who run this place. Besides, dogs have to be leashed, and that's tough while you're *whooshing* downhill.

Many dogs love every part of this adventure except for the grated stairs that lead to the gondolas. There's something about looking down and seeing nothing except air that makes even the bravest beast feel like he's on the bad end of a Road Runner cartoon.

The fee for adults is $10. Children are $5. Dogs go for free. To get here, exit US 395 at the Mammoth Junction exit and drive west along Highway 203/Main Street, through the town of Mammoth Lakes. Once past town, follow the signs to the mountain. Call (619) 934-2571 for schedules and more information.

WALKER

PARKS, BEACHES & RECREATION AREAS

•**Mono County Park** 🐾 🐾

There's not much in the way of year-round green grass in these parts, so a visit to this little county park will add a bit of color to your dog's day (providing he doesn't see only in black and white). The grassy strip in back of the tennis courts is pretty spacious and it's well-protected from the few cars that zip by. Dogs are supposed to be leashed here anyway.

From US 395, go west on Hacking Drive (there will be a sign). You'll be in the park almost immediately. (619) 932-5248. → *See #11 on map p. 246.*

MARIPOSA COUNTY

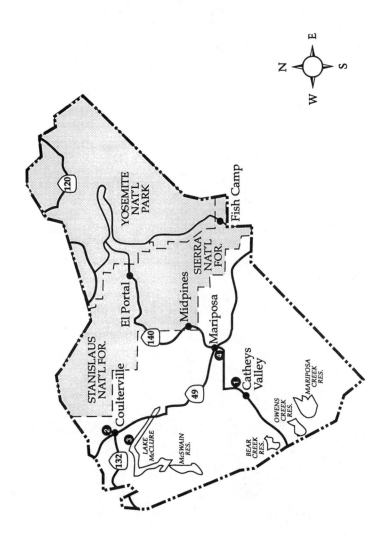

26
MARIPOSA COUNTY

It's bad enough that dogs are pretty much banned from Yosemite National Park. But to have to endure the attitude of a couple of administrators with this county parks system is enough to make a grown dog growl.

"Yep," said a razor-voiced woman on the other end of the phone. "We allow leashed dogs. But we don't like 'em." A voice in the background started cackling with sadistic laughter. "You tell her!" her cohort chortled.

"Nope, we don't like them at all." Click.

Don't pay any attention to those county parks people, dogs. You've got the law on your side. It's a leash law, but just the same, it's the law. Exercise your right to exercise your legs. Don't let the snarling civil servants get you down.

NATIONAL FORESTS

See the National Forests/Wilderness Areas chapter starting on page 801 for important information and safety tips for visiting national forests with your dog. The following two national forests make up for Yosemite National Park's lack of canine hospitality.

- **Sierra National Forest** 🐾🐾🐾🐾 🐾 🐕
  See page 809.
- **Stanislaus National Forest** 🐾🐾🐾🐾 🐾 🐕
  See page 810.

NATIONAL PARKS

- **Yosemite National Park** 🚹 🐾
  Ask just about anyone who's ever visited this park about what they've seen, and they'll gush about the impossibly beautiful geography, the dramatic waterfalls, the sheer cliffs, the pristine wildlife and every other detail they can dredge up. It's not hyperbole. This fantastic park is bigger than the imagination, bigger than life. It inspires even the most reticent parkgoer to sing its praises.

Then ask the same question of people who've visited with dogs. They'll be able to tell you all about the lovely car campsites here. They can even expound on the glories of the commercialization of Yosemite Village and the clever way the parking lots are set up. If they're just back from vacation, their faces will show just what kind of adventure they had. It's pretty much the same disgusted, disheartened scowl their dog is wearing.

Dogs are not allowed on any trails, in meadows or in the backcountry of Yosemite. About all they can do is camp at certain campgrounds, and putter around Yosemite Village with you as you while away the hours until your human friends get back from a breathtaking hike. Dogs can also stay at the park's kennel from late May to mid-October. We're not talking luxury suites here. We're talking your basic cage-like contraptions that make you feel incredibly guilty for leaving the little guy behind.

Some folks think they can get away with leaving their dog tied up to their campsite for a few hours while they go exploring. But remember, if the ranger doesn't catch up with you, there's always the chance that a mountain lion or other cunning critter might catch up with your tethered dog. "We call one of these camping areas Coyote Point," a park employee told me. "You'd be a fool to leave your dog behind even for a little bit."

Joe and I each give a thumbs down to the idea of bringing your dog on a Yosemite vacation. But if you insist, here are the campgrounds that permit pooches:

In the valley, there's the Upper Pines Campground. Along Highway 120, you can stay at Hodgdon Meadow Campground, Crane Flat Campground (section A), White Wolf Campground (section C), Yosemite Creek Campground (front section) and the west end of the Tuolumne Meadows Campground. Along Glacier Point Road and Highway 41, you can stay at the Bridalveil Creek Campground (section A) and the Wawona Campground.

The kennel costs $6 per day. They will not board dogs overnight. The campsites cost $12 a night. Call MISTIX at (800) 365-CAMP for reservations, or (209) 372-0302 for park information.

CATHEYS VALLEY

PARKS, BEACHES & RECREATION AREAS

•**Catheys Valley County Park** 🐾 🐾 🐾

Dogs like to gambol around the fenced-in ball field here. It's adjacent to some big, open cattle land, which makes a dog feel at home on the range. A few dogs have jumped over the fence in pursuit of a steak dinner, so make sure you hang on tight to that leash. If it's warm, other parts of this park have plenty of trees to shade you and your pal. We like to stop here for a picnic while traveling on Highway 140.

It's on the south side of the highway at 2820 Highway 140. There is no cross street. (209) 966-2498. ➤ *See #1 on map p. 258.*

COULTERVILLE

Dogs, listen up. Without your kind, this tiny, Old West town may never have even made it onto the map. Here's why: Back in 1850, a certain George Coulter started a tent store here to keep roofs over the heads of the local gold miners. This fellow also built the first hotel, which helped attract a more civilized sort. But the place needed water. So Coulter convinced a couple of Newfoundland dogs to pump water from the well. The hotel is now home to the Northern Mariposa History Center. You'll have to stop in for a visit to learn the rest of this shaggy-dog tale.

PARKS, BEACHES & RECREATION AREAS

• **Coulterville County Park** 🐾 🐾 1/2

This isn't a big park, but it's fenced on three sides, which makes it a convincing place to take an overly zealous leash puller. Dogs are supposed to be leashed, but just in case your leash slips out of your hand, at least you probably won't have to go searching the streets for your dog.

The park is grassy, with a few picnic tables, a playground and a swimming pool. It's conveniently located just off Highway 49, in the center of "town." Just pull off the highway and park. Or take Highway 49 to Main Street, head east and make an immediate left onto Park Lane. (209) 966-2498. → *See #2 on map p. 258.*

• **Lake McClure** 🐾 🐾 🐾 1/2

With 7,100 surface acres of water, this beautiful lake is a water dog's dream. But it's not bad for landlubbers either. The lake is surrounded by the kind of perfect, green land you only see around model-train sets and in picture puzzles your old aunt used to give you.

The lake has several recreation areas with decent places to walk a leashed dog and even better campsites. Some of the sites are on the water. The 110 sites at the Horseshoe Bend Recreation Area at the northeast corner of the lake are filled with trees and provide plenty of privacy. During the off-season, you might even have the place to yourselves. The ranger here recommends walking your dog by the hanglider area when no one else is around. It's far from cars and has ample acreage.

The Bagby Recreation Area, on the Merced River section of the lake, has a pretty good trail along the river, across from the camping spots. Campsites here get more secluded the farther you drive down the winding road. All told, there are 25 sites. Watch out for the resident kittens. There always seems to be a litter here.

The day-use fee for the recreation areas is $4 per car. Campsites are $7 to $12. All are available on a first-come, first-served basis. Dogs are $2 extra, day or night. To get to the Horseshoe Bend Recreation Area from Highway 49 just south of Coulterville, go west on Highway 132 for about three miles. The entrance will be on your left. Call (800) 468-8889 for a brochure or directions to other parts of the lake. →*See #3 on map p. 258.*

PLACES TO STAY
Lake McClure camping: See above.

EL PORTAL

PLACES TO STAY
Yosemite View Lodge: If your dog wants to spend the night somewhere other than a tent when you visit Yosemite National Park, try this motel. None of the park's lodgings permit pooches, but with this reasonably priced motel just over the border on Highway 140, it doesn't matter. Rates are $62 to $135. Dogs cost $5 extra. The lodge is located on Highway 140 at Parkline Road. The mailing address is P.O. Box D, El Portal, CA 95318; (209) 379-2681 or (800) 321-5261.

FISH CAMP

DIVERSIONS
Gonna take a sentimental journey: If you're hankering to ride the old Logger Steam Train through some of Sierra National Forest's most magnificent scenery, you don't have to worry about waving goodbye to your dog. Leashed, calm dogs are welcome aboard the quaint old trains of the Sugar Pine Railroad.

We discovered on an earlier locomotive trip that Joe is not especially keen on the sound of a train's powerful blasts of steam. He cringes, tail down, until someone picks up his 70-pound body and holds him in a lap. He looks embarrassed afterward, but appears to have no regrets.

If your dog is shy of loud noises, get as far back from the engine as possible, or simply take the railroad's "Model A"-powered trip. It's quieter, shorter (30 minutes as opposed to 45 minutes) and cheaper ($6.50 per adult, not $9.50) than the Logger train.

The train station is located at 56001 Highway 41. It's about 12 miles past Oakhurst, two miles before the town of Fish Camp. And there's a terrific fringe benefit: It's right next to a couple of trailheads into dog-friendly Sierra National Forest. (209) 683-7273.

MARIPOSA

If you're on your way to Yosemite with your dog (not the kindest act in the world—see page 259), take time to stop at this historic town. It's the county seat, but it looks nothing like most governmental centers we've seen. It's full of historic Gold Rush buildings and antique shops. The restaurants aren't bad either.

PARKS, BEACHES & RECREATION AREAS

• **Mariposa Park** 🐾 🐾 🐾

This tiered park is kind of like a wedding cake, with something delectable on every layer. Your dog will want to sink her teeth into it.

The top of the park is green and grassy, with picnic tables, a small playground and excellent views of the town of Mariposa. A dirt road leads you to the lower levels, which have plenty of shade, picnic tables and a decent walking path. Dogs must be leashed.

From Highway 49/140 going south, turn right on 6th Street. In one block, jog right on Strong Street and make a quick left onto County Parks Road. (209) 966-2948. *See #4 on map p. 258.*

RESTAURANTS

Frost Shop: Your dog may find canine company at the outdoor tables—plenty of dogs bring their people here for a bite of burger. 5087 Highway 140; (209) 966-5557.

High Country Health Foods: This restaurant sports attractive white wrought-iron chairs and glass-top tables on its patio. If you and your dog like tasty veggie burgers and healthy shakes, you'll want to stop here every time you visit Yosemite. 5176B Highway 49 North; (209) 966-5111.

Mariposa Coffee Trading Company: "Taste your own" is the motto, and you'll want to do that since they have great gourmet coffees and baked goods. Dine with your dog at the outdoor tables. On Saturday nights, you can get all-you-can-eat smoked meats. ("You" here means you, not your dog.) 2945 Highway 49 South; (209) 842-7339.

Underdog Gourmet Hot Dogs and Ice Cream: There's no need to fear—Underdog is here, and it's got great hot dogs for you and your hungry dog. Dogs (the furry kind) like to hang out with their people at the outdoor tables. 5103A Highway 140; (209) 966-3647.

PLACES TO STAY

The Guest House Inn: Rent this place and you're renting the entire three-bedroom house. The rate is $98, plus a pooch deposit. It's at 4962 Triangle Road, and the mailing address is P.O. Box 1848, Mariposa, CA 95338; (209) 742-6869.

Motherlode Lodge: Rates are $28 to $68. The physical address is 5051 Highway 140, and the mailing address is P.O. Box 986, Mariposa, CA 95338; (209) 966-2521 or (800) 398-9770.

MIDPINES

PLACES TO STAY

The Homestead Guest Ranch: When you stay here, the house is all yours. It comes with a fireplace, a barbecue and a well-stocked kitchen. Rates are $95 per couple plus $35 for each additional person. As of press time, there was no fee or deposit for dogs, but that may change. Regardless, this if a wonderful place to stay, and the owners are sweet, dog-loving folks. The ranch is on 13 acres of land located about a half mile off of Highway 140. The mailing address is P.O. Box 113, Midpines, CA 95345; (209) 966-2820.

BAY AREA/DELTA COUNTIES

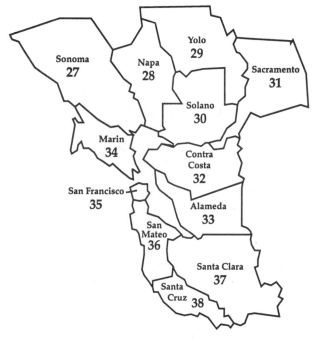

SONOMA COUNTY

27
SONOMA COUNTY

The horticulturalist Luther Burbank, who made his home in Santa Rosa and Sebastopol from 1875 to 1926, called Sonoma County "the chosen spot of all the Earth as far as nature is concerned." Practically anything will grow in Sonoma County. It's the Bay Area capital for trees, flowers and vegetables, as well as goats, sheep, cattle, chickens, pigs and probably a few farm animals that are just now being invented.

But there's an irony in Bay Area dogdom: Often, the more bucolic the area, the stiffer the penalties for an unleashed dog. On every inch of unincorporated Sonoma County land, and in every single public park, your dog must be on a six-foot leash. At last check, there wasn't a single off-leash beach or public dog run in the county.

If you think about it, though, it makes sense—dogs and farm animals don't mix. Some Sonoma sheep ranchers have been known to impose the ultimate penalty on loose dogs that they see near their livestock: They shoot them.

They're not acting under the law of the Wild West, either: It's a county ordinance that dogs harassing livestock in unincorporated areas or on private property may be shot by the property owner.

But fear not. Sonoma County has many enchanting places where the only shot your dog will experience is a shot of adrenaline when he lays eyes on the stunning scenery.

BODEGA BAY

PARKS, BEACHES & RECREATION AREAS

• **Doran Beach Regional Park** 🐾 🐾 🐾

This Sonoma County Regional Park offers leashed dogs access to marshland full of egrets, herons and deer, and to the Pinnacle Gulch Trail. The plain but serviceable beach has almost no surf (which is great for dog swims), and there are picnic tables near the beach.

The fee for day use is $3. Campsites are $14 ($12 for Sonoma County residents), plus $1 for each dog. The campground, which has 134 sites, is on a first-come, first-served basis. On Highway 1, one mile south of Bodega Bay. (707) 875-3540. → *See #1 on map p. 268.*

•Westside Regional Park 🐾 🐾

This is an undistinguished but handy park and campground built on landfill right on the water, with picnic tables and barbecues. Spud Point Marina, just to the north, also allows leashed dogs.

The fee for day use is $3. There are 47 campsites here, costing $14 ($12 for Sonoma County residents), plus $1 for each dog. It's first come, first served. On Westshore Road, a westward turn off Highway 1 in town. Call (707) 875-3540 for reservations, or (707) 527-2041 for park info. ➜*See #2 on map p. 268.*

RESTAURANTS

The Boat House: This restaurant in downtown Bodega Bay will allow you to sit with your dog as you eat fish and chips, oysters and calamari at one of the six unshaded tables on their patio. But alas, they won't let you take him along on one of their rental boats. If fish isn't your dog's wish, he can order a burger. 1445 Highway 1; (707) 875-3495.

PLACES TO STAY

Holiday Inn–Bodega Bay Resort: Rates are $75 to $180. Dogs are $10 extra. 521 Coast Highway/Highway 1, Bodega Bay, CA 94923; (707) 875-2217.

Doran Beach Regional Park camping: See page 269.

Westside Regional Park camping: See above.

FESTIVALS

Bodega Bay Fisherman's Festival: Annually on the third or fourth weekend in April, the fishing fleet is blessed at the beginning of the salmon season. Surrounding the traditional blessing is a parade of more than 100 decorated boats. You can also join in a 6K run, a bathtub race, kite flying contests—all the usual silliness. Live music varies every year—in the past it has been provided by a Navy band, an oompah band and Scottish bagpipes; lamb and oysters are barbecued.

The festival is held at Westside Regional Park, off Highway 1 at Bodega Bay. Turn west on Westshore Road to the park. (707) 875-3422.

COTATI

DIVERSIONS

Check out a canine country club: If Kamp K-9 isn't an exclusive country club, it's the closest thing to it. It's just that no dogs have actually been excluded. Any dog is welcome as long as she's had her shots. Since owner Randy Ashton opened K-9's doors to the "elite with four feet" in 1992, about 1,500 dogs have passed through. (They have to maneuver around three resident sheep.)

Set on a lush five-acre converted dairy farm, K-9 offers lots of open space for dogs to romp in. There's also an obstacle course for exercise, including a plank walk, a swinging bridge, a slide, a shoe tied to a pole (for teething) and many excellent jumps. After your dog's workout, you can give your pooch a good scrubbing in a spa-like tub room, actually a converted barn. Ashton hopes to put in an outdoor swimming pool (well, a cement pond) sometime in the near future.

The camp is open from 9 a.m. to 5 p.m. most of the year, until 7 p.m. in summer. You're welcome to stay with your dog or leave him for the day. It's $10 for a full day, $6 for a half day or $3 an hour. Baths are $8 extra, with everything provided but the elbow grease. For more information, call (707) 795-5995.

CLOVERDALE

PARKS, BEACHES & RECREATION AREAS

• **Lake Sonoma Recreation Area** 🐾 🐾 🐾 🐕

This is the only recreation site in the nine counties of the Bay Area run by the U.S. Army Corps of Engineers, and it's too bad. The Corps has a liberal attitude toward dogs, and this park is beautifully developed and managed, and it's clean. It's also free. You must keep your dog on a six-foot leash, and he's not allowed on the swimming beach at the north end, but rangers told us there's no rule against dogs swimming anywhere else.

A large lawn with picnic tables, some shaded, is located at the visitors center. You can rent a boat from the private concession on the lake, which allows dogs—leashed—on all boats. Follow signs from the visitors center. To reserve a boat, call (707) 433-2200. Waterskiing and camping are also popular here.

For a good dog hike, pick up a map at the visitors center and drive west on Dry Creek Road to the trailheads, which have their own parking lots. There are 40 miles of trails. Here are two of our favorites: There's a bit of shade at the Digger Pine Flat Trailhead. This smooth foot trail goes down to the lake through an unusual forest of digger pines, madrone, manzanita and blooming desert brush. The buzz of motorboats on the lake blends with the hammering of woodpeckers. You get a good view of the lake fairly quickly. If you'd prefer less of a climb back to the trailhead, take the Little Flat Trail, which starts lower down.

Horses are allowed on these trails, but bikes aren't—a plus for your dog's safety. Unfortunately, it's bone-dry here in summer, and poison oak is common.

Developed, primitive and boat-in campsites are available. Liberty Glen Campground has 113 individual campsites. Sites are $6 to $12. To use the primitive sites (no water, but no fee either), you must get a permit from the visitors center. There are 15 secluded sites reachable only by boat. They're also free. All these sites are first come, first served. Dogs must be leashed or "restrained" in the campgrounds, which in this case means you can put them on a generous rope tether. The idea is to keep them from invading other campsites.

Take Highway 10 to the Canyon Road exit. Go west to Dry Creek Road and turn right into the entrance. Take a right at the only fork. (707) 433-9483. ➡ *See #3 on map p. 268.*

PLACES TO STAY

Lake Sonoma Recreation Area camping: See above.

FREESTONE

PLACES TO STAY

Green Apple Inn: This is a homey bed-and-breakfast in the midst of meadows and redwoods. "Sometimes dogs are our favorite guests. People who have dogs are the nicest people," says owner Rosemary Hoffman. Rosemary and her husband, Rogers Hoffman, offer a relaxed atmosphere and good conversation. You can also pet their goats, Emily and Charlotte. "The goats love dogs, and the dogs are fascinated by the goats," says Rosemary.

All the rooms have separate entrances, and there's one stand-alone cabin with a yard. Rates are $85 to $92, including breakfast. Breakfast includes plenty of delicious apple-based dishes. As at any lodging, you should never leave your dog alone in your room. In this case, it tears Rosemary's heart apart to hear a scared and lonesome dog crying for his folks. 520 Bohemian Highway, Freestone, CA 95472. (707) 874-2526.

GUALALA

PARKS, BEACHES & RECREATION AREAS

•**Gualala Point Regional Park** 🐾 🐾 🐾 🐾

This is the pristine, driftwood-strewn beach you can see from the town of Gualala, just over the Mendocino County border from Sonoma. The small, friendly visitors center offers displays of shore life, Pomo Indian artifacts and old machinery. Outside is a sandstone bull sea lion. From there, it's a half-mile walk to the beach on a smoothly paved trail.

You and your leashed dog will stroll through mixed grasses, ferns, berries, dunes and rows of pines and cypresses. At the beach, you can take a trail through a marsh or along a coastal bluff. On the beach you'll find driftwood and piles of kelp bulbs, good for jumping on for their satisfying pop.

The day-use fee is $3. Campsites are $14 (for up to two vehicles), with overnight dogs costing $1. Sonoma County residents pay only $12 per site. There are 26 sites, available on a first-come, first-served basis only. From Highway 101, turn just south of Gualala at the sign announcing the park and the Sea Ranch Golf Links. (707) 527-2041. ➡ *See #4 on map p. 268.*

PLACES TO STAY
Gualala Point Regional Park camping: See above.

GLEN ELLEN

PARKS, BEACHES & RECREATION AREAS

• **Jack London State Historic Park** 🐾 🐾 🐾 🐾

The extensive backcountry trails here are off-limits to dogs, but the parts of historic interest are not: You're free to take your dog (leashed) the half mile to Wolf House, visiting Jack London's grave en route, and around the stone house containing the museum of Londoniana (open 10 a.m. to 5 p.m., no pets inside). The trail is paved and smooth up to the museum, but then becomes dirt and narrow.

Oaks, pines, laurels and madrones cast dappled light, and the ups and downs are gentle. Signs warn against poison oak and rattlesnakes. The ruins of the huge stone lodge that was London's dream Wolf House are impressive and sad. A fire of unknown origin destroyed it in 1913. London planned to rebuild it, but he died three years later.

Dogs are also allowed in the picnic areas by the parking lot and the museum. From Highway 12, follow signs to the park: Turn west on Arnold Drive, then west again on London Ranch Road. The fee is $5 for day use, $1 for dog. (707) 938-5216. ➡ *See #5 on map p. 268.*

• **Sonoma Valley Regional Park** 🐾 🐾 🐾

This large, welcoming park has a paved, level trail that winds alongside a branch of Sonoma Creek. Better yet for dogs who like to roll, it sports many dirt trails that head off into the oak woodlands above. Varied grasses and wildflowers, madrones and moss-hung oaks make this a scenic walk. Dogs like to chew some of the grasses, roll on the wildflowers (don't let them do this!) and do leg-lifts on the madrones and oaks. They may enjoy it even more than you.

If you start at the park entrance off Highway 12 and walk westward across the park to Glen Ellen, about a mile, you'll end up at Sonoma Creek and the old mill, with its huge working waterwheel.

The park is just south of Glen Ellen between Arnold Drive and Highway 12. The entrance is off Highway 12. The parking fee is $1. (707) 539-8092. →*See #6 on map p. 268.*

GUERNEVILLE
PARKS, BEACHES & RECREATION AREAS

• **Armstrong Redwoods State Reserve** 🐾 🐾

As is usual in state parks, you can take a dog only on paved roads and into picnic areas. But here you can give your dog and yourself an exceptional treat. The picnic grounds are a cool, hushed redwood cathedral. You can walk on Armstrong Woods Road, which winds along Fife Creek (usually lush, but dry in the heart of summer) all the way to the top of McCray Mountain, about three miles.

The drive is fairly terrifying, so you may prefer to walk anyway. Hikers, bicycles and autos all share the road, so be very careful. Your dog must be leashed everywhere in the park. From Guerneville, go about 2.5 miles north on Armstrong Woods Road. The day-use fee is $5. Dogs are $1. (707) 869-2015 or (707) 865-2391. →*See #7 on map p. 268.*

• **Vacation Beach** 🐾 🐾 🐾 🐾 🐕

Vacation Beach is not really a beach, but an access point where the Russian River is dammed by two roads across it. It's one of several public spots where you and your dog can legally jump into the drink. Here, people picnic, swim, put in canoes and let their dogs cool their paws. It's free and there are no posted leash rules, but watch out for cars going over the dam roads. No overnight camping is allowed.

From Highway 116 between Guerneville and Monte Rio, turn south at the unmarked road where you see Old Cazadero Road veering north. You can park at the approaches to the dams, but not on the crossing itself. →*See #8 on map p. 268.*

HEALDSBURG

RESTAURANTS

Costeaux French Bakery: Stroll around Healdsburg's good-looking town square, with its old buildings and benches for shady rest stops, and then drop in here for dinner or a wonderful pastry snack at an outdoor table. 417 Healdsburg Avenue; (707) 433-1913.

PLACES TO STAY

Best Western Dry Creek Inn: Rates are $55 to $70. They want small dogs only. 198 Dry Creek Road, Healdsburg, CA 95448; (707) 433-0300.

JENNER

PARKS, BEACHES & RECREATION AREAS

• **Sonoma Coast State Beaches** 😺 😺 😺 1/2

A string of beautiful, clean beaches runs from Jenner south to Bodega Bay. From Goat Rock Beach south to Salmon Creek Beach, you can't go wrong: Gorgeous bluff views, stretches of brown sand, gnarled rocks and grassy dunes welcome you. Always keep an eye on the surf and a leash on your dog.

Dogs are not allowed on any of the trails that run on the bluffs above the beaches, on Bodega Head, in the Willow Creek area east of Bridgehaven, or in the seal rookery upriver from Goat Rock Beach. (Watch for the warning sign.) No camping is permitted on any of the beaches, except Bodega Dunes and Wright's Beach, which have campgrounds. These two also charge a $5 day-use fee. Day use of all other beaches is free. For beach info: (707) 875-3483.

The Bodega Dunes Campground has 98 developed sites. Wright's Beach Campground has 30 developed sites. Sites at Bodega Dunes are $12 a night and sites at Wright's $17; during peak season, they each charge $2 more. There's always a $1 fee for each dog. They're open year-round. Advance reservations are highly recommended in summer and early fall (you may reserve up to eight weeks in advance). Call MISTIX for reservations at (800) 444-PARK. For general beach information, call (707) 875-3483. ➡ *See #9 on map p. 268.*

PLACES TO STAY

Bridgehaven Campground: This friendly place welcomes dogs, leashed or not, as long as they are under control. It's in the hamlet of Bridgehaven, where Highway 1 crosses the Russian River south of Jenner. For a day-use fee of $3, you and your dog can swim together—"and if he doesn't make a mess, I'll forget the $3," says the campground owner. Campsites are $10. Dogs are free. There are 23 sites. Open year-round. P.O. Box 59, Jenner, CA 95450. (707) 865-2473.

Sonoma Coast State Beach camping: See page 275.

OCCIDENTAL
PLACES TO STAY
Negri's Occidental Lodge: There's no official street address here, but it's in the middle of town—you can't miss it. Rates are $35 to $50. Dogs are $5 extra. P.O. Box 84, Occidental, CA 95465; (707) 874-3623.

PETALUMA
Petaluma is a captivating Sunday afternoon stroll, with its tree-lined streets and pocket parks for your dog's pleasure. Victorian buildings, old feed mills and a riverfront that remains mostly original, but not dilapidated, complete the charming picture. Several eating places will gladly serve you and your dog along the riverfront at outdoor benches and tables (see Restaurants).

PARKS, BEACHES & RECREATION AREAS
•**Helen Putnam Regional Park** 🐾🐾 1/2

This county regional park is, and will remain, a minimally developed stretch of converted cow pasture with oak trees. A wide paved trail shared by hikers and bicyclists runs between the main entrance and the Victoria housing development (to enter from that end, go to the end of Oxford Court). Dogs must be leashed. There's no shade from the scrub oaks and it can get mighty windy. The paved trail has gentle ups and downs. Some other dirt trails give you steeper hill climbs. About one-quarter mile in from the main entrance is an old cattle pond good for a dog swim (if the dog stays on a leash—quite a feat).

Parking is $1. Next to the lot is a kids' playground and a picnic gazebo, by a creek that's only a gully in summer. Drive south on Western Avenue. Turn left on Chileno Valley Road. After a half mile, you'll see the turn-off to the park. (707) 527-2041. ➡*See #10 on map p. 268.*

•**Lucchesi Park** 🐾🐾

This is a well-kept, popular city park with a postmodern community center that impresses people, but doesn't stir dogs much. Dogs prefer strolling through empty sports fields, picnicking at shaded tables, watching ducks at the large pond, and strolling along the paved paths here. No dog swimming is allowed in the pond, but that's a rule Joe "The Water Hater" dog can live with just fine.

Dogs are supposed to be leashed. The park is at North McDowell Boulevard and Madison Street. (707) 778-4386. ➡ *See #11 on map p. 268.*

•**Petaluma Adobe State Historic Park** 🐾 🐾

Leashed dogs are welcome here, if they behave well around goats and such, and if you avoid the farm animals' courtyard. From the parking lot, walk across a wooden bridge over a wide, willow-lined creek (dry in summer) to the house, built in 1836 as headquarters for General Mariano Vallejo's 66,600-acre Rancho Petaluma. Clustered around the house are tempting displays of animal hides, saddles and tallow makings, as well as sheep, chickens and a donkey. Dogs must use their best manners. If you see them starting to think of lamb chops for dinner, make sure you hang on hard to that leash.

The park is southeast of Petaluma at Adobe Road and Casa Grande Road. From Highway 101, you'll see an exit sign for the Petaluma Adobe. Admission is $2 for adults, $1 for children. (707) 762-4871. ➡ *See #12 on map p. 268.*

RESTAURANTS

Apple Box: A store of antiques and housewares, this charmer also serves good desserts, teas and coffee. There's a bookshop next door and ten tables outside, right by the river. Joe's dog buddy Dabney loves the smell here of sun on river water, mixed with baking cookies. 224 B Street; (707) 762-5222.

Que Pasa: At this Mexican place on the river, you can tie your dog up outside the patio fence and munch tacos close by. 54 East Washington Street; (707) 769-8396.

Perry's Charburgers: Order a burger, onion rings, mozzarella sticks and a milk shake to wash it down. (Healthier fare is also available.) The eatery furnishes around 10 tables, or pick a park bench at the pretty Putnam Plaza Park next door (say that 10 times fast). 139B Petaluma Boulevard North; (707) 762-9559.

Rocket Cafe: On weekends, the dog-loving owners offer barbe-cue and live music. Other times, enjoy light meals at the outdoor tables here. 100 Petaluma Boulevard, Number 104; (707) 763-2314.

The Old River Inn: This elegant spot in a restored Victorian serves Italian and French brunch, lunch and dinner on a sunny riverfront patio. The owner, very fond of dogs, regrets that the board of health frowns on dogs on the patio, but she'll let you tie yours on the nearby shaded lawn while you eat. It's by the walk-across floating bridge, at 222 Weller Street; (707) 765-0111.

DIVERSIONS

Yikes! What a dog!: If your dog is so ugly that the fleas flee when they see his face, you'll want to know about this one. Petaluma's annual Ugly Dog Contest is a good time for you and your dog, ugly or not. (Beautiful dogs are welcome, so long as they don't mind losing.) It's held on the last day of the Sonoma-Marin Fair and it's open to any dog owner for a $3 entry fee. For your $3, you get free admission to the fair for that day, but your dog is allowed only in the contest area. Water and shade are provided; bring your own pooper scooper.

A winner is chosen in the Mutt and Pedigreed categories. These winners square off for the Ugly Dog of the Year award. Then there's the Ring of Champions division, in which past winners compete for the title of World's Ugliest Dog. Don't miss it. Held at 12:30 at the Grandstand Park Stage on a Sunday in late June, at the Sonoma-Marin Fairgrounds. Call for this year's date: (707) 763-0931.

ROHNERT PARK

PARKS, BEACHES & RECREATION AREAS

•**Crane Creek Regional Park** 🐾 🐾

For years, this 128-acre patch of grazing land in the middle of nowhere has been undeveloped open space for your dog's pleasure. Recent improvements include an upgraded parking lot, the addition of picnic tables and the widening of 2.6 miles of hiking trails. Unfortunately, the leash law is enforced here, and a sign tells you why: "Dogs Caught in Livestock May Be Shot." Carry water; you may get thirsty just trying to find the place in your car.

From Rohnert Park, drive east on the Rohnert Park Expressway to Petaluma Hill Road. Turn south on Petaluma Hill Road to Roberts Road, and go east for two miles on Roberts Road. Shortly after Roberts turns into Pressley Road, there's the park. A machine hopes to collect a $1 parking fee from you. (707) 527-2041. ➡*See #13 on map p. 268.*

SANTA ROSA

Santa Rosa no longer looks quite as it did in Hitchcock's *Shadow of a Doubt*, but it's still a decent town with neat, green city parks that get good use. All require that dogs be leashed.

PARKS, BEACHES & RECREATION AREAS

• Doyle Park 🐾 🐾 1/2

This is a perfect small-town park, much appreciated on summer evenings, when kids play softball under huge oaks and mariachi music fills the air. Even in summer, there's water in Spring Creek for your leashed dog to enjoy. Besides the big softball diamond, there are volleyball courts, a parcourse and a kids' gym.

From Sonoma Avenue, turn south on Doyle Park Drive to the parking lot. (707) 524-5116. ➔See #14 on map p. 268.

• Hood Mountain Regional Park 🐾 🐾 🐾

Dogs and people love the trails in this park, but it's open only on weekends and holidays and closes every summer when fire danger gets high. It usually reopens only in late September. Make sure your dog wears a leash. If a sign appears at the Los Alamos Road turn-off saying that the park is closed, believe it.

To get to the only entrance, from Highway 12, turn east on Los Alamos Road (not Adobe Canyon Road, which leads only to Sugarloaf Ridge State Park—where dogs aren't allowed on trails). The road is long, winding, steep and narrow for the last two miles. It's not for nervous drivers or car-sick pooches, but it's a beautiful four-mile drive, with a good close-up of Hood Mountain's bare rock outcropping "hood."

A machine in the parking lot will ask you to pay $1. Call to make sure the park is open before driving here. (707) 527-2041. ➔See #15 on map p. 268.

• Rincon Valley Community Park 🐾 🐾

This city park has a softball field, picnic tables, a parcourse and a kids' gym, and ponds in which three happy dogs were swimming (with leashes on, like good dogs) the day we visited. There's an attractive picnic area with shade trees by one pond. On Montecito Boulevard, west of Calistoga Road. (707) 524-5116. ➔See #16 on map p. 268.

• Spring Lake Regional Park 🐾 🐾 🐾

In winter, this county park doesn't offer much more than a pleasantly dutiful on-leash trot around the lake. But in summer, it's leafy and full of the summer sounds of kids yelling and thumping oars. It's more fun here for people than dogs, who must be leashed. This is a good spot for a picnic, roller skating, a parcourse workout, a boat ride or human swimming (no dogs allowed in the swim area). The path around the lake is paved for skaters, strollers and bicycles, and there are short dirt paths off into the open oak and brush woods. You can fish from the banks, where they're cleared of tules and willows.

The parking fee is $3 in winter, $4 in summer; the large lot has some shady spots. Campsites are $14, plus $1 extra for a dog. Ten sites are reservable; 21 are first come, first served. Dogs must have proof of rabies vaccination. The campground is open daily between May 15 and September 15, weekends and holidays only after September 15.

From Highway 12, the Farmer's Lane portion in Santa Rosa, turn east on Hoen Avenue. Take Hoen four stoplights to Newanga Avenue. Turn left on Newanga, which goes straight to the entrance. (707) 539-8092. ➜ *See #17 on map p. 268.*

PLACES TO STAY
Best Western–Garden Inn: Rates are $48 to $75. Dogs are $10 extra. 1500 Santa Rosa Avenue, Santa Rosa, CA 95404; (707) 546-4031.

Best Western Hillside Inn: Rates are $46 to $54. 2901 Fourth Street, Santa Rosa, CA 95409; (707) 546-9353.

Los Robles Lodge: Rates are $75 to $95. 925 Edwards Avenue, Santa Rosa, CA 95401; (707) 545-6330.

Santa Rosa Travelodge: Rates are $50 to $65. A $5 dog deposit is required. 1815 Santa Rosa Avenue, Santa Rosa, CA 95407; (707) 542-3472.

Spring Lake Regional Park camping: See page 278.

SEA RANCH
PARKS, BEACHES & RECREATION AREAS
• **Sea Ranch Beach Trails** 🐾 🐾 1/2

Sea Ranch is a private development, but seven public foot trails cross the property leading to the beach, which is also public property. The smooth, wide dirt trails are managed by the Sonoma County Regional Parks. They offer incomparable solitary walks through unspoiled grassy hills.

All the trails are clearly marked on Highway 1. Each trailhead has restrooms and a box where you are asked to deposit $3 for parking. No motorcycles, bicycles or horses are allowed. Keep your dog on-leash.

Here are the distances to the beach, listing trails from north to south: Salal Trail, .6 mile; Bluff-Top Trail, 3.5 miles; Walk-On Beach Trail, .4 mile; Shell Beach Trail, .6 mile; Stengel Beach Trail, .2 mile; Pebble Beach Trail, .3 mile; Black Point Trail, .3 mile. Call (707) 527-2041 for more info. ➜ *See #18 on map p. 268.*

SEBASTOPOL

PARKS, BEACHES & RECREATION AREAS

• **Ragle Ranch Park** 🐾 🐾 🐾 1/2

This Sonoma County regional park, right in the town of Sebastopol, is surprisingly large and wild, once you pass the fields and picnic areas. Unlike most urban parks, it's not very crowded, except during ball games on weekends. Level hiking and equestrian trails wind alongside vineyards and apple orchards, which are in bloom beginning in early April. Waterfowl breed in marshy spots around the creek, so don't yield to the temptation to let your dog off the obligatory leash. The landscape is gently rolling, with reeds and willows lining the creek and oaks with mistletoe on the higher rises. Woo woo, it's kissy stuff.

At Healdsburg Avenue and Ragle Road. Admission is $1 per car. (707) 527-2041. ➡ *See #19 on map p. 268.*

RESTAURANTS

So-N-So's: Don't miss the truly delicious burgers, fries and shakes at this roadside drive-in. 915 Gravenstein Highway/ Highway 116; (707) 823-3398.

FESTIVALS

Apple Blossom Festival: This festival isn't a thrill for dogs, who must be leashed everywhere and mind their manners impeccably. But if your dog likes jumping in and out of the car, and behaves well in crowds on leash, by all means bring her along. Stroll through town and browse the arts and crafts and food displays. This two-day festival is usually held in April. Call the Chamber of Commerce for details: (707) 823-3032.

Gravenstein Apple Fair: You'll see plenty of leashed pooches here. The begging is excellent. Listen to country-western or bagpipes, shake paws with someone in a cow costume, watch cooking demonstrations and pet farm animals (only you—not your dog). Held one weekend in early August, in Ragle Ranch Park. For admission prices and exact dates: (707) 829-GRAV.

DIVERSIONS

Sniff out the farm trail: If you're serious about buying homegrown produce and dairy products, or just like farms—and your dog wears a leash at all times and won't do leg lifts on the vegetables—pick up a Farm Trails map from Sonoma County Farmtrails, (707) 996-2154, or from the Chamber of Commerce, P.O. Box 178, Sebastopol, CA 95473; (707) 823-3032.

SONOMA

Sonoma's historic buildings and Town Plaza are a fine stroll with a canine on a summer day. But even on-leash dogs aren't permitted in the square park, which on a good day is full of picnickers wolfing down fine wine and Sonoma jack cheese.

PARKS, BEACHES & RECREATION AREAS

•Maxwell Farms Regional Park 😊 😊 1/2

This park offers playing fields, picnic tables, a generous kids' playground, smooth paths and a large undeveloped area where paths follow Sonoma Creek under huge laurels wound with wild grapevines. The creek is dry in summer, but leashed dogs like to sniff it anyway.

The entrance is off Verano Avenue, west of Highway 12. Day-use fee is $1. (707) 527-2041. ➡ *See #20 on map p. 268.*

RESTAURANTS

The Feed Store Cafe & Bakery: Delicious breakfast, lunch and late afternoon snacks, coffee and desserts, and beer and wine can be enjoyed by both of you at cafe tables in front or on the roomy and beautifully landscaped back patio, with almost 20 umbrella-topped tables. A fountain provides the soothing sound of flowing water (don't worry, there's a bathroom here) and also serves as an elegant water dish. The owners welcome well-behaved dogs. 529 First Street West; (707) 938-2122.

PLACES TO STAY

Best Western Sonoma Valley Inn: Rates are $80 to $150. Small dogs only, please. 550 Second Street West, Sonoma, CA 95476; (707) 938-9200.

TIMBER COVE

PARKS, BEACHES & RECREATION AREAS

•Salt Point State Park 😊 😊 😊

Leashed dogs are allowed only on South Gerstle Cove Beach—south of the rocky tide pool area, which is an underwater reserve—and in the Gerstle Cove, Woodside and Fisk Mill Cove picnic areas and campsites. Gerstle Cove picnic area is right above the portion of the beach where dogs are allowed, so that's your best bet. The surf is usually gentle here, but if in doubt, you can call an ocean-conditions recording: (707) 847-3222.

The parking fee is $5. Dogs are $1 extra. Dogs are allowed at all campsites here except the walk-in, group and environmental sites.

The park has about 30 tents in the upland portion of the park. East of Highway 1 are 80 family sites. Sites are $14 per night. The dog fee is $1. Between March 2 and November 30, reserve through MISTIX: (800) 444-PARK. The rest of the year, it's first come, first served.

The park is about five miles north of Timber Cove and six miles south of Stewarts Point, off Highway 1. For park info, call (707) 847-3221. →*See #21 on map p. 268.*

• **Stillwater Cove Regional Park** 🐾 🐾 1/2

This is a tiny but delightful beach at the foot of spectacular pine-covered cliffs. Park in the small lot beside Highway 1, leash your dog and walk down. There is a larger picnic area above the highway, where a $3 day-use fee is charged. From here, you have to cross the highway to get to the cove. Look both ways!

There are 23 campsites, available on a first-come, first-served basis. Sites are $14 per night for up to two vehicles ($12 for Sonoma County residents). Dogs are $1 extra. The turnout is about one mile north of Fort Ross State Park (where dogs are banned). (707) 527-2041. →*See #22 on map p. 268.*

PLACES TO STAY

Salt Point State Park camping: See page 282.
Stillwater Cove Regional Park camping: See above.

NAPA COUNTY

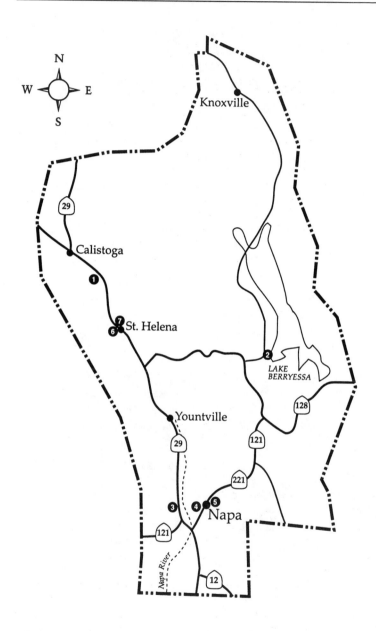

28
NAPA COUNTY

Napa dogs don't whine. They wine. And since there are plenty of dog-friendly restaurants here, they often wine and dine.

This is the home of California's most famous wine-making valley, and dogs get to experience some of the fringe benefits of this productive area. A few attractive wineries invite well-behaved dogs to relax and sniff at wines with their owners (see page 295). Just don't let your dog do leg lifts on inappropriate items, because Bacchus will get you. And your little dog, too.

The county's parks come up a little on the dry side. With the county's lush, fertile and inviting vineyards, it seems like there's so much land that dogs would be in heaven here. Not true.

Only nine public parks and a few miscellaneous sites in Napa County allow dogs. The city of Napa has four parks where dogs are allowed, and all permit them off leash in certain sections. You may incur the grapes of your dog's wrath if you don't take her to visit one of these leash-free lands next time you're in town.

CALISTOGA

PARKS, BEACHES & RECREATION AREAS

Dogs aren't allowed in either of Calistoga's municipal parks, but if you're camping, or visiting one of two private roadside attractions (see pages 289 and 290), your dog will feel at home here. One campground actually has a lake where your dog is welcome to take a dip. The only public park that allows dogs is in the nearby Bothe-Napa State Park, and the rules there are so strict it's barely worth a sniff.

• **Bothe-Napa State Park** 🐾 🐾

Dogs are relegated to paved roads and campgrounds here and it's a crime because of all the alluring trails. Hiking the highways can be fun, though: Joe seemed especially captivated by a man who was burning bacon over the campfire, his wife yelling that this was some vacation.

A wilderness haven this park is not, at least for you and your dog. Dogs must be leashed at all times. One of the two roads they're allowed on parallels Highway 29 and is so close you can see the drivers' eyes, bloodshot from too much wine-tasting.

On the positive end, the roads are stunning in autumn when the leaves change color. And dogs are allowed to camp with you, on leash. Dogs are also allowed in some of the picnic areas just off the roads.

The day-use fee is $5. Dogs are an additional $1. There are 50 campsites. Fees are $12 a night, plus $1 extra for the dog. Call MISTIX at (800) 444-PARK for reservations. The park is on Highway 29, halfway between St. Helena and Calistoga, just north of Bale Lane. The entrance is on the west side of the road, and the address is 3801 North St. Helena Highway (Highway 29). (707) 942-4575. → *See #1 on map p. 286.*

RESTAURANTS

Calistoga Drive Inn: Plenty of outdoor tables for dining on good drive-in food. 1207 Foothill Boulevard (Highway 128); (707) 942-0543.

Home Plate: Far from the tourist parking woes in town, this inexpensive, unassuming short-order restaurant makes some of the best grilled cheese sandwiches that ever melted in a mouth. Dine at one of three big outdoor tables. 2448 Foothill Boulevard (Highway 128); (707) 942-5646.

Lord Derby Arms English Pub and Restaurant: You drink one of 11 import beers offered on draft here, and your dog can drink a fine bowl of water supplied by the staff. The outside deck, also known as the beer garden, has 10 shaded tables and is comfortable on all but the hottest of afternoons. Food is served until late at night, and you can choose from typical English pub grub like fish and chips or bangers and mash; 1923 Lake Street. (707) 942-9155.

PLACES TO STAY

Bothe-Napa State Park camping: See above.

Calistoga Ranch Campground RV Resort: There's a lake here where dogs love to swim, but otherwise you're asked to keep them on leash on the hiking trails and in the camping areas. The owners keep guinea hens to keep the rattlesnakes away, and you don't want your puppy to tangle with either creature. There are 144 sites. Fees are $16 to $18 a night. It's $1 extra for a dog. 580 Lommel Road. (707) 942-6565.

Napa County Fairgrounds: A far cry from the great outdoors, this flat landscape with few trees is at least a good, inexpensive campground if all the motels are booked. There are 50 sites. It costs $10 to $13 to stay a night. Dogs (one per site) are $1 extra. 1435 Oak Street. (707) 942-5111.

Pink Mansion: This lovely old place is an 1875 Victorian—very picturesque and very pink. The owners love dogs—they have a huge one themselves. But if you have a bird dog, think twice about staying here: Also in residence are chickens and doves. Rates are $85 to $160. 1415 Foothill Boulevard (Highway 128), Calistoga, CA 94515; (707) 942-0558.

Washington Street Lodging: Relax in any of several cabins, each with its own little kitchen. You're just a couple of blocks from Calistoga's main drag here. The owner has a cat and a friendly dog, but she says if the cat doesn't like your dog, he'll make himself scarce. Rates are $80 to $90. There's a $15 fee for your pooch. 1605 Washington Street, Calistoga, CA 94515; (707) 942-6968.

FESTIVALS

Calistoga Community Christmas Bazaar: Go Christmas shopping with your leashed dog at this big sale with dozens of booths. It's the first Saturday of every December at the Napa County Fairgrounds. (707) 942-5111.

DIVERSIONS

The two places dogs can actually roam among the trees in this town happen to be at two private roadside attractions. Call them kitschy, call them tacky—they're more fun to explore than most public parks in this county.

Sniff out a petrified forest: You and your leashed dog can roam among trees entombed by a volcanic explosion 3.4 million years ago.

During a summertime visit, Joe found out why they call it the Petrified Forest. For him, it had nothing to do with the fact that we were surrounded by trees of stone. The sign announced in big bold letters, "Once Towering Redwoods—Now the Rock of Ages." But Joe didn't know the true meaning of petrified until we encountered—the elves.

They were the Elves of Ages, the ceramic kind you find on suburban lawns and know beyond a doubt they'll be discovered by archeologists a million years from now...The ones with the leering grins and bewitching eyes that children find enchanting by day and have nightmares about at night. They appeared everywhere Joe looked—sitting beside giant ceramic storybooks, standing beside stony trees.

The elves were at eye level for an Airedale, and they were all staring at him. Every time he saw a new one, he backed away with his tail between his legs and twisted his head around to make sure it wasn't following him. I couldn't help wondering how Airedales have remained so popular for frontline duty during wars.

But then came the petrifying elf. He didn't look any different from the others. But as soon as Joe laid eyes on him and his donkey companion, his tail went down and he turned 90 degrees. For at least two minutes, he was too frightened to look at the elf, growling instead at a manzanita tree. When he peeked and the elf was still staring at him, he decided enough was enough and bolted—leash and all.

He was waiting by the wishing well when I finally caught up to him. He would have left the park if he could have negotiated the turnstile by himself.

The Petrified Forest is at 4100 Petrified Forest Road, off Highway 128. It's actually in the outskirts of Sonoma County, but its address is in Calistoga. The unpaved trail is a quarter-mile loop. Admission is $3 for adults. There are dozens of tables around the gift shop, so pack a picnic. Open from 10 a.m. to 5:30 p.m. in summer, 10 a.m. to 4:30 p.m. in winter. (707) 942-6667.

See Old Faithful in your own back yard: You know you're in for a treat when a big sign greets you at the entry to Old Faithful Geyser: "Many Notable People Have Come to SEE HEAR AND LEARN the mysteries of this WONDER OF NATURE which captures the imagination. IT'S AMAZING."

And indeed, when dogs see the 350-degree-Fahrenheit plume of water gushing 50 to 70 feet into the air, they generally stare for a few seconds with their mouths agape. But the sight of tourists jumping in front of the geyser for a quick photo before the eruption subsides quickly bores them. Dogs then try to wander to the snack bar and persuade the person on the other end of the leash to buy a couple of hot dogs. But even more fascinating is the scent of goat and pig in nearby pens.

If your dog is the brave sort, don't hesitate to bring him to visit Clow, the fainting goat, or Valentino, the Vietnamese pot-bellied pig. Clow butts her head against her fence at first, but she's only playing. After a few minutes, she was calming Joe's fears by licking him on the nose. Soon he was in love. But he never quite got used to the big black pig. When Valentino grunted a swinish hello, Joe trembled and ran away backwards.

Old Faithful erupts every 40 minutes, and the eruptions last about two to three minutes. Picnic tables are plentiful, so bring a snack or buy one here between eruptions. A sign at the site warns that dogs aren't allowed in the geyser viewing area, but you can bring your dog—securely leashed—within a safe distance of the geyser and not get scolded or scalded.

The geyser and its menagerie are between Highways 128 and 29, on Tubbs Lane. Open 9 a.m. to 6 p.m. in summer, 9 a.m. to 5 p.m. in winter. Admission is $4.50 for adults. (707) 942-6463.

LAKE BERRYESSA

PARKS, BEACHES & RECREATION AREAS

• Lake Berryessa 🐾 🐾

Lake Berryessa offers 165 miles of shoreline for human and canine enjoyment. All the resort areas on the lake allow leashed dogs. Better yet, most allow them to swim off leash. The summer heat is stifling here, so your dog will want to take advantage of that.

Most resorts rent fishing boats and allow dogs to go along on your angling adventure. The fishing is fantastic, especially for fall trout. It's cooler then, too, so you won't have to contend with so many waterskiers, and your dog won't roast.

If you just want to hike and swim for an afternoon, explore the Smittle Creek Trail. The entrance is just north of the lake's visitor center, on Knoxville Road. The trail takes you up and down the fingers of the lake. Dogs must be leashed, except when swimming.

To get to Lake Berryessa from the Rutherford area, take Highway 128 and turn left at the Lake Berryessa/Spanish Flat sign. It's a very curvy route, so take it easy if you or your dog tend toward car-sickness. For more information about the lake, call the Bureau of Reclamation Visitor Information Center at (707) 966-2111. For questions about lakeside businesses, call the Lake Berryessa Chamber of Commerce at (800) 726-1256. ➡ *See #2 on map p. 286.*

PLACES TO STAY

Here is a partial list of Lake Berryessa resorts. Prices and amenities vary depending on the season and the extent of the drought, so call the individual resorts for information. Dogs stay free unless otherwise indicated.

Berryessa Marina Resort: $1 extra per day for a dog. (707) 966-2161.

Markley Cove Resort: (707) 966-2134.

Pleasure Cove Resort: Dogs are $2 extra a day. (707) 966-2172.

Rancho Monticello Resort: (707) 966-2188.

Spanish Flat Resort: Dogs aren't allowed on rental boats here. (707) 966-7700.

Steele Park Resort: Dogs are allowed in the campground here, but not in the motel. (800) 522-2123.

NAPA

The city of Napa has some 40 parks. Dogs are allowed in a whopping four, each of which has an off-leash section. You'll see dogs in some of the bigger parks, such as the Lake Hennessey Recreation Area, but they're not officially sanctioned, so we can't officially mention them.

PARKS, BEACHES & RECREATION AREAS

• Alston Park 🐾 🐾 🐾

With 157 acres of rolling hills surrounded by vineyards, Alston Park seems to stretch out forever. The lower part of the land used to be a prune orchard, and these prunes are just about the only trees you'll find here.

From there on up, the park is wide-open land with a lone tree here and there. Without shade, dogs and people can fry on hot summer days. But the park is magical during early morning in the summer or any cooler time of year.

Miles of trails take you and your dog to places far from the road and the sound of traffic. Dogs are supposed to be off-leash only in the lower, flat section of the park. Signs mark the area. It's better than nothing, and it's reasonably safe from traffic. A water fountain and a water closet also grace the entrance.

From Highway 29, take Trower Avenue southwest to the end, at Dry Creek Road. The parking lot for the park is a short jog to your right on Dry Creek Road, and across the street. (707) 257-9529.
→See #3 on map p. 286.

• John F. Kennedy Memorial Park 🐾 🐾 🐾 1/2 🐕

Throw your dog's leash to the wind here and ramble along the Napa River. Dogs are allowed in the undeveloped areas near the park's boat marina. The only spot to avoid is a marshland that's more land than marsh during dry times.

Dogs enjoy chasing each other around the flat, grassy area beside the parking lot. There's also a dirt trail that runs along the river. You can take it from either side of the marina, although as of this writing, the signs designate only the south side as a dog-exercise area. The scenery isn't terrific—radio towers and construction cranes dot the horizon—but dogs without a sense of decor don't seem to mind.

Dogs like to amble by the river, which is down a fair incline from the trail. But be careful if you've got a water dog, because jet-skiers and motor boaters have been known to mow over anything in their path. There's no drinking water in the dog area and it gets mighty hot in the summer, so bring your own.

Take Highway 221 to Streblow Drive, and follow the signs past the Napa Municipal Golf Course and Napa Valley College to the boat marina/launch area. Park in the lot and look for the trail by the river. (707) 257-9529. → *See #4 on map p. 286.*

• **Shurtleff Park** 🐾 🐾 🐾 🦴

The farther away from the road you go, the better it is in this long, narrow park. It gets shadier and thicker with large firs and eucalyptus trees. Dogs are allowed off leash as soon as you feel they're safe from the road.

The park is almost entirely fenced, but there are a few escape hatches. Two are at the entrance and two others are along the side that lead you into the schoolyard of Phillips Elementary School. This isn't normally a problem, unless your dog runs into the day-care center at lunch time, as Joe once did. A teacher escorted him out by the scruff of his neck before he could steal someone's peanut butter sandwich.

On Shelter Street at Shurtleff, beside Phillips Elementary School. (707) 257-9529. → *See #5 on map p. 286.*

RESTAURANTS

Brown's Valley Yogurt and Espresso Bar: Cool off with a cold frozen one at the outside tables shaded by a wooden awning. 3265 Brown's Valley Road; (707) 252-4977.

Dawg Patch: If your dog likes hot dogs, then these dogs are your dog's. Eat them at the bench outside, on the way to John F. Kennedy Memorial Park (see page 292). 1453 West Imola Avenue; (707) 255-8656.

Honey Treat Yogurt Shop: The non-fat frozen yogurt here will make you feel 10 pounds lighter and 10 degrees cooler after a long walk with the dog. 1080 Coombs Street; (707) 255-6633.

Rio Poco: Great burritos and easy take-out packages make eating on the outside bench a pleasure. Veteran's Park may beckon from across the street, but unfortunately you're not allowed with your dog. 807 Main Street; (707) 253-8203.

Napa Valley Traditions: Enjoy fresh baked goods and cappuccino at four outside tables shaded by two trees and an awning. Your dog will find as much to enjoy here as you will: Inside, they also sell dog biscuits and dog soap. 1202 Main Street; (707) 226-2044.

PLACES TO STAY

Best Western Inn: Small dogs are welcome here. Rates are $50 to $149. 100 Soscol Avenue, Napa, CA 94559; (707) 257-1930.

Sheraton Inn Napa Valley: Rates are $65 to $120. A $25 deposit is required for dogs. 3425 Solano Avenue, Napa, CA 94558; (707) 253-7433.

FESTIVALS

Napa has several street fairs throughout the year, but most are so crowded that we recommend dogs stay home. The only exception:

Christmas Kickoff Parade: Santa visits the wine country and winds through downtown Napa on the day after Thanksgiving. (707) 257-0322.

ST. HELENA

PARKS, BEACHES & RECREATION AREAS

• **Baldwin Park** 🐾 🐾

Baldwin Park has everything you could want in a park, except size. But what it lacks in acreage, it makes up for in dog appeal. Set off a small road, it's almost entirely fenced in and full of flowering trees, oaks and big pines. A dirt path winds through green grass from one end of the park to the other, passing by a water fountain and a conveniently placed garbage can.

Unfortunately, dogs must be leashed, but it's still a pleasant place to stretch all your legs after a tour through Wine Country. On Spring Street between Stockton Street and North Crane Avenue. (707) 963-5706. ➡ *See #6 on map p. 286.*

• **Lyman Park** 🐾 🐾

You'll think you're on a movie set for some old-time village scene when you and your dog wander into this small, cozy park on historic Main Street. Leashes are mandatory, but the park has a gazebo, lots of trees and benches, a flower garden and—best of all for dogs—an antique horse/dog water fountain. The top part is for horses, the lower bowl for dogs. Horses aren't allowed here anymore, so if your dog is huge, he might as well sip from the equine bowl.

The park is nestled snugly between the police station and a funeral home, at 1400 Main Street. (707) 963-5706. ➡ *See #7 on map p. 286.*

RESTAURANTS

Showley's at Miramonte: "West Coast fresh" is how this place describes their sumptuous food. At 1327 Railroad Avenue; (707) 963-1200.

Taylor's Refresher: Dine on ice cream and burgers at the many outdoor tables here. And get this: They have milkbones for your dog. Wow! 933 Main Street; (707) 963-3486.

Valley Deli: Eat good deli food at a couple of sidewalk tables. 1138 Main Street; (707) 963-7710.

PLACES TO STAY

Harvest Inn: Dogs who stay in this tudor-style lodging can wander the inn's 21 acres of gardens, vineyards, fields and ponds (on leash). Rates are $100 to $350. Dogs are $10 extra. They prefer small dogs here. At One Main Street, St. Helena, CA 94574; (707) 963-WINE.

Hyphen Inn: Stay in one of two country cottages, each with a patio, in the middle of this large, lush country estate. Dog-friendly owners serve up a fresh European breakfast. Cottages are approximately $135. Since this is a private residence, the owners don't give their address unless you stay here. The mailing address is P.O. Box 190, St. Helena, CA 94574; (707) 942-0434.

DIVERSIONS

Grape Expectations: There are miles and miles of lush vineyards in Napa Valley and more than 70 wineries. But sadly, despite all the fine wine tours available, you probably won't be able to introduce your dog to the joyous process of fermentation. I have yet to find a winery that welcomes canines inside its doors. However, many do have outdoor areas where you may be allowed to brunch with your pooch and have your own private wine tasting (provided your dog isn't planning on driving home).

Finding a dog-friendly winery can be hit-or-miss, so call ahead if you have a particular place in mind. For general info on Napa Valley, call (707) 226-7455. Here are three vintners that wholeheartedly allow well-behaved dogs to picnic on their grounds:

Bergfield 1885 Wine Cellar: Four large, umbrella-shaded picnic tables on sprawling park-like grounds. Water is available. Open 10 a.m. to 5 p.m. Thursday through Monday. 401 Highway 29 in St. Helena. (707) 963-7293.

Cuvaison: Three small picnic areas with a total of 11 outdoor tables. Water is available. The person I spoke with even said, "Dogs are welcome in the tasting room if it's not too crowded." Open 10 a.m. to 5 p.m. daily. 4550 Silverado Trail in Calistoga. (707) 942-6266.

Folie a Deux Winery: Six tables in a rustic farmhouse setting. (The name, by the way, is a psychological term which translates as "shared delusion.") Water is available. 3070 Highway 29 in St. Helena. (707) 963-1160.

YOUNTVILLE

Unlike the Yountville town government, which bans dogs from its parks, restaurateurs here have the right idea. Several exquisite restaurants welcome dogs to their patios, which are generally shaded and very accommodating to people and their canines. The only word of warning is to avoid these restaurants when they're packed with people from the tour buses that occasionally descend on the town. It's just too crowded for dogs, who usually get tripped on and later photographed as tourist souvenirs.

RESTAURANTS

California Cafe Bar & Grill: California cuisine reigns here, with fresh seafood as the focal point. Several outdoor tables with oversized umbrellas keep you and your dog cool. 6795 Washington Street; (707) 944-2330.

Compadres Mexican Bar & Grill: Tropical landscaping, intoxicating jasmine and honeysuckle, and umbrellas over tables make this one of the most pleasant restaurants for spending a few hours with your dog. Try the *pollo borracho*, a whole chicken cooked with white wine and tequila. 6539 Washington Street, at the Vintage 1870 complex; (707) 944-2406.

Java Express: This place sells espresso drinks, bakery goods, sandwiches, granola, fresh lemonade—anything you and your dog would want after being kicked out of local parks. Eat, drink and relax at the outdoor tables. 6795 Washington Street; (707) 944-9700.

Red Rock Vintage Cafe: A great place for people who love burgers or omelets. Eat with your dog at the deck in back of the cheery, ivy-covered brick building. 6535 Washington Street, at the Vintage 1870 complex; (707) 944-2614.

Yountville Market: This Old West-style building houses a general store where you can grab some edibles and snack at the benches out front. 6770 Washington Street; (707) 944-1393.

Yountville Pastry Shop: Eat pastries, sandwiches or pizza on the wooden outdoor patio. 6525 Washington Street, at the Vintage 1870 complex; (707) 944-2138.

PLACES TO STAY

Vintage Inn: Stay here and you're located right next door to some of the Bay Area's best restaurants that take dogs. Rates are $144 to $204. Dogs are $25 extra. 6541 Washington Street, Yountville, CA 94599; (707) 944-1112.

YOLO COUNTY

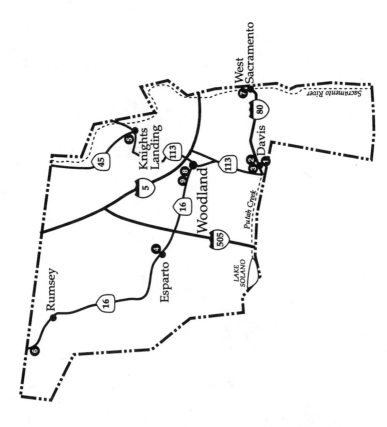

29
YOLO COUNTY

The little towns along the winding Sacramento River haven't changed much since the early 1900s. That's good news for you, but it's not necessarily what your dog wants to hear. Restaurants with outdoor dining are rare, and dog-friendly parks are equally uncommon. You'll see mile after mile of wide open land and dense forests, but most of it is privately owned and off-limits. For information on the one state wildlife area here (the Sacramento Bypass), call the California Department of Fish and Game at (916) 355-0978.

The Sacramento River is so integral to life here that many of the county's parks are formed around public boat ramps that charge nominal launching fees. If you have a dog who loves to go angling for salmon, stripers or shad, this is a great place to bring her to show off your fishing skills.

Davis and Woodland are the only two cities with off-leash dog areas and a fair number of outdoor dining establishments. Some of the parks are close to major highways, so they're a blessing when your dog starts moaning and getting that bulgy-eyed look on a long trip.

DAVIS

This home to a University of California campus is a very friendly town, especially where dogs are concerned. There are three parks that have sections for leashless dogs. Joe and I didn't know about these parks the first few times we visited Davis, and we spent our time slinking leashlessly around the shadows of city parks where leashes are the law. Joe feels much better now that we've discovered these other parks and his scofflaw days are over.

PARKS, BEACHES & RECREATION AREAS

•**Pioneer Park** 🐾 🐾 1/2 🐕

This park is good for kids, with playgrounds and basketball hoops, but the dog-exercise area is a little too close to the road for our comfort. It's also very small. If you have a very obedient dog who needs to stretch his legs off leash, but doesn't need to stretch them very far, this will do. It's clean, green and has some shade. Fortunately it's on a quiet road, so the danger from cars is low.

Pioneer Park is convenient for dogs traveling through on the freeway. Heading east on Interstate 80, take the Mace Boulevard exit and go left on Chiles Road. Take a right on El Cemonte Avenue. Go left on Swingle Drive and you'll be at the park. The dog walk area is just to the right, about halfway down the block on Hamel Street. (916) 757-5626. ➡ *See #1 on map p. 298.*

•**Slide Hill Park** 🐾🐾🐾 1/2 🐕

The off-leash portion of this diverse community park is toward the back, protected from most traffic. It's also partly shaded and it has green grass, even in the middle of summer! What more could a city dog want? More room? Possibly, but this off-leash area is Davis' largest, so why be picky?

The park is also a great place to take kids. There are playgrounds and tennis courts, and there's even a decent-sized swimming pool in the front.

To get to the dog area, park in the lot at Temple Drive and walk into the park on the paved path, heading left past the tennis courts until you reach the back. The dog spot, under a small grove of trees, is marked by a garbage can and a sign. (916) 757-5626. ➡ *See #2 on map p. 298.*

•**Sycamore Park** 🐾🐾🐾 🐕

If your dog won't be tempted to join in the fun and games of the playground on his right and the sports field on his left, the off-leash portion of this park will suit her just fine. It's green, grassy and fairly safe from traffic.

Park along Sycamore Lane between Villanova and Bucknell drives, not in the parking lot of West Davis Intermediate School. Go into the park's grassy field to the right of the school as you face it from Sycamore Lane. The dog exercise area is to the left of the playground and is clearly marked. (916) 757-5626. ➡ *See #3 on map p. 298.*

RESTAURANTS

Most of the city's best restaurants are downtown. Dog owners in Davis say that because so many students have let their dogs run loose around here, there's a kind of backlash going on against all dogs in the downtown area. We've never seen evidence of it, though.

The following restaurants are still dog-friendly. Be extra courteous and you can help resuscitate the sullied reputation of dogs here.

The Crepe Bistro: It's crepes, crepes and more crepes at this small outdoor cafe in a gazebo-like setting. And are they ever scrumptious. From the fruit-filled breakfast crepes to dinner crepes filled with beef bourguignon, chicken, ham and cheese, and spinach, everything is first-rate here. 234 E Street; (916) 753-2575.

Domenic Cafe: Completely covered outdoor dining for that constantly shaded feel makes the Vietnamese and American cuisine here taste even better than it would in the sweltering sun. At least that's what dogs say. 234 E Street; (916) 753-2575.

London Fish 'n Chips: 129 E Street; (916) 753-7210.

Steve's Place Pizza: Dogs love to sleep at your feet as you eat yummy pizza on the covered wood deck here. 314 F Street; (916) 758-2800.

Subway: Eat subs at a couple of outdoor tables. 130 G Street; (916) 756-1440.

PLACES TO STAY

Best Western University Lodge: When your dog needs to go see someone graduate or consult with a professor on some "arcanine" matter, this motel one block off campus (and a few blocks from Central Park, a good spot for leashed dogs) is a convenient place to stay. Rates are $50 to $70. Dogs are $10 extra. 123 B Street, Davis, CA 95616; (916) 756-7890.

Econo Lodge: Rates are $45 to $55. Dogs are $5 extra. 221 D Street, Davis, CA 95616; (916) 756-1040.

Motel 6: Rates are $30 for the first adult, $6 for the second. All Motel 6s allow one small dog per room. 4835 Chiles Road, Davis, CA 95616; (916) 753-3777.

FESTIVALS

Picnic Day/Doggie Day: Dogs are always welcome on leash on the University of California campus. But on Picnic Day in mid-April, there's more than a mere welcome mat for them. There's a red carpet.

Dachshunds can run their stubby legs off at race designed especially for them. If you've never seen these little hot dogs going all out against the clock, it's a sight you shouldn't miss. There's also a contest for frisbee catchers, and even some sheep dog trials.

Besides dog events, 70,000 people attend the festivities and watch the extravagant opening parade, eat good food, listen to bands and talk to university professors about their research at departmental demonstrations. (These are usually in the buildings, so dogs have to stay out.) (916) 752-2222 or (916) 752-1990.

Whole Earth Festival: Old hippie dogs like this springtime affair. They can wear their best tie-dye, buy beads and crafts, eat healthful food, dance their four legs off and listen to lectures on living in harmony with the environment. Merchants are usually very friendly here, offering melting ice and cool water to hot and dusty dogs. Call (916) 752-2568 for location and dates.

ESPARTO

You could get your hopes up if you're hungry when entering the main street to this tiny old-time town. A sign bigger than most around here announces that the Dogtown Diner is dead ahead. When we arrived late one Monday afternoon, it was indeed dead. In fact, all three of the town's eateries were closed.

It turns out that even when they're open, only the Burger Barn (see below) has outdoor seating. About the only place to get hot food around here after 5 p.m. is at the Cache Creek Indian Bingo & Casino center, a few miles west on Highway 16. There are no outdoor tables, but if you're traveling with another human companion, one of you can walk the dog around the area outside the incongruously large building while the other goes inside and orders a three-piece fried chicken dinner with beans and mashed potatoes and gravy for $4.50. Be sure to order an extra mashed potato cup for your dog. While you're in there, you can take your change and try your luck at the video slot machines on the other side of bingoland. (Whatever you do, don't leave your dog alone in the car here. It is often mortally hot.)

PARKS, BEACHES & RECREATION AREAS

•Esparto Community Park 🐾 🐾

A brochure announces that this four-acre park is "mainly used for passive recreation." That suits most dogs just fine, since they have to be on leash here anyway. It's a convenient stop on the long and scenic Highway 116.

The park, which is loaded with shade trees, is about five miles west of Interstate 505, on Highway 116. (916) 666-8115. ➡ *See #4 on map p. 298.*

RESTAURANTS

Burger Barn: Eat big burgers at this eatery's lone, shaded picnic table. 17090 Yolo Avenue; (916) 787-3720.

KNIGHTS LANDING

PARKS, BEACHES & RECREATION AREAS

•Knights Landing Boat Ramp 🐾 🐾

When you and your dog launch your boat here, you'll be gliding into movie history: In 1932, this once-bustling riverside community was the backdrop for the Mississippi River scenes in *Showboat.* Your dog may not be impressed, but it's something to think about when motoring out of Sycamore Slough into the Sacramento River.

The town is a mere shadow of what it once was, but it still retains that old-time river town feel. The three acres of trees and grassy glades that surround the boat ramp are open to you and your on-leash dog for such good old-fashioned activities as fishing from shore, swimming in the slough and taking an easy stroll. There's even a dilapidated wood bridge to add to the Huck Finn ambience.

The entry fee is $3. Going north on Highway 113, make a left at 4th street in downtown Knights Landing. After you pass the first bridge, make your first left. It's a sharp one and easy to miss. (408) 666-8115. → *See #5 on map p. 298.*

RUMSEY

PARKS, BEACHES & RECREATION AREAS

• **Cache Creek Canyon Regional Park** 🐾 🐾 🐾

This 700-acre park is flat in the developed sections and very hilly when you get away from people. Couch potato canines enjoy picnicking at any of three car-accessible sites, as well as "ruffing" it at the campground. More adventurous dogs prefer hiking over the creek and into the woods with their human friends on a self-guided nature walk.

We've found that some park hosts don't know about the trails, so it's best to get a map of the nature walk before you go. Write for one from the Yolo County Parks Division at 625 Court Street, Woodland, CA 95695.

Very feisty dogs may want to continue their treks onto federal land, where they're allowed to be off leash. More than 15,000 acres—some of it inaccessible because of the steep terrain—is out there for your leashless bliss. It can be tricky to find. Contact the Bureau of Land Management, Clear Lake Resource Area, 555 Leslie Street, Ukiah, CA 95482; (707) 462-3873.

Camping at Cache Creek Canyon Regional Park costs $10 to $15. Dogs are $1 extra. There are 45 sites, all first come, first served. The day-use fee is $3. The first of the three park turnoffs is about six miles west of Rumsey on Highway 16. All sites are on the south side of the road. (916) 666-8115. → *See #6 on map p. 298.*

PLACES TO STAY

Cache Creek Canyon Regional Park camping: See above.

WEST SACRAMENTO

PARKS, BEACHES & RECREATION AREAS

• **Elkhorn Regional Park** 🐾 1/2

This is a lush 55-acre park along the Sacramento River. Sounds nice. But unless you and your leashed dog are willing to get out your sickles and blaze a trail through the thick bramble and trees that make up most of this park, you'll be relegated to a very small developed portion.

Joe and I arrived at the park just as some kids were coming out of the woods, yelling that they had been attacked by poison oak. Joe still wanted to check out the possibilities, but we remained on terra firma, near the shaded picnic tables at the top of the boat ramp.

The park is convenient to Interstate 5, and if you're passing through with your boat looking for a launch ramp, this is as good as any.

The day-use fee (includes the boat ramp) is $3. From north-bound Interstate 5 four miles north of West Sacramento, take the Elkhorn exit. Go right on Old River Road and follow it for about two miles. The park entrance is on the left, just after the railroad tracks. (916) 666-8115. → *See #7 on map p. 298.*

WOODLAND

Churches and saloons—this little city has them both in unusually high numbers. An interesting phenomenon, but neither should be vying for your dog's dollar. Dogs are better off investing their allowance in a permit to run leashless in the city's parks. For a mere $10, Woodland can be The Land of the Free for your dog. Call the Woodland Department of Parks and Recreation at (916) 661-5880 for details.

PARKS, BEACHES & RECREATION AREAS

The following two Woodland parks are rated based on their enjoyability with an off-leash permit from the city Department of Parks and Recreation.

•**Crawford Park** 🐾 🐾 🐾 🐾 🐕 (with permit)

You and your dog will enjoy the year-round green grass and the abundance of shade trees here. You can run the fitness course and play catch without being attached by a leash if you have a special permit. If you're at all worried about safety, try the side of the park bordered by a big wood fence.

This park is a great place to come to exercise your human and canine children at the same time. There's a pint-sized railroad village in the middle of the playground. Kids love it.

Exit Interstate 5 at East Street and go south for several blocks. Make a right on Gibson Road. After a few blocks, go left on College Street and you'll find the park at the corner of College Street and El Dorado Drive. (916) 661-5880. → *See #8 on map p. 298.*

•**Woodside Park** 🐾 🐾 🐾 1/2 🦴 (with permit)

There's plenty of green, flat open space here for your dog's running pleasure. The park also has several shaded picnic tables for your dog's dining pleasure. Most pleasurable of all for your dog is the off-leash freedom he can experience if he goes out and buys a permit.

The park is on the corner of Cottonwood Street and El Dorado Drive, just six blocks west of Crawford Park (see page 304). (916) 661-5880. →*See #9 on map p. 298.*

RESTAURANTS

Depot Burgers: Dogs like to sit with you at the two umbrella-topped tables here while you munch on hot dogs and hamburgers. 628 Main Street; (916) 661-2345.

The Grind: Eat tasty sandwiches under the shade of umbrellas or a roof overhang. 608 Main Street; (916) 666-3774.

PLACES TO STAY

Cinderella Motel: Dogs gloat at this little motel because they're the only pets allowed. Cats are just plain not welcome. Rates are $35 to $42. 99 West Main Street, Woodland, CA 95695; (916) 662-1091.

Comfort Inn: The owners here have had a great deal of bad luck with dogs and their owners, so be sure to be on your absolutely, positively best behavior here, or they may not allow dogs much longer. Rates are $45 to $65. A $6 deposit is required for dogs. 1562 East Main Street, Woodland, CA 95695; (916) 666-3050.

SOLANO COUNTY

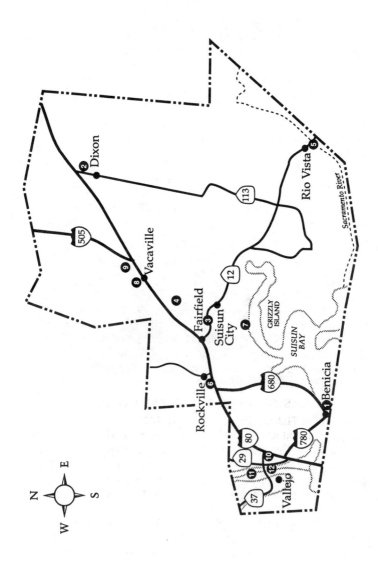

30
SOLANO COUNTY

One park saves Solano County from being devoid of leash-free areas. And what a park it is—8,600 acres of nature as dogs would have created it. The Grizzly Island Wildlife Area (see page 313), in the thick of the Suisun Marsh, is absolutely worth the trip to Solano County.

The rest of the county offers a mix of small to medium-sized neighborhood parks. Some are enchanting. Many are mundane. All demand leashes.

BENICIA

Drive into this quaint town, and you're immediately greeted by the friendly sign: "Welcome to Benicia—A California Main Street City." The sign stands in front of a park straight out of Disneyland's Main Street U.S.A., white gazebo and all.

You'll feel like jumping out of your car and bounding to the nearest green space with your dog to wait for the marching band. But wait! Read the other signs—the ones in every single Benicia town park: "NO DOGS." The nerve!

But all isn't lost. There's a decent fishing area at the end of First Street. It's not dog heaven, but at least it smells good.

The one consolation for being in Benicia with your dog is that the First Street area is full of some of the most dog-friendly restaurants around. Your dog can eat here and use some other city's park to powder his nose.

PARKS, BEACHES & RECREATION AREAS
• **Point Benicia Fishing Pier Area** 🐾 🐾 1/2

Park and fish at this big drive-on pier at the end of First Street that juts into the Carquinez Strait. It's a popular spot among local anglers. If you're not up for fishing, bring a lunch from a nearby restaurant and park yourself on one of the benches near the old train station here. You'll be amazed at the numbers of seagulls vying for your crusts.

Dogs enjoy the smells of the strait. While the pier itself isn't conducive to dog exercise, there's an area of undeveloped land nearby where they can cut loose as much as their leashes will allow.

At the southern end of First Street, just past A Street. (707) 746-4285. → *See #1 on map p. 308.*

RESTAURANTS

Java Bay: The owners will bring your dog a bowl of water while you're awaiting your order at the outdoor tables. They love dogs. They also make a mean bowl of minestrone soup—some of the best we've ever sampled. We sometimes like to take our meal down to the end of First Street, where dogs can sniff the Carquinez Strait and watch people fishing. 122 First Street; (707) 747-6860.

Morgan's Grill: If your dog slips his leash anywhere in Benicia, check for him here first. They've got great burgers (digna-fried, says owner Lynda Morgan), and they'll cut them in quarters for dogs who dine at their outdoor picnic tables. They even cook them to order. Morgan says, "We love dogs! We encourage people to bring them!" 1034 First Street; (707) 745-4466.

Pacifica Pizza: Choose from a large selection of pizzas to eat at tables shaded by umbrellas. 915 First Street; (707) 746-1790.

PLACES TO STAY

Best Western Heritage Inn: Rates are $60 to $65. Dogs require a $50 deposit. 1955 East Second Street, Benicia, CA 94510; (707) 746-0401.

FESTIVALS

Benicia Peddler's Fair: This August antique sale is held on First Street, starting at the waterfront. Leashed dogs are permitted, but with the valuables they're peddling here, make absolutely, positively certain your dog isn't lifting his leg on anything but a tree. For this year's dates, call (707) 745-8680.

DIXON

Although it's no more stringent than most, the pooper-scooper law in Dixon has such a formidable name we had to pass it on. It's called the "Canine Defecation Ordinance." Beware.

PARKS, BEACHES & RECREATION AREAS

•Hall Memorial Park 🐾 🐾

If you have to conduct business with city government and you want your dog to conduct business, too, you couldn't have asked for a better location for a park. It's right behind City Hall.

There's not much in the way of shade here, but on cooler days this park proves a decent stroll for dogs, provided they're leashed or at very firm heel. The park also has a playground, a swimming pool, tennis courts and picnic areas with barbecues, so it's even better for people.

At Hall Park Drive and East Mayes Street. (916) 678-7000. ➔*See #2 on map p. 308.*

FESTIVALS

Lambtown Festival: Dixon claims the title of having once been the Lamb Capital of the World. The town still celebrates its sheep industry every year with a two-day festival of events that will bring a grin to your dog's face. Young children get to ride sheep rodeo-style. People race the clock to dress sheep in boxer shorts. And there are wool shearing, spinning and weaving displays, live music and lots of food. (Lamb dishes are big here, of course.)

Dogs have to be leashed, even on the dance floor. If you've got any kind of herding dog, you may want to leave her at home or risk a dislocated shoulder.

The fair is held the first full weekend in August at the Dixon Fairgrounds, 655 South First Street. Admission is $5 for teens and adults, $3 for children and senior citizens. Toddlers are admitted free. (916) 678-2650.

FAIRFIELD

PARKS, BEACHES & RECREATION AREAS

• **Dover Park** 🐾 🐾

The atmosphere here is right for relaxing. It's a fairly small park, but it has two ponds with lots of ducks, and big, shady willows, oaks and firs. It's the place to go if you want to take a stroll with your leashed dog, then sit against a willow tree to read your favorite book.

On the other hand, if your dog doesn't feel like relaxing, this park can be a little too stimulating: Chaseable ducks abound. And the picnic areas are so popular that the smells just beckon dogs. We saw one unleashed mixed-breed fellow swipe a toddler's bag lunch and run away to eat it in peace. He came to the right place.

At Travis Boulevard and Flamingo Drive. (707) 428-7428. ➜ *See #3 on map p. 308.*

• **Laurel Creek Park** 🐾 🐾 1/2

Remember the kind of park you used to play in as a kid—the big neighborhood park with a great playground where the ice-cream truck visited several times a day? This is it. Only it's better, because there's some room for leashed dogs to roam.

The entire west side of this 40-acre park is open fields and undeveloped land. It's the right environment for running around with a dog, but the wrong place for keeping cool on hot days—there's no shade.

The park is on Cement Hill Road at Peppertree Drive. (707) 428-7428. ➜ *See #4 on map p. 308.*

PLACES TO STAY

Holiday Inn of Fairfield: Rates are $60 to $86. 1350 Holiday Lane, Fairfield, CA 94533; (707) 422-4111.

RIO VISTA

Humphrey the humpback whale visited this Delta town, and so should your dog. This is a real, dusty Old West town—not one of those cute villages loaded with boutiques and "shoppes." It's refreshing to find a town with more bait shops than banks.

Rio Vista isn't bursting with dog amenities. In fact, it's really appropriate to visit with your dog only if you're on a fishing holiday. Then you can slip your boat into the water and take off on the Delta for a few hours. Come back with your catch and eat dinner at the county park as the sun goes down on another Delta day.

PARKS, BEACHES & RECREATION AREAS

•**Sandy Beach County Park** 🐾 1/2

Dogs can't just jump into the Sacramento River here. They have to be in the right day-use area. One section is completely off-limits, while in the second area, dogs can take a dip, provided that they stay leashed on land and in the surf.

Your dog has another chance of getting wet if he follows you into the showers at the campground. Dogs are allowed at the campground, but it's not a very hospitable place. It's flat and dry, and its trees are more like bushes. With the campsites as close together as they are, and no foliage to give you privacy, it's like sleeping in one big commune. There are 42 sites. Fees are $10 a night. Dogs are $1 extra. All sites are first come, first served.

Take Highway 12 all the way to Rio Vista; follow Main Street to Second Street and go right. When the street bears left and becomes Beach Drive, the park is within a quarter mile. Bring proof of a rabies vaccination. (707) 374-2097. ➜ *See #5 on map p. 308.*

RESTAURANTS

Delta Deli: After a long day of fishing, there's nothing like the homemade barbecued beef, ribs and chicken they serve at the outdoor tables here. 659 Highway 12; (707) 374-6539.

Food Farm: They've got every kind of fast food you could ever want here, and several picnic tables for your feast. Try the southern fried chicken, but watch that your leashed dog doesn't dispose of the bones for you. 650 Highway 12; (707) 374-2020.

PLACES TO STAY
Sandy Beach County Park camping: See page 312.

DIVERSIONS
Roll on the river: Hire a houseboat. There's nothing like cruising around the Delta in your very own house. Your dog can feel right at home, and nothing makes her happier than having you home all the time. Just remember that, as on land, you have to walk your dog—only you have to dock to do it. Call the Rio Vista Chamber of Commerce at (707) 374-2700 for information on houseboat rentals in the Delta.

ROCKVILLE

PARKS, BEACHES & RECREATION AREAS
• **Rockville Hills Recreation Center** 🐾 🐾 🐾

Hike, fish and enjoy nature in this 500-acre park filled with trees and trails. The main trail is fairly steep and takes you to the top of the park, where you'll find two small ponds for fishing. After this hike on a summer afternoon, many dogs jump in when they reach the summit. A man told me that a small beagle once disappeared for several seconds and came up with a tiny fish flailing in her mouth. Could this be just another flagrant flailing fish story?

Once you enter the park, you're safe from traffic. But dogs are supposed to be leashed anyway, since the park is officially run by the city of Fairfield, which has a strict leash law. Check out the nature trail that a local Eagle Scout troop has created.

For the most vigorous workout, try the main trail. It's the one that bends slightly to the left and up a steep hill as you enter from the parking lot. The park is often desolate, so use judgment about hiking alone.

It's on Rockville Road, just west of Suisun Valley Road. (707) 428-7433. ➤ *See #6 on map p. 308.*

SUISUN CITY

PARKS, BEACHES & RECREATION AREAS
• **Grizzly Island Wildlife Area** 🐾 🐾 🐾 🐾 🐾

This is what dogs have been praying for since they started living in cities: 8,600 acres of wide-open land where they can run—leashless—among the sort of wildlife you see only in PBS specials.

This sprawling wetland, in the heart of the Suisun Marsh, is home to an amazing array of fauna including: tule elk, river otters, waterfowl of every type, jackrabbits, white pelicans and peregrine falcons.

Of course, walking in marshy areas has its pros and cons. But you don't have to get muddy feet here; the landscapes are as varied as the animal life. Dry upland fields are plentiful. You can also canoe down a slough with your steady dog or hike on dozens of dirt trails. Many folks bring dogs here to train them for hunting, which brings us to the unfortunate subject of the park's schedule.

Because of hunting and bird-nesting seasons, Grizzly Island Wildlife Area is open for you and your dog only between mid-January and March 1, July and early August, and part of September. (Call for exact dates. These are approximate and are subject to change.)

If your dog helps you hunt for elk, ducks or pheasant, she's allowed to join you during some of the hunting seasons. Department of Fish and Game staff also occasionally open small sections to people during the off-season, but it's unpredictable from one year to another when and if they'll do it. Even when the park is open, certain sections may be off-limits to dogs. Check with staff when you come in.

To get to the Grizzly Island Wildlife Area, exit Interstate 80 at Highway 12 heading toward Rio Vista. Turn onto Grizzly Island Road at the stoplight for the Sunset Shopping Center. Drive 10 miles, past farms, sloughs and marshes, until you get to the headquarters. You'll have to check in here and pay a $2.50 fee. Then continue driving to the parking lot nearest the area that you want to explore (staff can advise you). Don't forget your binoculars. (707) 425-3828. → See #7 on map p. 308.

VACAVILLE

PARKS, BEACHES & RECREATION AREAS

• Andrews Park 🐾 🐾 1/2

If you need a shopping cart, try this park first. For some reason, the creek that cuts through the west end of the park contains more shopping carts than most supermarkets.

The chunk of park to the east of the creek is graced with gentle rolling hills, picnic areas, barbecues, deciduous trees and a lawn as green and smooth as a golf course. But dogs must be leashed.

The west side of the creek is just a shady trail that officially stops at the first overpass and can get pretty seedy if you continue.

The best parking for the east side is on School Street, near Davis Street. For the west side of the creek, park in a lot at Kendal Street, off Dobbins Street. (707) 449-5390. → See #8 on map p. 308.

• **Lake Solano County Park** 🐾 🐾 1/2

It's no picnic here for dog owners. In fact, dogs aren't allowed in the picnic/day-use area at all. The only way to visit this isolated county park with a dog is to use the camping area across the street. It costs $12 per vehicle weekdays and $15 weekends during peak season, $10 weeklong during off-peak season, and $1 per dog—fares higher than the day-use section.

But for dogs who love to swim, it's worth the price of admission. The big freshwater lake here is an ideal respite on a hot summer day. Dogs are allowed off leash for swimming—and only for swimming. There are a couple of narrow trails along the shore, but they're very short.

The camping here is typical "pack 'em in" camping. Sites are so close together you can hear your neighbors unzip their sleeping bags. But if you scout it out, you may be able to nab a site that has a little more privacy. There are even a few sites on the lake. There are 50 sites, with fees ranging from $10 to $15 a night.

Don't forget to bring proof of rabies vaccination for your dog. This can be his certificate or just his up-to-date tag. The park is at Highway 128 and Pleasant Valley Road, about five miles west of Interstate 505. For park info or to make camping reservations, call (916) 795-2990. ➡ *See #9 on map p. 308.*

FESTIVALS

Onion Festival: You're allowed to bring your dog to this onion lover's extravaganza (as if she didn't have bad enough breath already!), but she must be left with SPCA dogsitters volunteering at the gate. They'll keep your dog comfortably shaded from the September sun, and provide lots of water and companionship. Call (707) 448-4613 for this year's dates.

PLACES TO STAY

Lake Solano County Park camping: See above.

Best Western Heritage Inn: Only very small dogs are allowed here. Don't try to pass your Saint Bernard off as a lap dog, even if he is your lap dog. Rates are $42 to $48. 1420 East Monte Vista Avenue, Vacaville, CA 95688; (707) 448-8453.

Gandydancer RV Park: The office here is made up of old cabooses. It's situated among groves of eucalyptus trees. Sites are $16. Dogs must be leashed. Take Interstate 80 to the Midway exit. 4933 Midway Road, Vacaville, CA 95688; (707) 446-7679.

DIVERSIONS

Eat, drink and look in strange mirrors: Most people who visit the Nut Tree come here for the shopping or the Western-style cuisine. But dogs and their people visit exclusively to enjoy the unusual array of activities in front of this giant complex.

Vain dogs get offended, but most dogs seem highly amused by the funhouse mirrors perched on the restaurant's outer wall. From one moment to the next, your dog becomes fat and thin and distorted beyond belief. (Joe was initially taken aback. Cautiously, he sniffed behind the mirror to see what horrible creature lurked on the other side of the glass. Then he got brave and started barking at his image. A dalmation/basset hound mix joined him with howls and pranced back and forth, never taking his eyes off his reflection.)

Some dogs pass the time watching the mini-train steam its passengers around the grounds of the Nut Tree. Others like to romp in the shaded, grassy portion that runs parallel to the parking lot. But all dogs love at least one of the many outdoor food concessions in front of the restaurant.

The Sandwich Garden offers dozens of shaded tables and live entertainment on weekends, weather permitting. There are also ice cream shacks, places to buy popcorn, cookies and drinks, and plentiful benches.

If your dog doesn't like crowds, you may want to avoid the Nut Tree on weekends and during school breaks. But even in the busiest times, there's always an empty spot of grass.

Exit Interstate 80 at Monte Vista Avenue. Open 7 a.m. to 9 p.m. daily. You can't miss it. (707) 448-1818.

VALLEJO

PARKS, BEACHES & RECREATION AREAS

• Dan Foley Park 🐾 🐾 🐾

You won't often see this at Marine World Africa USA—professional waterskiers practicing their acts over sloping jumps, then landing head first in the water when everything doesn't work out perfectly.

You and your dog will be treated to this unpolished spectacle if you visit this park on the right day. The park is directly across Lake Chabot from Marine World, so you get to witness a good chunk of the goings-on there. Since dogs aren't allowed at Marine World, this is an ideal place to walk them if your kids are spending a few hours with more exotic animals. You still get to hear the sound of jazz bands and the roar of amazed crowds.

Dan Foley Park is so well maintained we initially were afraid it was a golf course. Willows and pines on rolling hills provide cooling shade, and there's usually a breeze from the lake. Leashed dogs are invited everywhere but the water. Even humans aren't supposed to swim in it. Picnic tables are located right across from the waterski practice area, so if your dog wants entertainment with his sandwich, this is the place.

The park is on Camino Alto North just east of Tuolumne Street. There is a $1 parking fee. (707) 648-4600. →*See #10 on map p. 308.*

• River Park 🐾 🐾 🐾

With goldenrod as high as an elephant's eye and a preponderance of low brush, this waterfront park looks like a huge abandoned lot. That's actually one of its charms—you don't have to worry about your dog mowing over children in a playground or digging up a plug of green grass. The only park-like features here are a couple of benches along the Mare Island Strait.

A wide dirt path leads you toward the water and far from traffic danger. Unfortunately, the leash law is in effect here. And unless your dog is inclined to wade through several yards of mucky marsh to get to the water, he's not going to go swimming. It's still fun to walk along the water and watch the ships at the Mare Island Naval Shipyard across the strait. One ship looks straight out of central casting for *McHale's Navy*. (Visit before this military base is closed for good, as it's slated to be soon.)

There are two entry points. If you're driving, use the south entrance on Wilson Avenue, just north of Hichborn Street, which has a small parking lot. Otherwise, you can enter at Wilson Avenue just across the street from Sims Avenue. (707) 648-4600. →*See #11 on map p. 308.*

• The Wharf 🐾 🐾 🐾

This is the place for hip Vallejo dogs and it's not even an official park. The paved path along the Mare Island Strait looks toward the Mare Island Naval Shipyard on the other side of the strait. There's a real nautical atmosphere here.

It's also the perfect place to take your dog while you're waiting for your ship to come in: This is where the Vallejo-San Francisco ferry stops.

There's a substantial strip of grass beside the path where dogs like to take frequent breaks. Here, they can socialize without getting under joggers' sneakers. Leashes are a must.

The wharf area covers almost the entire length of Mare Island Way, starting around the Vallejo Yacht Club. Your best bet is to park at the public parking area of the ferry terminal. (707) 648-4600. →*See #12 on map p. 308.*

RESTAURANTS

Gumbah's Beef Sandwiches: Here's the beef. If your dog is your lunch partner, this meaty place is where he'll ask to go. Dine at the tables out front. 138 Tennessee Street; (707) 648-1100.

Sardine Can: Get a view of the strait while you eat some of the freshest seafood available. Dogs get great treatment here, including a big bowl of water. Dine at the two outdoor tables. It's at 0 (as in zero) Harbor Way; (707) 553-9492.

PLACES TO STAY

Best Western Royal Bay Inn: Rates are $30 to $55. Dogs are $5 extra. 44 Admiral Callaghan Lane, Vallejo, CA 94591; (707) 643-1061.

Holiday Inn—Marine World Africa USA: While the kids are being entertained by dolphins and big cats at the nearby theme park, you and your dog can curl up, read a book and enjoy the peace. Rates are $55 to $80. Dogs are $25 extra. 1000 Fairgrounds Drive, Vallejo, CA 94590; (707) 644-1200.

Ramada Inn: Rates are $61 to $98. Dogs cost $20 extra. 1000 Admiral Callaghan Lane, Vallejo, CA 94591; (707) 643-2700.

FESTIVALS

Whaleboat Regatta: Enjoy live entertainment, food and crafts at the fair celebrating the annual race of these big, old, eight-person rowboats. It's sponsored by the California Maritime Academy and is usually held along the waterfront during the first weekend in October. For this year's dates, call (707) 648-4216.

SACRAMENTO COUNTY

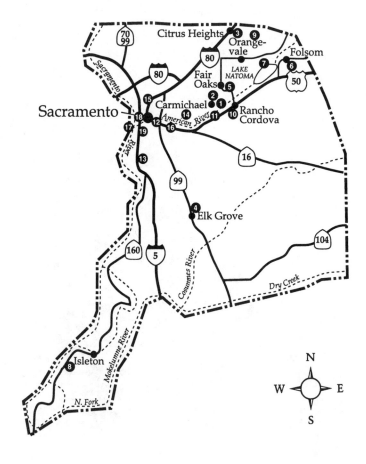

31
SACRAMENTO COUNTY

The American River Parkway is one of the finest county park systems I've come across. This riverside greenbelt extends 23 miles from Discovery Regional Park to Folsom Lake, encompassing 20 recreation areas and 5,000 acres. A bike trail connects it all together.

If your dog were a bike, you'd be all set.

Unfortunately, dogs aren't allowed on the bike trails here. They're also banned from the numerous horse trails. That leaves them with a few small hiking trails, plenty of open land and the riverbank. It's not a bad fate, but it could be much better. Three of the American River Parkway recreation areas are described in this chapter. For more information, call the county Parks Department at (916) 366-2061.

If you and your dog have a hankering to visit the state capitol building together, you'll get as close as the front door before you're ushered away. But it's more attractive from the outside anyway.

The park surrounding the capitol (called Capitol Park, strangely enough—see page 327) is an exquisite place, with hundreds of trees from around the world. If you're tired of high taxes and crooked politicians, you'll get vicarious pleasure watching your he-dog do leg lifts here.

Dogs who like alternative modes of transportation enjoy this county. Sacramento's historic district is the base for an enchanting horse-and-buggy ride that welcomes dogs (see Diversions, page 331). And in Folsom, it's "all aboard" for dogs who want to ride on an old-style miniature steam train (see Diversions, page 325). These entertaining asides don't make up for the lack of leash-free parks in Sacramento County, but chances are they'll bring a grin to your dog's snout.

CARMICHAEL

PARKS, BEACHES & RECREATION AREAS

• **Ancil Hoffman Park** 🐾 🐾 🐾 1/2

This 393-acre park is part of the grand American River Parkway. It has plenty of wooded areas for dogs who like to sniff trees and dozens of acres of open grassy land.

Our favorite part is toward the back of the park, near the picnic area. This section is full of shade trees, and sports a wonderful dirt trail along the upper banks of the American River. It's also where you can easily access the river. When we visited, a few folks were picnicking at the tables above, but not a soul (canine or human) was down by the river. If you don't mind walking on small, smooth rocks, you can have a good riverside hike. Dogs are supposed to be leashed, but water dogs have no problem taking a short dip. And as with all county parks, dogs are not permitted on any bike or horse trails.

A $4 vehicle entry fee is usually charged. You can park at an outside street and walk in fee-free if you don't mind a bit of a hike. From Fair Oaks Boulevard, drive east on Kenneth Avenue a few blocks, south on California Avenue one block, then east again on Tarshes Drive, into the park. (916) 366-2061. ➔*See #1 on map p. 320.*

•**Carmichael Park** 🐾 🐾
This is a flat park with some shade trees for those warmer days. It's a pretty good size for a morning stroll with your leashed beast. The park is at Fair Oaks Boulevard and Grant Avenue. (916) 485-5322. ➔*See #2 on map p. 320.*

RESTAURANTS
Made Rite Hamburgers: Eat burgers and barbecued meats with your drooling dog at the covered patio. 7836 Fair Oaks Boulevard; (916) 944-7180.

CITRUS HEIGHTS
PARKS, BEACHES & RECREATION AREAS
•**Rusch Community Park** 🐾 🐾 1/2
When a park is made up mostly of ball fields, it doesn't bode well for dogs. But this park has some pretty, tree-filled land on the edges of its recreational sections. The ball fields themselves are enclosed, so if you have dog who's an escape artist, it's a good place to exercise him.

A winding cement path leads you around the park. Dogs must be leashed. Exit Interstate 80 at Antelope Road and drive east to Rosswood Drive. Turn left on Rosswood, and within a block, turn right on Busch Drive. Park in the lot. (916) 725-1585. ➔*See #3 on map p. 320.*

ELK GROVE
PARKS, BEACHES & RECREATION AREAS
•**Elk Grove County Park** 🐾 🐾
This 125-acre park is much better for people than for dogs. If you bring a dog, you'll have to avoid 12 busy ball fields, a pool, a

horse arena, soccer fields and a playground. What's left is a paved pathway that winds through green grassy areas. You and your dog can frolic on the grass, or sit under a tree or near the little lake and read *Call of the Wild* together. It's about as close to wilderness as you're going to get in this very developed park. Here's a real surprise: Dogs must be leashed.

The vehicle entry fee is $4, but if you walk in or get here before or after rangers are working the entry station, you can avoid that fee. The entry is on Elk Grove-Florin Road, just off Highway 99. (209) 366-2061. ➡️*See #4 on map p. 320.*

FAIR OAKS

PARKS, BEACHES & RECREATION AREAS

•**Fair Oaks Park** 🐾 🐾 1/2

Dogs run around here with frisbees in their drooling mouths, but since they're supposed to be leashed, they can't go too far. The park has some rolling hills and trees. If you're going to be waiting for someone at the library located on the park grounds, it's a fine place to bring your dog.

The park entrance is on Fair Oaks Boulevard at Temple Park Drive. (916) 966-1036. ➡️*See #5 on map p. 320.*

RESTAURANTS

Java Java: People come here for a variety of gourmet coffees, but the place is really known for its mochas. Try one at an umbrella-topped table while your dog snoozes at your feet. 5262 Sunrise Boulevard; (916) 863-0201.

Sunflower Drive-In Restaurant: We love this natural foods drive-in. So do many other people, judging by the crowds it attracts. You and your dog can eat a variety of healthful, tasty dishes at the two picnic tables here, but watch out for the chickens who like to hang out. If the tables aren't available, just walk next door to Village Park and eat at one of the picnic tables there. At least the chickens won't be hen-pecking you. 10344 Fair Oaks Boulevard; (916) 967-4331.

FOLSOM

Thanks in part to Johnny Cash, most folks who aren't from the area know of Folsom because of the imposing Folsom State Prison.

But this is a charming Gold Rush town, which boasts in its motto that it's "Where the West Came and Stayed." A walk down historic Sutter Street will prove this slogan right. The wealth of antique shops, art galleries and restaurants make it a popular place for tourists. Grab a tasty lunch with your dog at Taste of the Rainbow (see page 325) and make an afternoon of it.

•**Folsom City Park** 🐾 🐾

If you and your dog are with a friend who's visiting the unusual gift shop (or an inmate) at the Folsom State Prison, this is the perfect place to wait. It's next door to the maximum security prison grounds. Even though your dog must be leashed, she'll feel free compared with the folks inside that gray granite structure.

The park is flat and grassy, with ball fields, playgrounds, picnic areas and a zoo (which is not the most appealing place, if the sight of wild animals in small cages bothers you). Dogs can't go to the zoo, but they revel in sniffing the air that wafts out of it.

Dogs here get a real bonus—they get to ride a mini-steam train. If you have a train-loving pooch, see Diversions, page 325. The park is at East Natoma and Stafford streets. (916) 355-7285. ➜ *See #6 on map p. 320.*

•**Folsom Lake State Recreation Area** 🐾 🐾 🐾 1/2

The bulk of this 12,000-acre reservoir is located in Placer and El Dorado counties, but its Folsom entrance is popular and easy to find. With four million visitors every year, this park is one of the busiest recreational lakes in the state park system.

Fortunately, that doesn't stop the rangers from permitting leashed pooches on the 80 miles of trails here. The farther you get from the water, the better, at least during crowded months. It can get really crazy around the lake. The operative word here is *party*. But the hiking and horse trails that meander through the recreation area should give you and your dog a little peace.

You'll wander through valley oaks, oracle oaks, digger pines and toyon here. In the spring, wildflowers are everywhere. You'll see Indian paintbrush, California poppy and countless other colorful varieties. It's the best time to visit this park, because it's usually not too crowded or hot.

Bring your binoculars. You may come across such winged beauties as quail, grebes, red-tailed hawks and eagles. Many are visible from the lake's edge. Dogs aren't allowed on the swim beaches here, but with 75 miles of shoreline (when full), you're bound to find a few lakeside spots. You might even want to try your paw at fishing, which can be mighty good here.

The day-use fee is $5 per vehicle. Camping at one of the 182 sites costs $12 to $14. Dogs are $1 extra. All sites are available on a first-come, first-served basis, except in summer, when reservations are required. Call MISTIX at (800) 444-PARK to reserve a site. There are many ways to access the park. To get to the park headquarters from the town of Folsom, go a couple of miles north on Folsom-Auburn Road. (916) 988-0205. →*See #7 on map p. 320.*

RESTAURANTS

Taste of the Rainbow: This coffeehouse welcomes dogs to eat with their owners at the handmade outdoor tables on this historic street. And the eating is good, with homemade soups, quiche, scones and a vast variety of coffee drinks. 611 Sutter Street; (916) 355-1903.

DIVERSIONS

Get steamed together: The folks who run the miniature steam train at City Park boast that it's the only coal-fired locomotive that runs a regular schedule west of the Rockies. They're also proud that it may soon be the largest miniature railroad (is that like jumbo shrimp?) in the United States. The ride, now one mile long, could become a three-miler soon, if all goes as planned.

Regardless of all these records, dogs love this train. That's partly because Terry Gold, the train's engineer, loves dogs. "We've had Saint Bernards, Great Danes, all kinds of dogs," says Gold. "We've never had a problem. They have the best time. It's so much fun to watch their faces."

If the train looks familiar to you, you probably visited Berkeley's Tilden Park between 1950 and 1970. It's the very same one-third-scale, narrow-gauge locomotive that was so popular there for two decades before Tilden's new train came along. The Folsom train was built in 1950, but was modeled after a train that ran around 1875.

Dogs and their people get to ride in the open-air cattle cars, gondolas and hopper cars. The ride takes about 10 minutes and costs $1 per human. Dogs go free. The train runs Tuesday through Sunday. It's in City Park, at East Natoma and Stafford streets. Call for a schedule. (916) 355-7285.

ISLETON

PARKS, BEACHES & RECREATION AREAS

• **Brannan Island State Recreation Area** 🐾 🐾 1/2

Most people come to this Delta haven to fish or windsurf. Those activities may not be among your dog's favorites, but even if your dog is not the sporting sort, this park is pleasing enough. You and your dog can dip your paws in a cool slough, walk around open grassy land (on leash), or picnic in the shade of a eucalyptus. If you get tired, you can just saunter back to your tent and take a nap. It's a dog's life.

The day-use fee is $5. They have 102 campsites. Fees are $12. Dogs are $1 extra. Reservations are required in summer and on holiday weekends. From Highway 160 a few miles south of Isleton, go east at the signs for the park. Call MISTIX at (800) 444-PARK to reserve a campsite. For park info, call (916) 777-6671. →*See #8 on map p. 320.*

ORANGEVALE

PARKS, BEACHES & RECREATION AREAS

One of the movers and shakers in this city has been trying to get some land devoted to a dog park, where dogs can run leash-free in an enclosed area. Last we'd heard, she'd given up for a while. But if you hear any rumblings about the issue, check with the parks department to find out what you can do to help. Such a park is long overdue in this county.

•**Orangevale Community Park** 🐾 🐾 🐾

The northwest corner of this park looks more like it belongs in the northwest corner of the United States. It's wild, and filled with trees and tiny dirt trails. It's not a huge area, but it's far enough from the more civilized parts of this park that you and your dog might actually feel as if you're in a rural setting (for at least 30 seconds, until the tennis courts or the street comes into view).

Enter the park on Hazel Avenue. The parking lot entrance is south of Oak Avenue. (916) 989-0266. →*See #9 on map p. 320.*

RANCHO CORDOVA

PARKS, BEACHES & RECREATION AREAS

•**Community Park Two** 🐾 🐾

This is a flat and grassy park with a name about as creative and unusual as the park itself. It's a good place to visit if your leashed dog needs the basics and you just don't feel like paying $4 to get into Goethe Park (see below).

Exit Highway 50 at Sunrise Boulevard and drive north a few short blocks to Zinfandel Drive. Turn left, drive a few blocks and turn right on Benita Drive. Take your first right, Mapola Way, and you're there. (916) 362-1841. →*See #10 on map p. 320.*

•**Goethe Park** 🐾 🐾 🐾

This chunk of the American River Parkway has a dirt trail that runs along a segment of bank above the American River. It's one of the few trails here where dogs are actually permitted. All county parks ban dogs from bike trails and equestrian trails—and this one has both in abundance. In fact, it's not easy to get around here without them.

You'll find some very well-shaded picnic areas here, but they don't make up for the lack of legally walkable places.

The vehicle fee is $4. You can park on the street a few blocks from the entrance and get in for free. Boat launching will cost you $8. Exit Highway 50 at Bradshaw Road, head north and follow the signs to the park. (916) 366-2061. →*See #11 on map p. 320.*

PLACES TO STAY

Comfort Inn: Rates are $49 to $74. A $100 pooch deposit is required. 3240 Mather Field Road, Rancho Cordova, CA 95670; (916) 363-3344.

Economy Inns of America: The rooms that are set aside for pets here face the highway. (Only the best for dogs!) This inn is located about a mile from the American River. Rates are $35 to $43. 12249 Folsom Boulevard, Rancho Cordova, CA 95670; (916) 351-1213.

SACRAMENTO

This is a capital place to have a dog who doesn't mind being on a leash. In addition to the 23-mile American River Parkway, which begins in Sacramento (see page 321), the city has some real dog-pleasing parks of its own. The restaurants with outdoor tables aren't bad either.

PARKS, BEACHES & RECREATION AREAS

• Capitol Park 🐾 🐾 🐾 👟

Your boy dog will be overwhelmed if you bring him here for the Capitol Park Tree Tour. It's a self-guided tour of this 40-acre park's magnificent assemblage of trees, which represent the continents and climates of the world. On the tour brochure, each tree is numbered, and its scientific and common names are given. So when your leashed dog sniffs at or does a leg lift on a dawn redwood tree, you can impress him by saying, "That's quite a Metasequoia glyptostroboides, eh Spot?"

The park extends from the front of the state capitol building to several blocks behind it. It's a great excuse to get up close and personal with the capitol. Take a picnic and relax under the shade of a Calocedrus decurrens (incense cedar).

Warning: If your dog is anything like Joe, you may not want to bring him here. Squirrels are everywhere. He pulled my arm so hard I thought I wouldn't be able to drive home. And the squirrels are probably still talking about the loud howling shrieks that emanated from this refined-looking Airedale's face.

The park runs from the capitol back to 15th Street, between L and N streets. Call (916) 324-0333 to receive a tree-tour brochure. →See #12 on map p. 320.

• Chorley Park 🐾🐾🐾 1/2

If you and your dog are waiting to pick up a loved one at Sacramento's Executive Airport, a visit to this nearby park is a wonderful way for your dog to expend some energy so she won't maul the homecomer with jumps of adulation.

This park is a real find. At first it looks just like so many other neighborhood parks, with a small playground and a little grassy area. But as you walk in, you'll see that it has the potential to be Land of the Dogs. The back of the park is extremely wide, far from traffic, and fenced from the adjacent golf course. Tall firs provide some shade. During wet months, there's even a tiny creek back here.

Even when we've visited on beautiful Saturday mornings, the place has been empty. If it stays this way, it's actually a better place to visit than many of the sprawling county parks, which get heavier use and charge a fee. Dogs are supposed to be leashed here.

Exit Interstate 5 at Florin Road and drive east just a little more than a mile to 20th Street and turn left. Drive to the end and park on the street just outside the park. (916) 277-6060. →See #13 on map p. 320.

• Del Paso Park 🐾🐾🐾

This park is a real find if you have reason to walk your dog near the McClellan Air Force Base or the American River College. Leashed dogs like the horse trail that runs in the back of the park by Arcade Creek.

A couple of smaller dirt trails branch off from the main trail, and they're fun to try, especially if there are too many horses on the main path for your dog's taste (or if your dog likes the taste of horse manure). A shaded picnic area adds a different culinary dimension to the park.

Exit Interstate 80 at Watt Avenue and drive south to Auburn Boulevard. Turn left on Auburn Boulevard and drive a little less than a half mile to Bridge Road. Park past the ball field, and you'll see the trail. (916) 277-6060. →See #14 on map p. 320.

• Discovery Regional Park 🐾🐾🐾

Lots of leashed urban dogs stroll down here for their early evening walks, dragging their work-weary people behind them. The park has 275 acres of green open space, and although much of it is devoted to human activities like archery and softball, there's more than enough room for your average dog to take an average walk. It's nothing your dog will write home about, but since he can't write anyway, it's no fur off his back.

Unfortunately, because it's a county park, dogs are not permitted on the equestrian trails or the bike path here. That cuts down on easy walking. But the park is well-manicured, so there aren't any bushes or dense tree groves to get in your way. You won't want to let that leash slip out of your hand here, as roads wind throughout the park.

Water dogs enjoy Discovery Regional Park because it's at the confluence of the American and Sacramento rivers. The banks are steep here, so it's hard to reach out and touch the rivers. But they sure do look good.

Many people walk here with their dogs and avoid the $4 entry fee that is occasionally charged. If you're driving from the north end of the city, take Highway 5 to the Garden Highway, drive east and take the first road to the right, Discovery Park Road. (916) 366-2061. ➡See #15 on map p. 320.

• **McKinley Park** 🐾🐾 1/2
You can tell lots of dogs visit here just by the signs everywhere. They shout at you to clean up after your dog.

The park has 38 acres of picnic tables, grassy fields, baseball diamonds and tennis courts. It's at H Street and Alhambra Boulevard, just east of the business loop of Interstate 80. (916) 277-6060. ➡See #16 on map p. 320.

• **Miller Park/Sacramento Marina** 🐾🐾 1/2
You and your leashed dog can stroll along a path overlooking the marina here or picnic under big shade trees while you watch the mighty Sacramento River flow by. You can dip your paws in or even do some casting for your supper. It's a very relaxing way to spend a dog-day afternoon.

Drive west to the end of Broadway (past all the lovely refinery tanks) and turn left on Marina View Drive. (916) 277-6060. ➡See #17 on map p. 320.

• **Southside Park** 🐾🐾 1/2
Water dogs grimace here, but the truth is that the little lake is fenced off and shows no signs of being made accessible. About the only way to take a dip here is with a fishing pole.

Landlubbing dogs think this is a decent park. There's plenty of shade, grass and walkways to keep a leashed dog happy. There's even a fitness course so dogs can keep their youthful figures.

The park is about eight blocks south of the capitol, at T and 8th streets. (916) 277-6060. ➤*See #18 on map p. 320.*

•**William Land Park** 🐾 🐾 🐾

As you enter this 236-acre park, you may be struck by the thought that it looks just like a golf course. Now hold onto that thought and look around very carefully. See those shiny sticks glimmering in the background, and those people in white-and-green outfits walking forward at a determined pace or standing around scratching their heads? Those are golfers. Joe, Nisha and I learned this the hard way one day when we bounded out of our car and directly into the line of fire of a golfer quite some distance away. Nisha immediately tried to eat the ball. It was not a walk I care to remember, nor, I'm sure, was it a game the golfer remembers fondly.

The golf course is not fenced off from most of the rest of the park, so you really do have to be careful here. A safe, shaded section of the park is the north end. Since dogs must be leashed, it doesn't matter that a couple of little roads run fairly close. If you brought along the kids and someone to watch them, they can go explore the zoo and the amusement park located on the other side of the park.

You can access the park's north side by taking Riverside Boulevard (parallel to Interstate 5) to 12th Avenue and turning east. (916) 277-6060. ➤*See #19 on map p. 320.*

RESTAURANTS

Cafe La Salle: This restaurant is located in charming Old Sacramento (a.k.a. "Old Sac"). Dine with your dog on the terrace, enjoying American-French cuisine and gourmet coffees. 1028 Second Street; (916) 442-4775.

Capitol Garage Coffee Company: Pooches and their human partners come here all the time to enjoy the ambience and great food. Ask Jim or George, the owners, about the dog-friendly bookstore nearby. 1427 L Street; (916) 444-3633.

Kane Coffee Company: This fine coffee cafe is located directly across the street from beautiful Capitol Park (see page 327). Dogs can watch you become caffeinated at the outdoor tables. 1007 L Street; (916) 447-8855.

New Helvetia Roasters and Bakers: Talk about dog-friendly! This place even has a dog biscuit dispenser. And your dog won't even have to have a dime or quarter to use it. Dogs like to join their people when they dine outside in the little courtyard. Try the foccacia. 1215 19th Street; (916) 441-1106.

A Shot of Class: Dine on fine continental cuisine at the outdoor tables, right in the heart of Sacramento. 1120 11th Street; (916) 447-5340.

PLACES TO STAY

Beverly Garland Hotel: Rates are $55 to $95. Huge dogs require a deposit. 1780 Tribute Road, Sacramento, CA 95815; (916) 929-7900.

Canterbury Inn: Rates are $55 to $65. You must leave a $100 deposit for your dog. 1900 Canterbury Road, Sacramento, CA 95815; (916) 927-3492.

Crossroads Inn: If you want to splurge, you can get a room here with a sauna or a Jacuzzi. Rates are $38 to $100. Small pets only, please, and they require a $20 deposit. 221 Jibboom Street, Sacramento, CA 95814; (916) 442-7777.

Howard Johnson Hotel: Rates are $60 to $65. Dogs require a $50 deposit in case of doggy indiscretions. 3343 Bradshaw Road, Sacramento, CA 95827; (916) 366-1266.

La Quinta Inn: Rates are $52 to $68. Dogs require a $25 deposit. 200 Jibboom Street, Sacramento, CA 95814; (916) 448-8100.

Motel 6: Rates are $30 for the first adult, $6 for the second. All Motel 6s permit one small pooch per room. 1415 30th Street, Sacramento, CA 95816; (916) 457-0777.

Radisson Hotel: Some rooms here provide a water dog with views of the ultimate temptation—a small lake on the hotel's property. But sorry, dogs. No paddling is allowed around here. Rates are $72 to $82. Dogs require a $50 deposit. 500 Leisure Lane, Sacramento, CA 95815; (916) 922-2020.

Red Lion Hotel: Rates are $82 to $143. 2001 Point West Way, Sacramento, CA 95815; (916) 929-8855.

Sacramento Hilton Inn: Rates are $100 to $250. There's a $25 pooch deposit. 2200 Harvard Street, Sacramento, CA 95815; (916) 922-4700.

DIVERSIONS

A moveable beast: If you and your dog want to get a feel for Sacramento before you start exploring on your own, Joe highly recommends a carriage ride through the charming old part of town.

The folks who run the Top Hand Ranch carriage company are more than happy to take you and your well-behaved dog on a carriage tour around the quainter section of Sacramento. As long as your dog doesn't interfere with the horse who's pulling this old-style carriage, he'll be welcome on any of the rides offered by Top Hand Ranch.

You'll find the carriage somewhere on the streets of Old Sacramento just about every day, and on weekend nights. The price for a 10- to 15-minute ride is $10 for a small family (including a dog). For a higher fee, you can arrange to go just about anywhere in the carriage. The capitol building is a frequent request. That tour takes roughly one hour and will cost you about $50. Call (916) 655-3444 for locations and prices.

CONTRA COSTA COUNTY

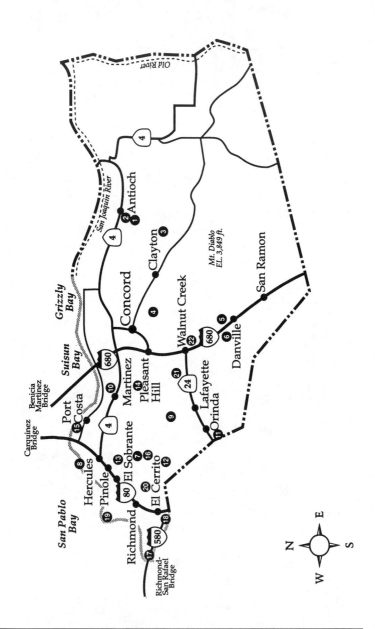

32
CONTRA COSTA COUNTY

Although much of Contra Costa County is considered a sleepy bedroom community for San Francisco, it's a rip-roaring frontier-land of fun for dogs.

From the renowned off-leash dog haven of Point Isabel Regional Shoreline (see page 345) to the leash-free inland nirvanas such as the Morgan Territory (see page 337), this county enables every dog to have her day, day after day.

For dogs who like long hikes through highly diverse lands, 10 long regional trails lace Lafayette, Walnut Creek and the other urban areas of the Diablo Valley. There are 60 miles of trails in all, linking together a dozen towns and many beautiful parklands. Dogs must be leashed, but with all the horses and bikes that can visit here, it's a sensible rule.

The Briones to Diablo Regional Trail is one of the more popular trails. It's about 12 miles long, and it snakes through some terrific parkland, including the off-leash wonderlands of the Acalanes Ridge Open Space Recreation Area and the Shell Ridge Open Space Recreation Area (see page 348). The trail, which is part paved/part dirt, starts at Briones Regional Park's Lafayette Ridge Staging Area, located on Pleasant Hill Road just north of Highway 24.

The Contra Costa Canal Regional Trail is a good one for dogs who like to look at water but not set foot in it. Joe loves this 12-mile trail that follows the off-limits canal. For information and a trail map of all 10 regional trails, call (510) 635-0135.

ANTIOCH

Antioch is pretty much a desert for dogs, but south of town are two charming spots of relief.

PARKS, BEACHES & RECREATION AREAS

• **Black Diamond Mines Regional Preserve** 😊 😊 😊 😊 🐕

Leash-free dogs, especially leash-free dogs of the male persuasion, think this park is an excellent place to visit. The coal miners who worked and lived here in the 1860s and 1870s planted a variety of drought-tolerant trees not usually found in the East Bay, including something called trees of heaven. Dogs who sniff these trees seem to know why they're called "trees of heaven." Their noses just can't get enough as they press them deep into the bark.

The hills of Black Diamond Mines are jumbled and ragged, looking a lot like the Sierra foothills. From the parking lot, it's a moderate climb to the Rose Hill Cemetery, where Protestant Welsh miners (the tombstones bear the names Davis, Evans and Jenkins) buried victims of mine accidents and many of their children, who died of diphtheria, typhoid and scarlet fever.

Plenty of tunnel openings and piles of tailings have been preserved by the park for walkers to examine. A brochure marks mine sites. You should be alert for rattlers during warm seasons, although any rattler not actually snoozing will probably get out of your way before you even know he's near.

You can walk into this East Bay Regional Preserve from the Contra Loma Regional Park just below it (see next listing). But from that direction, the trails are too hot and dry for a dog in summer. Instead, enter from the north by car via Somersville Road and park in the last lot, which has some shady trees.

From Highway 4 at Antioch, exit at Somersville Road and drive south to the park entrance. Keep driving for a bit more than one mile if you want to park in the lot farthest in. You'll pass wonderful old mining-era houses and barns, now used as park headquarters and offices. (510) 635-0135. → *See #1 on map p. 334.*

• **Contra Loma Regional Park** 🐾 🐾

This 776-acre park is so well hidden amid barren hills north of Black Diamond Mines that you might not ever know it was here. A few attractive trails, including a trail leading into Black Diamond Mines Regional Preserve (see previous listing), rise into the surrounding hills for you and your leash-free dog to explore.

Unfortunately, as in all regional parks, your dog may not accompany you in the swimming area. Nor can he take an informal swim himself in the fishing areas, since the park managers want to protect his feet from stray fishhooks. It's probably better not to bring your dog here on a hot day. Instead, save the trip for winter or for spring, when the wildflowers burst open.

From Highway 4, take the Lone Tree Way exit. Go south on Lone Tree, then turn west on Fredrickson Lane to the entrance. The fee for parking is $3 or $4, depending on season. The dog fee is $1. (510) 635-0135. → *See #2 on map p. 334.*

CLAYTON

Stop in Clayton on the way to Morgan Territory and walk through its Old Town. You'll discover quite a few funky old Victorian buildings around Main Street. If you're lucky enough to be free on Wednesdays during the summer, the town holds a farmers market from May through October on Main Street from 3 p.m. to 8 p.m. You and the pooch can listen to music and buy fresh produce and flowers.

PARKS, BEACHES & RECREATION AREAS

• **Morgan Territory Regional Preserve** 🐾 🐾 🐾 🐾 ⬤ 🐕

Morgan Territory, named after a farmer who owned the land long before it became part of the East Bay Regional Parks System, is as far away from the Bay Area as you can get while still being in the Bay Area. From its heights, on a rim above the Central Valley, you see the San Joaquin River, the Delta, the valley and, on a clear day, the peaks of the Sierra. Eagles and hawks soar above as you and your leash-free pooch explore ancient twisted giant oaks and lichen-covered sandstone outcroppings below. Morgan Territory is close to the end of the earth, and well worth the journey.

One way to approach this faraway place with the strange-sounding name is through Clayton, but the preserve really isn't near any town. As the crow flies, it's equidistant from Clayton, Danville, San Ramon, Livermore, Byron and Brentwood. And "distant" is the key word.

This 2,164-acre preserve has miles of hiking and riding trails. If you don't want to climb much, but want great views of the Central Valley, try the Blue Oak Trail that starts at the entrance. You'll even see the "backside" of Mount Diablo. It's an unusual vantage point for Bay Area folks.

Most of the creeks are dry in the summer, though your dog can splash into cattle ponds, if he's so inclined. Watch for wicked foxtails in these grasses. These are the stickety widgets that help make veterinarians a well-off breed.

The easiest access is from Livermore in Alameda County: From Interstate 580 take the North Livermore Avenue exit and drive north on North Livermore; go left on Manning Road, then right onto Morgan Territory Road to the entrance. Or, for a longer but more picturesque drive: From the intersection of Highway 24 and Interstate 680 in Concord, exit at Ignacio Valley Road, go east on Clayton Road to Clayton and continue east on Marsh Road. Take a right on Morgan Territory Road to the entrance. (510) 635-0135.
➡ *See #3 on map p. 334.*

RESTAURANTS

Skipolini's Pizza: The folks here serve New York-style pizza, as well as salads and sandwiches. They welcome dogs at their outdoor tables. It's at Main Street and Diablo Road; (510) 672-5555.

CONCORD

PARKS, BEACHES & RECREATION AREAS

Most of Concord's parks are run-of-the-mill on-leash parks. But for a real treat, try this one:

•**Lime Ridge Open Space Recreation Area** 🐾🐾🐾🐾 🐕

This open space reserve is huge, sprawling across parts of both Walnut Creek and Concord. It's undeveloped and open to lucky leash-free dogs. You can sometimes find a creek, depending on time of year and status of drought, and that's a real relief during the long, hot summers here.

The only entry point from Concord is from the parking lot on Treat Boulevard west of Cowell Road. (510) 256-3560. ➡️ *See #4 on map p. 334.*

PLACES TO STAY

Best Western Heritage Inn: Rates are $60 to $65. Dogs are $50 extra. 4600 Clayton Road, Concord, CA 94521; (510) 686-4466.

Holiday Inn Concord: Rates are $60 to $95. 1050 Burnett Avenue, Concord, CA 94520; (510) 687-5500.

Sheraton Hotel and Conference Center: Rates are $75. 45 John Glenn Drive, Concord, CA 94520; (510) 825-7700.

DANVILLE

PARKS, BEACHES & RECREATION AREAS

•**Oak Hill Park** 🐾🐾 🦴

Oak Hill Park is a very clean, beautiful park run by the city of Danville. It's about as decent as a park designed for people can get. Among its human-oriented amenities are picnic tables, a pond with ducks and geese and waterfalls, volleyball and tennis courts, and an unusually attractive kids' play area with swings, a slide and its own waterfall.

The rest of the park—the part that dogs care about—is natural oak-studded hillside laced by an equestrian/hiking/exercise dirt trail. You can get an excellent view of Mount Diablo from here. Dogs enjoy this path, but must remain on-leash. They also can't wiggle their little tootsies in the pond.

At Stone Valley Road and Glenwood Court. (510) 820-6074. ➡️ *See #5 on map p. 334.*

•**Las Trampas Regional Wilderness** 🐾🐾🐾🐾 🐕

This regional wilderness is remarkable for its sense of isolation from the rest of the Bay Area. You can experience utter silence at this 3,298-acre park, and the views from the ridgetops are breathtaking.

Rocky Ridge Trail (from the parking lot at the end of Bollinger Canyon Road) takes you and your leash-free pooch on a fairly steep three-quarter-mile ascent to the top of the ridge, where you'll enter the East Bay Municipal Utility District watershed. Since dogs aren't allowed here, and permits are even required for humans, it's better to head west, on any of several trails climbing the sunny southern flanks of Las Trampas Ridge.

Creeks run low or dry during the summer, so bring plenty of water. Your dog should know how to behave around cattle, deer and horses.

From Interstate 680 about six miles north of the intersection with Interstate 580, take the Bollinger Canyon Road exit and head north on Bollinger Canyon Road to the entrance. (Go past the entrance to Little Hills Ranch Recreation Area, where dogs aren't allowed.) (510) 635-0135. ➡ *See #6 on map p. 334.*

PLACES TO STAY

Econolodge of Danville: Rates are $60 to $90. 803 Camino Ramon, Danville, CA 94526; (510) 838-8080.

EL SOBRANTE

• **Sobrante Ridge Regional Preserve** 🐾 🐾 🐾 🐾 🐕

Sobrante Ridge is such a well-kept secret that we might never have found our way without advice from kind rangers at Kennedy Grove. After a brief climb up a fire trail, through grass, dwarf manzanita, oaks and coyote brush, you and your leash-free dog have a choice of several ridgetop trails that don't loop. It's a tough choice, but someone's got to make it. Have your dog flip a coin or something.

This 277-acre preserve is the habitat of the extremely rare Alameda manzanita. Don't let your boy dog do anything the manzanitas wouldn't want him to do.

From Interstate 80 in Richmond, exit at San Pablo Dam Road, drive south to Castro Ranch Road. Turn left on Castro Ranch, then left at Conestoga Way, going into the Carriage Hills housing development. Take another left on Carriage Drive and a right on Coach Drive. Park at the end of Coach and walk into the preserve. Or from Pinole, exit Interstate 80 at Pinole Valley Road, south; Pinole Valley will become Alhambra Valley Road. Then bear right on Castro Ranch Road, and left on Conestoga Way. (510) 635-0135. ➡ *See #7 on map p. 334.*

HERCULES

PARKS, BEACHES & RECREATION AREAS

• **San Pablo Bay Regional Park** 🐾🐾🐾 1/2 🐕

This tiny, undeveloped East Bay Regional Park shoreline is just right if you happen to be in Hercules exploring the old Santa Fe Railroad yard. A paved trail runs about one-eighth of a mile along the tracks. New housing developments and interesting restored Victorian railroad workers' housing surrounds a small but pretty area of grass, swamp and eucalyptus trees. Best of all, you and your dog can check it all out without a leash.

If you follow Railroad Avenue to its end, across the line into Pinole, there's a very small and beautifully-landscaped city park behind the waste water treatment plant (which smells fresh as a rose). You must keep your dog on leash here.

From Interstate 80, exit at Pinole Valley Road and travel north. Pinole Valley Road becomes Tennent Avenue, then Railroad Avenue. Park somewhere around the Civic Arts Facility, a cluster of Victorian buildings in a grove of palms and eucalyptuses. Call (510) 724-9004 or (510) 635-0135. ➤*See #8 on map p. 334.*

LAFAYETTE

PARKS, BEACHES & RECREATION AREAS

• **Briones Regional Park** 🐾🐾🐾🐾 🦴 🐕

From both main entrances to this park, you can walk one-quarter of a mile and be lost in sunny, rolling hills or cool oak woodlands. Unless you stick to the stream areas, it's not a good park for hot summer days. But with a good supply of your own water, you and your dog, who may run blissfully leash-free, can walk gentle ups and downs all day on fire roads or foot trails.

The north entrance requires an immediate uphill climb into the hills, but you're rewarded with a quick view of Mount Diablo and the piping of ground squirrels, all of whom are long gone safely into their burrows by the time your dog realizes they might be fun to chase (much to Joe's chagrin). If your dog is a self-starter, this end of the park is fine for you. The Alhambra Creek Trail, which follows Alhambra Creek, does offer water in the rainy season. Stay away from the John Muir Nature Area (shaded on your brochure map), where dogs aren't allowed.

When we're feeling lazy, we prefer the south entrance at Bear Creek, just east of the inaccessible (to dogs) Briones Reservoir. Here you have an immediate choice of open hills or woodsy canyons, and the land is level for a few miles. The Homestead Valley Trail leads gently up and down through cool, sharp-scented bay and oak woodlands.

Watch for deer, horses and cattle. Some dogs near and dear to me (they shall remain nameless, Joe and Bill) love rolling in fresh cow patties—an additional hazard of the beasts existing in close proximity.

From Highway 24, take the Orinda exit; go north on Camino Pablo, then right on Bear Creek Road to Briones Road, to the park entrance. The parking fee is $3 and the dog fee is $1. (510) 635-0135. ➤*See #9 on map p. 334.*

RESTAURANTS
Geppetto's Cafe: Gourmet coffee, gelati and pastries may be enjoyed at sidewalk tables. Dogs are welcome. It's a good spot for a cool drink after a hot summer hike in Briones. 3563 Mount Diablo Boulevard; (510) 284-1261.

MARTINEZ
Martinez has a charming historic district right off the entrance to its regional shoreline park, so spend some time walking with your dog around the Amtrak station and antique shops. You'll see plenty of fellow strollers taking a break from the train.

PARKS, BEACHES & RECREATION AREAS
• **City of Martinez Hidden Lakes Open Space** 🐾 🐾 🐾
Although the city park called Hidden Valley Park doesn't allow dogs, the open space to the south of it does. It's crossed by one of the East Bay Regional Parks' trails (the California Riding and Hiking Trail) on its way from the Carquinez Strait Regional Shoreline to where it connects with the Contra Costa Canal Trail. (Call (510) 635-0135 to order a map of the Contra Costa Regional Trails.)

One entrance to Hidden Lakes is off Morello Avenue, where it intersects with Chilpancingo Parkway. (510) 313-0930. ➤*See #10 on map p. 334.*

ORINDA
PARKS, BEACHES & RECREATION AREAS
• **Robert Sibley Volcanic Regional Preserve** 🐾 🐾 🐾 🐾 🐕
We're not exactly talking Mount St. Helens here, but this 371-acre park has some pretty interesting volcanic history. Geologically-inclined dogs can wander leash-free as you explore volcanic dikes, mud flows, lava flows and other evidence of extinct volcanoes.

The preserve is actually closer to Oakland than Orinda, but it lies in Contra Costa County. From the entrance on Skyline Boulevard, you can get on the Skyline National Trail and walk north to Tilden Regional Park (see page 358 in the Alameda County chapter) or south to Redwood Regional Park (see page 372 in the Alameda County chapter). Or, for a shorter stroll, take the road to Round Top, the highest peak in the Berkeley Hills. Round Top is made up of volcanic debris left over from a 10-million-year-old volcano.

More attractive and less steep is the road to the quarries. It's partly paved and smooth enough for a wheelchair or stroller, but it becomes smooth dirt about halfway to the quarries. Both trails are labeled for geological features. (Pick up a brochure at the visitor center.) At the quarry pits, there's a good view of Mount Diablo. This is a dry, scrubby and cattle-grazed area, but in the rainy season your dog may be lucky enough to find swimming in a pit near the quarries. In the spring, look for poppies and lupines.

From Highway 24 east of the Caldecott Tunnel, exit on Fish Ranch Road and drive north to Grizzly Peak Boulevard, then take a left. Go south on Grizzly Peak to the intersection with Skyline Boulevard. Go left on Skyline. The entrance is just to the east of the intersection. (510) 635-0135. ➤ *See #11 on map p. 334.*

• **San Pablo Dam Reservoir** 🐾 🐾 🐾 1/2 🐾

This reservoir is a top fishing spot in the Bay Area. It's stocked with more trout than any lake in California. That's great news for humans, but dogs could care less. They're not allowed to set paw in this magnificent body of water (and neither are people), so hanging out alongside a human angler is almost out of the question. You can't even take your pooch out on your own boat.

The paved and dirt trails around the reservoir are lovely and often empty once you and your leashed dog wind into the hills. The dirt trails get rougher as you leave the popular fishing areas. You'll have to ford some creek beds or streams, and there's too much poison oak for comfort if your dog doesn't step daintily right down the middle of the trail. The trails are wild and woodsy, though, and dogs recommend them highly.

From Interstate 80, exit at San Pablo Dam Road and drive east about six miles. From Highway 24, exit at Camino Pablo/San Pablo Dam Road and go north about 5.5 miles. The entrance fee, year-round, is $4.50 for parking and $1 for dogs. You can buy a season ticket for $60 a car or $80 a boat. (510) 223-1661. ➤ *See #12 on map p. 334.*

PINOLE

PARKS, BEACHES & RECREATION AREAS

• **Pinole Valley Park** 🐾🐾🐾

This city park is fortunate enough to be contiguous with Sobrante Ridge Regional Preserve (see page 339). The paved bike path off to the right past the children's playground leads to Alhambra Creek—a good plunge for your dog, if he can negotiate the banks wearing a leash. The path then becomes a fire trail and ambles through brush, oaks and nicely varied deciduous trees. This trail is quite wild and litter-free. It ends at an outlet on Alhambra Road.

The entrance is at Pinole Valley Road and Simas Avenue. (510) 724-9062. → *See #13 on map p. 334.*

PLEASANT HILL

PARKS, BEACHES & RECREATION AREAS

• **Paso Nogal Park** 🐾🐾🐾🐾 🐕

This large park has smooth dirt trails along gentle oak-dotted slopes. Dogs must be on leash in the park, but the lawn area here is used as a leash-free dog run by locals. Owners are expected to carry a leash, clean up after their dogs (there are no scoopers available) and cooperate with park rangers if there's a complaint. But "no complaint, no problem" is the operable phrase here. At Morello Avenue and Paso Nogal Road. (510) 682-0896. → *See #14 on map p. 334.*

PORT COSTA

Port Costa is a sleepy, picturesque town of Victorian cottages. In the 19th century, it was a booming wheat export dock. Of course, if your dog remembers Frank Norris' book *The Octopus*, he already knows this.

PARKS, BEACHES & RECREATION AREAS

• **Carquinez Strait Regional Shoreline** 🐾🐾🐾🐾 🐕

This regional shoreline, run by the East Bay Regional Parks, lies just east of Crockett. From the Bull Valley Staging Area, on Carquinez Scenic Drive, you can choose one of two leash-free hillside trails. The Carquinez Overlook Loop, to the right, gives better views of Port Costa, the Carquinez Bridge and Benicia. We surprised a deer here sleeping in the shade of a clump of eucalyptus.

The eastern portion of the park, east of Port Costa, is contiguous with Martinez Regional Shoreline. But beware: You can't get there from here. (Carquinez Scenic Drive is closed at a spot between Port

Costa and Martinez. You must turn south on twisty McEwen Road to Highway 4 instead.)

To get to the Carquinez Strait Regional Shoreline from Interstate 80, exit at Crockett and drive east on Pomona Street through town. Pomona turns into Carquinez Scenic Drive, from which you'll see the staging area. (510) 635-0135. →See #15 on map p. 334.

RICHMOND

Point Richmond, the Richmond neighborhood tucked between the Richmond-San Rafael Bridge and Miller-Knox Regional Shoreline, is a cheerful small-town hangout for you and your dog. Consider stopping here for a snack on your way to some of the magical, four-paw shoreline here.

Sit on a bench in the Point Richmond Triangle, the town center. You'll be surrounded by nicely preserved Victorian buildings, the Hotel Mac and many delis and bakeries, some with outdoor tables. We were asked not to mention one by name because it welcomes cats as well as dogs. Grrrr. The Santa Fe Railroad rattles past periodically, blowing the first two notes of "Here Comes the Bride."

From Interstate 580, on the Richmond end of the Richmond-San Rafael Bridge, exit at Cutting Boulevard and drive west to town. Bear right on Richmond Avenue. The Triangle is at the intersection of Richmond, Washington Avenue and Park Place.

PARKS, BEACHES & RECREATION AREAS

•**Kennedy Grove Regional Recreation Area** 🐾 🐾 🐾

This is a large picnic and play area for folks who like softball, volleyball and horseshoes. Dogs must be leashed. A few short trails lead toward the San Pablo Dam. In the past, the East Bay Municipal Utility District unaccountably closed the connection between the jurisdictions, so you couldn't get to the reservoir trails from here. But apparently there has been some compromise and now the trails are open to dogs.

From Interstate 80, take the San Pablo Dam Road exit and go south; the entrance is a quarter-mile past the intersection of Castro Ranch Road. There's a $3 parking fee and $1 dog fee when the entrance is staffed on weekends and holidays. (510) 635-0135. →See #16 on map p. 334.

•**Miller-Knox Regional Shoreline** 🐾 🐾 🐾 🐾 1/2 🐕

Hooray! Wooooof! Yap! (The last utterance was from a dog-ette...the kind Joe likes to pretend is a cat.) Although your dog must be leashed in developed areas, she can run free on the hillside trails east of Dornan Drive in this 259-acre park.

West of Dornan is a generous expanse of grass, pine and euca-lyptus trees with picnic tables, a lagoon with egrets (so there's no swimming) and Keller Beach (dogs are prohibited). It's breezy here and prettier than most shoreline parks by virtue of its protecting gentle hills, whose trails offer terrific views of the Richmond-San Rafael Bridge, Mount Tamalpais, Angel Island and San Francisco. Ground squirrels stand right by their holes and pipe their alarms. Although you can't bring your dog onto Keller Beach, there's a paved path above it along riprap shoreline, where your dog can reach the water if he's so inclined. In the picnic areas, watch for discarded chicken bones!

You can also tour the Richmond Yacht Harbor by continuing on Dornan Drive south to Brickyard Cove Road, a left turn past the railroad tracks. Or, from Garrard Boulevard, drive south till you see the Brickyard Cove housing development. The paved paths lining the harbor offer views of yachts, San Francisco, Oakland and the Bay Bridge.

From either Interstate 80 or Interstate 580, exit at Cutting Boulevard and go west to Garrard Boulevard. Go left, pass through a tunnel and park in one of two lots off Dornan Drive. (510) 635-0135. →*See #17 on map p. 334.*

• **Point Isabel Regional Shoreline** 🐾 🐾 🐾 🐾 ✕

One exception to the East Bay Regional Parks' rule that dogs must be on leash in "developed" areas is Point Isabel Regional Shoreline. This is a decidedly unwild but terrific shoreline park with plenty of grass and paw-friendly paved paths. It's swarming with dogs. Unofficially, in fact, it's a dog park.

The large lawn area is designed for fetching, frisbee throwing and obedience training. People are often seen lobbing tennis balls for their expert retrievers, or hollering, "Hey! Run! Go!" at a dog like Joe who can't catch anything except an occasional cold. The dog owners police themselves and their dogs very effectively.

And owners, as in most parks frequented by dogs, love to socialize. Even the shyest person will feel brave enough to start a conversation with another dog owner. It's one of life's mysteries.

There are benches, picnic tables, restrooms, a water fountain for people and dogs, and many racks full of bags for scooping. A bulletin board posts lost-and-found dog notices, news of AARF (Area for Animals to Run Free) and its campaign for more open dog-run space, and membership information for the Point Isabel Dog Owners' Association, PIDO, which keeps the scooper dispens-ers full and otherwise looks out for dogs' interests in the park. If you're interested in volunteering or just want information, write to: Sylvia Schilb, 1321 Carlotta, Berkeley, CA 94703. Annual dues are $5 per family.

Cinder paths run along the riprap waterfront, where you can watch windsurfers against a backdrop of the Golden Gate and Bay bridges, San Francisco, the Marin Headlands and Mount Tamalpais. On a brisk day, a little surf even splashes against the rocks.

From Interstate 80 in Richmond, exit at Central Avenue and go west to the park entrance, next to the U.S. Postal Service Bulk Mail Center. (510) 635-0135. → *See #18 on map p. 334.*

•Point Pinole Regional Shoreline 🐾🐾🐾🐾 🐕‍🦺 🐕

Of all the East Bay Regional Parks' shorelines, this is the farthest from civilization and its discontents, and thus the cleanest and least spoiled. It's also huge and a heavenly walk for dog or owner, with its views of Mount Tamalpais across San Pablo Bay, and its docks, salt marsh, beaches, eucalyptus groves and expanses of wild grassland waving in the breeze. Some of the eucalyptus trees are so wind-carved they could be mistaken for cypresses.

The park has fine bike paths, and your dog should be leashed for safety on these, but on the unpaved trails he's free—even on the dirt paths through marshes, such as the Marsh Trail. Just make sure he stays on the trail and doesn't go into the marsh itself. Dogs may not go on the fishing pier or on the shuttle bus to the pier.

From Interstate 80, exit at Hilltop Drive, go west and take a right on San Pablo Avenue, then left on Atlas Road to the park entrance. A dog fee of $1 and a $3 parking fee are charged on weekends and holidays. (510) 635-0135. → *See #19 on map p. 334.*

•Wildcat Canyon Regional Park 🐾🐾🐾🐾 🐕‍🦺 🐕

This is Tilden Regional Park's (see page 358) northern twin. Tilden has its attractive spots, but it is designed for people; Wildcat seems made for dogs, because almost nothing is happening there except things growing, sun, fog and wind. And you can leave your dog's leash in your pocket.

Large coast live oaks, madrones, bay laurels and all kinds of chaparral thrive on the east side. And since the area was ranchland from the days of Spanish land grants, and traces of house foundations remain, it isn't surprising that a lot of exotic plants flourish here alongside the expected ones. You'll find berries, nasturtiums and cardoon thistle, which looks like an artichoke allowed to grow up. All kinds of grasses and wildflowers cover the western hillsides.

At the entrance parking lot is Wildcat Creek, which gets low but usually not entirely dry in summer. Then you can follow the Wildcat Creek Trail (actually an abandoned paved road); it travels gently uphill and then follows the southern ridge of the park. Or follow any of the nameless side trails, which are wonderfully wild and solitary. You can hear train whistles all the way up from Emeryville and the dull roar of civilization below, but somehow it doesn't bother you up here.

Other trails lead through groves of pines or follow Wildcat Creek. The park is roughly three miles long. If you come to the boundary with Tilden, remember that dogs aren't allowed in the nature area across the line. You can get on the East Bay Skyline National Recreation Trail (Nimitz Way), running along the park's north side. Don't branch off onto the Eagle Trail, however; it belongs to the East Bay Municipal Utility District, which requires a permit and frowns on dogs. But there's plenty of room here. You and your dog could spend several blissful days in Wildcat.

From Interstate 80, southbound, take the McBryde exit and turn left on McBryde Avenue to the park entrance. If you're northbound, take the Amador/Solano exit. Go three blocks left (north) on Amador Street and turn right (east) on McBryde to the entrance. No fees are charged. (510) 635-0135. → *See #20 on map p. 334.*

DIVERSIONS

Preaching for the pooch: Want to take your dog to church? If you don't think he's ready to pray in a pew, you can bring him along to attend a service in the comfort of your car. Since 1975, the First Presbyterian Church of Richmond has offered a drive-in service in a shopping mall parking lot. Held at 8:30 a.m. every Sunday outside the Pinole Appian 80 shopping center, the ceremony attracts about 40 worshippers every week.

Reverends Brian Reed and Calvin Polston transmit the service over shortwave radio from a mobile pulpit, complete with a sermon and choral music. Church elders bring communion around to each car on a silver platter and parishioners honk and flash their headlights at the pastors to say "Amen." It's quite a scene—and afterwards you can go shopping. Dogs are as welcome to attend as anyone. For more information, call (510) 234-0954.

SAN RAMON

PLACES TO STAY

San Ramon Marriott at Bishop Ranch: Rates are $65 to $120. 2600 Bishop Drive, San Ramon, CA 94583; (510) 867-9200.

WALNUT CREEK

Walnut Creek's big secret is its beautiful creeks and canals, former irrigation ditches that now adorn golf courses and housing developments. Walnut Creek, San Ramon Creek, the Contra Costa Canal and the Ygnacio Canal all pass through town. Dogs must be leashed everywhere, except in the undeveloped areas of city-owned open spaces.

PARKS, BEACHES & RECREATION AREAS

Acalanes Ridge Open Space Recreation Area 🐾 🐾 🐾 🐾 🐕

In 1974, the city of Walnut Creek set aside a few open spaces for a limited-use "land bank." Dogs must be "under voice or sight command." (Translation: off leash if obedient.) Hoo boy! The trails are open to hikers, dogs, horses and bicycles, however, so on a fine day, your dog may have competition.

Acalanes Ridge, close to Briones Regional Park (see page 340), is crossed by the Briones to Diablo Regional Trail. Like the others, it lacks water.

A good entry point is from Camino Verde Circle, reached by driving south on Camino Verde from the intersection of Pleasant Hill and Geary roads. For information on any of the open spaces, call (510) 256-3560. ➤ *See #21 on map p. 334.*

Shell Ridge Open Space Recreation Area 🐾 🐾 🐾 🐾 🐕

Dogs may run off leash everywhere but in the developed areas (parking lots, picnic grounds), but "must be under positive voice and sight command." The people who write these rules must be retired military document writers or part-time computer-manual writers.

Within the Shell Ridge Open Space is the Old Borges Ranch, a demonstration farm staffed irregularly by rangers. The ranch house itself is sometimes open on Sundays from noon to 4 p.m. Call first to check. For information or to make a reservation to visit, call (510) 943-5860.

You can enter by the Sugarloaf-Shell Ridge Trail at the north edge. From Interstate 680, take the Ignacio Valley Road exit, go east on Ignacio Valley Road to Walnut Avenue (not Boulevard), turn right and right again on Castle Rock Road. Go past the high school, turn right and follow signs. (510) 256-3560. ➤ *See #22 on map p. 334.*

RESTAURANTS

Walnut Creek's "downtown," your respite from mallsville, is Main Street. Here, you'll find several welcoming outdoor restaurants, benches for just sitting and good weather.

J.R. Muggs: Enjoy desserts and gourmet coffee with your pooch at your side at the outdoor tables here. The store also sells thousands of coffee mugs for all tastes. You can get a mug picturing Betty Boop, Garfield, the 49ers, your name or your horoscope. They love dogs here. 1432 North Main Street; (510) 256-9595.

La Fogata: You can sit on comfy Mexican barrel chairs outside with your dog, under a cool awning, and munch on burgers or Mexican food. 1315 North Main Street; (510) 934-8121.

Original Hot Dog Place: Every kind of hot dog is served in this tiny shop with a neat hot dog mural on the wall and a wooden Indian outside next to the tables. 1420 Lincoln Avenue at Main. (510) 256-7302.

Pascal French Oven: You and your dog will drool over the baked goodies. Waitresses often bring buckets of water out to dogs. 1372 North Main Street; (510) 932-6969.

PLACES TO STAY

Walnut Creek Motor Lodge: Rates are $50 to $90. 1960 North Main Street, Walnut Creek, CA 94596; (510) 932-2811.

DIVERSIONS

Do a doggone good deed: If you and your dog want to take a weekend stroll and raise money for a good cause, you should sign up for Canines Against Cancer. Started in 1993, the one-and-a-half-mile walk-a-thon is an annual event held one weekend in August at Walnut Creek's Heather Farm Park. Proceeds go to help the American Cancer Society's research and education programs. After the walk, there's an owner/dog look-alike contest and an ugliest dog competition. Agile, frisbee-catching dogs perform tricks for entertainment. Advance registration is $10, or $15 the day of the event. Your dog will get a doggy goody bag and a bandana. For information on the exact date, call (510) 934-7640.

ALAMEDA COUNTY

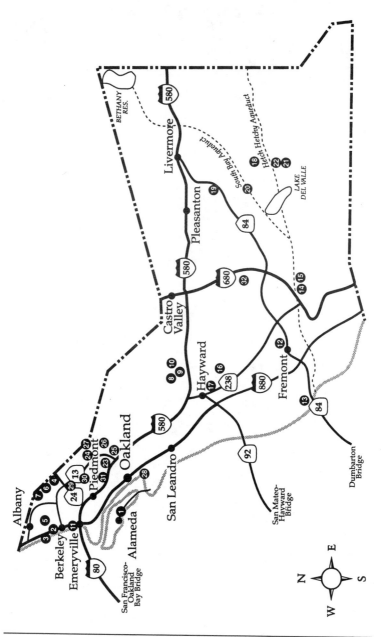

33
ALAMEDA COUNTY

From the hallowed hippie havens of Berkeley's Telegraph Avenue to the pleasing suburban pleasantries of Pleasanton, Alameda County is like California in miniature: It has nearly every level of population density and type, and nearly every temperate natural environment. Somehow, it all works.

Dogs dig it here, whether they're rasta dogs or shaved Shih Tzus. The county is like the creek it's named after—it's been lined with concrete, filled with trash and dammed into oblivion, yet it still manages to gush joyfully onward. Some of the wildest country in the Bay Area is located in this county, full of hidden gems of nature. So many of these parks are off-leash havens that your dog may think he's dreaming.

The 12-mile Alameda Creek Regional Trail (see page 363) is a favorite among dogs. They can run off leash on most of the trail, but where signs say leashes are required, heed the message.

An even more invigorating trail is the East Bay Skyline Trail. Well-behaved, leash-free dogs are welcome on the entire 31-mile length of this trail. Wowza wowza and arrooooo! The trail stretches from the northern end of Wildcat Canyon Regional Park in Contra Costa County (see page 346) to the southern end of Anthony Chabot Regional Park (see page 361). Plenty of horses also use this trail, so if your dog is a hoof chaser, keep him leashed.

As if all this wasn't enough good news, your dog's hair will stand on end when he learns that unless he's a pit bull, he's allowed to run leash-free on thousands of acres of parkland within the East Bay Regional Parks District. Some 50 parks and recreation areas and 20 regional trails—75,000 acres in all—fall under the district's jurisdiction.

If the fact that dogs can trot around leash-free sounds too good to be true, you may be right. The district board has been going through a lengthy process of deciding whether to make owners tether their dogs when other visitors are nearby. If you want to help board members make up their minds in favor of the dogs, you can write the district at 2950 Peralta Oaks Court, P.O. Box 5381, Oakland, CA 94605.

The only places where dogs must be leashed within the district's parks are in developed areas, parking lots, picnic sites, lawns and in posted Nature Areas. They aren't permitted on beaches, wetlands, marshes or in the Tilden Nature Area. Entry fees range from free to $3.50, depending on the park and the time of year. Dogs are normally charged $1 extra, but they can buy their own annual passes for $50. It comes with 100 disposable pooper scoopers. Such a clean deal!

ALAMEDA

PARKS, BEACHES & RECREATION AREAS

•Washington Park 🐾 🐾

Washington Park, next to Robert Crown Memorial State Beach (sorry, pooches—no can go), is Alameda's largest park. It has lots of great amenities for people and leashed dogs enjoy the wide green expanses, the bike path, the picnic areas and the edge of the marsh here.

From downtown, take Central Avenue toward Webster Street. The park is at the corner of Central and 8th Street. For the beach, continue on 8th Street. Call (510) 635-0135 for beach information or (510) 748-4565 for park information. *→See #1 on map p. 352.*

FESTIVALS

Alameda Park Street Fair: This is a family-style street fair. Leashed dogs who are comfortable in crowds are welcome. You'll find music, arts and crafts and a wide array of ethnic foods. It's held on the first weekend in August each year, both days, from 10 a.m. to 6 p.m. On Park Street. (510) 521-8677.

ALBANY

RESTAURANTS

For a pleasant street where people are dog-friendly, and at least a couple of restaurants have outdoor tables, try Albany's Solano Avenue.

Marco Polo's Deli Cafe: Dogs enjoy watching you eat tasty sandwiches at the outdoor tables here. 1158 Solano Avenue; (510) 524-5667.

Barney's Gourmet Hamburgers: While its street address is in Berkeley, it's just over the border from Albany. Dogs drool while watching you eat gourmet burgers at the outdoor tables here. 1591 Solano Avenue, Berkeley; (510) 526-8185.

FESTIVALS

Solano Stroll: Your well-behaved and crowd-friendly dog is welcome at this street fair on Solano Avenue. It's held yearly in

September. For this year's date, call (510) 525-1771.

BERKELEY

Berkeley, well-known for its tolerance of eccentricity, is equally eccentric when it comes to dogs. Like most of Alameda County, it features strict leash laws: Your first, second and third infractions net you fines of $10, $25 and $50 respectively, plus court costs assessments of $17 for each $10 (or fraction thereof) of the fines. That adds up to $27 for the first offense and $76 for the second. For a fourth infraction, you must appear personally in court.

But there is a unique loophole. If your dog is obedience trained, Berkeley doesn't require him to be leashed. If an animal control officer sees you with your unleashed dog, you'll be asked to demonstrate that your dog is under absolute voice control. If the officer is not persuaded, you'll be cited and asked to appear in court with your dog, where you'll have another chance to prove it. (I can just picture Joe sitting, lying down and rolling over in court…Well, maybe if a treat were involved…Nahhh.)

Whether they're all under absolute voice control or not, you'll see a lot more unleashed dogs in Berkeley than in any other Bay Area city. The University of California at Berkeley also has a leash law, but the campus is swarming with loose dogs, too. The only leashed animal you'll see is a local pet pig whose owner walks him there. Go figure.

Berkeley created the country's first official dog park, Ohlone Dog Park (see page 357). Still, it's been slow in approving a plan to allow dogs to run free on paths in the 40 undeveloped acres of Waterfront Park in the marina. A citizens' group that calls itself AARF (Area for Animals to Run Free) has been lobbying the city to convert the space since 1988. Its efforts have met with resistance from other groups, including the Sierra Club and Audubon Society, which claim that dogs off leash are incompatible with wildlife. (AARF points out that the space, a converted landfill, *has* no wildlife.) A study of the environmental impact the plan would have on the current and future wildlife in the area is ongoing. If you're interested in finding out more about the park or how to get involved, contact AARF founder Susan Fleisher at (510) 527-0793.

Despite the controversies involving dogs in Berkeley, Joe loves it here. His rasta-dog hair fits right in on Telegraph Avenue, where the '60s still reign. He gets special treatment all over town—a phenomenon I attribute to his mellow California-dog demeanor and to his bandanas, especially his red one. The last time Joe wore his red bandana in Berkeley, he got a free slice of Blondie's pizza, an apple and a child-sized tie-dyed T-shirt from a street vendor.

Joe and I were even invited into a clothing store while window shopping. The store clerk's boyfriend offered to watch him so I could try on a dress. "I love good dogs—good hairy dogs who wear red," he said, looking up at me and brushing his own long wisps out of his eyes.

"Well, this is a very good dog," I said, more warning Joe that's what he'd better be than telling the boyfriend that's what Joe really was.

Everything was going well until, standing with no clothes on in the tiny dressing room, I heard a cry from the boyfriend. "Oh my God! Not the silk pants!"

I was trapped, but I think I preferred it that way to facing the scene that lurked outside my curtain. I prayed fervently that perhaps the boyfriend was answering a question about what looked good on a customer. But with his next words, I knew the truth, and it was not good.

"Bad dog. Bad, bad dog!"

Eventually, I slithered out of the dressing room and surveyed the damage. A pair of purple silk pants, one leg slimy wet and dented from Joe's fangs. I apologized and drew out my checkbook, but the clerk said, "Don't worry. We get a lot of shoplifters here. We'll hide it and the manager won't know the difference."

With that, the clerk cut off the unscathed leg and tied it in a bow around Joe's neck.

Several doors down, a shopkeeper watched Joe from the doorway of her clothing store. "Oh, come in!" she said. "He looks soooo good in purple. Come take a look inside if you want. I'll watch him for you."

I smiled, nodded my head in thanks and walked on. Even in Berkeley, tolerance must have its limits.

PARKS, BEACHES & RECREATION AREAS

• **Aquatic Park** 🐾 🐾 🐾

Take advantage of this city park for a quick stroll by the water. Conveniently located off Interstate 80, it's fairly tranquil, even with the lagoon's power boats and waterskiers whizzing by. The lagoon's banks are planted with a mixture of grass, willows, cypress and eucalyptus. Boy dogs have lifted many a leg in homage here.

Thanks to its greenery, birds are plentiful. Dogs like to birdwatch from the paved paths and the parcourse. Leashed dogs enjoy splashing around the shallow, calm lagoon water here.

From Interstate 80, take the Ashby exit and turn north on Bay Street. There's a small parking lot and no fee. (510) 644-6530. →*See #2 on map p. 352.*

• **Berkeley Marina Park** 🐾 🐾 1/2

If you and your dog feel like whiling away the hours conversing with each other along a rocky shoreline or in grassy hills, this pine-filled bayside park is your kind of place. There's one tiny sandy beach where people and dogs can swim, but y'all are supposed to be leashed for now.

If AARF's plan to create a leash-free dog run in the North Waterfront Park section of the marina goes through (see page 355), this could become a four-paw park in a snap.

Take University Avenue west past the Interstate 880 interchange and follow the signs. (510) 644-6371. →*See #3 on map p. 352.*

• **Claremont Canyon Regional Preserve** 🐾 🐾 🐾 🐾 🏃

This large park is full of steep hillside trails that lead to crests with stunning views of the university and the surrounding hills and valleys. If your dog likes eucalyptus trees and doesn't like leashes, take him here. It's one of those tree-filled, leashes-optional parks.

From Highway 13 (Ashby Avenue), drive north on College Avenue. Turn right on Derby Street, past the Clark Kerr Campus. The trailhead is at the southeast corner of the school grounds, near the beginning of Stonewall Road. (510) 635-0135. →*See #4 on map p. 352.*

• **Ohlone Dog Park** 🐾 🐾 🐾 🐾 🏃

Since 1979, when it opened as the first leash-free dog park in America, Ohlone has provided a model for other cities willing to experiment with the concept. Even after years of unflagging popularity, the park still seems to be in good shape. This can be credited in large part to a conscientious park upkeep committee which keeps an eye on facilities and provides plastic bags for cleaning up after your dog. You'll find a water faucet, complete with a dog bowl set in concrete, and two picnic tables for owners who want to relax while their dogs socialize. The grass isn't always green here, but it's definitely better than what's on the other side of the fence.

At Martin Luther King Jr. Way and Hearst Street. (510) 644-6530. →*See #5 on map p. 352.*

• **Strawberry Canyon** 🐾 🐾 🐾

This canyon is located between Claremont Canyon and Tilden Park on the University of California campus. It's classified as an

Ecological Study Area by the university, which owns it. Dogs must be leashed, but at least they're allowed.

Adventurous dogs like the Grizzly Peak Trail, which starts below the Botanical Gardens (sorry, pooches, no dogs at the gardens). You'll cross three small creeks that pour into Strawberry Creek farther down. They're great for cooling your paws.

From the Berkeley campus, follow Centennial Drive to the gate near the Botanical Gardens. (510) 643-6720. ➜ *See #6 on map p. 352.*

• **Tilden Regional Park** 🐾 🐾 🐾 🐾 🐕‍🦺

Humans and dogs alike give Tilden a big thumbs-up (dewclaws-up). Leash-free dogs find the scents from its western ridge delectable and humans find the ridge's breathtaking views of the entire San Francisco Bay equally enticing.

Escapes from civilization are everywhere in this 2,078-acre park. Try the trails leading east from South Park Drive. They connect with the Skyline National Recreation Trail.

You can pick up the Arroyo Trail at the Big Springs sign and take it all the way to the ridgetop. There's a great stream at the trailhead which you can follow through laurel, pine, toyon and scrub on your low-grade ascent. Your dog may want to take a dip in the stream for refreshment.

After the trail veers from the stream, it steepens and leads into cypress-studded meadows and eucalyptus groves. Eventually it feeds into the Skyline National Recreation Trail, also known as the Sea View Trail, offering vistas over the Bay along the way.

Dogs aren't allowed in the large nature area at the northern end, or in the Lake Anza swimming area. Leashes are required in all the developed areas, including picnic grounds and ball fields. Remember to watch your step in the areas frequented by dogs, as some owners neglect to clean up after their furry friends. There's nothing like stepping in a steaming pile of dog dung to put a damper on a day of exploring nature.

Speaking of steaming, be sure to check out Tilden's miniature steam train for a riveting good time. (See Diversions, page 360.)

From Highway 24, take the Fish Ranch Road exit north (at eastern end of the Caldecott Tunnel). At the intersection of Fish Ranch, Grizzly Peak Boulevard and Claremont Avenue, take a right on Grizzly Peak and continue north to South Park Drive. One more mile north brings you to Big Springs Trail. During peak season, continue on Grizzly Peak to the Shasta Gate. (510) 635-0135. ➜ *See #7 on map p. 352.*

RESTAURANTS

Just north of University Avenue, a three-block stretch of Shattuck Avenue is home to several restaurants with outdoor seating.

Bubi's After Hours: If you like light Armenian fare, and your dog likes to watch you eat it, try the outdoor tables here. Joe loves the creamy rice pudding. 1700 Shattuck Avenue; (510) 549-1759.

Cafe Ariel: This cafe has a pleasant deck where you and your dog can avoid sidewalk traffic while you dine on tasty Israeli-style food. 1600 Shattuck Avenue; (510) 845-4300.

Clarinet Cafe: You'll love the croissants and lattes. 1908 Shattuck Avenue; (510) 644-1070.

The French Hotel Cafe: Someone sneaked Joe a saucer of espresso and he barked at feet for the rest of the day. It's the real stuff—good and strong. Sip it at the outside tables, but let your dog stick with water. 1540 Shattuck Avenue; (510) 548-9930.

Mama's Bar-B-Q: The motto here is "Walk in, pig out." They specialize in low prices and huge helpings of ribs, chicken, burgers and baked beans. Munch them outside with your dog at your side. 1686 Shattuck Avenue; (510) 549-2316.

Smokey Joe's Cafe: A tie-dyed and true local establishment, the menu gives the address as Berzerkley. Try the Mexican breakfast and the matzoh brie. The outdoor tables are 1620 Shattuck Avenue; (510) 548-4616.

Elsewhere in Berkeley, you'll find many other outdoor options, including:

Berkeley Cheese: The fresh pasta, cheese, produce and prepared foods are delicious here. Eat these tasty treats at the outdoor tables with your dog. 1601 Martin Luther King Jr. Way; (510) 841-7737.

Burnaford's Produce: There are six sidewalk tables here, but the streets have heavy foot traffic. If it's a quiet day, bring your dog and enjoy coffee and a pastry. 2635 Ashby Avenue at College Avenue; (510) 548-0348 or (510) 548-7720.

College Avenue Delicatessen: Dogs enjoy watching you eat standard deli fare at the outdoor tables here. 3185 College Avenue; (510) 655-8584.

La Mediterranee: This delicious and inexpensive Middle Eastern restaurant has built up quite a following; there's usually a line on weekends when Cal is mid-semester. The folks here will let your dog sit quietly at your feet at the outdoor tables, which have the added benefit of an outdoor heater on cool nights. You might want to tie your dog up on the sidewalk outside the fence separating the tables if it's especially crowded. 2936 College Avenue; (510) 540-7773.

Noah's New York Bagels: Noah's has benches on the sidewalk, but no tables—but it's still a must-visit for you and your dog, if bagels are your yen. Very popular on Sunday mornings. 3170 College Avenue; (510) 654-0944.

Peet's Coffee: Not only Peet's but the *Bread Garden Bakery* and various other cafes and shops encircle a sunny patio with benches in the small Village Square shopping center. Nearly every morning, crowds of hungry bicyclists and amblers congregate to sit in the sun, argue (this is Berkeley), eat pastries and sip Peet's coffee, which many call the best in the Bay Area. Dogs' noses don't stop quivering and they can often meet other frustrated dogs. 2916 Domingo Avenue off Ashby. Peet's: (510) 843-1434. Bread Garden: (510) 548-3122.

Sea Breeze Market and Deli: Smack in the middle of the Interstate 880 interchange, you won't even notice the traffic as you and your dog bask at sunny picnic tables, where crab claws crunch underfoot and begging is outstanding. Dogs are perfectly welcome so long as they don't wander into the store itself. You can buy groceries, beer, wine, classy ice cream or a meal from the deli: fresh fish and chips, calamari, prawns, scallops, chicken and quiche. The deli serves croissants and coffee early; if you live in the East Bay, you can zip in for a quick croissant and a dog walk in the Marina (see page 356) before work. At the foot of University Avenue, past the Interstate 880 entrance—598 University Avenue; (510) 486-8119.

PLACES TO STAY

Berkeley Marina Marriott: Rates are $100 to $155. 200 Marina Boulevard, Berkeley, CA 94710; (510) 548-7920.

Golden Bear Motel: Small dogs only, please. Rates are $45 to $50. 1620 San Pablo Avenue, Berkeley, CA 94702; (510) 525-6770.

DIVERSIONS

Ride a dog-sized train: If your dog's not an escape artist or the nervous type, he's welcome to ride with you on Tilden's miniature train. The open-car train takes you for a 12-minute ride through woods and past stunning views of the surrounding area. Adventurous dogs like it when the train toots its whistle as it rumbles past a miniature water tower, a car barn and other such train accessories.

The Redwood Valley Railway Company runs trains between 11 a.m. and 6 p.m. weekends and holidays only, except during spring and summer school vacations, when it runs weekdays, noon to 5 p.m. and weekends until 6 p.m. Tickets are $1.50; kids under two and dogs ride free. You must keep the dog on a tight leash and make sure he doesn't jump out. It's in the southeast corner of Tilden Regional Park. From the intersection of Grizzly Peak Boulevard and Lomas Cantadas, follow the signs. (510) 548-6100.

Flea to the Market: If your dog has the itch to shop, and promises not to do leg lifts on furniture even when it's outdoors, you can have a relaxed time at the Ashby Flea Market. Crowds will be tolerant, but keep him on a short leash and watch out for chicken bones and abandoned cotton candy. Joe's friend Dabney, for instance, is a dog who knows how to shop for scraps, nose to the ground for hours. He's been to his last flea market.

Good dogs love the easy camaraderie they'll find here. If it's hot, though, keep it short. This market is held every Saturday and Sunday at the Ashby BART Station parking lot.

From Interstate 80, take the Ashby exit and drive about 1.5 miles east to the intersection of Adeline Street.

Go shopping in 1967: You and your dog can shop in the autumn of love when you stroll through the sidewalks of Telegraph Avenue near the UC Berkeley campus. Street vendors sell tie-dye clothes, crystals, pottery and T-shirts airbrushed with clouds. Street performers sing, juggle, beg for money, or do whatever else comes naturally. Incense and other herbaceous odors waft through the air, but dogs prefer the scents of all the non-deodorized humans.

Dogs who reminisce about the 1960s really dig it here. They're perceived as totally cool dudes, and given major amounts of love from people who like to hug dogs hard. A palm reader made friends with Joe on a recent visit, but since Joe isn't a believer in soothsaying, he steadfastly refused to give her his paw. (Actually, he only gives a paw for food, not friendship. He's a very pragmatic Airedale.)

Some dogs—and humans—may find the weekend crowds a sensory overload. If your schedule allows, try a cool afternoon. From Interstate 80, take the Ashby exit, go about two miles east to Telegraph and turn left (north). The street-merchant part begins around the intersection of Dwight Way. On weekends, parking is challenging.

CASTRO VALLEY

PARKS, BEACHES & RECREATION AREAS

• **Anthony Chabot Regional Park** 🐾 🐾 🐾 🐾 🦴

You and your leash-free dog can throw your urban cares to the wind when you visit this 4,684-acre park filled with magnificent trails and enchanting woodlands. Except for the occasional sounds of gunfire, you'll scarcely believe you're in the hills east of metropolitan Oakland. But fear not—the guns you'll hear here are merely being used for target practice at the park's marksmanship range.

The trails here are so secluded that if no one is firing a gun, the only sounds you may hear are those of your panting dog and the singing birds. Adventure-loving dogs like to take the Goldenrod Trail, starting at the southern terminus of Skyline Boulevard and Grass Valley Road. It connects with the East Bay Skyline National Trail, which winds through Grass Valley and climbs through eucalyptus forests. Lucky dogs can be off leash everywhere but in developed areas.

Campsites are $13 to $18. Dogs are $1 extra. Reserve by calling the East Bay Regional Parks reservations department: (510) 562-CAMP. No reservations are taken between October 1 and March 31, when the 23 sites are first come, first served.

From Castro Valley, go from the intersection of Redwood Road and Castro Valley Boulevard north on Redwood about 4.5 miles to Marciel Gate. (The campground is about two miles inside the gate.) From Oakland at the intersection of Redwood Road and Skyline Boulevard, go about 6.5 miles east on Redwood to Marciel Gate. For general park info, call (510) 635-0135. *→ See #8 on map p. 352.*

•**Cull Canyon Regional Recreation Area** 🐾 🐾 🐾 1/2 🐕

Dogs may be off leash up on the grassy slopes laced with eucalyptus stands, but they have to wear their leashes in the areas designed for human fun. It's not such a bad fate, considering that there are plenty of grassy slopes away from developed areas.

In summer, fishing and swimming are popular here. But pooches may not go near the swimming complex, which includes an attractive pavilion and sandy beach. Leashed dogs may visit picnic areas, the Cull Creek area and the willow-lined reservoir that sports a wooden bridge and a handful of ducks and coots.

From Interstate 580, take the Center Street/Crow Canyon Road exit. Go left on Center Street and take a right on Castro Valley Boulevard. Follow it to Crow Canyon Road and take a left. Take another left on Cull Canyon Road. It's a half mile to the park entrance. (510) 635-0135. *→ See #9 on map p. 352.*

•**Greenridge Park** 🐾 🐾 🐾

This is a small, very pleasant neighborhood park in the hills above the city. Its only drawback is that it isn't very accessible, but that's a benefit for dogs who don't like to hike among hordes of people. From the green ridge that gives it its name (at least in the rainy season), you can see the bay on one side, suburbs and hills on the other. There are basketball courts, swings and a slide for children, and a stream at the eastern end. Dogs must be leashed.

Take the Crow Canyon Road exit off Interstate 580 and turn left (north) on Cold Water Drive. (510) 881-6715. → *See #10 on map p. 352.*

PLACES TO STAY
Anthony Chabot Regional Park camping: See page 361.

EMERYVILLE

PARKS, BEACHES & RECREATION AREAS
• **Emeryville Marina Park** 🐾 🐾

If you're a human, this is a fine park. If you're a leashed dog, it's just so-so. A concrete path follows the riprap shoreline past cypress trees and through manicured grass. A quick and scenic stroll down the north side will give you a fine view of the marina and a miniature bird refuge where egrets, sandpipers, blackbirds and doves inhabit a tiny marsh. Dogs who like to birdwatch think it's cool here.

Dogs who like to fish don't have it so easy. Pooches aren't allowed on the fishing pier. But if you console them with an offer to picnic at tables with grand views of the Bay Bridge, they usually snap out of their funk.

From Interstate 80, take the Powell Street exit at Emeryville and go west on Powell to the end of the marina. There's lots of free parking. (510) 596-4340. → *See #11 on map p. 352.*

PLACES TO STAY
Holiday Inn-Bay Bridge: Rates are $75 to $100. 1800 Powell Street, Emeryville, CA 94608; (510) 658-9300.

FREMONT

PARKS, BEACHES & RECREATION AREAS
• **Alameda Creek Regional Trail** 🐾 🐾 🐾 🐕

This 12.4-mile trail runs from the bayshore to the East Bay hills and dogs can actually be off leash in many sections. But they may be disappointed when they discover that it's not as pristine a trail as the name might imply. First of all, the trail is paved. Second of all, the creek is paved. (You'll see what I mean.) But more important, the trail doesn't just pass through farmland and greenbelt areas. It also runs alongside railyards, industrial lots and quarries. Junkyard dogs like it. Wilderness dogs just shrug their hairy shoulders. A scenic stretch of this paved trail is at the Niles Canyon end. Dogs find it especially interesting in winter after a storm, when there's actually water in the concrete-lined creek and ducks and coots splash around.

You may enter this trail at many points between the creek's mouth—in the salt flats of the bay by Coyote Hills Regional Park. The trail officially begins in Fremont's Niles district, at the intersection of Mission Boulevard (Highway 238) and Niles Canyon Road (Highway 84).

Although the East Bay Regional Park District's usual liberal leash rules apply here, it has posted a good many areas with "leash up" symbols. If you see one, do so. On this trail, as on any you share with other hikers, horses and bicycles, just use common sense. (510) 635-0135. → *See #12 on map p. 352.*

•Coyote Hills Regional Park 🐾 🐾 🐾 🐾 🐕

This park is a paradox. It's a working research project on Ohlone Indian history, a teeming wildlife sanctuary and a family picnic and bicycling mecca—all rolled into 966 acres.

Dogs may run leash-free in the small hills that give the park its name. You'll see red-tailed hawks, vultures and white-tailed kites that swoop down on unsuspecting squirrels. Joe hasn't ever seen one of these kite-gets-squirrel incidents, but since he's never even come closing to capturing a squirrel, he'd give his canine teeth to witness such a spectacle.

The beautiful Bayview Trail climbs quickly up behind the visitors center. From the crest of Red Hill—green even in the dry season because its ground cover is drought-tolerant—you look down on varied colors of marsh grasses, waterfowl and wading birds, and the shallow salt ponds in the bay. Most of the park is a fragile sanctuary, and dogs must stay on the little hills or on leash at the picnic by the visitors center.

From Interstate 880, take the Decoto Road/Highway 84 exit in Fremont. Go west on Highway 84 to the Thornton Avenue/Paseo Padre Parkway exit. Go north on Paseo Padre about one mile to Patterson Ranch Road/Commerce. A left on Patterson Ranch Road brings you to the entrance. When the kiosk is staffed, the parking fee is $3. The dog fee is $1. For information on tours and activities, call (510) 795-9385. For general information: (510) 635-0135. → *See #13 on map p. 352.*

•Mission Peak Regional Preserve 🐾 🐾 🐾 🐾 🐕

Smart Fremont dwellers take their dogs to this 2,596-acre park. It's a huge expanse of grass, dotted with occasional oak groves and scrub. Unfortunately for humans who get short of breath, the foot trails head straight up: Trails to the top rise 2,500 feet in three miles. (Pant, pant.)

Leash-free dogs love this place. The entrance at Stanford Avenue offers a gentler climb than the entrance from the Ohlone College campus. You'll pass Caliente Creek if you take the Peak Meadow Trail, but in hot weather, there won't be much relief from the sun. Be sure to carry water for yourself and your dog. The main point of puffing up Mission Peak is the renowned view stretching from Mount Tamalpais to Mount Hamilton. (On very clear days, you can see to the Sierra's snowy crest.) Your dog may not care much for the scenery, but she'll probably appreciate the complete freedom of the expanse of pasture here.

From Interstate 680, take the southern Mission Boulevard exit in Fremont (there are two; the one you want is in the Warm Springs district). Go east on Mission to Stanford Avenue, turn right (east), and in less than a mile, you'll be at the entrance. (510) 635-0135.
→ *See #14 on map p. 352.*

• **Sunol Regional Wilderness**

You and your leash-free dog will howl for joy when you visit this large and deserted wilderness treasure. It's like going to a national park without having to leave your poor pooch behind.

One of the best treats for canines and their companions is a hike along the Camp Ohlone Trail (which you get to via the main park entrance, on Geary Road). The trail takes you to an area called Little Yosemite. Like its namesake, Little Yosemite is magnificent. It's a steep-sided gorge with a creek at the bottom, lofty crags and outcrops of greenstone and basalt that reveal a turbulent geological history. Its huge boulders throw Alameda Creek into gurgling eddies and falls. There's no swimming allowed here, much to Joe's relief.

You can return via the higher Canyon View Trail or head for several other destinations: wooded canyons, grassy slopes, peaks with peaks of Calaveras Reservoir or Mount Diablo. The park brochure offers useful descriptions of each trail. Dogs may run free on trails except for on the Backpack Loop.

Dogs are allowed only at the Family Campground site at headquarters, and not at the backpacking campsites farther in. Sites are $13. The dog fee is $1. Dogs must be leashed in the campground or confined to your tent. (Anyone whose dog has ever chased off after a wild boar in the middle of the night understands the reason for this rule, and this park has plenty of boars.) Call (510) 636-1684 to reserve. Reserved sites are held until 5 p.m.

From Interstate 680, take the Calaveras Road exit, then go left (east) on Geary Road to the park entrance. The park may be closed or restricted during fire season, from June to October. (510) 635-0135.
→*See #15 on map p. 352.*

RESTAURANTS

Big Daddy's: After a trek along the Alameda Creek Regional Trail or an appetite-arousing hike through the Sunol Regional Wilderness, the outdoor tables here are the perfect spot for a little snack. This is a cheerful, old-fashioned cafe that serves all-American food. Big Daddy's boasts painted murals featuring Niles street scenes on the walls and water birds on the ceiling. (Watch out for bird dogs. Sometimes they get a glimpse of one of the water-bird paintings and stare up during your whole meal.)

At Mission Boulevard (Highway 238) and Niles Canyon Road (Highway 84). Open 24 hours, whenever your dog is hungry; (510) 790-9155.

PLACES TO STAY

Sunol Regional Wilderness camping: See page 365.

HAYWARD

PARKS, BEACHES & RECREATION AREAS

• **Garin Regional Park &**
  Dry Creek Regional Park (contiguous) 🐾 🐾 🐾 🐾 🐕

Garin Regional Park is about one mile and one century away from one of the busiest streets in Hayward. It's a fascinating place for you and your dog to learn about Alameda County farming and ranching. The parking lot next to Garin Barn—an actual barn, blacksmith's shop and tool shed that is also Garin's visitors center—is strewn with antique farm machinery.

A total of 20 miles of trails, looping among the sweeps of grassy hills, beckon you and your dog. Off-leash dogs are fine on the trails once you've left the visitors center. Dogs seem to like to think they're on their own farm here, looking for all the world like they're strutting down their very own property and watching out for evil feline intruders.

Dry Creek, which runs near the visitors center, was a delightful small torrent one day when we were there after a March storm. There isn't much shade on hot days, though. That's when you might want to try cooling your paws at tiny Jordan Pond. It's stocked with catfish, should your dog care to join you on his kind of fishing excursion.

From Highway 238 (Mission Boulevard), Tamarack Drive takes

you quickly up the hill to Dry Creek Regional Park. Garin Avenue takes you to Garin, or you can enter Garin from the California State University, Hayward campus. The parking fee is $3 on weekends and holidays. Dogs are $1 extra. (510) 635-0135. ➜*See #16 on map p. 352.*

• **Hayward Memorial Park Hiking & Riding Trails** 🐾 🐾 🐾

For humans, Memorial Park offers all kinds of amenities, including an indoor pool, tennis courts, kids' swings and slides, picnic tables, a band shell and even a slightly funky cage full of doves. But really, if you're a dog, the big question is "Who cares?"

The fun for dogs begins when you get on the Wally Wickander (poor guy) Memorial Trail and enter the greenbelt portion of the park, laced with dirt fire trails designed for hikers and horses. Dogs must remain leashed, but the trail is so beautiful that it doesn't seem to matter. It follows a steep-sided creek lined with a thick tangle of oak, laurel, maple and lots of noisy birds. The trash pickup is a little lax, but if you're looking for solitude in a city park, you'll find it here.

You can enter through Hayward Memorial Park, at Mission Boulevard (Highway 238) just south of the intersection of Highway 92. You can also enter at the parking lots on East Avenue, through East Avenue Park on the north end; or on Highland Boulevard through Old Highland Park on the south end. (510) 881-6715. ➜*See #17 on map p. 352.*

PLACES TO STAY

Vagabond Inn: Rates are $50 to $65. 20455 Hesperian Boulevard, Hayward, CA 94541; (510) 785-5480.

LIVERMORE

PARKS, BEACHES & RECREATION AREAS

• **Del Valle Regional Park** 🐾 🐾 🐾 🐾 🐕

This popular reservoir is best known for swimming, boating, fishing and camping. Like Anthony Chabot Regional Park (see page 361), it's primarily a manicured and popular human recreation area, with neat lawns and picnic tables (where dogs must be leashed).

But, glory be to dog, the park sports several unspoiled trails for leash-free hiking in the surrounding hills. And, unlike at Lake Chabot, here you're permitted to take a dog on a rented boat. Every dog can have his day here.

From this recreation area, you can enter the Ohlone Wilderness Trail—29 miles of gorgeous trail through four regional parks. (See

Ohlone Regional Wilderness, page 369.)

The 150 sites at Family Camp allow dogs, but only on leash or confined to your tent. Sites are $13 to $18. Reserve through the East Bay Regional Parks reservation number: (510) 562-CAMP.

From Interstate 580, take North Livermore Avenue from downtown Livermore. It will become South Livermore Avenue, then Tesla Road. Take a right (south) on Mines Road, then turn right on Del Valle Road. The parking fee is $3, $4 from March through October. The dog fee is $1. (510) 635-0135. ➡ *See #18 on map p. 352.*

•**Livermore Canine Park** 🐾 🐾 🐾 🐾 🐕

If it weren't for the efforts of local vet Martin Plone, Livermore wouldn't have this slice of dog paradise in Max Baer Park. After seeing leash-free dog parks in Marin, Dr. Plone asked himself, "Why don't we have one in Livermore?" Then he asked the city. In spring of 1993, Livermore agreed to try it on a six-month trial basis, provided that the park be privately funded. Dr. Plone raised the needed cash from other local veterinarians and it's been a smashing success ever since.

The half-acre, fenced-in park is level and grassy, with lots of shady trees. Inside the run are disposable scoopers, a water fountain and bowls, and chairs where people can hang out while their dogs romp. On summer evenings, as many as 25 to 30 dogs enjoy the park. "Everybody loves it," Plone says. "It's become a meeting place for people. While their dogs are playing, people form friendships." Jerry Ingledue, the city's parks superintendent, is just as pleased with response to the dog park. He has received over 20 enthusiastic thank-you notes—more than a few co-signed with paw prints.

From Interstate 580 east, take the Portola exit. Go south on Murietta Boulevard. Turn right on Stanley Boulevard and follow it to Murdell Lane. Turn left on Murdell and go about two miles to the park. To get to the dog park area, park at the far end of the lot and follow the concrete path. (510) 373-5700. ➡ *See #19 on map p. 352.*

•**Sycamore Grove Regional Park** 🐾 🐾 🐾

Sycamore Grove is an unusual and attractive streamside park. In rainy times, it can look semi-swampy, as most of the Central Valley used to look. In fact, it is Lake Del Valle's flood plain, and federal flood controllers occasionally send runoff into this park's stream, Arroyo Del Valle, when Lake Del Valle rises too high.

With its low hills, tall grass and loud sounds of birds and squirrels, it's almost an African savanna. Blackbirds and swallows swoop over the stream and marshy spots, grabbing insects. Poppies are plentiful in spring. Kids wade in the stream pools near the picnic tables (and so may dogs, but technically they must be leashed). Follow the paths far enough, though, and the place becomes satisfyingly wild.

The park is quite flat, perfect for dogs who don't do well in low gear. Take Interstate 580 to Livermore; exit to Portola Avenue. Go east to North Livermore Avenue and turn right. After 2.5 miles, North Livermore turns into Arroyo Road. Turn right on Wetmore Road. There's a $2 fee. (510) 373-5700. → *See #20 on map p. 352.*

• **Ohlone Regional Wilderness** 😺 😺 😺 😺 🐾

The centerpiece of this magnificent parkland is the 3,817-foot Rose Peak—only 32 feet lower than Mount Diablo. Leash-free dogs are in heaven on earth as they explore the surrounding 6,758 acres of grassy ridges. Wildlife is abundant, so if your dog isn't obedient, it's best to keep her leashed. The tule elk appreciate it, and your dog will appreciate it too, should you run into a mountain lion.

The regional parks system shares the wilderness with the San Francisco Water District, which wants to limit the human presence here. Dogs may not stay overnight in the campgrounds.

To enter this wild and breathtaking area east of Sunol Regional Wilderness, you must pick up a permit (which includes a detailed trail map and camping information) for $1 at East Bay Regional Parks headquarters or at the Del Valle, Coyote Hills or Sunol kiosks. (510) 635-0135. → *See #21 on map p. 352.*

• **Ohlone Wilderness Trail** 😺 😺 😺 😺 🐾

Some of the area's most remote and peaceful wilderness areas are accessible only by way of this 29-mile trail. The trail stretches from Mission Peak, east of Fremont, through Sunol Regional Wilderness and Ohlone Regional Wilderness to Del Valle Regional Park, south of Livermore. You and your occasionally leash-free dog (signs tell you when it's allowed) will hike through oak and bay woods and grassy uplands that are carpeted with wildflowers in spring.

You'll also see abundant wildlife—if you're quiet and lucky, you might even see an endangered bald eagle. If your dog can't take the pressure of merely watching as tule elk and deer pass by, you should keep him leashed.

A permit is required. Because of some restrictions, you won't be able to do all 29 miles at once with your dog. That's okay. In fact, that's probably just fine with your dog. (510) 635-0135. → *See #22 on map p. 352.*

PLACES TO STAY
Del Valle Regional Park camping: See page 367.

Holiday Inn-Livermore: They like pooches here. Rates are $53 to $65. 720 Las Flores Road, Livermore, CA 94550; (510) 443-4950.

OAKLAND

Oakland, the most urban city in the East Bay, is also blessed with a collection of generous and tolerant city parks. Unfortunately, what we call the "white gloves" part of Oakland—the parklands ringing Lake Merritt and the Oakland Museum—is off-limits to dogs. But read on.

PARKS, BEACHES & RECREATION AREAS

•Dimond Park 🐾 🐾 🐾

Dimond Park is a small jewel of a canyon, dense and wild in the midst of the city. Your leashed dog's eyes will sparkle when she sees this lush place. The Dimond Canyon Hiking Trail begins to the east of El Centro Avenue. There's a small parking lot at El Centro where it bisects the park. A short foot trail goes off west of El Centro, ending quickly at the Dimond Recreation Center and an attractive jungle gym for children.

The main trail is wide and of smooth dirt. It starts on the east side and follows Sausal Creek about one-quarter mile up the canyon. At that point, the trail becomes the creekbed, so you can continue only in dry season. But what a quarter mile! The deciduous tangle of trees and ivy make the canyon into a hushed, cool bower, and the creek is wide and accessible to dogs longing for a splash. When the water level is high enough, there are falls and, except in the driest months, there's enough for a dog pool or two. After the trail goes into the creekbed, the going is a little rougher, but you can follow it all the way to the ridge at the eastern end.

From Interstate 580, take the Fruitvale Avenue exit north to the corner of Fruitvale and Lyman Road, the eastern entrance. Or, to park at the trailhead, take the Park Boulevard exit from Highway 13 and turn left (south) on El Centro Avenue. (510) 238-7100. ➡ *See #23 on map p. 352.*

•Joaquin Miller Park 🐾 🐾 🐾 🦴

This large, beautiful city park is nestled at the western edge of the huge Redwood Regional Park (see page 372). If it weren't for the Oakland city parks' rule that dogs must always be leashed, Joaquin Miller would be dog heaven.

Dogs can't enter some of the landscaped areas, such as around Woodminster Amphitheater. On the deliciously cool and damp creek trails below, however, you and your dog will feel like you own the place.

The West Ridge Trail, reachable from Skyline Boulevard, is popular with mountain bikers. It's waterless, but it's still a good run. The best trails can be entered from the ranger station off Joaquin Miller Road. The Sunset Trail descends about one-eighth of a mile to a cool, ferny stream winding through second- and third-growth redwoods, pines, oak and laurel. It then ascends to a ridge overlooking cities and the bay. In spring, the ridge is peppered with wildflowers. Plenty of picnic tables and water fountains are scattered throughout the park.

From Highway 13 in Oakland, take the Joaquin Miller Road exit and go one-half mile east to the ranger station. (510) 238-7100. →*See #24 on map p. 352.*

•Leona Heights Park 🐾 🐾 🐾 1/2

This park is a miniature version of the incomparable Redwood Regional Park (see page 372), which is most dogs' idea of nirvana. Leona Heights would be among the best parks in the city, if not for Oakland's leash law. Few bikes can negotiate the trails here and few people know about the secluded areas of the park. You're likely to find yourselves on your own in this lush setting.

Park at the entrance on Mountain Boulevard. There are plenty of paths on both sides, but we recommend walking east on Oakleaf Street, past Leona Lodge. The street is actually the York Trail, which follows boulder-lined Horseshoe Creek, with falls and plentiful dog pools. The dirt path is passable for about a quarter mile, over wooden bridges and through glades of eucalyptuses, ferns, oaks, pines, redwoods, bay and French broom. When you reach the stream crossing that's lacking a bridge, don't continue unless you're prepared to clamber, slide and grab trees the rest of the way. Unfortunately, there's a distinct lack of trail maintenance here. Several spots on the York Trail are downright dangerous, and the lack of railings next to steep creek banks and slippery boulders rules out bringing any young kids along.

Take the Redwood Road exit from Highway 13 and go south on Mountain Boulevard. Park when you see the sign for Leona Lodge. There is also a fire trail starting behind Merritt College's recycling center—at the first parking lot on the right on Campus Drive (off Redwood Road). A new hiking trail will soon be open leading down into the park from this lot. (510) 238-6888. →*See #25 on map p. 352.*

•Leona Heights Regional Open Space 🐾 🐾 🐾 🐕

Unmarked on most maps, this open space stretches from Merritt College south to Oak Knoll, and from Interstate 580 east to Anthony

Chabot Regional Park. Since it's part of the East Bay Regional Parks system, your dog need not be on leash. A bumpy fire trail goes from Merritt College downhill to the southern entrance, just north of Oak Knoll.

The best way to enter is to park at a lot off Canyon Oaks Drive, next to a condominium parking lot. Right at this entrance is a pond, but you won't see any more water as you ascend. It's a dry hike in warm weather.

The fire trail leads gently uphill all the way to Merritt, through coyote brush and oak woodland. In spring, it's full of wildflowers and abuzz with the loud hum of bees. Watch out for poison oak.

From Interstate 580, exit at Keller Avenue and drive east to Campus Drive. Take a left (north), then a left on Canyon Oaks Drive. (510) 635-0135. ➔*See #26 on map p. 352.*

• **Redwood Regional Park** 🐾 🐾 🐾 🐾 👣 🐕

Many dogs rate this as their all-star, four-paw park. It's less frequented than Tilden Regional Park (see page 358), and our favorite spots are easy to find. The cool redwood canyons are filled—even through most summers—with ferny pools for dog swims. We've seen the larger pools hold three or four blissed-out golden retrievers at once. Off leash once you leave the parking lot, your dog can spend hours on the trails, sniffing, swimming and gathering burrs.

This is also one of the most naturally beautiful and varied of the regional parks, with its majestic redwood, pine, eucalyptus, madrone and flowering fruit trees. A human being won't want to go home from here either.

Mud is inevitable if you follow the Stream Trail and stop at the pools, but fortunately it dries quickly and falls off. The only real hazards on these trails are ticks and poison oak.

No parking fee is charged at Skyline Gate at the north end (in Contra Costa County—the park straddles Contra Costa and Alameda counties). Entering here also lets you avoid the tempting smells of picnic tables at the south end. The Stream Trail takes you steadily downhill, then takes a steep plunge to the canyon bottom. It's uphill all the way back, but it's worth it.

To get to the Skyline Gate, take the Joaquin Miller Road exit and head east. Turn right on Skyline Boulevard and take it four miles to the entrance. The Redwood Road entrance charges a $3 parking fee and a $1 dog fee. (510) 635-0135. ➔*See #27 on map p. 352.*

• **San Leandro Bay Regional Shoreline** 🐾 🐾 1/2

The Oakland shoreline doesn't have much to offer a dog besides this park, which is well maintained by the East Bay Regional Parks system. And it has a major flaw: The parks system classifies the whole thing as a developed area, so you must leash. The kinds of fun a dog most wants—running full-out across grass, swimming in the bay or chasing ground squirrels—is illegal.

But you can have a genteel good time on a sunny day that's not too windy, ambling together along the extensive paved bayside trails. Amenities for people are plentiful: picnic tables, a few trees, fountains, a parcourse, a tiny beach and a huge playing field.

There's a wooden walkway over some mudflats for watching shorebirds and terns fishing. For birdwatching, go at low tide. Keep your dog firmly leashed and held close to you and hike along the San Leandro Creek Channel to Arrowhead Marsh. If you enter from Doolittle Drive, walk along the Doolittle Trail. There's a small sandy beach here, but dogs aren't allowed to swim. (The usual East Bay Regional Parks rules apply: No dogs allowed on beaches.)

From Interstate 880, exit at Hegenberger Road in Oakland. Go west on Hegenberger and turn on Edgewater Drive, Pardee Drive or Doolittle Drive. Parking is free at each of these entry points. (510) 635-0135. ➡ *See #28 on map p. 352.*

• **Temescal Regional Recreation Area** 🐾 🐾 🐾

Lake Temescal, a small, natural-looking reservoir in North Oakland, is popular for swimming, fishing and picnicking. In warm weather, it's swarming with happy families from every part of the world, cooking up smells that will drive your poor leashed dog wild. We've seen Japanese group games, outdoor church services and pinata parties.

Dogs love the paths through woods around the lake. Because this is a regional recreation area and not a park, they're supposed to be on leash even on the trails, and park staffers are strict about dogs in the water. In winter, however, you may have the park nearly to yourself. One drawback is a hearing the low-key whoosh of traffic from highways 13 and 24. The pine and willow trees on the steep-sided hills on a misty winter day can remind you of a Japanese watercolor. The terrible fire of 1991 burned about 20 acres of trees on the western hillside, but they were well on their way back by spring of '94.

Day-use fees are $2 to $3.50. Dogs are $1 extra. From Highway 24, take the Broadway exit and follow signs to Highway 13. You'll see the parking area on the right. From Highway 13, take the Broadway Terrace exit and drive west a short distance to the park entrance. (510) 635-0135. ➡ *See #29 on map p. 352.*

RESTAURANTS

Oakland's College Avenue, in the Rockridge District, has a tolerant family atmosphere. Lawyers with briefcases buy flowers on the way home from the BART station, and students flirt over ice cream. I've never seen anyone in this neighborhood who didn't love dogs. Even so, you should leash for safety on this busy street.

The avenue is known to be a food lover's paradise, and among the attractions are a string of restaurants with outdoor tables.

Cactus Taqueria: Tacos, burritos, beer and wine are served cafeteria-style, surrounded by Yup-Mex decor. Eight tables in a tiled space set off from the sidewalk are inviting to dogs. But since health departments are ambivalent about dogs in any enclosed space, you'll do the owners a favor if you offer to tie your dog up on the other side. 5525 College Avenue; (510) 547-1305.

Cafe Rustica: The pizza here is elegant. Eat it at the outdoor tables with your drooling dog. 5422 College Avenue; (510) 654-1601.

Oliveto Cafe: This cafe and Peaberry's, next door, share a building with the Market Hall, God's own food emporium. The food's the best, but for a dog, the atmosphere is congested. It's not for nervous dogs. Oliveto serves very classy pizza, tapas, bar food, desserts, coffees and drinks, but alcohol is not allowed at the sidewalk tables. 5655 College Avenue, just south of Rockridge BART; (510) 547-5356.

Peaberry's: Enjoy coffees, pastries and desserts at the outdoor tables here. This is a favorite with BART commuters. 5655 College Avenue; (510) 653-0450.

Royal Coffee: This is a cheery and popular place with very good coffee and tea, in the bean or in the cup, and supplies. On weekend mornings, it's dog central. 307 63rd Street at College Avenue; (510) 653-5458.

Salty Dog: Located at the end of the pier in Jack London Square, this sandwich shop has four outside tables where you and your dog can chow down. (When asked what their specialties are, the owner said, "We make 25 different sandwiches and they're all special.") On Sundays in the summer, after strolling through the farmers market, you might enjoy their barbecued burgers and spare ribs while watching the sailboats cut across the estuary. 53 Jack London Square; (510) 452-2563.

PLACES TO STAY

Days Inn-Oakland Airport: Small dogs only, please. Rates are $60 to $84. Dogs require a $10 deposit. 8350 Edes Avenue, Oakland, CA 94621; (510) 568-1880.

Oakland Airport Hilton: They prefer the tinier pooches here. Rates are $120 to $160. Dogs are $10 extra. At 1 Hegenberger Road, Oakland, CA 94614; (510) 635-5000.

PIEDMONT

Piedmont, the incorporated town in the midst of Oakland, is almost entirely residential and very proper and clean. This means you won't be able to find a stray scrap of paper to scoop with, so be prepared. Its quiet streets are delightful for walking, offering views from the hills.

Piedmont has no official park curfews. "We don't have the kind of parks people would be in after dark," says a woman at the city's recreation department, and it's true.

PARKS, BEACHES & RECREATION AREAS

• **Dracena Park** 🐾 🐾 🐾 🐾 🐕

Dracena is a woodsy oasis for a 15-minute leashed walk and sniff. Signs say you must pick up after your dog, and they mean it. There is an off-leash dog run here which is clearly marked. At Blair and Dracena avenues. (510) 420-3070. ➡ *See #30 on map p. 352.*

• **Piedmont Park** 🐾 🐾 🐾

The city is restoring Piedmont Park to its 19th-century elegance after years of neglect, clearing and re-lining the creekbed and building attractive new salmon-pink concrete pathways. The stream, fed year-round by a spring higher in the hills, creates a cool canyon of ivy and redwoods, pines, eucalyptuses and acacias. Even in the driest summer, you and your dog can enjoy a genteel stroll past pools and waterfalls.

Enter this charming urban park at the main gate, on Highland Avenue. (You can also enter through the Piedmont High School playing fields, but the school would rather you didn't bring your dog that way during school hours.) Be sure to keep your dog leashed at either end: The city animal control headquarters and a police station flank the main entrance, and Piedmont is strict! Police make periodic sweeps and cite owners who've forgotten that they aren't in Berkeley.

The park's main entrance is at Highland Avenue and Magnolia Avenue. (510) 420-3070. ➡ *See #31 on map p. 352.*

FESTIVALS

Piedmont Fourth of July: Well-behaved dogs are welcome to watch Piedmont's old-fashioned parade, but—as with all Fourth celebrations—leave your dog at home if he's afraid of firecrackers and other loud noises. Joe, for instance, celebrates our nation's birth from under the bed. The Piedmont parade begins with a cannon shot and a fire truck siren. (510) 420-3040.

PLEASANTON

PARKS, BEACHES & RECREATION AREAS

• **Pleasanton Ridge Regional Park** 🐾 🐾 🐾 🐾 ➤

This fairly recent and beautiful addition to the East Bay Regional Parks system is an isolated treat: Dogs may run off leash on all the secluded trails here as soon as you leave the staging area.

You can access Pleasanton Ridge from either Foothill or Golden Eagle roads. At the Foothill staging area, there are fine picnic sites at the trailhead. Climb up on the Oak Tree fire trail to the ridgeline, where a looping set of trails goes off to the right. The incline is gentle, through pasture (you share this park with cattle) dotted with oak and—careful—poison oak. Wildflowers riot in spring. It's a hot place in summer. At the bottom of the park, however, is a beautiful streamside stretch along Arroyo de la Laguna. There's no water above the entrance, so be sure to carry plenty.

From Interstate 680, take the Castlewood Drive exit and go left (west) on Foothill Road to the staging area. (510) 635-0135. ➡ *See #32 on map p. 352.*

PLACES TO STAY

Doubletree Hotel: Rates are $60 to $100. Dogs are $15 extra. 5990 Stoneridge Mall Road, Pleasanton, CA 94588; (510) 463-3330.

Holiday Inn: Rates are $60 to $90. A $100 deposit is required for dogs, in addition to a $10 fee. 11950 Dublin Canyon Road, Pleasanton, CA 94588; (510) 847-6000.

SAN LEANDRO

DIVERSIONS

Hustle your tail for a good cause: Each October, the Oakland Society for Prevention of Cruelty to Animals holds a fundraising dog run. You and your dog can do a two-mile run or a scenic one-mile walk, watch the World Canine Frisbee Champs perform, or enter contests—goofy pet tricks, tail-wagging, that sort of thing. It's held in the San Leandro Marina. For this year's date and info on fees, call the Oakland SPCA at (510) 569-0702.

MARIN COUNTY

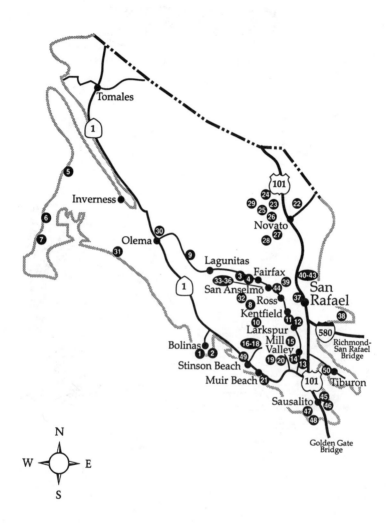

34
MARIN COUNTY

Long-known as the home of hot tubs, backrubs and ferny pubs, this comfortable, green county is also a heavenly place for the canines among us.

As you cross over the Golden Gate Bridge into this magical land, look to your left. See those hills overlooking the ocean and the bay? Some of this spectacular turf is open to off-leash dogs (see Marin Headlands Trails, page 399). A few magnificent beaches also permit buck-naked (leashless) pooches. Most are run by the Golden Gate National Recreation Area (GGNRA). To get a GGNRA "Pet Trail Map," phone (415) 556-0560.

In addition to those off-leash havens, Marin County operates 25 Open Space District lands. The landscapes include grassy expanses, wooded trails, redwood groves, marshes and steep mountainsides. The idea is to set aside bits of land so that Marin never ends up looking like the Santa Clara Valley. The Open Space parks are free, completely undeveloped and open 24 hours. As long as your obedient dog stays away from designated wildlife protection areas, you don't have to keep her leashed. To order free maps, call (415) 499-6387.

Most dogs are surprised to discover that if they wear a leash, they're permitted to explore a bit of beautiful Mount Tamalpais. (See Mount Tamalpais State Park, page 386, and Mount Tamalpais-Marin Municipal Water District Lands, page 387.)

Their mouths also tend to drop open when you mention they can visit parts of the Point Reyes National Seashore. Because it's a delicate ecosystem and a national treasure, dogs are banned from campgrounds, most backcountry trails and several beaches. Kehoe Beach (see page 381) is Bill's favorite dog-friendly Point Reyes National Seashore beach.

The Marin County ordinance doesn't specifically require dogs to be on leash. It states, "Dogs must be under the control of a responsible person at all times." But most towns—and even the parks within unincorporated areas—have their own leash laws that supersede this laid-back law. Bolinas is a refreshing exception (see page 380). If dogs could live in any town in Marin, this mellow hamlet would surely be their paws-down pick.

Dog-owning residents of Novato and San Rafael are trying to

make their communities even more dog-friendly than they are. See the introductions to these cities for more on these commendable efforts. Joe is applauding right now. Bravo.

BOLINAS

Bolinas is famous for hiding from curious visitors—thereby drawing hordes of them. They keep coming, even though town citizens regularly take down the turnoff sign on Highway 1. So if you're coming from the east (San Francisco area), turn left at the unmarked road where Bolinas Lagoon ends. If you're coming from the west, turn right where the lagoon begins.

Sometimes it seems as if half the inhabitants of Bolinas are dogs, most of them black. They stand guard outside bars, curl at shop owners' feet, snooze in the middle of the road. There's no city hall in Bolinas, an unincorporated area, and no Chamber of Commerce. Dogs are always welcome here, but cars, horses, bicycles and too many unleashed dogs compete for space. Be thoughtful and keep your pooch leashed in town.

PARKS, BEACHES & RECREATION AREAS

•**Agate Beach** 🐾 🐾 🐾 🐾

The county ordinance applies here: dogs must be on leash or under voice control. There are lots of dogs on this narrow beach flanked by rock cliffs. Kelp bulbs pop satisfyingly underfoot. Watch that the high tide doesn't sneak up on you.

From the Olema-Bolinas Road (the Bolinas turnoff from Highway 1), turn west on Mesa Road, left on Overlook Drive, right on Elm Road, all the way to the end. (415) 499-6387. ➜ *See #1 on map p. 378.*

•**Bolinas Beach** 🐾 🐾 🐾 🐾 1/2 🐕

At the end of the main street, Wharf Road, is a sand and pebble beach at the foot of a bluff. Dogs are free to run off leash. But watch for horses—with riders and without—thundering past without warning. It's animal anarchy here, and not the cleanest beach in Marin. We give it points for fun, though. (415) 499-6387. ➜ *See #2 on map p. 378.*

RESTAURANTS

Bolinas Bay Bakery and Cafe: Eat pizza, salads, desserts and baked goodies, and sip espresso on the deck with your dog. The ramp up to the deck tables renders them wheelchair- and dog-accessible. 20 Wharf Road; (415) 868-0211.

The Shop: This is a very friendly spot for breakfast, lunch and dinner, beer, wine and ice cream. It's across the street from Smiley's bar, only one of the establishments where dogs run around naked. 46 Wharf Road; (415) 868-9984.

FAIRFAX

PARKS, BEACHES & RECREATION AREAS

• **Cascade Canyon Open Space Preserve** 🐾🐾🐾🐾 🐕

As on all of Marin's open space lands, dogs can be leashless in this undeveloped area. The trail sticks close to San Anselmo Creek, which is reduced to a dry creekbed in summer. A no-bicycles trail branches off to the right and disappears into the creek; the left branch fords the creek. When the water's high, you may be stopped right here. But in summer, you can walk a long way.

Side trails lead you into shady glens of laurel and other deciduous trees, but there's lots of poison oak, too. Stay on the trail, and if your dog isn't the staying-on-trail type, it might pay to leash her.

The fire road (left fork) is the same as Cascade Canyon Road, vehicle-free except for rangers. It leads all the way into the Marin Municipal Water District lands of Mount Tamalpais. (Once you enter these, you must leash.)

The park is at the end of Cascade Drive. Park on the street at the very end of Cascade. There's a Town of Fairfax sign saying "Elliott Nature Preserve," but it's official open space. (415) 499-6387. ➡ *See #3 on map p. 378.*

• **Deer Park** 🐾🐾🐾

This is one of only three county parks to which you may bring a dog. "Leash Law Enforced" screams a sign at the entrance. Welcome!

A level dirt trail bordered with bay laurels, redwoods and oaks follows a creek, which is dry in summer. Later, the trail grows twisted and rougher—not good for casual strollers—and heads into the deeper woodlands. Watch toddlers and crazy pups carefully; there are some unprotected dropoffs by the creek. Even on weekends, you may be alone here. The delicious smell of bay is thick. Park in the lot at the end of Porteous Avenue. (415) 499-6387. ➡ *See #4 on map p. 378.*

INVERNESS

PARKS, BEACHES & RECREATION AREAS

• **Kehoe Beach** 🐾🐾🐾 1/2 🐕

This is our favorite of the Point Reyes National Seashore beaches that allow dogs, since it's both the most beautiful and the least accessible. The only parking is at roadside. You take a half-mile cinder path through wildflowers and thistles, with marsh on one side and hill on the other. In the morning, you may see some mule deer. Then, you come out on medium-brown sand that stretches forever. Since the water is shallow, the surf repeats its crests in multiple white rows, as in Hawaii. Behind you are limestone cliffs. Scattered rocks offer tide pools filled with mussels, crabs, anemones, barnacles, snails and sea flora.

In such a paradise of shore life, the leash rule makes sense. The chief reasons for leashing dogs (or banning them altogether) at the Point Reyes National Seashore beaches are the harbor seals that haul out onto the beaches. They're in no position to get away fast from a charging dog. Snowy plovers, a threatened shorebird that nests on the ground, also appreciate your dog obeying the leash law.

From Inverness, follow Sir Francis Drake Boulevard to the fork; bear right on Pierce Point Road and go about four miles; park beside the road where you see the sign and walk about one-half mile to beach. (415) 663-1092. *See #5 on map p. 378.*

•**Point Reyes Beach North** 🐾 🐾 🐾 1/2 🐾
Point Reyes Beach North is a generous, functional beach. There's no long trail from the parking lot, no special tidepools or rocks, just a long, clean, beautiful running beach for the two of you. Officially, however, the dog must be leashed.

From Inverness, take Sir Francis Drake Highway. Follow signs for the lighthouse. Go about 10 miles. The turnoff for the beach is well marked. (415) 663-1092. *See #6 on map p. 378.*

•**Point Reyes Beach South** 🐾 🐾 🐾 🐾
Point Reyes Beach South is a little narrower and steeper than Point Reyes Beach North, and it has a few interesting sandstone outcroppings with wind-carved holes. It has a bit less of that wide-open feeling. Leash the dog.

Follow the directions for Point Reyes Beach North; it's the next beach southward. (415) 663-1092. *See #7 on map p. 378.*

PLACES TO STAY

Manka's Inverness Lodge: Often, humans and their dogs spend the night here, eat breakfast and decide never to return home. It's an old hunting lodge, surrounded by woods and the beaches and mudflats of Tomales Bay—and the owners love dogs. Dogs can stay in the cabins or the garden suite. Rates are $65 to $160. Dogs are $20 extra for the length of their stay.

The food here is exceptional. The lodge's restaurant was recently given a four-star rating by the *Marin Independent Journal*. With all the wild game dishes, dogs vote it a four-paw restaurant. If they accompany you for a meal at the outdoor tables here, they'll drool over every mouthful you eat. Monday nights are excellent nights to come here for a bite, because the wild game dishes are a mere $5 to $7 each.

Look for the uphill turn off Sir Francis Drake Boulevard and take Argyle Way about 400 yards to the lodge. P.O. Box 1110, Inverness, CA 94937; (415) 669-1034.

RESTAURANTS

Manka's Inverness Lodge: This magnificent lodge is also home to a mouth-watering restaurant, if wild game is the type of dish that makes your mouth water.

KENTFIELD

PARKS, BEACHES & RECREATION AREAS

• **Northridge/Baltimore Canyon Open Space Preserve** 🐾🐾🐾🐾 🐕

From this spot, access is good for a lot of fire trails through the ridges connecting with Mount Tamalpais and water district lands. Leashes aren't required, but bikes are also allowed on these trails, so be careful. You'll be starting out fairly high on the slope.

Two access points are at the ends of Crown Road and Evergreen Drive. (415) 499-6387. ➤*See #8 on map p. 378.*

LAGUNITAS

PARKS, BEACHES & RECREATION AREAS

• **Samuel P. Taylor State Park** 🐾🐾🐾 🐾

An exception among the state parks: Dog access is generous. You can take a dog into the picnic areas, and that's worth doing here. The main picnic area right off Sir Francis Drake Boulevard is cool and often lively with the grinding call of jays. It's an easy place to bring out-of-state visitors who may just want to eat a sandwich, hug a redwood and go home. There are hollow trees stretching 20 feet across that you can actually stand inside.

But best of all, you and your dog may spend a whole day here on the wide fire trails—roughly 10 miles of them—clearly differentiated on the map you get at the entrance. Dogs may not go on the foot trails, but the fire trails are delightful enough. You can take the bicycle/horse trail from near the entrance along Papermill Creek, rising for four miles to Barnabe Peak, at 1,466 feet. Unfortunately, your dog must stay leashed, but you may actually appreciate that when you see the excellent artist's drawing of a poison oak cluster on the park's map—it's everywhere.

The park has 60 campsites. Sites are $14. Dogs are $1 extra. Call MISTIX for reservations, at (800) 444-PARK. The park's day-use fee is $5 for parking, $1 per dog. The entrance is on Sir Francis Drake Boulevard about two miles west of Lagunitas. (415) 488-9897. ➡ *See #9 on map p. 378.*

PLACES TO STAY

Samuel P. Taylor State Park camping: See above.

LARKSPUR

PARKS, BEACHES & RECREATION AREAS

• **Blithedale Summit Open Space Preserve** 🐾 🐾 🐾 🐾 ⬤ ➤

The access point at the end of Madrone Avenue—the north end of this open space—is a delightful walk in hot weather, through cool redwoods that let some light filter through. This isn't one of those really dark, drippy canyons; you're at a medium-high altitude on the slopes of Mount Tamalpais. The trail follows Larkspur Creek, which retains some pools in summer. Cross the footbridge and follow the slightly rough foot trail.

The drive up narrow Madrone Avenue is an adventure in itself; redwoods grow right in the street. According to a sign at the entrance, the part of this space belonging to the city of Larkspur requires dogs to be leashed. (415) 499-6387. ➡ *See #10 on map p. 378.*

• **Creekside Park** 🐾 🐾 1/2

This is the small, attractive county park where the multi-purpose Bon Air Path starts. The 1.8-mile paved trail goes from Bon Air Road, following Corte Madera Creek, westward to the town of Ross and eastward to the Larkspur Landing shopping center, near the ferry terminal. There are lots of paths by Corte Madera Creek, as well as a kids' gym. You must leash your dog and be sure to keep him out of marshy areas. A bulletin board displays excellent bike trail maps and descriptions of local flora and fauna. (415) 499-6387.

From Sir Francis Drake Boulevard, turn south on Bon Air Road; from Magnolia Drive, turn north. The park entrance is across from Marin General Hospital. You can get more information on the county's bike trails from the Bicycle Trails Council of Marin: (415) 456-7512. ➡ *See #11 on map p. 378.*

• **Piper Park** 🐾 🐾 🐾 1/2 ➤

Here's an ordinary people-style city park—athletic facilities, playground, picnic tables, community garden, the works—that has also included what your dog needs! It's got a small fenced area next to the community garden called Canine Commons, and it's just the ticket if your dog is a fetcher or an escape artist, or hates the leash, or loves to meet other dogs. The drawback is its small size, a mere third of an acre. There's only one striving little tree. Still, it's better than nothing. A water dish and metal scoopers are supplied.

An informative bulletin board posts useful information on where dogs are allowed in the county. The info is published by the Marin County Humane Society. Send for it: 171 Bel Marin Keys Boulevard, Novato, CA 94949. (415) 883-4621.

The Larkspur City Recreation Department runs Piper Park. You can play or watch softball, volleyball, tennis and even cricket. Outside Canine Commons, dogs must be leashed. Between Doherty Drive and Corte Madera Creek. (415) 927-5110. →*See #12 on map p. 378.*

MILL VALLEY

PARKS, BEACHES & RECREATION AREAS

• **Bayfront Park** 🐾🐾🐾🐾 🐟 🐕

This good-looking park is well designed for every kind of family activity and for dogs. There's an exercise course, lawns are green and silky, and picnic areas clean and attractive. The multi-use trails for bicycles, strollers and what-not may be used only by leashed dogs. (There are bikes galore.) But here's the canine payoff: It has a special dog run next to an estuary, where dogs are free to bathe.

The dog-use area starts where the brown grass begins. Beware, owners of escape artists: The area is huge, but not fenced. No scoops or water are furnished, but the Richardson Bay Estuary is right there to jump into.

At the end of the run there's even a marsh that dogs can explore, if you're willing to put a very mucky friend back into the car with you. Luckily, this marsh is all organic muck, free from the dangerous trash that fills many unprotected bay marshes.

For a dog park, this one offers an unparalleled view of Mount Tam. Horses and bikes pass by harmlessly on their own separate trail in the foreground, and mockingbirds sing in the bushes.

The parking lot is on Sycamore Avenue, just after you cross Camino Alto, next to the wastewater treatment plant. Keep your dog leashed near the steep-sided sewage ponds; dogs have drowned in them. Also, be sure to keep your dog leashed until you've left the parking lot and crossed the bike path. Some riders really whiz through here. (415) 383-1370. →*See #13 on map p. 378.*

• **Camino Alto Open Space Preserve** 🐾🐾🐾 1/2 🐕

In this accessible open space, your dog may run free on a wide fire trail along a ridge connecting with Mount Tamalpais. You'll walk through bay laurels, madrones and chaparral, looking down on soaring vultures and the bay, Highway 1, the hills and the headlands. A small imperfection is that you can hear the whoosh of traffic. Just pretend it's the wind. Park at the end of Escalon Drive, just west of Camino Alto. (415) 499-6387. ➔ *See #14 on map p. 378.*

• **Cascade Park** 🐾🐾🐾 1/2

Just driving to this verdant place on the slopes of Mount Tamalpais is a treat in itself—along park-like, redwood-filtered Cascade Drive. Because it borders Marin Municipal Water District land, you and your leashed dog can walk forever into its redwood and mixed-deciduous forest. The paths are wild, but well-maintained. Cascade Creek is accessible, and wet even in summer.

The very small, informal parking area is off Cascade Drive near its western end. (415) 383-1370. ➔ *See #15 on map p. 378.*

• **Mount Tamalpais State Park** 🐾🐾🐾

Generally, dogs are restricted to paved roads here. But dogs may stay in one of the campgrounds and there are also a few spots near the summit where you can take your dog. The views from here are something you'll certainly appreciate on a clear day.

Stop for lunch at the Bootjack Picnic Area, west of the Mountain Home Inn on Panoramic Highway and about a quarter mile east of the turnoff to the summit, Pantoll Road. The tables are attractively sited on the hillside under oak trees. This picnic ground is an access point for the Bootjack Trail and Matt Davis Trail. The Matt Davis Trail is off-limits, but you and your dog may—hallelujah!—use the 100 feet of Bootjack Trail that leads you into Marin Municipal Water District land, where leashed dogs are allowed. (You must travel north on the Bootjack Trail, though, not south; it's all state park in that direction.)

Heading northward, you can hook up with the Old Stage Fire Road and the Old Railroad Grade Fire Road, which are water district roads going almost the whole distance to the summit. You can also enter the Old Stage Fire Road right across from the Pantoll Ranger Station, at the intersection of Panoramic Highway and Pantoll Road. Pooches have special permission to cross the 100 feet or so of state park trail approaching water district trail.

The Bootjack Picnic Area parking lot charges $5 to park. (Once you pay in any state park lot, your receipt is good for any other spot that you hit that day.) The park has 16 developed walk-in campsites that allow dogs. They're at the Pantoll Station Campground. Sites are $14 plus $1 for your dog. All sites are first come, first served. (415) 388-2070. ➤*See #16 on map p. 378.*

• **Mount Tamalpais Summit** 🐾 🐾 🐾 🐾

The summit of Mount Tam is worth the $5 fee that you're charged merely to drive here. But in addition to the magnificent views, you may also take your dog on one trail up here ($1 dog fee).

You'll find a small refreshment stand, restrooms, visitors center and viewing platforms. On clear days, you can see nine counties, whether you want to or not. In summer, white fingers of fog obscure a good part of your view as they creep between the "knuckles" of Marin's ridges.

It's too bad if your leashed dog doesn't care about views. But he will take eagerly to the smoothly paved Verna Dunshee Trail, about one mile long, running almost level around the summit. About three-quarters of this trail is also wheelchair-accessible.

From Highway 101, take the Stinson Beach/Highway 1 exit. Follow Highway 1 to Panoramic Highway, which will be a right turn. Continue on Panoramic to the right turn off to Pantoll Road; Pantoll soon becomes East Ridgecrest Road and goes to the summit, then loops back for your trip down. (415) 388-2070. ➤*See #17 on map p. 378.*

• **Mount Tamalpais-Marin Municipal Water District Land** 🐾 🐾 🐾

Your very best bet for a dog walk high on the mountain is to find one of the water district fire roads near the summit. Your dog must be leashed, but at least she can go on the trails with you, and you both can experience the greenness of this wonderful mountain. At this elevation, the green comes from chaparral, pine and madrone.

Just below the summit on East Ridgecrest Boulevard, watch for the water district's gate and sign. This is the Old Railroad Grade Fire Road, which descends 1,785-feet from the entry point just west of the summit. On the way it intersects with Old Stage Fire Road, then emerges at the Bootjack Picnic Area. En route, you'll cross three creeks. For obvious reasons, you'll be happier in warm weather taking this road down, not up; get someone to meet you in a car at the Bootjack picnic site.

Another spot to pick up a water district trail is off Panoramic Highway just west of the Mountain Home Inn. Look for the Marin Municipal Water District sign by the fire station. Park at the state park parking lot west of Mountain Home Inn and walk east along this fire road, called Gravity Car Road (though it's unmarked), through mixed pines, redwoods, fir, madrone and scrub. Keep your eyes open for fast-moving mountain bikes. (415) 924-4600. ➤*See #18 on map p. 378.*

•Mountain Theatre 🐾 🐾

For a very short but lovely walk that's legal for dogs—on-leash—turn right off East Ridgecrest Boulevard just after Pantoll Road becomes East Ridgecrest, at the Rock Springs Picnic Area. Park in the lot beside the road and take the paved trail to the Mountain Theatre (officially the Sydney B. Cushing Memorial Theatre). It's an attractive five-minute walk through madrone, oak and redwoods to the theater, with its stone "bleachers." Dogs are even allowed to attend some performances with you, so long as they're leashed. Call for details: (415) 388-2070. ➤*See #19 on map p. 378.*

•Old Mill Park 🐾 🐾 🐾

Refresh your dog under cool redwoods right in the town of Mill Valley. The old mill, built in 1834, was recently restored. A wooden bridge over Old Mill Creek leads to well-maintained paths that run along the creek. The creek is dog-accessible, though pooches are supposed to be leashed.

One picnic table here sits within the hugest "fairy ring" we've ever seen—40 feet across. Boy dogs like to imagine the size of the mother tree whose stump engendered this ring of saplings. On Throckmorton Avenue at Olive Street, near the public library. (415) 383-1370. ➤*See #20 on map p. 378.*

RESTAURANTS

The Depot Cafe and Bookstore: This place is Mill Valley's town square and everybody's backyard. You and your dog may sit at cafe tables, benches or picnic tables and snack or just bask in the sun—if you don't mind skateboarders, bikes, chess players, crying kids, telephones, frisbees, hackeysack and guitar music happening right next to you. These are Marin kids, the kind who will reach out to your dog's face without a moment's hesitation. Mellow is the watchword here. Both sun and shade available, at least after midafternoon. On the Plaza; (415) 383-2665.

Dipsea Cafe: Enjoy breakfast, lunch and snacks at one of the five outdoor tables here (all but one are shaded). The food is American-style and everything is homemade, from omelets and sandwiches to lemon meringue pie. You get a scenic view onto a canal, and there's a bike path that runs right in front of the restaurant. You and your dog can stroll on it after a bite or two or three. In Tam Valley at 200 Shoreline Highway; (415) 381-0298.

Piazza d'Angelo: This Italian lunch and dinner spot has 15 tables on two outside patios, one shaded, the other not. Dogs are welcome at either. The premier dish for people here is the tortelloni della casa, and they'll even bring a bowl of agua for your dog. 22 Miller Avenue; (415) 388-2185.

PLACES TO STAY
Mount Tamalpais State Park camping: See page 386.

MUIR BEACH
PARKS, BEACHES & RECREATION AREAS
• **Muir Beach** 🐾 🐾 🐾 1/2 🐕

Muir Beach allows leashed dogs only. It's small, but a real gem, with rugged sand dunes spotted with plants, a parking lot and large picnic area, a small lagoon with tules, and its share of wind. Redwood Creek empties into the ocean here.

You can reach Muir Beach the long way, hiking about five miles from the Marin Headlands Visitor Center (see Rodeo Beach listing, page 399), or the easy way, via Highway 1. From Highway 1, watch for the turnoff for the beach. (415) 331-1540. ➔*See #21 on map p. 378.*

NOVATO
Novato is one of the Marin cities whose dog ordinance is the county's: Dog must be on leash or under verbal command. Its city parks require leashes, though.

But that last rule may soon have an exception in the form of a leash-free dog-run area. As of press time, a group called D.O.G.B.O.N.E. was working with Novato to garner a small bit of land so dogs can run around like the dogs they were meant to be. To get involved, write D.O.G.B.O.N.E, c/o Lauren Cobb, 1337 Denlyn Street, Novato, CA 94947, or phone (415) 898-5843.

PARKS, BEACHES & RECREATION AREAS
• **Deer Island Open Space Preserve** 🐾 🐾 🐾 🐾 🐕

This leash-free preserve is called an island because it's a high point in the flood plain of the Petaluma River, an oak-crowned hill surrounded by miles of dock and tules. You can easily imagine it surrounded by shallow-water Miwuk canoes slipping through rafts of ducks. The trail is a 1.8-mile loop of gentle ups and downs above ponds and marshy fields. There are some sturdy old oaks among the mixed deciduous groves, and lots of laurels. The trail is partly shaded and bans bikes.

From Highway 101, exit at San Marin Drive/Atherton Avenue; drive east about 1.5 miles and take a right on Olive Avenue, then a left on Deer Island Lane. Park in a small lot at the trailhead, by a small engineering company building. (415) 499-6387. ➤ *See #22 on map p. 378.*

• Miwuk Park 🐾🐾🐾 🦴

This is one of the best city parks we've visited. Dogs must be on-leash, but it offers a great combination of dog pleasures and human amenities. Paved paths, good for strollers, wind through pine trees. There are bocce ball courts, horseshoes, a kids' gym and a lovely shaded picnic area with grills.

Outside the Museum of the American Indian, located in this park, is an intriguing display of California native plants that the coastal Miwuk used for food, clothing and shelter.

Best of all for canines, Novato Creek flows deep and 30 to 40 feet wide—even in summer. A woman we encountered with a golden retriever told us that the muddy bottom can sometimes be soft and treacherous, so keep a close eye on your dog if he goes swimming.

At Novato Boulevard and San Miguel Drive. (415) 897-4323. ➤ *See #23 on map p. 378.*

• Mount Burdell Open Space Preserve 🐾🐾🐾🐾 🐕

Mount Burdell is the largest of Marin's open space preserves. You'll share it with cattle, but there's plenty of room. There are 8 or 10 miles of cinder and dirt paths, including part of the Bay Area Ridge Trail, that wind through its oak-dotted grasslands.

About one-eighth of a mile up the trail starting at San Andreas Drive there's a creek, but it's dry in summer. In winter, you might find the preserve's Hidden Lake. Dogs may run "under voice control" here, but as in all these open spaces, it's a good idea to carry a leash in case you meet a herd of cattle or mountain bikes. In summer, there are lots of foxtails and fire danger is high. No fires are ever allowed. Camping is allowed by permit, but there are no facilities.

From San Marin Drive, turn north on San Andreas Drive. Park on the street. (415) 499-6387. ➤ *See #24 on map p. 378.*

• Indian Tree Open Space Preserve 🐾🐾🐾 1/2 🐕

This open space and Verissimo Hills Open Space Preserve (see page 391) are good to know about because they're just east of Stafford Lake County Park. You needn't leash, but watch out for horses.

From Highway 101, exit at San Marin Drive/Atherton Avenue; drive west on San Marin. After San Marin turns into Sutro Avenue, take a right onto Vineyard Road. Park along the dirt county road that begins at the trailhead. (415) 499-6387. →*See #25 on map p. 378.*

•**Indian Valley Open Space Preserve** 😺😺😺😺 🐾

Lots of dogs come here to run in leashless ecstasy. The trail is partly sunny, partly shaded by laurels, and much-revered by canines.

From Highway 101, exit at DeLong Avenue and go west on DeLong, which becomes Diablo Avenue. Take a left on Hill Road and a right on Indian Valley Road. Drive all the way to the end; park on this road before you walk left at the spur road marked "Not a Through Street," just south of Old Ranch Road. Cross Arroyo Avichi Creek right at the entrance (dry in summer). (415) 499-6387. →*See #26 on map p. 378.*

•**Loma Verde Open Space Preserve** 😺😺😺 1/2 🐾

There are two access points to this open space where dogs are allowed off leash. One, south of the Marin Country Club, is a waterless, tree-covered hillside with a fire trail. Bikes are allowed. It's good if you like easily reachable high spots; there are fine views of San Pablo Bay. Exit Highway 101 at Ignacio Boulevard. Go west to Fairway Drive and turn left (south), then left on Alameda de la Loma, then right on Pebble Beach Drive. Access is at the end of Pebble Beach.

The second access point is through the Posada West housing development. From Alameda del Prado, turn south on Posada del Sol. The trail opening is at the end of this street. (415) 499-6387. →*See #27 on map p. 378.*

•**Lucas Valley Open Space Preserve** 😺😺😺😺 🐾

This space of rolling, oak-dotted hills affords great views of Novato and Lucas Valley developments. There are a dozen access points, most from Lucas Valley and Marinwood.

One access point is reached by turning left (north) off Lucas Valley Road on Mount Shasta Drive, then a brief right turn on Vogelsang Drive. Park near this dead end and walk in. (415) 499-6387. →*See #28 on map p. 378.*

•**Verissimo Hills Open Space Preserve** 😺😺😺 🐾

The golden hills with clumps of oak here have narrow foot trails only; bikes are prohibited. As you enter the area, you'll see a fork in the trail. Take the trail uphill to the left. This path features fine views of the hills as well as nearby residential areas. (Note that this open space preserve is co-managed by the Marin Municipal Water District, which means that if you're in doubt, leash. Be sure to close the gate to keep cattle inside.)

From Highway 101, exit at San Marin Drive/Atherton Avenue; drive west on San Marin. Turn right (west) on Center Road. Go all the way to the end, where you can park. (415) 499-6387. →*See #29 on map p. 378.*

OLEMA

PARKS, BEACHES & RECREATION AREAS

• **Bolinas Ridge Trail** 🐾 🐾 🐾

This Golden Gate National Recreation Area trail, part of the Bay Area Ridge Trail, is not for sissies—canine or human. It climbs steadily up for 11 miles from the Olema end, giving you gorgeous views of Tomales Bay, Bolinas and the ocean, ending up at the Bolinas-Fairfax Road below Alpine Lake.

You must keep your dog leashed. One good reason for this is that there are cattle roaming unfenced along the trail. And the trail is very popular with non-sissy mountain bicyclists. (The trail is wide, but made of dirt and rock.) From the western end, you'll walk through rolling grassland with cypress clumps. Rock outcrops sport crowns of poison oak, so watch it.

You may be able to cope with 11 miles of this, but remember your dog's bare pads and don't overdo it. Also, it isn't much fun for man or beast to walk 11 miles attached by a leash.

Unfortunately, only the Bolinas Ridge Trail is open to dogs; you can't take any of the spur trails going south.

The western end begins about one mile north of Olema on Sir Francis Drake Boulevard. There's roadside parking only. (415) 556-0560 or (415) 663-1092. →*See #30 on map p. 378.*

• **Limantour Beach** 🐾 🐾 🐾 🦴

This bountiful beach at Point Reyes National Seashore is most people's favorite, so it's often crowded. From the main parking lot, walk one quarter-mile through tule marsh, grasses and brush and scattered pines, past Limantour Estero. (Dogs are prohibited on the side trails.)

Rules for leashed dogs are clearly marked—a refreshing exception to the obscure and contradictory rules in so many parks. For example, approaching Limantour Beach on the path, you'll see a sign that says dogs are prohibited to your right, allowed to your left. This beach is plenty big, so it's an excellent arrangement that keeps dog owners and dog-avoiders equally happy. You may walk with your dog to Santa Maria Beach.

From Highway 1, look for the turnoff to Bear Valley Road, which runs between Olema and Inverness Park. Take Bear Valley from either direction to Limantour Road; turn south on Limantour all the way to the beach. (415) 663-1092. ➤*See #31 on map p. 378.*

ROSS

PARKS, BEACHES & RECREATION AREAS

• **Natalie Coffin Greene Park** 😺 😺 😺

Leashed dogs are welcome at this enchanted mixed forest of redwood and deciduous trees. The picnic area has an old-fashioned shelter built of logs and stone.

The park borders generic Marin Municipal Water District land, and from the park, you can pick up the wide cinder fire road leading to Phoenix Lake, a five-minute walk. Bikers, hikers and leashed dogs are all welcome on this road, but the lake is a reservoir, so no body contact is allowed—for man or beast.

The road continues, depending how far you want to walk, to Lagunitas Lake, Bon Tempe Lake, Alpine Lake and Kent Lake. (No body contact in any of them: sorry, dogs.) Combined, the water district offers 94 miles of road and 44 miles of trail in this area, meandering through hillsides, densely forested with pine, oak, madrone and a variety of other trees. For a trail map, send a self-addressed, stamped envelope to: Sky Oaks Ranger Station, P.O. Box 865, Fairfax, CA 94978, Attention: Trail Map.

At the corner of Sir Francis Drake Boulevard and Lagunitas Road, go west on Lagunitas all the way to the end, past the country club. You'll find a parking lot and some portable toilets. (415) 453-6020. ➤*See #32 on map p. 378.*

SAN ANSELMO

San Anselmo Avenue provides you and your mellow pooch with a laid-back stroll, and you can both cool your paws in San Anselmo Creek, which runs through town. Your well-behaved pooch can even be off leash, provided she's under voice control.

PARKS, BEACHES & RECREATION AREAS

• **Creek Park** 😺 😺 😺 😺 🐕

San Anselmo Creek runs between Sir Francis Drake Boulevard—which has a wide variety of antique shops—and San Anselmo Avenue, the main shopping street. A bridge connects the two streets.

Creek Park is small, but handy and clean. It's next to a free public lot with some shady spaces. Along the creek banks on the Sir Francis Drake side are picnic tables on a lawn with beautiful willows and maples. Lots of people lounge on the grass. Wooden steps lead down to the water. Dabney, a water-loving friend of Joe, loves to jump in on a hot summer day. He plunged in once next to some children catching minnows, helping herd the fish into their hands.

There's plenty of shade in which to picnic, or lie on the grass, while resting between shopping binges for antiques. "No un-leashed dogs except at heel," reads the polite sign.

Turn into parking lot from Sir Francis Drake Boulevard, near "The Hub" (intersection of Sir Francis Drake and Red Hill Avenue). (415) 258-4645. ➡ *See #33 on map p. 378.*

•Loma Alta Open Space Preserve 🐾🐾🐾🐾 🐕

A little canyon amid bare hills, lined with oaks, bay laurel and buckeye, this is an exceptional open space preserve. There's plenty of shade. The trail follows White Hill Creek, which is dry in the summer. No leash is required.

You can park at the trailhead at the end of Glen Avenue, a turn north off Sir Francis Drake Boulevard. (415) 499-6387. ➡ *See #34 on map p. 378.*

•Memorial Park 🐾🐾🐾🐾 🐕

This pleasant and popular city park has tennis courts, three baseball diamonds and a children's play area. Next to the diamonds is a fenced dog-exercise area, where leash-free dogs romp joyfully, fetching, chasing frisbees or socializing. There's even a creek next to the dog run. A volunteer group, Memorial Park Dog Owners Association, publishes a newsletter and keeps an eye out for scooper-scofflaws.

The park is off Sunnyhills Drive. (415) 258-4645. ➡ *See #35 on map p. 378.*

•Sorich Ranch Park 🐾🐾🐾🐾 🐕

The biggest and by far the wildest city park in San Anselmo is Sorich Ranch Park, an undeveloped open space soaring up to a ridgetop from which you can see a distant make-believe San Francisco skyline across the bay. From the very top of the ridge, you also can see Mount Tamalpais and most of San Rafael, including the one-of-a-kind turquoise and salmon Marin County Civic Center, designed by Frank Lloyd Wright. (Some Marinites are glad there's only one.)

The entrance from the San Anselmo side is at the end of San Francisco Boulevard, and the path is pretty much straight up. But if you aren't up to a 10-minute puffing ascent, you can just stroll in the meadows at the bottom. No leash is required, and the park is uncrowded and often pleasantly breezy. There's no water available, and it can be scorching in summer. (415) 258-4645. ➡ *See #36 on map p. 378.*

RESTAURANTS

The Arbor: They're friendly toward dogs here, but they prefer that you chain them outside the fence next to your table. The Arbor is an inviting all-around cafe with some umbrella-shaded tables on a wooden deck. 636 San Anselmo Avenue; (415) 459-5708.

SAN RAFAEL

This charming town may soon go to the dogs, thanks to an enterprising organization called Field of Dogs. The goal of this group of 200 dog-loving folks is to get a dog-run area somewhere in town. "It's been a real battle," says founder Mario Di Palma. But it looks like the dog people are winning. As of this printing, local government entities were in the process of considering a two-acre site at the end of Smith Ranch Road, north of McInnis Park.

To help support the cause, you can buy a T-shirt with the group's logo, a dog bone, and motto, "When you build it, they will come," inspired by the movie *Field of Dreams.* Or you can be involved in more direct ways. Write Di Palma at 34 Heritage Drive, San Rafael, CA 94901, or call (415) 454-4851.

PARKS, BEACHES & RECREATION AREAS

• Boyd Park 🐾 🐾 1/2

This is not a very doggy park, until you drive past the Dollar mansion (now the Falkirk Community Cultural Center) into the hills on Robert Dollar Scenic Drive to the undeveloped portion. The only parking is at a turnout off the drive, but at that spot, the drive becomes a dirt fire trail, closed to autos, that mounts the ridgecrest in a steady uphill climb through brush, oak and madrone.

Leash your pup and start walking. You'll get a breathtaking view of the Richmond-San Rafael Bridge, the Bay Bridge, the Oakland skyline and Mount Tam. Robert Dollar Scenic Drive begins at the end of Laurel Place. (415) 485-3333. ➡ *See #37 on map p. 378.*

• China Camp State Park 🐾 🐾 🐾 🐾

You shouldn't miss a drive through this lovely park, although it's not terribly hospitable to dogs except at Village Beach, the site of the 1890s Chinese fishing village for which the park is named. As you drive in, you'll see a rare piece of bay, marsh and oak-covered hills as the Miwuks saw it. The hills, like islands, rise from saltmarsh seas of pickleweed and cordgrass. You'll see the "No Dogs" symbol at every trailhead, in case you're tempted. However, with your dog, you may visit any of three picnic grounds on the way, via North Point San Pedro Road: Buckeye Point and Weber Point both have tables in shade or sun overlooking San Pablo Bay, mudflats at low tide, and the hills beyond the bay. Bullhead Flat lets you get right next to the water, but there's no shade at the tables.

Watch for the sign to China Camp Village, a left turn into a lot, where there's some shade. You'll see the rickety old pier and the wood-and-tin village. Park, leash your dog and walk down to the village and the beach. On weekdays, this park is much less crowded. There are more picnic tables overlooking the water by the parking lot, an interpretive exhibit (open from 10 a.m. to 5 p.m., and open to the air so that your dog can casually stroll in with you if it isn't crowded), and, on weekends, a refreshment stand serving shrimp, crab and beer. You can eat at picnic tables right on the beach—small, but pleasantly sheltered by hillsides, with gentle surf.

Swimming is encouraged here, and it's often warm enough. Derelict fishing boats and shacks are preserved on the beach. You can walk all the way to a rocky point at the south end, but watch out for the luxuriant poison oak in the brush along the beach. You may also find occasional broken glass.

There are 31 primitive walk-in campsites here. As in all state parks, dogs must always be leashed or confined to your tent. Sites are $12 to $14. Dogs are $1 extra. Reserve through MISTIX at (800) 444-PARK. From Highway 101, take the North Point San Pedro Road exit and follow it all the way into the park. (Don't go near McNears Beach County Park just south of China Camp. Dogs are strictly forbidden.) (415) 456-0766. → *See #38 on map p. 378.*

•**Jerry Russom Memorial Park** 🐾 🐾 🐾 🐾 🐕‍🦺
Finding this undeveloped piece of leash-free land run by the city isn't easy. It's on the map, off Lucas Valley Road, but there are no signs. You enter by parking at a roadside turnout and walking around a locked gate designed to keep vehicles out. This is the paved Old Lucas Valley Road, now a foot trail. Blackberries to your left at the start of the road are an unexpected treat in season.

This is a good running track, if you don't mind asphalt, and it's good for strollers, too. But stay on the road, because there's poison oak aplenty. In some spots, the creek paralleling the road is dog-accessible and full, even in summer. A dirt path winds off into the hills, too. One small drawback: You can hear traffic noise from the highway.

Drive west on Lucas Valley Road past Las Gallinas Avenue. Turn left on Canyon Oak Drive. It's 200 yards to the unmarked turnout for the park. Leashes aren't mandatory, but if your dog is the type to crash recklessly through clumps of poison oak, you'd be wise to leash up. (415) 485-3333. → *See #39 on map p. 378.*

• **John F. McInnis County Park** 😺😺😺 🐾
This is an all-around, got-everything park for people. Among it's riches are two softball fields, two soccer fields, tennis courts, picnic area, a scale-model car track, a nine-hole golf course, miniature golf, batting cages and a dirt creekside nature trail.

Best of all for trustworthy dogs, they can be off-leash, so long as they're under verbal command and out of the golf course at all. This park isn't particularly pretty, but it's very utilitarian. From Highway 101, exit at Smith Ranch Road. (415) 499-6387. → *See #40 on map p. 378.*

• **San Pedro Mountain Open Space Preserve** 😺😺😺 1/2 🐾
A narrow footpath rises moderately but inexorably upwards through a madrone forest. But if you make it up far enough, you'll be rewarded with terrific views of the bay and Marin's peaks. Deer are plentiful, so it's kind to leash your dog if you don't trust him completely to stay by your side.

Park at the entrance at the end of Woodoaks Drive, a short street off North Point San Pedro Road just north of the Jewish Community Center of Marin. (415) 499-6387. → *See #41 on map p. 378.*

• **Santa Margarita Island**
   Open Space Preserve 😺😺😺😺 🌊 🐾
What a wonderful, secret place this is: Gallinas Creek, fortified by levees, is lined with rickety piers and small boats, like a bit of the Delta. You can cross to a tiny island via a footbridge and climb the hill you'll find here, covered with oaks and boulders, or walk around the edge on a dirt path. Watch for poison oak on the hill. Though of course it isn't true, you can feel as if no one has been here before you except Coast Mi-wuks.

From North Point San Pedro Road, turn west on Meadow Drive. Where it ends, at the western end of Vendola Drive, is the footbridge. You can park on the street. Carry water if you plan to stay long. (415) 499-6387. → *See #42 on map p. 378.*

• **Santa Venetia Marsh Open Space Preserve** 😺😺😺😺 🐾
This is one of only a few saltwater marshes where dogs may go unleashed, but they must stay on the trails. Unless you have a real water dog, that won't be a problem; it's a good spot for an escape artist to be off leash, since he can't get far on solid ground. It's cool and breezy here, but gentler than any San Francisco Bay shore park. The grasses and pickleweed make a pretty mixture of colors,

and swallows dart above the ground hunting insects.

Vendola Drive has two distinct parts, and you can get to the marsh from the end of either. At the western end of the creekside segment of Vendola, at the corner of Meadow Drive, is a footbridge leading to Santa Margarita Island (see page 396). (415) 499-6387.
➡️*See #43 on map p. 378.*

• **Terra Linda-Sleepy Hollow Divide**
  Open Space Preserve 🐾 🐾 🐾 1/2 🐕

There are many entrances to this ridgeline preserve, but generally the best are the highest on the ridge. We'll describe the one that starts you at a good high point, so that you don't have to climb. From the entrance at the end of Ridgewood Drive, you can walk into Sorich Ranch Park (see page 394).

From this ridge, you can see the city of San Rafael, Highway 101, the wonderful turquoise-roofed Marin County Civic Center, the bay and the hills of Solano County. No leash is necessary, unless you're worried about your dog tangling with deer.

Park near the very end of Ridgewood Drive. The entrance is unmarked, and you have to step over a low locked gate. (415) 499-6387. ➡️*See #44 on map p. 378.*

RESTAURANTS
Le Chalet Basque: On your way to China Camp, stop here for lunch. The restaurant features European-style cooking, both fancy and *ordinaire*. Wine and beer is served at a large number of umbrella-shaded tables behind an iron gate. The proprietor welcomes well-behaved, quiet dogs, but they must be tied up on the other side of the fence. They'll still be close enough to smell the beef bourgignon. 405 North Point San Pedro Road; (415) 479-1070.

PLACES TO STAY
China Camp State Park camping: See page 395.
Holiday Inn: Rates are $90 to $120. Dogs require a $50 deposit, plus a $10 fee. 1010 Northgate Drive, San Rafael, CA 94903; (415) 479-8800.
Villa Inn: Rates are $60 to $83. They prefer small pooches here, but they'll consider your larger dog if he's an angelic kind of guy. Dogs require a $20 deposit. 1600 Lincoln Avenue, San Rafael, CA 94901; (415) 456-4975.

SAUSALITO
Even if you live here, you should play tourist and stroll around Sausalito's harbor in the brilliant sea light (or luminous sea fog). On weekends, it's especially pleasant early in the day, before the

ferries disgorge their passengers. You can visit bookstores and cafes with your dog tied up outside; we didn't find any with outdoor tables, probably because the weather is often too cool. But the city's attitude toward dogs is relaxed. And if you're on your way to the blustery Marin Headlands, fortify yourself with a big breakfast.

PARKS, BEACHES & RECREATION AREAS

• Dunphy Park 🐾 🐾 🐾

This is a small but accessible park by the bay, and it comes complete with grass, willows, picnic tables and a volleyball court. Best of all, there's a small beach, and canine swimming is fine. You can watch sailing and windsurfing from there, too. Dogs officially must be on leash. The parking lot is at Bridgeway and Bee streets. (415) 289-4125. → *See #45 on map p. 378.*

• Remington Dog Park 🐾 🐾 🐾 🐾 🐕

Sausalito's new Remington Dog Park is named after the dog whose owner, Dianne Chute, raised the money to put the park together. It's more than an acre, all fenced, on a grassy slope with trees. An informative bulletin board, leash rack, benches, scoopers and water are furnished.

From the day it was finished, Remington and his dog friends have made terrific use of this place. "It's the social hub of Sausalito," says cartoonist Phil Frank, "where the elite with four feet meet."

What a boon to freedom-loving Sausalito dogs, who otherwise must be leashed everywhere in town. D.O.G. (Dog Owners Group) of Sausalito maintains the park and publishes a newsletter. Write to: D.O.G., 690 Butte Street, Sausalito, CA 94965, or call (415) 332-6086. The dog park is on the grounds of Martin Luther King Park, on Bridgeway at Ebbtide Avenue. Park in the large lot at the end of Ebbtide. → *See #46 on map p. 378.*

• Rodeo Beach and Lagoon 🐾 🐾 🐾 🐾 🐕

Rodeo Lagoon is lined with tules and pickleweed. Here, ocean water splashes into the lagoon in winter and rainfall swells it until it overflows, continually mixing salt and fresh water. Birds love this fecund lagoon.

It's one of the few marshes to allow dogs, who delight in the sheltered swimming. They needn't be leashed. Be courteous if you see birders, though. Birdwatching and dogs don't mix. An attractive wooden walkway leads across the lagoon to the beach.

Rodeo Beach is small but pretty, made of the dark sand common in Marin. Large rocks on shore are covered with "whitewash," birders' polite name for guano. Letting your dog swim in Marin

County surf is always risky—currents are strong, and trying to rescue a dog who is being swept away is to risk your own life. Not only that: While on the beach, watch your dog like a hawk and don't turn your own back on the surf. Especially in winter, a "sneaker" wave can sweep you and your dog away.

From the Marin Headlands Visitor Center, follow the sign west. (415) 331-1540. ➤*See #47 on map p. 378.*

•**Marin Headlands Trails** 🐾🐾🐾🐾 🐾 🐾

From Rodeo Beach, you can circle the lagoon or head up into the hills. You're in for a gorgeous walk—or a gorgeous and challenging walk, depending on the weather. Look at a map of the Bay Area, and it will be obvious why the headlands' trees all grow at an eastward slant. In summer especially, cold ocean air funnels through the Golden Gate, sucked in by the Central Valley's heat—chilling the headlands and the inhabitants of western San Francisco with fog and wind. The Bay Area may be "air-conditioned by God," but the headlands sit right at the air inflow, and it's set on "high." Never come here without at least one jacket.

Your dog will love the wind. The combination of fishy breeze and aromatic brush from the hillsides sends many into olfactory ecstasy. What looks from a distance like green fuzz on these headlands is a profusion of wildflowers and low brush. Indian paintbrush, hemlock, sticky monkeyflower, ferns, dock, morning glory, blackberry, sage and thousands more species grow here—even some stunted but effective poison oak on the windward sides. (On the lee of the hills, it's not stunted.) Groves of eucalyptus grow on the crests. You hear a lovely low rustle and roar of wind, surf, birds and insects—and the squeak and groan of eucalyptuses rubbing against each other. Pinch some sage between your fingers and sniff; if you can ever leave California again after that, you're a strong person.

From the beach and lagoon, you can hike the circle formed by the Mi-wuk Trail starting at the eastern end of the lagoon, meeting the Wolf Ridge Trail, then meeting the Coastal Trail à la the Pacific Coast Trail), back to where you started. Or you can pick up the Coastal Trail off Bunker Road near Rodeo Beach. There are trailhead signs.

Sights along these trails include World War II gun emplacements, the Golden Gate Bridge and San Francisco. As the trail rises and falls, you will discover a blessing: You'll be intermittently sheltered from the wind, and in these pockets, if the sun warms your back, you'll think you've died and gone to heaven. Your dog can run off leash on all these trails.

If you want to hike from Rodeo Beach to Muir Beach (see page 389), you must put your pooch on leash at the point where the Coastal Trail branches off westward. But the great thing is that you can travel nearly the whole width of the headlands with your dog. This is tick country, so search carefully when you get home. (415) 331-1540. ➡ *See #48 on map p. 378.*

STINSON BEACH

It's fun to poke around Stinson, which is swarming with surfers and tourists on beautiful days. There's a relaxed attitude toward dogs at the outdoor snack shop tables. Bolinas Lagoon, stretching along Highway 1 between Stinson Beach and Bolinas, is tempting but environmentally fragile, so you should picnic along the water only if your dog is controllable. You'll also be taking a chance with muddy paws in your car. Don't go near Audubon Canyon Ranch, where herons and egrets nest.

PARKS, BEACHES & RECREATION AREAS

• **Stinson Beach** 🐾 🐾 🐾 1/2 🐕

Highway 1 to Stinson and Bolinas is worth the curves you'll negotiate. Don't be in a hurry. On sunny weekends, traffic will be heavy. Try it on a foggy day—it's otherworldly. Anyway, dogs often don't care whether or not the sun is shining.

Before setting out, we asked around. "Go to Stinson," said a friend. "There are dogs everywhere." "Dogs aren't allowed on Stinson Beach," said a Golden Gate National Recreation Area ranger. "Stinson is swarming with dogs," said another friend.

A kind woman in the Muir Woods bookstore solved the mystery. "No dogs on Stinson," she said sternly, "but there's this little part at the north end that isn't Stinson. We call it Dog Beach."

Indeed, the county-managed stretch where private houses are built at the north end does allow dogs on leash. Which is itself a bit of a contradiction, because as you walk along with your obediently leashed dog, dogs who live in the houses lining the county stretch, and who don't have to wear leashes, come prancing out like the local law enforcement to check out the new kid. Leashed and leashless, dogs are indeed everywhere at Stinson. It's merry and there's plenty of room for them.

You and your dog will be equally happy on Stinson Beach, with its backdrop of low hills and lining of dunes. Keep the dog off the dunes where they're roped off, being "repaired" by the forces of nature. Dogs are allowed in Stinson Beach's picnic area by Eskoot Creek, a pretty setting redolent with tantalizing smells.

Take the beach turnoff from Highway 1. Turn right at the parking lot and park at the far north end. Walk right by the sign that says "No Pets on Beach"—you can't avoid it—and turn right. Where the houses start is the county beach. You'll see a sign dividing the two jurisdictions saying "End of Guarded Beach." (415) 868-0942. ➡ *See #49 on map p. 378.*

TIBURON

The town of Tiburon is almost too Disneyland-perfect, with its green lawns and fountains, brick sidewalks and lack of smells. On a sunny day you can't beat the clean, safe street atmosphere for eating and strolling. Dogs, of course, must be as polite and well-behaved as their owners. Tiburon did a good job of planning for parking: There's almost none except for one large lot costing $2 just for the first hour, which means that cars aren't driving around searching for a spot. Just give up and park there.

The town has also arranged for fog banks to lie harmlessly to the west—usually over Sausalito. You and your dog can walk onto the ferry dock and watch boats of the Red & White Fleet come in and out, destination San Francisco or Angel Island. Dogs aren't allowed on Angel Island, but they can take pleasure with you sniffing the exciting scent of boat motor oil on the dock.

If you get a sudden impulse to take off for San Francisco, do it! One recreational secret of the Bay Area is that you may take your dog with you on the Red & White Fleet ferries, except to Angel Island or Alcatraz (see Diversions, page 430).

PARKS, BEACHES & RECREATION AREAS

• **Richardson Bay Park** 🐾 🐾 🐾

Generally known as the Tiburon Bike Path, this is a terrific multi-use park, unusual because it can be safely enjoyed by both bicyclists and dogs. It stretches two-thirds the length of Tiburon's peninsula and has parking at both ends. The larger lot is at the northern end. A dirt road, Brunini Way (no vehicles), leads into the park at the north end. You'll find a quiet, natural bay shoreline with a bit of marsh. There's some flotsam and jetsam, but only the highest quality, of course.

Keep walking and you'll enter McKegney Green, the name of the wide bike path that runs for two miles along Tiburon Boulevard toward downtown. (It doesn't go all the way, though.) Your dog must be leashed. The path, marked for running trainers, swings past benches overlooking the bay and a kids' jungle gym.

Soon the path splits and goes past both sides of a stretch of soccer fields, fenced wildlife ponds (no dogs) and a parcourse. You can take your dog on either side, but be aware that bicyclists use both. You'll also share this path, on a fair weekend day, with roller skaters and parents pushing strollers. On the green are sunbathers and kite fliers.

The view: Mount Tamalpais and Belvedere, with the Bay Bridge, San Francisco and the Golden Gate Bridge peeking out from behind it. Bring a jacket—it can be breezy here—and carry water for your dog if you're walking far. The only fountains are for people.

The park parallels Tiburon Boulevard. (415) 435-7373. ➡*See #50 on map p. 378.*

RESTAURANTS

Paradise Hamburgers and Ice Cream: This place furnishes bike racks and lots of outdoors tables. There's always a Fido bowl of water outside the door. The owners adore dogs. 1694 Tiburon Boulevard; (415) 435-8823.

DIVERSIONS

Brunch and munch: Only in Marin? Could be: Brunch with your dog at the For Paws pet store in Tiburon. On the first Sunday of every summer month at noon, champagne for you and kibble quiche for your dog are served at outside chairs with umbrellas. It's free, unless you wish to donate to the Marin Humane Society. Brunches are served from June through September. For Paws is at 90 Main Street. (415) 435-9522.

Have your dog blessed: For Paws pet store also holds a Blessing of the Animals ceremony on the first Sunday in May. In past years, blessings have been bestowed by ordained Episcopal priests; a woman once brought a bottle of water from the River Jordan. 90 Main Street. (415) 435-9522.

Dress for trick-or-treating: Dogs certainly take naturally to the treating part of Halloween. For Paws presents an annual Doggy Costume Contest on the Sunday before Halloween. The competition is fierce for four costume awards; some 400 dogs attended last year, and owners work all year on their canine costumes. If your dog thinks dressing up is beneath her, there's a special Nude Beach area for water dogs and sophisticates—inflatable pools supplied with balls. In 1991, one of the judges was Grace Slick. So long as your dog likes crowds of other dogs looking silly, you shouldn't miss this. A $5 donation is requested for the Marin Humane Society. 90 Main Street. (415) 435-9522.

SAN FRANCISCO COUNTY

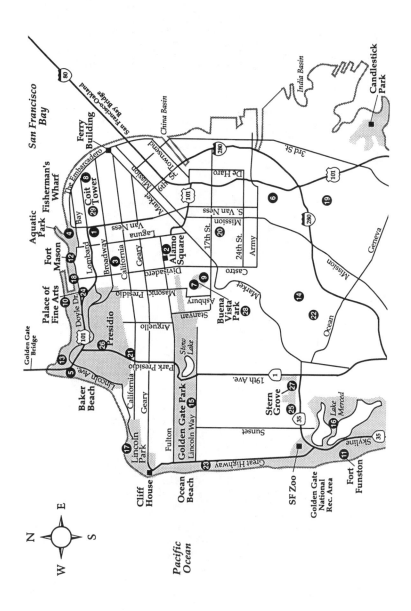

35
SAN FRANCISCO COUNTY

DOGLAND

(Best when read by someone who doesn't know
whether to become a rapper or a cheerleader.)
Keep it simple, keep it sweet.
San Francisco can't be beat.
For dogs who like to dig in sand
Or scout the land, it's the most grand
City in the world.
With tongues unfurled
And leashes off
No dog could ever get enough
Of the finest city on the earth
For making a dog know what he's worth.
(Ooh ooh arf, uh-huh-uh-huh oh, woof,
Ooh ooh arf, uh-huh-uh-huh oh, woof.)
From cable cars to ferries fast
This city makes a dog feel first, not last.
Twenty-five places to explore leash-free
So a dog can live in utter ecstasy.
Saint Francis, I wish that you could see
Just how kind your namesake town turned out to be.
(Ooh ooh arf, uh-huh-uh-huh oh, woof,
Ooh ooh arf, uh-huh-uh-huh oh, woof.)

SAN FRANCISCO

San Francisco is the only city in San Francisco County, but it's
the only city this magical county needs.

PARKS, BEACHES & RECREATION AREAS

• **Allyne Park** 🐾 🐾
This one's known as one of the most romantic little parks in the
city; your dog may get into trouble here if she doesn't watch her
step. On sunny days or moonlit nights, you're almost sure to find
friends and lovers lazing around on the grass, gazing into each
other's eyes, blissfully unaware that your dog is about to swipe the
French bread from their picnic basket.

We like this park because it's enclosed by a tall wooden fence.

But watch out if you have small dogs; they can escape underneath certain sections of the fence and gate. Because of the cultivated gardens, and because people frequently leave the park's two gates open, dogs must be on leash.

At the corner of Green and Gough streets. (415) 666-7200. →*See #1 on map p. 406.*

• **Alamo Square Park** 🐾 🐾 1/2

A postcard comes to life here for you and your leashed dog. This is where the famed Painted Ladies hold court over the city. These six brightly colored Victorian homes are even better in person than they are on a postcard.

Walk up the east side of the park, near Steiner Street, to enjoy the view of the old houses with the modern city skyline in the background. If your dog doesn't care about architecture, she'll love the fields and hills that make up this park. There's plenty of room to roam and she'll find plenty of other dogs cavorting.

The park is bordered by Fulton, Hayes, Scott and Steiner streets. (415) 666-7200. →*See #2 on map p. 406.*

• **Alta Plaza Park** 🐾 🐾 🐾 1/2 🐕

Smack in the middle of Pacific Heights, this park is where all the best breeds and most magnificent mutts gather daily. They flock to the hill on the north side of the park and conduct their dog business in the most discriminating fashion. It's not uncommon to see 25 dogs trotting around the park. Owners often address each other by their dogs' names—"Shane's mom! How *are* you?"

Make sure to visit the Dog Park Walk of Fame while you're up there—two long cement gutters with dozens of dog names carved into them. For two days after the cement was poured alongside the paved path in 1991, dog owners with sticks or keys got down on hands and knees and engraved their dogs into immortality.

The park's off-leash run is actually on the other side of the playground and tennis courts, on the second level up from Clay Street. You can distinguish it by the two cement trash cans that warn non-dog owners, "Dog Litter Only." Bushes line the paved walkway, and it's far enough from traffic that you don't have to worry about cars.

The park is bordered by Jackson, Clay, Steiner and Scott streets. (415) 666-7200. →*See #3 on map p. 406.*

• **Aquatic Park** 🐾 🐾 1/2

You've got tourist friends in town and don't feel like taking them for the usual amble through Fisherman's Wharf? Here's a great plan that lets you be semi-sporting about the whole thing while you take your dog for a jaunt. Drop them off at Aquatic Park, point them toward the tourist attractions and walk your dog right there.

Aquatic Park is just a few minutes from Ghirardelli Square, Fisherman's Wharf, a cable car line and the Hyde Street Pier. It's also a decent place for a leashed dog to romp, with its large grassy field and plenty of pine trees, benches and flowers. But stay away from the little beach—dogs aren't allowed. If you feel like shopping for T-shirts, jewelry or arts and crafts, you can take your dog along Beach Street, where dozens of sidewalk vendors sell their wares (see page 431).

The park is on Beach Street between Hyde and Polk streets. (415) 556-2904. →*See #4 on map p. 406.*

•**Baker Beach** 🐾 🐾 🐾 🐾 🐕

This beach brings your off-leash dog as close as she can get to the ocean side of the Golden Gate Bridge. And what a sight it is. Though in summer you shouldn't hold out much hope for a sunny day here, this sandy shoreline is ideal for a romp in the misty air. And dogs really appreciate Baker Beach in the summer. It's almost always cool and breezy.

If you like to sunbathe without a bathing suit and want to take your dog along, the very north end of the beach (closest to the bridge) is perfect. It's the only official nude beach in Northern California where dogs are welcome (as long as they're under voice control). But just make sure he doesn't get too up close and personal with your exposed co-bathers.

The south end is also intriguing, but dogs must be on leash. There are trails to explore and lots of picnic tables behind both ends of the beach. Leashes are required here, too. Also behind the beach is Battery Chamberlain, with its 95,000-pound cannon aimed toward the sea.

From either direction take Lincoln Boulevard to Bowley Street, then make the first turn into the two parking lots. The first one will put you closer to the off-leash area, which starts at the north end of the lot, closest to the Golden Gate Bridge. (415) 556-8371. →*See #5 on map p. 406.*

•**Bernal Heights Park** 🐾 🐾 🐾 1/2 🐕

The last time we visited this park, a dozen wolf-shepherds were the only dogs atop the amber hill. They ran and played in such pure wolf fashion it was hard to believe they weren't the genuine item. The icy wind hit the powerlines overhead and made a low, arctic whistle. The scene left an indelible impression that even in the middle of a city like San Francisco, the wild is just beneath the surface.

The rugged hills here are fairly rigorous for bipeds, but dogs have a magnificent time bolting up and down. Humans can enjoy the view of the Golden Gate and Bay bridges. The vista makes up for the austere look of the treeless park. Dogs are allowed off leash on the hills bordered by Bernal Heights Boulevard. It can be very windy and cold, so bundle up.

Enter at Carver Street and Bernal Heights Boulevard, or keep going on Bernal Heights Boulevard until just past Anderson Street. (415) 666-7200. ➡ *See #6 on map p. 406.*

• **Buena Vista Park** 🐾🐾🐾🐾 🐕

The presence of vagrants who sometimes congregate at the front of the park has scared off lots of would-be park users, but it shouldn't. They're generally a friendly lot, posing no threat to folks exploring the park's upper limits with a dog.

This park is a real find for anyone living near the Haight-Ashbury district. Hike along the myriad dirt and paved trails winding through the hills, enveloped by eucalyptus and redwood trees. Some of the gutters are lined with pieces of tombstone from a nearby cemetery. Its occupants, who died in the 1800s, were moved to the oh-so-quiet town of Colma earlier this century. The gutters give the park a historical, haunted feeling.

From the top of the park, you can see the ocean, the bay, the Marin headlands and both the Golden Gate and Bay Bridges. Birds sing everywhere. And there are lots of benches to rest on. Dogs are allowed off-leash at the woodsy west side of the park, near Central Street.

A note: Sometimes people meet for assignations at the top of the park. If this bothers you or your dog, avoid this lovers' lane.

Enter at Buena Vista Avenue West and Central Street, or from Haight Street. Open (415) 666-7200. ➡ *See #7 on map p. 406.*

• **Coit Tower** 🐾🐾 👞

Dogs enjoy a nocturnal romp here as much as people do. And since they aren't allowed inside the tower, you're not missing anything but a traffic jam if you visit here after dark.

The giant lighted column must look like a huge fire hydrant to dogs; when they see it, their noses go wild. It was erected with the funds of Lillie Hitchcock Coit, a woman who had a penchant for firefighters, so maybe our pooches are onto something.

But don't let your leashed dog use the building as a source of relief. There are plenty of trees and bushes he can try to extinguish instead, while you gaze at the sparkling city lights in every direction.

We like to park at the bottom of Telegraph Hill, at Lombard Street, and walk up the winding inner path to the top. You can also continue up Lombard as it becomes the winding Telegraph Hill Boulevard and leads you to the tower. (415) 666-7200. ➡ *See #8 on map p. 406.*

• Corona Heights Park/Red Rock Park 🐾🐾🐾🐾 🐕

The rust-colored boulders atop this park cast long, surreal shadows at dawn. If you and your dog are early risers, it's worth the hike to the summit to witness this. And there's a fine view any time of day of downtown and the Castro district.

Unfortunately, dogs aren't allowed off leash on hikes up the hill. Their off-leash area is a roomy square of grass at the foot of the park. Your best bet is to park at Museum Way and Roosevelt Avenue, and let your dog run with other dogs in the leash-free section there. Then you can go together up the hill. Fences keep dogs and people from falling down the steep cliffs. Keep in mind that there's virtually no shade, so if you have a black rug of a dog, think twice about climbing the hill on hot, sunny days.

At Museum Way and Roosevelt Avenue. (415) 666-7200. ➡ *See #9 on map p. 406.*

• Crissy Field 🐾🐾🐾🐾 🦴 🐕

There's nothing quite like Crissy Field at sunset: As the orange sun disappears behind the Golden Gate Bridge, you'll be viewing one of the most stunning blends of natural and man-made wonders in the world.

Crissy Field is a jewel of a park any time of day. Obedient, leash-free dogs can chase and cavort up and down the beach, and jump into the bay whenever they feel like it. It's one of very few spots in the Bay Area where they are allowed to swim in the bay. This is a particularly good place to bring a dog who has no desire to brave the waves of the Pacific. The surf here doesn't pound—it merely laps.

As you walk westward, the Golden Gate Bridge is before you, Alcatraz and bits of the city skyline behind you. Sailboats sometimes glide so close you can hear the sails flagging in the wind. There's a stretch of trees and picnic tables a few minutes into your walk, where you'll find water and a good place to relax while your dog investigates the scents. There's also a heavily used jogging/biking path parallel to the beach, but we don't advise you to take your unleashed dog there. He's likely to get underfoot.

If the tide is low, you can walk to the end of the beach, put your dog on the leash and continue to Fort Point (see page 413).

Enter on Mason Street in the Marina district, driving past the warehouses. Go right on Mitchell Street and through a big, rough parking lot. If you go too far to the east, you'll run into a sea of windsurfers, so try starting your walk close to the western edge of the parking lot. The beach is bordered by delicate dunes which are undergoing restoration in many places, including the entrance, so keep canines off. (415) 556-0560. ➡ *See #10 on map p. 406.*

• Fort Funston 🐾 🐾 🐾 🐾 ➡ 🐕

If there were a heaven on Earth for dogs, this would be it. This scenic ocean park lives up to its nickname—Fort Fun. It combines trails through wooded and dune areas, an eerie walk through an old military battery, and miles of ocean and sand. The best part is that even on gloomy days, you're sure to find other dogs cruising the park for a good time. It's the perfect mingling of environment and companionship, and it's all *sans* leash.

Starting from the main parking lot, next to the take-off cliff for hang gliders, you can bring your dog to the watering hole—actually a bowl underneath a drinking fountain—and fill her up. From the take-off cliff you can follow a steep trail down to the beach, but we recommend exploring above first.

Take the first trail to the north of the parking lot, the Sunset Trail, and you'll meander through dunes and ice plant, encountering every kind of dog imaginable. You'll soon come to the main entrance to Battery Davis, which was built in 1939 to protect San Francisco from enemy ship bombardment. It's now very dark and empty, and you can still enter the chambers hidden within. Bring your flashlight, a friend, your dog and some bravery. Local kids can do some great ghost imitations. Your dog is good for warding off bogeymen, unless she won't go in at all.

Or you can skip the battery and continue along on trails on either side. Both eventually end up in the same place. If you take the trail at the rear of the battery, you'll quickly be able to see the Golden Gate Bridge and the Cliff House. At that point, you'll also see a trail that takes you back into a mini-forest. Don't go all the way down, though, or you'll end up on Highway 35.

Back on the main trails, continue past a little grove of redwoods, near the merging of the two trails. If you keep going north, there's actually a way to walk all the way to the Golden Gate Bridge. But be forewarned: It's a long haul—almost eight miles to Baker Beach alone, and more than another mile after that to the bridge.

You can get to the beach at Fort Funston by following the

narrow trails through the dunes shortly after the cypress groves. You'll notice that one takes you between two cliffs. Take it all the way down to the beach. Depending on the tide, you can walk for miles or just a few feet.

You can go back the way you came, or walk along the ocean and take the steep trail back up to the main parking lot. By this time, you and your dog will both be thirsting for that water fountain.

To get to Fort Funston, follow the brown signs on the Great Highway. It's about one-half mile south of the turnoff to John Muir Drive. Once on the main drive, bear right, past a little building painted with hang gliders, and drive into the main parking lot. (415) 556-8371. ➤*See #11 on map p. 406.*

•Fort Mason 🐾 🐾 🐾

This park, perched high above the bay, is full of surprises. Depending on the disposition of your dog, some of the surprises are great fun. One can be downright frightening.

The best stands right in the middle of the wide open field that constitutes the main part of the park. It's a fire hydrant, and it sticks out like a sore yellow thumb from its flat green surroundings. Joyous male dogs bound up and pay it homage time and time again.

The object that seems to take dogs aback, although people find it riveting, is a gigantic bronze statue of Phillip Burton. Several feet taller and broader than life, with outstretched hand, it can send a dog fleeing as far as his mandatory leash will allow.

Lower Fort Mason is also interesting to investigate. You can walk alongside the piers and sniff the bay, or peer at the liberty ship Jeremiah O'Brien.

Enter the lower Fort Mason parking lot at Buchanan Street and take the stairs all the way up to upper Fort Mason. (Huff, puff.) Or park along Bay Street or Laguna Street and walk in. (415) 556-0560. ➤*See #12 on map p. 406.*

•Fort Point National Historical Site 🐾 🐾 🐕

Beneath the Golden Gate Bridge, this mid-19th-century brick fortification stands as a reminder of the strategic military significance San Francisco once had. Now it serves as a tourist attraction and one of the best places to view the skyline, Alcatraz and the bridge. It's also a magnificent spot for your dog to stand mesmerized by the crashing surf.

By itself, Fort Point doesn't offer much for dogs. They must be leashed and there's only a small patch of grass. We recommend Fort Point as the goal of a long hike that starts at Crissy Field (see page 411). After walking to the west end of Crissy Field, leash your dog and follow the Golden Gate Promenade toward the bridge.

Along the way, you'll come to an old pier. There are actually two piers, but the one you're allowed on is closer to the bridge. Stroll to the end for a close-up view of sailboats being tossed about on the bay. When you finally reach Fort Point, it's a tradition among dog people to continue to the westernmost point and touch the fence. There's no telling why, but you may as well try it.

To get to Fort Point without a long hike, follow the signs from Lincoln Avenue as you approach the Golden Gate Bridge. (415) 556-1693. ➡ *See #13 on map p. 406.*

•Glen Canyon Park 🐾 🐾 🐾

From the redwood forests to the streams and grassy hills, this park was made for you and your dog. The nature trail in the middle of the park follows a muddy creek and is so overgrown with brush and bramble that at times you nearly have to crawl. It's as though the trail were blazed for dogs. There are so many dragonflies of all colors and sizes near the creek, and so much lush vegetation, that you may wonder if you've stepped back to the age of the dinosaurs.

Park at Bosworth Street and O'Shaughnessy Boulevard and walk down a dirt trail past a recreation center, through the redwoods and loud birds. Stay away from the paved road—it can look deserted for hours on end, then a car whizzes by. Your dog is supposed to be leashed, but you should still be aware of the road. In a few minutes, you'll come to a long, low building. At this point, you can go left and up a hill for some secluded picnic spots, or keep going and take the nature trail. When you finally emerge from the dragonflies and dense greenery, take any of several trails up the open, rolling hills and enjoy a panorama of the park.

At Bosworth Street and O'Shaughnessy Boulevard. (415) 666-7200. ➡ *See #14 on map p. 406.*

•Golden Gate Park 🐾 🐾 🐾

This famed city park provides much dog bliss, but only in the places where dogs are supposed to be leashed. Four areas are set aside for leashless dogs, but dogs-in-the-know try not to go to those places, for good reason. For information about any area in the park, call (415) 666-7200. ➡ *See #15 on map p. 406.*

•Golden Gate Park Dog Run 🐾 🐾 1/2 🐕

This fenced-in dog exercise area has the dubious distinction of being located right next to a field full of buffalo. It's a grassless, dusty, chain-linked pen designed for owners who'd rather go for a talk than a walk. Dogs tend to sniff each other and sit, sniff each other and take a drink from the water bowls. But since it's the city's only fenced-in dog park, it provides a good service.

We've found more amorous dogs here than in any other park, so if your dog isn't in the mood (or you don't want her to be), this isn't the place to take her.

But just in case, it's at 38th Avenue and Fulton Street. Park on Fulton Street and walk in, or take 36th Avenue into the park and go right at the first paved road. Drive all the way to the end, and there it is.

• Golden Gate Park (northeast corner) 🐾 🐕

Then there are the narrow fields at the northeast corner of the park, up by the horseshoe courts. It's a strange little area with hills and dales and dirt paths. Homeless people live here and some don't keep good house. You'll see the campfire remains, old sleeping bags and trash of every type. It's best to avoid this place, except in the middle of the day.

Enter at Stanyan and Fulton streets.

• Golden Gate Park (south side) 🐾 🐾 🐕

The two other areas set aside for dogs are slivers along the south end of the park. One is between Fifth and Seventh Avenues, and bounded on the north and south by Lincoln Way and Martin Luther King Jr. Drive. The other is on the south side of the polo field, between 34th and 38th Avenues, and Middle Drive and Martin Luther King Jr. Drive. Bring your dog to these sections if he's very good off leash. They're too close to busy traffic for less disciplined dogs.

• Golden Gate Park (Stow Lake/Strawberry Hill) 🐾 🐾 🐾

One of the in places in Golden Gate Park is the summit of the man-made mountain at Stow Lake. It's truly a sniffer's paradise. Dogs who like to look at ducks will also enjoy it. The path winds up Strawberry Hill to a breathtaking 360-degree view of the city. Unfortunately, dogs are not supposed to be off leash. It's best to avoid this walk on weekends, when bikers and hikers are everywhere.

Stow Lake is between 15th and 19th avenues. From John F. Kennedy Drive or Martin Luther King Jr. Drive, follow the Stow Lake signs.

• Golden Gate Park (by the Polo Field) 🐾 🐾 🐾

Dogs who prefer playing frisbee (on leash) go to the meadow just east of the polo field. It's known for wide-open dells, good bushes and plenty of gopher holes for old sports. Your best bet here is to go early in the morning.

•Golden Gate Park (horse paths) 🐾🐾🐾

Dogs who like to promenade—to see and be seen—take to the horse paths that radiate out from the stables. Or you can simply walk along the track that circles the field. One word of caution: The stables are rife with cats. Dogs need to know this. Leashes are mandatory, and remember—the mounted police station is uncomfortably close by.

•Golden Gate Park (The Panhandle) 🐾🐾

That long, thin strip of park that extends eight blocks from the east end of the park to Baker Street, is a great hangout for cool dogs. It's got a real Haight-Ashbury influence in parts, and although dogs must be leashed, they love to saunter around visiting other dogs wearing bandanas.

•Lake Merced 🐾🐾 1/2 🐕

As the city's largest body of water, Lake Merced is favored by Labrador retrievers, Irish setters and the like. An ideal spot to explore is the footbridge area near the south end of the lake. There are a couple of sandy beaches there that are safe from traffic, but dogs are supposed to be leashed anyway. Once you cross the bridge, you'll come to an inviting area with lots of little trees.

You'll enter a small grassy section and come to a narrow dirt trail overlooking the lake's northeast bowl. We don't recommend letting dogs off the leash until you're at least a couple of hundred feet into the park, because menacing traffic is so close by. There are birds galore and purple wildflowers in spring. The park is a tease, though, because there's no way to get to the lake—it's down a very formidable slope covered with impenetrable brush.

The off-leash section of Lake Merced is at the north end, at Lake Merced Boulevard and Middlefield Drive. Park at Middlefield Drive and Gellert Drive, and cross Lake Merced Boulevard—very carefully. At times it's like a race car track. (415) 666-7200. ➤*See #16 on map p. 406.*

•Land's End/Lincoln Park 🐾🐾🐾🐾 🦴 🐕

This is probably the most spectacular park in San Francisco. You won't believe your eyes and your dog won't believe his nose. And neither of you will believe your ears—it's so far removed from traffic that all you hear are foghorns, the calls of birds and the wind whistling through the redwoods and eucalyptus. The best part: No leashes.

The towering cliffs, high above the crashing tide below, overlook virtually no civilization. For miles, all you can see is ocean, cliffs, trees, wildflowers and boats. It looks more like Mendocino did 100 years ago—at least until you round one final bend and the Golden

Gate Bridge jars your senses back to semi-urban reality.

If you want to venture the entire length of the dirt trail, keep two things in mind: Don't wear tight pants—you'll have to do some high stepping in some spots, and you don't want your legs packed into your Levi's—and don't bring a young puppy or out-of-control dog. The cliffs here can be dangerous, especially where the trail becomes narrow.

There are many entrance points, but we like to start from the parking lot at the end of Camino del Mar. Go down the wooden steps to the wide dirt trail and turn right. As you hike, you'll come to occasional wood benches overlooking wildly beautiful sea-scapes. Take a moment to sit down. Your dog will appreciate the chance to contemplate the wondrous odors coming through her bulbous olfactory sensor.

As you continue, you'll pass a sign that makes its point efficiently and effectively: "Caution! Cliff and surf are extremely dangerous. People have been swept from the rocks and drowned." You'll have no problem if you proceed on the main trail and ignore the temptation to follow the dozens of tiny paths down the cliff face. (Naked men often hang out at a beach or two down there, so if your dog blushes easily, you'll have extra reason to stay on the wider paths.)

In a little while, you'll come to the second such sign. This time, instead of continuing on the main path (it gets extremely precarious, even for the most sure-footed), take the trail to your right. It's a fairly hard slope, but it's safe and gets you where you want to go.

Rest at the bench halfway up, if you feel the need. The trail will soon bring you down and around to an incredible view. Keep going and turn around when you're ready to go home. Try not to end up on the golf course, though. Golfers don't appreciate canines at tee-off time.

At the end of Camino del Mar. (415) 556-8371. ➡️*See #17 on map p. 406.*

• **Marina Green** 🐾 🐾 1/2

The clang of halyards against masts creates a magical symphony from the nearby marinas here on windy days. Your dog's first reaction may be a puzzled 30-degree head tilt.

Most of us know the Marina Green for its high-flying kites and hard-running joggers. But it's also a decent place to take your dog, as long as he's leashed. It's too close to the rush of cars on Marina Boulevard to be comfortable off leash, anyway.

The grass is always green here, as the park's name indicates. It's a treat for eyes overdosed on dry yellow grass and paws laden with foxtails. There's also an attractive heart parcourse and a great view of Alcatraz.

Enter on Marina Boulevard, anywhere between Scott and Buchanan streets. (415) 556-0560. → *See #18 on map p. 406.*

•**McLaren Park** 🐾 🐾 🐾 🐕

You and your dog can enter this park anywhere and find a trail within seconds. The surprise is that most of the trails run through remote wooded areas and windswept hills with sweeping views.

It's an ideal place to visit if you're taking someone to play soccer or softball at the Crocker-Amazon Playground. They play, you walk up a hill behind the soccer fields and roam with your leashed dog. Better yet, drive to the northern part of the park, to the section bounded by John F. Shelley Drive. Dogs are allowed off leash here, where they're far enough from traffic. Certain parts can be crowded with schoolchildren or company picnickers, so watch where you wander.

There are many entry points, but we prefer Brazil Avenue, which turns into Mansell Street in the park. (415) 666-7200. → *See #19 on map p. 406.*

•**Mission Dolores Park** 🐾 🐾 🐾

You can get a little history lesson while walking your dog here. A statue of Miguel Hidalgo overlooks the park, and Mexico's liberty bell hangs at the Dolores Street entrance.

History may not impress your dog, but a wide-open space for running off leash will. It's behind the tennis courts.

There are two problems with this area, though. One: It's easy for your dog to run into the road. Even if she's the voice control type, she could find herself in Church Street traffic just by running a little too far to catch a ball.

And two: You have to be on the lookout that your dog doesn't run over people who live in the park. Joe once slid into a sleeping homeless woman and scared her so badly she screamed and ran away.

Enter anywhere on Dolores or Church streets, between 18th and 20th streets. (415) 666-7200. → *See #20 on map p. 406.*

•**Mountain Lake Park** 🐾 🐾 🐾 1/2 🐕

In this sociable park, your dog can cavort with other dogs while you shoot the breeze with other dog people. The off-leash area is between two signs on the east side of the park. There's a bench for humans, and a pretty good safety net between dogs and the outside world.

The favorite game among dogs here involves a big green bush.

One dog usually starts running around it for no apparent reason. Circle after circle, he'll attract more and more dogs into chasing him until almost every dog is swirling around in a dizzying loop. Watch too closely and you can get seasick.

Dogs find the rest of the park mildly entertaining, although they have to be leashed. The lake that's the park's namesake is little more than a pond. Ducks and a couple of swans live here, and the temptation may be too much for your dog. We've seen dogs drag their owners ankle-deep into the muddy pond in pursuit of a duck dinner. The park is also home to an attractive playground and a decent heart parcourse.

For the dog-run area, enter on 8th Avenue at Lake Street. (415) 666-7200. ➡ *See #21 on map p. 406.*

•Mount Davidson 😺 😺 😺

Hiking to the peak of this park can be a religious experience—literally. As you emerge from the tall pine and eucalyptus trees leading to the 927-foot summit, a concrete structure looms in the distance. As you get closer you'll see that it's a gigantic cross, 103 feet tall. It's so huge, and in such a prominent spot—at the end of a long, wide path surrounded by trees—that it can be a startling sight. On his first vision, Joe backed out of his collar and collided with a tree. Since leashes are the law here, we had to quickly put him back together.

In 1934, President Roosevelt became the first person to flick the switch and light the cross. It's visible for miles, especially vivid under its nighttime floodlighting. On a night hike up Mount Davidson, you can follow the glow to the top.

Since you enter the park at such a high altitude, it's only about a 10-minute pilgrimage to the peak. But you can make it a much longer walk by experimenting with different trails.

Enter at Dalewood Way and Lansdale Avenue. (415) 666-7200. ➡ *See #22 on map p. 406.*

•Ocean Beach 😺 😺 😺 😺 🐕

This broad, four-mile-long beach with a crashing surf isn't exactly Palm Beach. It's usually cold and windy, and full of seaweed, jellyfish, jagged bits of shells and less savory deposits from the Pacific. In other words, it's a dog's dream come true.

There are usually very few bathers here, so let your dog run off-leash and have the time of his life. If you walk for an hour, you'll probably run into at least two dozen other dogs. They seem especially inspired to frolic here, so it's possible to give your dog all the exercise he needs while you sit on the sand and read a book.

By the end of Chapter 2, you'll have a thoroughly pooped pooch. Bring water for him, though. We've seen too many dogs try to drink from the ocean, thirsty after playing so hard.

You can park along the ocean, between the Cliff House and Balboa Street. Walk south on the sidewalk until you hit the beach. Or park in the spaces between Fulton Street and Lincoln Way. There's also a parking lot at Sloat Boulevard. (415) 556-8371. ➡ *See #23 on map p. 406.*

• **Palace of Fine Arts** 🐾 🐾 🐾 🐾

The glory of ancient Rome embraces you even as you approach this relic of the 1915 Panama-Pacific Exposition. From the huge colonnaded rotunda to the serene reflecting pool, the place drips with Romanesque splendor.

The Palace is especially grand under its night lighting. It's also an ideal place to take your dog while the kids go to the Exploratorium, located inside. Walk around the paved path that winds through the grand columns and around the pond. But keep your eyes peeled for people feeding the multitudes of pigeons, ducks and geese. Dogs like Joe love to break up the feeding frenzy with an abrupt tug on the mandatory leash. Feathers fly and dried bread scatters everywhere.

The best place to enter for the full Roman effect is on Baker Street, between North Point and Jefferson Streets. (415) 666-7200. ➡ *See #24 on map p. 406.*

• **Pine Lake Park** 🐾 🐾 🐾

Adjacent to Stern Grove (see page 421), its more famous cousin, Pine Lake Park can be even more fun for dogs because it has Laguna Puerca, a small lake at the west end of the park. Swimming isn't allowed, but there's always the muddy shore for wallowing.

The lake is in a valley at the bottom of steep slopes, so there's not much need to worry about traffic. Leashes are supposed to be on at all times, in any case. At the lake's east end, there's a big field where dogs can really cut loose—as far as leashes allow.

Enter at Crestlake Drive and Wawona Street and follow the paved path, which quickly turns into a dirt trail. (415) 666-7200. ➡ *See #25 on map p. 406.*

• **Presidio of San Francisco** 🐾 🐾 🐾

Dogs and their people like to pretend that the Presidio is their very own country estate, acre after rolling acre of secret pathways, open meadows and dense groves of eucalyptus and redwoods. The park will be much closer to being your own once the Army moves out and it becomes a national park (scheduled for late 1994).

Dogs are supposed to be leashed at all times and pooper scooper laws apply, but despite the Presidio military police's reputation as overzealous traffic enforcers, we've never seen anyone busted for walking a leashless dog. But there's always a first, so be warned.

Our favorite tour is to park just north of the Arguello Boulevard entrance, at a roadside parking area on the west side of Arguello. Follow the path in and go down the hill as it gets wider. It will loop past wildflowers and seasonal sweetpeas. Bear left at the first major fork and hike through a thick forest area, then bear right when that path gives you a choice. You'll hike up and down a gentle sequence of hills. Pull over and enjoy the larger hills to the west. Dogs thrill at speeding up and down them for no apparent reason. You'll run into a few more side trails along the way. Explore them as you wish, watching out for traffic on nearby roads.

In these hills, in the spring, you'll come across patches of bright yellow jonquils, many of them in formations resembling letters of the alphabet. An elderly British fellow who kept a good rapport with other dog owners used to plant them as a memorial to dogs who have died. There's a "G" for George at the foot of the first large hill. The man, now deceased himself, liked to plant the flowers in the spots favored by the deceased dogs, whose spirits still live on their very own 1,500-acre country estate. (See also "Explore a Military Pet Cemetery," page 430.) (415) 561-2211. *→See #26 on map p. 406.*

• Stern Grove 🐾 🐾 🐾

Until the 1991 concert season, dogs were welcome at all Stern Grove music festivals. Unfortunately, complaints about hygiene and noise changed this policy. Though dogs aren't allowed at the concert meadow, as of this printing, they are still tolerated around the peripheral hills, on leash. Bring a picnic, a bottle of wine, a rawhide bone and, of course, a pooper scooper.

Stern Grove is a treasure of trees, hills, meadows and birds. There's even a spot where dogs are allowed off leash. Unfortunately, it's one of the least attractive areas in the park—very close to the street—although trees act as an effective barrier. And if you perch on the inner edge, the dog-run area isn't a bad place to listen to a concert. The violins get a little tinny at that distance, but your dog won't care.

For the dog-run area, enter on Wawona Street between 21st and 23rd avenues. (415) 666-7200. *→See #27 on map p. 406.*

• Twin Peaks 🐾 🐾 🐾

So dogs aren't allowed at the Top of the Mark. So what. The view from up here will put all those "No Dogs Allowed" establishments to shame, and it's cheaper to entertain guests up here—it's free, in fact.

The summits of the twin peaks are higher than 900 feet. It's usually cold up here, so bundle up. You can drive to the northern peak and park in the lot. It's very touristy, but on this peak, signs tell you what you're looking at—Tiburon, Nob Hill, Mount Diablo, Japantown and Mount Tamalpais. Your dog won't get much exercise, though, since all he can do is walk around the paved viewing area on leash. And frankly, Joe is bored by the marvelous vistas.

For your dog's sake, try exploring the other peak. It's a bare hill with wooden stairs up one side. While dogs must be on leash, it's not bad exercise. And the view—at almost 20 feet higher than the first peak—is magnificent. From here you can see other potential walks for you and your dog on the lower hills, where the views are almost as dynamic and the air is a little warmer. Be sure to keep your dog on leash, because the road is never far away.

On Twin Peaks Boulevard, just north of Portola Drive. (415) 666-7200. ➤ *See #28 on map p. 406.*

• **Washington Square** 🐾 🐾

Grab a gelato, leash your dog and relax in this park in the middle of North Beach. There are plenty of benches, and enough trees to make your dog comfortable with his surroundings. The park is only about one block square, but it's great for a stroll when you're hitting the cafes of San Francisco's Little Italy. And if you have a child with you, so much the better. There's a small playground that's popular with local parents.

Washington Square is right across from the ornate Saints Peter and Paul Catholic Church, and the Transamerica pyramid looks close enough to reach out and touch.

Enter the park at any of its four borders: Columbus, Union, Stockton or Filbert streets. Try not to drive to North Beach. Even during the day, parking's a bear. (415) 666-7200. ➤ *See #29 on map p. 406.*

RESTAURANTS

Angelina's Caffe: Conveniently located one-half block from Cal's Discount Pet Supply, Angelina's is a good place for you and your dog to take a break from shopping. It's got everything from soup to pine nuts, and a large variety of coffees. Enjoy them at one of six sidewalk tables. You can also stock on up on Italian souvenirs here, but watch out for the red, white and green hats. 6000 California Street; (415) 221-7801.

Bakers of Paris: Eat French on a bench here. The croissants are out of this world. 3989 24th Street; (415) 863-8725.

Bepples Pie Shop: Joe thinks their cherry pie is tops. So do I. Eat a piece at the bench outside. 2142 Chestnut Street. (415) 931-6226.

Blue Danube Coffee House: Have your cake and eat soup and sandwiches, too, at five tables outside this charming cafe. You can even indulge in a wide selection of beer or wine, but you'll have to drink alone if your dog is under 21. On sunny days, it may be hard to find an empty spot. 306 Clement Street; (415) 221-9041.

Boudin Sourdough Bakery and Cafe: Boudin sourdough bread has few rivals in San Francisco. This bakery is smack in the middle of all the Fisherman's Wharf activity and has three outdoor tables. 156 Jefferson Street; (415) 928-1849.

Bugatti's Espresso Cafe: A popular spot with neighborhood dogs, Bugatti's has some of the best espresso and light food in town. 3001 Webster Street; (415) 922-4888.

Cafe Espresso: Sip a cappuccino while you and your dog enjoy the Anchorage Shopping Center's afternoon entertainment. Every day from noon to 5 p.m., you can hear jazz, blues, folk or a special surprise musical guest. Anchorage Shopping Center, 2800 Leavenworth Street; (415) 776-3420.

Cafe Rustico: This eatery in Potrero Hill features pizza, pasta, panini, soup and salads. There are lots of outside tables. (415) 252-0180. Right next door is *Sally's Deli and Bakery* which serves brunch on the weekends in addition to breakfast and all kinds of salads and sandwiches during the week. 300 DeHaro Street; (415) 626-6006.

Caffe Freddy's: This is a real find in North Beach, especially if you want a touch of California influence to your Italian food. Pizzettas are the specialty here. A favorite has goat cheese and smoked salmon, but there are eight other kinds. 901 Columbus Avenue; (415) 922-0151.

The Cannery: This old Del Monte packing plant is home to several restaurants with courtyard tables for you and your dog, and there's often entertainment here. Some of the restaurants don't have courtyard service after dark because it's too cold, so call first to find out. The Cannery is at 2801 Leavenworth Street. Here are three to get you started:

Le Garden Caffe: German, American, Italian—just about any kind of food you feel like. And there are plenty of tables, right next door to the courtyard's stage. (415) 928-4340.

Cafe Rigatoni: Eat delicious Italian food outside with your dog here. (415) 771-5225.

Las Margaritas Restaurant: Seven kinds of margaritas, mesquite-grilled shark and a great view of the courtyard below make this one of the more popular Mexican restaurants this side of the Mission district. (415) 776-6996.

Cleo's: Two sidewalk tables provide you with a front-row view of the lower Haight. The food is good, and mostly vegetarian, and outdoors the atmosphere's...er...funky. 698 Haight Street; (415) 252-7912.

Coffee Merchant: Lots of people come here to wake up with their dogs. We see them downing caffeine at the outside benches at any hour. 1248 9th Avenue; (415) 665-1915.

Coffee Roastery: They roast their own coffee here and you can drink it on one of the benches outside. 2191 Union Street; (415) 922-9559.

DDJ's: This places serves great Mideast food and you can enjoy it at one of their sidewalk tables—"so long as your dog isn't dangerous," says one of the owners. 624 Irving Street; (415) 681-5858.

Curbside Cafe: The servers here are very dog-friendly, and the continental cuisine is top-notch. Try not to let your dog block the sidewalk. It's a tight squeeze here. 2417 California Street; (415) 929-9030.

Double Rainbow Dessert Cafe: Dave Fong, the owner of this Sunset District ice cream parlor, loves dogs. In fact, since 1994 is the Year of the Dog according to the Chinese calendar, the store is hosting a unique (and tasty) special all year. Bring your dog to the store with you, or even just a photo of your dog, and get a free scoop of your choice. Already they've got a good many photos of dogs smiling from the walls—add yours! 2116 Irving Street; (415) 665-3090.

Embarcadero Center: If you take your dog when you go to work in the financial district, you can brown bag it at the dozens of tables and chairs and decks in the center's huge concrete courtyard, or choose from any of several restaurants with outdoor tables. Be aware, though, that some eateries aren't open on weekends. Embarcadero Center is at the foot of Market Street, between Clay and Sacramento Streets. Here are a couple of the restaurants:

> *Harbor Village Restaurant:* If you've never had dim sum with your dog, this is the place to try it. 4 Embarcadero Center. (415) 781-8833.
>
> *Marcello's Pizza:* The calzones here are among the best we've ever tasted, and the gourmet pizzas are deliciozo. 5 Embarcadero Center. (415) 781-1300.

Ghirardelli Square: What was once a chocolate factory is now one of the classiest tourist shopping centers in the country. More important than that, it's got a lot to offer residents and their dogs. Ghirardelli Square is at 900 North Point Street. Here are some restaurants with outdoor cafes:

Boudin Sourdough Bakery & Cafe: Dine on pastries, croissants, cheesecake or huge sandwiches as you gaze across Beach Street at the bay. (415) 928-7404.

Compadres Mexican Bar & Grill: The terrace outside this second-floor restaurant provides you and your dog with a first-rate view of the bay, the boats at Hyde Street Pier and Alcatraz. The food is as good as the scenery, and if it's too sunny, you can dine at tables with umbrellas. (415) 885-2266.

Ghirardelli Fountain & Candy: Here's where you can get some of that famous rich Ghirardelli ice cream with all the fixings. Just remember: The more of it your dog gets, the fewer sit-ups you have to do. Stay away from chocolate, though. It can be very bad for dogs. (415) 474-3938.

Ghirardelli's Too!: A healthier alternative to the previous entry, Ghirardelli's Too offers non-fat yogurt desserts. (415) 474-1414.

Gino Gelateria: This cafe, with its own gelato factory and some of the best tartufo and tiramisu in the region, is a must for anyone doing the North Beach scene with a dog. An older woman visits every day with her little white dog to eat gelato at one of the sidewalk tables. She brings a plastic bowl with ice, and the owners fill it with water. Both dog and woman down their refreshments in bliss. The owners say they'll do the same for anyone else with a dog. 701 Columbus Avenue; (415) 981-4664.

Horse Shoe Cafe: Enjoy good coffee and pastries at a down-to-earth cafe with two sidewalk tables. 566 Haight Street; (415) 626-8852.

Hyde Street Bistro: This is one of only a few fancy Bay Area restaurants where dogs are allowed. Two outdoor tables are covered with white tablecloths. A superb selection of Austrian and Northern Italian dishes make dining here—even with the most unkempt mutt—a delight. 1521 Hyde Street; (415) 441-7778.

Java Beach: After a morning of combing Ocean Beach, you can catch some rays and eat some lunch on one of the benches outside this mellow soup, sandwich and salad shop. 1396 La Playa at Great Highway; (415) 665-5282.

La Canasta: This Mexican take-out restaurant is where we get our favorite burritos. When Joe is with us, we like to sit on the bench outside while we wait—and often while we eat. 2219 Filbert Street; (415) 921-3003.

La Mediterranee: Dog owners are lucky—there are two of these top Mideast/Greek restaurants in the city and both put tables outside in decent weather. Joe highly recommends the vegetarian plate, even for meat eaters. At 2210 Fillmore Street, (415) 921-2956, and at 288 Noe Street, (415) 431-7210.

Martha & Bros. Coffee Company: Strong coffee on a hard bench may not be an ideal way to start the day, but it will wake you up enough to take your dog for a long walk. 3868 24th Street; (415) 641-4433.

Nob Hill Noshery: Eat hearty deli food at the tables outside. 1400 Pacific Avenue; (415) 928-6674.

The Orbit Room: Situated between Hayes Valley and the Castro, this trendy spot serves sandwiches, bagels and salads, and coffee drinks and beer all day and until midnight. They have two outdoor tables where dogs are welcome. There are glassed-in windows so you and your hip pooch can see the hipsters as they mix and mingle. 1900 Market Street; (415) 252-9525.

Pier 39: If your dog doesn't mind flocks of tourists, there's a wide selection of decent eateries with outdoor tables for the two of you here. Your dog gets to smell the bay and sniff at the sea lions below. Pier 39 is off the Embarcadero, near Jefferson Street. These are some of the restaurants where you and your dog are allowed:

Burger Cafe: Every burger imaginable is waiting for your dog to drool over. The mushroom cheeseburger is a big hit. (415) 986-5966.

Chowder's: Fried seafood and several types of chowder make Pier 39 really feel like a pier. (415) 391-4737.

Eagle Cafe: Eggs, potatoes, burgers, cheese—good heavy food for a cold day is yours for the asking. Management asks that you tie your dog to a pole near the tables, rather than have him underfoot. (415) 433-3689.

Le Carousel: The next best thing to being on the carousel at the end of the pier (where no dogs are allowed) is this restaurant with a carousel theme, with painted ponies everywhere. It also has a large deli with a selection of cakes and pastries, and plenty of outdoor tables. (415) 433-4160.

Sal's Pizzeria: You and your dog can get a real taste of San Francisco by biting into any of Sal's special pizzas. There's the 49er Special, with sausage, pepperoni, onions and mushrooms. The Earthquake, with sausage, salami, mushrooms and tomatoes, was a hit with Joe. (415) 398-1198.

Polly Ann Ice Cream: Here, dogs are treated like people, in the best sense. Every dog gets a free mini-doggie cone. Since dogs can't order for themselves, the owners usually give them vanilla, but the dogs rarely complain. Even if you have several dogs, the owners welcome them all and dole out the goods with a smile. They're especially happy if you buy some ice cream for yourself, of course. The doggie cone tradition has been alive for 30 years. (Joe's and Nisha's first date together was videotaped here as part of KRON-TV's delightful *Outdoor Journal* show. Little did they know…) 3142 Noriega Street; (415) 664-2472.

Pompei's Grotto: If your dog likes the smell of seafood, he probably won't mind joining you at an outdoor table here. The fish is fresh and the pasta delicious. And if your dog is thirsty, she'll be offered a cup of water. 340 Jefferson Street; (415) 776-9265.

Real Food Deli: You'd think a place like this would have only the healthiest, most vegetarian cuisine. It does have gourmet natural food, like grilled tofu brochettes, but it also has decadent dishes, like prosciutto sandwiches. Desserts soar to the same extremes. Three outdoor tables make eating with your dog a pleasure. 2164 Polk Street; (415) 775-2805.

Savoy Tivoli: Come to this North Beach bar/cafe on weekday afternoons if you want your dog to be your date. Otherwise, it's too crowded for dogs to be comfortable. 1434 Grant Avenue; (415) 362-7023.

Simple Pleasures Cafe: This is a quaint cafe with a warm and cozy atmosphere, and food to match. You and your dog can sit at the outdoor tables and catch live folk and jazz music Wednesday through Saturday nights. It may be cold, so bring lots of money for hot chocolates. 3434 Balboa Street; (415) 387-4022.

Tart to Tart: If you want to satisfy a sweet tooth (with your dog as accomplice), the outdoor tables are perfect for your desires. 641 Irving Street; (415) 753-0643.

Tassajara Bread Bakery: The goods here are as wholesome and natural as the bread Tassajara made famous. Although the place is usually crowded, there are plenty of outdoor tables. 1000 Cole Street; (415) 664-8947.

Toy Boat Dessert Cafe: You may not be able to say it 10 times fast, but you and your dog won't feel a need to speak when you're at the outside bench eating rich and creamy desserts. 401 Clement Street; (415) 751-7505.

Trio Cafe: Sandwiches, soups and salads—the basics here are some of the best. 1870 Fillmore Street; (415) 563-2248.

PLACES TO STAY

Best Western Civic Center Motor Inn: Rates are $65 to $95. 364 9th Street, San Francisco, CA 94103; (415) 621-2826.

Campton Place: Dogs over 25 pounds are not allowed at this luxury hotel, located a half block from Union Square. For small pooches, the fee is $25 per night. "We have to clean the room extra thoroughly, deodorize it, and put flea powder around—so it costs money," a manager explained. "We love dogs, but we want the people who stay in the room after them to be happy, too."

Joe promised to wear his best aftershave, but he was still too big to get in. Maybe they knew he couldn't afford it: Rates are $195 to $850. 340 Stockton Street, San Francisco, CA 94108; (415) 781-5555.

Four Seasons Clift Hotel: They prefer small dogs here, but large ones are welcome if they're quiet. After all, the hotel recently had a pig as a guest. Your dog can get on the Very Important Pet list— and every VIP gets a basket of pet treats sent to their room on arrival. Rates are $160 to $655. 495 Geary Street, San Francisco, CA 94102; (415) 775-4700.

Laurel Motor Inn: Rates are $72 to $98. 444 Presidio Avenue, San Francisco, CA 94115; (415) 567-8467.

Mansions Hotel: Step back in time in this mysterious old mansion, circa 1890. It's full of art treasures and beautifully attired mannequins. People tell tales of a resident ghost. Dogs are allowed in a few of its 21 rooms, but because the hotel itself is a work of art, bring only a very docile dog. Rates are $129 to $350. 2220 Sacramento Street, San Francisco, CA 94115; (415) 929-9444.

Rodeway Inn: Rates are $65 to $135. Dogs require a $20 deposit. 1450 Lombard Street, San Francisco, CA 94123; (415) 673-0691.

San Francisco Marriott: Rates are $140 to $185. The higher priced the room, the higher in the sky your room will be in this towering pink downtown hotel. If your dog has vertigo, you'll save yourself some money. But the views from the top are magnificent. The city skyline, the bay and the Bay Bridge are all in your scope. Dogs have to sign a liability form, but there's no deposit. 55 Fourth Street, San Francisco, CA 94103; (415) 896-1600.

Sheraton at Fisherman's Wharf: Only one block from the wharf area, this is an ideal hotel for tourists with well-behaved dogs. Rates are $170 to $200. 2500 Mason Street, San Francisco, CA 94133; (415) 362-5500.

The Westin St. Francis: At this luxurious Union Square hotel, "small, well-behaved dogs are as welcome as anybody," according to a manager. Rates are $180 to $275. 335 Powell Street, San Francisco, CA 94102; (415) 397-7000.

FESTIVALS

Cherry Blossom Festival: You'll run into lots of Akitas at this late April festival at the Japan Center. You'll also encounter Japanese food, dance and martial arts demonstrations. It's one of the largest celebrations of Japanese culture this side of the Pacific. Dogs must be leashed. (415) 922-6776.

Folsom Street Fair: Proceeds from this South of Market fair always go to a worthy local charity. From rock-and-roll to funk, this large street party in autumn has music for the modern, leashed dog's ears. (415) 648-FAIR.

Nihonmachi Street Fair: Another big affair in Japantown, this time in August. It's a lively festival, with music, dance and food from all of San Francisco's Asian communities. Bring your leashed dog and an appetite. (415) 922-8700.

DIVERSIONS

Be a stage parent: Anyone who watches KOFY-TV 20 is familiar with the hairy beasts who sit in easy chairs every half hour for station identification. Maybe you've longed to launch your own dog into the living rooms of thousands of viewers, but never thought you had a chance.

The good news is that your dog doesn't need connections, an agent or a Screen Actors Guild card to be a star. Just send KOFY-TV a photo of your dog, along with your daytime phone number. If they're interested, they'll call and set up a taping date. "They're always looking for unique breeds," advises Frank Pappas, a.k.a. the TV 20 Dog Guy, but any mutt with a lovable face can qualify.

An added benefit to being taped is that you can finally find out just what makes those TV dogs whirl their heads toward that TV set at the perfect moment. Write to KOFY-TV 20, Attention: Pets, 2500 Marin Street, San Francisco, CA 94124.

Catch a rising star: If your pooch has his paws on the ground but his head in the stars, you should give the San Francisco Sidewalk Astronomers a call. Since 1986, once or twice a month, depending on what's happening in the sky, astronomer John Dodgson and friends have been setting up telescopes at city intersections (often at Haight and Clayton streets or at 4th and Clement) and hosting stargazing parties. Passersby can scan the universe through Dodgson's 18-inch telescope lens. (The telescope is so big it requires climbing up a six-foot ladder to peer through it.)

The group sets up at dusk, sometimes positioning telescopes on three different corners, and stays out for hours. On a given night, more than 100 people might check out the constellations. "If people want to walk by with their dogs, they're welcome to join in," Dodgson says. Best of all, it's free. To find out when and where the Sidewalk Astronomers will be stargazing next, call (415) 567-2063.

Celebrate great music and dance: Your dog's in for culture shock if you bring him to Golden Gate Park to catch top artists Saturday afternoons in the summer. Grab a picnic blanket, a leash and lunch and head for the Golden Gate Park Music Concourse, in front of the Academy of Sciences. You'll see top dancers from around the world and hear some of the best jazz, classical and ethnic music around. Just be considerate, and if your dog is the barking type, leave her at home. Admission is free. For more information, call Summer Festival at (415) 474-3914.

On Sundays from noon to 3 p.m., the Golden Gate Band serenades parkgoers with a wide range of music. The band is a lively group with talent for both oompah rhythms and delicate tunes. For more information on the band, call (415) 666-7200.

Explore a military pet cemetery: If only human cemeteries were so full of bright flowers (albeit many made of plastic or silk) and thoughtful epitaphs, death might not seem so somber. When you enter the little cemetery, surrounded by a white picket fence, a sign tells you, "The love these animals gave will never be forgotten." You'll want to bring your leashed dog friend with you.

"Sarge," reads one simple epitaph. "Our pet George. George accepted us people," says another. Several markers bear only a large red heart, which means the pet was unknown but loved even after death. This is where cats, birds, dogs and even Freddy Fish— whose grave is marked by a lone plastic rose—can live together in harmony. Take Lincoln Boulevard and turn north onto McDowell Avenue. The cemetery is just south of the corner of McDowell and Crissy Field avenues. (415) 561-4516.

Go organic: The California Harvest Ranch Market, known for its wide selection of fresh organic produce, has a healthy attitude toward dogs. The owners installed two clamps in the front just for dogs. The idea is to hook your dog's leash to the clamp and go shopping, knowing your dog is safe and secure. As always, though, don't leave him unchecked for long. They're open from 9 a.m. to 11 p.m. 2285 Market Street. (415) 626-0805.

Have a ferry, ferry nautical experience: Dogs wag their tails hard and fast when they learn that the Red & White ferry system permits them on all its lines, free. You must leash your pooch or carry her in a traveling box, and if there's an "accident" on board, you're responsible for the cleanup. Two destinations are forbidden—Angel Island and Alcatraz, both state parks that don't allow dogs. That leaves you a choice of voyages between Fisherman's Wharf in San Francisco (Piers 41 and 43) and Tiburon, Belvedere, Sausalito or Vallejo, and a bay cruise. Phoning (415) 546-2896 will give you fares, daily schedules and departure locations.

Unfortunately, the Blue & Gold Fleet (running between San Francisco and Alameda and Oakland) and the Golden Gate Transit Ferry Service (between San Francisco and Sausalito and Larkspur) don't allow dogs on board.

Help someone with AIDS: PAWS (Pets Are Wonderful Support) is dedicated to preserving the relationship of people with AIDS and their pets. If you've ever been comforted by your dog while ill, you have a glimpse of the importance of the work PAWS does. PAWS needs people to do office work, deliver pet food, and walk and care for pets. And if you have room for another dog in the house, PAWS usually has some special animals for adoption. Write them at 539 Castro Street, San Francisco, CA 94114, or call (415) 241-1460.

Pay homage to a teacup poodle: One of the oddest pieces of art in the city is near the foot of the Filbert steps, at Montgomery Street. It's a mural, at dog's-eye level, of a tiny poodle in a semi-desert setting. A sign in the painting says, "No dogs. Teacup poodles OK." The exhibit also contains a real fire hydrant, lots of real live ferns, and a brass plaque about Ginger the poodle. Among the biographical details is that Ginger flunked out of obedience school. Tsk, tsk. And such a polite-looking thing, too. To drive to the mural, go to the end of Union Street and turn left on Montgomery Street. The art is easy to miss, so keep your eyes low to the ground.

Shop on Beach Street: You can shop for baubles, bangles and T-shirts with your leashed dog at any of dozens of little stands up and down this Fisherman's Wharf area street. You can even get your dog's caricature done by a local artist. Make sure to take him to nearby Aquatic Park while you're there, especially if he's sat patiently for the artist's rendition. The bulk of the stands on Beach Street are between Hyde and Polk streets.

Hop on a bus: Dogs are allowed on Muni buses and cable cars anytime they're running. Only one dog is permitted per bus. Dogs must be on a short leash, and muzzled, no matter how little or how sweet. Bus driver Tom Brown told us about the creative, but ineffective, ways some people muzzle their dogs. "This one man had a part pit-bull dog, and he put a little rubber band around its mouth," said Brown. "No way that dog was getting on my bus."

Dogs pay the same fare as owners. If the owner is a senior citizen, the dog pays senior citizen rates. Lap-sized dogs can stay on your lap, but all others are consigned to the floor. Keep your dog from getting underfoot and be sure he's well walked before he gets on. Call (415) 673-MUNI for more information.

Ride halfway to the stars: As far as cable cars are concerned, opinions vary widely about whether dogs should ride inside or outside. Some drivers feel the outside is better because the cable noise isn't so amplified, and dogs don't get so nervous. Others say the outside is too dangerous—that a dog could panic and jump off.

If you do decide to do the full San Francisco experience and ride outside, have your dog sit on a bench, and hold her securely by the leash and by the body. The standing area is very narrow and precarious. And you never want to go on a crowded cable car with your dog, so stay away from the popular tourist areas during the peak seasons. (For rules, see above.) Call (415) 673-MUNI for more information.

Joe was so terrified when he first boarded a cable car that he got in no trouble at all after barking at the bell. How much mischief could he get into hiding his head under my coat?

But after a while, with the coaxing of our personable California Street cable car drivers Louie and Dave, he started peeking out at the sights. As they regaled us with stories of dogs they'd known, and flea remedies that work, Joe loosened up. He got so relaxed by the middle of our trip that he fell off his seat as the cable car descended the steep hill in Chinatown. Fortunately, we were seated inside.

No one seemed to want to sit next to Joe. In fact, the deeper we rode into the financial district and the more suits and ties we encountered, the more people avoided even looking at him. Joe got off at the end of the line with his feelings hurt, but his bravery intact.

Take a dog to the animal fair: The Great San Francisco Dog Fair is one of the few indoor dog events that actually welcomes the dog himself. But even though they're the guests of honor, dogs still have to wear short leashes.

But while at the fair, there are plenty of diversions to distract them from being tethered. They can eat at the Dogitessan or in a separate dog dining area called the Bow House. They can also participate in dozens of events or just watch, from dachshund races to dog glamour parades. The fair is held at Pier 2, Fort Mason's Festival Pavilion and benefits the San Francisco SPCA. For more information, call the hotline at (415) 554-3096. If the hotline is giving information about a different event, call the SPCA at: (415) 554-3000.

Walk with thousands of dogs: Get your dog's walking shoes and stroll from one to five miles in what's probably the largest dog walk-a-thon in the world. Dogs and people of all shapes and breeds gather for the PetWalk every May in Golden Gate Park to raise money for the San Francisco SPCA. The walks can get very crowded, so think twice if your pooch can't handle thousands of dog and human legs strutting by. Otherwise, it's probably one of the funnest dog events in the country. After the walk, there are howling contests, athletic competitions, owner/pet look-alike events and lots of refreshments. For an application, write the San Francisco SPCA PetWalk, 2500 16th Street, San Francisco, CA 94103. The number is (415) 554-3000. A few months before the event, a special hotline can answer your basic questions: (415) 554-3096.

Wash your socks with your dog: A jug of wine, a loaf of bread, your dirty laundry, your dog and you. Bring all this and feast at one of four tables outside Star Wash Laundry, while your wash is in the rinse cycle. This is a very popular spot among dog owners with dirty clothes, and since the laundromat owners adore dogs, chances are your pet won't be alone. It's especially enjoyable for your dog after a sprint in nearby Mission Dolores Park (see page 418). Don't forget water for your dog. 392 Dolores Street. (415) 431-2443.

Watch a big-screen flick: Picture this—you, your date, a romantic drive-in movie. The plot thickens, your date takes your hand, the lead characters start to kiss, lips locking…. You feel hot breath on your neck and turn in dreamy anticipation. And there, only millimeters from your face, is your dog's big black nose, sniffing away and asking for more popcorn.

Still, taking a dog can to a drive-in theater can be fun. At the Geneva Drive-In Theater, a resident cat prowls around cars looking for a handout, or a dog to tease. The Geneva is on Carter Street, off Geneva Avenue, next to the Cow Palace. (415) 587-2884.

Wear your Easter bonnet: Now you and your dog have an excuse to dress to the nines for a high society Easter Parade in Presidio Heights. Held the day before Easter in the parking lot next to Ken Grooms Pet Supply and Gifts, the parade is a benefit for the SPCA. It's a real blast and draws quite a crowd. Each year about 100 pets stroll by a panel of three judges, competing for prizes. First place wins a silver trophy and a $100 gift certificate for pet goods and goodies from Grooms' store. In 1993, the winner was a basset hound named Morty who came dressed as the Pope. (He was accompanied, of course, by two hound cohorts in the guise of Cardinals.) Donations of any amount earn the right to enter the parade. Even if your dog isn't competing, it's fun and for a good cause. 3429 Sacramento Street. For more info, call (415) 673-7708.

Walk across the Golden Gate: Like their people, dogs thrill to a jaunt across San Francisco's most famous landmark. The bridge spans 1.9 miles from the city to Marin County. It's open to pedestrians, both humans and dogs, from 5 a.m. to 9 p.m. daily. There's no fee.

The only thing that the Golden Gate Bridge Authority asks is that your dog wear a leash. You both probably will want to wear sweaters, too—it can be a little nippy when making your way across. But don't let that stop you. The spectacular views at daybreak and sunset make it all worthwhile. Take the last San Francisco exit before the bridge tollway. Free street parking is available on the west side of the bridge, next to the GGBA employee parking lot. For more info, call (415) 921-5858.

SAN MATEO COUNTY

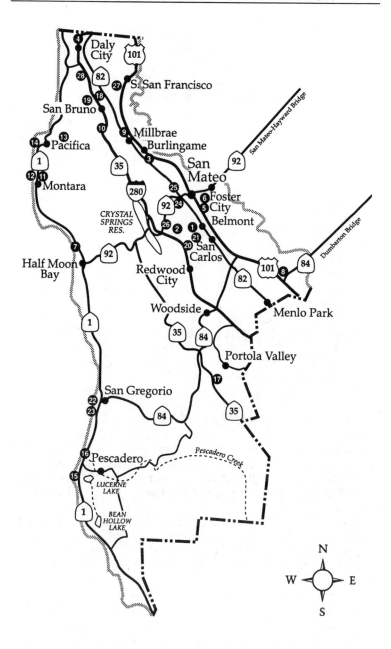

36
SAN MATEO COUNTY

Joe and I were stuck in Redwood City on business all day. After a while, he began to glare at me. His brow wrinkled. His eyes got wide and seemed to float in extra liquid. Then he started groaning like a door in a bad horror movie. It was all too clear. This was a dog urgently in need of a park.

So we got in the car and drove until we found a little city park. I let Joe out and he bounded for a private spot behind a bush. But just as he was getting into position, a woman with a baby stroller bustled up. "No! Bad dog! No dogs allowed. Tell your mother that," she yelled and shot us an angry look.

Joe ran back to the car in a more cowardly manner than I care to admit, tail down, head low. Instead of arguing, we left. Besides, there was a big county park at the other end of Redwood City that looked even better.

Joe was so desperate that by the time we got there he was crossing his legs. But it seemed worth the wait. The park was big and grassy with lots of pine trees and bushes essential for Joe to do his thing. Birds and wildflowers were everywhere. It was one of the more alluring parks we'd ever seen.

But just as we entered, three words on a sign stopped us in our tracks. They were big, bold and mean: "NO DOGS ALLOWED."

Joe lifted his leg on the sign and we were gone. Thus was our unsavory introduction to San Mateo County.

Once we started exploring San Mateo County, we realized that it wasn't quite as bad as our first impression had led us to believe. There are many parks that allow dogs. Four even allow them off leash. But some of the biggest and best have an outright ban on canines.

The worst offender here is the county Department of Parks and Recreation. There are 15,000 acres of county parklands in San Mateo County, but none of the county's 65,000 licensed dogs may set paw in them. "All of our parks are wildlife preserves and we consider dogs predators, unfortunately," says Parks Superintendent Bob Emert, who has two big dogs himself. As a result, dozens of desperate dog owners have formed an organization called DOGS— Dog Owners for Green Space. Their goal is modest—to get the county to open one or two of its parks to dogs on leash. Thousands of residents have signed a petition requesting this. Members of DOGS are even willing to pay an annual user's fee to help defray costs.

But county officials have continued to stubbornly deny their request. They fear liability, they say. They fear for threats to wildlife. They fear the expense of signs and enforcement.

DOGS members are themselves concerned about wildlife, saying that dogs should be allowed only in areas where people, and even bikes and horses, are already allowed. As for the other worries the commissioners have, DOGS members remind them that San Mateo County is the only regional park district in the Bay Area that bans dogs.

"It's time to give dog owners the same rights as bikers and hikers and horses," says Terry Robertson, chairman of DOGS. "This county is just full of bad excuses. For the sake of our dogs, I hope these excuses crumble soon."

For more information, call the county Department of Parks and Recreation at (415) 363-4020, or Terry Robertson, of DOGS, at (415) 595-1026.

BELMONT

PARKS, BEACHES & RECREATION AREAS

•Twin Pines Park 🐾 🐾 🐾

This park is a hidden treasure, nestled among eucalyptus trees just outside the business district of Belmont. You'd never guess the dog wonders that await within. Your dog may hardly notice she's leashed.

The main trail is paved and winds through sweet-smelling trees and brush. A clear stream runs below. In dry seasons, it's only about two feet deep, but in good years it swells to several feet. Dogs love to go down to the stream and wet their whistles. Past the picnic area are numerous small, quiet dirt trails that can take you up the woodsy hill or alongside the stream.

It's located at 1225 Ralston Avenue, behind the police department. (415) 595-7441. ➡ *See #1 on map p. 436.*

•Water Dog Lake Park 🐾 🐾 🐾

Dogs and their people seem magically drawn to this large, wooded park with a little lake in the middle. Maybe it's the way the moss drips off the trees at the bottom of this mountainous area, or the way the lake seems to create a refreshing breeze on the hottest days.

Or maybe it's got something to do with the name. We asked

several dog owners how the park came to be called Water Dog Lake Park.

"I think the lake is kind of shaped like a dog. Actually, it's more like a kangaroo, isn't it?" said the proud owner of a beagle/terrier mix.

"It would be a good place to water your dog, if that were allowed," said a woman with a black lab.

"When dogs and people were allowed to swim here, you couldn't get the labs and all those water dogs out of this lake," explained a man with an Irish setter.

We hate to burst the romantic fantasy that a park as alluring as this one is named after man's best friend. But after some searching through historical records, we discovered the biting truth: Water Dog Lake Park was named after salamanders. A colloquial name for a salamander is "water dog," and apparently the little critters used to wriggle all over the place around here.

We still think the park is great. Too bad dogs have to be leashed.

One other thing that we discovered about this park: If people would follow their dogs, perhaps a lot fewer would stumble onto the wrong trail—the one that goes up to the top of the park never comes near the lake and leads you more than a mile away from where you started. Joe tried tugging in the other direction, but I ignored him. We got a ride back to the entrance from a teenage boy who felt sorry for us.

Upon entering the park from the Lake Road entrance, take the wide path that goes straight in front of you. It will lead you down to the lake. Neither you nor your dog can go in the water, but you can have a great picnic there, or even go fishing off the little wooden pier.

If you start off taking the smaller trail that veers to the right, you'll get good exercise and a great view of the Bay, but we don't recommend it, unless you enjoy getting lost and suffering heat fatigue in the summer. A final word of warning: Watch out for bikers. They're fast here.

Enter on Lake Road, just off Carlmont Drive. Try to come back to the same place. (415) 595-7441. ➤*See #2 on map p. 436.*

RESTAURANTS
The Coffee Club: This is an international coffee nook with a wooden bench in front. It's a great place to visit on a morning walk in Twin Pines Park. 1035 Ralston Avenue; (415) 591-9888.

FESTIVALS
Belmont Art and Wine Festival: This festival is held each May in

Twin Pines Park. Dogs must be leashed. With roughly 10,000 people attending, this festival isn't as crowded as some, but it's not for dogs who are squeamish about masses of people. To get this year's date or more information, call (415) 595-7441.

BURLINGAME

PARKS, BEACHES & RECREATION AREAS

•**Washington Park** 🐾🐾

This relatively small park has the look of an old college campus. Its trees are big and old and mostly deciduous, making autumn a particularly brilliant time. Bring a lunch and eat it on the thick, knotty old redwood picnic tables. They're something out of the Enchanted Forest. Joe is intrigued by the abundance of squirrels, but he doesn't get too far with his pursuits, since leashes are the law.

At 850 Burlingame Avenue below Carolan Avenue. (415) 696-7245. → *See #3 on map p. 436.*

RESTAURANTS

Coffee Bistro: A charming little cafe below street level, Coffee Bistro is just a few blocks from Washington Park. Dogs must be tied to something sturdy when you dine at any of the outdoor tables. A good snack is the strawberry fruit shake. At the Avenue Arcade, 1110 Burlingame Avenue; (415) 347-1208.

PLACES TO STAY

Days Inn-Airport: Rates are $72 to $82. Dogs are $10 extra. 777 Airport Boulevard, Burlingame, CA 94010; (415) 342-7772.

San Francisco Airport Marriott: Rates are $125 to $138. Small pooches only, please. 1800 Old Bayshore Highway, Burlingame, CA 94010; (415) 692-9100.

Radisson Hotel-San Francisco Airport: "Very tiny pets only," says a clerk. Rates are $125 year-round. 1177 Airport Boulevard, Burlingame, CA 94010; (415) 342-9200.

Vagabond Inn, Airport: Rates are $63 to $85. Dogs are $5 extra. 1640 Bayshore Highway, Burlingame, CA 94010; (415) 692-4040.

FESTIVALS

Broadway Merchants Street Festival: If your dog appreciates an old-fashioned, small-town atmosphere, he'll like this festival. Strolling musicians, barbershop quartets and dozens of locals fill Broadway during early August. (415) 588-2933.

DIVERSIONS

Slurp it up: Does your dog get the urge to down a cold one with the boys while you're strolling around Burlingame together? We've got just the oasis for him. There are two popular "pet fountains" in front of the pet store Feast Your Beast. Dogs are welcome to drink all the fresh water they can hold, and there's no cover charge. At 1223 Donnelly. (415) 343-2378.

DALY CITY

We called the Daly City parks department to find out what its rule is regarding leashes. A helpful woman read the city ordinance: Animals must be "under control of owner by being saddled, harnessed, haltered or leashed by a substantial chain, lead rope or leash, which chain, lead rope or leash shall be continuously held by some competent person capable of controlling such an animal."

So Joe wore a leash during our Daly City visits. But he put his paw down when it came to donning the saddle and halter.

PARKS, BEACHES & RECREATION AREAS

•Gellert Park 🐾 1/2

The best feature of this flat, square park is that it's right behind the Serramonte Library. It's also conveniently located if you are going to pay homage to someone at the Chinese Cemetery, right across the street. The park is made up of a few sports fields—watch out for flying baseballs, soccer balls and softballs. The park's trees, which surround two sides, aren't even accessible—they're on top of a very steep little ridge. Your dog may become frustrated, especially since he must wear a leash through all this.

On Wembley Drive at Gellert Boulevard. (415) 991-8006. → *See #4 on map p. 436.*

FESTIVALS

Daly City Fall Festival: Take your dog for a stroll and get your Christmas shopping done early. This crafts fair is held each September outside the Westlake Shopping Center. Call (415) 755-8526 for more information.

DIVERSIONS

Ask your dog for a date to a movie: It's greasy. It's hokey. But going to the Burlingame Drive-In Theater is a great way to catch a movie and spare yourself the guilt of leaving your dog home alone. And it's cheap. Dogs are free—unless, like Joe, they have a thing for popcorn. We saw a real classic here: *Don't Tell Mom the Babysitter's Dead.* Joe loved it. He couldn't take his eyes off the screen, except to lick the sound box. 350 Beach Road. (415) 343-2213.

FOSTER CITY

John Oliver, former mayor of Foster City, isn't the sort to beat around the bush. When he describes the older women who set out to improve the town by getting recreational vehicles off the streets and enforcing the leash law, he's not kind.

"They are the forces of darkness," he says. "They're a couple of little old ladies right from central casting for their nit-picking roles."

Oliver's feathers are ruffled for good reason. In 1988—a year after he stopped being mayor, and shortly after the "forces of darkness" started crusading for more dog patrols—a cop cited him for walking his little dog, Topper, off leash. The ticket was only $25. It was the principle that distressed him—not to mention the newspaper story. "Topper was an angel of a dog and in a totally empty park. Come on, let's get sensible here," he says.

This is the dog who used to break out of Oliver's truck and run into City Council chambers to find him during meetings. She's the same 20-pound mutt who stayed by Oliver's side during a recent bout of bad luck that forced them into homelessness. "She made life a lot easier when we were living in that truck," he says.

Oliver has always voted for leash laws, but he believes the real issue is control. "If you can control your dog in a safe area, and there's no one around to disturb, why not let her loose for a few minutes?" he asks. "It's a shame it has to cost you if you're caught."

PARKS, BEACHES & RECREATION AREAS

•**Boothbay Park** 🐾 🐾 🐾 🦮

It's off with the leash once you find the right section of this park, which is the grassy area behind the tennis courts. It's surrounded on two sides by a tall wooden fence, and is comfortably far from the road. This little corner of the park is nothing fancy, but it does allow dogs some freedom. The park is at Boothbay Avenue and Edgewater Lane. (415) 345-5731. ➤*See #5 on map p. 436.*

•**Foster City Dog Exercise Area** 🐾 🐾 🐾 🦮

This enclosed dog run has great potential, but it's a disappointment. Dogs are allowed off leash here, but as soon as they get down to having fun with each other, they kick up clouds of dust. The ground is pretty much packed dirt, with little bits of grass trying to push through.

The view isn't any more attractive, with powerlines overhead, the back of City Hall in the foreground and rows of look-alike townhouses in the distance. What this place needs is a few good trees. And some water for the dogs.

There are two good points, though: The fences are very high, so if you have an escape artist for a dog, this place is about the safest around. And there are plenty of large trash cans—six, to be exact—and no shortage of pooper scoopers.

At 600 Foster City Boulevard. Park in the lot behind City Hall. (415) 345-5731. ➤*See #6 on map p. 436.*

FESTIVALS

Foster City Art and Wine Festival: Ferris wheels, merry-go-rounds, crafts, food and wine surround you at this early summer event in Leo J. Ryan Park. Dogs must be leashed and can't go on the rides, but there's plenty to interest them on the ground. Be aware it can be very crowded. (415) 573-7600.

Fourth of July: Start with a pancake breakfast at Leo J. Ryan Park and peruse arts and crafts with your leashed dog for the rest of the day. Make sure to take your dog home before the fireworks start. Even the bravest mutt can fall to pieces hearing all that noise. (415) 573-7600.

HALF MOON BAY

PARKS, BEACHES & RECREATION AREAS

• **Half Moon Bay State Beach** 🐾🐾🐾 1/2

This is the beach air-conditioned by the god of sheepdogs. No matter how steaming hot it is elsewhere, you can almost always count on brisk weather here. It's cool and foggy in the summer, wet and windy in the winter, and moderate in the fall and spring.

The three-mile crescent of beach is actually made up of four beaches. From north to south, along Highway 1, they are: Roosevelt Beach, Dunes Beach, Venice Beach and Francis Beach.

Dogs aren't permitted on Francis Beach, but they are allowed at the campground and picnic area above it. If you can ignore all the RVs and crowds of tents, this is a stunning camping spot. Perched on ice plant-covered dunes above the Pacific, it's one of the most accessible beach camp areas in the Bay Area. All of the 53 campsites are available on a first-come, first-served basis. Sites are $12 to $14. Dogs are $1 extra.

Dogs are allowed on leash on all other beaches, but this isn't the place to come for a 15-minute romp: It costs $4 per car and $1 per dog.

The beaches are all clean and each is almost identical to the next, so your choice of beach should depend on which entry is most convenient. Rangers roam year-round. If you're thinking of breaking the leash law, this is a bad place to try it.

From Highway 1, follow the brown and white signs to the appropriate beach. (415) 726-6203. ➡ *See #7 on map p. 436.*

RESTAURANTS

Cameron Inn: Rich and creamy fountain treats are the specialty here, but burgers are big sellers, too. There are two outdoor picnic tables for dining with friends and dogs. 1410 South Cabrillo Highway; (415) 726-5705.

Taqueria La Mexicana: Fast burritos, tacos, enchiladas, burgers and fried chicken are just a few of the items you can eat at picnic tables under a bright orange awning. On Highway 1 just north of Kelly Avenue; (415) 726-1746.

Pasta Moon: This restaurant offers several sidewalk tables and every type of pasta imaginable. 315 Main Street; (415) 726-5125.

PLACES TO STAY

Half Moon Bay State Beaches camping: See page 443.

The Zaballa House: This 1859 country Victorian is the oldest standing house in Half Moon Bay. Some of the nine quaint bedrooms have fireplaces and Jacuzzis. Breakfasts are fresh and out of this world. Cats are occasionally guests here, so if your dog likes cats for lunch, you may want to inquire as to their presence when you make your reservation. The average double room is about $90. They ask that you only bring one dog per room. 324 Main Street, Half Moon Bay, CA 94019; (415) 726-9123.

MENLO PARK

PARKS, BEACHES & RECREATION AREAS

• **Bayfront Park** 🐾 🐾 🐾

This place used to be a dump—literally. It was the regional landfill site until it reached capacity in 1984. Then the city sealed the huge mounds of garbage under a two-foot clay barrier and covered it with four feet of soil, planted grass and trees, and *voilà*— instant 160-acre park!

Now it's a land of rolling hills with a distinctly Native American flavor. The packed dirt trails take you up to majestic views of the bay and surrounding marshes. There's no sign of garbage anywhere, unless you look down from the top of a hill and spot the methane extraction plant. Fortunately, very few vista points include that.

Our favorite part of the park is a trail studded with large, dark rocks arranged to form symbols, which in series make up a poem. The concept was inspired by Native American pictographs—a visual language system for recording daily events. At the trailhead, you'll find a sign quoting part of the poem and giving a map of the trail, showing the meaning of each rock arrangement as it corresponds to the poem.

Here's the entire poem:

Evening good
weather clear with stars.
I walk with the wind behind me
inspired with glad heart.
Come,
discover many animals,
grass, sun, canyons and earth.
No hunger, no war, no fear
Making peace and strong brothers.
Climb this way,
over mountain or hill.
Go in four directions—
up, down, close or far away,
to places hidden or bright,
under rain or cloud, night or day,
reaching to see
birds, plants, water and trees,
as you walk this trail and cross this path.
Rest here.
Talk here.
Flee your troubles to the sky
holding firm to harmony, virtue and peace,
barring evil,
strong with wisdom and healing,
reaching out with supplication
to the Great Spirit everywhere.

Although leashes are required, dogs seem really fond of this park, sniffing everywhere, their tails wagging constantly. Perhaps they can sense the park's less picturesque days deep underground. Or they may be touched by the Native American magic that imbues these hills.

The park starts at the end of Marsh Road, just on the other side of the Bayfront Expressway. To get to the beginning of the rock poem trail, continue past the entrance on Marsh Road to the second parking lot on the right. (415) 858-3470. → *See #8 on map p. 436.*

RESTAURANTS

Garden Grill: This is one of the very best. In an old English garden, under the canopy of an enormous 400-year-old oak tree, you can eat like a king—an English king, to be precise. While Garden Grill specializes in traditional English dishes and a charming afternoon tea, it's especially proud of its medieval cuisine. Try the 14th-century soup. It was one of King Richard II's favorites. And your dog will salivate when your server brings you elk, venison or squab with a hearty fruit and wine sauce. Unlike medieval tourist traps, Garden Grill encourages the use of fork and knife. There are 18 tables outside this English cottage restaurant. 1026 Alma Street; (415) 325-8981.

MILLBRAE

PARKS, BEACHES & RECREATION AREAS

•**Central Park** 🐾

A long, inviting line of trees runs down the middle of this park. Leash your dog and explore. Other than the trees, Central Park isn't too distinctive, except for a popular children's playground at one end. The park is on Lincoln Circle at Laurel Avenue. (415) 259-2360. ➡ *See #9 on map p. 436.*

•**San Andreas Trail** 🐾 🐾 🐾

We should probably feel lucky to even be allowed inside the Crystal Springs Reservoir area with dogs. But though this two-mile trail past sparkling San Andreas Lake provides a view of nature at its best, it's probably not a place your dog will long to return to. He's got to be on a leash, and the trail is often so crowded with joggers, walkers and bikers that you'll have to keep the leash very short. Besides, you're separated by fence from all but a narrow strip of land and you're right next to the roaring freeway for most of the trail.

But on the good side, the San Andreas Trail is a stone's throw from several areas with a distinct shortage of parks that allow dogs. And you can still see eagles here, if you're lucky.

There are a few entrances off Highway 280. We prefer to exit at Highway 35 (Skyline Boulevard). Some like the Millbrae Avenue exit. For either, get as close to the trail (to the west) as you can and park on the side of the road. We don't list a phone number because responsibility for the trail is unclear. ➡ *See #10 on map p. 436.*

RESTAURANTS

Angela's Italian Deli: "Mamma mia!" was Joe's reaction to the side order of pesto pasta spilled all over the sidewalk. He must have looked thirsty after he wolfed it down, because the cashier came out and gave him a bowl of water. 310 Broadway Avenue; (415) 697-2617.

Leonardo's Delicatessen: Just a few blocks from Central Park, this truly Italian deli has plenty of outdoor tables, all comfortably far from sidewalk traffic. 540 Broadway Avenue; (415) 697-9779.

PLACES TO STAY

Clarion Hotel: Rates are $69 to $89. Dogs must be brought in via cage, so think twice if your Saint Bernard needs a place to stay. 401 East Millbrae Avenue, Millbrae, CA 94030; (415) 692-6363.

MONTARA

PARKS, BEACHES & RECREATION AREAS

• McNee Ranch State Park 🐾 🐾 🐾 1/2 🐾

State parks usually ban dogs completely, or at least from all but paved roadways, but McNee is a refreshing exception to the rule.

At McNee, you can hike at the same level as the soaring gulls and watch the gem-blue ocean below. The higher you go up Montara Mountain, the more magnificent the view. Hardly a soul knows about this park, so if it's peace you want, it's peace you'll get.

And if it's a workout you want, you'll get that, too. Just strap on a day pack and bring lots of water for you and your dog. If you do the full hike, you'll ascend from sea level to 1,898 feet in a couple of hours. As you hike up and away from the ocean and the road, you lose all sounds of civilization, as Highway 1 fades into a thin ribbon and disappears below.

As soon as you go through the gate at the bottom of the park, follow the narrow trails to the left up the hills. You may be tempted to take the wide and winding paved road from the start, but to avoid any bikers, take the little trails. Besides, they lead to much better vistas.

Eventually, you'll come to a point where you have a choice of going left or right on a wider part of the trail. It's a choice between paradise and heaven. Left will lead you to a stunning view of the Golden Gate Bridge and the Farallon Islands. Right will bring you to the top of the ridge, where you see Mount Diablo and the rest of the San Francisco Bay.

This would be Joe's favorite park, but dogs are supposed to be leashed. Still, he always manages to slide down several steep grassy hills on his back, wriggling and moaning in ecstasy all the way.

It's easy to miss this park: There aren't any signs and there's no official parking lot. From Highway 1 in Montara, park at the far northern end of the Montara State Beach parking lot and walk across the road. Be careful as you walk along Highway 1, because there's hardly any room on the shoulder. You'll see a gate on a dirt road just north of you and a small state property sign. That's where you go in. A few cars can also park next to the gate, on the sides of the dirt road. But don't block the gate or your car probably won't be there when you get back. (415) 726-8800. ➡ *See #11 on map p. 436.*

•**Montara State Beach** 😺 😺 😺 1/2

This long, wide beach has more nooks and crannies than your dog will be able to investigate. Around mid-beach, you'll find several little inlets carved into the mini-cliffs. Take your dog back there at low tide, and you'll find all sorts of water, grass, mud and beach flotsam. It's a good place for her to get her paws wet, while obeying the leash law.

The water is very still back there. This is where Joe first dared to walk in water. It was only a centimeter deep, but he licked his paws in triumph all the way home.

Off Highway 1, park in the little lot behind the Chart House restaurant. There's also a parking area on the north side of the beach, off Highway 1. (415) 726-6203. ➡ *See #12 on map p. 436.*

PACIFICA

PARKS, BEACHES & RECREATION AREAS

•**Milagra Ridge** 😺 😺 😺 1/2

Follow the trail up to the top of the tallest hill, and you'll end up with both an incredible view of the Pacific and a perfect plateau for a picnic. There are hillsides covered with ice plant and even a few small redwoods along the way. Despite the leash law, dogs really seem to enjoy this park. Make sure to keep them on the trail, as the environment here is fragile. And keep your eyes peeled for the Mission Blue butterfly: This park is one of its last habitats.

Milagra Ridge is especially magical at night. You've never seen the full moon until you've seen it from here.

Enter on Sharp Park Road in Pacifica, between Highway 1 and Skyline Boulevard. (415) 556-0560. ➡ *See #13 on map p. 436.*

•**Pacifica State Beach** 😺 😺 1/2

This surfer's paradise has mixed messages for canines. First the bad news: Dogs must be leashed, picnickers abound and the temptation to sneak a chicken leg can be too much for even the best dog. The beach isn't very wide, leaving little room for exploration.

Now the good news: The setting alone warrants a visit. With green rolling hills in the distance behind you and the pounding sea before you, you and your dog won't regret stopping here. On Highway 1, park between Crespi Drive and Linda Mar Boulevard. (415) 726-6203. ➡See #14 on map p. 436.

• **Sweeney Ridge** 🐾 🐾 🐾 1/2
See page 452.

RESTAURANTS

Beach Cafe: After a walk on the chilly beach, there's nothing like a hot espresso and homemade croissant at the outdoor tables here. The owners have two Samoyeds, so it's a very dog-friendly place. Highway 1 at Rockaway Beach Avenue, next to Kentucky Fried Chicken; (415) 355-4532.

Sam's Deli: Sam's is a refreshing spot to hit after an afternoon at Pacifica State Beach. It has good sandwiches at low prices and two outdoor tables. It's at the Linda Mar Shopping Center, just behind the beach. It's on the same side as Denny's and the shoe stores, about halfway down the row of shops. 1261 Linda Mar Shopping Center; (415) 359-5330.

PESCADERO

PARKS, BEACHES & RECREATION AREAS

• **Bean Hollow State Beach** 🐾 🐾 🐾 1/2
The rocky intertidal zone here is terrific for tidepooling, but only if you and your dog are sure-footed. To get to the best tidepools, you must perform an amazing feat of team coordination—climbing down 70-million-year-old rock formations while attached to each other by leash. It's not that steep, just awkward. The pitted rocks can be slippery. This maneuver is not recommended for dogs who go deaf and senseless when the alluring ocean beckons them to swim. Besides, the surf can be treacherous in this area.

If you reach the tidepools, you're in for a real treat. But make sure your canine companion doesn't go fishing—we've seen a dog stick his entire head in a tidepool to capture a little crab. Fur and fangs aren't natural in the delicate balance of this wet habitat, so please keep dogs out of the tidepools. The mussels will thank you.

If you decide to play it safe and stay on flat land, you can still see the harbor seal rookery on the rocks below the coastal bluffs. Bring a pair of binoculars and you can really get a view of them up close and personal.

Off Highway 1 at Bean Hollow Road. (415) 726-6203. ➡See #15 on map p. 436.

• **Pescadero State Beach** 🐾 🐾 🐾 1/2

There are three entrances to this two-mile beach and each one leads to a unique setting on the Pacific. The prime attractions at the southernmost entrance, on Highway 1 at Pescadero Road, are the small cliffs that hang over the crashing ocean. There are even a few picnic tables on the edges of the mini-cliffs, for those who like lunch with a built-in thrill. Hold onto your leash!

The middle entrance, reached from the small parking lot, will lead you to a secluded and untamed rocky area. Take one of the less steep trails down, and you'll find yourself in the middle of lots of rocks, rotting kelp, driftwood and a few small tidepools. This is an eerie place to come on a very foggy day. Joe loves it here during pea-soupers.

Perch atop the vista point at this central entrance and you'll get a great view of the Pescadero Marsh Natural Preserve, just across Highway 1. Unfortunately, you can't explore the preserve with your dog.

The north entrance is the only one that charges a fee for use—$4 per car and $1 per dog. But many people park beside the road and walk over the sandy dunes to escape the cover charge. This is the most civilized—and mundane—entrance, with a wide beach and lots of kite fliers. Dogs must wear leashes on all parts of the beach.

The south entrance is at Pescadero Road and Highway 1. Follow the signs to the north for the other entrances. (415) 726-6203. ➤ *See #16 on map p. 436.*

RESTAURANTS

Arcangeli Grocery Company: There's always fresh-baked bread here—still hot—waiting for you after a cold day at the beach. We like to buy a loaf of steaming herb-garlic bread and eat it on the bench out front. 287 Stage Road; (415) 879-0147.

Tony's Place: For homemade pies, Greek food and french-fried artichokes, this diner with three big wooden tables outside is the best. If you tie your dog to a table with a short leash, she's welcome to join you. 1956 Pescadero Road; (415) 879-0106.

PLACES TO STAY

McKenzie House: Any dog who ever longed for his own comfy cottage by the sea, with his own private beach and fenced-in dog run, will howl with joy when he hears about this place. It's utterly spectacular. No wonder, since it was designed by owner Christie Keith with dog lovers in mind.

Inside the lone cottage, you're treated to a wood-burning stove and a Jacuzzi tub in the bathroom. But what's outside is the real jaw dropper: Your backyard leads to a two-acre fenced-in bluff with a gazebo, overlooking two small private beaches to which you and your dog have access. Keith can also tell you about a couple of hush-hush, off-leash dog walks in the area, as well as some pleasant on-leash ones. The cabin rents for only $75 a night, with weekly rates available. If you or your dog have been very good lately, you deserve a break here. To ensure privacy, the address is not advertised. But to get information or make reservations, you can call (415) 879-1240 or write to Keith at 443 Dearborn Park Road, Pescadero, CA 94060.

PORTOLA VALLEY

PARKS, BEACHES & RECREATION AREAS

•**Windy Hill Preserve** 🐾 🐾 🐾

You can look out from the top of the first big hill you come to and see for miles all around—and though you're on the edge of the suburbs, you'll see hardly a house. This 1,130-acre preserve of the Midpeninsula Regional Open Space District has as many different terrains as it has views, including grassland ridges and lush wooded ravines with serene creeks.

There are more than three miles of trails that allow you and your leashed canine companion. But watch out for foxtails. The park is so dry that foxtails seem to proliferate all year.

Start at Anniversary Trail, to the left of the entrance. The hike is a vigorous three-quarters of a mile uphill, and that may be enough, especially when it's baking. But you can continue down the other side of the hill and loop right, onto Spring Ridge Trail. Near the end of this two-and-a-half-mile path, you'll come to a wooded area with a small, very refreshing creek. This is a good place to sit a spell before heading back.

Park at the lot on Skyline Boulevard, two miles south of Highway 84 and five miles north of Alpine Road. You'll see the big sign for the preserve and three picnic tables. (415) 691-1200. ➡ *See #17 on map p. 436.*

REDWOOD CITY

No dogs are allowed in any of Redwood City's parks.

RESTAURANTS

Cafe Figaro: Polenta and risotto are big here. So is opera. From your table outside, you and your dog can feast your ears on recordings of some of the best vocal cords in the world. 2635 Broadway; (415) 365-1223.

FESTIVALS

Sunflower Festival: Considering Redwood City's anti-dog attitude in its parks, this is as close as your dog will ever come to having a good time in a public place here. Sunflowers are the theme, but there's plenty of wine tasting and food sampling as well. The festival is usually held on Broadway in late September. Call (415) 364-1722 for more details.

SAN BRUNO

PARKS, BEACHES & RECREATION AREAS

• **San Bruno Dog Exercise Area** 🐾🐾🐾🐾 🐕

This is a gem of a fenced-in park, where dogs can run their tails off—without a leash. The grass always seems to be green. There's plenty of water, pooper scoopers galore and benches for two-legged beasts. As an extra bonus, it has a great view of the bay. And for those who can't get enough of it while driving north on Highway 101, there's an unparalleled view of that strange sign: "SOUTH SAN FRANCISCO—THE INDUSTRIAL CITY."

The park opened in 1989 after local dog trainer Mal Lightfoot was fined for walking his notoriously obedient dogs off leash. "I spend all my life training dogs to be good citizens, and I was treated like a criminal," says Lightfoot, who runs the San Bruno Dog Training School. "It was the last straw." It took him and dozens of other frustrated dog owners nearly two years of working with—and against—city officials to get the park of their dreams.

Some detailed directions are necessary for finding this out-of-the-way park, even for locals. From El Camino Real, take Sneath Lane west. Just past Highway 280, turn right on Rollingwood Drive. Go right again at the first possible right, Crestwood Drive. Go left on Valleywood Drive and take a sharp right at Evergreen Drive. The park is in a few blocks, at Maywood and Evergreen drives in back of the old Carl Sandburg School. Once at the school driveway, take the first road to the right and drive until you see the dog park. (415) 877-8868. ➔ *See #18 on map p. 436.*

• **Sweeney Ridge** 🐾🐾🐾 1/2

If your dog appreciates breathtaking vistas of the Bay Area, with a rainbow assortment of wildflowers in the foreground, this 1,000-acre park is a rare treat. But if your canine is like most, he can take or leave such a magnificent panorama.

If you like a vigorous uphill climb, take the Sneath Lane entrance. It may be toasty when you start, but bring a couple of thick wool sweaters if you plan to hike along the ridge—it's cold and often foggy up there. The furrier your dog, the more she'll take to the invigorating conditions.

The Skyline College entrance is ideal if you want a more moderate grade, but both trailheads will take you to the same place. The leash law here can come in handy if your dog is of the pulling mentality. Just say "mush" on those steep slopes.

From different parts of the ridge, you'll be able to see the ocean (and the Farallon Islands, on a good day), as well as Mount Tamalpais in Marin, Mount Diablo to the east and Montara Mountain to the south. Judging by all the canines with flaring nostrils, the scents from all four directions must be as enticing as the views.

For the Sneath Lane entrance, take San Bruno's Sneath Lane all the way to the end. There's usually plenty of parking. The Skyline College entrance, off College Drive, is in the southeast corner of campus, near Lot 2. (415) 556-0560. ➡ *See #19 on map p. 436.*

SAN CARLOS
PARKS, BEACHES & RECREATION AREAS
• **Big Canyon Park** 🐾 🐾

The big canyon here is more like two steep hills, with you sandwiched between. There's a short trail that takes you and your leashed dog to the back of the park, but it's barely worth the walk, unless the creek is dry. If it is, you can keep walking beyond the trail, along the creek bed. Bring your insect repellent, because the farther back you go, the more voracious the mosquitoes.

On Brittan Avenue, just east of Crestview Drive. (415) 593-8011. ➡ *See #20 on map p. 436.*

• **Heather Park** 🐾 🐾 🐾 1/2 🐕

This is the only fenced-in dog park I've ever seen that comes complete with rolling hills, wildflowers, old gnarled trees and singing birds. Your dog will have the time of his life here, bounding up and down hills or trotting down the winding paved path to the bottom of the park—*sans* leash. You may be tempted to take some of the tiny dirt trails up the steep hills, but they tend to end abruptly, leaving you and your dog teetering precariously. The only thing the park lacks is water, usually a given at dog runs.

If you have a dog who likes to wander, watch out: There are a couple of potential escape routes near the park's two gates, at the far ends of the park. Also on the down side: I've been told the place is infested with ticks, although I've never had a problem.

At Melendy and Portofino drives. (415) 593-8011. ➡ *See #21 on map p. 436.*

RESTAURANTS

Coffee Club Two: Lots of dogs come here with their owners for a sip of coffee and a pastry on weekend mornings, sitting in any of several chairs outdoors. There's heavy socializing among dog people. 749 Laurel Street; (415) 592-9888.

SAN GREGORIO

PARKS, BEACHES & RECREATION AREAS

• **San Gregorio State Beach** 🐾 🐾

This place is usually a little too crowded with families for a comfortable dog walk, even a leashed one, which is the rule. It's sometimes just too difficult to negotiate through all the barbecuers, sunbathers, children and sand castles. The beach is so popular in part because of a lagoon that often forms at the mouth of San Gregorio Creek. The still water is an ideal depth for children, but dogs tend to enjoy wading through, too. Watch out for crumbling cliffs above. And don't forget the $4 entry fee, plus $1 per dog.

On Highway 1 just south of Highway 84. (415) 726-6203. ➡ *See #22 on map p. 436.*

• **Pomponio State Beach** 🐾 🐾

This one-and-a-half-mile beach is fine for sunbathing, but you can also go surf fishing for striped bass, search for driftwood or walk to the south end of the beach and watch nesting ravens along the craggy bluffs. Dogs must be leashed, but they seem to feel right at home here. One of Joe's favorite pastimes is picking up long pieces of driftwood and "accidentally" tripping whoever is walking him as he trots merrily along. There's a $4 fee per car. Dogs are $1 extra.

On Highway 1, just south of San Gregorio State Beach. (415) 726-6203. ➡ *See #23 on map p. 436.*

SAN MATEO

PARKS, BEACHES & RECREATION AREAS

• **Beresford Park** 🐾 🐾

The bulk of this park is made up of sports fields. But venture behind the garden center, and you and your pooch can enjoy a pleasant little leashed romp on a large grassy field. A dozen or so adolescent pine trees are trying to grow despite dozens of daily assaults from male dogs. Several picnic tables and a children's play area near the field make this an adequate spot for a weekend afternoon with the family. People are friendly here—we were twice offered soda and beer by locals, who wanted Joe to "hang" with them.

On Parkside Way at Alameda de las Pulgas. (415) 377-4640. →*See #24 on map p. 436.*

• **Central Park** 🐾 🐾 🐾

Bring plenty of quarters if you want to fully experience this strange park on the edge of downtown. It costs a quarter to park in the underground lot; a quarter to put your finger in the pulse machine; a quarter to watch the chicken lay a plastic prize egg; a quarter for the Pen Vendorama; it even costs a quarter for a cup of water at the refreshment stand, although smart shoppers know there's a water fountain within 20 feet.

As you enter the park from the 5th Avenue side, you immediately encounter the concession stand and surrounding dispensers that rival any at state fairs. The stand has good ice cream and tolerable pizza.

The rest of the park is a lush, green, miniature version of Golden Gate Park. There's a Japanese garden, and although no dogs are allowed inside, the Japanese ambience spills outside. The days we've visited, there was always something going on at the outdoor stage in back of the recreation center. A couple of large meadows are bordered by big shady redwoods. There's even a pint-sized railroad that takes up part of a small field. Someone told us that dogs have been known to chase the cars as they chug along the track. Leashes are a must, a rule you'd be well-advised to follow: The fine for loose dogs is not a quarter.

East 5th Avenue at El Camino Real. (415) 377-4640. →*See #25 on map p. 436.*

• **Laurelwood Park** 🐾 🐾 🐾

A small, clear stream winds the length of this rural park in the suburbs. Joe won't have anything to do with the water and jumps from one side to the other without getting a toenail damp. But normal dogs delight in its fresh scents and enticing sounds. Follow the bike trail—heeding the leash law, as this is a popular spot for bikers—along the stream, and enjoy tree-covered hillsides in a virtually suburb-free environment. Only a few blocks from the Laurelwood Shopping Center, this park is an ideal getaway after a quick shopping trip. The kids can use the playground at the foot of the bike trail.

At Glendora and Cedarwood drives. (415) 377-4640. →*See #26 on map p. 436.*

RESTAURANTS

Norby's Frozen Yogurt: If you'd rather indulge in yogurt than in Central Park's ice cream, this shop has some of the best. There are two benches on the sidewalk. 239 East 3rd Avenue; (415) 344-3863.

PLACES TO STAY

Dunfey San Mateo Hotel: Rates are $59 to $89. Small dogs only, please, and they require a $75 deposit. 1770 South Amphlett Boulevard, San Mateo, CA 94402; (415) 573-7661.

Residence Inn by Marriott: Rates are $129 to $155. Dogs are $6 extra, plus a $50 deposit. 2000 Winward Way, San Mateo, CA 94404; (415) 574-4700.

Villa Quality Hotel: Rates are $77 to $87. Dogs require a $50 deposit. 4000 South El Camino Real, San Mateo, CA 94403; (415) 341-0966.

FESTIVALS

Victorian Days: You and your dog may feel as though you've traveled back in time a century or so. This fair has mock Civil War skirmishes, duels, historic plays, entertainment and, of course, arts and crafts. Victorian Days is held at the end of August at Central Park. Call (415) 574-6441 for more information.

SOUTH SAN FRANCISCO

PARKS, BEACHES & RECREATION AREAS

•Orange Memorial Park 🐾 🐾

Hidden behind the park's large baseball field is a big square of land surrounded on all sides by tall trees. It's good for a quick on-leash romp. There seem to be all kinds of sniffs around the large weeping willow tree in the middle of the field.

It's on Orange Avenue at Tennis Drive. (415) 877-8560. ➡ *See #27 on map p. 436.*

•Westborough Park 🐾 🐾

This is a hilly little park with many picnic tables, a tennis court and a children's playground. Your best bet is to take the narrow, paved path along the back of the park. It's lined with trees, and far from the madding baseball field below. Leashes are required. It's on Westborough Avenue at Galway Drive, just west of Highway 280. (415) 877-8560. ➡ *See #28 on map p. 436.*

PLACES TO STAY

Ramada Inn San Francisco International: Rates are $59 to $110, but they could soon go up because of recent renovations. 245 South Airport Boulevard, South San Francisco, CA 94080; (415) 589-7200.

La Quinta Motor Inn: Rates are $54 to $78. 20 Airport Boulevard, South San Francisco, CA 94080; (415) 583-2223.

WOODSIDE

RESTAURANTS

Alice's Restaurant: You can get almost anything you want at this restaurant, including a table for you and your dog on the large porch. Weekends here are packed with bikers, especially for Alice's colossal breakfasts. If your dog rides in your motorcycle sidecar, this is the place for you. It's at 17288 Skyline Boulevard, on the corner of highways 35 and 84, just two miles north of Portola Valley's Windy Hill Preserve; (415) 851-0303.

King's Mountain Country Store: This store has everything from candles and books to dog food, crafts and camping items. There's even a deli. Classical music plays all the time. You and your dog can grab a sandwich and sit at an outside table. 13100 Skyline Boulevard, adjacent to Purisima Creek Open Space Preserve (no dogs are allowed there); (415) 851-3852.

SANTA CLARA COUNTY

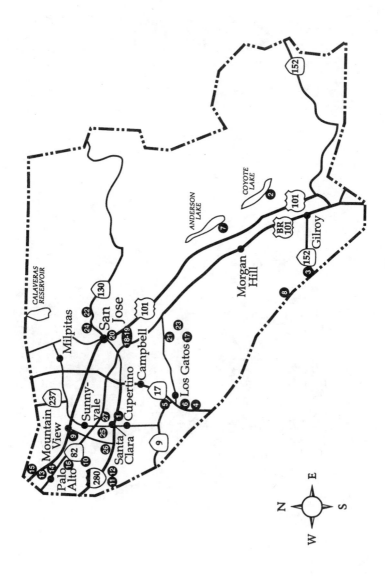

37
SANTA CLARA COUNTY

While some parts of Santa Clara County are quite scenic, dogs have to face the facts: The place still revolves around Silicon Valley. It's not a pretty sight. Cookie-cutter duplexes and townhouses abound. So do suburban-style office buildings, strip shopping centers and low-lying metal warehouses. Even dogs with questionable taste wince.

But if you get your dog out of the more populated areas and into the quieter county parks, you'll scarcely know you're in the middle of a megabyting, microchipping mecca.

The Midpeninsula Regional Open Space District manages nearly 30 preserves in San Mateo and Santa Clara counties, but only three in Santa Clara County permit pooches: St. Joseph's Hill (see page 465), Fremont Older (see page 462) and Foothills (see page 469) open space preserves are the ones lucky enough to have leashed dogs come to pay homage to the land. For maps and more information, call (415) 949-5500.

The county-run parks are the most attractive ones here, if you like plenty of land with a dash of wildlife mixed in. Mount Madonna (see page 463) and Coyote Hellyer (see page 472) county parks are the jewels in the county's canine crown. But the county's rules are confusing. Most of the park brochures say "Dogs prohibited except in designated areas," which doesn't help much. You might see a "No Pets" sign on a given trail, while a recently printed dog information sheet tells you that dogs are allowed on all trails in that park. If you find a ranger, you might be told something else entirely. But heed the ranger's words, because the rangers are the ones who will fine you if you make a mistake.

A few off-leash parks keep dogs from going out of their minds here. Palo Alto has three and Santa Clara has one. Mountain View has several that are open to leashless dogs who have special permits. But the best off-leash park of all is one of the newest: Sunnyvale's beautiful Las Palmas Park dog exercise area (see page 474) comes complete with picnic tables, plenty of shade trees and a dog toilet—okay, it's really just a fire hydrant. A toilet wouldn't have worked anyway, because all the dogs like Joe would drink out of it, then go running up and giving their loving people big slobbery kisses.

CAMPBELL

PLACES TO STAY
Campbell Inn: Rates are $90 to $175. Dogs are $10 extra. 675 East Campbell Avenue, Campbell, CA 95008; (408) 374-4300.

FESTIVALS
Highland Games: Put on her tartan collar and dance a fling with your dog. Scotties and other breeds are welcome to attend Campbell's Highland Games. The bagpipe competitions may be hard on the ears, but the meat pies make up for that. Dogs must be leashed, of course. Adults are $7, children $5. Held on the third Saturday in August at the Campbell Community Center Stadium on the corner of Campbell and Winchester boulevards. (408) 378-6252.

DIVERSIONS
You doity dog: Even if your dog hates a bath more than anything, he'll surely like it a bit better if it's you working him over, and not some stranger. Shampoo Chez (pronounced "Shampoochers") is a wash-him-yourself dog grooming establishment with two branches in the Bay Area.

The current owners say they've done 10,000 self-service washes in the two-and-a-half years they've been in business. The branch in Santa Cruz has been open 10 years. A shampoo for any size dog is $10 for 30 minutes of wash time, and an additional $1 for each five minutes after that. 523 East Campbell Avenue. (408) 379-WASH.

CUPERTINO

PARKS, BEACHES & RECREATION AREAS
•Fremont Older Open Space Preserve 🐾 🐾 🐾
This park smells sweet and clean, but that doesn't disappoint dogs. They've got enough trees and ground-level odors to keep them happily trotting along on their mandatory leashes.

Once you park in the small lot, you'll walk several hundred feet on a paved roadway, but be sure to turn right at the first sign for hikers. Otherwise you'll find yourself in the middle of a bicycle freeway. The narrow dirt trail to the right takes you on a three-mile loop through cool woodlands and rolling open hills up to Hunters Point via the Seven Springs Loop Trail. The view of Santa Clara Valley from the top is incomparable.

Signs at the entrance warn of ticks, so be sure to give your dog (and yourself) a thorough inspection after your hike.

From Highway 101 or Interstate 280, take Highway 85 (Saratoga-

Sunnyvale Road) south to Prospect Road. Go west on Prospect Road to the park entrance. (415) 691-1200. ➡ *See #1 on map p. 460.*

GILROY

PARKS, BEACHES & RECREATION AREAS

• **Coyote Lake Park** 🐾 🐾 🐾

This county park is full of wildlife no matter how high or low the lake. In fact, when we last visited, we saw foxes, wild turkeys and a grazing deer—and there wasn't a drop of water in the reservoir. The reservoir had been bone dry for so long that it looked like an enormous open field. Brush and a few trees were starting to emerge from the hard, dry ground.

When it's in this drought condition, the lake bed is a favorite stomping ground for leashed canines—who are usually relegated to picnic areas, the campground and the one-mile trail connecting them.

The campsites are roomy and several are shaded by large oak trees. Others look out on the lake—or field, depending on the water level. We like to visit the nearby picnic areas after stopping at one of Gilroy's garlic stores for lunch supplies. Joe has a penchant for garlic-flavored pistachios.

There are 75 sites here. Sites are $8, plus $1 extra for a dog. The day-use fee is $3. From Highway 101, exit at Leavesley Road and follow the signs to the park. (408) 842-7800. ➡ *See #2 on map p. 460.*

• **Mount Madonna County Park** 🐾 🐾 🐾 1/2

This magnificent park is midway between Gilroy and Watsonville (in Santa Cruz County). No matter where you're coming from, it's worth the drive. The mountain, covered with mixed conifers, oak, madrone and bay and sword ferns, is wonderfully quiet and cool—which is especially appreciated by San Jose dwellers, whose parks are almost never far from the roar of freeways. You may hear the screech of jays and little else.

Try driving on Valley View Road (to the right from the ranger station) to the Giant Twins Trail, where you can park in the shady campsite of the same name—at least, when no one is camping there. (When we were there on a perfect Indian summer day in late September, the park was deserted.) Two huge old redwoods, green with lichen, give the trail its name. After one-half mile, the trail becomes Sprig Lake Trail and continues for another two miles. Sprig Lake, really a pond, is empty in summer, but in spring it's stocked for children's fishing.

This walk isn't much of a strain. If you'd like more exercise, there are plenty of longer and steeper trails—18 miles in all, and as of this writing, your dog may enjoy every one of them. From the Redwood Trail or the Blackhawk Canyon Trail, you'll be rewarded with views of the Santa Clara Valley, the Salinas Valley and Monterey Bay. For a walk almost completely around the park, try the Merry-Go-Round Trail.

The park's deer are only one of many reasons you should keep your dog securely leashed, tempting as it might be to let her off. "Dogs have instincts," a friendly ranger said.

Your dog might enjoy a camping vacation here. There are 117 large, private campsites available on a first-come, first-served basis. Sites are $8 per night, $1 for each dog.

A $3 day-use fee is always charged on weekends and seven days a week from Memorial Day through Labor Day. From Highway 101, exit at Highway 152 west to Gilroy. Continue on 152 (Hecker Pass Highway) through part of the park. The entrance is a right (north) turn at Pole Line Road. Call (408) 842-2341 for park and campground information. → *See #3 on map p. 460.*

PLACES TO STAY

Coyote Lake Park camping: See page 463.

Leavesley Inn: Rates are $38 to $50. 8430 Murray Avenue, Gilroy, CA 95020; (408) 847-5500.

Mount Madonna County Park camping: See page 463.

Sunrest Inn: Rates are $42 to $50. 8292 Murray Avenue, Gilroy, CA 95020; (408) 848-3500.

LOS GATOS

PARKS, BEACHES & RECREATION AREAS

•**Lexington Reservoir County Park** 🐾 🐾

When the reservoir is full, this park is full of life. Birds sing and the foliage is bright green. But in drought years, everything here— trees, grass, brush—is covered with silt. This death mask must frighten birds away to better nesting areas, because it's utterly silent, except for a few cars kicking up dust on a nearby road.

It can really bake during summer months, too. And since there's no swimming allowed, dogs get miserable fast. (To cool himself off here, Joe rolled on the dusty ground until his entire body was coated with ash-colored silt. He looked like some kind of moving statue on a mandatory leash.)

Exit Highway 17 at Montevina Road and drive east a quarter mile. You can stop at any of several parking areas along the road. There is no entrance fee. (408) 691-1200. → *See #4 on map p. 460.*

• **Vasona Lake County Park** 🐾🐾🐾

This is a perfectly manicured park, with grass like that of a golf course. Dogs find it tailor-made for rolling, although they tend to get tangled in their leashes—which the county demands they wear here.

Several pathways take you through this 151-acre park and down to the lake's edge. But no swimming is allowed. And dogs aren't allowed to visit the children's playground either. You can picnic in the shade of one of the large willows or lead your dog up to the groves of pines and firs for a relief session.

From Highway 17, take Highway 9 (Saratoga-Los Gatos Road) west to University Avenue. Go right and continue to Blossom Hill Road. The park will be on your left. Enter at Garden Hill Drive. The parking fee is $3. (408) 356-2729. ➤*See #5 on map p. 460.*

• **St. Joseph's Hill Open Space Preserve** 🐾🐾🐾 1/2

This small preserve in the foothills just south of Los Gatos allows dogs on leash. There are no facilities for you here, and no water; bring your own. The grassy meadows are actually overgrown vineyards. From the public parking areas east of the Lexington Reservoir dam, you can find the trailhead to St. Joseph's Hill. It starts opposite the boat launch beyond the dam.

You may encounter horses on the dirt trails, but you and your dog will probably have the place to yourselves, with views of the reservoir, the valley and the Sierra Azul range.

From Highway 17, take the Alma Bridge Road exit and follow the signs. Parking is a quarter mile off the highway. (415) 691-1200. ➤*See #6 on map p. 460.*

PLACES TO STAY

Los Gatos Motor Inn: Rates are $58 to $70. 55 Saratoga Avenue, Los Gatos, CA 95032; (408) 356-9191.

FESTIVALS

Eastfield Ming Quong Strawberry Festival: You and your dog can get just about anything strawberry-flavored (except a rawhide chew) at this festival, held the first weekend in June on the Los Gatos Civic Center grounds. The strawberry pancakes are a great breakfast and dogs like to get there early, while it's still cool. Lots of dogs line up with their owners. Be sure to leash. 110 East Main Street. (408) 379-3790.

MILPITAS

PLACES TO STAY

Best Western/Brookside Inn: Rates are $39 to $44. Dogs are $10 extra, and it's requested that they not weigh more than 20 pounds. (Instead of putting your paunchy pooch on a crash diet, try Economy Inns.) 400 Valley Way, Milpitas, CA 95035; (408) 263-5566.

Economy Inns of America: Rates are $40 to $50. 270 South Abbott Avenue, Milpitas, CA 95035; (408) 946-8889.

MORGAN HILL

PARKS, BEACHES & RECREATION AREAS

• Anderson Lake County Park 🐾🐾 1/2

When there's enough water to keep the reservoir open to the public, dogs love to go along on fishing trips. But when it's low, dogs take solace in dipping their paws in the shady, secluded stream that runs between picnic areas.

Call the rangers to find out if the reservoir is open, because if it isn't, it may not be worth a trip. You can't get anywhere near the lake if it's too low.

The only trail connects picnic areas, and it isn't even a half mile long. There are plenty of picnic tables with lots of shade, but dogs tend to get bored unless hunks of hamburger happen to fall from the grills. The picnic areas can be rowdy, with lots of beer and loud music, so if your dog doesn't like rap, take him somewhere else.

From Highway 101, follow Cochrane Road east to the park. (408) 779-3634. ➔ *See #7 on map p. 460.*

• Uvas Canyon County Park 🐾🐾🐾 1/2

In the past, there was a lot of confusion about which trails in this park allowed dogs. Happily, the Santa Clara County Parks decided in 1992 to open all the trails to leashed dogs. You can get a map when you drive through the entrance kiosk.

This is a pretty, clean park of oaks, madrone and Douglas firs in cool canyons. The Uvas Creek Trail is a favorite trail. Dogs always appreciate a creek on a warm summer day, and this one doesn't dry up in hot weather. You might also try the wide, dirt Alec Canyon Trail, one-and-a-half miles long, within sight of Alec Creek, or the Nature Trail Loop, about one mile long, beside Swanson Creek. You may see some waterfalls in late winter and early spring.

Dogs are allowed in the campgrounds and picnic areas of Uvas Canyon. The park has 25 campsites, available on a first-come, first-served basis, for $8 a night. The campground is open daily from April 15 to October 31; and Fridays and Saturdays from November through March. It's crowded on weekends during late spring and summer—arrive early, or camp during the week.

From Highway 101, exit at Cochrane Road; go south on Business

101 to Watsonville Road, then right (west) on Watsonville to McKean-Uvas Road. Turn right on Uvas (past Uvas Reservoir) to Croy Road. Go left on Croy to the park. The last four miles on Croy are fairly tortuous. (408) 779-9232. → *See #8 on map p. 460.*

RESTAURANTS
Country Kitchen: This place has only two or three tables outside, but it specializes in homey dishes like spaghetti and hamburgers. There's a different special every night. 10980 Monterey Road; (408) 779-2928.

PLACES TO STAY
Best Western Country Inn: Rates are $54 to $76. 16525 Condit Road, Morgan Hill, CA 95037; (408) 779-0447.

Uvas Canyon County Park camping: See page 466.

MOUNTAIN VIEW
PARKS, BEACHES & RECREATION AREAS
• **Rengstorff Park** 🐾 🐾

This park is typically neat, green and interesting for people, and it has another excellent feature. A sign reads, "Dogs must be on leash (except by permit)." This means that you can get a permit from the city that allows you to train a dog off leash, with the understanding that he'll be under control, in any of Mountain View's parks. Be forewarned, though: If you don't bring the permit along with you when training, you will be ticketed.

Rengstorff Park is at Rengstorff Avenue between California Street and Central Expressway. (415) 903-6331. → *See #9 on map p. 460.*

RESTAURANTS
Blue Sky Cafe: This is a popular neighborhood restaurant in a small house with outdoor tables. Ingredients are strictly fresh, with vegetarian dishes a specialty. Dogs are happy to know that meat is served, too. The owners will be glad to seat your dog on the sidewalk just next to the outside tables. 336 Bryant Street; (415) 961-2082.

PLACES TO STAY
Best Western Tropicana Lodge: Rates are $55 to $80. 1720 West El Camino Real, Mountain View, CA 94040; (415) 961-0220.

FESTIVALS
California Small Brewers Festival: Mountain View hosts this annual festival late in early July. It's open to owners and dogs, even if most of the latter aren't 21 yet. The festival sets up live music,

beer-tasting booths and food booths, serving all kinds of dishes with chili predominating. Proceeds from the festival benefit local nonprofit organizations. At The Tied House Cafe and Brewery, 954 Villa Street, north of Castro Street; (800) 300-BREW.

PALO ALTO

For dogs, this town is the county's garden spot. Here, you'll find lots of other dog lovers and well-behaved dogs, enticing city parks—all of which allow dogs—and no fewer than three leash-free dog runs. At the Baylands, you and your leashed dog can watch birds and get a good workout at the same time. And many student-oriented restaurants with outdoor seating welcome your dog. If you're lucky enough to have a Palo Alto address, or a friend with one, you may bring your dog to the glorious Foothills Park on weekdays.

PARKS, BEACHES & RECREATION AREAS

• **Esther Clark Park** 🐾 🐾 🐾 🐾

This is a beautiful piece of undeveloped land with some dirt paths, right on the border of Los Altos Hills. The city leash rule applies—dogs must be leashed everywhere, except in official dog runs. There are no facilities, but plenty of meadow and eucalyptus trees. A creek bed promises water in wet season.

Where Old Adobe Road bends to the left and makes a cul-de-sac, the park is the undeveloped land on your right. (415) 496-6950. ➔ *See #10 on map p. 460.*

• **Foothills Park** 🐾 🐾 🐾 1/2

To use this park, privately owned by the city of Palo Alto, you must prove you're a resident or be the guest of one. And dogs are allowed only on weekdays, and on leash, but they can go on all the trails.

There's a large lake surrounded by unspoiled foothills, and 15 miles of hiking trails of varying difficulty. At sundown, deer are plentiful. The park's sole creek, Los Trancos Creek, has been dry for several years, but someday it will fill up again. This park is heaven on Earth for dogs and people alike. If you don't pass the entry test, though, don't despair—drive one mile down Page Mill Road to Foothills Open Space Preserve (see page 469).

To find Foothills Park from Interstate 280, exit at Page Mill Road and drive about 2.5 miles south. As usual, when you're searching for a really good Santa Clara County park, the road will become impossibly narrow and winding, and you'll think you're lost. But you aren't. The entry fee for Palo Alto residents is $2 per car, $1 for hikers and bicyclists. (415) 329-2423. ➡ *See #11 on map p. 460.*

• Foothills Open Space Preserve 🐾 🐾 🐾

This is pretty country, too, but dry and completely undeveloped—as in all open spaces, there's not even a portable toilet. You'll walk through lovely oak and brush with views of wooded hills and the populated valley below. The somewhat rough dirt trail is full of deer tracks, and your dog will be fascinated by mysterious rustlings. Leashes are the rule. The place is often full of ticks, but to your dog, it's worth the trouble.

Follow the directions to Foothills Park (see page 469) and go one mile farther down Page Mill Road. Watch carefully for the obscure turnout on the left (south) side. The worst feature of this park is that there is barely room for two cars at the turnout that constitutes the entrance, and turning around in the winding road is dangerous. (415) 691-1200. ➡ *See #12 on map p. 460.*

• Greer Park 🐾 🐾 🐾 1/2 🐕

This is one of Palo Alto's parks with an off-leash dog run, but it isn't the largest (see Mitchell Park, below). The park is green and pleasant, as are all the city's parks, but it's somewhat noisy from nearby Bayshore Road. Dogs have to be leashed outside the dog run. There are athletic fields, picnic tables and two playground areas. The dog run, near the Bayshore side, is small and treeless, but it's entirely fenced, if that's what your dog needs. Bring your own scoopers and water.

At Amarillo Street and West Bayshore Road. The parking lot is off Bayshore, conveniently near the dog run. (415) 496-6950. ➡ *See #13 on map p. 460.*

• Mitchell Park 🐾 🐾 🐾 🐾 🐕

This generous, green park has some unusual amenities, including two human-size chess boards and a roller-skating rink. This park is also a standout in the canine book: Its dog run is the largest and best of the three that Palo Alto offers. It's completely fenced and has a row of pine trees on one side, water dishes on the other, and scrappy tennis balls everywhere. The dog run is a short walk from the parking lot.

The park itself has plenty of shade to delight a dog. Remember to leash outside the dog run. For kids, the playground area has sculptured bears for climbing and a wading pool (sorry, no dogs). On East Meadow Drive just south of Middlefield Road. (415) 496-6950. ➡ *See #14 on map p. 460.*

• Palo Alto Baylands 🐾 🐾 🐾

This is the best-developed wetlands park in the Bay Area for adults, children and dogs. It's laced with paved bike trails and levee trails. Along the pretty levee paths, benches face the mudflats. Don't forget your binoculars on a walk here. A cacophony of mewling gulls, mumbling pigeons and clucking blackbirds fills the air. Small planes putt into the nearby airport and your dog will love the fishy smells coming from the marshes. This seems to be a popular spot for dog exercise. Keep your pooch leashed and on the trails.

Dogs shouldn't go near the well-marked waterfowl nesting area, but they are welcome to watch children feed the noisy ducks and Canada geese in the duck pond, as long as they don't think about snacks à l'orange.

From Highway 101, exit at Embarcadero Road East and go all the way to the end. At the entrance, turn left for the trails, ranger station and duck pond. A right turn takes you to a recycling center. (415) 496-6997. → See #15 on map p. 460.

• **The Stanford Dish** 🐾 🐾 🐾
"The Stanford Dish" is not a park but Stanford University property, surrounding the satellite dish used by the physics department. Stanford lets dog owners enjoy it, so long as dogs stay on leash and on the trails, and their owners pick up after them. The hill is quite popular, with its grasslands reclaimed from cattle pasture and dotted with oaks. A reforestation project is under way, so in the future it will be even nicer. Cattle still graze on the Interstate 280 side, so there's good reason for the leash rule. A ranger patrols to enforce it.

You can park on campus across the street from the Tressider Student Union and walk up a path to Junipero Serra Boulevard. The dish property borders Junipero Serra. Don't park in the nearby residential areas. (415) 723-2862. → See #16 on map p. 460.

RESTAURANTS
Downtown Palo Alto is walker-friendly and dog-adoring. It's full of benches and plazas for sitting, and quite a few restaurants will serve both of you out on the sidewalk or patio. Here are several from the Stanford end of University Avenue. You may find plenty of students who'll hug your dog and feed him treats. Then again, your dog might find the students and hug them.

Il Fornaio: Enjoy fine coffee and pastries here. There are about seven sidewalk tables subject to heavy foot traffic, but most of the feet will be of students who miss their dogs and want to stop and make a fuss over yours. "Dogs encouraged!" says the manager. 388 University Avenue; (415) 325-9353.

Rodger's Plaza Ramona: Snack on gourmet sandwiches and coffee. You're welcome at the relatively quiet sidewalk tables with your dog. On Ramona Street, off University Avenue; (415) 324-4228.

PLACES TO STAY

Holiday Inn—Palo Alto: Rates are $124 to $152. Dogs require a $50 deposit. 625 El Camino Real, Palo Alto, CA 94301; (415) 328-2800.

Hyatt Rickeys: Rates are $85 to $150. A $50 deposit is required for pooches. 4219 El Camino Real, Palo Alto, CA 94306; (415) 493-8000.

DIVERSIONS

Jog that dog: The city of Palo Alto stages an annual Dog's Best Friend Run at the Palo Alto Baylands. The five-kilometer (3.1-mile) course, which you may run or walk with your leashed dog, begins and ends at the athletic center. Rules are as follows: You must have your dog on a regular six-foot leash, not a retractable one; you can't carry the dog; and she must cross the finish line before you do. (The idea of this last rule is to restrain hot-dog owners who drag their poor dogs across the finish line.) The record will show your dog's racing time, not yours. Nearly 500 dogs now show up every year, yet the organizer, recreation supervisor Tom Osborne, says he's never seen a dogfight in all the years he's hosted the race.

For your entry fee of $15, you get a T-shirt and the dog gets a bandana and plenty of treats. Winners receive plaques and photos. At the Palo Alto Baylands (see page 469), around the second week of April. Call (415) 329-2380 for this year's date.

Shop with a best friend: It's perfectly legal to bring your dog to the huge, open-air Stanford Shopping Center, so long as he stays outside the stores. Dogs haven't quite mastered the art of shopping without wearing out the merchandise. "No deposits," the managers plead. This mall has plenty of outdoor snacking places. On El Camino Real and University Avenue, next to Stanford University. (415) 617-8585.

SAN JOSE

We visited San Jose's downtown center hoping to find plenty of dog-friendly outdoor eateries and shopping malls, but we were disappointed. Only one mall—The Pavilion, next to the Fairmont Hotel, with an inviting array of shops and outdoor tables—looked as if it might allow dogs, but it didn't. The same went for outdoor restaurants. But a dog can drink from a fountain featuring wrought-iron fish in elegant St. James Square Park or gaze at 20 terrific pillars of water shooting from the fountain at Park Plaza. Keep your eye on the area if you have a boulevardier-type dog.

Any day now, San Jose may change into his kind of place.

Dogs are welcome in most of the city's parks. Leashes are mandatory in all the parks, and there are no leash-free dog runs.

San Jose residents must enjoy most of their city parks—even the best ones—in the shadow of freeways (some literally) and under the buzz of airplanes landing at the central airport. This listing describes several of the larger, clean, green parks. Many others are undistinguished or full of litter. Call the parks department at (408) 277-4573 for more information.

PARKS, BEACHES & RECREATION AREAS

• **Almaden Quicksilver County Park** 🐾 🐾 🐾 1/2

This rustic, 3,600-acre park allows dogs on about half of its 30 miles of trails. Some of these trails are popular for horseback riding, so watch out, because although leashes are the law here, they don't always stop dogs who like to chase hooves.

In the spring, the hills explode with wildlife and wildflowers. Any of the trails will take you through a wonderland of colorful flowers, and butterflies who like to tease safely leashed dogs.

Dogs are allowed on: the Guadalupe Trail, the Hacienda Trail, portions of the Mine Hill Trail, the Mockingbird Picnic Area, the No Name Trail and the Senator Mine Trail.

Call the park for more information about the trails and the locations of their trailheads. You can enter the park at several points. We prefer the main park entrance, where New Almaden Road turns into Alamitos Road, near Almaden Way. (408) 268-3883.
➡ *See #17 on map p. 460.*

• **Coyote-Hellyer County Park** 🐾 🐾 🐾 1/2

Dogs are not officially allowed in this park's best feature—Coyote Creek—or in the lake. They can't go on athletic fields, either, and they must be leashed everywhere. But visit the beautiful picnic area beside the creek, lined with big sycamores and other trees.

It's a generous, rustic park, popular with bicyclists. The best deal for dogs is the El Arroyo del Coyote Nature Trail, which by some miracle allows dogs. Walk to the left at the entrance kiosk and cross under Hellyer Avenue on the bike trail to find the entrance to the nature trail. Cross the creek on a pedestrian bridge to your right; once across, take the dirt path to your left. Bikes aren't allowed, making it all the nicer for dogs.

Willows and cottonwoods are luxuriant here, and in spring, poppies bloom. There's occasional shade from eucalyptus groves. Watch out for bees and poison oak. Otherwise, this is heavenly territory for your dog. It is ridiculous that he's not allowed to dip his paws in the largest creek in the Santa Clara Valley, but them's the rules.

From Highway 101, exit at Hellyer Avenue and follow prominent signs to the park. A parking fee of $3 is charged every weekend and on weekdays from Memorial Day to Labor Day. (408) 255-0225. →*See #18 on map p. 460.*

•**Coyote Creek Multiple-Use Trail** 🐾 🐾 🐾
When this trail is completely paved, it will furnish your dog with 13 miles of trail, if she doesn't mind sharing space with bicycles. Some pooper-scooper dispensers are being installed, too. You may take your dog, leashed, on any portion between the Coyote-Hellyer County Park end and Parkway Lakes, a private fishing concession at the south end, close to Morgan Hill. (Your only reason to go there would be to pull in some of the club's stocked trout or to enter one of its fishing derbies.)

See the directions to Coyote-Hellyer County Park above. (408) 255-0225. →*See #19 on map p. 460.*

•**Emma Prusch Park** 🐾 🐾 🐾 🖐
This park, one of San Jose's most attractive working farms, is a museum. Like a symbol of the county, it lies in the shadow of the intersection of three freeways. Yet it's a charming place and, surprisingly, it allows your leashed dog to wander around the farm with you so long as he stays out of the farm-animal areas. A smooth paved path, good for strollers and wheelchairs, winds among a Victorian farmhouse (which serves as the visitors center), a multicultural arts center, farm machinery, a barn, an orchard and gardens. There are picnic tables on an expanse of lawn with trees.

During the summer and through October, a farmers market is held here every Saturday from 8:30 a.m. to 1 p.m. Also here, the city's K-9 Corps of trained police dogs occasionally shows off for children. If you think your own dog won't be intimidated by dogs in uniform, call the park to find out when they'll be there.

The entrance is on South King Road, near the intersection of Highway 101 and Interstate 680/280. (408) 926-5555. →*See #20 on map p. 460.*

•**Guadalupe Oak Grove Park** 🐾 🐾 🐾 1/2 🖐
This park is a pleasant exception to most of the others in San Jose—it's undeveloped, beautiful and doesn't allow bicycles—and sure enough, it may not be open to dogs forever. For years we've been hearing it may "soon" be declared an oak woodlands preserve. It still hasn't been, so go there and enjoy it.

Dirt trails wind through hills, alternately semi-open and covered with thick groves of oaks. Birds are plentiful and noisy. Be aware of high fire danger in the dry season, and don't even think of letting your dog off leash. The park's ranger loves dogs, but she'll ticket you, and she's heard all the excuses—from "He just slipped out of his collar for a moment..." to "I couldn't get my dog through the gate with his leash on..."

Guadalupe Oak Grove Park is at Golden Oak Way and Vargas Drive. (408) 277-4661. → *See #21 on map p. 460.*

• Joseph D. Grant County Park 🐾 🐾 🐾

Here's another huge, gorgeous, wild park that your dog may barely set foot in. Dogs are limited to the campgrounds, picnic areas, Edwards Field Hill and the Edwards Trail. But if you don't mind a long, winding drive for one short—albeit satisfying—trail hike, by all means try this park. Stop in at the homey old ranch house that is now the visitors center for directions to the Edwards Trail, which isn't easy to find.

Or try these directions: On Mount Hamilton Road midway between the intersection with Quimby Road and the park border is a white barn on your right as you're heading out of the park. Just past the white barn is an unmarked pedestrian gate on the left. This is the trailhead. This trail is a fine walk through a deciduous forest.

There are 22 campsites, available first come, first served. Sites are $8 and dogs are $1 extra. Open daily from April 1 to October 31; open weekends in November and in March; closed from December to February.

To get to the park from Interstate 680, exit at the Capitol Expressway and drive south to Quimby Road. Turn left (east) on Quimby and wind tortuously to the park entrance. It's a long six miles and the road is often a one-lane cliffhanger. Alternatively, you can get to the park from Interstate 680 via Highway 130 (Mount Hamilton Road). It's similar, but at least it's a two-lane. (408) 274-6121. → *See #22 on map p. 460.*

• Los Alamitos-Calero Creek Park Chain 🐾 🐾 🐾

Six miles of multi-use trail, both dirt and paved, run along Los Alamitos Creek and Arroyo Calero from the southern end of Almaden Lake Park (which doesn't allow dogs) south to the western entrance of Santa Teresa County Park. San Jose dogs love these trails for their easy creek access. There's plenty of shade.

Two small adjacent city parks, Graystone Park and Carrabelle Park, have picnic tables and drinking fountains for a break, if you and your dog are making a trek of it. Keep your dog leashed and watch for bicycles and horses sharing the trail with you. You can park on a neighborhood street, but not along Camden Avenue.

From Camden Avenue at Villagewood Way or Queenswood Way, you can pick up a new segment of the Bay Area Ridge Trail that runs all the way to Santa Teresa County Park's western entrance, about 1.3 miles. Where the trail forks, take the westernmost fork—the trail paralleling Camden Avenue—westward across Harry Road and continuing to Santa Teresa County Park.

The creek park chain runs parallel to the southern end of the Almaden Expressway. The trails run along the north side of Camden Avenue and along the east side of Queenswood Way. (408) 277-4573. ➤ *See #23 on map p. 460.*

• **Penitencia Creek County Park** 🐾 🐾 🐾

This county park is largely a four-mile paved streamside trail designed for hikers, bicyclists and rollerskaters. Leashed dogs are welcome, and it usually isn't dangerously crowded. From the western end, at North King Road, you can connect with the Coyote Creek Multi-Use Trail (see page 473). The Penitencia Creek Trail is paved from end to end, but it is not designed to go under roads like the better bicycle trails in Walnut Creek, for example. You will have to scramble your way across highways or around fenced portions. Or you'll be confronted with a locked gate protecting water district equipment.

At the Jackson Avenue end, large walnut trees line the creek and shelter some picnic tables. Restrooms are scattered along the route.

There are parking lots on Penitencia Creek Road and on Jackson Avenue. This is the best portion of the trail for a dog, because there's a dry lake bed. (408) 358-3741. ➤ *See #24 on map p. 460.*

PLACES TO STAY

Best Western San Jose Lodge: Rates are $55 to $68. 1440 North First Street, San Jose, CA 95112; (408) 453-7750.

Holiday Inn Park Center Plaza: Rates are $72 to $90. 282 Almaden Boulevard, San Jose, CA 95113; (408) 998-0400.

Joseph D. Grant County Park camping: See page 474.

Red Lion Hotel: Rates are $90 to $150. A $50 dog deposit is required. 2050 Gateway Place, San Jose, CA 95110; (408) 453-4000.

DIVERSIONS

Be a fundraiser: You and your dog can raise money for cancer research by taking part in San Jose's Canines Against Cancer walk-a-thon, held annually in the fall, usually in October. For a $10 registration fee, you get a T-shirt and your dog gets a goody bag (last year's included dog biscuits, a pooper scooper and discount coupons). After the walk, there are a grab-bag collection of contests—everything from dog and owner look-alikes to best dressed dog. Ninety percent of the proceeds benefit the American Cancer Society and the other 10 percent go to UC Davis' Center for Companion Animal Health, which does medical research on animals' cancer-related illnesses. For the exact date and location of the event, call (408) 287-5973.

FESTIVALS

Tapestry in Talent: Visual, performing and culinary arts are all on display at this multicultural arts festival. Six stages feature every kind of live music. You can watch modern, ethnic, square and folk dancing. There are potential dog treats here from all over the world. Your leashed pup will love this festival, no matter what his ancestry. Just make sure he doesn't mind crowds and the occasional firecracker, and that the weather isn't too warm for him. Held on Labor Day weekend in downtown San Jose. (408) 293-9727.

SANTA CLARA

PARKS, BEACHES & RECREATION AREAS

•**Central Park** 🐾 🐾

This Santa Clara city park, like most of the others, has a sign that reveals a certain slant: "No Dogs Allowed Except on Leash." If you can get past that, the park is large and has a wide assortment of trees. Its creek is large and deep, but dry in summer. A beautiful round picnic pavilion has tables fully shaded by wisteria vines, the most we've ever seen in one place.

On Kiely Boulevard between Homestead Road and Benton Street. (408) 984-3223. *→See #25 on map p. 460.*

•**The Dog Park** 🐾 🐾 🐾 1/2 🐕

It's not much, but this 200-foot by 200-foot fenced dog run is the only leash-free option in Santa Clara. Located on the grounds of what used to be Curtis Intermediate School, it's a flat stretch of grass bordered by stands of shady trees. Inside you'll find water, pooper scoopers and benches to sit on. And it has been popular with dog owners since it opened in the fall of 1993, with up to 20 dogs using it at a time in the evenings. That's what you get for being the only game in town.

At the corner of Pomeroy Avenue and Locknivar Street, near Lawrence Expressway and Homestead Road. (408) 984-3223. *→See #26 on map p. 460.*

PLACES TO STAY

Econo Lodge: Rates are $50 to $90. Dogs are $5 extra. 2930 El Camino Real, Santa Clara, CA 95051; (408) 241-3010.

Santa Clara Travelodge: Rate are $45 to $55. Small dogs only, please, and they're $5 extra. 3477 El Camino Real, Santa Clara, CA 95051; (408) 984-3364.

The Vagabond Inn: Rates are $44 to $55. Dogs are $5 to $8 extra, depending on the dog's size. 3580 El Camino Real, Santa Clara, CA 95051; (408) 241-0771.

DIVERSIONS

Go on a pilgrimage: Mission Santa Clara, on the Santa Clara University campus, allows leashed dogs on its grounds. You might make it part of your walk if you're exploring the campus. The building, dating from 1929, is a replica of one version of the old mission, which was first built in 1777 but was destroyed five times by earthquake, flood and fire. Preserved fragments of the original mission, and the old adobe Faculty Club, are the oldest college buildings standing in the western United States. The mission is on campus, off El Camino Real. (408) 554-4023.

SUNNYVALE

PARKS, BEACHES & RECREATION AREAS

• **Las Palmas Park** 🐾 🐾 🐾 🐾 🐕

With its paved paths, green grass and beautiful pond, this park used to be the best in town for a walk among rolling hills. Now it's really the best, because of its brand new dog run. Opened in 1993, this two-acre run has everything a dog could possibly desire—shade, water, pooper scoopers and even a fire hydrant. It's a kind of fenced-in nirvana. Dogs get deliriously happy when they visit.

At Danforth and Russet drives. (408) 730-7350. ➡ *See #27 on map p. 460.*

PLACES TO STAY

The Vagabond Inn: Rates are $40 to $55. Dogs are $5 extra. 816 Ahwanee Avenue, Sunnyvale, CA 94086; (408) 734-4607.

SANTA CRUZ COUNTY

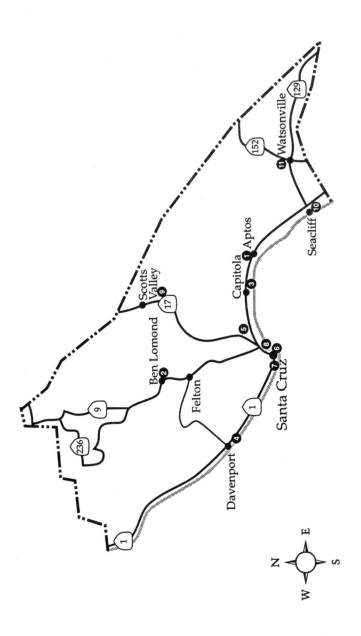

38
SANTA CRUZ COUNTY

Despite the leash that so obviously attaches Joe to me, my strange little Airedale pretends he's an orphan dog when he visits Santa Cruz County's beach towns. He puts on his best "I'm abandoned" face and gets pity from everyone he eyes. And at beaches, he eyes only girls in bikinis.

I don't know how he can tell a bikini from a one-piece, but when he spots someone walking around in a double-decker bathing suit, he stops in his tracks and sits while his eyes grow big and blank. Usually he'll hang his head low, all the time maintaining eye contact. When the object of his attention says "Awwwww," which she inevitably does, he gets up and smells her legs. If he likes her sunscreen, he tastes it. But alas, before he can sample more, he finds himself unceremoniously dragged away by his ruthless leash holder. His pitiable face freezes into a scowl—until his next paramour comes along.

If you have a beach-loving dog, Santa Cruz County is a great place to take him. The beaches here rarely get too warm, and while some are packed beyond belief (dogs are generally not allowed at the popular beaches), most are on the quieter side. One of the best ways to get to the beach from mid-county is to take the turn-of-the-century steam train, run by the Roaring Camp & Big Trees Railroad. The same company runs an 1880s narrow-gauge railroad through the redwoods. Both trips can be the thrill of a dog's life (see Diversions, page 485).

Despite his penchant for beach bunnies, Joe's favorite beaches are the more desolate ones along the northernmost coast of Santa Cruz County. Only one (Bonny Dune Beach) is detailed later in this chapter because there are so many of them and they're relatively small, with parking only on the shoulder of the road. But they're wonderful for getting away from the crowds, especially if you're also looking at getting away from day-use fees.

These beaches run from Scott Creek in the north to Wilder Ranch State Park in the south. Davenport is the mid-point. Many of the beaches are hidden from Highway 1, so sometimes the only way to tell if there's a beach at all is to look for a few other cars parked on the roadside.

A word of warning about those big green patches you'll see

when you look at a map of the county: They're mostly state parks and they ban dogs from doing everything but camping with you and hanging out on the paved portions of road (not a safe habit).

APTOS

If all suburbs could be like Aptos, this country would be a much better looking place. While Aptos is falling victim to the suburban sprawl of its neighbors to the north, it still retains a core of grace in its old village section. Check out the rustic Redwood Village, whose quaint stores were originally built in 1928 with redwood hewn from trees on the property.

While exploring Aptos, if you run into Loma Prieta Drive, don't sit around with your dog and wonder why someone would name a street after the deadly 1989 earthquake. This is the area of the epicenter of that quake, which measured 7.1 on the Richter scale. If your dog starts acting restless around here, you may want to move on. It could be fleas. It could be boredom. It could even be gas. But why take a chance? Actually, people around here say the pressure along the fault line was relieved by the quake, so there's probably little chance that another big one could be centered here again for a while.

If you do hear any rumbling, most likely it will be the sound of your empty stomach growling. That's a quaking that can be calmed easily by eating at a few Aptos restaurants that welcome dogs at their outside tables (see page 483).

PARKS, BEACHES & RECREATION AREAS

Don't be fooled by the map handed out by the Aptos Chamber of Commerce! That big patch of green that says Polo Grounds Regional Park is not a place where the public is welcome. In fact, it looks like a gigantic empty lot. The county says it's trying to figure out what to do with the land, but for now it's off-limits. If you're without a dog and are looking for a real patch of green, just move on to the gigantic Forest of Nisene Marks State Park, only a couple of miles away. Unfortunately, like most state parks, this one is so strict that a dog won't have much fun there. If you're with a dog, and that dog is desperate, try the Aptos Village Park.

• Aptos Village Park 🐾 🐾

The grass here is perfectly manicured. The trees are perfectly shaped. The gazebo is perfect...the picnic tables are perfect...the playground is perfect. Even the people who use the park seem perfect. It's all a bit much for a dog who's just trying to go about the business of being a dog. About the only place where leashed dogs can let it all hang out in this park is on the nature trail.

The park is just off Soquel Drive, about 50 yards east of The Veranda restaurant. There's a road to the right that's unmarked except for the sign "Aptos Station." Go right and make an immediate left into the long and winding park driveway. (408) 454-2800. ➤*See #1 on map p. 480.*

RESTAURANTS

Cafe Sparrow: Eat your croissant sandwich on the bench in front of this little restaurant. 8042 Soquel Drive; (408) 688-6238.

Jorie's: This deli serves big enough portions to satisfy even the heartiest appetite. We like the mashed potatoes with gravy. Dine at the outdoor tables topped with umbrellas. 7957 Soquel Drive; (408) 685-2627.

The Veranda: This is an old, wonderful, huge mansion. Dogs are allowed to dine with you out in front, at two charming tables. 8041 Soquel Drive; (408) 685-1881.

FESTIVALS

Aptos Pancake Breakfast and World's Shortest Parade: On July 4 in Aptos, you can start the day at 7 a.m. by sharing a pancake with your dog friend, then watch a parade that lasts all of a half mile. After the excitement, head to the Aptos Village Park for an afternoon of family fun, including food (in case your dog snatched all your pancakes), games, music and children's activities. (408) 688-1467.

BEN LOMOND

PARKS, BEACHES & RECREATION AREAS

•Quail Hollow Ranch 🐾 🐾 🐾

This 300-acre ranch-style park is the largest county park in Santa Cruz. It's also one of the least developed, making it a good area for a dog. There's plenty of wildlife around, so bring your binoculars and hold on tight to that leash. Deer and coyotes abound certain times of year. You'll also see a few quail, but don't get any ideas about dinner: No hunting is allowed.

From Highway 9, go east on Graham Hill Road and then north (left) on East Zayante Road. Turn left at Quail Hollow Road. The park is on the right. The official address is 800 Quail Hollow Road. (408) 454-2800. ➤*See #2 on map p. 480.*

CAPITOLA

This beautiful resort area's main beach, Capitola City Beach, is off-limits to dogs. But just down the road, New Brighton State Beach more than makes up for the loss.

If you feel like a beautiful stroll by Soquel Creek, take your leashed dog to the Esplanade, just off Opal Cliff Drive. It's the paved walk that usually has flowers at the entrance, east and inland of the Capitola Wharf (which also doesn't allow dogs).

PARKS, BEACHES & RECREATION AREAS

• **New Brighton State Beach** 😺 😺 😺 1/2

Is your dog bored of the same old beach scene? Is she tired of sand and surf and surf and sand, bored of sitting around getting tan? Bring her here! There's much more to this place than beach. The trails above the beach allow leashed dogs, who are usually grateful for a break in the routine.

Take her on the trail that leads up to big pines and eucalyptus trees. It starts to the left of the main beach entrance. If you walk along the forest/dune area, you'll be able to see Capitola as birds see it. Dogs like to sit up here and let their nostrils quiver over scents drifting in from around the world.

From Highway 1, take the New Brighton Beach exit west. Day-use fees are $6 per car, $1 per dog. More than 100 campsites, set on dunes and surrounded by trees, are also available. Rates are $14 to $16 per night, $1 extra for dogs. For campground reservations, phone MISTIX at (800) 444-PARK. Call (408) 475-4850 for beach information. → *See #3 on map p. 480.*

RESTAURANTS

Caffe Lido: It's a kind of small outdoor area, but if you keep your dog from getting underfoot, you'll enjoy a relaxed California-Italian meal. 110 Monterey Avenue; (408) 475-6544.

Souza Cones Ice Cream & Candy: 200 Monterey Avenue; (408) 475-9339.

PLACES TO STAY

New Brighton State Beach camping: See above.

DAVENPORT

PARKS, BEACHES & RECREATION AREAS

• **Bonny Dune Beach** 😺 😺 😺

This beach is hidden from Highway 1 by bluffs, so few people know it exists. That's good news for dogs, even though they're still supposed to be leashed. Some days, you won't find a soul here. Other times, the crowd will consist of a couple dozen folks. You still won't even notice they're around.

See the introduction to this chapter for info on other small beaches along the north coast of Santa Cruz County. Bonny Dune

Beach is at Highway 1 and Bonny Dune Road. There's a small, dirt parking lot on the side of the road. ➡ *See #4 on map p. 480.*

RESTAURANTS

Whale City Bakery, Bar & Grill: Smell fresh ocean breezes on the other side of Highway 1 as you and your quiet dog dine on tasty baked goods. 490 Highway 1; (408) 423-9803.

FELTON

PLACES TO STAY

Henry Cowell Redwoods State Park: This being a state park, dogs aren't allowed to explore any of the magnificent trails here. They're restricted to pavement, the campgrounds or the picnic area. That's rather limiting for dogs who love to run around the redwoods and the mountains. The 112 campsites are surrounded by the big old trees, if that's any comfort to your canine. Fees are $14 to $16. Dogs are $1 extra. From Felton, take Graham Hill Road southeast about two miles to the park. The entrance is on the right. Phone (408) 335-4598 for park information or call MISTIX at (800) 444-PARK for campsite reservations.

DIVERSIONS

All aboard for some dog training: Riding on the antique Roaring Camp & Big Trees Narrow-Gauge Railroad through a redwood forest was one of Joe's favorite adventures ever—except whenever the engineer released loud bellows of steam. And whenever the railroad car moved.

Eventually he did get used to the chug-a-lug motion. Toward the end of the one-and-a-half hours, he was thoroughly enjoying himself, nose in the air, sucking in the smells of the primeval redwood forest from our open train car. But he still wouldn't leave my lap.

Most dogs are ecstatic on the train. Nisha smiled the whole time and her tail never stopped wagging. When the steam let loose, she followed it with her eyes as if it were a beautiful white bird. She slept the rest of the day. Joe just stared blankly at the sky, trying to sort out what had happened to him.

The railroad company offers another trip, to the Santa Cruz city beach. But since dogs aren't allowed in that area, we recommend the excursion through the redwoods. Besides, halfway through the redwood trip, dogs and their people get to walk around the ancient forest a little before clambering back aboard.

At the end of either train journey, nothing beats spreading out a picnic at the old-fashioned depot's picnic tables. There's plenty of room for walking your leashed dog around the grounds. And humans have fun shopping at the antique general store. It's hard to leave the little shop without buying the kids a miniature train car, so if you don't want to spend extra money, you'd better not even go in.

Rates for the redwood trip are $11.50 for adults, $8.50 for children ages 3 to 15. Rates for the Santa Cruz beach excursion are $14 for adults, $9 for kids ages 3 to 15. Dogs go free.

From Highway 1 in the Santa Cruz area, take Highway 17 north toward San Jose. Exit at the Scott's Valley/Big Basin exit, and drive west on Mount Hermon Road 3.5 miles to Graham Hill Road. Turn left onto Graham Hill Road. Roaring camp is one-half mile ahead on the right. They often offer special trips, such as moonlight steam train parties and chuckwagon barbecue rides. Call for details and schedules. (408) 335-4484.

SANTA CRUZ

When I told Joe and Nisha that we were going to visit Santa Cruz, they started whining and running around in circles. Joe began moaning what sounded like the word "cool." I figured somehow the dogs knew that this laid-back, liberal town had to be, like, *totally* relaxed about dogs.

I was wrong. Now that I look back on it, the dogs were probably whining with anxiety about driving for two hours to a place where they would not only have to stay on leash, but would be completely banned from certain beaches. Joe's "cool" moan was more likely a resounding "nooo!"

We'd been to Santa Cruz several times before and had survived just fine at some of the more remote beaches when we weren't aware of the rules. But now that we were trying to be law-abiding creatures, it was tough.

There are a couple of beaches that allow dogs off leash during limited hours. We're very grateful for those. But somehow we didn't think dogs would be outcasts at such hangouts as Santa Cruz Beach, the Boardwalk and the Municipal Wharf.

If this were any other city, it wouldn't be such a disappointment. But this is Santa Cruz, land of the free, home of the unusual. The dogs had that "bummer" look the whole way back. Even their bandanas drooped.

PARKS, BEACHES & RECREATION AREAS

Two beaches and one field allow dogs off leash. Most city parks permit leashed dogs. San Lorenzo Park is a notable exception. So is Nearys Lagoon City Park, a popular wildlife sanctuary you may be tempted to visit with your canine friend. But since dogs aren't part of the natural scenery here, they're not allowed.

• De La Veaga Park 🐾🐾🐾

When you get past all the golf courses here, this large park and its trails are remote and not widely used. That means party time, even for leashed dogs.

Many trails lead you through fields, into woods and back through lush meadowland. Just watch out for flying arrows at the archery range on the east side of the park. If you like sitting down and resting every few hundred feet, this park provides benches. At the top of the park, you can see forever.

From Highway 1, exit at Morrissey Boulevard and go south for one block. Turn right at Fairmount Avenue. Within two blocks, go right on Brancifort Avenue. As you cross back over the highway and enter the park, the road turns into La Veaga Park Road. Bear right and then left. You'll pass through what will seem like an eternity of golf courses, then you'll finally see your destination. (408) 429-3663. ➡ *See #5 on map p. 480.*

• Lighthouse Field State Beach (two sections)

This beach area is divided into two parts, both of which allow dogs to run off leash during limited hours:

• Lighthouse Field 🐾🐾 1/2 🐕

Dogs can run off leash at this field between 6 a.m. and 9 a.m. from May 1 to September 30, and from 6 a.m. to 10 a.m. the rest of the year. It's a great dog privilege, but the field itself is no prize. It's not large enough for escape artist dogs to be safe from traffic, and there's barely any shade. But the view of the ocean is a winner. Unless your dog likes traipsing through eye-high dry grass, which is what this place has most of the year, you're better off taking him to West Lighthouse Beach on the other side of West Cliff Drive (see below).

Don't worry if signs tell you only that dogs must always be leashed, without mentioning the off-leash hours. The field is on the north side of West Cliff Drive, west of Point Santa Cruz. (408) 429-3777. ➡ *See #6 on map p. 480.*

• West Lighthouse Beach/It's Beach 🐾🐾🐾🐾 🐕

Dogs are allowed to run leash-free between 6 a.m. and 9 a.m. from May 1 to September 30, and from 6 a.m. to 10 a.m. the rest of the year. While that's not many hours, it's enough to keep your dog happy. The beach is narrow and not nearly as heavily used as Santa Cruz Beach. It's just below the famed Lighthouse Field State Beach Surf Museum, which houses the largest collection of surfing books on the West Coast. The beach is perfect if you want to hang out on the sand with your cool dog while a surfing dude friend checks out the museum. The beach is on the south side of West Cliff Drive, west of Point Santa Cruz, and just west of the Surf Museum. (408) 429-3777. ➤*See #6 on map p. 480.*

• **Mitchell's Cove Beach** 🐾 🐾 🐾 🐾 🐕

This is the place locals come with their dogs when they want to get away from the tourist scene. The beach is small, attractive and conveniently located next to Lighthouse Field State Beach. But for some reason, hardly anyone uses it.

Dogs may run off leash between 6 a.m. and 9 a.m. from May 1 to September 30, and from 6 a.m. to 10 a.m. the rest of the year. The beach is between Almar and Woodrow avenues, on the south side of West Cliff Drive. It's unmarked. (408) 429-3777. ➤*See #7 on map p. 480.*

• **Twin Lakes State Beach** 🐾 🐾 1/2

The beach here is wide and inviting for leashed dogs and their people. But unfortunately, even more inviting is a section that dogs should stay away from: Schwan Lagoon, a wildfowl refuge full of ducksch and geesch and, they say, even a few schwans.

Twin Lakes State Beach is on both sides of the Santa Cruz Small Craft Harbor, on East Cliff Drive and 7th Avenue. (408) 688-3241. ➤*See #8 on map p. 480.*

RESTAURANTS

The Coffee Vault, Inc.: Humans like the bagels here, and dogs love to beg for them when they're slathered with cream cheese. 3701 Portola Drive; (408) 476-4729.

Cole's Bar-B-Q: 2590 Portola Drive; (408) 476-4424.

Harbor Deli: The Mexican food and burgers are satisfying here. 460 7th Avenue; (408) 479-1366.

Pleasure Pizza: 4000 Portola Drive; (408) 475-4999.

Polar Bear Ice Cream: Dogs are welcome to eat with you under the awning in back of this ice creamery. 1224 Soquel Avenue; (408) 425-5188.

Tony & Alba's Pizza: Dogs like hanging out under the shade of a cool umbrella-covered table while you enjoy pizza and pasta. 817 Soquel Avenue; (408) 425-8669.

PLACES TO STAY

Comfort Inn: This new hotel has some rooms with Jacuzzi and fireplaces. But ewww—only dogs who are smaller than 10 pounds are allowed! That's smaller than most of the cats Joe stalks. Rates are $39 to $150. 110 Plymouth Street, Santa Cruz, CA 95060; (408) 426-2664 or (800) 228-5150.

Edgewater Beach Motel: There's a one-time doggy fee of $10 and a $40 doggy deposit. A rude and abrupt member of the staff told us they "sometimes, sort of" take dogs, so beware. Rooms are $48 to $100. 525 Second Street, Santa Cruz, CA 95060; (408) 423-0440.

Motel Continental: Five blocks from the beach, this is a decent nighttime hangout for you and your dog. Pooches are allowed only at the manager's discretion. Rates are $40 to $140. 414 Ocean Street, Santa Cruz, CA 95060; (408) 429-1221.

Sunny Cove Motel: Your dog is welcome here as long as he isn't "big as a giraffe," says a staffer. Rates are $30 to $100. Dogs are $5 extra. 2-1610 East Cliff Drive, Santa Cruz, CA 95062; (408) 475-1741.

Sunset Inn: Rates are $40 to $95. 2424 Mission Street, Santa Cruz, CA 95060; (408) 423-3471.

Terrace Court Motel: This oceanfront motel is across the beach from the Municipal Wharf—the one that doesn't allow dogs. Small dogs only, please. Rates are $62 to $105. 125 Beach Street, Santa Cruz, CA 95060; (408) 423-3031.

FESTIVALS

Shake, Rattle & Roll: Leashed pooches are welcome at this springtime music festival, usually held in April. Performers try to break odd records, such as the largest band and the band with the most guitar players. Locals make up most of the talent, but big names often drop in to perform and help raise money for music in the schools. At Pacific Avenue and Cathcart Street; (408) 427-0670.

DIVERSIONS

Enjoy the dog day of summer: Each August, the Santa Cruz SPCA holds a summertime dog festival called The Mutt Show, complete with contests for the waggiest tail, the muttiest mutt and the best celebrity look-alike. It's a terrific event, and it's especially fun for dogs who don't mind a little socializing. Call (408) 475-6454 for dates and details.

Go to the movies: The Skyview Drive-In Theatre, like its cousin theater in Salinas, is one of those rare drive-in joints that dares to call itself a theatre. A tip for you and your doggy date: Put the speaker on the side of the car where the human will be sitting. Dogs have been known to knock off the speakers in a fit of boredom or lick them if they hear an appealing sound. 2260 Soquel Drive. (408) 475-3405.

SCOTTS VALLEY

PARKS, BEACHES & RECREATION AREAS

The developed parks here don't allow dogs, but the city has one undeveloped park where your dog can romp. When it is developed, by mid-1995, dogs will still be allowed.

•**Lodato Park** 🐾 🐾 1/2 🐕

Since this is the only park in town that allows dogs, it's a welcome sight for many a canine. It's a decent size for your dog to get exercise, but where the workout really comes in is on the trails, which can be quite steep and rough. Dogs are allowed to roam off leash in this 40-acre site for now, but the city has big plans for the park. That means the brushy, ticky land will be cleaned up and improved, but it also means leashes will be mandatory. The park is on Green Hills Road, just east of Highway 17. (408) 438-3251. ➜ *See #9 on map p. 480.*

RESTAURANTS

Rosie's Espresso Bar and Cafe: From Cajun food to pasta, pastries, muffins and all sorts of sweet eats, the dining here is delectable. At Victor Square in Scotts Valley Junction; (408) 438-1735.

PLACES TO STAY

Best Western Inn: Small dogs and exemplary larger dogs are welcome. Room rates are $58 to $125. 6020 Scotts Valley Drive, Scotts Valley, CA 95066; (408) 438-6666 or (800) 528-1234.

SEACLIFF

RESTAURANTS

Sno-White Drive-In: Dogs can sit with you at picnic tables as you dine together on calamari, burgers and fries. 223 State Park Drive; (408) 688-4747.

PLACES TO STAY

Seacliff State Beach: If you, your RV and your dog need a place to spend the night, try this scenic RV campground. While dogs are allowed to camp with you here at the 26 sites in the area overlooking the ocean, they're not allowed on the beach below. They're also banned from the cement boat/fishing pier that juts into Monterey Bay. Sites are $23 to $25. Dogs are $1 extra. The campground is six miles south of Santa Cruz, west on the Seacliff Beach exit. Call (408)

688-3222 for beach information or call MISTIX at (800) 444-PARK for reservations.

WATSONVILLE

PARKS, BEACHES & RECREATION AREAS

• **Palm Beach** 🐾 🐾 🐾 1/2

Dahling! What a mahvelous place! And not a sign of Jackie O., or anyone rich and famous, for that matter.

This may not be the Palm Beach of Robin Leach fame, but it's a heavenly, remote place that has considerably more to offer down-to-earth dogs and their people. A trail takes you through a large eucalyptus grove where you and your dog can stop for a cool, relaxing picnic. Then it's onward to the large beach, where your dog has to remain leashed, but he can still have a jolly old time sniffing and walking and walking and sniffing.

Even on perfect summer afternoons, this unit of Sunset State Beach gets very little use, probably because of its location at the end of the county. Fees are $3 per car and $1 per dog. Exit Highway 1 at Riverside Drive/Highway 129 and follow the signs to Beach Road, past huge farms. The beach is at the end of the road. (408) 688-3241. ➤*See #10 on map p. 480.*

• **Pinto Lake County Park** 🐾 🐾 1/2

If you and your dog like to fish on small lakes, have we got a small lake for you! There's a reason so many anglers, young and old, sit on their lounge chairs with their lunches by the lakeside: They're actually catching fish. The stories they tell aren't just fish stories. They're taking home bass, bluegill, catfish, crappie and trout.

Even dogs have a decent day here when it's not too warm. They lay under the big trees watching their best friends land dinner. Sometimes they'll get their paws wet. When their owners walk them (on leash), there's enough space to stretch all their legs. And if it happens to be summer, they can stroll to the boat house and drool over the candy, cookies and bait.

Paddleboats are available to humans for $5 an hour. It's perfect if the rest of the family wants to do something other than fish.

There's camping for RVs and trailers, but no tents are allowed. It costs $16 nightly for complete motor home hookup at the 25 sites here. Dogs are $1 extra. Day-use fees are $2 May through October. There's no fee during the off-season. Driving from Santa Cruz, exit Highway 1 at Airport Boulevard. Make a left at Green Valley Road. The entrance is well marked. (408) 722-8129. ➤*See #11 on map p. 480.*

PLACES TO STAY

Country Sunrise Bed-and-Breakfast: Dogs are welcome to relax at this quiet, peaceful mini-"Tara," on a private hillside. If you like sunrise, this is the place for you. The view of the sun coming up over the easterly mountains is inspiring. There are two rooms where dogs may stay. Each has an outside entrance, so if your dog likes camping out, you can leash him up and put his bed outside the door. Note: There are two cats who wander the premises, and since the owner is trying to maintain a serene atmosphere, you should definitely consider staying elsewhere if your dog finds cats yummy. Rates are $70 to $95. 3085 Freedom Boulevard, Watsonville, CA 95076; (408) 722-4793.

Motel 6: This one's only a couple of miles from Palm Beach. All Motel 6s allow one small dog per room. Rates are $34 for one adult, $6 for the second adult. 125 Silver Leaf Drive, Watsonville, CA 95076; (408) 728-4144.

Sunset State Beach: The main unit of Sunset State Beach allows dogs to camp, but doesn't allow them on the beach. Water-loving dogs should cruise down to Palm Beach (see page 491). This campground is a good one, though, with 90 sites set on a bluff over the Pacific. There's a decent amount of exercise area for your dog to survive without trying to sneak down to the beach. Sites are $15 per night. Dogs are $1 extra. From Santa Cruz, exit Highway 1 at San Andreas Road and go right at Sunset Beach Road. For campsite reservations, call MISTIX at (800) 444-PARK. For beach information, call (408) 724-1266.

CENTRAL AREA COUNTIES

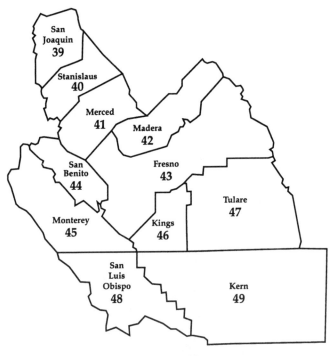

SAN JOAQUIN COUNTY

MAP PAGE

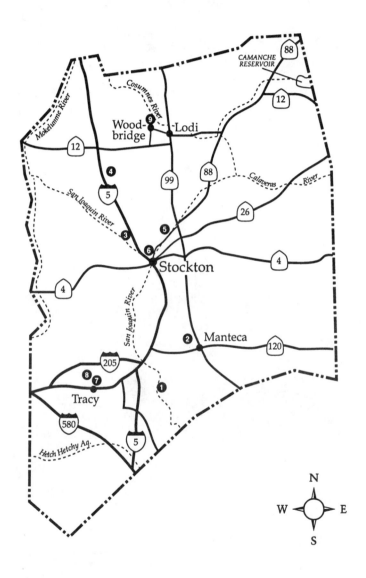

39
SAN JOAQUIN COUNTY

Chances are that you won't be driving a few hundred miles just to vacation here with your dog. That's good. In fact, your dog is probably reading over your shoulder right now and slobbering in gratitude.

It's not that San Joaquin County is a terrible place for dogs. It certainly has its share of attractive parks. But since dogs aren't permitted off leash around here, and since this isn't exactly the wilderness capital of California, it's just not a great doggy destination.

A good rule of thumb to remember if you don't want to come away with a ticket for a dog offense: Tempting as it may be, don't let your dog walk on the paths and trails in the county-run parks. It's an offense punishable by a few dollars out of your dog bone fund. It's a ridiculous rule. What would have happened to Toto if he hadn't been permitted to walk on the Yellow Brick Road?

LODI

Dogs are allowed in this city's parks, but only on the paved areas. Joe doesn't think the parks are even worth describing. With these kinds of rules, he prefers to stroll on the sidewalks. At least with garbage cans and cats, the scenery is more scintillating.

RESTAURANTS

Geoffrey's Cafe: In the summer, when there is no threat of rain, Geoffrey's sets up tables outside where you may dine on delicious California cuisine, pastries and fancy coffees. 1110 West Kettleman Lane, Suite 2; (209) 369-6995.

PLACES TO STAY

Best Western Royal Host Inn: Small pooches only, please. Rates are $45 to $56. There's a varying deposit for dogs. 710 South Cherokee Lane, Lodi, CA 95240; (209) 369-8484.

MANTECA

PARKS, BEACHES & RECREATION AREAS

• **Durham Ferry State Recreation Area** 🐾 🐾

If dogs were permitted on the trails here, the paws rating would be higher. The park is adjacent to the San Joaquin River and it's quite attractive. But because this state recreation area is run by the county parks department, it falls prey to the county's rotten regulations. Dogs can only be where there are no trails.

That means the park's nature area is pretty much off-limits to dogs. And that's a shame. It's separated from the main park area by a levee and it has a surprising amount of wildlife. The best way through the nature area is via the equestrian and hiking trails. Otherwise, it's cut-and-slash time through the vegetation. Since most dogs we know don't carry scythes with them, it's pretty much an impossible situation.

What's left for dogs is the more civilized section of the park, with picnic tables, mowed grass and plenty of people on the weekends—despite the $4 day-use fee imposed on weekends and holidays. The day-use fee during weekdays is $2 per car. Camping at the popular 70-site campground is $11. Dogs are $1 extra. Campsites are available on a first-come, first-served basis. Reservations can be made for some of the sites, an additional $5 reservation fee is charged.

From Highway 120, take Airport Way south about six miles. The entrance will be on your right. (209) 953-8800. ➤ *See #1 on map p. 496.*

• Northgate Park 😺 😺 1/2

If your dog wants to meet the hounds of Manteca, come to Northgate Park. This is where Manteca dogs gather for long afternoons of leisure. The setting is grassy and fairly flat, with softball fields and picnic tables. It's not exactly Yosemite National Park, but dogs have more fun here.

Dogs are supposed to be leashed. The park is at Northgate Drive and Hoyt Lane. (209) 239-8470. ➤ *See #2 on map p. 496.*

PLACES TO STAY
Durham Ferry State Recreation Area camping: See above.

STOCKTON

PARKS, BEACHES & RECREATION AREAS

• Louis Park 😺 😺 😺

The address of this park is the intersection of the San Joaquin River and Smiths Canal. It's where the whole watery world converges—where freighters move their bulk alongside waterskiers, where tugboat captains wave to shoreline anglers.

You and your leashed dog will enjoy watching all the action from the comfort of this 70-acre park. It's slightly contoured, so some sections provide better views than others. Because the park was established in the 1920s, it has plenty of large trees for shade. Conifers, cottonwoods, native valley oaks and broadleafs abound.

The park is also home to softball diamonds, tennis courts, a free boat ramp and Pixie Woods, a children's play area complete with carousels and a miniature train. Louis Park is at the western end of Monte Diablo Avenue, at Occidental Avenue. (209) 937-8206. ➡️ *See #3 on map p. 496.*

• Oak Grove Regional County Park 🐾 🐾 🐾

This 180-acre park is home to more than 1,500 oak trees. If you want shade, or your boy dog wants a target for his leg lifts, you've come to the right place.

You can easily get around the park without use of the wonderful one-and-a-half-mile nature trail, and it's a good thing, because dogs aren't allowed to set a paw on it. As with all San Joaquin County parks, dogs aren't permitted on trails or paths. But this park has enough open land so it won't matter much except on muddy days.

Dogs must be leashed. There's a $2 vehicle entry fee on weekdays, $4 on weekends and holidays. (209) 953-8800. ➡️ *See #4 on map p. 496.*

• Oak Park 🐾 🐾 🐾

This park is notorious for confusing people who are supposed to meet each other at Oak Grove Regional County Park, and vice versa. "I asked this girl I'd just met to meet me at Oak Park and she never showed up," teenage dog walker Frankie Ramirez told me. "She was new in town, so I had this idea and raced over to the Oak County Park, and there she was, waiting for me with her big dog. Now I love her and her dog, but these parks could have screwed up a great love story. Tell your readers to be careful out there." Awww. I couldn't have said it better myself.

This park is just as pretty as the county park, but it's free. It's actually a large canopy valley oak grove. Hundreds of these lovelies are packed into 60 acres. Leashed dogs love to hike on the shaded walkways through the park, sniffing the bark of these trees.

The park is also home of the Stockton Ports, the farm team for the Milwaukee Brewers. Dogs aren't permitted at games, but they tilt their heads at the roar of greasy popcorn and the smell of the crowd. The park is between Alpine Avenue and Fulton Street, at Sutter Street. (209) 937-8206. ➡️ *See #5 on map p. 496.*

• Victory Park 🐾 🐾 🐾

This is where local dogs come to mingle. It's an attractive park, full of large oaks and conifers. There's a paved walkway around the park's 27 acres. A hike around it makes for an excellent exercise routine.

Weekdays after work are the best times to visit if you want your leashed dog to hang out with other leashed dogs. Too bad the city couldn't set aside a couple of acres as a fenced-in dog exercise area, so dogs could play as they really want to—*sans* leash.

The park is at Pershing Avenue and Picardy Drive. (209) 937-8206.
→*See #6 on map p. 496.*

RESTAURANTS
Manny's Drive-In: Eat burgers with your hungry dog here. 1945 South El Dorado; (209) 464-8207.

Safari Coffee & Tea, Inc.: Eat sandwiches, drink coffee and be merry with your dog at the outside tables. 2529 West March Lane, Suite 101; (209) 473-7223.

Soupeddler: The all-you-can-eat salad bar here comes with soups and fresh muffins for a healthful, filling and tasty meal. But don't let your dog trick you into giving her a snack as she watches you eat on the patio. "All you can eat" does not mean "all you and your bottomless-pit pooch can devour." 7562 Pacific Avenue; (209) 477-7687.

PLACES TO STAY
Best Western Charter Inn: Small dogs are fine here, but large dogs need the approval of the manager. Rates are $45 to $62. 550 West Charter Way, Stockton, CA 95206; (209) 948-0321.

La Quinta Inn: They prefer small to medium-sized dogs here. Rates are $51 to $60. 2710 West March Lane, Stockton, CA 95219; (209) 952-7800.

TRACY

PARKS, BEACHES & RECREATION AREAS
• Lincoln Park 🐾 🐾
The trees here are big and the walkways are flat. It's just how lazy leashed dogs like it. The park is an old, attractive one in the downtown area. It's at Eaton Avenue and East Street. (209) 832-1274. →*See #7 on map p. 496.*

• Pescadero Park 🐾 🐾
If your leashed buddy likes to roll on the grass, he'll be happy to know that this grassy 15-acre park is ideal for canine rollers. It's not completely flat, because that isn't conducive to truly fine rolling. It's slightly contoured, making those upside-down wiggling maneuvers much more invigorating. And there aren't many trees to

crash into should the roll get out of hand.

The park is at Kavanagh and Louise avenues. (209) 832-1274. *→See #8 on map p. 496.*

RESTAURANTS

Banta Inn: Dogs are welcome at the patio tables while you dine on charbroiled sandwiches, steaks and fish. 22563 South Seventh Street; (209) 835-1311.

Taco Bell: If you need a quick bite, you can eat it on the patio with your pooch here. 2320 Tracy Boulevard; (209) 835-9939.

WOODBRIDGE

PARKS, BEACHES & RECREATION AREAS

•**Woodbridge Regional Park** 🐾 🐾 🐾

A quarter-mile stretch of the Mokelumne River is yours at this undeveloped riparian park. It's good for fishing or for dipping your paws on a warm day. It gets much less use than other county parks and it's free. Just keep your dog on a leash, and keep him off the trail here. It's the law. We don't like it, but what can you do?

The park is on East River Meadows Drive at the Mokelumne River, just north of Woodbridge Road. (209) 953-8800. *→See #9 on map p. 496.*

STANISLAUS COUNTY

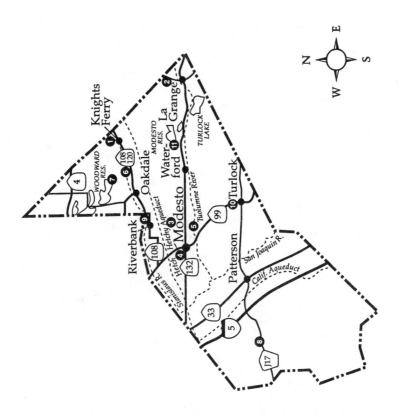

40
STANISLAUS COUNTY

Chambers of commerce in these parts boast that "Summer Lasts Longer" here. Longer than what? When we asked, they weren't too sure. But when it's late September and your dog's tongue is unfurled just as long and bologna-like as it was in July, you may find the answer yourself: Summer lasts longer than hell here.

Fortunately, there are plenty of decent parks near the county's rivers. Dogs like to cool their fuzzy heels in the water.

Director George Lucas grew up here, surviving one sweltering summer after another. In his film *American Graffiti* (inspired by his younger years in Modesto, but not set there), a drive-in diner played a key role in the lives of his characters. It was a cool place to go on hot summer nights. If you and your dog want to dine *alfresco* here, you'll find a respectable number of outdoor restaurants. The most fitting is Modesto's very own A&W Root Beer drive-in restaurant, where carhops on rollerskates will take your dog's order lickety split. Just don't let your dog do naughty things to any passing poodle skirts. See page 507.

KNIGHTS FERRY

PARKS, BEACHES & RECREATION AREAS

• **Knights Ferry Recreation Area** 🐾 🐾 🐾

You and your leashed dog can swim, fish, hike or just relax under a big oak tree at this popular riverside park. A historic covered bridge takes you from one side of the Stanislaus River to the other. You'll find picnic tables and room for a little walking on either side.

It's crowded on weekends, but during weekdays, it's a relaxing getaway. From Highway 108/120, head north on Kennedy Road to the river. (209) 881-3517. → *See #1 on map p. 504.*

LA GRANGE

PARKS, BEACHES & RECREATION AREAS

• **La Grange Regional Park** 🐾 🐾 🐾 1/2

This 750-acre park has an undeveloped trail system that takes you along the Tuolumne River and through a delicate wilderness area. Woodpeckers, eagles, bobcats, deer and all their friends make the park their home at different times of the year. Bring your binoculars and keep your dog leashed. (It's a real trick to birdwatch with a dog who's tugging on your arm to visit a nearby tree, but it can be done.)

The park is located in the historic town of La Grange, and contains ancient adobe buildings, an old jail, a schoolhouse, a cemetery and an abandoned gold dredge. It makes for an interesting pit stop.

There are several parcels of La Grange Park. We like to start at the Basso Bridge Fishing Access. Exit Highway 132 at Lake Road and follow the signs. You'll be there in a snap. Park in the lot and head upriver. You can continue walking for a few miles and have a pleasant riverside hike. Or you can cross the street when you see a sign for the wilderness area and pay a visit to a more pristine setting. (209) 525-4107. →*See #2 on map p. 504.*

MODESTO
PARKS, BEACHES & RECREATION AREAS
•**Dry Creek Regional Park** 🐾 🐾 🐾

A well-maintained bike/pedestrian trail leads you and the leashed dog in your life for more than three miles along the south side of Dry Creek. This park is actually a few parks strung together, so you'll find different terrain as you stroll merrily along. If your dog likes sniffing big trees or meditating at a riverside, he'll be happy here.

The park runs between La Loma Avenue and Claus Road. The section from El Vista Avenue east to Claus Road is not used much because it's a very undeveloped area. You may want to stick with the western part of the park. (209) 577-5344. →*See #3 on map p. 504.*

•**Roosevelt Park** 🐾 🐾 1/2

Liquid ambers and horse chestnuts dot this pleasant neighborhood park. These colorful old trees provide a shaded setting for all the leashed dogs who visit. Roosevelt Park is known as one of the more popular places to take a dog around here, but when we visited, we didn't even see pawprints in the mud. Of course, it was pouring rain, so that may have had something to do with it.

The park is at Orangeburg and Bronson avenues. (209) 577-5344. →*See #4 on map p. 504.*

•**Tuolumne River Regional Park** 🐾 🐾 🐾 1/2

It's rare that you find a city park that's even a couple of miles long. But here's one that spans six miles—dogs think it's the cat's meow.

It has just about everything a dog could want, except permission to run around off leash. It's mostly undeveloped, meaning few softball fields or playgrounds to get in the way of a dog's endeavors. It's on the banks of the Tuolumne River, so water-loving dogs can cool their paws where they're able to reach the river. And it has an appealing blend of wide-open meadows, oak knolls and natural riparian riverside land.

The park is on the north side of the Tuolumne River, and runs from Ohio Avenue on the west to Mitchell Road on the east. It has a golf course where dogs are verboten. It's also broken up by the occasional road and some sections of parkland that aren't too appealing. Try the area east of Tioga Drive. (209) 577-5344. ➔ *See #5 on map p. 504.*

RESTAURANTS

A&W Root Beer: It's not the same diner as the one in *American Graffiti* but the carhops still come by on rollerskates, and poodle skirts are still in. Come here on a summer afternoon and slurp down a root beer served in a frosted mug. Your dog can join you at the shaded patio here. In the winter, the patio is heated. That's the time to try two piping-hot cheeseburgers, one for you, one for you-know-who. (Joe made me write that.) 1404 G Street; (209) 522-7700.

Mediterranean Market & Grill: Dine on tasty Italian food at one of the outdoor tables with your dog at your side. 1222 H Street; (209) 544-6433.

Piccadilly Deli: You and your dog will enjoy the deli fare here and you'll be grateful for the covered patio area during Modesto's long, hot summers. 941 Tenth Street; (209) 523-0748.

PLACES TO STAY

Motel 6 South: All Motel 6s allow one pooch per room. Rates are $25 for the first adult, $4 for the second. 722 Kansas Avenue, Modesto, CA 95351; (209) 524-3000.

Red Lion Hotel: This is one of the better Red Lions. Small to medium-sized dogs are preferred. Rates are $85 to $365. 1150 9th Street, Modesto, CA 95354; (209) 526-6000.

OAKDALE

PARKS, BEACHES & RECREATION AREAS

• **Valley Oak Recreation Area** 🐾 🐾 🐾

Some of the most pristine river woodland left in California lies along the Stanislaus River and you should be able to see a sampling when you and your leashed dog visit this park. A hiking trail here offers a short tour of the lush river woodland. Moisture-loving trees such as cottonwoods, alders and willows will keep you shaded while you dip your toes in the cool river.

This isn't a well-known park, so it doesn't get as crowded as some of the other riverside parks in the area. There are 16 boat-in campsites available for $6 per site. There is also one group site available ($25 fee). Reservations are required. From Highway 108/120, go north on County Road J9 and cross the river. Turn right at Rodden Road and follow it east to the park. (209) 881-3517. → *See #6 on map p. 504.*

•**Woodward Reservoir Regional Park** 🐾 🐾 🐾

Although this is the largest county park in the system, dogs generally prefer Frank Raines Regional Park (see below). Raines Park is 1,800 acres smaller, but it's got a lot more of the natural stuff that some dogs need.

Woodward is more barren, and yet much more developed. By virtue of its 3,800 acres of land (not including the 2,900-acre reservoir), it's a fine place to take the leashed dog in your life. If someone in your family has the urge to waterski or fish, you and your dog can dip your paws in the reservoir and stroll around the park's rolling hills while you wait.

Since there are no official trails here, most people walk around on the small dirt roads. But when the park gets extremely crowded, as it's wont to do on some weekends, you and your dog won't feel safe on these roads. Stick to the meadowy sections of the park.

The day-use fee is $5 per vehicle. Camping fees range from $10 to $14 per site. Dogs are $2 extra day or night. There are 152 sites available on a first-come, first-served basis. If you want to launch your boat here, you'll pay an additional $5. From Highway 101/120, drive north on 26 Mile Road for about six miles to the park's entrance, which will be on your right. (209) 525-4107. → *See #7 on map p. 504.*

PLACES TO STAY

Valley Oak Recreation Area camping: See above.
Woodward Reservoir Regional Park camping: See above.

PATTERSON

PARKS, BEACHES & RECREATION AREAS

•**Frank Raines Regional Park** 🐾 🐾 🐾 1/2

This 2,000-acre county park is remote, mountainous and full of wildlife you don't see much around these parts any more. Leashed dogs love to hike among junipers, oaks and digger pines on the many dirt trails that wind through the park.

Springtime is the best season for a visit. The wildflowers are fantastic and the creek looks splendid when it's full.

About 640 acres of parkland are set aside for off-highway vehicle use from November 1 to April 30 each year. Dogs should avoid that area during the off-highway vehicle season. There's also 43 acres of lawn with barbecues, a baseball diamond and a playground. Dogs actually seem to like this manicured section because of the enchanting little nature trail here.

Tempting as it may be to slip your dog's leash off in the backcountry, you really shouldn't. If I can't inspire you to listen to the law, perhaps the tarantulas, rattlesnakes, bobcats and occasional mountain lions can.

Campsite fees range from $10 to $14. Dogs are $2 extra. There are 54 sites available on a first-come, first-served basis. From Interstate 5, exit at Del Puerto Canyon Road and head west. You'll reach the park in about 18 winding miles. Follow the signs. (209) 525-4107. ➤*See #8 on map p. 504.*

PLACES TO STAY
Frank Raines Regional Park camping: See above.

RIVERBANK

PARKS, BEACHES & RECREATION AREAS
•**Jacob Meyers Park** 🐾

At first glance (say at 7 a.m. on a fresh spring day), this is a lovely park. There are lots of big trees and plenty of places to access the river. If you were so inclined, you and your leashed dog could go down to the Stanislaus River and dip your toes or fish for the catch of the day.

Unfortunately, many of the folks who hang out here go down to the river and do drugs and paint graffiti later in the day. It kind of puts a damper on the whole feel of the park.

If you're in town and your dog's gotta go, take Highway 108 to First Street and drive north to the park. If you're visiting later in the day, tell him to put on his best snarl. (209) 869-7101. ➤*See #9 on map p. 504.*

TURLOCK

PARKS, BEACHES & RECREATION AREAS
•**Donnelly Park** 🐾 🐾 1/2

One day, the adolescent trees here will be massive and shady, but for now, your dog will have to bring his own umbrella if he wants shelter from the sun. A pond takes up about half of the park.

Ducks like it, and so do water dogs. But the latter aren't allowed.

The park is conveniently located in the middle of town. From Highway 99, exit at Fulkerth Road and drive east about 1.5 miles. (Fulkerth Road turns into Hawkeye Avenue, but keep going.) The park will be on your left, between Del's Lane and Donnelly Drive. (209) 668-5545. → *See #10 on map p. 504.*

RESTAURANTS

La Crème: You and your pooch can sit together under an umbrella while you dine on sandwiches, burgers and ice cream. The setting isn't scenic (it's located in a mini-mall), but it's the only dog-friendly restaurant around. 310 East Main Street; (209) 667-2293.

PLACES TO STAY

Best Western Orchard Inn: Medium or small pooches are preferred here. If you're especially exhausted, you could even get a room with a Jacuzzi. Just don't let your dog try to rescue you from all those scary, dangerous bubbles. Rates are $47 to $63. 5025 North Golden State Boulevard, Turlock, CA 95382; (209) 667-2827.

WATERFORD

PARKS, BEACHES & RECREATION AREAS

•**Modesto Reservoir Regional Park** 🐾 🐾 🐾

Leashed dogs are welcome to explore the dry rolling foothills in this 6,000-acre park. (2,800 of these acres are the reservoir, but it's still a big place.) It's not the prettiest park around. There's little shade and not much in the way of trails, but dogs seem to enjoy themselves in the cooler months.

You can get around this park by dirt roads. They can get very crowded on popular weekends, so you and your dog may find yourselves navigating a course around the grassy hills. It's not such a bad fate. When you get warm, you can head to the reservoir and dip your toes. (It seems dogs might not be allowed to do this for much longer. Ask the ranger when you enter if dog contact with the water is still permitted.)

The day-use fee is $5 per vehicle. Campsites are $10 to $14. Dogs are $2 extra day or night. There are 92 campsites available. No reservations are necessary. If you want to launch your boat, it's an additional $5. From Highway 132 just east of town, go north on Reservoir Road. You'll reach the park in about one mile. There, you'll have a choice of going left on Rio Linda Drive or continuing to the right on Reservoir Road. Joe highly recommends taking the right fork. The inlet area makes for a good dog hike. (209) 525-4107. → *See #11 on map p. 504.*

MERCED COUNTY

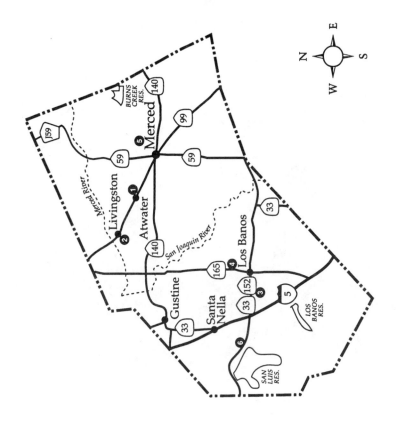

41
MERCED COUNTY

The county parks here ban dogs. The national wildlife refuges ban dogs. Even some of the smaller cities ban dogs from their parks. It can make a dog howling mad.

But clench not thine paws, canines. Merced County is rescued from the recesses of rottendom by the state wildlife areas here. Most are huge and permit off-leash pooches for at least a few months of the year. Two of these areas, Los Banos and O'Neill Forebay, are discussed in this chapter. For information on the others, call (209) 826-0463.

ATWATER
PARKS, BEACHES & RECREATION AREAS
• **Ralston Park** 🐾 🐾

If you're window shopping in the antique stores a few blocks away and you need to rest your weary paws, Ralston Park is a decent park to set a spell. It's got lots of lawn and plenty of trees for you and your leashed pal to snuggle up to and relax.

The park is between Grove and Fir avenues, on 3rd Street. (209) 357-6320. ➡ *See #1 on map p. 512.*

RESTAURANTS
Out to Lunch: Enjoy quiche, sandwiches, soups and salads on the covered patio with your dog. 1301 Winton Way; (209) 357-1170.

GUSTINE

Dogs are banned from Gustine's parks. That smarts. But at least they can eat at a couple of restaurants. They're not exactly Jeremiah Tower's Stars, but the food hits the spot when you and your dog get hungry on the road.

RESTAURANTS
Burger Hut: Eat cheeseburgers at the outside tables with your favorite pooch. 380 Fourth Street; (209) 854-6903.

Pizza Factory: Pooches prefer pepperoni. Dine at the outdoor tables. 479 Fifth Street; (209) 854-3777.

LIVINGSTON

PARKS, BEACHES & RECREATION AREAS

• **Arakelian Park** 🐾 1/2

The trees here are young, and the picnic benches and playground equipment is new. It's an okay place to take a leashed dog, but when the trees grow big and muscular, it will be much better. It doesn't usually get crowded except on perfect weekends, so it's a pretty safe bet that if you want seclusion, you'll get at least a small dose of it.

The park is at the westernmost end of J Street, about a block west of Prusso Street. (209) 394-8041. ➡ *See #2 on map p. 512.*

RESTAURANTS

Taco Bell: Dine with your dog at the outdoor tables here. 229 Simpson Avenue; (209) 394-4077.

LOS BANOS

PARKS, BEACHES & RECREATION AREAS

• **County Park** 🐾 1/2

If your dog is walking away from this book and scratching his fuzzy head in confusion, he has a right to. Just a few pages ago we mentioned that Merced County parks ban pooches, and now we're recommending one for a visit. Vot's goink on?

Fortunately, although the park is officially the county's, the city of Los Banos actually runs it and makes the rules. That means leashed dogs are welcome to explore the 11-acre park's proliferation of trees, which include pines, sycamores and elms. It's not a large park, but it's the biggest one in the city.

The park is on the south side of Pacheco Boulevard, at Seventh Street. (209) 827-7000. ➡ *See #3 on map p. 512.*

• **Los Banos Wildlife Area** 🐾🐾🐾🐾 👟 🐕

Dogs are allowed to roam leash-free here during certain times of the year, and the terrific news is that they don't have to be hunters' companions to do it. Unlike so many other state wildlife areas, even dogs who just like to walk around and watch the birds fly by are permitted to experience this leash-free bliss.

The wildlife area is 5,568 acres of flat, grassy land with intermittent marshlands and ponds. You and your dog can walk just about anywhere on the dirt roads and levees here. With more than 200 species of birds, plenty of reptiles (including the rare giant garter snake) and many mammals, you'll have plenty to watch. Bring your binoculars and a good pair of walking shoes. Don't forget a towel for your dog. It can get muddy.

Camping is available from mid-January to mid-September. While there are no developed campsites here, the Department of Fish and Game can suggest areas where you might find a good primitive site. There's no fee for camping. The day-use fee is $2.50, but that's waived if you have a valid hunting, fishing or trapping pass (eeks!) or a California Wildlands Pass.

From Highway 152, exit at Mercey Springs Road/Highway 165 and drive north for three miles to the wildlife area. Call first for a schedule of when it's open to leashless pooches, because dog visitation days are limited. You don't want to drive all the way here and find out that the entire wildlife area is closed for nesting season. Your dog will never forgive you. At least not until you take her to the nearest national forest. (209) 826-0463. ➡ *See #4 on map p. 512.*

RESTAURANTS
Chubby's: This fun, '50s-style diner is ideal for travelers with dogs. It comes complete with a grassy area to walk your leashed dog. It also sports a faucet, where the owner's son likes to make sure thirsty dogs get plenty of water! The fare is your basic burgers and fries, and there's even music to relax you after a long drive. 1341 Pacheco Boulevard; (209) 826-1674.

Fosters Old-Fashioned Freeze: There are two picnic tables outside for you and your dog. 906 Pacheco Boulevard; (209) 826-4195.

Ron & Terry's Drive-Thru: If you and your pooch can get a seat at the outdoor table here, you'll enjoy a quick bite. 609 West Pacheco Boulevard; (209) 826-1555.

Sam's Dairy Queen: Rick, the dog-loving/owning manager of Sam's, wants to be sure your dog gets lots of water at the faucet outside when you arrive after a long, hot car ride. Then you can both settle down and eat. 502 Pacheco Boulevard; (209) 826-0662.

PLACES TO STAY
Los Banos Wildlife Area camping: See above.

MERCED
Dogs of the male persuasion, rejoice! Merced is designated as a Tree City U.S.A. by the National Arbor Association. It's not exactly a forest, but the city does have an abundance of trees. It gives a dog plenty to sniff at, even if he's just accompanying you on a short walk.

PARKS, BEACHES & RECREATION AREAS

A Class-A bike path runs through town and passes many of the city's tree-shaded parks. You and your leashed dog are welcome to use the path, as long as you stay out of the way of things that could run you over. It's a great way to check out the various parks around the city.

If you get a chance, swing by the Courthouse Museum. It's a striking Italian Renaissance-style structure with columns, sculpted window frames and a magnificent cupola. Dogs can't hang out in the museum, but the park just outside is fine for leashed dogs.

• **Applegate Park** 🐾 🐾 🐾

More than 60 varieties of trees grace this lovely 23-acre park that borders Bear Creek. Boy oh boy, do boy dogs adore this place! Kids like it, too. The park is home to a small zoo and the Kiwanis Kiddieland mini-amusement park.

The city's 12-mile bike path runs through Applegate Park, so if you and your leashed dog want to saunter off to other parks, just follow the path to the next clump of greenery. Applegate is between M and R streets, on the south side of Bear Creek. (209) 385-6802.
➡ *See #5 on map p. 512.*

RESTAURANTS

Jack-in-the-Box: Eat outside with your drooling dog. 595 West Olive Avenue; (209) 723-7806.

PLACES TO STAY

Motel 6: Merced has three Motel 6s. Rates at this centrally located one are $24 for the first adult, $6 for the second. All Motel 6s permit one small pooch per room. 1215 R Street, Merced, CA 95340; (209) 722-2737.

FESTIVALS

Farmers Market: On Thursday evenings from spring through fall, you and your leashed dog can have a delicious time eating your way down Main Street. You can get just about anything you want here, from farm-fresh produce to delectable hot snacks. There's usually musical entertainment to accompany your munchings. The festival runs from 6 p.m. to 9 p.m., and is on Main Street between M and K streets. You may want to call before you bring your dog, because the local health department has been pondering the possibility of banning dogs. It's a shame, but it's reality. (209) 383-6908.

SANTA NELLA

This town is alive because of Interstate 5, which spews visitors into and out of town as quickly as they can get some gas and a bowl of Andersen's Split Pea Soup (which, in turn, can give folks enough of a different type of gas to last them clear to the Oregon border). If you want your pooch to have a sip of the delectable soup, go easy on it. Remember, you may be traveling in an enclosed vehicle together for many hours.

PARKS, BEACHES & RECREATION AREAS

•O'Neill Forebay Wildlife Area 🐾 🐾 🐾 🐾 🐕

If your dog's just aching to get out of the car and have a really good stretch, try this 700-acre grassland just to the west of Interstate 5. It's a terrific place if your obedient dog needs to run around without her leash for a while.

You'll find some marshy sections, but you'll be able to access most of the wildlife area by fire roads and levees. The wildlife viewing from here is wonderful.

But before you get your hopes up, call first and find out if the place is even open when you're planning to be here. At certain times of year, it's off-limits, even to leashed dogs. And you may not want to be hanging around during hunting season, unless you plan to hunt.

Exit Interstate 5 at Highway 33 and drive about two miles south to the entrance, which will be on your right. (209) 826-0463. *→See #6 on map p. 512.*

PLACES TO STAY

Holiday Inn Mission de Oro: Rates are $40 to $65. 13070 Highway 33 South, Santa Nella, CA 95322; (209) 826-4444.

Motel 6: Rates are $32 for the first adult, $6 for the second. All Motel 6s permit one small pooch per room. 12733 South Highway 33, Santa Nella, CA 95322; (209) 826-6644.

San Luis Reservoir State Recreation Area: Since dogs aren't permitted on trails here or on boats or even in the water, about all that's left is camping. There are approximately 130 developed campsites and many primitive sites. Sites are $12 to $14. Dogs are $1 extra. Exit Interstate 5 at Highway 152 and drive west about four miles to the entrance road on the left. Call MISTIX for reservations at (800) 444-PARK. Or phone the park at (209) 826-1196 for more information.

MADERA COUNTY

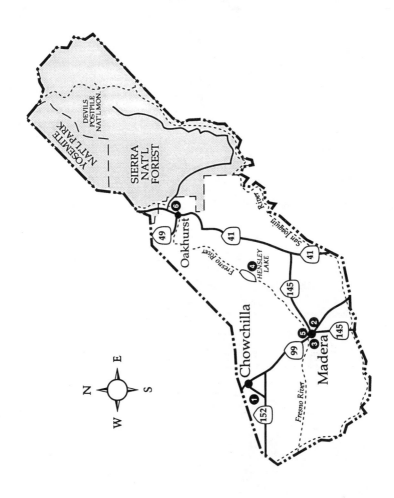

42
MADERA COUNTY

A farm that looks like a pizza is one of the most dog-friendly places we've encountered in our travels through California. Dogs have to be leashed, but it's worth a stop to watch their jaws drop when the cows start mooing up-close and personal. See page 523.

Between the Pizza Farm, Sierra National Forest and a couple of lakes where dogs can go leashless, Madera County is a hidden gem for dogs and their people. Okay, so it's more like a tourmaline than a diamond. It still outshines many of the nearby areas.

NATIONAL FORESTS

See the National Forests/Wilderness Areas chapter starting on page 801 for important information and safety tips for visiting national forests with your dog.

• **Sierra National Forest** 🐾🐾🐾🐾 🦴 🐕
See page 809.

NATIONAL MONUMENTS

• **Devil's Postpile National Monument** 🐾🐾🐾 1/2 🦴
See page 252 in Mono County for a description of this park. You can't get there from here, even though the park is officially in Madera County.

NATIONAL PARKS

• **Yosemite National Park** 🏛 🦴
See page 259 for the disheartening news about dogs in this otherwise amazing park.

CHOWCHILLA

PARKS, BEACHES & RECREATION AREAS

• **Sports and Leisure Community Park** 🐾🐾
Dogs like the second half of this park's name better than the first. Besides, even sporting dogs are not allowed to play on the soccer and softball teams that often congregate here. If no sporting teams are using the park, you and your leashed pal will have 20 acres for your leisurely pursuits.

The park is at Fifteenth Street and Ventura Avenue. (209) 665-8640.
➡ *See #1 on map p. 520.*

PLACES TO STAY
Safari Motel National Inn: Rates are $32 to $40. 220 East Robertson Boulevard, Chowchilla, CA 93610; (209) 665-4821.

MADERA
PARKS, BEACHES & RECREATION AREAS
As you'll note by the names of the three smaller parks, this is a very civic-minded area. Joe just wants to know where the Shriners' park is—and what about those Masons?

• **Courthouse Park** 🐾
This is a perfect example of how well Madera's county parks masquerade as city parks. Courthouse Park is all of two acres, and is just as flat, grassy and square as any typical, tiny municipal park.

Despite its size, it's a pleasant place to visit. It's got some fairly large elms and there are picnic tables waiting for you and your leashed dog to visit with a lunch. It's a good spot for relaxing while waiting for a friend to check a book out of the nearby library, or to bail a buddy out of the nearby sheriff's headquarters.

The park is nestled between Yosemite Avenue and West 6th Street, at Gateway Drive. (209) 675-7904. ➡ *See #2 on map p. 520.*

• **Lions Town and Country Regional Park** 🐾🐾 1/2
There are lots of places to roam in this charming park. The rolling hills and shaded meadows make it a fine park for an afternoon walk with your leashed dog.

A little canal runs through the park. Arched wooden footbridges take you over the waterway to more romping room. As long as there's not a baseball game going on, you won't have to worry about crowds.

The park is in the southwest part of town, at Howard Road, just east of Granada Drive. (209) 661-5495. ➡ *See #3 on map p. 520.*

• **Hensley Lake** 🐾🐾🐾🐾 🐕
This 1,500-acre lake provides some choice fishing opportunities for you and your angling dog. But if you're the types who prefer to stick around terra firma, you'll be happy to know that the lake is surrounded by 1,500 acres of hilly land that you and your well-behaved dog can roam without a leash.

Visit in the springtime during the wildflower bloom if you really want a piece of paradise. If it's a tad warm, you'll find refreshing shade under the many oaks here. If it's still too warm for you, take a dip in the lake. Dogs are permitted to swim here, as long as they're not on the official beach areas.

The only day-use fee here is for the swim beaches, so you and your dog won't have to worry about forking over your dough. There are 52 campsites available on a first-come, first-served basis. Camping costs $6 to $12 per site. Dogs must be leashed at the campsites and other developed areas.

From Madera, drive northeast on Highway 145 for about six miles. Turn left on County Road 400 and drive 10 miles north to the lake. (209) 673-5151. ➤*See #4 on map p. 520.*

(For information on Eastman Lake, located just northwest of Hensley Lake, call (209) 689-3255. The setting, prices and rules are pretty much the same as Hensley's, but hydrilla weeds can prevent swimming.)

• **Rotary Park** 🐾🐾

If you're cruising along Highway 99 and your dog starts crossing his legs and humming an unintelligible tune while avoiding direct eye contact with the bottle of water you've wedged between the seats, pull over here. The park has plenty of trees and lots of grass, even for the most discriminating dog's needs.

If you have time, try to visit the very dog-friendly Pizza Farm, located just across the highway in the Madera County Fairgrounds (see Diversions, below). Exit Highway 99 at Cleveland Avenue and drive east about a block to Gateway Drive (just before the railroad tracks). Turn right. The park will be on your right almost immediately. Snap on that leash and trot, don't walk, to the nearest tree. (209) 661-5495. ➤*See #5 on map p. 520.*

RESTAURANTS

Burger King: Do the King thing at their outdoor tables. 1103 Country Club Drive; (209) 673-7806.

Eppie's: Dogs like to eat the good diner food at Eppie's outdoor tables. 1101 Country Club Drive; (209) 674-0368.

PLACES TO STAY

Best Western Madera Valley Inn: Small pooches only, please. Rates are $52 to $107. 317 North G Street, Madera, CA 93637; (209) 673-5164.

Gateway Inn: Rates are $35 to $49. 25327 Avenue 16, Madera, CA 93637; (209) 674-8817.

DIVERSIONS

One half-acre pizza, please: Hold the anchovies! As long as your leashed dog doesn't poop on this gigantic pizza or try to terrorize the pepperoni pigs, she'll be mighty welcome at the Pizza Farm.

The point of the Pizza Farm is to show folks how integral farming is to the food we eat. The half-acre, circular Pizza Farm is divided into eight triangular "slices." Each slice contains something that's growing (or grazing for) the ingredients of a pizza. One slice has tomatoes. Another has cows who supply the milk for the cheese. Another has piggies for pepperoni. Other slices vary seasonally. Visiting all the slices is a fun, educational and mouthwatering way to spend an hour or two.

The Pizza Farm is surrounded by a couple more acres of land, where your dog may stretch her legs and contemplate if she wants deep dish or regular crust for dinner. You'll never look at a pizza the same way again. (Sorry, hungry dogs. You can't get pizza here, but the farm has a produce stand that might satisfy your pangs.)

The farm is open seven days a week and it's always free. Spring and fall are great times to visit. It's located in the Madera County Fairgrounds. Exit Highway 99 at Cleveland Avenue and drive west. The farm/fairgrounds is on your left almost immediately. Call (209) 674-2391 for hours and more information.

OAKHURST

PARKS, BEACHES & RECREATION AREAS

•Oakhurst Community Park 🐾 🐾 1/2

This is a really green, meadowy park that you can get to by crossing over a wooden footbridge from the Chamber of Commerce parking lot. It's very convenient for people on the go with a dog who's got to go.

A little dirt path encircles the park. You can walk around the park a few times to stretch all of your legs, or relax in the gazebo or at a picnic table. The park is just off Road 426 on Civic Circle. Follow the signs for the Chamber of Commerce. (209) 683-7766.
➡ See #6 on map p. 520.

RESTAURANTS

The Daily Grind: Besides great coffee, they make one mean chocolate shake here. Slurp it on the porch with your pooch at your feet. 40879 Highway 41; (209) 683-8815.

Fosters Freeze Jr.: This place sees plenty of dogs during the tourist season. The deck has a few tables with umbrellas where you can have your choice of a wide variety of fast-food items. 40713 Highway 41; (209) 642-2600.

Subway Sandwiches and Salads: Eat subs at the outdoor tables here. 425A Stagecoach Road; (209) 683-3066.

PLACES TO STAY

Best Western Yosemite Gateway Inn: This inn is located 17 miles from the south gate of Yosemite. Small dogs only, please. Rates are $44 to $80. 40530 Highway 41, Oakhurst, CA 93644; (209) 683-2378.

Pine Rose Inn: This bed-and-breakfast inn welcomes doggy guests. It's a beautiful place in a quiet mountain countryside setting just 12 miles from the south gate of Yosemite and two miles from Bass Lake.

Owner Anita Griffin has had some unusual guests. She once played hostess to a baby leopard who was so young his spots hadn't come out yet. A chimpanzee also made the inn his home for a few days while acting in a movie filmed in the area. "Obviously, good dogs are no problem at all," says Griffin.

You and your dog can stay in the main house or in one of five cottages. The rooms are full of country antiques, and some rooms even have fireplaces for those cold wintry nights. This is the perfect place to get away from it all. Rates are $40 to $100. There's a $50 deposit for dogs. The street address is 41703 Road 222. The mailing address is P.O. Box 2341, Oakhurst, CA 93644; (209) 642-2800.

FRESNO COUNTY

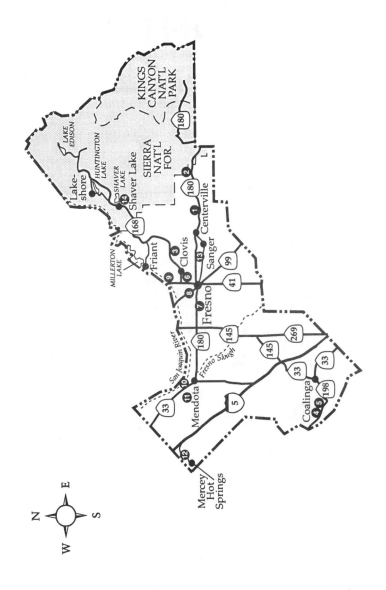

43
FRESNO COUNTY

At first glance, Fresno County seems like both an agricultural wonderland and a doggy wasteland. But your dog doesn't have to bite his toenails when he hears you're going to be spending some time exploring the area. The county has something for just about every dog's taste.

Rugged canines will enjoy the leashless freedom they'll experience in the national forest and the Bureau of Land Management areas. And those who prefer their toenails painted and their bouffants fluffed will enjoy the tinier, well-manicured city parks.

Dogs with a taste for olfactory offenses will appreciate visits to the pungent section near the zoo at Fresno's Roeding Park (see page 533) and to the stinky creek at Coalinga Mineral Springs (see page 531). You may not be crazy about the odors, but it's worth a few moments of holding your breath to see that enraptured expression on your dog's quivering snout.

NATIONAL FORESTS / NATIONAL PARKS

See the National Forests/Wilderness Areas chapter starting on page 801 for important information and safety tips for visiting national forests with your dog.

• **Sierra National Forest** 🐾 🐾 🐾 🐾 ⬤ 🐕

The cross-country skiing in some areas of this forest is first-rate. Leashless dogs love to bound along beside you as you slice through the snow. See page 809 for more information.

• **Kings Canyon National Park** 🔥 ⬤

See page 573 for information on this not-so-dog-friendly park.

CENTERVILLE

PARKS, BEACHES & RECREATION AREAS

• **Avocado Lake County Park** 🐾 🐾 🐾

Although there are no real trails around this 83-acre fishing lake, you and your dog can still manage to walk around just about the entire lake with little difficulty. That's because almost all 127 acres of county park land surrounding the lake are more like lawns than wilderness.

It's a flat park, so if you don't like hills, you've got it made—in fact, you've got it made in the shade, because the park is full of trees. Just don't let your dog slip into the lake. Pooches aren't permitted, even if they wear a bathing cap.

From Centerville, exit Highway 180 at Piedra Road and follow it about five miles northeast to the lake. There's a $3 entry fee per car. (209) 488-3004. ➡ *See #1 on map p. 528.*

• **Pine Flat Lake Recreation Area** 🐾 🐾 🐾

Lakemeisters tell us there's about 120 acres of land for camping and hiking around Pine Flat Lake. But the lake itself is often extremely low—sometimes down to 10 percent of its capacity— because its water is being directed to farmland. When this happens, there's much more acreage for dogs and their leashed people to explore. But the loss of water isn't worth it. The lake is a sorry sight when it's in a depleted state.

But when it's full, it's a pleasure to hike around it. You'll amble through land dotted with digger pines, cottonwoods, oaks and willows. The land is fairly flat, and some of it is grassy. If you like to fish, you might try your luck on the spotted bass who hang out in the lake

The day-use fee is $3. Campsites are $10.50. From Centerville, exit Highway 180 at Trimmer Springs Road and drive about 12 miles northeast to the lake. (209) 488-3004. ➡ *See #2 on map p. 528.*

CLOVIS

PARKS, BEACHES & RECREATION AREAS

• **Letterman Park** 🐾 🐾

If you can't visit Johnny Carson Park in Burbank, why not give Letterman Park a try? So what if it's not named after TV's top late-night gap-toothed guy. Maybe someday it will be. Anyway, it's just as well, because he might not take kindly to his statue being on the receiving end of doggy leg lifts.

Leashed dogs are welcome to poke around at this shady, eight-acre park. There's plenty of grass and a couple of small rolling hills. The park is at Villa Avenue and West 9th Street. (408) 297-2320. ➡ *See #3 on map p. 528.*

RESTAURANTS

Deli Beans: If you're bringing your dog here, the manager prefers that you come after 2 p.m., when the place is less packed. You can eat sandwiches and slurp gourmet coffee on the patio. 2141 Shaw Avenue; (209) 323-8054.

Taco Bell: This Taco Bell has tables outside with umbrellas for shade. 434 West Shaw Avenue; (209) 299-0084.

Villa Cafe: "We have everything," says Maritza, of the Villa. And she means it—you can choose from turkey sandwiches, burgers, Mexican or Middle Eastern cuisine. There's plenty of outdoor seating for you and your pooch. 200 West Shaw Avenue; (209) 298-8881.

COALINGA

PARKS, BEACHES & RECREATION AREAS

• **Coalinga Mineral Springs Recreation Area** 🐾 🐾 1/2

Question: What smells like rotten eggs and attracts both man and beast? Answer: This park.

Leashed dogs love to come here because of the sulfur stench given off by the mineral-laden creek that runs through the park. Whenever Joe starts staring at the ground as if he's just had an epiphany, I know we're either getting near one of these sulfur heavens or approaching a piece of roadkill.

Humans enjoy this flat 35-acre park because it's full of pines, and surrounded by mountains. There are warnings against drinking the stinky creek water, but a local woman in her 80s has been drinking it for decades and she looks mahhhvelous.

The camping here is very secluded, primitive and cheap. It's used mostly by hunters during wild boar season and you have to bring your own water and get prior written permission from the county parks department. You could stay back in the campground for a few days and never see a soul. From Coalinga, drive northwest on Highway 198 for about 18 miles and turn right on Coalinga Mineral Springs Road. Continue five more miles to the park. (209) 488-3004. ➡ *See #4 on map p. 528.*

• **Coalinga Mineral Springs Scenic Trail** 🐾 🐾 🐾 🐾 🐕

Adjoining the county park (see above) are 9,000 acres of open land run by the dog-friendly Bureau of Land Management. If the 35-acre county park doesn't satisfy you or your dog, continue on to the adjacent BLM land and let the good times roll you through the grasslands. Just watch out for the occasional rocky outcropping.

The best part of this adventure is that if your dog is very obedient, you can let him run around leashless. But the 2.5-mile trail is also an equestrian trail, so if your dog thinks horses are giant dogs just waiting to be chased, keep him on his leash. Also be aware that deer live in the area surrounding the trail. If you aren't absolutely certain that your dog won't bound off after one, do everyone a favor and don't unleash him.

The hike is not for the fair of paw. It can be steep. But if you and your dog are in good shape, it's worth the exertion. The trail leads you to Kreyenhagen Peak, where you'll have wonderful views of the southern Diablo Mountains. Come in the spring and watch the wildflowers go wild.

We've heard that ticks can be a real problem at times. Call (408) 637-8183 for information, advice and a schedule of when hunters might be shooting at the deer and other critters you're avoiding with your dog. The trail starts where the county park leaves off. See page 531 for directions to the county park. ➤ *See #5 on map p. 528.*

RESTAURANTS

Harris Ranch Restaurant: This enormous beef restaurant has outdoor tables where you can eat the food you ordered inside. Or if you prefer, you can bring a blanket, order your food inside and bring it out for a cozy picnic on the lawn with your drooling dog. (You'd better order more than you can eat, because your dog will likely pull out all the stops for her begging routine.) Harris Ranch claims to be the largest beef company on the West Coast, so if you like red meat, you've struck gold. 24505 West Dorris Street; (209) 935-0717.

PLACES TO STAY

Coalinga Mineral Springs camping: See page 531.

The Inn at Harris Ranch: Ahh, Spanish-style architecture and the smell of broiling beef wafting into your room from the famed steak-o-rama next door. What more could a dog want? The only smell that could make this place more appealing to dogs is that of the Harris Ranch feed lot, but it's eight miles away. Unless the wind is just right, dogs are out of luck.

Rates are from $83 to $225. Dogs are $10 extra. It's just off Interstate 5, at the Highway 198/Hanford-Lemoore exit. The location is 24505 West Dorris Street, and the mailing address is Route 1, P.O. Box 777, Coalinga, CA 93210; (209) 935-0717.

FRESNO

In the midst of the region's raisin growers and cattle rustlers lies Fresno, the heart of the Central Valley. And like all hearts that are anatomically correct (not like the kind you get on a Valentine's Day card), it's functional and essential, but not too attractive.

Rest assured, there are some pretty good-looking parks in the midst of the malls and the cookie-cutter developments. If you have time to visit the charming Tower District, you may even start looking at Fresno in a different way. Or at least you'll start looking at Fresno.

PARKS, BEACHES & RECREATION AREAS

• Einstein Park 🐾 🐾 1/2

There's a completely fenced-in section in the southwest part of this grassy park, and you don't have to be a genius to figure out why dogs and their people like it. We can say no more here. Go visit for yourself. Just a word of warning: There really is a leash law.

The park is at East Dakota Avenue, just west of North Millerbrook Avenue. (209) 498-1551. ➡ *See #6 on map p. 528.*

• Kearney Park 🐾 🐾 🐾

People who visit this tree-filled 225-acre park may well think that the man for whom this park is named was a philanthropic sweetheart. After all, his huge mansion is in the middle of the park, and the land for the park had been his yard essentially, surrounded by thousands of acres of his farmland. Anyone who would give that kind of property to the city must be a kindly gent, right?

But according to Dave Caglia, head of parks and grounds operations for the county, English-born Martin Kearney was an ornery, racist farmer who acquired his land through crooked deals. He was jilted by the love of his life and became richer and more bitter over the years. The raisin mogul turned into a woman-hating recluse, and built this mansion, complete with 18-inch-thick walls.

When he died in the early 1900s (on a transatlantic ocean crossing, no less), he left some of the land to the University of California. In 1949, the university gave it to the county. It was the start of the Fresno County Park System.

The old guy may have been mean, but he sure knew how to make a pretty park. It's very popular—too popular for a dog's taste, at times. Don't come here with your dog on beautiful week-end afternoons unless you want to share it with the masses.

The park is filled with 100-year-old trees, including maples, palms, oaks and eucalyptus trees that are seven feet across and 200 feet tall! Boy dogs can barely contain themselves. But they can't go too wild, because leashes are the law here.

There's a $3 day-use fee. The park is on Kearney Boulevard, seven miles west of Fresno. (209) 488-3004. ➡ *See #7 on map p. 528.*

• Roeding Park 🐾 🐾 🐾 🐾

Before you and your dog look at your map and start drooling over this 157-acre chunk of land, you should know that it's much better for humans than for dogs. That's not to say dogs don't have a good time here. They have to be leashed, but they do enjoy the grass and trees in the sections where they're actually allowed.

But dogs are fairly restricted because of all the fun activities for humans. Between such dog-banning attractions as the Fresno Zoo, Storyland, Playland and the park's numerous tennis courts and playgrounds, a dog could get to feeling like he's not a real person. But when he walks near the zoo and gets a whiff of the elephant and zebra poop, he'll be so enraptured that he'll probably forget all about his dejection.

There's a $1 parking fee from February through October. You can walk in free of charge. The rest of the year, there's no fee for parking. Exit Highway 99 at Belmont Avenue or Olive Avenue and drive east to the park's main entrance. (209) 498-1551. ➡ *See #8 on map p. 528.*

• **Woodward Park** 🐾 🐾 🐾 1/2

At times, the line of cars trying to get into this park is so long that traffic in the area forms gridlock. It's obvious why the park is so popular. With 299 acres of grassy meadows, rolling hills, big trees, trails, streams, lakes and ponds, Woodward Park provides a much-needed refuge from life in Fresnoland.

The park actually started out as a bird refuge. The sanctuary remains virtually untouched, but the surrounding parklands are burgeoning. It's not the kind of place your dog will want to visit on a weekend or just about any decent summer day. But if you pick the right time, you can pretty much have the run of the park. Early mornings are almost always a safe bet. Rainy days aren't bad either.

Dogs have to be leashed here, and they're not permitted in the Japanese garden. The parking fee from February through October is $2 per car, but you can walk in for free. The rest of the year, there's no charge. Driving north on Highway 41, exit at North Friant Road and drive northeast to East Audubon Drive. You'll be at the southeast corner of the park. Turn left and follow East Audubon Drive to the main entrance. (209) 498-1551. ➡ *See #9 on map p. 528.*

RESTAURANTS

Babe's Cafe: This cafe serves mouth-watering sandwiches. Enjoy one with your dog at the outdoor tables here. It's located in the Fig Garden Village. 5076 North Palm; (209) 224-0326.

The City Cafe: Sometimes customers with canines order plain meat for their dogs while they dine on the tasty sandwiches served at the patio. Dogs also get a bowl of water here. 5048 North Blackstone Avenue, Suite 108; (209) 224-4399.

PLACES TO STAY

Blackstone Plaza Inn: This is more of a motel than an inn, but it does permit pooches, with a $15 deposit. Rates for humans are $30 to $42. 4061 North Blackstone Avenue, Fresno, CA 93726; (209) 222-5641.

Brooks Ranch Inn: "Of course dogs are allowed. They are man's best friend!" exclaimed inn employee Richard, a dog owner himself. They don't have room, though, for "huge" dogs. Rates are $29 to $43. Dogs require a $30 deposit. 4278 West Ashlan Avenue, Fresno, CA 93722; (209) 275-2727.

Fresno Hilton: Rates are $65 to $120. Dogs are $25 extra. 1055 Van Ness Avenue, Fresno, CA 93721; (209) 485-9000.

Holiday Inn Airport: Rates are $76 to $105. 5090 East Clinton Avenue, Fresno, CA 93727; (209) 252-3611.

Holiday Inn Centre Plaza: Rates are $72 to $80. 2233 Ventura Street, Fresno, CA 93721; (209) 268-1000.

Phoenix Lodge: Rates are $25 to $33. Dogs are $4 extra. 2345 North Parkway Drive, Fresno, CA 93705; (209) 268-0711 or (800) 621-0808.

FRIANT

PLACES TO STAY

Millerton Lake State Recreation Area camping: Since dogs aren't permitted on the trails here, or in the lake, or on a boat, about all you can do together is hang around one of the 138 campsites here. Sites are $8 to $14. Dogs are $1 extra, and should only camp here if someone will be with them if the rest of your party splits to do more interesting things. Call MISTIX at (800) 444-PARK for reservations. Or call the park at (209) 822-2332 for more info.

LAKESHORE

PLACES TO STAY

Lakeshore Resort: The managers at this Huntington Lake resort are a little gun-shy about allowing dogs. They've had people leave destructive pooches alone in the rooms only to find ruined furniture and torn apart curtains and rugs. But more responsible dogs and their people might renew their faith in the canine species.

It's an old 1920s-style mountain resort. And if you have a pup sitter and want to party, there's a saloon and dance hall on the premises. Rates are $55 to $120. Dogs are $10 extra. The street address is 61953 Huntington Lake Road, and the mailing address is P.O. Box 197, Lakeshore, CA 93634; (209) 893-3193.

MENDOTA

PARKS, BEACHES & RECREATION AREAS

• **Delta Mendota Canal Fishing Access** 🐾🐾🐾

If you and your favorite leashed dog don't mind whiling away the hours conversing with the fishies, you'll enjoy this 12-mile stretch along a farmland irrigation canal.

The scenery wouldn't make a top-selling postcard. It's open land and the canal isn't pretty. But the fishing isn't bad, if you crave critters like catfish. Some folks bring a barbecue and make a day of it. Don't try this in the summer, though. There's no shade at all, and you can't cool off in the off-limits canal. Besides, the fishing isn't the greatest then anyway.

If you do plan to spend the day, be aware that there were no bathrooms here last time we checked. Park officials say every time they put some restrooms out for public use, they get shot up and thrown in the canal. At $500 a pop, it adds up fast.

From Highway 33 just north of town, go east on Bass Road (just past the railroad tracks). In about 1.5 miles, you'll come to something called Mendota Pool Park. There are bathrooms there, should you plan ahead enough to need to use them before you fish. As you exit the park, you'll go up a little embankment. Turn left and you'll find the parking for the canal fishing. (209) 488-3004. ➡ *See #10 on map p. 528.*

• **Mendota Wildlife Area** 🐾🐾🐾🐾 🔫 🐕

Your dog doesn't have to be a hunter in order to enjoy off-leash privileges at this 11,802-acre wildlife haven. As long as she's an obedient pooch, she can gambol at your side as you hike on trails and levees through the wetlands and grasslands here.

Bring your binoculars if you want to get up close and personal with the waterfowl and shorebirds who hang around the area. And watch out for skunks. We know one dog who got blasted here, and he's never quite smelled the same.

Follow the signs from Highway 180. Call (209) 655-4645 for a schedule of when the park is off-limits, because of nesting seasons, and for information on hunting seasons. ➡ *See #11 on map p. 528.*

MERCEY HOT SPRINGS

PARKS, BEACHES & RECREATION AREAS

• **Panoche Hills** 🐾🐾🐾🐾 🐕

These 30,000 acres of rolling hills and grasslands are heaven to dogs who need more than just your average community park to make them feel like real dogs. Because the Bureau of Land Management operates it, obedient dogs are allowed to run around leash-free. Be extra sure to keep a close eye on your dog, because the hills are home to endangered species such as the San Joaquin kit fox and the blunt-nosed leopard lizard.

Hilltops, some of which are more than 2,500 feet tall, give you great views of the lush San Joaquin Valley and the dramatic Sierra Nevadas. And if you visit in the spring (by far the best time of year to come), you'll be treated to a spectacular wildflower bloom. The hilltops are also excellent for setting up a telescope and watching other worlds go by. Bring a hearty dinner and a blanket for your dog, and you couldn't ask for a better viewing station.

The hills are near Mercey Hot Springs, off County Road J1. You'll see the signs. Call before you visit so you can find out about any hunting that might be going on and any closures due to fire danger. (408) 637-8183. → *See #12 on map p. 528.*

SANGER

PARKS, BEACHES & RECREATION AREAS

Dogs aren't allowed in Sanger parks—not unless you get written permission from the director of community services. Then you can let your dog run around the parks without a leash! It's kind of a strange setup, but it's definitely worth a try. Call (209) 875-7513 for more information.

• **Greenwood Park** 🐾🐾🐾 🐕 (with permit)

This is your typical green, grassy, somewhat hilly community park with picnic tables and plenty of trees. Only dogs with written permission from the city can visit here, and then they can do so off leash. The park is at Fifth Street and Academy Avenue. (209) 875-7513. → *See #13 on map p. 528.*

SHAVER LAKE

PARKS, BEACHES & RECREATION AREAS

• **Shaver Lake** 🐾🐾🐾🐾 🐕

Although some of the land immediately surrounding this attractive lake is run by the county, even more of it is administered by the U.S. Forest Service. In fact, Sierra National Forest pretty much surrounds the lake. And you know what that means for dogs: No mandatory leashes on national forest land!

The lake is set at an elevation of 5,000 feet. There are 320 camping sites, ranging in fees from free (at a nearby Sierra National

Forest campground; phone 209/841-3311) to $22 per site (at Camp Edison; phone 209/841-3444). Reservations are recommended at both camps. From the town of Shaver Lake, follow Highway 168 north to the lake. ➡ *See #14 on map p. 528.*

RESTAURANTS

Shorthorn Bar & Grill: Dogs bring their owners here all the time to hang out on the deck. You can eat burgers, steaks, chili, burritos and a whole host of other hearty foods while you watch your dog shoot the bull with his buddies. 41790 Dorabella Road; (209) 841-7175.

PLACES TO STAY

Shaver Lake camping: See page 537.

Shaver Lake Village Hotel and Cabins: This is the oldest lodge in Shaver Lake, circa 1940. The rooms at the hotel are wood-paneled and feel like cabins themselves. Separate cabins are also available. Rates are $60 to $85. The street address is 42135 Toll House Road and the mailing address is P.O. Box 118, Shaver Lake, CA 93664. (800) 695-7368.

SAN BENITO COUNTY

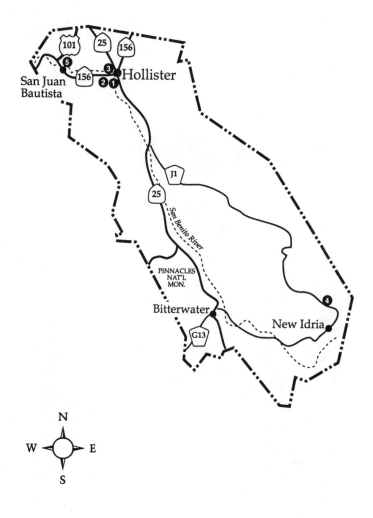

44
SAN BENITO COUNTY

If you look at a map of this county, you may wonder, "What's a dog to do here?" Joe looked as if he were being sent to purgatory when I told him we were going to visit San Benito County. He sat at the front door of the house and wouldn't budge. When I tried pulling him, he tugged back and slipped out of his collar. But since I have longer legs, a stronger body and a box of desiccated liver treats, I won the battle. He gulped down the bait, frowned and succumbed to his fate.

He must have remembered those vast stretches of privately-owned nothingness we once drove across on the way from no-where to not-much-of-any-place-else. Even I wanted to be any-where but there. But this time our visit was different. It wasn't heaven, but it wasn't hell either. At the end of our time in this county, even Joe had a smile on his boxy snout.

BITTERWATER

PLACES TO STAY

Pinnacles National Monument: Dogs are permitted only in picnic areas, parking lots and the campground at this park, so they miss all the fascinating pinnacle-shaped volcanic rock formations within. It's not much fun for your pooch, but if she's with someone who's not in the mood to hike around and explore the caves and trails here, the campground isn't a bad place to hang out for a day.

There are 90 sites at the privately-operated campground that you can get to from San Benito County, costing $6 per person. Campsites are available on a first-come, first-served basis. Reservations are required for groups of 10 or more. From Highway 25 about 13 miles north of Bitterwater (26 miles south of Hollister), take Highway 146 southwest to the park. The park-operated campground costs $10 per night, but can be accessed only from its west side, on Highway 146. The east and west ends of Highway 146 don't connect, so you can't drive on it from one side of the park to the other. The private campground phone is (408) 389-4462. The park number is (408) 389-4485.

HOLLISTER

PARKS, BEACHES & RECREATION AREAS

• **Dunne Park** 🐾 🐾

This downtown-area park is the city's oldest, and though it's only about four acres, your leashed dog may feel like he's in a significantly larger space. Dogs of the leg-lifting persuasion enjoy the sycamore, olive and bay trees throughout the park.

The park is at 6th and West streets. (408) 636-4370. ➡ *See #1 on map p. 540.*

• **San Justo Reservoir County Park** 🐾 🐾 🐾

You and your leashed dog are free to hike on the dirt trail/fire road that encircles this 580-acre park. Many folks like to come here to fish at the 200-acre reservoir, but dogs generally prefer to amble through the open land. It's not the most attractive place in the world, but it beats the backyard.

The day-use fee is $4 per vehicle. The park is west of town. Exit Highway 156 at Union Road and drive south. The park will be on your right in a little less than a mile. The park's hours are limited. Call (408) 638-3300 for a schedule. ➡ *See #2 on map p. 540.*

• **Vista Park Hill** 🐾 🐾 🐾

This hilltop park overlooks town, and has plenty of undeveloped acres for your leashed dog to explore. In this case, though, undeveloped means dry grass, weeds and, yes, foxtails in the wrong time of year. Be careful out there. You may want to stick with the green open spaces and the eucalyptus-lined walkways that are also in this park.

From Highway 156, go west on Hill Street for a long block to the park's entrance. This is also where the Bureau of Land Management's local office is located. It's a good place to stop in and pick up information on the nearby BLM lands (see Griswold Hills, page 543, for information on one of these off-leash areas). The city park department's phone number is (408) 636-4370. ➡ *See #3 on map p. 540.*

RESTAURANTS

Casablanca: Dine on Mexican food on the patio with your pooch. 1274 San Juan Road; (408) 637-1833.

Hollister Coffee Roasting Company: You and your dog can sit at the sidewalk tables here and enjoy fine coffee and pastries. 420 San Benito Street; (408) 636-0240.

PLACES TO STAY

Best Western San Benito Inn: Rates are $40 to $55. Dogs are $2 extra. 660 San Felipe Road, Hollister, CA 95023; (408) 637-9248.

NEW IDRIA

PARKS, BEACHES & RECREATION AREAS

• **Griswold Hills Recreation Area** 😺 😺 😺 😺 🐾

Some small city parks I've explored are run by departments that tell you the parks' acreage down to the hundredth of an acre. When you're dealing with parks that are 3.21 acres, you want to count every inch.

But then along comes the Bureau of Land Management. In its written material, it says Griswold Hills has "several thousand acres." We're not talking exact measurements here. But that's the charm of these off-leash BLM havens. Precision and rules are left at the gate (when there is a gate). Rules exist, but few restrict a well-behaved dog's good time.

This recreation area is made up of rugged canyons of scrub oak, juniper and chaparral. Some trails take you up to ridgetops for good views of the surrounding valleys. Others take you to the riparian zone at Griswold Creek. Not many people know about this area, so if you and your dog need to get away from it all, there's a good chance you can.

The park isn't as big or as scenic as the BLM's nearby 50,000-acre Clear Creek Management Area. But we don't recommend that area for people who worry about things like asbestosis, mesothelioma or cancer. Because of naturally occurring asbestos, you and your dog are supposed to wear protective clothing and respirators when setting paw on much of the land. It's not worth it.

The main entrance to Griswold Hills is three miles south of Panoche Road on New Idria Road. Watch out for hunters during deer and quail seasons. Call (408) 637-8183 for hunting dates and more information on local BLM lands. → *See #4 on map p. 540.*

SAN JUAN BAUTISTA

Be sure to swing by the Mission San Juan Bautista when you visit this town, especially if you or your dog are fans of Alfred Hitchcock. The mission (the largest of the old California missions) starred in the Hitchcock classic, *Vertigo*. It's worth a peek, but dogs have to stay firmly planted on the ground outside. Jimmy Stewart would have envied the stance.

If you're hungry, don't let all the restaurants with outdoor tables fool you. We couldn't find any eateries that would permit pooches. But as the pendulum swings, we don't expect that to last for long.

PARKS, BEACHES & RECREATION AREAS

•San Juan Bautista State Historic Park 🐾🐾 1/2

Leashed dogs who like local history are welcome to accompany you as you tour this small state park. You'll see buildings like the old Plaza Hotel, which was a popular stagecoach stop, and the Castro House, at one time the administrative headquarters of Mexican California.

But since dogs must stay outside such buildings, they prefer to tour the livery stables, gardens and orchards. The park is on the plaza in the center of town. Admission is $2 per adult. Call (408) 623-4881. ➡ *See #5 on map p. 540.*

PLACES TO STAY

San Juan Inn: It's quiet here. Rates are $42 to $60. Dogs require a $20 deposit. The inn is located at 410 Alameda Street, and the mailing address is P.O. Box 1080, San Juan Bautista, CA 95045; (408) 623-4380.

MONTEREY COUNTY

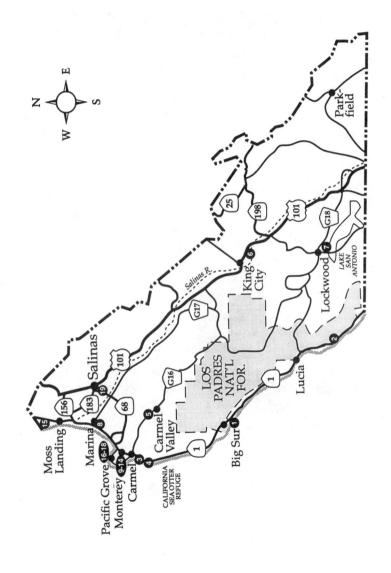

45
MONTEREY COUNTY

Native son John Steinbeck and his fearless blue poodle, Charley, visited here during their cross-country journey recorded in the 1961 classic, *Travels with Charley*. The Gentle Reader is never sure what Charley did while his master paid homage to old bars and old memories in Monterey and Salinas, but wherever Charley went in this county, he probably felt as accepted as his human friend. Monterey County is as warm and welcoming as an old Italian aunt.

The county is a wonderland for dogs and their drivers. People get part of the vast agricultural sweeps in the east part of the county and the rugged mountain coast along the mighty Pacific in the west. Dogs get the pungent odor of fresh fertilizer in the east and the tantalizing scents carried miles by the Pacific winds in the west.

If going leashless is your dog's fantasy, Carmel, Carmel Valley and Pacific Grove are ideal stopping points. Their designated off-leash romping grounds are as picturesque as their cozy inns. And your dog would never forgive you if you forgot the northern segment of the magnificent Los Padres National Forest for a hearty leashless hike.

NATIONAL FORESTS

See the National Forests/Wilderness Areas chapter starting on page 801 for important information and safety tips for visiting national forests with your dog.

•Los Padres National Forest 🐾 🐾 🐾 🐾 🐕

This spectacular, rugged terrain in the Big Sur area is great for an outing with a spectacular, rugged dog. Actually, even spectacular couch-potato dogs can enjoy some of the hikes here in the Ventana Wilderness. See page 806 for a description of Los Padres National Forest.

BIG SUR AREA

As the two-lane ribbon of Highway 1 winds 90 miles up and down what many think is the most spectacular coastal scenery in the world, your dog may be praying for the end of the trip—or at least wishing for a dose of Dramamine.

Car-sick dogs are not uncommon as mountains shoot up 1,000 feet over the crashing Pacific, only to curve and slope down again, roller coaster fashion. It's a good idea to take your time and stop at as many vista points as you can along the road. Your dog will thank you for it, and you'll get to breathe the exhilarating Pacific air and study the rugged shoreline.

A must-stop vista point is at the Bixby Creek Bridge, 260 feet high and more than 700 feet long. There are pullouts on either side.

Whatever you do when you're making these stops along Big Sur, make sure your dog is securely leashed and in no danger of stepping too close to the edge of the world. There's usually not much room between Highway 1 and the hazardous cliffs.

PARKS, BEACHES & RECREATION AREAS

Unfortunately, there are plenty of state parks along the way, and few beaches. This isn't so bad for people without dogs, but canines are extremely restricted in state parks. Most allow dogs only where they allow cars: paved roads and drive-in campsites. It's not worth the price of admission, unless you're planning an overnight stay.

•**Pfeiffer Beach** 🐾 🐾 🐾 🐾 🐾

You and your leashed dog will be stunned at the natural beauty of this white, sandy beach. Surrounded by sea caves, steep cliffs and natural arches, you won't know what to marvel at first. Your dog will be so thrilled that he won't even notice he's leashed.

From the north, take the second right turn (Sycamore Canyon Road) off Highway 1 south of Big Sur State Park. It's a sharp turn. At the end of the narrow, two-mile road is a sandy trail under a canopy of cypress trees. It leads to the beach. (408) 385-5434. ➡ *See #1 on map p. 546.*

•**Sand Dollar Picnic Area and Beach** 🐾 🐾 🐾

Your dog will enjoy the romance of a picnic among the cypress trees here. After downing your French bread, Brie and white wine, take one of the trails across the field and follow it down to the beach. Although dogs must be leashed, this is one of Joe's favorite spots. It's toward the southern end of Big Sur, so it's at a perfect place to take a break in the driving. The picnic area is about 11 miles south of Lucia, west of Highway 1. (408) 385-5454. ➡ *See #2 on map p. 546.*

PLACES TO STAY

Here are just a few of the many private and public campgrounds along the Big Sur coast:

Big Sur Campground: If you're into family-oriented camping, this is your kind of place. This privately owned campground in the redwoods along the Big Sur River features basketball courts and a playground for the kids. Tent camps are $20 a site, and dogs are $3 extra. The more exclusive tent-cabins have queen-size beds, and cost $38 a night for two people, dogs an additional $8. The campground is on Highway 1, about 24 miles south of Carmel. For reservations, contact the campground at Highway 1, Big Sur, CA 93920; (408) 667-2322.

China Camp: It's fun to camp here if you're planning on hiking in the Ventana Wilderness (see page 806) but you're not quite sure about camping in the wilderness itself. There's a trail that leads directly from the camp into the Ventana Wilderness. Dogs are permitted on leash at the campsite, but they can put their leashes in their doggy backpacks as soon as they're in the wilderness area. There are six sites that are available on a first-come, first-served basis. Campsites are $10. The campground is inland, about 20 miles southwest of Carmel Valley, on Tassajara Road. Call the Los Padres National Forest main office at (408) 385-5434.

Kirk Creek Campground: You'll love the view from the bluffs above the beach here, and your dog will appreciate the cool Pacific breezes. You can bring your leashed dog down to the beach on a couple of steep trails, or you can take a trail from here that leads into the Ventana Wilderness. That's where your dog can legally remove his leash. There are 33 campsites available at Kirk Creek. Campsites are between $10 and $15. The campground is west of Highway 1, about four miles south of Lucia. Call the Los Padres National Forest main office at (408) 385-5434.

Pfeiffer-Big Sur State Park: Of the 821 acres of redwoods, some near Big Sur River, dogs are permitted only in the camping area. It's not so bad—each of the 218 campsites has a picnic table where your dog can join you for gourmet outdoor cooking or sleep under when the shade of the redwoods isn't enough. Sites are $14 to $16. Dogs are an extra dollar. The park is east of Highway 1, about 26 miles south of Carmel. Call park headquarters at (408) 667-2315 for information. For reservations, call MISTIX at (800) 444-PARK.

Ventana Campground: This privately owned campground, set in a redwood canyon, is ideal for getting away from motor home campers without getting too primitive. There are 70 sites available. No reservations are necessary but they are recommended for summer weekends. It's more rustic than many campgrounds you'll find around here, which is something Joe appreciates. Sites are $20. Dogs are an extra $2. The campground is about 2.5 miles south of Pfeiffer Big Sur State Park. P.O. Box 206, Big Sur, CA 93920; (408) 667-2688.

CARMEL

Dogs feel more welcome in this picturesque village than almost anywhere in the world. Maybe there's an aura emanating from dog-lover Doris Day's Cypress Inn (see page 551). Or perhaps it's the "doggie hitching posts" attached to shops around Ocean Avenue, Carmel's main street. The hook-and-snap devices make it possible for you to shop while your dog relaxes in the shade outside, without being forced to hear the incessant ringing of cash registers. Or maybe that welcome feeling comes from knowing that its city beach, one of the most enticing beaches in California lets them run leashless (see Carmel City Beach, below).

Whatever the case, your dog can't help but be happy in Carmel, which in these busy times still shuns the idea of street addresses. You won't have a problem finding your destinations, though, because the village is small enough and the people are friendly enough that it's very hard to stay lost for long.

PARKS, BEACHES & RECREATION AREAS

•Carmel City Beach 🐾 🐾 🐾 🐾 🐾

The fine white sand crunches underfoot as you and your leash-free dog explore this pristine beach. It's the only beach for many, many miles that allows dogs off their leashes, so it's a real gem for dog travelers. Bordered by cypress trees and a walking trail, the beach is also popular among humans, especially on weekends. So if your dog is the type to mark beach blankets and eat things out of other peoples' picnic baskets, you may want to leash him until you find a less crowded part of the beach.

From Highway 1, take the Ocean Avenue exit all the way to the end, where you'll find a large parking area that's not large enough on summer weekends. (408) 624-3543. → *See #3 on map p. 546.*

•Carmel River State Beach 🐾 🐾 🐾

Dogs can enjoy this large stretch of beach as far as their leashes will allow. It's convenient if you're stuck south of Carmel, but most dogs prefer the Carmel City Beach (see above) because of its leash-free policy.

The state beach is accessible from many points, including Ribera Road, off Highway 1. (408) 624-4909. → *See #4 on map p. 546.*

RESTAURANTS

Le Bistro: How could a restaurant born and bred out of the dog-accepting French tradition not allow pets? Dogs are more than welcome on the patio. They'll drool over the beef brochette. At San Carlos Street and Ocean Avenue. (408) 624-6545.

Plaza Cafe and Grill: They've got everything a dog owner could want, from fresh fish to pizza. Dine at one of the many umbrella-shaded tables. At Carmel Plaza, at the corner of Ocean Avenue and Junipero Street; (408) 624-4433.

PLACES TO STAY

Cypress Inn: Dogs get the royal treatment here, in part because actress and animal activist Doris Day owns this sumptuous hotel. The Mediterranean-style inn is very elegant, with fine oak floors and delicate antiques, but you never feel out of place with your dog. Day's staff makes sure your dog feels especially welcome, right down to offering pet beds and pet food for your four-legged friend. There's no doggy spa yet, but *que sera, sera.*

Rates are from $90 to $190, and dogs are $15 extra each night. At Lincoln Street and 7th Avenue. The mailing address is P.O. Box Y, Carmel, CA 93921; (408) 624-3871.

Happy Landing Inn: This bed-and-breakfast is out of a fairy tale. The home-turned-inn was built in 1925, and still retains the warm feel of a cozy cottage. The gardens are from Eden, complete with lush flowers, a gazebo and a pond. Dogs who stay here (lap-sized pooches only, please) may never want to leave, but that's okay, because neither do the people who bring them. Rates are $95 to $150. The inn is at Monte Verde Street and 6th Avenue. The mailing address is P.O. Box 2619, Carmel, CA 93921; (408) 624-7917.

Wayside Inn: Part inn, part motel, this is a charming old ivy-covered brick building well off the beaten path. What it lacks in divine exterior grace it makes up for inside, with comfortable country-style surroundings. Some rooms come with kitchenettes or fireplaces. Rates are $95 to $225. At Mission and 7th streets. The mailing address is P.O. Box 1900, Carmel, CA 93921; (408) 624-5336.

FESTIVALS

Carmel Bach Festival: Dogs aren't allowed in the theater, which is where the performances are held, but they can trot by and listen to the brass ensemble that often plays on the terrace before the festival. It's usually held for three weeks in July and August, at the Sunset Cultural Center. (408) 624-1521.

CARMEL VALLEY

Only 10 miles inland from Highway 1, this is one of the hidden jewels of the Central Coast. Carmel Valley boasts an average of 283 sunny days a year—quite a feat for anyone so close to the ocean. The peaceful country setting isn't marred by the little Carmel Valley Village, the "city center" that's chock full of outdoor cafes that put out the welcome mat for dogs.

Joe was disappointed to learn that when Charley and John Steinbeck reached Carmel Valley in their travels, the human half of the team wasn't happy. In *Travels with Charley,* Steinbeck wrote of a conversation he had with his old friend Johnny Garcia in a Monterey bar: "I went to the Carmel Valley where once we could shoot a thirty-thirty in any direction. Now you couldn't shoot a marble knuckles down without wounding a foreigner. And Johnny, I don't mind people, you know that. But these are rich people. They plant geraniums in big pots. Swimming pools where frogs and crayfish used to wait for us."

Joe, who hates swimming, agrees there are too many swimming pools here. But frogs and their friends still make Carmel Valley their home. You just have to visit Garland Ranch Regional Park (see below) to get a sampling of what was once wild and wonderful about the entire Carmel Valley area.

On your way here on Carmel Valley Road, you'll run across several small flower and vegetable farms, some of which occasionally allow dogs to tiptoe through the tulips with you. When you find one that appeals to you, stop in and check the rules. Many tend to be friendly to dogs who promise not to do leg lifts on their geraniums.

PARKS, BEACHES & RECREATION AREAS

• **Garland Ranch Regional Park** 🐾 🐾 🐾 🐾 ⬅ 🐕

This 4,500-acre park is heaven for any dog who has ever dreamed of living in the country. From the maple-filled canyons to the dense oak woodlands to the willow-covered banks of the Carmel River, you can find almost any environment you and your dog like.

Nine miles of trails can take you and your leash-free dog from just above sea level to 2,000 feet. The wildlife here is plentiful. At the visitor center, you can pick up trail maps as well as species lists of common birds, mammals and plants to look for while on the trails. Make sure your dog is kind to nature and doesn't disturb the creatures of the woods. Your dog should also know that this is horse country—if he's thinking of spooking any equines, he'd better be leashed.

While the park has its wild side, it also can be downright civilized. You'll find restrooms and oodles of picnic tables near the visitor center.

Take Carmel Valley Road about 10 miles east from Highway 1. The park will be on your right. Park in one of the lots and follow any of the narrow trails over the Carmel River and to the visitors center. The visitors center is the convenient trailhead for all the park's trails. (408) 659-4488. ➡ *See #5 on map p. 546.*

RESTAURANTS

Bon Appetit: Dine with your dog at tables with big umbrellas, where you can enjoy food with a Belgium-California flair. 7 Delfino Place; (408) 659-3559.

The Iron Kettle Restaurant: This is our favorite spot, at least as far as ambience. The home cooking is good, and the setting is out of this world. It's in the Old Milk House, an enchanting farmhouse-style building complete with cupola, built in 1890. When it's hot out, this is the place to cool your heels and paws. You and your dog can dine in the shade of the front porch, or in the shade of a variety of towering trees out back.

If afternoon tea is your bag, The Iron Kettle has one of the best, for one of the best prices: $4.25. It may not be the Sheraton-Palace, but at least your dog can sit with you. English dogs, like some springer spaniels and yes, Airedales like Joe, get all misty eyed when they hear the tinkling of a teaspoon in a dainty cup, especially if there's a chance they can mooch some of your scone by looking sentimental. On a good day, dogs are actually provided with water and their own biscuits. 9 Carmel Valley Road; (408) 659-5472.

The King & I: The Thai food here is refreshing and delicious. Dogs love it here, because the owners will serve them water under the umbrella tables. 3 Delfino Place; (408) 659-2126.

Village Pizzeria: 10 Delfino Place; (408) 659-3112.

PLACES TO STAY

Carmel Valley Inn: The hospitality and grace of the best of country inns awaits you and your dog at this inn/tennis resort. Dog aren't allowed to play tennis or jump in the heated pool, but other than that they're about as welcome as anybody. Rates are $59 to $109. At Carmel Valley and Los Laureles roads. P.O. Box 115, Carmel Valley, CA 93924; (408) 659-3131.

Valley Lodge: This quiet, secluded country inn is a great place for dogs to get away from city life. The redwood buildings, some with fireplaces, kitchenettes and private decks, are the perfect place to relax after a long day of hiking at Garland Ranch Regional Park. At Carmel Valley and Ford roads. The mailing address is P.O. Box 93, Carmel Valley, CA 93924; (408) 659-2261.

KING CITY

This is a fine place to stop with your dog, but a word of warning: It's also a good place to get caught speeding. The California Highway Patrol seems omnipresent on this stretch of US 101, so watch yourself. They don't take kindly to the old "my dog *really* has to go to the bathroom" excuse.

PARKS, BEACHES & RECREATION AREAS
•San Lorenzo Regional Park 🐾 🐾 🐾
Conveniently located just off US 101 almost midway between San Francisco and Los Angeles, this is a great park for your dog to get out and stretch his legs on a long journey. The park has an intriguing Agricultural and Rural Life Museum which tells the story of Salinas Valley agriculture. Although dogs aren't welcome in the buildings, humans are invited to enter a one-room schoolhouse and farmhouse.

If you want to make a night of it, you can camp at any of the park's 190 campsites. Reservations are only necessary for group sites. Sites are $12 to $14. Dogs cost an extra dollar. Exit US 101 at Broadway and follow the signs. (408) 385-5964. ➜ *See #6 on map p. 546.*

PLACES TO STAY
Motel 6: Rates are $23 for the first adult, $6 for the second. All Motel 6s allow one small pooch per room. 3 Broadway Circle, King City, CA 93930; (408) 385-5000.

Palm Motel: Rates are $20 to $24 a night. Dogs are $10 extra. 640 Broadway, King City, CA 93930; (408) 385-3248.

San Lorenzo Regional Park camping: See above.

LOCKWOOD

PARKS, BEACHES & RECREATION AREAS
•Lake San Antonio 🐾 🐾 🐾 🐾
Dogs who love water love this park because of its narrow, 16-mile-long reservoir. We've seen dogs on bass boats, dogs on houseboats and dogs on rowboats, and they've all looked blissed out. Authorities here discourage dogs from jumping in the water. It's pretty tough for dogs to swim around here anyway, since they're required to be leashed.

On land, you'll find more than 600 campsites, plenty of playgrounds and picnic areas, and even a few hiking trails. The campsites are available on a first-come, first-served basis. The lake is usually very busy in the summer, and very tranquil in the winter.

The day-use fee ranges from $1 to $3. Camping fees range from $10 to $20, and pets are $1 extra.

From US 101 in King City, take the Jolon Road exit. Jolon Road puts you onto County Road G14. Follow County Road G14 for 45 miles and then take either the North Shore or South Shore entrance into the park. (408) 755-4899. ➡ *See #7 on map p. 546.*

PLACES TO STAY

Lake San Antonio camping: See page 554.

MARINA

PARKS, BEACHES & RECREATION AREAS

•**Marina State Beach** 🐾 🐾 🐾

This is one of the largest state beaches on the Central Coast. Dogs have to be leashed, but they can still enjoy an exhilarating day here. It may be tempting to unleash your dog, but beware: The ranger's residence is always within eyeshot.

The main entrance is at the foot of Reservation Road, just off Highway 1. Park in the lot here and walk down the 2,000-foot-long boardwalk to the beach. (408) 384-7695. ➡ *See #8 on map p. 546.*

PLACES TO STAY

Motel 6: Rates are $32 for the first adult, $6 for the second. All Motel 6s allow one small pooch per room. 100 Reservation Road, Marina, CA 93933; (408) 384-1000.

MONTEREY

Although there's nowhere to legally let your dog off leash here, Monterey is still a grand stomping ground for dogs and their people. A few activities you can enjoy with your dog include taking in the sights of old/new Cannery Row, fishing off Municipal Wharf No. 2, and watching sea otters frolic about Monterey Bay.

Alas, dogs are not allowed on Fisherman's Wharf, home to some of the world's most dog-friendly scents. Joe visited a few times before we learned of the rule, and he never got into trouble, except when he tried to eat the calamari out of somebody's carry-out cup. And then there was the time he stuck his nose in a kid's cotton candy and set the kid to wailing so hard that her parents rushed to her thinking Joe had taken a bite out of *her.*

PARKS, BEACHES & RECREATION AREAS

The only city park that allows dogs is El Estero Park. Keep that in mind while strolling past the small parks along the Recreation Trail. Leashed dogs are welcome on city beaches and county parks near Monterey.

• El Estero Park 🐾 🐾 🐾

Dogs are advised to stay away from this park's best feature, Dennis the Menace Playground (designed by the comic's creator, Hank Ketcham). But while the kids frolic on the playground's steam engine, roller slide and giant swing ride, you and the dog can walk around El Estero Lake.

It's a fun walk for leashed dogs and their people. If you like birdwatching (and what dog doesn't?), you'll enjoy the ducks and migrating birds who hang out on the lake. Benches and picnic tables are scattered around this well-manicured park, so you can really make an afternoon of it.

If you're heading from Highway 1 to the Cannery Row area of Monterey, you'll run right into the park. Exit Highway 1 at the central Monterey exit. Stay in the right lane and go right on Camino Aguajito. The park will be immediately on your left. You'll get to the best parking area by going left on 3rd Street. (408) 646-3866. →*See #9 on map p. 546.*

• Jack's Peak Regional Park 🐾 🐾 🐾 1/2 🐾

Some of the most stunning views of the Monterey Bay, Carmel Valley and Santa Lucia Mountain Range can be seen from the 1,068-foot peak, the highest point on the Monterey Peninsula. You and your leashed dog will love the cool Pacific Ocean breezes that sweep through the pine-covered ridges and cathedral-like forests here.

On the eight-and-a-half miles of intersecting trails (including a self-guided nature trail), you and your dog can make a day of it or just take in a little fresh air for a half hour. Joe enjoys the Pine Trail, which starts at the Jack's Peak parking area. This is also where you'll find one of the last three remaining native stands of Monterey pine in the world.

The best time to visit here is the spring, when the meadows are blanketed with wildflowers, but this park is worth a visit any time of year.

Fees are $1 Monday through Thursday, and $2 Fridays through Sundays. From Monterey, take Highway 68 east a couple of miles and go right on Olmstead Road. Then turn left on Jack's Peak Road, and follow the signs to the park. (408) 755-4899. →*See #10 on map p. 546.*

• Laguna Seca Recreation Area 🐾 🐾 🐾

Dogs may not jump for joy at the prospect of spending a couple of days at this county park, but if you're a sports car racing fan, you sure will. This is a race car enthusiast's heaven. Chances are good that almost any time of year you visit, you'll be able to see some kind of race car driving on the world-famous Laguna Seca Raceway in the middle of the park.

Joe was hoping to see Mario Andretti the last time we visited, but he had to settle for the Paul Newman Racing Team doing test laps. Many of the park's 180 camping sites for RVs or tents provide a prize-winning view of the track, where excitement-loving leashed dogs can also watch stock cars, motorcycles and monster truck shows.

The park isn't known for its wild and scenic trails, but there are enough adequate spots on the oak-covered hills for a little exercise. There are also plenty of picnic tables for dining before or after the big race.

The day-use fee is $2 per car Monday through Thursday and $4 Friday through Sunday. There are 180 campsites available. Camping is $15 per site per night, with dogs costing $1 extra. If no race is scheduled reservations are required only five days in advance. If a race is scheduled you must buy a race ticket to camp here. If your dog is gun shy, you won't want to spend time here. One segment of the park is devoted to a rifle/pistol range.

From Monterey, follow Highway 68 about seven miles east to the signs for Laguna Seca Recreation Area, which is on the north side of the highway. For racetrack information and competition dates, call (408) 648-5111. You can phone the park at (408) 755-4899.
➡ *See #11 on map p. 546.*

•**Macabee Beach** 🐾 🐾

This is a very small beach, but it serves an important purpose: When the kids are holed up in the Monterey Bay Aquarium and you and your dog are taking in the sights of Cannery Row, the beach makes an excellent pit stop. Since your dog won't be able to smell the Cannery Row sardines of the early century, she'll be happy to sniff at some of the marine critters who call the Monterey Bay their home.

It's also a fun place for you and your leashed dog to get away from the throngs of weekend tourists and settle in for a picnic. But because it's so small, you wouldn't want to come here just for exercise.

The beach is between McClellan and Prescott avenues, just off Cannery Row. (408) 373-1902. ➡ *See #12 on map p. 546.*

•**Monterey State Beach** 🐾 🐾 1/2

This beach is actually in two segments, and neither is very large. We prefer to hit the Marina State Beach (see page 555) if we have to find a beach in the area. It's much larger, and usually less widely used.

But if you're strolling along the Recreation Trail (see below) and your dog needs to go roll in some sand, try the section on Del Monte Avenue, at the foot of Park Avenue. You can make your stroll and roll last longer by extending your walk to Monterey Beach Park, just east of the Municipal Wharf (see Diversions, page 560). This tiny beach also requires that your dog wear a leash. (408) 649-2836. ➡ *See #13 on map p. 546.*

•Recreation Trail 🐾 🐾 🐾 🐾

Stretching five miles from Lover's Point in Pacific Grove (no dogs allowed in the little Lover's Point Park) past Cannery Row and into Seaside, this paved bike and walking path is a great way to see Monterey.

You and your leashed dog can get your fill of sightseeing and exercise here. You can sit on one of the many benches that dot the trail and watch some of the world's most fascinating marine life. Joe likes to check out the mama otters wrapping their babes in kelp before they swim off to forage for food. He could stare for hours at the bobbing babes, but fortunately, the mothers return pretty quickly.

You can start the trail anywhere, but many folks like to start at Fisherman's Wharf. Although dogs aren't allowed on the Wharf, this is where smaller dogs get to embark on one of the funnest adventures known to canines: Riding on a bike, while you pedal. (See Diversions, page 559.) ➡ *See #14 on map p. 546.*

RESTAURANTS

Hoagies Cafe: Dogs get a bowl of water when they dine at the picnic tables here, and humans can choose from a variety of tasty treats, including baked potatoes, veggie burgers and fat deli sandwiches. 529 Lighthouse Avenue; (408) 649-0320.

Kalisa's Restaurant, Coffeehouse and Deli: This is a great place to come with a dog while waiting for the rest of the gang to get done at the Monterey Bay Aquarium, located just across the street. You and your dog can sit at the chairs outside and wile away the minutes eating ice cream, one of Kalisa's more popular treats. 851 Cannery Row; (408) 372-8512.

Monterey Coffeehouse: This bookshop/cafe in the heart of downtown Monterey is popular among erudite pooches. Dine on croissants, bagels, lasagna and cakes at the big, umbrella-topped tables. 472 Alvarado Street; (408) 647-1822.

Monterey Brewing Company: They love dogs here. Your pooch

will get the royal treatment when you sit down at the little tables out front. Besides great beer, the place serves a mean clam chowder. 638 Wave Street; (408) 375-3634.

Monterey Peninsula Winery: Buy your favorite wine and toast your favorite dog at the little chairs outside. 786 Wave Street; (408) 372-4949.

PLACES TO STAY

Cypress Garden Motel: Dogs are allowed as long as they're smaller than the guests. Rates are $50 to $100. 1150 Munras Avenue, Monterey, CA 93940; (408) 373-2761.

Laguna Seca Recreation Area camping: See page 556.

Monterey Beach Hotel-Best Western: This is one of Joe's favorites. From his first-floor room (dogs are restricted to ground level) he can see the beach, gulls walking around, and girls in bikinis. But what he likes even more is the easy access to Monterey State Beach (see page 557). Rates are $100 to $170. 2600 Dunes Drive, Monterey, CA 93940; (408) 394-3321.

Motel 6: Rates are $40 for the first adult, $6 for the second (but slightly cheaper on weekdays). All Motel 6s allow one small pooch per room. 2124 North Fremont Street, Monterey, CA 93940; (408) 646-8585.

Victorian Inn: If you're willing to pay a one-time doggy fee of $25 and a $100 deposit, this beautifully furnished Victorian-style inn is as relaxing as it is attractive. Dogs love to curl up in front of the marble fireplaces here. 487 Foam Street, Monterey, CA 93940; (408) 373-8000 or (800) 232-4141.

FESTIVALS

Monterey's Birthday Party: This two-day festival, usually held in early June, features four blocks of fine arts and crafts, and gourmet and ethnic foods along historic Alvarado Street. It's not held every year, but when it is, leashed dogs have fun. (408) 655-8070.

DIVERSIONS

Take someone furry on a surrey: Chicks and ducks and geese better scurry when you take your dog on a bicycle-powered surrey from Heritage Harbor Bikes. The surreys come complete with a fringe on the top. The best part is that they also come with baskets in the front, perfect for small or medium-sized dogs. You and a friend can pedal up and down Monterey's scenic Recreation Trail (see page 558) while your dog just sits back and takes in the scents and sights. Folks who know recommend bringing a jacket or

something soft for your dog to sit on. Wire baskets don't make for the most comfortable ride.

The surreys rent for about $12 an hour. Heritage Harbor Bikes is located just off Fisherman's Wharf, at 255-C Heritage Harbor Center. (408) 655-0242.

Fish for your supper: The Municipal Wharf No. 2, built in 1926, is one of the best places in the Monterey Bay for landlubbers and their dogs to nail perch and other catches of the day. It's also ideal for watching commercial fishing boats unload their bounties— everything from anchovies to salmon. The wharf is at the foot of Figueroa Street. (408) 646-3950.

MOSS LANDING

PARKS, BEACHES & RECREATION AREAS

• **Salinas River State Beach** 🐾 🐾 🐾

With 246 acres of sand and steep dunes, this is our favorite beach of the three in the Moss Landing area. Because the beach is so large, the beachgoers are more spread out, so it rarely seems crowded. This beach is renowned for its excellent clamming and fishing.

There's easy access at the end of Portrero Road, off Highway 1. (408) 384-7695. ➡ *See #15 on map p. 546.*

PACIFIC GROVE

This quaint town on the rocky coast is a good place to get away from the crowds that can sometimes smother you and your dog during the peak tourist season in its neighboring city, Monterey. And if you like Monarch butterflies, this is your kind of town: It's known as "Butterfly City, USA" because of the millions of Monarch butterflies who winter here every year. Check out the annual Butterfly Parade in early October (see Diversions, page 562).

PARKS, BEACHES & RECREATION AREAS

• **Asilomar State Beach** 🐾 🐾 🐾

The beach here is great fun for leashed dogs. Not only do they get to romp on prime beach land, they can watch whales in the fall and winter, and see what real tidepooling is all about year-round.

Tucked in and around this rugged shoreline is a vast variety of marine critters representative of the Central Coast. I've seen dogs try to eat the contents of tidepools—a dining activity which should be strictly forbidden. And for your dog's safety, don't take him on slippery rocks or let him get too close to the surf. There are hazardous rip currents here.

Park along the shore on Sunset Drive, across from the infamous Asilomar Conference Grounds. For sandy beach, park along the south end of Sunset Drive. (408) 372-8016. →*See #16 on map p. 546.*

• **George Washington Park** 🐾 🐾 🐾 🐕

If you're dining at any of Pacific Grove's many outdoor eateries in the village center and your dog starts crossing his legs, have no fear, this park is near. And better yet, part of the park is devoted to off-leash dogs during certain times of the day.

Dogs may run leash-free from sunrise to 9 a.m. and from 4 p.m. to sunset. During winter, those hours can be a little restrictive, but it's better than nothing.

The segment of the park for leashless canines is bounded by Short Street, Melrose Avenue, Alder Street and Pine Avenue. Dogs are allowed on leash in the entire park at any time during the day. (408) 648-3100. →*See #17 on map p. 546.*

• **Lynn "Rip" Van Winkle Open Space** 🐾 🐾 🐾 🐾 🐕

This scrub oak haven near Pebble Beach is large enough so that even dogs who tend to wander out of sight aren't in much danger of wandering into the road. Dogs may be leashless from sunrise to 9 a.m. and 4 p.m. to sunset.

You'll find many a dog and many a dog person here during the off-leash hours. They tend to congregate near the park's entrance, but if your dog would prefer walking to talking, there are plenty of trails leading through the twisted scrub oaks and the small clear areas of the park.

The entrance can be hard to find. Follow the non-toll portion of Seventeen Mile Drive south and go left on Sunset Drive. Go right on Congress Avenue. Pass Forest Grove Elementary School on your left. Within a few hundred yards, on your right you'll see a dirt parking area. There's no sign, but this is the main entrance to the open space. (408) 648-3100. →*See #18 on map p. 546.*

PLACES TO STAY

Andril Fireplace Cottages: In these homey cottages, it's easy to get away from it all or to be on top of it all: All the separate cottages in this quiet area have cable TV, with VCRs for the asking. They also have wood-burning fireplaces, perfect for snuggling up with a human friend and a dog friend after a long day exploring the nearby beach. Rates are $64 to $100. 569 Asilomar Boulevard, Pacific Grove, CA 93950; (408) 375-0994.

Bide-A-Wee: This motor inn with lots of cottages from the 1930s is in a very quiet setting, very close to the spectacular Asilomar State Beach. While the inn is a very dog-friendly place, be forewarned: The owners also allow cats. Rates are $49 to $89. 221 Asilomar Boulevard, Pacific Grove, CA 93950; (408) 372-2330.

Butterfly Trees Lodge: You want cottages, a pool, Jacuzzi and tasty continental breakfasts? This is the place for you and your dog. Rates are $60 to $110. 1150 Lighthouse Avenue, Pacific Grove, CA 93950; (408) 372-0503.

Olympia Motor Lodge: You and your dog can sit on your private balcony and contemplate life while staring at the ocean. Rates are $50 to $90. 1140 Lighthouse Avenue, Pacific Grove, CA 93950; (408) 373-2777.

RESTAURANTS

Fandango: Dine on Mediterranean country-style cuisine at this romantic wood cottage with quiet tables on the front patio. Try the paella. 223 17th Street; (408) 372-3456.

Fishwife Seafood Restaurant at Asilomar Beach: Dogs like to grab a quick bowl of soup with their people at the bench outside. 1996 1/2 Sunset Drive; (408) 375-7107.

Lighthouse Cafe: The benches outside this quaint cafe are just begging for you and your dog to visit for breakfast or lunch here. 602 Lighthouse Avenue; (408) 372-7006.

Rocky Coast Ice Cream Company: 708 Lighthouse Avenue; (408) 373-0587.

FESTIVALS

Butterfly Parade: You and your leashed dog will be wowed by the sight of hundreds of Pacific Grove elementary school kids costumed as butterflies and colorful critters marching through downtown. The festival is in celebration of the annual migration of thousands of Monarchs to Pacific Grove, and is usually held the second Saturday of October. (408) 646-6520.

Feast of the Lanterns: Each July, on a Friday night before the dramatic "feast" (the story of a princess and her lover), local kids and their dogs march through Pacific Grove in a pet parade. It's an uplifting spectacle. If you're not from here, all your pooch can do is cheer from the sidelines. (408) 373-3304.

DIVERSIONS

Tie the knot, bring Spot: If, while saying your wedding vows at this tiny red chapel, you begin to feel someone's cold nose nuzzling your ankle, don't blame a fresh guest or an eager spouse. It's just your dog. Probably.

The Special Moments Wedding Chapel is a cute old place where your well-behaved dog is welcome to take part in the ceremonies. Owner Elena Young can set you up with a minister, a photographer, flowers, the appropriate licenses and the right music so you can get married as quickly as California law allows—and in some cases, that means lickety split. About the only thing Young doesn't provide is the dog food.

Young, a bridal consultant, can also arrange for your wedding to be outside at some secluded, enchanting location on the Monterey Peninsula, if your dog prefers that kind of setting. That will save you the $50 chapel fee, plus a possible security deposit in case your dog gets overly emotional on the chapel carpeting.

For more information, contact the chapel at 610 Laurel Avenue, Pacific Grove, CA 93950; (408) 624-5925.

Out, damned spot: At the Pacific Grove Wash-a-Pet, scrubbing your dog need not be a dramatic production. For $12 ($10 if you bring your own shampoo), your dog walks up some steps to a waist-level bathtub, and dirt and grime are history. You can blow dry him to look good enough for even the fanciest Monterey Peninsula event. The pet wash is in a convenient location for travelers with dirty dogs, just blocks from the beach. 167 Central Avenue; (408) 375-2477.

SALINAS

The "Salad Bowl of the World" is one of Joe's favorite places to visit on a Sunday drive. Most other city dogs we've talked to agree that it's a grand olfactory experience. When Joe smells the chicken manure spread across great fields of green, and sees horses readying for the rodeo, his nostrils shiver and his eyes bug out. Afterward, he's always exhausted.

PARKS, BEACHES & RECREATION AREAS

• Toro Regional Park 🐾 🐾 🐾

This is the only park in the Salinas area where you and your dog can really take a hike. More than 4,500 acres of wilderness awaits leashed dogs. About 12 miles of hiking and horse trails are etched into the rolling foothills of Mount Toro. As you climb, you'll occasionally be rewarded with shade from oak trees. In the summer it can be very hot, so be sure to bring extra water for you and your dog.

The views up high are spectacular. You can see both the Salinas Valley and the Monterey Bay, depending on where you hike. The park also features a self-guided nature trail adjacent to a gentle creek, as well as many picnic sites and play areas in the flat green valley near the parking lots.

From Salinas, follow Highway 68 west about five miles to the signs for the park. The park's entrance is just a few hundred yards from the highway. Fees are $2 per car Monday through Thursday and $4 Friday through Sunday. (408) 755-4899. ➜*See #19 on map p. 546.*

PLACES TO STAY

The lodgings that accommodate dogs here may not be fancy, but they're excellent places to relax and watch bad TV with your dog after a day of traveling.

Motel 6: There are two of these motels in Salinas where dogs are welcome. All Motel 6s allow one small pooch per room. Rates are $28 for the first adult, $6 for the second. One motel is at 1010 Fairview Avenue, Salinas, CA 93905; (408) 758-2122. The other is at 1257 De La Torre Boulevard, Salinas, CA 93905; (408) 757-3077.

Vagabond Inn: Close to US 101, this is where Joe and I once stayed and encountered at least five other dogs who were also guests. There's a $5 charge for dogs. Rates are $55 to $65. 131 Kern Street, Salinas, CA 93905; (408) 758-9835.

DIVERSIONS

Go to a movie: The Skyview Drive-In Theatre is one of the few drive-in theaters that dares to call itself a thea*tre*. It must be the tasty popcorn they serve here, because they sure don't show Ingmar Bergman flicks. Good, non-barking, non-howling dogs are welcome. The theater is open Friday, Saturday and Sunday nights. At North Sanborn Road and Garner Avenue. (408) 424-6510.

KINGS COUNTY

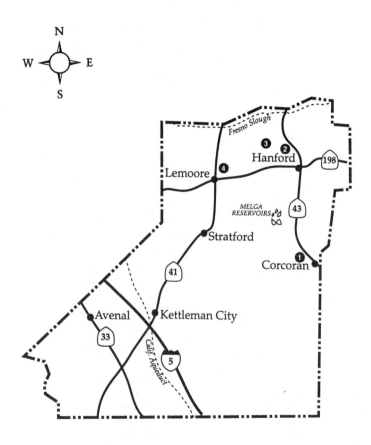

46
KINGS COUNTY

This is farm country, the kind of land that drives dogs crazy around the time the fertilizer's being spread. But despite all the open fields and rural surroundings, it's tough to find a place to take a dog for a good time. Dogs would love to roll in the cow patties, but between your objections, the farmers' objections and that killer look on Bessie's face, they quickly realize it's not the best idea in the world.

Ironically, the most appealing areas for dogs are in the small cities, especially Lemoore and historic Hanford. Off-leash parks are nonexistent, but pooches still manage to stretch their legs a little.

CORCORAN

You'll see plenty of dogs here, but they're usually in the backs of big pickup trucks parked at local bars and convenience stores. The dogs like to bark, especially at each other.

To want to drive all the way out here with your dog, you either have to be a Renaissance Faire fan (see below) or have a loved one at the maximum security Corcoran State Prison. Dogs aren't allowed to visit any of the prison's 5,500 inmates, so they'll be sorely disappointed if that's the only reason they came with you.

PARKS, BEACHES & RECREATION AREAS
• **Community Park** 🐾 🐾
This is exactly what it sounds like—a park for the community, featuring picnic tables, ball fields and children's playgrounds. It's the only game in town if your dog needs to relieve her bladder, and it can be quite crowded with local kids. The park is at Dairy and Patterson avenues. (209) 992-4514. ➡ *See #1 on map p. 566.*

FESTIVALS
Renaissance Faire: Of all the Renaissance Faires in California, this is the newest and it allows dogs. It's so new that as of this book's press time, many details weren't available, except that it will be held in Community Park, probably the second weekend of May, and the year will be 1559. (209) 992-4514.

HANFORD

Anyone looking for a set for *The Music Man*? You couldn't find a more perfect one than the turn-of-the-century town square in the middle of the old part of Hanford. It's got all the charm and permanence of River City, Iowa, and you won't have to put up with a freckle-faced kid with a bad lisp. The city has some of the grandest old buildings in California. Most of them are in or around Civic Center Park, where your leashed dog can enjoy green grass and big, stately trees (see below).

In July, a chunk of Hanford is transformed into the old English village of Hanfordshire, circa 1520, and the place comes alive for the Renaissance of Kings Cultural Arts Faire (see page 570).

Dogs also seem to enjoy walking down China Alley, the center of an area which in its heyday boasted one of the largest populations of Chinese immigrants in the United States. The Taoist Temple, built in 1893, still retains its position as the centerpiece of China Alley. It's now a theater, and dogs have to stay outside, but it's still amazing to see something like this in the middle of San Joaquin Valley.

If you stray out of the old core of town, you'll be transported to Wal-Mart world—not a pretty sight. A hefty chunk of Hanford is a fairly major suburban-style shopping area, complete with the biggest chains and fast food restaurants. Dogs highly recommend staying in the historic district, especially since their kind isn't always appreciated in department stores.

PARKS, BEACHES & RECREATION AREAS

• Civic Center Park 🐾🐾🐾 🐾

If you were to find yourself in the middle of a park with huge shade trees, flowers, an antique carousel, a fire engine from 1911 and a neoclassical courthouse building, in what year do you think you'd be? 1920? 1930? It's hard to believe, but this old charmer exists today.

It must be something about the clock on the front of the Civic Auditorium across the street. The impressive classical revival building's big clock actually works. The whole thing is reminiscent of *Back to the Future*—clock, columns and all. But the title of this ideal town square would have to be *Back to the Past*.

The place is very friendly to leashed dogs. The courthouse has been converted to quaint shops and offices. There's even a deli with outdoor tables (see page 569) where dogs can join you for an afternoon club sandwich. And if your dog is really lucky, she'll get to accompany you for a meal behind the courthouse at the Bastille, an enchanting building that was Hanford's original jailhouse (see page 569).

Exit Highway 198 at 11th Avenue, drive north a few blocks and go right on Seventh Street. The park is at Irwin and Seventh streets. (209) 585-2500. → *See #2 on map p. 566.*

• **Hidden Valley Park** 🐾 🐾 🐾

At first, this extremely well-manicured park with low rolling hills seems like a golf course. Everything is so beautifully landscaped that it's hard to believe people and dogs can play anything but 18 holes here. Willow trees abound, and there's even a pond and a gazebo for that old-time flavor this town cultivates.

Leashed dogs are welcome at this six-block-long park. Beware: The grass is so low that if you don't clean up after your dog, the stuff will stick out like a mountain. Exit Highway 198 at 11th Avenue and drive north about two miles. The park is on your left. For good parking lots, turn left at West Cortner Street. (209) 585-2500. → *See #3 on map p. 566.*

RESTAURANTS

The Bastille: Alfresco dining, entertainment on the patio, live blues and dishes like artichoke quiche—all outside a gigantic castle-like brick building. What more could a dog want? If you promise your dog won't sing with the entertainment and show proof of a pooper scooper, you'll be welcome. 113 South Court Street; (209) 583-9544.

Hot Dog Stand: Eat franks at beautiful old picnic tables at Civic Center Park, just outside the old courthouse. 300 North Irwin Street; (209) 582-6531.

Port of Subs: Munch good deli food outside with your pooch. 729 West Lacey Boulevard; (209) 582-7651.

PLACES TO STAY

Downtown Motel: This is the only dog-friendly hotel anywhere near Civic Center Park. Rates are $30 to $42. 101 North Redington Street, Hanford, CA 92320; (209) 582-9036.

FESTIVALS

Deck the streets with bow-wows of howling: Set around the old Courthouse Square district, the Hanford Christmas Parade is about as old fashioned a Christmas parade as they come. It's at night, so you can spend your day exploring Hanford. You can even get your Christmas shopping done without the kids on the afternoon of the parade because they'll be entertained by a special fun film at the historic Hanford Fox Theater. Admission price that day is two cans of food, which goes to the local Salvation Army. It's best if two adults go, so you can take turns shopping and keeping the dog company. The parade is held at the end of November, usually on the day after Thanksgiving. (209) 582-0483.

Revel with the villagers: The year is 1521, and there's a major party. You and your dog can join in the two-day Renaissance of Kings Cultural Arts Faire and celebrate something or other with knights, lords, ladies, maidens, village trash and Renaissance musicians. Dogs like the food the best. There's plenty of meat—rough and finger-licking good.

Once you start visiting every July, you'll come to know the characters, who evolve in soap opera-style from year to year. Dogs get the royal treatment here, often but not always being offered water by some servant-type. Bring ye olde doggy bowl and fill it up frequently, as dogs can get hot here. And be even more careful than you usually are about cleaning up after your dog. There was a big stink last year because someone didn't take care of their dog's mess. Another incident like that could jeopardize pooches' future visitation rights to the past. (209) 585-2527.

KETTLEMAN CITY

PLACES TO STAY

Best Western Olive Tree Inn: This is a convenient stop a half block east of Interstate 5. Rates are $56 to $62. There's a $40 deposit for dogs. 33415 Powers Drive, Kettleman City, CA 93239; (209) 386-9530.

LEMOORE

Besides the gigantic Harris Ranch (a must-smell for dogs), Lemoore is the first civilization you come to driving east on Highway 198 from Interstate 5. It's got a cute town center, lined with trees and antique stores.

PARKS, BEACHES & RECREATION AREA

Unfortunately, the large Heritage Park was still in the development stage as this book went to press, so we couldn't rate it. The park was scheduled to be ready for leashed dogs sometime in mid-1994. It's on the corner of Hanford-Armona Road and Avocado Drive. To find out the status of Heritage Park, phone (209) 924-6767.

• City Park 🐾🐾

This square-block park is usually green and grassy, which makes it ideal for dogs who like to roll. Willows and palms abound, so even in hot summer, you and your dog can survive. Kids like it here because of the special playground.

Take the Lemoore/Fresno exit (Highway 41) from Highway 198 and go north to West Bush Street. Go right on West Bush Street and drive for about 12 blocks. The park is on your left. (209) 924-6767.

➡ *See #4 on map p. 566.*

TULARE COUNTY

SNIFF!
SNIFF!

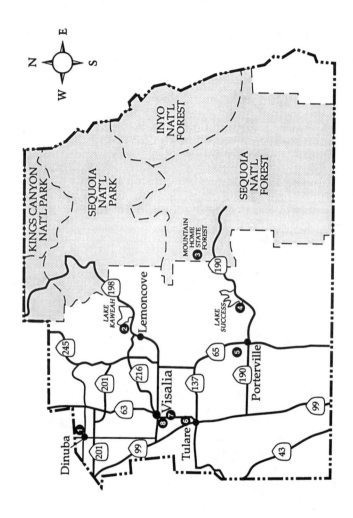

47
TULARE COUNTY

Don't worry if you don't find your thrills in the civilized parts of Tulare. About one-third of the county belongs to the U.S. Forest Service, the Bureau of Land Management and the California Department of Forestry. In dog-speak, that translates to "Look, ma, no leash!"

The BLM's dog-friendly Chimney Creek Recreation Area is split between Tulare County and its southern neighbor, Kern County. While Tulare County contains the best portion of the recreation area, it's more easily reached from Kern County. Please see page 607 in Kern County for a description.

NATIONAL FORESTS

See the National Forests/Wilderness Areas chapter starting on page 801 for important information and safety tips for visiting national forests with your dog.

• **Inyo National Forest** 🐾 🐾 🐾 🐾 🥾 🐕
See page 804.

• **Sequoia National Forest** 🐾 🐾 🐾 🐾 🥾 🐕
See page 808 for more information on this remarkable land of big trees.

NATIONAL PARKS

• **Sequoia and Kings Canyon National Parks** 🏛 🥾
If you were a chocoholic, your idea of hell would probably include being chained to the middle of a small island surrounded by a sea of unreachable, creamy Ghirardelli, Godiva and Guittard chocolates.

If you were an ice skater, purgatory might include being relegated to gravel driveways for the rest of your life, never being able to set a blade on the ice that's all around you.

And if you were a dog, your idea of hell would probably involve a visit to these two exquisite national parks. Sequoia National Park contains the thickest concentration (and the biggest individual specimens) of giant sequoia trees in the world. And while Kings Canyon doesn't have the huge trees, it's wild and untamed, just begging to be sniffed at by an inquisitive dog snout.

Dogs, however, must be cloistered in the car-camping areas and the little villages here, far from the trails and the madding trees. This is bad news. This makes boy dogs moan. This is hell.

Fees for sites where dogs can camp are $8 to $12. There are approximately 1,300 sites available on a first-come, first-served basis. The parks are connected, and stretch for almost 60 miles from north to south. Because of their sizes, we can't provide specific directions here. Call the parks at (209) 565-3134 for information on what areas might be best for you and your traveling dog. And if no one in your traveling party is going to be around to hang out with your dog while you explore the parks, leave him home with a friend. Too many dogs get stuck in cars here, and that can be dangerous as well as a crashing bore.

DINUBA

PARKS, BEACHES & RECREATION AREAS

• **Rose Ann Vuich Park** 🐾 🐾

Leashed dogs are welcome to stroll through this grassy, tree-filled park. It's in the middle of town, so if you've got business to attend to, you can take your dog here for some doggy business afterward.

The park is at East El Monte Way at McKinley Avenue. (209) 591-5921. → *See #1 on map p. 572.*

LEMONCOVE

PARKS, BEACHES & RECREATION AREAS

• **Lake Kaweah Recreation Area** 🐾 🐾 🐾

A few dirt trails will lead you and your favorite dog around various parts of the lake. These trails are not for the soft of paw, though. This is foothill country, and it can be rough going, with some trails taking you over rocks and through steep turns.

The lake itself is adequate for dipping your paws. Since dogs have to be leashed, they can't turn into fuzzy little Mark Spitzes here, but just a dip'll do them good.

Summer is the worst time to visit the lake. The fishing is cold and the temperatures are hot. Joe likes winter best. The farther he can get from scorching weather, the better.

Campsites are $6 per night, and you'll find a decent trail running right through the campground. There are 80 sites available on a first-come, first-served basis. The lake is on Highway 198, just north of Lemoncove. (209) 597-2301. → *See #2 on map p. 572.*

PLACES TO STAY
Lake Kaweah Recreation Area camping: See page 574.

MOUNTAIN HOME

PARKS, BEACHES & RECREATION AREAS

•**Mountain Home State Forest** 🐾 🐾 🐾 🐾 🔊 🏃

If you and your leash-free pooch want to see the seventh-largest tree in the world, you'd better make nice with the rangers here. The tree isn't on any maps and rangers prefer to point it out only to the folks they like.

If the ranger just doesn't dig you or your dog enough to let you check out that tree, don't worry. There are plenty of other trees to make up for your loss. The forest's 4,800 acres are filled with trails that take you past other giant sequoias in addition to ponderosa pines, sugar pines, cedars and firs.

Some of the rangers aren't keen on the forest's leash-free policy, and they recommend it only for the best-trained dogs. They say they've seen too many dogs get lost or chase down critters which would be best left alone. But chances are if you and your dog aren't used to elevations around 6,500 feet, neither of you will be in the mood to run far. In the words of one ranger: "People just suck for oxygen until they get accustomed to the air up here."

Campsites are free, but dogs must be leashed. Sites are available from June through October. From Highway 190 in Springville, drive north on Balch Park Drive for three miles and turn east on Bear Creek Road for 15 to 21 miles, depending on your destination within the forest. Mobile homes should take an alternate route, continuing up Balch Park Road for about 30 more miles to the park. Be sure to get a trail map and some ranger advice before venturing into the forest. (209) 539-2855. → *See #3 on map p. 572.*

PLACES TO STAY
Mountain Home State Forest camping: See above.

PORTERVILLE

PARKS, BEACHES & RECREATION AREAS

•**Lake Success Recreation Area** 🐾 🐾 🐾

The nature trails and wildlife areas around this waterski haven make life more than tolerable for dogs and their tranquility-seeking people. Dogs do best here in the non-summer months, when temperatures are cooler and loud boats are rarer. If you visit in the spring, you might have a shot at some good bass fishing.

When the water in the lake is down, there's even more land for hiking. It's pretty much open foothill land, but your dog won't complain if you make sure he doesn't get too warm.

Camping is available for fees ranging from free to $10 per site. From Porterville, drive eight miles east on Highway 190 to the lake. (209) 781-0215. → *See #4 on map p. 572.*

• **Veterans Park** 🐾 🐾 🐾

This L-shaped park has a nature trail that leashed dogs are welcome to sniff out. It runs the length of the park, so you get to hike a total of almost two miles in one direction. You'll walk by cottonwoods and huge oaks. If you get tired, you can relax at the picnic tables or under the shade trees here.

The really interesting part of this park is the big HU1B dust-off helicopter that's mounted about 20 feet up in the air on the park's north side. It's in a landing position, and it's meant to symbolize the end of the Vietnam War.

This town was hard-hit by the war. A local veteran told me that the Porterville area is home to the highest number of men per capita killed in Vietnam. In addition to the chopper, the memorial is encircled by several young redwood trees—one per local hero killed in the war. This end of the park is at Henderson Avenue and Newcomb Street. (209) 782-7536. → *See #5 on map p. 572.*

PLACES TO STAY
Lake Success Recreation Area camping: See page 575.

TULARE

PARKS, BEACHES & RECREATION AREAS
• **Live Oak Park** 🐾 🐾 1/2

If you happen to be passing through town and stopping at the carry-out Foster Freeze down the street, be sure to visit this green park with your leashed canine companion (and your ice cream cones).

After that ice cream cone, you and your dog may want to take a siesta under a shade tree. Then, when your snacks are digested, try out the fitness course here. It's not gruelling, so it's a pleasant way to work off those free-floating fat calories.

The park is close to Highway 99. Take the Tulare Avenue exit east a few blocks and turn left on Laspina Street. In a few more blocks, you'll be at the park. It's right beside the Live Oak Middle School. (209) 685-2380. → *See #6 on map p. 572.*

VISALIA

PARKS, BEACHES & RECREATION AREAS

• **Blaine Park** 🐾 🐾 1/2

This is a very attractive park in a lovely neighborhood. There are enough trees, ball fields and picnic tables for even the most suburban of dogs.

The park is on the west side of South Court Street, just a few blocks north of Caldwell Avenue. (209) 738-3365. ➡ *See #7 on map p. 572.*

• **Plaza Park** 🐾 🐾 1/2

If you and your dog are staying at the Holiday Inn across the street, you couldn't ask for a more conveniently located park. Although the park is full of activities for humans, there's lots of room for leashed dogs to hike on the trail, relax under a big shade tree or watch kids fish in the little pond.

The crowd here can swell on weekends and during softball and baseball games, but it's generally less packed than the city's other large park. It's located west of town, at Highway 198 and Road 80, just east of Highway 99. (209) 738-3365. ➡ *See #8 on map p. 572.*

RESTAURANTS

Le Croissant de France: Poodles adore this restaurant, but any breed is welcome to join you at the outdoor tables for some savory French cuisine. If someone in your crew likes burgers, they're available, too. 120 West Main Street; (209) 739-0708.

Java Jungle: They've had dogs "act like apes" here, say the managers. But as long as your pooch behaves with the decorum befitting a high-class canine, she's welcome. Eat bagel sandwiches and pie, and sip coffee on the lovely tiled patio. 208 West Main Street; (209) 732-5282.

PLACES TO STAY

Best Western Visalia Inn Motel: Rates are $53 to $62. Small pooches only, please. 623 West Main Street, Visalia, CA 93291; (209) 732-4561.

Holiday Inn Plaza Park: Rates are $66 to $89. 9000 West Airport Drive, Visalia, CA 93277; (209) 651-5000 or (800) 821-1127.

SAN LUIS OBISPO COUNTY

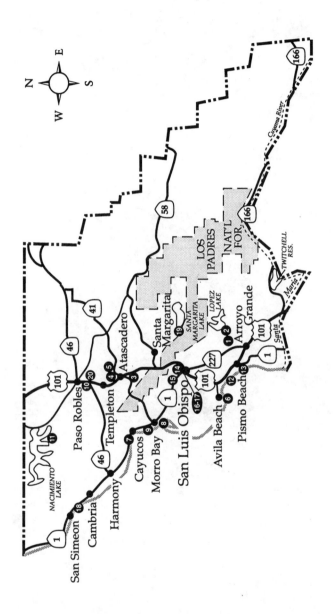

48
SAN LUIS OBISPO COUNTY

Home of Hearst Castle, spectacular beaches, quaint seaside hamlets and the mighty Pismo clam, this county is one of the state's most popular getaways. Dogs appreciate the olfactory beauty—the fishy piers, the farm-fresh soil, the suntan lotion—as much as their drivers enjoy the scenery and history.

Dog activities are numerous. Your dog can dine with you at countless restaurants with outdoor tables. She can trot alongside you at most of the county's beaches. She can camp with you, fish with you and tour wineries with you. She can even be the flower dog if you get married in a chapel in a teeny town appropriately named Harmony (see page 586).

Two of the county's most popular attractions don't allow dogs. Hearst Castle unfortunately doesn't offer a tour of the grounds from the outside, so your dog can't go anywhere near this architectural wonder (see the section on Cambria, page 585, for help with this problem). And dogs are banned from the city of San Luis Obispo's spectacular Thursday night farmers market. This is one giant street party with some of the best food and freshest produce available in these parts. If you do go without your dog, don't try to appease her with fresh flowers from the farmers market. Bring her part of your leftover burger from one of the barbecue grills here and she just might let you back in the house again.

NATIONAL FORESTS

See the National Forests/Wilderness Areas chapter starting on page 801 for important information and safety tips for visiting national forests with your dog.

• **Los Padres National Forest**

Both the Santa Lucia Wilderness and the Manchesna Mountain Wilderness, east of the city of San Luis Obispo, are ideal for dogs who like their wilderness spelled with a capital W. See page 806.

ARROYO GRANDE

PARKS, BEACHES & RECREATION AREAS

• **Biddle Regional Park** 1/2

Cows graze in the pastures adjacent to this secluded county park. That's all you have to tell your dog to get her excited about visiting this park. To avoid the crowds who can occasionally descend here (and to avoid the weekend entry fee), the best time to visit is on weekdays. Between the draw of the softball fields, the group picnic areas and the shaded creek, this quiet park can be too popular for your leashed dog to feel comfortable just being a dog.

The entrance fee is $1 per car and $1.50 per dog on Saturdays, Sundays and holidays and is charged only in summer. Exit US 101 at Grand Avenue and travel northeast, following the signs to Lopez Lake. You'll find Biddle Regional Park on the right a couple of miles before the lake. (805) 781-5930. ➡ *See #1 on map p. 580.*

• **Lopez Lake Recreation Area** 🐾 🐾
The rules at this county-run park are just like those at state parks: Dogs are not allowed anywhere but at campsites and paved areas. It's a restrictive, frustrating place for dogs. All the trailheads are marked by something that looks like a horse with a slash through it. Rangers swear it's a dog, though a big one. But if you sneak your dog onto a trail and get caught, don't try the old "I thought it meant 'No Great Danes'" excuse. They've heard it before and it didn't work then either.

The 940-acre lake is off-limits to dogs, unless they fish in your boat with you. In fact, most of the 4,200-acre park bans dogs. Plenty of dogs do camp here though, at any of the 359 sites set in oak woodlands. Reservations are recommended. Leashes are mandatory, and dogs are supposed to sleep in your tent or camper at night. There's a resident bear here and plenty of deer.

The entrance fee is $4 per car, $1.50 per dog. Campsites are $12. As always, be prepared with proof of your dog's rabies vaccination. Exit US 101 at Grand Avenue and travel northeast, following the signs to Lopez Lake. (805) 489-2095. ➡ *See #2 on map p. 580.*

RESTAURANTS
Burnardo'z Candy Kitchen & Ice Cream Parlor: 114 West Branch Street; (805) 481-2041.

Vic's Hamburger Haven: You don't have to eat beef to eat here. They've got veggie burgers that even dogs seem to enjoy. 803 Grand Avenue; (805) 473-1727.

PLACES TO STAY
Best Western Casa Grande Inn: Rates are $50 to $90. Dogs are $10 extra, which is worth it because there's a grassy area with a little creek in the back. 850 Oak Park Road, Arroyo Grande, CA 93420; (805) 481-7398.

Econo Lodge: Rates are $42 to $60. 611 El Camino Real, Arroyo Grande, CA 93420; (805) 489-9300.

Lopez Lake Recreation Area camping: See page 582.

ATASCADERO

PARKS, BEACHES & RECREATION AREAS

• **Atascadero Lake Park** 🐾 🐾 1/2

Great blue herons, ducks of every shape, bluebirds and even red-tailed hawks are just a few of the birds you may see during a visit to this large city park. Dogs have to be on leash to explore the lake and surrounding lawns and picnic areas, but they seem to enjoy themselves despite the constraints.

This is *the* place to take your dog in Atascadero. While they aren't allowed to swim or rent a paddleboat, they revel in life's simple pleasures, like sniffing each other end to end.

The Charles Paddock Zoo is next door. Instead of those typical zoo odors, this place smells like fresh jasmine when you walk by. It's good if you're trying to fool your dog into thinking you just dropped off the kids at some botanical garden and not at the home of wild and smelly animals.

From US 101, take Santa Rosa Road west for three long blocks. The park is on your right, between Mountain View Drive and Morro Road. For the best parking, turn right on Morro Road and make another right into the park. (805) 461-5001. → *See #3 on map p. 580.*

• **Sunken Gardens Park** 🐾 🐾 1/2

Pat St. Clair of the Atascadero Chamber of Commerce is proud of how friendly her city is to animals. In fact, she says, this lush strip of green with fountains and statues in front of the grand old city administration building is where some of the strangest looking creatures go for walks.

One day she saw a pig wandering around, who she assumed was an escapee from a nearby farm. "It's a beautiful park. I thought he had good taste," she says. But on inquiring, it turned out that the pig was someone's pet. He was off his leash and having a grand old time rooting around. Since then, the pig has become a regular, scaring dogs away, or at least making them freeze in their tracks with curiosity. Dogs, unlike Mr. Piggy, are supposed to be leashed.

From US 101, exit at Traffic Way and go northeast for a block. Turn right on El Camino Real. The park will be on your left in four blocks, at West Mall Street. (805) 461-5001. → *See #4 on map p. 580.*

• **Traffic Way Park** 🐾 🐾

The only reason to come to this park is if you have to play softball or walk the dog. The park is made up of two ball fields.

Since each is very well fenced, even at the entrances, dogs who tend to run away are safe here. Of course, they're supposed to be leashed anyway, but dogs can do the darndest things if a cat beckons from down the street.

Exit US 101 at Traffic Way and drive northeast for about six blocks. The park is on your right. (805) 461-5001. ➡See #5 on map p. 580.

RESTAURANTS

Atascadero Donuts Plus: 8790 Morro Road; (805) 466-8636.

Felicia's Deli By the Lake: This great soup and sandwich eatery is right on the lake, in Atascadero Lake Park (see page 583). Try the fresh, hot cinnamon rolls. 9315 Pismo Avenue; (805) 466-0783.

Yogurt Shack: They've got hot dogs, chili dogs and even corn dogs here, so your dog, whatever her breed, should feel right at home. There's even yogurt. The Yogurt Shack is located just across from Sunken Gardens Park (see page 583). 6450 El Camino Real; (805) 466-2063.

PLACES TO STAY

Motel 6: Rates are $25 for one adult, $6 for the second adult. All Motel 6s allow one small pooch per room. 9400 El Camino Real, Atascadero, CA 93422; (805) 466-6701.

AVILA BEACH

This small coastal community is about the farthest north you'll find the Southern California beach lifestyle. And if you hear three siren blasts, prepare to have the beaches to yourself—the Diablo Canyon Nuclear Plant, which sits on a fault six miles north of town, just may have had a little boo-boo.

PARKS, BEACHES & RECREATION AREAS

Dogs are allowed on leash at Avila State Beach, which you'll see just as you enter town. It's okay for dogs, but it's far more crowded than the Olde Port Beach. What's more, Olde Port Beach has a mighty dog-friendly attitude (see below).

•**Olde Port Beach** 🐾 🐾 🐾 🐾 ➤🐕

Shhh. Don't tell anyone about this beach! It's the only off-leash beach in this part of California! It's not exactly colossal, but it's more than adequate for your dog to run around and enjoy himself without crashing into beachcombers or sunbathers.

The beach, run by the Port San Luis Harbor District, is particularly picturesque, looking out on fishing boats moored offshore. The occasional jet-skier can mar the tranquility here, but nothing gets in the way of a good time when your dog is freed from his shackles.

From Highway 1/US 101, take the Avila Beach exit west. Once in town, continue west, on Harford Drive. The beach is on your left. If you reach the Port San Luis Pier (not the modern, very long Union Oil pier you'll come to first, but the woody old one in the harbor), you've gone too far. It's not so bad, though. You can either turn right around and find the beach, or hang out at the pier and harbor area for a while. Dogs are fond of those fishy breezes and you'll enjoy looking at the old boats. (805) 595-2381. ➡ *See #6 on map p. 580.*

CAMBRIA

This charming village can be a fun stroll for you and your dog, but it serves a more important purpose: It's the home of the Tail Wag's Inn, a quality kennel where you can board your dog for part of a day while you visit Hearst Castle about nine miles north in San Simeon.

The owners of this kennel heard of too many dogs who had been left unattended in sweltering cars as their caretakers sauntered around the magnificent castle for hours. So they created a relatively inexpensive, yet absolutely luxurious package to encourage people not to risk the lives of their dogs. For $10, your dog gets at least two good walks and drinks Crystal Springs bottled water. Hey, what the heck, if you're spending the day among opulence, why shouldn't your pup?

Dogs can arrive as early as 7 a.m. and leave as late as 5 p.m. The kennel is at the Village Service Center, 2419-A Village Lane. Call (805) 927-1589 for more information.

Unfortunately, despite all the human hotels and inns in Cambria, we couldn't find any that allow dogs. The same goes for restaurants.

CAYUCOS

A funkier coastal community would be hard to find. Cayucos, about eight miles north of Morro Bay, provides a great escape from summer crowds. Even on holiday weekends, the place doesn't get packed. The Old West stores and saloons are a real find, but if you'd rather fish than shop and drink, try the old pier on Cayucos State Beach. It was built in 1875, and those in charge figure a few dogs aren't going to hurt it now. Besides, the fishing is great, and what dog wouldn't enjoy watching you reel in a mackerel or a salmon?

PARKS, BEACHES & RECREATION AREAS

• **Cayucos State Beach** 🐾 🐾 🐾 1/2

The beach is wide and wonderful. Dogs have to be leashed, but they still enjoy a long walk here. Since there are a couple of good greasy-spoon take-out joints nearby, we like to order lunch and bring it to the beach, where dogs pray hard that you'll drop a french fry in the sand.

The south end of the beach has fewer people and more seaweed—the stuff of fine dog outings. From Highway 1, go southwest on Cayucos Drive and turn left at Ocean Drive. You can enter almost anywhere between Cayucos Road and E Street, west of Ocean Drive. (805) 549-3312. ➡ *See #7 on map p. 580.*

HARMONY

"Living in Harmony" was a classic episode of Patrick McGoohan's science fiction TV series, *The Prisoner*. But here in this two-acre dairy town-turned-artist's colony several miles south of Cambria, all 18 residents live in Harmony and there's nothing odd about it. They thrive on being off the beaten track. And there's good news for dogs: People in these parts are as dog-friendly as they come. If your dog is of the well-behaved ilk, she might be invited into some of the businesses here. Be aware that this is an equal-opportunity town and felines frequent just about every nook.

RESTAURANTS

Harmony Pasta Factory: They make their own pasta here, and boy is it delicious. The patio features umbrella-covered tables, heat lamps and cats. This is something your dog should know, because if he can't keep harmony with the kitties here, he won't be a welcome guest. 2 Old Creamery Road; (805) 927-5882.

DIVERSIONS

Get me to the church on leash: Folks around here say that if you wed in the town of Harmony, your lives together will be blessed with harmony. Fortunately, your dog can be part of the ceremony at the Harmony Wedding Chapel, so you should never again have a problem with him barking or chasing the cat, if all this harmony stuff is true.

This unique chapel was built as a cold storage facility in 1914. The door is the bottom of a huge wine cask. The walls are two feet thick. Inside, the pews are oak, the floors are pine and the walls are whitewashed. With all this and stained glass windows, the chapel seems like a shrunk-down mission. There's not a hint of froufrou anywhere, unless your dog decides to wear a ruffled shirt under his tuxedo.

Weddings, including the minister's fee, run between $175 and $275. For more information, write the Reverend Denise Mikkelson, P.O. Box 1523, Morro Bay, CA 93443. There is no street address, but you'll find the chapel in the northeast corner of Harmony, behind a restaurant. (805) 995-3178.

MORRO BAY

The landmark Morro Rock draws more visitors to this seaside community than its beaches and quaint stores. This 576-foot-tall, 50-acre-wide extinct volcano peak juts into the Pacific and beckons anyone who gets a glimpse. In fact, in 1512 it attracted explorer Juan Rodriguez Cabrillo, who named the rock which has become a landmark for ocean navigators and tourists.

Dogs have a number of reactions to this unusual formation. Most ignore it. Some give it only a sideways glance. But others stare at it, sniffing the air in fascination. Maybe they smell the scents of the eons. Or maybe they're just contemplating what a challenge it would be to leave their own unique mark on such a gigantic chunk of rock.

PARKS, BEACHES & RECREATION AREAS

• **Coleman City Park** 🐾 🐾 1/2

This is the park to visit if you forgot your sunscreen. At the right time of day, the shadow of Morro Rock will loom over you and protect you from those wrinkling rays.

Walking through the dunes here while under the spell of the volcanic mound can be a hypnotic experience. Don't let the otherworldly quality of it all make you forget that your dog is supposed to be leashed.

The park is to the north of Morro Rock. For easy access to both Coleman City Park and the southern portion of Morro Strand State Beach, park in the Morro Rock lot, after Embarcadero turns into Coleman Drive. There's another lot for the park on the north side of Coleman Drive just before the rock. (805) 772-6200. ➡ *See #8 on map p. 580.*

• **Morro Strand State Beach** 🐾 🐾 🐾 1/2

This three-mile beach doesn't get heavy use, so it's a good place to take your leashed dog in this popular tourist haven. Dunes aren't abundant, but there are enough to keep your walks interesting.

The beach is an especially appealing stop for Highway 1 travelers because it comes complete with a 104-site campground. The campground is nothing fancy or rustic. It's actually a converted day-use parking lot. But it's right over the beach, so if sounds of crashing surf send you to sleep, you'll get your eight hours here.

Camping costs $14 to $16. Dogs are $1 extra. There's no day-use fee. The beach is west of Highway 1 between Atascadero Road and Yerba Buena Avenue. For camping reservations, call MISTIX at (800) 444-PARK. For beach information, phone (805) 772-8812. →*See #9 on map p. 580.*

RESTAURANTS
Dorn's Original Breakers Cafe: The specials here include clam chowder, fresh seafood and New York steaks. Many of the tables are shaded by umbrellas. 801 Market Avenue; (805) 772-4415.

The Gourmet Chalet: The beautiful outdoor area is surrounded by etched glass windows. Enjoy coffee, tea and sweet little things here with your pooch. 500 Embarcadero; (805) 772-2739.

PLACES TO STAY
Best Western El Rancho: Rates are $50 to $90. Dogs must be under 25 pounds, and are $4 extra—"to cover the bug bomb," the manger told us. 2460 Main Street, Morro Bay, CA 93442; (805) 772-2212.

Gold Coast: Small or medium-sized dogs only, please. Rates are $30 to $85. Dogs are $5 extra. 670 Main Street, Morro Bay, CA 93442; (805) 772-7740.

Morro Bay State Park camping: This verdant state park overlooking Morro Bay has 115 campsites set in pine woodlands. Dogs are banned from the park's trails and from every other natural wonder. Campsites and paved roads are their only stomping grounds. Sites are $14 to $16. Dogs are $1 extra. Take Highway 1 to the south end of Morro Bay and follow the signs to the park. This campground gets crowded, so call MISTIX at (800) 444-PARK for reservations. Phone (805) 925-9583 for park information.

Morro Strand State Beach camping: See above.

Motel 6: Rates are $34 for one adult, $6 for the second adult. All Motel 6s allow one small pooch per room. 298 Atascadero Road, Morro Bay, CA 93442; (805) 772-5641.

DIVERSIONS
Knight to King-Dog 3: Did you ever wonder what it would be like to play chess with your dog? Ponder no more. At the giant chessboard just a block from the bay, you, your friends and even your dog can play chess—literally. You can be king, if you want. Your stepmother can be a pawn. Your dog can occasionally sub for people getting tired of standing around acting like a bunch of

bishops. One man, a local named Bob, told me his dog plays queen, so she gets a lot of action and doesn't become bored. He gives her a treat every time she captures a piece or checks the king. But Queen Janey, his cocker spaniel, is not brilliant enough to figure out the moves for herself, so Bob guides her along.

Fill in the empty squares, or all the squares for that matter, with the giant pieces you can borrow from the city. If you bring your dog along for a short game, make sure it's cool enough and she moves around as much as Queen Janey. To reserve the giant chess pieces, call (805) 772-6275.

Don't you hurry in that furry surrey: Dogs seem to be highly entertained watching their caretakers push the pedals in these fringed surreys/bikes. Dogs can afford to be entertained, since all they have to do is sit down in the front basket and watch. They don't have to lift a paw. Just bring them a blanket to cushion the hard basket and make sure they're secured so they can't zip out after a passing kitty.

Small dogs are most comfortable. Large dogs just don't fit. "Any dog is better than a lot of the teenage boys we get here," a surrey rental agent told me as he watched a surrey full of teens swerve down the road. Surrey rental fees range from $10 an hour for the small ones to $18 an hour for the large sizes. The Morro Bay Surrey Company is located at 850 Embarcadero. There is no phone.

PASO ROBLES

PARKS, BEACHES & RECREATION AREAS

Dogs are not allowed at the charming City Park in the middle of the old part of Paso Robles.

•Pioneer Park 🐾 1/2

This is a decent neighborhood park, with enough grass, trees and dirt to satisfy any leashed dog in need of some exercise. For human entertainment, there's a playground, a ball field and a tiny historical museum.

From US 101, exit at Highway 46 and go west at the off-ramp. In two blocks, turn left at Riverside Avenue. The park is on your left, just past the fairgrounds. (805) 237-3875. → *See #10 on map p. 580.*

•Lake Nacimiento 🐾 🐾 1/2

While this oak-lined lake has 165 miles of shoreline, only the portion run by Lake Nacimiento Resort is open to the public. And with the resort's limited dog areas, that means just a so-so vacation for canines. Dogs are allowed on leash in the meadows and picnic areas here. They're also allowed to camp with you at any of the resort's 350 sites. But unless your dog enjoys helping you fish for white bass and smallmouth bass from your boat, a visit here probably won't be the highlight of her year.

Campsites are $20 a night. From US 101, exit at Highway 46 and go west at the off-ramp. Follow this road, known for most of its span as Nacimiento Lake Road, for eight miles. When you get to County Road G-14, make a hard right and drive another eight miles. The resort is on the left. (805) 238-3256. ➡ *See #11 on map p. 580.*

RESTAURANTS

Bakery Works Cafe: Enjoy three meals a day under the shade of an umbrella-topped table. Spring Street at 17th Street; (805) 239-1070.

DK's Donuts: 1740 Spring Street; (805) 238-9371.

Good Ol' Burgers: Dogs and their people have to sit at the farthest possible rugged wood tables, but that's okay. You can smell the charbroiled beef from hundreds of yards away. 1145 24th Street; (805) 238-0655.

Skinny Dippers Frozen Yogurt & Fruit Shakes: Dog heaven! Everyone here seems to love dogs. So everyone with a dog comes here. You can often see 4-H'ers hanging out at the benches with their pooches. The manager here trains dogs. And the place is close to a park that allows dogs. 1131 Creston Road; (805) 238-3477.

PLACES TO STAY

Lake Nacimiento Resort camping: See above.

Paso Robles Travelodge: Rates are $40 to $80. Dogs are $4 extra. 2701 Spring Street, Paso Robles, CA 93466; (805) 238-0078.

DIVERSIONS

A loaf of bread, a glass of wine, and thee dog: When you think of Wine Country, Paso Robles may not be the first place that comes to mind. But there are some fine wineries east of town, and a few allow your dog to hang out with you at their serene picnic areas while you sip your newly bought wine. Eberle Winery and Meridian Vineyards, both east of town on Highway 46, welcome dogs in their picnic areas. Eberle has the added advantage of a water spigot handy dandy for your dog. Call Eberle at (805) 238-9607. Meridian's number is (805) 237-6000. Just down the road a bit, in Templeton, you'll find the beautiful Mastantuono Winery, complete with gazebos and horseshoe pits in its dog-friendly picnic area. (805) 238-0676.

PISMO BEACH

The Chumash Indians, who lived here for at least 9,000 years, referred to this area as the place to find *pismu*, or tar. History has changed this once-pristine land to a busy seaside community, but your dog might show you that there's one thing that hasn't changed: This is still the place to find tar. Joe found it all over his paws when he was exploring one of the beaches. Later, despite cleaning his feet, I found it all over the inside of the truck. Even the dry cleaner found it—he found it amusing that the jacket I'd left inside the truck was covered with indelible paw prints.

This never happened again, and it has never happened to any other dogs we talked to on the beaches, so fear not. Pismo Beach is a good place for you and your dog to share some quality time. Most of the beaches here allow leashed dogs, who can be champion partners in clamming for the famous Pismo clams. They don't need a fishing license, but you will.

Pismo Beach is usually cool and foggy. It's ideal if you have a dog who melts in the heat. When we drive to Southern California, this is a must-stop area for Joe. Although there are no leash-free areas, he always appreciates land that is naturally air conditioned.

PARKS, BEACHES & RECREATION AREAS

City parks here don't allow dogs. The 1,250-foot pier in the middle of the beach area also bans them. But there are a couple of beaches that more than make up for these places.

•**Pismo Beach City Beach** 🐾 🐾 🐾

Does your dog like watching people in bathing suits play volleyball? Does she enjoy sniffing at bodies slathered with coconut oil? If so, this beach is for her. It's rarely so crowded that it's uncomfortable, but it's rarely so uncrowded that it's a bore for a social butterfly dog.

The farther north you walk, the fewer people you'll encounter. Dogs have to be leashed everywhere, though. But this shouldn't stop the digging breeds from helping you uncover prize Pismo clams (fishing licenses are required for the human half of the team). We once saw a dog who would thrust his entire snout into the wet sand and come up with a clam every time. His owner didn't even have to use his clam fork.

One of the many access points is west of Highway 1, at the foot of Main Avenue, near the recreation pier. (805) 773-4658. ➔ *See #12 on map p. 580.*

•**Pismo Dunes/Pismo State Beach** 🐾 🐾 🐾 1/2

It's hard to tell what dogs enjoy more here—exploring the long, wide beach or wandering through the great dunes above. Your leashed dog can get all the exercise he needs by trotting down the miles of trails on the unspoiled dunes. If he likes cold ocean spray, take him down to the beach for a romp among the gulls.

Camping is available at a couple of sections of the beach. Fees are $6 for the on-beach camping area south of the Grand Avenue entrance (four-wheel-drive vehicles are recommended), and $16 for camping among the trees at the Pismo State Beach North Beach Campground. There a 225 campsites here. Dogs are $1 extra at both. Call MISTIX for reservations at (800) 444-7275.

To avoid the $6 day-use fee at the Grand Avenue entrance, drive west from Highway 1 and park on Grand Avenue before the ranger kiosk. Once at the beach, head north. Walking south will put you in the middle of a busy off-highway vehicle recreation area—not the best place for a dog. (805) 473-7230. ➡ *See #13 on map p. 580.*

RESTAURANTS
Eclair Bakery & Delicatessen: 221 Pomeroy Avenue; (805) 773-4145.

Old West Cinnamon Rolls: 861 Dolliver Street; (805) 773-1428.

Pierside Shack: Dogs like the extremely casual ambience here. They also like the nachos. 100 Pier Avenue; (805) 773-1953.

The Scoop Ice Cream Parlor: 607 Dolliver Street; (805) 773-4253.

The Splash Cafe: They adore dogs here. While you eat your fish and chips, clam chowder and shrimp at the outdoor benches, your dog will get his own water bowl. 197 Pomeroy Avenue; (805) 773-4653.

PLACES TO STAY
Motel 6: Rates are $30 for one adult and $4 for the second adult. All Motel 6s allow one small pooch per room. 860 4th Street, Pismo Beach, CA 93449; (805) 773-2665.

Quality Suites: No huge dogs, please. Rates are $79 to $128. Dogs are $6 extra. 651 Five Cities Drive, Pismo Beach, CA 93449. (805) 773-3773.

Sandcastle Inn: This one's on the beach. Even dogs enjoy an ocean view. Rates are $75 to $225. Dogs are $10 extra. 100 Stimson Avenue, Pismo Beach, CA 93499; (805) 773-2422.

Sea View: They're picky about the pets they'll allow here, but give it a try. Rates are $29 to $49. Dogs are $6 for every three nights. 230 Five Cities Drive, Pismo Beach, CA 93499. (805) 773-1841.

Spyglass Inn: This is a great place for the family, from the breakfast to the pool to the miniature golf course. Many of the rooms here have an ocean view. The managers don't like gigantic dogs as guests, but they're pretty generous about the size of the pooches they'll accept. Rates are $75 to $125. Dogs are $10 extra. 270 Spyglass Drive, Pismo Beach, CA 93449; (805) 773-4855.

Travelodge: Rates are $34 to $75. They advertise that they allow only small dogs here, but "no elephants" is actually the rule of the house, the manager told us. Dogs are $4 extra. 2701 Spring Street, Paso Robles, CA 93446; (805) 238-0078.

SAN LUIS OBISPO

This city is the big jewel of the Central Coast. Some of the smaller gems like Pismo Beach and Morro Bay can be more lustrous for dogs, but there's so much history here, and so much to do, that you're both bound to enjoy your visit.

If the past interests you at all, be sure to stop at the Chamber of Commerce and pick up a Heritage Walks pamphlet showing the fascinating buildings where much of California's history was shaped. Dogs may yawn as they trot by some of the ice-cream-colored Victorians and whitewashed adobes, but when they arrive at Mission Plaza, the good times roll.

The Plaza is the heart of the city and the home of Mission San Luis Obispo de Tolosa, built in 1772. Dogs aren't allowed inside, but it's the world outside that will interest them more anyway: That's where the beautiful Mission Plaza tantalizes with scents and sounds dogs love. A brick path follows a cool stream nestled in conifers full of songbirds. The path takes you by a few delicious-smelling restaurants with tables on the wood patios overlooking the stream (see the restaurant section starting on page 593 for descriptions).

But beware: The reason dogs like it here so much isn't necessarily for the food or ambience. They're wild about all the four-legged creatures who slink around here meowing for handouts of food and attention. If you have a cat-crazed canine, either avoid this area or keep a very tight hold of her leash.

PARKS, BEACHES & RECREATION AREAS
•Cuesta Canyon County Park 🐾 🐾 1/2

This park would be a peaceful place to visit, if not for the constant barking of dogs at the adjacent veterinary hospital and the non-stop drone of nearby US 101. Even with these distractions, the atmosphere isn't bad. Between the cool creek, the singing birds and the large trees, Cuesta Canyon County Park is a decent place to take a dog in need of a short romp. The playing field area in the back of the park is almost completely fenced and well-protected from the freeway.

The park is conveniently located near California Polytechnic State University. Exit US 101 at Grand Street and go east immediately onto Loomis Street. Follow Loomis Street as it runs parallel to US 101. The road ends in the park's parking lot. (805) 781-3000. →*See #14 on map p. 580.*

• **El Chorro Regional Park** 🐾 🐾 🐾 1/2

For some reason, very few people visit this 1,730-acre park, except on holidays and some summer weekends. You'll rarely find others on the four miles of trail here, but you may well run into deer, so keep your dog leashed.

It's not even that common to see people using the many group picnic areas. There are 24 developed campsites and an overflow area that accommodates an additional 12 sites. The best part about all this solitude is that even when all the other campgrounds in the area are full, you may still be able to find a spot at the park's 25 primitive sites. Hardly anyone knows they exist, contact park rangers for their locations.

Entry fees are $1 per car and $1.50 per dog, and are charged only on weekends and holidays. Campsites are $12. Exit US 101 at Santa Rosa Street/Highway 1 and drive northeast about seven miles. The park is on the right. (805) 781-5219. →*See #15 on map p. 580.*

• **Laguna Lake Park** 🐾 🐾 🐾 1/2

Early morning is the best time to visit this beautiful, large city park shaded by willows, pines and eucalyptuses. That's when it's most peaceful and coolest. The moist morning air and the smell of pine and clean earth, fresh lake water intermingle and make for a relaxing outing for you and your fine furry friend.

During days when the park is a little crowded (it rarely gets this way), there are still plenty of spots for you and your dog to escape from the masses. If you follow the Fitness Trail around, and bear right after Fitness Stop Number 8, you'll come to secluded fields abutting a marshy part of the lake. If you're not doing the Fitness Trail, you'll find this quiet area by walking to the other side of the long line of eucalyptus trees past the gazebo.

From US 101, take the Los Osos Valley Road exit northwest for several blocks and turn right on Madonna Road. In a few blocks, go left on Dalido Drive and park at any of the several lots in the park. (805) 781-3000. →*See #16 on map p. 580.*

• **Santa Rosa Park** 🐾 1/2

With its playgrounds, ball fields and basketball courts, this park is great for kids. But dogs are relegated to the section in the back of the park, where tall trees and a little grass make a so-so rest area.

From US 101, go north on Santa Rosa Street/Highway 1. For the part of the park dogs can visit, turn right at Montalban Street in about three blocks. The entrance is on your left. (805) 781-7300.
→See #17 on map p. 580.

RESTAURANTS

Brubeck's: The best place to eat at this restaurant is on the patio facing Mission Plaza. And the best section of patio is the one closest to the creek on the lowest level. It's less crowded there and more entertaining for dogs. The rule is that your dog has to sit on the other side of the railing, so be sure to get an outer seat. Then you can enjoy the fresh fish specials without a twinge of guilt in your heart, because your dog will still be at your feet. 726 Higuera Street; (805) 541-8688.

Cisco's Restaurant: This is by far the most beautiful patio restaurant in this part of California. It even has great sandwiches and live music every day. Dogs feel relaxed here, not at all cramped. Enter from the Mission Plaza side and try to get a table overlooking the creek. 778 Higuera Street; (805) 543-5555.

Country Yogurt Culture: Enter from the Mission Plaza side, and you and your dog can enjoy creekside tables and eight flavors of award-winning yogurt. The friendly service here makes dogs feel right at home. 746 Higuera Street; (805) 544-9007.

Garland's Hamburgers: 1065 Olive Street; (805) 541-4671.

Old Country Deli: A lot of people come here and give their dogs a bone as they eat the fresh barbecued meat the staff cooks out front. That's often not a good idea, but it's especially bad if you don't clean up after your dog eats. The owners here still allow pooches, but they won't if people don't mind the mess their pets make. 600 Marsh Street; (805) 541-2968.

Rudolph's Coffee & Tea Company: Enjoy a spot of tea, coffee or hot chocolate while your dog guards your muffin for you. 670 Higuera Street; (805) 543-4902.

San Luis Fish & Barbeque: 474 Marsh Street; (805) 541-4191.

San Luis Obispo Donuts: Open 'round the clock, you can sit at the umbrella-covered tables and eat donuts, pastries and even egg rolls as your dog looks on. 1057 Monterey Street; (805) 544-8580.

PLACES TO STAY

Best Western Royal Oak Motor Hotel: Rates are $61 to $85. 214 Madonna Road, San Luis Obispo, CA 93405; (805) 544-4410.

Campus Motel: They want only small dogs here. Rates are $44 to $80. Dogs are $4 extra. 404 Santa Rosa Street, San Luis Obispo, CA 93405; (805) 544-0881.

El Chorro Regional Park Campground: See page 594.

Howard Johnson Lodge: Huge dogs aren't allowed here, but smaller dogs enjoy all the open space around this mountainous locale. Rates are $50 to $75. Dogs are $10 extra. 1585 Calle Joaquin, San Luis Obispo, CA 93401; (805) 544-5300.

Motel 6: There's a big field in back where dogs are allowed at least for now. All Motel 6s allow one small pooch per room. Rates are $28 for one adult, $4 for the second adult. 1625 Calle Joaquin, San Luis Obispo, CA 93401; (805) 541-6992.

Sands Motel & Suites: Small dogs only, please. Rates are $49 to $99. 1930 Monterey Street, San Luis Obispo, CA 93401; (805) 544-0500.

Vagabond Inn: Rates are $44 to $73. Small dogs are preferred, and they're $5 extra. 210 Madonna Road, San Luis Obispo, CA 93401; (805) 544-4710 or (800) 522-1555.

DIVERSIONS

Catch a fur flick: The Sunset Drive-In Theater allows quiet dogs for no extra charge (it's $6 per car). Some pooches really enjoy a movie starring a dog, so be sure to bring your best friend if you notice one playing. 255 Elks Lane; (805) 544-4475.

SAN SIMEON

Dogs aren't trusted anywhere near the gilded towers of William Randolph Hearst's castle, so if you're thinking of visiting while your dog is with you, forget it. He'll have to wait in the car for at least three hours while you tour the castle, and that's a very bad idea.

But that doesn't mean you have to forgo this spectacular attraction. The Tail Wag's Inn, about nine miles south in Cambria, will board your dog for as long as your tour takes. With all the frills they provide your pet, she may come back thinking she should be living in Hearst Castle (see page 585 for details).

PARKS, BEACHES & RECREATION AREAS

•**San Simeon State Beach** 🐾 🐾 🐾

This rocky beach stretches for two miles between Cambria and San Simeon. Beachcombing and tidepooling can be first-rate, depending on the tide.

The beach is very popular because of its proximity to Hearst Castle. Even more popular here is the developed San Simeon Creek Campground and the more primitive Washburn Creek Campground. There's nothing quite like setting up a tent among 200 other tents just after you've visited Hearst's 38 lavish bedrooms. Sweet dreams!

Campsites range from $7 to $16. Dogs are $1 extra. The beach and campgrounds are about six miles south of Hearst Castle, along Highway 1. For reservations (essential during the summer), call MISTIX at (800) 444-7275. For beach information, phone (805) 927-2035. ➤ *See #18 on map p. 580.*

PLACES TO STAY

Motel 6: In keeping with the posh castle nearby, the rates at this Motel 6 are the most expensive of the entire chain. The beach is so close you can understand why. The rate for one adult is $42. The second adult is $6. All Motel 6s allow one small pooch per room. 9070 Castillo Drive, San Simeon, CA 93452; (805) 541-6992.

San Simeon State Beach camping: See page 596.

SANTA MARGARITA

PARKS, BEACHES & RECREATION AREAS

• **Santa Margarita Recreation Area** 🐾 🐾 🐾

You and your dog don't have to like swimming or fishing to enjoy this park, centered around Santa Margarita Lake. If hiking is more your style, try the 10 miles of trails that weave through the area. Keep your dog leashed and watch out for horses.

For the rest of the family, there are playgrounds, horseshoe pits and a swimming pool. And if you just can't help throwing a line in the water, you may well land supper.

The entry fee is $4 per car and $1.50 per dog. But there's plenty of parking just outside the park, if you want to avoid the vehicle fee. From Highway 101, take the Highway 58 exit and drive east about four miles. Follow the signs the rest of the way. (805) 438-5485. ➤ *See #19 on map p. 580.*

TEMPLETON

PARKS, BEACHES & RECREATION AREAS

• **Templeton Park** 🐾 🐾 🐾

This is among the most peaceful neighborhood parks we've visited. You could daydream the day away here under the huge shade trees, or kick back in the gazebo and read your favorite old book with another dog-eared friend (leashed). There's an old Southern Pacific railroad car on one corner and a fairly well-fenced ball field on the other.

The park is between Crocker Street and Old County Road, and Fifth and Sixth streets. (805) 781-5930. ➤ *See #20 on map p. 580.*

KERN COUNTY

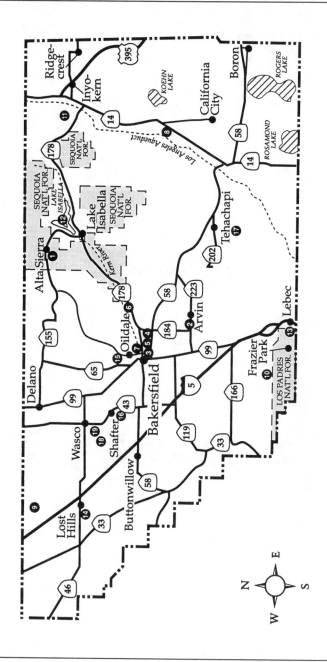

49
KERN COUNTY

This large southern San Joaquin Valley county is a diverse land o' plenty. There are plenty o' farms, plenty o' deserts, plenty o' mountains and plenty o' windmills—5,000 to be exact, enough to make Don Quixote quiver.

The county also has plenty of fertilizer, and that fact will jump right out at you as you cruise down certain roads during certain fertilizer seasons. Bring a gas mask or forever hold your breath. When we drove through one fine October afternoon, the humans in the car turned green on the extra ripe cow patty smell. Joe dog just sat there mesmerized, with a big smile on his snout.

NATIONAL FORESTS

See the National Forests/Wilderness Areas chapter starting on page 801 for important information and safety tips for visiting national forests with your dog.

•**Los Padres National Forest** 🐾 🐾 🐾 🐾 🖐 🐕

A sliver of this huge national forest pokes into the southwest edge of Kern County. See page 806.

•**Sequoia National Forest** 🐾 🐾 🐾 🐾 🖐 🐕

Only little segments of this grand forest dribble into Kern County from Tulare County. See page 808.

ALTA SIERRA

PARKS, BEACHES & RECREATION AREAS

•**Greenhorn Mountain County Park** 🐾 🐾 🐾 1/2

This rugged park is surrounded by extraordinary Sequoia National Forest land. While the park itself is a speck compared with the forest, it resembles the wooded wonderland in every other way except one: Dogs must be leashed. Joe likes the place, but it's really easy to drive down the road a bit and start on a real wilderness hike in the national forest.

Greenhorn is slightly more civilized, if that's what your dog prefers. It's got a playground and a picnic area. But most of the undeveloped forest areas at Greenhorn are as wild as the surrounding national forest land. Its 160 acres are set at 6,000 feet. Trails run through thick cedar and white fir forests.

The park is on Highway 155, about six miles west of Lake Isabella. (805) 861-2345. ➤*See #1 on map p. 600.*

ARVIN

PARKS, BEACHES & RECREATION AREAS

• **DiGiorgio Park** 🐾 🐾

Up until about 15 years ago, this 18-acre park was packed with trees. Then along came a big windstorm and blew about half of them to smithereens.

But fear not, dogs of the male persuasion: There are still plenty of trees here to claim as your own. There's also a ball field, a pool and a playground. The rest is flat and grassy. From Highway 233 (Bear Mountain Boulevard), go south on Meyer Street for four blocks. The park is at Haven Drive and Meyer Street. (805) 861-2345. ➤*See #2 on map p. 600.*

BAKERSFIELD

This is the country music capital of California. You'll know it when you turn on your car radio. Find yourself a good country station, and as you cruise past oil derricks and the surrounding agricultural land, you'll feel right at home.

Bakersfield also happens to be the hub of the southern San Joaquin Valley. It doesn't draw many tourists, but whether you live here or just do business here (with your pooch, of course), you'll find enough decently dog-friendly parks to make your friendly dog happy.

PARKS, BEACHES & RECREATION AREAS

• **Bakersfield Beach Park** 🐾 🐾

The grass is often so green and so short that you feel as if you're walking on crunchy AstroTurf here. This 27-acre park by the often-dry Kern River has ball fields, horseshoe pits, picnic tables and a playground, but where's the beach? It's there if you look hard, but it's difficult to recognize a beach when it doesn't touch some sort of water. Since dogs have to be leashed, they don't miss the river much during drought years.

The park is at 24th and Oak streets. (805) 326-3117. ➤*See #3 on map p. 600.*

• **Central Park** 🐾 1/2

"Stay out, stay alive," reads a sign next to the creek that runs through this 11-acre park. Even dogs who can't read will heed this advice: The creek is completely fenced off. It's not a pretty sight, but the parkees who put up the sign probably know what they're talking about. The park is flat and grassy, with plenty of trees, a playground and loads of picnic tables. It's located in the heart of the city's antique shopping district, at 19th and R streets. (805) 326-3117. *→See #4 on map p. 600.*

• **Jastro Park** 🐾

This nine-acre park has shade, manicured lawns and picnic tables to recommend it. Other than that, dogs don't care much for the other features like tennis and basketball courts and a swimming pool. It's at Truxton Avenue and Myrtle Street. (805) 326-3117. *→See #5 on map p. 600.*

• **Hart Park** 🐾 🐾 🐾

This park is actually part of the larger Kern River County Park. See below. *→See #6 on map p. 600.*

• **Kern River County Park** 🐾 🐾 🐾

Hart Park and Lake Ming make up the bulk of this 1,400-acre park. Hart Park is by far the better one for dogs, in a setting that's part-golf course and part-lunar landscape. The bare rock mountain on one edge of the park gives way to huge green meadows, with shaded paths running throughout. And if you're a food hound, you'll be happy to know you and your leashed dog are never more than a one-minute walk to a picnic table.

Down the road a bit is a huge soccer area. When no one's around, it's a terrific place to trot about with your pooch.

The easternmost section of the park is Lake Ming, a 100-acre lake with tolerable fishing in the cooler months and nothing in summer. At last look, only two tiny sections were open to anglers. Because of a parasite that can cause swimmer's itch, swimming and wading are often banned here. In all, it's not exactly a water dog's dream.

The 57 first-come, first-served campsites here are set in a remote, lush section of the Lake Ming area. Unlike the dry, dusty feel of most of the lake's shoreline, the camping here is a riparian riverside escape. Site are $8 to $12. Dogs are $2 extra.

From Panorama Drive in north Bakersfield, drive east to Alfred Harrell Highway, and follow it as it curves by the Kern River. Eventually the road will lead you through the gates of the park. Follow the signs to the areas that most interest you and your dog. (805) 861-2345. *→See #6 on map p. 600.*

• **Panorama Park** 🏕

If a park is going to have the guts to call itself "Panorama" Park, it had better supply a pretty decent view. Not so here. There's a view, all right, but it's not the kind you photograph, enlarge and hang on your living room wall as evidence of your enviable summer vacation.

The vista includes oil tanks, a refinery, smoke stacks and free-ways. Somehow, the few pastured horses by the river lose their rustic charm amid these surroundings.

The park is fairly narrow and follows the road closely. About all you and your leashed dog can do here is walk down the paved path and sit on the benches and admire the industrial scenery. The park is set along Panorama Drive from Union Avenue to Bucknell Street. The best parking is at the foot of River Boulevard. (805) 861-2345. → *See #7 on map p. 600.*

RESTAURANTS

Bakersfield has a real dearth of dog-friendly restaurants. Here's one:

Truxton Express Market: Picnic with your pooch at the outside tables. This casual place serves all kinds of hot and cold sandwiches. 1652 Oak Street; (805) 395-1163.

PLACES TO STAY

If only the city's restaurants were as open to dogs as its lodgings. Bakersfield has so many dog-friendly lodgings that it puts many larger cities to shame. We'll mention just a fistful of them here.

Best Western Hill House: "Not too big" dogs are welcome, says the manager. Rates are $52 to $72. Dogs are $5 extra. 700 Truxton Avenue, Bakersfield, CA 93301; (805) 327-1247.

Kern River County Park camping: See page 603.

La Quinta Motor Inn: Dogs under 35 pounds may sleep here. Rates are $50 to $62. There are no fees or deposits for dogs; you just have to sign a declaration accepting liability for doggy damage. 3232 Riverside Drive, Bakersfield, CA 93308; (805) 325-7400.

Motel 6: There are five Motel 6s in Bakersfield, all of which accept one small dog per room. This is an amazing per capita number. Lap dogs who don't need the lap of luxury will enjoy a night or two here. Call the national reservations number at (505) 891-6161 for the location nearest your destination.

Red Lion Hotel: This is one of the better Bakersfield accommodations. Rates are $100 to $140. 3100 Camino del Rio Court, Bakersfield, CA 93308; (805) 323-7111.

Rio Mirada Motor Inn: Bakersfield Beach Park is only about a mile from here. Rates are $48 to $64. Dogs are $10 extra. Efficiencies are available. 4500 Pierce Road, Bakersfield, CA 93308; (805) 324-5555.

Sheraton Inn Bakersfield: The folks here deliver *USA Today* to your room in the morning. Get your dog to retrieve it along with your slippers. Rates are $65 to $110. 5101 California Avenue, Bakersfield, CA 93308; (805) 325-9700.

BORON

Don't be surprised if your dog starts looking inquisitively at the empty sky here. Chances are that within a few moments the sky won't look so empty. This is the home of the Edwards Air Force Base, and they fly some mighty odd-looking experimental aircraft up yonder. Dogs usually seem to notice well before their people.

DIVERSIONS

Call out the 20-mule team: If your dog has fond memories of those puppyhood days when you sprinkled 20 Mule Team Borax on the rug almost daily to get out those "oops" odors, a trip to the 20 Mule Team Museum will be a journey down olfactory memory lane.

The town of Boron is the home of U.S. Borax, whose open pit mine is one of the major sources of borate in the world. The museum pays homage to the days when 20-mule teams hauled 36-ton wagonloads of borax across 180 miles of desert to waiting railroad cars in Mojave. On the museum's grounds, you'll find the oldest house in Death Valley, built in 1883 by a borax miner. Other features of the rather small museum include an early Boron beauty shop and tons of mining equipment.

Your dog is free to join you at the outdoor displays, and if the caretaker likes your dog (she says all a dog usually has to do is smile at her and she's hooked), your pooch can go inside the museum with you and look at the exhibits and the movies of the early days of borax mining. They haven't had any leg-lifting types of accidents yet, and although they've got access to tons of borax deodorizer, they'd prefer not to have to use it. In other words, if there's even a remote possibility of a squat or leg lift, don't bring your dog inside.

There's no fee, just a requested donation. From Highway 58, take the Boron Avenue off ramp and drive south about 1.5 miles. (619) 762-5810.

CALIFORNIA CITY

PARKS, BEACHES & RECREATION AREAS

No California City parks permit pooches, and the Bureau of Land Management would sure appreciate it if you wouldn't take your dog to the Desert Tortoise Natural Area here. Even leashed dogs can pose a threat to the tortoise population.

• **Red Rock Canyon State Park** 🐾 🐾 🐾 1/2

This magnificent park is known as "the Grand Canyon of the West." It lives up to the hype. The best time to be at this 10,384-acre park is at sunrise or at sunset. The low-lying sun dances with the red and white cliffs, and the results are magical. Dogs aren't permitted on the trails, but they can go along the small roads and seek out some of the stunning paleontological sites with you. Leashes are a must.

If you want to continue your education about borax (see Diversions, page 605), you'll be happy to know that this was an important watering hole for the 20-mule team freight wagons on their grueling journey hauling the stuff.

The day-use fee is $5. There are 50 camping sites available on a first-come, first-served basis for $7 per night. Dogs are $1 extra day or night. The park is located 25 miles northeast of the town of Mojave, on Highway 14. (805) 942-0662. ➤ *See #8 on map p. 600.*

DELANO

PARKS, BEACHES & RECREATION AREAS

• **Kern National Wildlife Refuge** 🐾 🐾 🐾 🐾 🐕

If your dog hunts waterfowl with you, she'll find this 10,618-acre refuge a four-paw destination. If your dog isn't a hunter, you'll have to keep her on leash, and your access to the refuge is quite limited. Non-hunting pooches give this place only about two-and-a-half paws.

There's a great auto tour route that goes around the natural valley grasslands and marsh areas. Wildlife watching is excellent. There are at least 200 species of birds here during the year, along with all sorts of other critters.

You may see snowy egrets, ring-billed gulls, warblers, peregrine falcons, endangered San Joaquin kit foxes and leopard lizards. Watch the life from the parking lots here, or walk a short distance from the lots if you want to get away from other cars and stretch out all six of your collective legs.

From Interstate 5 around the town of Lost Hills, take Highway 46 five miles east to Corcoran Road and turn north. Drive 10.6 miles and you'll be at the refuge. (805) 725-2767. ➤ *See #9 on map p. 600.*

FRAZIER PARK

The dusty little streets of this community near the interstate hide a fairly dog-friendly park. If your dog is crossing his legs on a long journey down the highway, it's not a bad place to stop.

PARKS, BEACHES & RECREATION AREAS

• **Frazier Mountain Park** 🐾🐾🐾

This 26-acre park is almost entirely fenced, but dogs are sup-posed to be leashed anyway. In addition to a grassy picnic area and a little pond, sections of the park have shrubs, shady oaks and scrubby fields. Dogs love the fact that it's not a perfectly manicured work of art.

Exit Interstate 5 at the Frazier Park exit and drive east about 3.5 miles. Turn left at the post office (Monterey Trail) and make an immediate right onto Park Trail Drive. Park on the street. (805) 861-2345. → *See #10 on map p. 600.*

INYOKERN

Friends who visited from New York could only call this town "Inyoface." It was amusing for at least a few seconds the first time they said it. But dogs find high amusement at the Chimney Peak Recreation Area, which lets them run around off leash and get rid of all that pent-up canine energy. See below.

PARKS, BEACHES & RECREATION AREAS

• **Chimney Peak Recreation Area** 🐾🐾🐾🐾 🥾 🐕

This large swathe of land is not the Mojave Desert and it's not the Sierra Nevadas. It's somewhere in between—a transition zone with less severe temperatures and an unusual mix of vegetation.

You and your well-mannered mutt will enjoy hiking through pinyon and juniper woodlands, digger pines, sage and desert needlegrass without the bondage of a leash. In the spring, wild-flowers explode with color and the place comes to life.

Speaking of coming to life, a brochure from the Bureau of Land Management describes another aspect of nature here: "Highlight-ing the wildlife attractions of the area are mule deer, black bear, mountain lion, bobcat..."

When I read this to Joe, he agreed that it might be best to keep him on a leash around here. Three out of those four critters make him a little antsy. If you have pooch who's less than perfect, as Joe is wont to be sometimes, it's best to keep him on a leash and not take a chance with lions and bobcats and bears. There's no scare-crow here to help your Toto out of a difficult situation.

The trails here join up with the surrounding dog-friendly national forest land, making this piece of dog heaven seem utterly vast. While there's plenty of good BLM turf in Kern County, the best portion of the Chimney Peak Recreation Area is in Tulare County to the north. You can get there by taking Highway 178 to

Canebrake Road and heading north. You may stop on the Kern side of the border if you wish, but the Tulare side has the good campgrounds and trails. (805) 861-4236. ➤*See #11 on map p. 600.*

LAKE ISABELLA

PARKS, BEACHES & RECREATION AREAS

• **Lake Isabella** 🐾 🐾 🐾

If what you want is a long hike with your leash-free dog, don't expect to find it right here. The land is surrounded by Sequoia National Forest, but there really aren't any trails around the lake. Just a short drive up the road, you'll find all the nude dog hiking you could imagine. Ask a ranger for directions to the national forest trails.

You can walk around some of the lake with your dog, but he must be leashed. With 38 miles of shoreline, this is the largest freshwater lake in Southern California, and it's worth taking a look around. The birdwatching is hot here, and so is the fishing for such goodies as largemouth bass.

There are 609 campsites. Some campsites are available on a first-come, first-served basis. Reservations are recommended for holiday weekends, call (800) 280-CAMP. Campsites are $8 to $12; there are four no-fee primitive sites available. Some offer blissful seclusion. The lake is located at highways 155 and 178. From Bakersfield, head east on Highway 178 for about 30 miles. Call the ranger office for directions to your particular destination within the lake area. (619) 379-5646. ➤*See #12 on map p. 600.*

PLACES TO STAY

Lake Isabella camping: See above.

LEBEC

PARKS, BEACHES & RECREATION AREAS

• **Fort Tejon State Historic Park** 🐾 🐾 🐾 1/2 🐾

The U.S. Army's First Dragoons established a camp here in 1854. Their mission was to protect white settlers and Native Americans in the Tejon Reservation from raids by other Indian groups, including the Paiutes, Chemehuevi and Mojave.

The buildings here are all restored versions of structures that were the backbone of the fort back then. There's even a miniature museum to get you up-to-date with the past.

Dogs like it here, but their pleasure has little to do with the buildings and lots to do with the land. There's plenty of land to peruse, on leash of course. If you get away from the main features of the fort and walk toward the backcountry (past the outhouses), you're in for a treat. Large valley oaks, blue oaks, black willows and cottonwoods are plentiful here, and critters like deer, rabbits, quail and several kinds of hummingbirds call the park home.

Admission is $2 for adults and $1 for kids and dogs. Exit Interstate 5 at the Fort Tejon exit and follow the signs. It's just west of the freeway. (805) 248-6692. →*See #13 on map p. 600.*

LOST HILLS

PARKS, BEACHES & RECREATION AREAS

• **Lost Hills Park** 🐾 🐾

There's nothing lost about this park. In fact, it's about as found as they come. A popular weekend haunt for locals, the park has barbecues, ball fields, playgrounds and acres of well-maintained grass. It's not exactly a doggy delight, but a dog could do a lot worse. Leashes are the law. The park is at the corner of Highway 46 and Lost Hills Road (only a few blocks southwest of the airport). (805) 861-2345. →*See #14 on map p. 600.*

OILDALE

If you like oil (the dark, inedible kind), you'll love this town. Grasshopper-like oil derricks are everywhere. Tanks, too. It's an interesting place to visit if you happen to be sick of forests and other forms of pristine landscapes.

PARK, BEACHES & RECREATION AREAS

• **Standard Park** 🐾 1/2

Old railroad cars and oil tanks clutter the area just to the east of the park. There's no mistaking where you are: You're in Oildale, land of much oil and many places named after the oil companies that have a stake in the town.

Standard Park is a flat 15-acre park edged with trees. If your leashed dog needs to get out of the car, it's a tolerable place for a little stretching and a few leg lifts. The park is a block south of Norris Road, just east of North Chester Avenue. (805) 392-2000.
→*See #15 on map p. 600.*

RIDGECREST

PLACES TO STAY

Heritage Inn: About a third of the 125 units are efficiencies. Bring your own utensils and you'll be all set out here in this remote city. Rates are $70 to $93. 1050 North Norma Street, Ridgecrest, CA 93555; (619) 446-6543.

Heritage Suites: This one is just around the corner from the Heritage Inn, and it offers kitchens with most units. Rates are $90 to $111. 919 North Heritage Drive, Ridgecrest, CA 93555; (619) 446-7951.

SHAFTER

Shafter is surrounded by agriculture, but its promotional brochure shows nothing but pictures of industrial parks and a nearby airport. A dog haven it is not.

PARKS, BEACHES & RECREATION AREAS
•**Richland School Park** 🐾

The park is just roomy enough for your leashed dog to have a good stretch. Try one of the open fields. The park is at Atlantic Avenue and Valley Street. (805) 746-6361. ➤*See #16 on map p. 600.*

TEHACHAPI

The Tehachapi area is home to thousands of windmills that supply more than one billion kilowatt-hours of electricity per year. Next time you're driving through some of the backroads with your dog, pull over and turn off your engine for a minute. The humming turbines provide an eerie contrast to the silence of the surrounding desert. Joe loves the strange noises, and tilts his head every which way to try to figure out who's making them. When he rules out the other passengers and the nearby rocks, he stares at me with an accusing look on his furled brow.

PARKS, BEACHES & RECREATION AREAS
•**Tehachapi Mountain Park** 🐾 🐾 🐾 1/2

We love coming to this 490-acre park in late autumn, when there's a little nip in the pure pine-scented air. With elevations up to 7,000 feet and dozens of different types of pines, firs and oaks, this park provides a stunning contrast to the desert surroundings.

Bill and Joe slid around on their butts last time we visited, because there was a good layer of slick snow in the upper reaches of the park. They had a great time slipping, sliding and sniffing the mountain sage that was poking out of the snow. Leashes are the law here, but you can still have a terrific time exploring this beautiful park via the trails that run throughout. And you may never run into another soul.

The camping is some of the best we've seen in any county park. Many of the 61 sites are 200 feet away from each other. Tall trees add a little more privacy. Sites are $6 to $10 and are available on a first-come, first-served basis. Pooches are $2 extra.

From Highway 58, exit onto Highway 202 and drive south, continuing straight onto Tucker Road when Highway 202 veers west. In about another mile, at Highline Road, turn right and drive about 1.5 miles to Water Canyon Road. Turn left. The park is another 2.2 miles. (805) 861-2345. ➡ *See #17 on map p. 600.*

PLACES TO STAY
Best Western Mountain Inn: Rates are $45 to $52. 416 West Tehachapi Boulevard, Tehachapi, CA 93561; (805) 822-5591.

Tehachapi Mountain Park camping: See page 610.

WASCO
PARKS, BEACHES & RECREATION AREAS
•**Barker Park** 🐾

We thought maybe, just maybe, this park was named for all the leash-free dogs who frequent it. But no one was barking for joy here. Leashes are the law at this eight-acre park. It has a small grassy area with some trees, but most of the park is filled with non-dog amenities, like swimming pools and playgrounds. The park is at Poso and Poplar streets. (805) 758-3081. ➡ *See #18 on map p. 600.*

•**Westside Park** 🐾🐾 1/2

Park staff labored hard to get some little hills built into this 17-acre park. "We didn't want it to be flat and boring like the rest of the landscape," a city worker told me. In addition to some contours, the park has many different adolescent trees, including rose hill ash trees, elms, oaks and even some redwoods.

The park is in the west end of town, just west of Beckes Street, at Parkside Drive. (805) 758-3081. ➡ *See #19 on map p. 600.*

RESTAURANTS
Teresa's Taco Villa: Get a taco for you, grab a burger for your best bud and dine together at the outdoor tables here. 441 F Street; (805) 758-2027.

SOUTH COAST COUNTIES

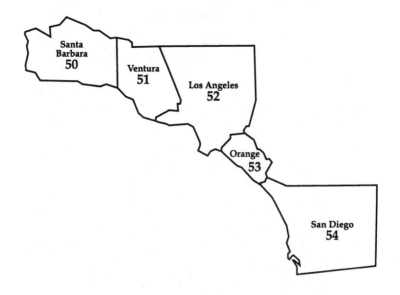

SANTA BARBARA COUNTY

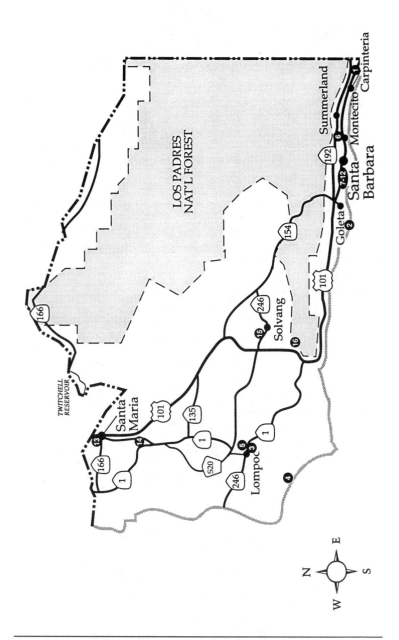

50
SANTA BARBARA COUNTY

If you're like most folks, when you hear the words "Santa Barbara," you probably think of a sun-drenched vacation paradise on the central California coast (unless you think of the soap opera first). Images of whitewashed, Spanish-style buildings, palm-lined beaches and big green resorts representing big green bucks may flash through your head. You can almost smell the suntan lotion and feel the warm sand caressing your body.

On the other hand, if you're a dog, when you think of Santa Barbara County, you'll likely think of a leash that never comes off outside your house or your hotel room. Images of "No Dogs" signs on the most glorious beaches will flash through your furry head. You may even try to convey to your owner, "Hey, I've got a great idea. Let's go to San Francisco!"

But despite the county's restrictive pooch policies, your dog can manage to have fun here. Many Santa Barbara restaurants welcome dogs to dine at their outside tables. Several beaches permit dogs on leash, and some of the inland areas, such as Solvang, make dogs feel right at home. And let's not forget magnificent Los Padres National Forest. It's the only public land in the county where dogs can be their doggy selves and cavort around off leash.

NATIONAL FORESTS

See the National Forests/Wilderness Areas chapter starting on page 801 for important information and safety tips for visiting national forests with your dog.

• **Los Padres National Forest** 🐾 🐾 🐾 🐾 🐾 🐕 🐕

Sections of the forest are near the Santa Barbara coast. The off-leash trails provide a much-needed breather from the strict leash rules around this county. See page 806.

CARPINTERIA

PARKS, BEACHES & RECREATION AREAS

The part of the city beach where dogs are permitted is fairly difficult to access, and it pretty much bans dogs during the harbor seal birthing season in the spring. It's much easier to go to the Rincon Beach County Park (see page 616), but if you really want to hit the small strip of city beach that permits dogs, call (805) 684-5405 and find out its status.

• **Rincon Beach County Park** 🐾 🐾 🐾

A wooden stairway takes you from a green blufftop picnic area down to the sandy beach. It's not a huge beach, but the Beach Boys sang about it and surfer dudes love it.

The bluff provides an excellent view of the ocean. Even though nude bathing is illegal, naked people flock here. Just cover your dog's eyes as you pass by the fleshy masses. (The nudists really appreciate it if your dog obeys the leash law.)

The park is at Bates Road and Highway 101, at the south end of Carpinteria. (805) 684-5405. → *See #1 on map p. 614.*

RESTAURANTS

The Coffee Grinder: This is an attractive place, with wooden outdoor tables for your dog's dining enjoyment. 910 Linden Avenue; (805) 684-5503.

Fish Barrel: Dogs can join you on the patio at the side of the restaurant. 509 Linden Avenue; (805) 684-2391.

Pacific Grill: Dogs dig the beautiful outdoor seating at this restaurant. It's on a half acre of lawn that goes right down to the beach. 3765 Santa Claus Lane; (805) 684-7670.

The Spot: This eatery is down by the beach. It's known for its great hamburgers and Mexican food. Your pooch can keep you company on the patio. 389 Linden Avenue; (805) 684-7120.

Toyland: You can't miss this store/restaurant. It's the one with the giant Santa Claus on top, staring longingly at US 101. Do your Christmas shopping at this oceanfront toy store, and then have your dog join you at the outdoor table for a date shake or hot chocolate and a piece of pumpkin bread. If you have kids, they can ride the rocking horse and elephant for a mere quarter while your dog watches and pulls on the leash, hoping for a chance to tame these mechanical beasts. 3821 Santa Claus Lane; (805) 684-3515.

PLACES TO STAY

Best Western Carpinteria Inn: Joe and I stayed here once while I was covering the aftermath of the big Santa Barbara blaze a few years back. We met this wonderful old woman who frequented the inn for long spells. She had us in for tea and biscuits, which made Joe's English heritage come bubbling up to the surface. He drank his water right out of a tea cup, and when it was time to leave, he offered our hostess a gracious paw. Rates at this charming inn are $85 to $115, and there's a $25 dog deposit. 4558 Carpinteria Avenue, Carpinteria, CA 93013; (805) 684-0473.

Carpinteria State Beach campsites: Camp along the Pacific Ocean at one of the 262 beachfront sites here. Dogs love it, but don't let them get any ideas about running around on the beach. They're banned. Sites are $14 to $22. Dogs are $1 extra. From US 101, take the Casitas Pass exit and drive west about a mile to the campground. Call (805) 684-2811 for information, or call MISTIX at (800) 444-PARK for reservations.

DIVERSIONS
Disguise your dog: Whenever there's a big parade in Carpinteria, the dogs come out of the woodwork for the costume contest held at the parade's tail end. A recent theme was "The West." The winner was a cocker spaniel who dressed up as a wild mustang, with a mane and all the right horse parts. Winners get free dog food or a gift certificate for some dog goodies.

The contests are usually held at the July 4th parade and the Christmas parade. Contestants meet at the Petcetera store and march into the parade together. Visit Petcetera at 890 Cactus Lane or call the store at (805) 684-9988 for dates and details.

GOLETA
PARKS, BEACHES & RECREATION AREAS
•Goleta Beach County Park 🐾 🐾 🐾
Leashed dogs enjoy strolling down the beach here. You and your pooch can enjoy a relaxing picnic under pine and palm trees in the small park area, then go get your paws wet as you saunter down the beach together. We prefer the section of beach near the Goleta Slough, which is wilder and more primitive.

From US 101, go west on Highway 217. Just before you get to the University of California, turn left onto Sandspit Road and follow it to the beach. (805) 568-2461 or (805) 967-1300. ➜*See #2 on map p. 614.*

RESTAURANTS
Taco Bell: Eat tacos at the outdoor tables here. 140 North Fairview Avenue; (805) 964-2485.

LOMPOC
It may be the home of a notorious federal penitentiary, but because of a few pooch-permitting parks, dogs don't feel imprisoned here.

PARKS, BEACHES & RECREATION AREAS
•Beattie Park 🐾 🐾 1/2
If you get away from the playing fields and basketball courts,

you and your leashed dog can experience a decent degree of solitude here. Follow the fitness course for a little extra calorie-burning activity or just hike up one of the mild-mannered hills.

Exit Highway 1 at 7th Street and drive south a few blocks to Olive Avenue. Turn right, drive two blocks to 5th Street and turn left into the park. The speed bumps on the way in get to be very annoying, so the sooner you park, the better. (805) 736-6565. → *See #3 on map p. 614.*

•**Jalama Beach Park** 🐾 🐾 🐾 1/2

The park may be only 24 acres, but there are so many ways to enjoy nature here that it seems much larger. Bring your binoculars and you won't regret it. Grey whale watching is excellent in February and March, and from September through November. Birdwatching is hot year-round, but springtime attracts many rare birds.

Joe's favorite activity is rock hounding, but he probably just likes the name. The beachcombing is great here, and since the park is within the Pacific Missile Range of the Vandenberg Air Force Base, you never know what you'll find. Wildlife watching and surf fishing are also first-rate. As long as your dog is on a leash and not harming the environment, she can accompany you anywhere here.

There's also camping at 110 campsites, some right by the beach. Sites are $12 to $16. Dogs are $1 extra. All sites are first come, first served. The beach is 15 miles off Highway 1, at the end of Jalama Road. The Jalama Road exit is about four miles south of the main part of Lompoc. (805) 736-6316. → *See #4 on map p. 614.*

•**La Purisima Mission State Historic Park** 🐾 🐾 🐾 1/2 🐾

This is a truly amazing place to bring a dog. Not only can they hike with you along 12 miles of trails here, they're actually allowed *inside* the restored mission. They have to promise not to do leg lifts, bark, throw up or any of those other activities that are not suited to the indoors. And they have to be on a leash at all times.

The original La Purisima Mission was founded in 1787, but an earthquake destroyed it in 1812. The mission was eventually picked up and moved across the Santa Ynez River to its present spot. During the 1930s, many of the mission's adobe buildings were restored. It was the largest mission restoration in California.

It's a treat to be able to take a dog inside such a historic place. But frankly, most dogs would rather be outside exploring this 967-acre park in their own doggy fashion.

The entrance fee is $5 per vehicle and it's good for up to nine people (and a dog). From Highway 1 in Lompoc, turn east on

Purisima Road. The park entrance will be on your left in a couple of miles. (805) 733-3713. ➡ *See #5 on map p. 614.*

PLACES TO STAY

Porto Finale Inn: Beattie Park is just three blocks away from here. Rates are $30 to $50. Dogs are $10 extra. 940 East Ocean Avenue, Lompoc, CA 93436; (805) 735-7731.

Quality Inn & Executive Suites: If you want a view of the Lompoc Airport, you've got it from this parking lot. Joy of joys. Rates are $46 to $70. Dogs are $15 extra. 1621 North H Street, Lompoc, CA 93436; (805) 735-8555.

Redwood Motor Lodge: Rates are $40 to $45. Dogs are $10 extra. 1200 North H Street, Lompoc, CA 93436; (805) 735-3737.

Tally Ho Motor Inn: Rates are $40 to $45. Dogs are $10 extra. 1020 East Ocean Avenue, Lompoc, CA 93436; (805) 735-6444.

MONTECITO

PARKS, BEACHES & RECREATION AREAS

• **Manning County Park** 🐾 🐾 🐾

It's beautiful here—lush and heavenly. This isn't a huge park, but with its narrow, ivy-covered walkways and ultra-green lawns and foliage, you may want to make a day of it. Bring your leashed dog, a picnic and a good book, and enjoy this verdant wonderland to it fullest.

A word to the wise: The ranger lives on the premises. If you're going to break a leash law, don't do it here.

Exit US 101 at San Ysidro Road and drive north for almost a mile. The park will be just after the school, on your left. (805) 568-2461. ➡ *See #6 on map p. 614.*

SANTA BARBARA

Dogs are not allowed on any city beaches in this exquisite community. But Joe doesn't get too upset about this. He likes the idea that of the city's five-member Animal Control Team, one of the members is a dog—an Airedale, to be exact. Her name is Rosa. She's a petite version of Joe, a little blonder, much more Southern California. Joe looked at a photo of her standing with the rest of the Animal Control Team and he licked it. It could be love. Then again, it could be the remnants of a cherry-flavored cough drop some kid had stuck on it a day earlier.

Although dogs can't visit the city beach, they can stroll very close to it. A wonderful walkway runs the entire beach length, along Cabrillo Boulevard. On Sundays and holidays, the Santa

Barbara Arts and Crafts Show makes its home under the grand palm trees here. It's a great opportunity to go shopping and take your dog along for advice on issues like which scarf would look best on Aunt Minnie.

An interesting way to spend a dog day is to walk around the historic sections of the city. While pooches aren't permitted inside buildings like Mission Santa Barbara or the city's historic adobes, they love having their pictures taken outside so their friends at home can envy their worldly ways.

(Although you'll see pooper scoopers beckoning you toward Mission Historical Park's rose garden across the street from the famed mission, the folks in the parks department beg you not to take your dog there. "We don't need any more foot traffic than we already have, especially foot traffic that has to go to the bathroom," says a parks supervisor. Looks like he wants us to take our business elsewhere.)

PARKS, BEACHES & RECREATION AREAS

• Alice Keck Park Memorial Gardens 🐾 🐾 1/2 🐾

There's an abundance of natural sniffables here for dogs and their human friends. This one-square-block park is a fragrant, voluptuous garden, complete with flowering trees, a pond, a gazebo and a stunning procession of brilliant flowers. Leashed dogs like it here, but most would rather be able to inspect a good, fresh cow patty than a dahlia.

The park is at Arrellaga Street and Carmelita Avenue, four blocks away from the court house. (805) 564-5433. ➡ *See #7 on map p. 614.*

• Arroyo Burro County Beach 🐾 🐾 🐾

Watch people with parachutes jump off a cliff above the back parking lot here. Better yet, walk your leashed dog on the beach. Around this city, the latter act is about as daring as parachuting. But it's actually legal to take your dog on the beach here, since it's a county beach. It's the only beach in the city where dogs are officially permitted.

Even though the beach here isn't very wide, it's good just to be able to take your dog for a sandy stroll. The beach is on Marina Cliff Drive, just west of Las Positas Road. (805) 568-2461. ➡ *See #8 on map p. 614.*

• Las Positas Friendship Park 🐾

If people are using the many sports fields here, you may as well pack up your dog and head for the nearest fire hydrant. This large park on a hill has some shrubby, earthy areas toward the bottom, but we hear those are soon to be made into more playing fields.

Leashed dogs are welcome to explore the many levels of this recreation-oriented park, but there's not nearly as much hikeable land as a map would have you believe. Most of the green splotch you'll see when you look at a map is very steep and impassable.

From US 101, exit at Las Positas Road and drive south about 1.2 miles to the park's entrance, which will be on your left. (805) 564-5433. → *See #9 on map p. 614.*

• **Plaza Del Mar Park** 🐾 1/2

This flat park is about a block from the beach, but it's nothing spectacular. It's a fairly good size, with enough grass and trees to please a leashed dog. Unfortunately, lots of people just hang out here, so the navigating can be difficult.

The park is on Cabrillo Boulevard at Castillo Street. (805) 564-5433. → *See #10 on map p. 614.*

• **Santa Barbara Botanic Garden** 🐾 🐾 🐾 1/2 🐾

As soon as you park your car, you'll be enveloped in the magical scents of lush vegetation and fresh earth. Dogs prefer to smell the compost heaps here, but what else would you expect?

This botanic wonderland is a rarity. Places like this usually exclude dogs without a second thought. But here, they actually like dogs. In fact, there's even a philanthropic doggy donor, a poodle named Sophie. This environmentally conscious gal has a bouffant hairdo and the distinction of being the garden's only canine member.

You and your leashed dog are welcome to explore this 65-acre garden on the five-and-a-half miles of trails that take you through the meadows, canyons and ridges here. The garden features more than 1,000 species of rare and indigenous California plants. The entry fee for adults is $3.

Exit US 101 at Mission Street and drive northeast. The road curves to the left after about 10 blocks (its name becomes Mission Canyon Drive). Continue to Foothill Road, bear right and then take a quick left on the continuation of Mission Canyon Drive. The park will be on your left in about a half mile. (805) 563-2521. → *See #11 on map p. 614.*

• **Shoreline Park** 🐾 🐾

Lots of dogs come here for their daily walks. Leashed dog are allowed on the green area here (not the beach). They walk the path, roll on the grass and smell the fresh ocean and the scent of the offshore oil rigs that dot the coast here.

The park is on Shoreline Drive, between San Clemente Street

and San Rafael Avenue, just south of Leadbetter Beach. (805) 564-5433. ➡ *See #12 on map p. 614.*

RESTAURANTS

Acapulco Mexican Restaurant and Cantina: This place sports an enchanting plaza setting with huge umbrellas and a fountain in the center. Your dog is welcome, as long as you sit at the outer perimeter of the patio, where he won't accidentally step in front of a busy waiter. 1114 State Street; (805) 963-3469.

Andersen's Danish Bakery and Restaurant: You and your pooch can sit under an umbrella at the edge of this patio and enjoy each other's company while dining on wonderful Scandinavian cuisine. 1106 State Street; (805) 962-5085.

Earthling Bookshop: This is a delightful place where you can get a huge variety of coffee and espresso drinks, along with good grub like quiche, lasagna, burritos and salads. The folks here get a lot of customers with dogs on their patio, and they find it especially endearing when customers come in with little dogs' faces peeking out of backpacks. 1137 State Street; (805) 965-0926.

Fat Burger: Come and savor a chubby burger with your drooling dog at one of the outdoor tables. 718 State Street; (805) 962-8955.

Hot Spots: Though your pooch may shy away if you tell her the name of this deli/coffee bar, you can assure her it's safe. Lots of dogs have come here with no adverse effects. 36 State Street; (805) 963-4233.

Moore Coffee: If you don't want more coffee, you can get more soups, salads and sandwiches here. The outdoor seating lies under an overhang, in case you don't want more Southern California sunshine. 1014 State Street; (805) 963-8060.

Nicky's Sports Pub: This is a fun place with lots of tables, grass and trees at its outdoor area. 217 State Street; (805) 963-6965.

Pierre La Fond Deli: You and your dog can sit at the sidewalk tables and watch the intriguing streets of Santa Barbara. 516 State Street; (805) 962-1455.

Santa Barbara Coffee Roasting Company: If you can find an empty table outside, you and your dog are welcome to relax and socialize at this hopping cafe. 321 Motor Way; (805) 962-0320.

Santa Barbara Nutrition Center: Enjoy health food and delicious smoothies at the sidewalk tables here. 15 East Figueroa; (805) 962-3766.

Sea Cove Cafe: This cafe has a special area where people and their pets are welcome. It sports two patios. The lower one is where you can go with your dog. The cafe borders the beach, so the views are outstanding. Too bad your dog can't stroll there afterward, but his kind is banned at local beaches. 801 Shoreline Drive; (805) 965-2917.

Surf and Sand: If you want a great cinnamon roll, this is your kind of place. Breakfast tastes extra good here, because the outdoor area is right across the street from the beach. A good sea breeze always gets the appetite going. At least that's Joe's excuse. 23 East Cabrillo Boulevard; (805) 966-1479.

PLACES TO STAY

Compared with the large number of lodgings available, the number that permit dogs is shamefully low.

Cachuma Lake campgrounds: Although Cachuma Lake has 42 miles of shoreline and numerous trails, dogs who visit here are stuck in the campgrounds. Trails ban dogs, and pooches and people aren't permitted to swim in the lake. Dogs can't be within 50 feet of the lake, and they're not even allowed to accompany their people on a boat here. Bummerooo, say the dogs.

Fortunately, there are plenty of campsites here—500 to be exact. You won't be roughing it, but at least you'll be with your dog. Sites are $12 to $17. Dogs are $1 extra. All are available on a first-come, first-served basis. From Santa Barbara, take the San Marcos Pass exit (Highway 154) off US 101 and drive about 20 miles to the entrance. (805) 688-4658.

Fess Parker's Red Lion Resort: This lovely, sprawling resort is across from the beach, but unfortunately, it's a beach you can't visit with your dog friend. Try the path that runs along the beach's edge. Rates are $190 to $290. There's also a $50 pooch deposit. 633 East Cabrillo Boulevard, Santa Barbara, CA 93103; (805) 564-4333.

Four Seasons Biltmore: This elegant oceanfront resort is renowned for its impeccable style. Its gracious, dog-friendly policy is the epitome of that style. Too bad other hotels and motels that ban pooches couldn't follow the example of the Biltmore: If this exquisite place accepts them, why can't so many cookie-cutter types of lodgings? Perhaps if you charge the steeper prices, you can afford to deal with the occasional canine *faux pas.* Rates here are $290 to $390. Dogs must stay in the cottages. 1260 Channel Drive, Santa Barbara, CA 93108; (805) 969-2261.

Motel 6: Rates are $40 for the first adult, $4 for the second. All Motel 6s allow one small pooch per room. 3505 State Street, Santa Barbara, CA 93108; (805) 687-5400.

DIVERSIONS

Hi ho, surrey, away!: Get your canine companion to hop up into your lap or onto the seat beside you, and drive away in your very own surrey with the fringe on the top. Don't you hurry, though, because there are plenty of dog-friendly spots where you can rent one of these pedal-powered vehicles.

One of our favorites is Beach Rentals, at 8 West Cabrillo Avenue. They want you to hang onto your dog, and for good reason: Cats and hamburgers are common sights on the oceanfront paths you're likely to use. Small surreys (for three adults and two small kids/one hefty dog) are $12 an hour. Large surreys are $22. (805) 963-2524.

SANTA MARIA

PARKS, BEACHES & RECREATION AREAS

• **Preisker Park** 🐾 🐾

If you're traveling south on US 101 and you've promised your pooch that you'd stop at the very first park you find when you cross the border from San Luis Obispo County into Santa Barbara County, this is it.

This park is right on the border. It's flat, with lush grass and plenty of places to barbecue those burgers you've been keeping in your cooler. (Joe asked me to say that last part.) It can get crowded with locals who sometimes hang out here all day, but since dogs must be leashed anyway, there's little danger of your dog crashing someone else's picnic.

Driving south from the northern edge of the county, exit US 101 at Highway 135. Drive southwest and take your first right, Preisker Lane. You'll be at the park within a few blocks. (805) 925-0951.
➡ *See #13 on map p. 614.*

• **Waller County Park** 🐾 🐾 🐾

This park is conveniently located next to the Santa Maria Public Airport. Parts of it look like a golf course, parts look like a miniature forest. Paths take you and your leashed dog past duck ponds and through quiet picnic areas.

We prefer to enter on the Waller Lane side. From Highway 135, take Waller Lane west about a half block, park on the street and walk in. (805) 688-3303. ➡ *See #14 on map p. 614.*

PLACES TO STAY

Howard Johnson Lodge: Waller County Park (see above) is fairly close to this motel. Rates are $39 to $60. 210 South Nicholson Avenue, Santa Maria, CA 93454; (805) 922-5891.

Hunter's Inn: Poodle-sized dogs (unfortunately, we're not talking standard-sized poodles) and smaller are okay here. Rates are $50 to $75. Dogs are $5 extra. 1514 South Broadway, Santa Maria, CA 93454; (805) 922-2123.

Ramada Suites: Rates are $55 to $150. Dogs require a $30 deposit. 2050 Preisker Lane, Santa Maria, CA 93454; (805) 928-6000.

SOLVANG

Solvang is a sweet Danish village, with architecture as authentically Danish as its baked goods. The place was settled in 1911 by Danish folks who missed their homeland. They bought property and perpetuated all the Danish customs they could.

After an article about the small community appeared in the *Saturday Evening Post* in 1947, entrepreneurs rushed in from all over the country and created something of a Danish theme park atmosphere here. Still, the town retains its core of true Danish charm.

For a little more on the history of the place, you and your dog can drop by the Solvang Visitors Center, at 1511-A Mission Drive (805) 688-0701. The people here love dogs and promise all visiting pooches a bone. "We like dogs better than babies," says representative Donna Keeler. "We just go nuts about them."

PARKS, BEACHES & RECREATION AREAS

•Hans Christian Andersen Park 🐾 🐾 🐾

When you tell a dog that he's going to get to visit a park that's half developed and half rough, you know which half he's going to want to explore. This 52-acre park has a good undeveloped section for dogs who could care less about refinement.

The area is full of brush, but there are enough trees and navigable walking areas for any dog to have a good time, even on the mandatory leash. If some human in your group insists on hanging out at the developed section of park, your dog will get along just fine.

From Highway 246, take Atterdag Road north. The arched gateway to the park is about three blocks on the left. (805) 568-2461.
➤ *See #15 on map p. 614.*

•Nojoqui Falls County Park 🐾 🐾 🐾 1/2 🐾

In non-drought springtimes, you'll be wowed by the Nojoqui (pronounced "Nah-ho-wee") Waterfall that plunges 100 feet. The rest of the year, you and your dog will still be in awe.

People often compare this 88-acre park with Yosemite National Park. It's kind of a miniature version, complete with thick forests and mini-mountains (also known as hills). Unlike Yosemite, dogs are allowed to explore the area. They have to be on leash, but they don't seem to mind.

From Solvang, go south on Alisal Road about 10 miles. After about six miles, the road will veer sharply to the right. Follow it for four more miles, and the park will be on your left. If you're on US 101 south of Buellton, you can exit at the signed marker for the park and follow the signs for about two miles. The park will be on your right. (805) 568-2461. → *See #16 on map p. 614.*

RESTAURANTS

Chase's Restaurant: Ahh, such an Italian name. "Chase's" just flows off the tongue like a good zabaglione. Dogs like to sit with their people under the umbrellas outside this charming Italian restaurant. The seafood specialties are terrific. 485 Alisal Road; (805) 688-3052.

Sally's Front Yard: This place has been a friend to dogs for years. In fact, Sally, the owner, told me that Ronald Reagan's Secret Service agents used to sit outside with their dogs. It makes one wonder just how well-disguised these sunglass-clad gents were. At least they had good taste. This is a fun little restaurant for dogs and their people. 475 First Street; (805) 688-7674.

The Touch: You and your pooch can share breakfast until 4 p.m. (try the Belgian waffles). Then, at dinnertime, The Touch becomes a Chinese food restaurant. The address is the same as Sally's Front Yard: 475 First Street; (805) 686-0222.

Trevi Espresso Bar: Enjoy coffee, biscotti and muffins at the sidewalk tables here. 1564 Copenhagen Drive; (805) 686-1418.

PLACES TO STAY

Hamlet Motel: Only small dogs are allowed here. Rates are $35 to $95. Dogs are $6 extra. 1532 Mission Drive, Solvang, CA 93463; (800) 253-5033.

Kronborg Best Western: If your dog is under five pounds (Egads! That's smaller than Joe's head!), she can stay here. Rates are $55 to $125. 1440 Mission Drive, Solvang, CA 93463; (805) 688-2383.

Meadowlark Motel: Rates are $35 to $60. Dogs are $5 extra. 2644 Mission Drive, Solvang, CA 93463; (805) 688-4631.

Viking Motel: Dogs under 60 pounds can stay here. Joe would really have to suck in his gut for a night at the Viking. Rates are $32 to $85. Dogs are $5 extra. 1506 Mission Drive, Solvang, CA 93463; (805) 688-1337.

SUMMERLAND

RESTAURANTS

Summerland Beach Cafe: As long as you stay along the perimeter, the brick patio here "is big enough for all kinds of dogs," says a dog-loving waiter. 2924 Lillie Avenue; (805) 969-1019.

VENTURA COUNTY

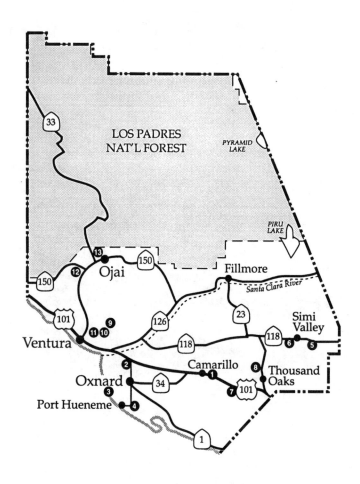

51
VENTURA COUNTY

This diverse coastal county is not a place to bring a dog who is seriously obsessed with swimming. Most beaches along the 42 miles of coastline here ban dogs, although some allow them in their camping or picnicking areas.

Even the big and bassy Lake Casitas makes sure dogs stay more than 50 feet from the lake's edge. We've seen water dogs tremble with genetic anticipation as they try to pull their owners close enough to dip a paw. A ranger told us about a dog who got so frustrated at not being able to swim that when he got back to the motel that night, he ran straight past the manager and into the swimming pool.

Oxnard State Beach is an exciting exception to the dry dog dilemma here. Not only can your dog take a dip, he will soon be able to go leashless. (Applause!) Wet and naked—now that's dog heaven. (See page 630.)

Dog hell, on the other hand, happens when you drive miles and miles to get to a county park, only to find Sir Ranger shaking his head at you, hands on hips, ready to do battle. County parks ban dogs from every inch of their terrain except campgrounds, which are generally not the most scenic spots in the world.

NATIONAL FORESTS

See the National Forests/Wilderness Areas chapter starting on page 801 for important information and safety tips for visiting national forests with your dog.

• **Los Padres National Forest** 🐾 🐾 🐾 🐾 🐆
   See page 806.

CAMARILLO

PARKS, BEACHES & RECREATION AREAS

• **Community Center Park** 🐾
   There's a decent-sized open green area here, and a few trees, but this park isn't anything your leashed dog will brag about to his buddies.

   Exit US 101 at Carmen Drive and go north several blocks. At Burnley Street, go right and park in the lot. (805) 482-1996. ➤ *See #1 on map p. 628.*

FILLMORE

RESTAURANTS

Dino's Frosty Mug and Car Hop: This is a great place to visit if you're dying for a root beer float. You can also get burgers, burritos and chili dogs while you hang out at the shaded picnic tables with your pooch. 650 Ventura Street; (805) 524-3577.

Margaret's Cocina Drive-In: The dog-friendly people here will give a thirsty canine customer a big bowl of water while she joins you for a bite on the patio. 446 Ventura Street; (805) 524-3638.

OXNARD

PARKS, BEACHES & RECREATION AREAS

I had a scintillating conversation with a parks department employee about the subject of dog doo-doo. He quoted from the scriptures (city code): "It says right here—'No person shall permit any dog to defecate on public property...without the consent of the person owning it.' That's the law."

"Okay, so you have to fax the parks commissioners, tell them your dog ate a whopper of a supper last night, and that you might be needing the use of their parks the next morning?" asked I. It took him a few minutes before he figured out that maybe there was more to this law than meets the eye. "Oh, right here it says that if you clean it up right away, you don't have to get permission," said he. "Whew!" said I. "Whew!" breathed Joe.

Another city law says that you must always carry a pooper scooper when with your dog. If you don't have one on hand, you could be fined. But what if your dog already did his business and you threw it out? "You'd better carry a spare just for show," another city employee told me.

The biggest park in the city, College Park, doesn't permit pooches because it's actually a county park. But with the wonderful new leash-free area scheduled to open at the Oxnard State Beach (see below), who needs it anyway?

• **Orchard Park** 🐾 🐾

It's not a large park, but it's attractive for its size. Even dogs seem to think the park is okay, but only early in the morning when less traffic is whizzing by. There are plenty of trees here.

The park is at Edelweiss Street and Erica Place, a few blocks west of Highway 1 and north of Gonzales Road. (805) 385-7950. ➡ *See #2 on map p. 628.*

• **Oxnard State Beach** 🐾 🐾 🐾 🐾 🐕

By the time you read this, a decent-sized stretch of this beach should be open to off-leash dogs. The city of Oxnard actually runs this state beach, so dogs are currently permitted on leash. But a city resolution allowing dogs to tear around leashless was poised to go into effect in the spring or summer of 1994.

This park is less developed than many other beaches in the area. It's about 62 acres and features dune trails and a picnic area.

There's currently no entry fee, but that could soon change. The beach is west of Harbor Boulevard, between Beach Way and Falkirk Avenue. As of this book's press time, the city had not designated which area would be for off-leash dogs. You can take your chances and go to the beach, looking for the proper signage, or call (805) 385-7950. ➜ *See #3 on map p. 628.*

RESTAURANTS

Fisherman's Wharf: This is a thoroughly charming, dog-friendly collection of old-fashioned shops and good restaurants. Little benches abound, but many of the restaurants have their own outdoor seating. We see at least a couple of dogs here each time we visit and we figure they're dogs of the nautical persuasion. They're in great shape, but their leashes seem to be boating line, and their owners have tan, leathery skin and a hint of salt on the hair. Here are two spots to check out with your pooch:

Buon Appetito: This place has lots of outdoor tables for you and your pooch. Come here if you want a meal that's a little elegant. The seafood, pasta and homemade desserts are doggone good. 2721 South Victoria Avenue; (805) 485-7754.

Marine Ice Cream & Candy: Share a treat with your best friend at the table near this shop. 2741 South Victoria Avenue; (805) 985-5532.

Popeye's Famous Fried Chicken and Biscuits: Eat at the outdoor tables here. (There's no spinach on the menu, in case your dog was wondering.) 1900 North Ventura Road; (805) 983-3928.

PLACES TO STAY

Vagabond Inn: Rates are $42 to $64. Dogs are $3 extra. 1245 North Oxnard Boulevard, Oxnard, CA 93030; (805) 983-0251.

PORT HUENEME

PARKS, BEACHES & RECREATION AREAS

Dogs are not allowed at this Navy city's beaches, but they can peruse the parks here.

• **Moranda/Bubbling Springs Park** 🐾 🐾 1/2

A stream runs through much of this park, and in the summer,

dogs love to dip their hot little toes in it to cool off. The park is actually two connected parks. Most of the Bubbling Springs Park, to the north, is a greenbelt area. Moranda Park is a chunk of green with trees, green grass, shaded picnic areas and playgrounds.

Many people and their leashed dogs hike from one end of the adjoining parks to the other. Going north to south (toward the beach), you can begin your walk at Bard Road and Park Avenue and follow the park as it winds south, crossing a few streets along the way. Your hike will end around Seawind Way. (805) 986-6555. ➡*See #4 on map p. 628.*

PLACES TO STAY

Point Mugu State Park campgrounds: Dogs aren't permitted on the magical trails in this spectacular park, even with a leash. "They're a hazard to wildlife and other park visitors," a young ranger told me in a monotone, robot-like voice. Creepy!

At least dogs are allowed to help you pitch a tent at one of their 131 campsites. Rates are $14 to $16. The park is about nine miles south of Port Hueneme Road, on Highway 1. For park info, call (818) 880-0350. Call MISTIX at (800) 444-PARK to reserve a site.

SIMI VALLEY

PARKS, BEACHES & RECREATION AREAS

•**Rancho Santa Susana Community Park** 🐾 🐾

Now *this* is suburbia. Parents in Volvo station wagons pull into the parking lot and out of the car pop a few little soccer demons raring to clobber whatever team they happen to be opposing. Neighbors greet each other with compliments about how fine their lawns look this year. Women push strollers up and down the walkway. Then they push them up and down again.

But when the talcum powder has cleared and it's just you and your leashed dog, you can actually have a decent time here. Between strolling on the path, checking out the bushes and running on the playing fields, your dog might even enjoy himself. The park is at Stearns Street and Los Angeles Avenue. (805) 584-4400. ➡*See #5 on map p. 628.*

•**Rancho Simi Community Park** 🐾 🐾 1/2

This park is pretty much one big field of green turf with some trees and shaded picnic tables. It's quite an attractive, decent-sized area for a community park. Despite a few sports courts and a playground, you can usually find some seclusion here. Just go the back section of the park. You'll know it when you see it.

Dogs would like to tear around chasing frisbees and softballs, but alas, they have to be leashed. The park is on Royal Avenue, about a block east of Erringer Road. (805) 584-4400. →*See #6 on map p. 628.*

PLACES TO STAY

Oak County Park campground: This county campground is located directly below some railroad tracks in what looks like a dirt parking lot with a few trees. It's not what you'd call a hot spot for getting back to nature. There are 55 sites. Rates are $10. Dogs are $1 extra, and they're not allowed on the park's trails or anywhere but the campground.

About halfway between Moorpark and Simi Valley on Highway 118, exit onto Los Angeles Avenue and drive southeast about 1.5 miles. The park entrance will be on your left, directly across from a really big, ugly contractor's storage facility. (805) 654-3644.

RESTAURANTS

Dinah's Famous Chicken and Rotisserie: Eat Dinah's famous chicken (which one?) at one of the outdoor tables here. 1464 Madera Road; (805) 583-8396.

Rasta Pasta and Salads: You'll enjoy eating healthful foods at the outdoor tables here with your pooch at your side. 464 Madera Road; (805) 520-4694.

Taco Tree: Besides decent Mexican food, you can also get teriyaki chicken. Dine on the patio with your favorite dog. 2161 Tapo Street; (805) 583-3556.

THOUSAND OAKS

PARKS, BEACHES & RECREATION AREAS

The Thousand Oaks area is home to thousands of acres of open space you can peruse with a leashed dog. Most of these areas are really difficult to access, though. A regular city map won't help much. As hard as I tried, when I visited I had no luck finding two of the three open space parks that interested me. When I called the open space district here, I was told, "Yes, they are hard to find. I don't know how to get there. There's no one who can help you at all. Why would you want people to come all the way here anyway?"

Maybe you'll have better luck. I hear they may soon be getting some decent maps. The number at the Conejo Open Space Conservation Agency is (805) 495-6471.

•**Borchard Community Park** 🐾 🐾 1/2

Pooches prefer this park's pretty paved path to plenty of places in this proximity. Say that 10 times fast, and you'll have something to occupy your time as you stroll through this attractive green park. There's not too much else here to occupy your attention, but boy dogs will give their attention to the many trees here.

From US 101, exit at Borchard Road/Rancho Conejo Road and follow Borchard Road southwest about a mile. The park will be on your right, at Reino Road. (805) 495-6471. *→See #7 on map p. 628.*

• **Wildwood Park** 🐾 🐾 🐾 1/2

It's not every day you and your dog get to hike to a 60-foot waterfall, so take advantage of this amazing 1,700-acre park. Joe likes to walk to the waterfall and stand there in awe that such waterworks can actually exist in what is otherwise dry land.

Several trails wind through the coastal sage and xeric scrub-covered hills that make up most of the park. In the spring, the wildflowers go wild in a burst of intoxicating color and scent.

You'll have to keep your dog leashed as you hike the many miles of trails. The wildlife appreciates it. After all, there's not much habitat around here for these animals anymore.

From US 101, exit at Thousand Oaks Freeway/Highway 23 and drive north about 2.5 miles to Avenida de los Arboles. Turn left and follow the road all the way to the end (about three miles). The parking area is on the left, next to the entry kiosk that holds maps and brochures of the park. (805) 495-6471. *→See #8 on map p. 628.*

PLACES TO STAY

Thousand Oaks Inn: Rates are $47 to $70. The doggy fee is $5 the first time you stay, after that there's no extra charge. 75 West Thousand Oaks Boulevard, Thousand Oaks, CA 91360; (805) 497-3701.

VENTURA

This seaside community has a wealth of parks for you and your leashed friend to sniff out. It's also home to the ninth—and last—mission founded by Father Junipero Serra. Dogs can't go inside, but they're more than happy to smile at the camera for an exterior shot.

PARKS, BEACHES & RECREATION AREAS

• **Arroyo Verde Park** 🐾 🐾 1/2

Most of this 129-acre park is on rugged land that's pretty much impassable by anyone but the critters of nature. There's a trail that takes you from the 14-acre open grass area into a tiny bit of the wilder area, but you'll barely get your paws moving when the trail loops you right back down the hill.

This is a better park for kids than for dogs (who must be leashed). The civilized segment of the park has a nature center, a playground, a wading pool and Fort Keller—a children's play fort. There's not even a fire hydrant for our four-legged friends.

There's a $1 fee per vehicle on Sundays and holidays. It's probably not worth it to take your dog on these days anyway, because it can be jam-packed. Exit US 101 at Victoria Avenue, and drive north on Victoria for about two miles. Where it ends, turn left on Foothill Road. In about two-thirds of a mile, the park will be on your right, at the corner of Foothill and Day roads. (805) 652-4550. → *See #9 on map p. 628.*

• **Camino Real Park** 🐾 🐾 1/2

When this 38-acre park isn't being used for ball games, it's a fine place to take a leashed pooch. The fields are really large, beckoning you and the leashed dog of your choice to run and jump and act like a couple of pups together.

The park has a refreshing eucalyptus smell. Enjoy the trees from the paved path that winds through much of the park. The park is at Dean Drive at Varsity Street, just a few blocks south of Ventura College. (805) 652-4550. → *See #10 on map p. 628.*

• **Grant Memorial Park** 🐾 🐾 🐾

In 1782, Father Junipero Serra raised a wooden cross on the mountain overlooking his newly built Mission San Buenaventura. That mountain is now part of this 107-acre park. A cross still sticks out of the top of the park, and if you go anywhere near it, you'll find wonderful views of the city, the Pacific and the Channel Islands.

Surrounding the cross is a little grassy area where you can unwind, take in the views or eat a relaxing picnic. But if you want to be kind to your dog, before you sit down to *ooh* and *ahh* at the scenery, turn around. On the other side of the parking lot you'll see a dirt trail heading up the adjacent hill. It's not shady, so your leashed dog won't be able to *ooh* and *ahh* at the trees, but it's a great way for you to get away from the park's never-ending trickle of visitors.

From Cedar Street (two blocks east of Ventura Avenue), turn east on Ferro Drive and follow it to the top of the park. (805) 652-4550. → *See #11 on map p. 628.*

• **Lake Casitas Recreation Area** 🐾 🐾 🐾

Don't bring a water dog here. She'll just stare at the water and weep. Dogs have to be kept 50 feet away from the lake, meaning they can't even go on a boat with you. With 50,000 people who rely on this lake for water, it's understandable how they wouldn't want a bunch of flea-bitten beasts floating around in their drink. But that's a hard one to explain to a quivering, frothing Labrador retriever. Actually, people aren't permitted to swim here either, but that news probably won't do much to console your dog-paddling pooch.

Once you enter this 6,200-acre park, your best bet is to bear to the right and follow the road to a dense, lush, oaky campground. Park wherever you can and walk with your leashed dog as far back as possible. You'll find some short trails winding through this part of the park, and some excellent places to relax and get away from the bulk of the people who visit here. (They're all at the water, like most normal folks.)

The day-use fee is $5. Dogs are $1. There are 480 campsites, with rates ranging from $12 to $18. Camping dogs cost $1.50. Reservations are not necessary. From the heart of Ventura, drive 11 miles north on Highway 33. Turn left on Highway 150 and drive about four miles to the main entrance. (805) 649-2233. →*See #12 on map p. 628.*

•**Ojai Valley Trail** 🐾 🐾 🐾 ◀▶
You and your leashed dog may have to share this nine-mile trail with a few fast bicycles, but don't let that stop you. It's a great way to see the valley east of Lake Casitas.

The trail will take you through little forested areas and quiet neighborhoods, past rolling hills and Christmas tree farms. For the fair of foot, there are plenty of shaded, tranquil resting spots along the way.

Even if you walk only one segment of the trail, it's worth the trip. When the trail first opened, dogs were banned, but the rule was so difficult to enforce that eventually pooches were given the okay. Take advantage of this! Rejoice! Take a hike!

The trail runs parallel to Highway 33. We like to start at Foster County Park (see page 637). It's the trail's staging area. But keep in mind that dogs are allowed at this park only at the trailhead and the campsites. Exit Highway 33 at Casitas Vista Road and follow the signs. As you head northeast on the trail, you can also access it from points such as San Antonio Creek, Santa Ana Boulevard, Barbara Street and Baldwin Avenue. (805) 654-3951. →*See #13 on map p. 628.*

RESTAURANTS
Beachside Pizzeria: This place has wood tables by the beach. You and your dog can enjoy the waves and eat gourmet pizza. Try the pesto and garlic varieties, but only if your dog doesn't have a hot date afterward. 1141 Seaward Street; (805) 648-7858.

Cafe Voltaire: This cute little cafe has a courtyard where you and your dog can dine on croissant sandwiches and other cafe-style food. 34 North Palm Street; (805) 641-1743.

Classic Carrot Cafe: Although there are two patios at this natural foods cafe, you and your dog can only dine out front, since the back patio has no outdoor access. But that's not a problem, because the sidewalk seating is a fine place to dine on all the delicious, healthful foods here. Homemade soups, killer burritos and hot sandwiches are popular lunch items. 1847 East Main Street; (805) 643-0406.

The Coastal Cone Company: 1583 Spinnaker Drive; (805) 658-2837.

Culinary Fantasies: If a Reuben or a grilled sandwich is your fantasy, dine here with your best doggy-friend at the sidewalk patio. 3737 Telegraph Road; (805) 644-6368.

Duke's Griddle 'n Grill: Your dog just might get a special treat from a waiter while you dine on the good grilled grub served at the outdoor tables here. 1124 South Seaward Avenue; (805) 653-0707.

Fiesta Restaurant: You and your beast can hang out together at the patio while you eat a hearty Mexican meal. 3114 Telegraph Road; (805) 642-4174.

Taco Jalisco: Despite its name, burritos are really the specialty here. Eat with your dog at the outdoor tables. 2292 East Main Street; (805) 643-2820.

Top Hat Burger Palace: You don't have to be of royal blood to enjoy this fast-food palace. All of the seating is outdoors; you just go to an order window to get your food, and then dine in leisure with your mutt. 299 East Main Street; (805) 643-9696.

PLACES TO STAY

Doubletree Hotel at Ventura: This hotel is a mere block from the state beach, where pooches are not permitted (alas). Rates are $90 to $130. Dogs are $50 extra. 2055 Harbor Boulevard, Ventura, CA 93001; (805) 643-6000.

Faria County Park campground: You're so close to the water here (you're actually at the ocean's edge), yet so very far away. Dogs aren't allowed on the beach, and that can be a bummer with a capital B. There are 42 sites, with fees ranging from $9 to $14. Dogs are $1 extra. From the main part of Ventura, drive seven miles northwest on US 101. For park info or campsite reservations, call (805) 654-3951.

Foster County Park campground: Some of the sites here are near oaks, but that's about the best thing we can say about this place, except that the park is the staging area for the Ojai Valley Trail (see page 636). Sites are $10. (805) 654-3951.

McGrath State Beach campsites: Your dog can't go on the beach with you here, but the camping area is pretty enough that it's not such a bad fate to hang out here together and read a good book. There are 174 sites. Rates are $14 to $16. Dogs are $1 extra. From US 101, take the Seaward Avenue/Harbor Boulevard exit and drive four miles west on Harbor Boulevard to the beach. For reservations, phone MISTIX at (800) 444-PARK. For park info, call (805) 899-1400.

Motel 6: Rates are $30 for the first adult, $4 for the second. You can bring one small pooch here. 2145 East Harbor Boulevard, Ventura, CA 93001; (805) 643-5100.

La Quinta Inn: This inn has had all sorts of nonhuman visitors— even birds and rabbits. Rates are $48 to $55. 5818 Valentine Road, Ventura, CA 93003; (805) 658-6200.

Vagabond Inn: Rates are $43 to $65. Dogs are $5 extra. 756 East Thompson Boulevard, Ventura, CA 93001; (805) 648-5371.

LOS ANGELES COUNTY

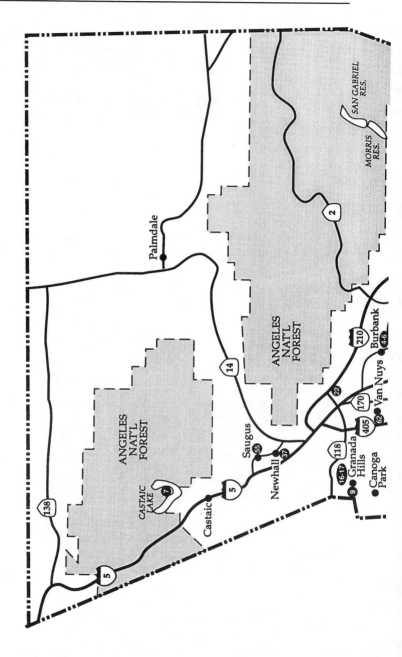

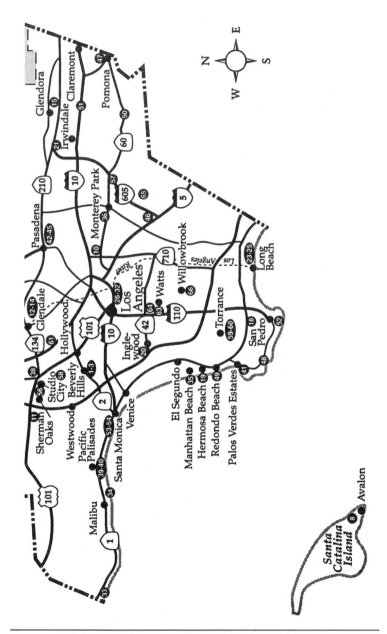

52
LOS ANGELES COUNTY

If you took all the "No Dogs Allowed" signs in this county, put them side by side and strung wire around them, you'd have a hell of a fenced-in dog-exercise area. The county could sure use it. There just aren't enough places to let your dog frolic off leash here.

In fact, even on-leash walks can be tough to find if you don't know where to look. Dogs are banned from all beaches except a few in the Malibu area. The rest of those 74 miles of shoreline are off-limits, verboten, badlands. Too bad the county or some of the cities here can't follow the lead of San Francisco or San Diego and open some of the less-used beach areas to leash-free dog traffic. The leash-free part of this dream may never happen because almost all of this county's beaches draw large crowds, but at least leashed pooches should be allowed to sniff out L.A.'s footprints in the sand.

The Los Angeles County Parks system is a good one, with dozens of large parks dotting the county. Most allow leashed pooches. But sadly, many parks are facing certain deaths with the fatal budget cuts of the last few years. In this chapter, I've tried to list only the parks that look as though they're going to make the cut. The more primitive ones that charge no money now may soon have to start collecting fees for trail use. If that doesn't work, they may not be open much longer either.

The devastating fires of 1993 didn't help matters, nor did the tragic earthquake and later mudslides. It's a minor consequence of this long string of disasters, but some parks that did permit dogs have been temporarily put out of business. In this edition, I've left out some of the parks that will be closed for a while. The directions to others may be a little askew now because of freeway closures. Please check updated maps before venturing far.

But the show must go on. With a little ingenuity, any dog can have his day in L.A. Dog parks such as Laurel Canyon Park in Studio City (see page 687) or the Recreation Park dog run in Long Beach (see page 663) are worth the drive if your dog needs to throw her leash to the wind. You can take a train ride with your dog at Griffith Park (see Diversions, page 670), and even take your extremely well-behaved poochum-woochums shopping at certain exclusive Beverly Hills stores (see Diversions, page 648).

Dogs can compare pawprints with the prints of Hollywood's biggest stars at Mann's Chinese Theatre (see Diversions, page 661). If you want a little exercise with your stargazing, pick up a map of the stars' homes and take a little walk around town. It's an extremely hackneyed, sometimes rude pastime, but most of the homes on these tours have long since changed hands so you're often just staring at a home where the star lived many moons ago. Anyway, it's a great excuse to walk your dog.

Anthony Shipp, a Beverly Hills veterinarian to the stars, says celebrities often feel that their dogs are the only ones who really love them for who they are. "So many people like them only for what they can get from them, or for the dazzle," says Shipp, who has ministered to the dogs of Frank Sinatra, Kirk Douglas, Peter Falk and even Richard Simmons, to drop a few names. (He says many years ago he helped Sinatra's and Douglas' disinterested dogs to mate, but the dogs would do it only after they put on a tape of the crooner's hits. "It seems even dogs get romantic to Sinatra's voice," he says.)

Chances are good that you'll see a star or two just by going to some of the cafes and restaurants that permit dogs at their outdoor tables. Joe and I aren't stargazers by nature, but when he saw Goldie Hawn saunter out of a Beverly Hills cafe that we were just about to walk into, he couldn't stop staring. It was embarrassing, even for him, but he just couldn't take his eyes off her. And when she glanced down at him and smiled, he melted. His mouth opened and he stared straight ahead, stunned. She walked on with her friend, never knowing the impression she had made on one lovestruck Airedale.

Joe and I usually prefer to stargaze in the direction of the heavens, in an open field on a clear night. Joe's favorite star (excluding Goldie Hawn) is the brilliant Sirius, part of the constellation Canis Major. If you or your dog enjoy dabbling in astronomy, the Los Angeles Astronomical Society may have some activities of interest (see Diversions, page 670).

This chapter separates some of the districts in the city of Los Angeles into their own sections. For instance, instead of listing Hollywood under "Los Angeles," it has its own heading. The city is too huge to lump all its districts together.

NATIONAL FORESTS

See the National Forests/Wilderness Areas chapter starting on page 801 for important information and safety tips for visiting national forests with your dog.

• **Angeles National Forest** 🐾 🐾 🐾 🐾 🐾 ➡ 🐕
  See page 803.

NATIONAL RECREATION AREAS

• **Santa Monica Mountains**
  National Recreation Area 🐾 🐾 🐾 1/2 ➡

Attention smog-coated dogs and city-weary people: You can breathe a sigh of relief. Nature is only a stick's throw away from the crowded freeways and urban sprawl of one of the largest cities in the world.

Contrary to what some local dog people have heard, leashed dogs really *are* allowed to explore portions of this 65,000-acre wonderland of mountains, canyons, woods and fern glens. This national recreation area is a patchwork of county, state and federal lands located throughout the Santa Monica Mountains. While dogs are banned from trails on all state lands and from all but a few Malibu-area beaches (see page 671) within the recreation area, they're welcome at 26 of the parks here.

The following are dog-friendly parks, from A to Z: Arroyo Sequit, Calabasas Peak, Castro Crest, Charmlee County Natural Area, Cheeseboro Canyon, Circle X Ranch, Coldwater Canyon, Corral Canyon, Franklin Canyon Ranch, Fryman Canyon, Laurel Canyon (includes an off-leash dog park, see page 687), Paramount Ranch, Peter Strauss Ranch, Rancho Sierra Vista/Satwiwa, Red Rock Canyon, Rocky Oaks, Runyun Canyon, San Vicente Mountain, Serrania Canyon, Solstice Canyon, Stuart Ranch, Tapia, Temescal Gateway, Wilacre, Wildwood Regional and Zuma Canyon.

The parks are too numerous to describe in detail in this book, but the Mountain Parks Information Service provides a free map showing all the parks, delineating which permit dogs. You can also get free brochures of many of the dog-friendly parks, which show trailheads and give descriptions and directions. They're essential for planning any enchanting back-to-nature outing with your dog. Call (800) 533-PARK to get your maps and brochures. For the National Park Service Visitors Center, call (818) 597-9192.

Spring is a terrific time to explore these lands. Wildflowers blossom white, bright yellow, orange, blue, red and every other color your dog might not be able to see if he's as color-blind as scientists claim. Birds sing their hearts out. The grasslands, normally a dead tan-brown color, get as green as green gets.

BEL-AIR

PLACES TO STAY

Hotel Bel-Air: Before you continue reading, it's only fair to give you the room/suite rates: The range is from $255 to $2,000 nightly. Dogs are $250 extra for the length of your stay. If you're still reading and haven't turned to the nearest Vagabond Inn listing, you'll be pleased to know that dogs are allowed to roam almost everywhere on the gorgeous, lush 11.5-acre garden setting that enfolds the captivating rooms and suites. You won't have to go to a park to exercise your pooch. The suites and rooms offer so many distinct decors that you should call and discuss your options with the very personable hotel staff. 701 Stone Canyon Road, Los Angeles, CA 90077; (310) 472-1211 or (800) 648-4097.

BEVERLY HILLS

As Joe, Bill and I rattled around this opulent city in our 14-year-old pickup truck on a recent research trip, we were the objects of unmasked curiosity and a smidgen of concern. Joe's head stuck out one side of the camper top in back, Bill's hung out the other, and the truck had hiccups at the time and was making obscene noises.

Park rangers and cops paid my little Beverly Hillbillies-mobile a visit three times as we stopped at park after park. "Just want to make sure you're not lost, Miss" was the general theme of their very cordial way of evaluating our menace potential.

I had a lunch date with a six-pound poodle and her owner, Elaine Young, known in these parts as one of the realtors to the stars. They were supposed to tell me about a couple of great places to take a pooch in Beverly Hills. Instead of taking the chance that Joe and Bill would take this tiny critter to be an appetizer, I left the boys with a friend in the area.

As it turns out, I could have brought them along. The teacup poodle, Mellow, couldn't make it. It seems Mellow wasn't of the housebroken persuasion, and rather than creating a stink, Young had left him home. Notorious San Francisco tort lawyer Melvin Belli had given Mellow to Young when they were an item, but she says she would have asked for a potty-trained dog if she'd been thinking. "For $1,500, you'd think they'd give you a pocket poodle who doesn't pee on everything," she whispered over salad.

Young is a glamourous, bouffant-haired 58-year-old woman who kisses and gets kissed by all the celebrities who walk into the restaurant near her office. She's had six husbands ("I love being married," she says) and three teacup poodles. Two of the poodles died under the wheels of Rolls Royces in separate accidents.

In between rubbing noses with actors and trying to sell a wealthy foreigner a big building on Sunset Boulevard, Young told me of a few dog-loving restaurants and a decent park. Unfortunately, there are no off-leash areas here. But judging by the fate of those two tiny poodles, it's just as well. Watch out for Rolls Royces and have a good time.

PARKS, BEACHES & RECREATION AREAS

Dogs aren't allowed in the stunningly beautiful Greystone Park. But then again, neither are cameras or picnics, so canines shouldn't feel too offended.

•Beverly Gardens Park 🐾 🐾 1/2

Stretching from Wilshire Boulevard to Doheny Drive, this narrow, 20-block-long park is great for dogs on the go. It runs along the north side of Santa Monica Boulevard, so if you and your dog are trying to sprint from one end of town to the other, you couldn't ask for a much greener way to go.

The strip of park has a path, so you're not relegated to the sidewalk. But since it does parallel the busy boulevard, it's not without its share of exhaust fumes and honking Mercedes. Dogs must be leashed. (310) 285-2541. ➡See #1 on map pp. 640-641.

•La Cienega Park 🐾 1/2

If your pooch wants to fraternize with the cream of the Beverly Hills canine corps, there are fancier places to take her. But this a passable neighborhood park with fenced-in ball fields and a playground. If the ball fields are in use, there's not much room for you and your leashed dog to roam, but you can always find a strip of grass.

The bulk of the park is on the east side of La Cienega Boulevard, between Gregory Way and Schumacher Drive. A smaller segment of the park is on the west side of La Cienega Boulevard. (310) 285-2541. ➡See #2 on map pp. 640-641.

•Will Rogers Memorial Park 🐾 🐾 1/2

Dogs and their elegantly clad people come to this lush park to lounge the afternoon away. Dogs have to be leashed here, and it's not a large park, but it is verdant and rich with the colorful sights and sounds of Beverly Hills. When Joe and Bill and I visited, we witnessed a tiny bit of a dog being led out of a Rolls by a chauffeur who had the same air of noble servitude as if he were escorting the Queen of England. He walked the little thing around once and said "Now, Emily." The dog did its little business on command. The chauffeur scooped and they sped off, no doubt to more pressing engagements.

The Will Rogers Memorial Park is a triangular chunk of fine real estate at the corner of Canon and Beverly drives and Sunset Boulevard, right across from the Beverly Hills Hotel. (310) 285-2541. ➡ *See #3 on map pp. 640-641.*

RESTAURANTS

California Pizza Kitchen: Your dog can dine outside with you here, but she has to be tied up on the other side of the wrought-iron fence. 207 South Beverly Drive; (310) 275-1101.

Celestino: The Italian food here is light and delicious. Dogs like joining their owners for lunch at the two outdoor tables. 236 South Beverly Drive; (310) 859-8601.

Chez Helene: If you like country French food, you must try this place. Not only is the food fantastique, the outside area is quite lovely, too. 267 South Beverly Drive; (310) 276-1558.

La Famiglia Restaurant: Eat Northern Italian-style food at the outside tables with your dog at your side. 453 North Canon Drive; (310) 276-6208.

The Hollywood Hotdog Co., Inc.: The manager tells us that not only do lots of dogs visit the outside tables with their owners, they also get to eat here. "People buy hot dogs for their dogs all the time. It's a good deal, one dog to another and all that," he says. For vegetarians, the place even serves a hearty veggie dog. 9527 Santa Monica Boulevard; (310) 278-4674.

Jacopo's Pizzeria: Besides pizza, you can get chicken, seafood and pasta at the outdoor tables here. 490 North Beverly Drive; (310) 858-6446.

Mulberry Street Pizzeria: 347 North Canon Drive; (310) 247-8100.

The Players: Dine on fish, pasta and steak under an awning in a very pretty outdoor setting. 9513 Santa Monica Boulevard; (310) 278-6669.

Royal Persis: If you like continental and Middle Eastern food, you'll lick your chops at the outdoor tables here. 362 North Canon Drive; (310) 281-0777.

Subway: 279 South Beverly Drive; (310) 278-7827.

Total Energy: They sell delicious, healthful drinks here, and the manager says people aren't the only ones who drink them. "We get some people who buy energy drinks for their dogs," she says. "Dogs love them." If your dog is thirsty but already has enough energy, they'll give the pooch a bowl of water, which he can sip under the awning here. 9533 Santa Monica Boulevard; (310) 246-9533.

Il Tramezzino: The eggplant parmesan here is delicioso. Eat it at an umbrella-topped table. 460 North Canon Drive; (310) 273-0501.

PLACES TO STAY

Beverly Hilton: If elegant hotels like this have few qualms about allowing dogs to spend the night, shouldn't others follow suit? Rates are $190 to $250. 9876 Wilshire Boulevard, Beverly Hills, CA 90210; (310) 274-7777.

L'Ermitage Hotel: If you can afford the first-class European elegance of this exclusive and very private hotel, you won't regret a night or two here. You will be pampered beyond belief. A chauffeur comes with your stay here, so you and the pooch (who will be treated like anything but a pooch) can hitch a ride to nearby locales. A wonderful array of goodies awaits you daily and nightly in your suite. The marble bathrooms alone come complete with a steam room, phones, a TV and a plush robe. All this and more can be yours for $290 to $630. (The hotel will be closed for renovation until autumn of 1994, and rates may change when it re-opens.) 9291 Burton Way, Beverly Hills, CA 90210; (310) 278-3344.

DIVERSIONS

Charge it with your wee doggy: If you can easily carry your well-behaved pooch under your arm, many top Beverly Hills shops will welcome your business (but not your dog's business, if you know what I mean—walk your dog first). "We have one customer who leaves her tiny dog with the doorman while she shops around, but most just carry their dogs around with them as they pick out what they want," says Ed Bodde, vice president and general manager of Saks Fifth Avenue on Wilshire. As far as Bodde knows, there's never been an "accident" on the premises and he'd like to keep it that way.

The Beverly Hills I Magnin has a general store policy against pooches, but security guards and regular dog-carrying customers tell us that if you can tote your dog, you're in. I couldn't try this with 70-pound groaning Joe, so you'll have to find out for yourself if they're as dog-friendly as local shoppers say.

Several small boutiques here also allow the occasional pooch, but they asked not to be mentioned for fear of being besieged with giant dogs and dogs with bad bathroom habits.

One place you'll have to avoid with your dog is Neiman-Marcus. A dog in another Neiman store recently bit a customer, and the Beverly Hills store has had to go along with a company policy banning all dogs. But they're discreet. Says a smooth-voiced representative: "We hand them a form that explains the situation, and they're usually very understanding. It can be a real disappointment."

I Magnin is at 9634 Wilshire Boulevard; (310) 271-2131. Saks' address is 9600 Wilshire Boulevard; (310) 275-4211.

BURBANK

PARKS, BEACHES & RECREATION AREAS

• **Izay Park** 🐾 🐾

Here it is: Not huge, but not tiny, a few ball fields, lots of grass and trees surrounding much of the park. We can't say much more, except leash your dog here. The park is at Glenoaks Boulevard between Andover and Amherst drives. (818) 953-9572. ➡ *See #4 on map pp. 640-641.*

• **Johnny Carson Park** 🐾 🐾 1/2

Remember all of Johnny Carson's lines about "beautiful downtown Burbank"? Since the former *Tonight Show* host did his best to put Burbank on the map, the city decided to do the same for him. Just across from the NBC studios where he hosted his show year after year, there's a decent little park named after him.

The park, which used to be called Buena Vista Park, is a great place to visit with your dog if you're dropping off a friend at NBC or at the nearby Disney studios. It's well-shaded and has many picnic tables and a footbridge that leads you to a fitness course. With Highway 134 roaring so close, it's not quiet, but who comes to this part of Burbank for tranquility?

A word of warning: Don't let your male dog lift his leg on the stone "sign" with Johnny Carson's mug engraved on it. We met a man who apparently sits on the grass all day watching for such indiscretions. He came running up to Joe after the dog did a quick leg left. I thought perhaps he knew Joe or was running up to say Joe was a fine dog, but something about the way he was screaming "No, no pee on this! Bad dog!" led me to believe he had another mission.

Exit Highway 5 at Alameda Avenue and drive southwest for about 20 blocks. At Bob Hope Drive, turn left. The park will be on your left in about a block. (818) 953-9572. ➡ *See #5 on map pp. 640-641.*

• **Wildwood Canyon Park** 🐾 🐾 🐾 1/2

The only way Joe would like this big park better than he already does would be if he could go leashless. It's beautifully manicured and surrounded by miles of forest. If he's in the mood to roll on the grass and enjoy a picnic near regal stone archways, we stay in the developed part of the park. If he's raring to explore nature and admire trees in his unique way, we take the myriad trails leading out from various points around the park.

His favorite kind of day involves a long hike through the hills, then a leisurely picnic at the serene, secluded, shaded picnic spots that dot the main area. You can't help but feel pampered in this lush park: It's run with such class that even the portable toilets are disguised to look distinguished.

Coming north on Interstate 5, take the Olive Avenue exit and head northeast. Turn left at Sunset Canyon Drive. In six blocks, turn right on Harvard Drive, which will take you into the park. Make sure you bear right once you come to a fork in the road, or you'll end up on the adjacent golf course. (818) 953-9572. *See #6 on map pp. 640-641.*

RESTAURANTS

Chez Nous: If you like California-continental cuisine, you'll enjoy dining under the canopies with your pooch. 10550 Riverside Drive; (818) 760-0288.

Toluca Garden: This is a good Chinese restaurant where you and the dog can dine at umbrella-topped outdoor tables. 10000 River-side Drive; (818) 980-3492.

El Mexicano: 3121 West Olive Street; (818) 567-0177.

Juicy Harveys: The AstroTurf here looks awfully realistic, so watch your dog closely lest he think it's a miniature park. 3203 West Alameda Avenue; (818) 846-9033.

Priscilla's: If you and your pooch want to feel really welcome at a restaurant, come here. "We *love* dogs, and would let them inside if we were allowed," says a manager. "We give them water, a little milk, whatever they want." You'll like the relaxed atmosphere on the patio with umbrella-shaded tables, as well as the gourmet coffees and tasty light fare. 4150 Riverside Drive; (818) 843-5707.

PLACES TO STAY

Burbank Airport Hilton: Rates are $106 to $171. 2500 Hollywood Way, Burbank, CA 91505; (818) 843-6000.

Holiday Inn: Rates are $96 to $135. Dogs can stay on the second floor. 150 Angeleno Avenue, Burbank, CA 91510; (818) 841-4770.

CASTAIC

PARKS, BEACHES & RECREATION AREAS

•Castaic Lake 🐾 🐾 🐾

At 9,000 acres, this is the largest of Los Angeles County's recreation areas. But before your dog starts drooling with excitement, you should be warned that there's not much for a dog to do around here.

Hiking trails are virtually nonexistent. Dogs must be leashed everywhere. They're never allowed in either the large Castaic Lake or the 180-acre Afterbay Lagoon, no matter how many trout or bass they see. (At this book's press time, humans were also banned from swimming because of a bacteria problem.)

Because there are no trails around Castaic Lake, it's pretty much impossible to hike its perimeter. The Afterbay Lagoon is a good sight easier for a dog jaunt, since it's developed. It has plenty of grassy areas, some trees, picnic tables and a couple of playgrounds.

If you and your dog aren't anglers, but you're with someone who is, it's a fine place to spend the day. But it's not the kind of destination you'd want to visit just to walk your dog.

There's a $6 fee per car. The fee is waived during weekdays from November through February. Boat launching is an additional $6. Campsites are being developed, so it might be a better place to take a pooch in the future. From Interstate 5, exit at Lake Hughes Road and follow it to the lake. (815) 257-4050. → *See #7 on map pp. 640-641.*

PLACES TO STAY

Comfort Inn: The lake is down the road a bit. Rates are $40 to $70; 31558 Castaic Road, Castaic, CA 91384; (805) 295-1100 or (800) 228-5150.

CATALINA

Contrary to popular belief, dogs are allowed on enchanting Santa Catalina Island. They're just not allowed at any parks, most beaches or along Crescent Avenue, the main drag here. As if that's not bad enough, if you're caught without a pooper scooper in your possession (regardless of whether you've already used it and won't be needing one), you can be fined.

Add to this scenario the fact that no hotels, motels or campgrounds permit dogs, making it pretty tough to spend the night together, and you'll see just what a challenge it can be to visit here with a dog.

For years, the no-dogs-at-hotels situation has made minor criminals out of dog-loving folks, forcing them to sneak their pooches into their rooms when eyes were diverted. When they were caught, their dogs would usually be banished to the car, or worse yet, the whole party had to return to the mainland on the next ferry.

But recently, the president of the Avalon Humane Society opened the Avalon Boarding Service, so dogs can now spend the night in their own accommodations. While it's not the same as snoozing the night away by your side, at least you know that first thing in the morning, you can arrange to pick up your dog and spend the whole day with him. Owner Neva Jennings knows dogs, loves dogs and will treat your pooch kindly and warmly. Even the most skittish dogs tend to feel content at her side.

Jennings says she's "very elastic" about pick-up and drop-off times, and she'll meet you somewhere other than the kennels if it's easier for you. She'll even just board your pooch for the day, if that's all you need. Dog boarding starts at $15 a day, which includes high-quality pooch food and some exercise. Contact Jennings at (310) 510-0852 or (310) 510-2221, or write her at P.O. Box 701, Avalon, CA 90704.

PARKS, BEACHES & RECREATION AREAS

If you don't know where to go, this place can be hell for a dog. It seems like every time you find a decent spot of green or beach, you also spot a "No Dogs Allowed" sign or a ranger with his hands on his hips and a frown on his lips.

The interior of the island is run by the Santa Catalina Island Conservancy and Los Angeles County. You'll need to get a permit to hike in these rugged natural areas. Call (310) 510-0688 to arrange one. We'd heard from some dog owners that muzzles might soon be required, but so far, so good. To get in touch with the Conservancy about this rule or other questions, call (310) 510-1421. Dogs aren't allowed anywhere near the campgrounds.

•**Pebbly Beach** 🐾 🐾 🐾 1/2

Pebbly Beach is where locals take their dogs. As the name implies, it's pebbly here, so you won't see dogs bounding around quite as they would in the sand. It's also not terribly conducive to sunworshipping either. But it's about the only game near town for dogs. They're supposed to be leashed here.

The beach is on Pebbly Beach Road, in the industrial part of town. It's just on the south side of Lovers Cove, about a mile from town. Call the county sheriff's department for information. (310) 510-0174. ➡️*See #8 on map pp. 640-641.*

RESTAURANTS

Shipwreck Joey's: Dine outside, overlooking Avalon Bay, at the base of the casino. The cuisine is of the burger-seafood-chicken variety. 2 Casino Way; (310) 510-2755.

DIVERSIONS

Nautical dog! Nautical dog!: Unless you have your own boat or care to hire a helicopter to sweep you to the island, you're going to have to rely on passenger ships to take you to Santa Catalina

Island. Although dogs must be leashed and muzzled, most seem to enjoy the scenes, smells and sounds they experience aboard these big boats. If lodgings in Catalina were as dog-friendly as the cruise services, dogs would give a Catalina Island vacation a four-paws stamp of approval.

Two lines offer dogs ship-to-shore hospitality. The Catalina Channel Express is the fastest passenger boat to the island's towns of Avalon and Two Harbors. The excursion takes only about an hour. Trips leave from San Pedro and Long Beach, and cost $35.50 roundtrip per adult. Call (310) 519-1212 for more information. Catalina Cruises offers a more leisurely experience, with cocktails and snacks available during the nearly two-hour trip. Adults are $28.50 roundtrip. Call (800) 228-2546.

Dogs go free on both excursions. If anyone in your party (dogs included) is prone to seasickness, it may be wise to choose the faster of the two. Every minute you spend with a green countenance and trembling gut can seem like an hour, and the Express boat will shave at least 50 of those eternal minutes off your trip.

CENTURY CITY

PLACES TO STAY

Century Plaza Hotel & Tower: Wow. This is some fancy joint. (That's what dogs say when they find out they're allowed here.) Small dogs are welcome and larger ones can sometimes stay here, too. Check with the manager. The hotel is right across the street from the ABC Entertainment Center, which won't matter to your dog since dogs aren't the kind of guests ABC seeks. Rates are $175 to $300. 2025 Avenue of the Stars, Century City, CA 90067; (310) 277-2000.

CHATSWORTH

PARKS, BEACHES & RECREATION AREAS

• **Chatsworth Park South** 🐾 🐾 🐾 1/2

Joe and Bill had a rollicking good time roaming and rolling in this very spacious park one sunny afternoon. Other dogs were having the same grand old time, and when they joined together, it was a major pooch party.

The park's 81 acres provide lots of leg room for dogs, but the creatures are supposed to be leashed. An Elysian green meadow stretches as far as you care to run with your dog. If tiptoeing through the grass isn't your idea of a good time, you can walk along the park's wide dirt hiking trail.

The craggy mountains towering north of the park make for an impressive backdrop. Enough trees grace the park that you can lounge in the shade while you admire the scenery and the friendly dogs who frequent the place.

Exit Highway 118 at Topanga Canyon Boulevard, and drive south for almost 1.5 miles to Devonshire Street. Turn right and drive a few blocks into the park. (818) 341-6595. *→ See #9 on map pp. 640-641.*

PLACES TO STAY

Summerfield Suites Hotel: If your dog is into fireplaces, big suites and big dog deposits, this is the place for her. Rates are $80 to $160. Dogs are $6 extra, and require a $250 deposit, at least $50 of which is nonrefundable. 21902 Lassen Street, Chatsworth, CA 91311; (818) 773-0707.

CLAREMONT

PARKS, BEACHES & RECREATION AREAS

If all goes as planned, by the time this book hits the stands Claremont is going to be home to a very dog-friendly dog-exercise area called **Bark Park**. Local dogs know that's not just good news for dogs, it's fantastic news. Until Bark Park, dogs haven't even been allowed to set paw in any Claremont park. Now all of a sudden (actually, it was a two-year process, but who's counting?), dogs will be able to run leashless on a rectangle of land about 50 by 80 yards. As of press time, officials weren't sure which city park was going to house the fenced-in Bark Park area, so call (909) 399-5490 if your dog looks like he could use a bit of off-leash freedom.

PLACES TO STAY

Howard Johnson: Rates are $50 to $75. 721 Indian Hills Boulevard, Claremont, CA 91711; (909) 626-2431 or (800) 654-2000.

EAST LOS ANGELES

PARKS, BEACHES & RECREATION AREAS

•**Belvedere Regional Community Park** 🐾 🐾 1/2

Although Highway 60 bisects this county park, it's still a decent place to take a leashed dog for a romp. In fact, the freeway's proximity makes it attractive to dogs on the go who find they have to go. Just exit Highway 60 at Atlantic, go north a block and turn west on 1st Street. Proceed on 1st Street about 10 blocks. The north half of the park will be on your right. Park in the lot and enjoy acres of green grass and a few trees. (213) 268-7264. *→ See #10 on map pp. 640-641.*

ENCINO

PARKS, BEACHES & RECREATION AREAS

• **Balboa Park** 🐾 🐾 🐾

This park is completely recreation-oriented, which is good news for leashed dogs, for once. Pooches are allowed on the many playing fields that make up this large city park. And they're welcome on the big empty fields where no sports are played. If your dog likes to hike on forested trails, this place won't be his idea of heaven, since there are none. But if he enjoys a good roll in the grass, take him here at once. If no one is playing soccer or softball, he's in for a real treat.

Exit US 101 at Balboa Boulevard, drive a couple of blocks north and you'll be at the park's entrance. (818) 343-4143. → *See #11 on map pp. 640-641.*

GLENDALE

PARKS, BEACHES & RECREATION AREAS

• **Brand Park** 🐾 🐾 🐾 1/2 🐾

If you feel as if you're on the estate of William Randolph Hearst when visiting this green and verdant park, you're not far off. It's actually the former property of the late real estate tycoon Leslie C. Brand, a.k.a. "The Father of Glendale."

Upon entering the park, you'll be greeted by a great white Moorish/Indian-style mansion. The mansion is now a library, surrounded by lush, shaded land. You and your leashed dog can pass an afternoon in perfect serenity here. Go ahead, pretend it's your estate. Relax, read, sniff the flowers and have a little picnic.

If you prefer a little exercise with your lounging, there's a fire road that takes you through the park and up to a ridge with a great view. This hike is not for the fair of foot: It's almost a six-mile roundtrip and, to put it mildly, it's not flat. But it's one of the more enjoyable hikes we found in the Los Angeles area. And if you want to keep going, there are ways to access the thousands of acres of open space that lie outside the park's perimeter. Unfortunately, the leash law applies in this area, too.

Exit Interstate 5 on Western Avenue and go northeast about 1.5 miles. The road will take you to the park's magnificent library entrance. (818) 548-2000. → *See #12 on map pp. 640-641.*

• **Dunsmore Park** 🐾 🐾 1/2

If, after a hike at the dusty, rugged George Deukmejian Wilderness Park (see page 656), you and your pooch are longing for mowed green grass, come here. It's only 10 blocks away, and has many signs of civilization, including water fountains, shaded picnic areas, a large playground and a fenced-in ball field.

The directions are the same as they are for George Deukmejian Wilderness Park, but you'll drive only four blocks north of Foothill Boulevard on Dunsmore Avenue. (818) 548-2000. ➔*See #13 on map pp. 640-641.*

•**George Deukmejian Wilderness Park** 🐾 🐾 🐾 1/2

When we first heard the name of this park, we thought someone was making a joke. The words "George Deukmejian" and the word "wilderness" were often used in the same sentence when he was governor, but more like: "That *George Deukmejian,* he should have been more concerned about *wilderness.*"

A couple of locals told us that back in the late '80s, the Duke was actually against setting aside this large parcel of land for a park. But he was finally sold on it when a clever environmentalist came up with an idea to name the park after him. Whether this is true or just a semi-urban myth, dogs can be grateful to the governor for making room for this 700-acre square of land.

It's not what you'd call a breathtaking park. It can be very dry and dusty, with only an occasional tree to provide relief from the sun in these chaparral-covered hills. But the dogs we've seen cavorting around the park really love it here. They seem to smile as they accompany their leashed people up and down the canyon.

Maybe they're smiling because of the lack of people or the abundance of singing birds. Maybe it's the scents of strange fauna on the couple of miles of dirt road here. Or perhaps they know that if they walk far enough, they'll be in Angeles National Forest, where they can run around in leashless ecstasy. (It will be 100 percent easier to get there once some trails connecting the two areas are completed.) Whatever the case, this is a park that you might not find aesthetically pleasing, but your dog will.

Exit US 101 on Pennsylvania Avenue. Go north a few blocks and turn left at Foothill Boulevard. Drive northwest about six blocks. Turn right on Dunsmore Avenue. The road will lead you into the park in about a mile, where you'll bear right after the sign for the park and drive up a narrow paved road to a dirt parking lot next to a horse corral. The wide, gated road just above the lot is where you'll start your hike. (818) 548-2000. ➔*See #14 on map pp. 640-641.*

RESTAURANTS

Hot Wings Cafe: This little restaurant has a shaded outdoor area and a loyal following of dog-toting patrons. 314 North Brand Boulevard; (818) 247-4445.

La Fontana Italian Kitchen: You and your dog will be surrounded by an impressive wrought-iron fence as you dine at one of their umbrella-topped tables. 933 North Brand Boulevard; (818) 247-6256.

Le Pafe Cafe Bakery: They allow dogs, cats, parrots and any other well-behaved animals to dine at the outdoor tables here. Try the pizza, if you're in the mood for lunch. 241 North Brand Boulevard; (818) 500-8777.

PLACES TO STAY

Days Inn: Rates are $47 to $57. Small pooches only, please. 450 West Pioneer Street, Glendale, CA 91203; (818) 956-0202.

Red Lion Hotel: They've got mini-bars in the rooms here, so you can have a glass of your favorite stuff while you and your dog watch David Letterman. Rates are $125 to $150. 100 West Glenoaks Boulevard, Glendale, CA 91203; (818) 956-5466.

Vagabond Inn: Rates are $61 to $81. Dogs are $3 extra. 120 West Colorado Street, Glendale, CA 91204; (818) 240-1700.

DIVERSIONS

Catch your dog kissing Santa Claus: Better yet, watch him be dumbfounded by a giant Easter Bunny. The Glendale Humane Society hosts year-round seasonal parties for pooches. A small donation is requested, but your dog gets plenty of goodies in return—like a picture of himself with Santa or the Easter Bunny, dog treats and lot of good canine companionship.

The Humane Society is planning to start Halloween bashes soon, so start thinking about your canine costumes. Education Director Eugena Olds is trying to get Elvira (the real one) to be the Halloween party guest any year she's available, and she says the Mistress of the Night is considering the offer. It's a good cause. The money goes to educating schoolkids about animal welfare and supplying thousands of students with a newspaper called *Kind News.* The Humane Society is located at 717 West Ivy Street. Call (818) 242-1128 for details.

GLENDORA

PARKS, BEACHES & RECREATION AREAS

Only one park allows dogs, but it's a doozy.

• **Big Dalton Canyon Wilderness Park** 🐾 🐾 🐾 1/2

This is among our favorite non-national forest parks in this part of Los Angeles County. It's so remote, so wild and so unused that you'll barely believe you're in a major metropolis. Big Dalton Canyon Wilderness Park is for people who don't want perfectly mowed park meadows, strict rules, tennis courts and droning freeways. The only hitch in this otherwise wild park is that dogs are supposed to be leashed.

The deeper you venture into the park, the farther you'll get from any signs of civilization. You can pull over at any of a few tiny (one- to two-car) parking areas near various trailheads. Since the park is part of a canyon, the trails won't always be easy, but they're rarely too rugged. The park is made up almost entirely of forest land, so you usually won't have to worry about the sun melting you.

What's especially wonderful about this park is that it extends into Angeles National Forest, a four-paw piece of dog heaven (see page 803). This particular section of the forest is the 27-square-mile San Dimas Experimental Forest, where watersheds from two acres to 9,000 acres are used to test land-management measures to increase water yield.

As usual in this area, be aware that mountain lions live and dine here. When we last visited, there were several signs posted for a poor lost dachshund who may have run into a hungry feline.

This park takes some patience to find, but it's well worth it. Exit Interstate 210 at Auto Centre Drive and follow the signs toward Glendora for a few blocks. Go right on Lone Hill Avenue. At Alosta Avenue, turn left. In just under a mile, turn right on Loraine Avenue. In about 20 blocks, go right on Sierra Madre Avenue. Drive about eight blocks to Glendora Mountain Road and go left. Finally, turn right at Big Dalton Canyon Road, which will take you into the park. Park officials say there's a possibility that the county will soon start charging a user fee for the trails it maintains. Call (818) 914-8228 to find out the latest. → *See #15 on map pp. 640-641.*

GRANADA HILLS
PARKS, BEACHES & RECREATION AREAS
•**Moonshine Canyon Park** 🐾 🐾 🐾 1/2

Our favorite part of this fairly narrow, twisty park is to the north of Highway 118. Within about two-thirds of a mile of the highway, you'll start to see the park, and entries into it, on your left.

Pull over and park on the road. (You'll see the parking possibilities on the southbound side of the street.) Enter the park at the trailheads that jut out of the edge of the canyon. You'll make a quick descent into the canyon bottom. Once there, it's best to go left on the trail. Going right will take you to a few dicey spots full of abandoned washing machines and cars, then to a busy road. The trail to the left, however, takes you alongside a creek past brushy hills and the occasional songbird.

The hike is fairly secluded, with only an occasional glimpse of a house on a ridge. This is good and bad. It's good if you and your dog need to get away from civilization and see hardly a soul on the trail. It's not so good if you're worried about who might be lurking in the bushes. Remember: At all large urban parks, it's better to hike with a human companion than alone with your pooch. If you feel at all unsure about the safety of the park, go with someone else or don't go at all.

Exit Highway 118 at Tampa Avenue. If you drive south, the park will be immediately on your right. It stretches to the south along Tampa Avenue for another mile. If you drive north on Tampa Avenue, the road doesn't come very close to the park until after the golf course. The park will be on your left. (818) 989-8188. → *See #16 on map pp. 640-641.*

•O'Melveny Park 🐾 🐾 🐾 1/2

This 672-acre park offers so many great hiking opportunities that your dog won't know which trail to try first.

Joe would like to suggest a fairly flat two-mile hike that takes you along a tree-lined creek at the bottom of the canyon here. It's often fairly green, and the creek actually has water in it, so it's not like so many dry L.A. County canyon parks.

Joe likes this park because he knows he's going to get a picnic after his leisurely hike. The picnic tables are plentiful, and they're at the beginning/end of this particular hike, so he knows if we don't eat upon entering, we'll definitely have a bite before leaving.

Exit Highway 5 at Balboa Boulevard and drive south about a mile to Orozco Street. Turn right and drive to the parking lot for the picnic area. The trail starts at the north end of the picnic area. For info on tougher hikes in this park, call (818) 989-8188. → *See #17 on map pp. 640-641.*

HARBOR CITY

PARKS, BEACHES & RECREATION AREAS

•Harbor Regional Park 🐾 🐾

This 210-acre park between Harbor City and Wilmington is right beside a huge oil refinery. Yum, yum. The air is often an other-worldly hue. It's not the most appetizing place, but you can manage to stomach a picnic here. To the park's credit, there's a good-sized lake along the east end. It may not be a prime fishing spot, but at least it's good old H_2O.

The best thing about this park is its proximity to Interstate 110. If you have a dog who's in dire need during a Sunday drive, a jaunt to this park won't take you far off course. Exit Interstate 110 at Highway 1/Pacific Coast Highway and drive west a short half mile. The entrance is on your left. (213) 548-7515. → *See #18 on map pp. 640-641.*

HERMOSA BEACH

PARKS, BEACHES & RECREATION AREAS
Dogs aren't allowed at any of Hermosa Beach's beaches.

•**Hermosa Valley Greenbelt** 🐾 🐾 1/2
This narrow, long strip of green runs 30 blocks—the entire length of the city. It's got a pleasant soft dirt/chipped bark path down the middle, which leashed dogs really enjoy treading on. It's shaded in parts and can be fairly quiet, considering that it's sandwiched by two roads. But it is quite narrow, not ideal for a dog who likes to do heavy-duty exploring.

You can enter the park almost anywhere along Ardmore Avenue or Valley Street. The park continues north into Manhattan Beach (see Manhattan Beach Parkway, page 672). (310) 329-4115. → *See #19 on map pp. 640-641.*

RESTAURANTS
Le Petite Cafe: Dogs can join you at the outdoor eating bar, where you can get a great omelet or a beefy burger. 190 Hermosa Avenue; (310) 379-1400.

Martha's 22nd Street Grill: They'll often let your dog sit beside you at the outside tables here, but if it's crowded you'll be asked to tie your dog up to one of the poles on the side. The food here is really good—and good for you, too. The menu includes apple pancakes, Monte Cristo sandwiches and veggie burgers. 25 22nd Street; (310) 376-7786.

HOLLYWOOD
Tinseltown just isn't what it used to be. The wealth of Art Deco architecture and grandiose theaters has faded. The half-mile Hollywood Walk of Fame is home to the homeless. But it's still worth visiting, for the myth and lure of Hollywood will never completely fade. And since a couple of sections are undergoing serious renovation, the stars may shine here again someday. Meanwhile, if you visit toward dusk, you may be glad you brought your dog.

RESTAURANTS

Melrose Cantina: Eat Mexican food under a cooling canopy at this delightful restaurant. 7164 Melrose Avenue; (213) 937-7788.

PLACES TO STAY

Best Western Hollywood: Rates are $55 to $80. A $25 to $50 deposit is required for pooches. 6141 Franklin Avenue, Hollywood, CA 90028; (213) 464-5181 or (800) 528-1234.

Holiday Inn: Small pooches only, please. Rates are $85 to $140. 1755 North Highland Avenue, Hollywood, CA 90028; (213) 462-7181.

Hollywood Celebrity Hotel: Huge dogs are welcome. The owners love dogs. In fact, you may run into the resident Great Dane here! Rates are $55 to $89. 1775 Orchid Avenue, Hollywood, CA 90028; (213) 850-6464.

DIVERSIONS

Compare paw prints: On a recent visit to the forecourt of Mann's Chinese Theatre, Joe found out his paws are as big as the heels of Gene Autry's boots. Since he's an old Western movie buff (we've caught him watching Westerns on TV when he's alone), it was doubtless a thrill for him to see that he could, if necessary, walk a mile in Autry's boots. You and your dog can spend part of a fun-filled Hollywood afternoon measuring your feet and paws against the footprints of the stars here. Be sure to bring a camera. Everyone else will have one and your dog is likely to have his mug snapped more than once. (213) 464-8111.

Walk on the stars: When you're done comparing shoe sizes with the stars at the Chinese Theatre, take your feet for a stroll down the Hollywood Walk of Fame. It's on Hollywood Boulevard, between Gower Street and Sycamore Avenue, and along Vine Street, from Sunset Boulevard to Yucca Street. More than 2,500 celebs are immortalized with stars planted into the sidewalk featuring their names. The walk is free, but be prepared for a barrage of homeless people and scam artists with their hands out. (213) 469-8311.

INGLEWOOD

PARKS, BEACHES & RECREATION AREAS

•**Centinela Park** 🐾 🐾 🐾

With 55 acres of hills, meadows and trees, this park is large enough for a good walk with your good leashed dog, but not so big that you're going to get lost. The path through the park is wide so you, your dog and a passerby all won't be squished together as you mosey along.

1

The best place to park is along Warren Lane, near Centinela Avenue. (310) 412-5370. ➡ *See #20 on map pp. 640-641.*

IRWINDALE

PARKS, BEACHES & RECREATION AREAS

• **Santa Fe Dam Recreation Area** 🐾 🐾 🐾

When you're approaching this large county park, you'll find it hard to believe anything but industry could exist here. The area is utterly fraught with unsightly evidence of rampant "progress."

But in the middle of it all is a big patch of green doing its best to fend off the onslaught of civilization. It's not the most attractive park in the world, but it's a commendable attempt.

The park's Santa Fe Reservoir is a decent place to share a picnic with your dog. You can also fish for trout or launch a boat here for a relaxing morning on the water. You won't exactly feel like you're in the middle of Wisconsin, but it's better than some water holes we've seen down here.

The best time you can have with your dog at this park is if you take a hike on the nature trail. Signs and pamphlets point out the flora and fauna you'll come across in the 1,000-acre nature area. The trail provides a good hike, but it's not without its sad side: As if the surrounding scenery were not enough of a reminder, signs tell you how humans have destroyed the habitat. Do your part to protect it, and make sure your dog is leashed and doesn't disturb the birds and beasts here.

There's a $6 fee per vehicle, which you can avoid by parking on a nearby street. (If you have the $6, keep in mind that the county park system is financially devastated and can use every penny to keep parks running.) Exit Interstate 210 at Irwindale Avenue and go south about 1.5 miles. Turn right at Arrow Highway, and within a few blocks turn right again at the signs for the park. To get to the nature trail, bear to the right after the entry kiosk and follow the signs. (818) 812-6375. ➡ *See #21 on map pp. 640-641.*

LAKEVIEW TERRACE

PARKS, BEACHES & RECREATION AREAS

• **Hansen Dam Recreation Area** 🐾 🐾 🐾 1/2

This is 1,400 acres of hills, trees, shrubs and grassy meadows. A lake used to be the center of attention here, but it's gone for a while during a long process of reclamation. The lake will probably be its old self again by 1997. Until then, try the equestrian trails or the bike path. Leashed dogs seem to prefer the horse trails. They just smell better, and they may find an occasional munchy along the way (but try as your dog might, don't let him nibble these morsels).

From Interstate 210, exit at Osborne Street and follow the signs for a couple of blocks. (818) 899-4537. →*See #22 on map pp. 640-641.*

PLACES TO STAY

Motel 6: Rates are $26 for one adult, $4 for the second adult. All Motel 6s allow one small dog per room. 43450 17th Street West, Lancaster, CA 93534; (805) 948-0435.

LONG BEACH

The downtown area used to be a pit stop (as in "the pits") for off-duty Navy folks. Porn shops, prostitutes and sleazy saloons were the big draw.

But in the last decade, the city has stripped these seedy-if-colorful images from its repertoire and become kind of a classy joint. At least parts of it have. Other sections are still dilapidated and somewhat shoddy. Fortunately, the waterfront really shines. These days, the worst problem here is the smog, which can be a choking green haze some hot afternoons.

The best new attraction here for dogs has nothing to do with the upgraded downtown or waterfront. It's a dog-exercise area where dogs are free to run around *sans* leash (see Recreation Park, below). It's the only park for many, many miles where you don't have to sneak to let your dog get the kind of exercise she craves.

PARKS, BEACHES & RECREATION AREAS

Dogs aren't allowed at any Long Beach beaches.

•El Dorado Regional Park 🐾 🐾 🐾 1/2

You and your dog can fish in the lakes here, watch dozens of ducks waddle around, stroll down shaded winding paths or frolic together on the park's numerous huge fields of green.

Pooches have to be leashed, so it's not quite as dog heavenly as it could be. But you don't find too many 450-acre parks in these parts, so your pooch will be pleased as punch to visit here.

Fees are $3 per vehicle on weekdays, $5 on weekends and holidays, but free street parking is available on some of the side streets. Exit Interstate 605 at Spring Street and drive west about a quarter mile to the park's entrance, which will be on your right. The nature study area of the park will be on your left and dogs are not allowed there. (310) 421-9431. →*See #23 on map pp. 640-641.*

•Recreation Park 🐾 🐾 🐾 🐾 🐕

Pooches passing through or living in Long Beach are extremely lucky dogs these days. The city recently opened its first leashless dog area, and it's an incredibly fun, attractive park for dogs and their people.

The fenced-in park has about two acres worth of grass with a few big old shade trees, a couple of picnic tables and bucketsful of drinking water. Dogs tremble with excitement as they approach. Because of the terrible lack of leashless areas in Southern California, many local dogs had never been off leash except in their own homes. It's a real treat to watch their joy as they bound from one end of the park to the other, somersaulting and crashing into each other with gleeful abandon.

If you have a herding dog, you may witness an interesting phenomenon: A golf course abuts two sides of the dog park, and collies and others of their ilk routinely run after the little golf carts that pass by, perhaps trying to get them back to their herd. It's amusing, and the cart drivers don't seem to mind since a fence separates them from the well-intentioned dogs.

Exit Interstate 405 at Bellflower Boulevard and drive south about two miles to 7th Street. Turn right and drive about another mile to the sign for the park's maintenance yard and dog park. Turn right again and park in the lot next to the dog run. Dogs are allowed in other parts of Recreation Park, but they must be leashed. (310) 434-2868 or (310) 597-4713. ➡ *See #24 on map pp. 640-641.*

• **Shoreline Park** 🐾 🐾 🐾

If your dog appreciates a good view, this park's for her. More likely, she'll appreciate the potent smells to be found here.

Eyes and noses have a feast at this 40-acre shoreline park. Among the sights you can see clearly, if the smog isn't like pea soup, are Shoreline Village, the marina and the Queen Mary. Among the smells dogs can snort are tracks from other dogs who frequent the park, fish being caught in the lagoon and enticing food from nearby restaurants.

The only trees here are palms, so there's little shade on hot days. If you're going to have a picnic at the many tables here, make sure you pick a cool day.

From downtown Long Beach, take Pine Street to its southernmost end and turn right. (310) 435-4960. ➡ *See #25 on map pp. 640-641.*

RESTAURANTS

Dogs are banned from the charming Shoreline Village shops and restaurants. Too bad, because it's the perfect atmosphere for well-behaved pooches and their people.

Biscotti Express: 200 Pine Avenue; (310) 983-9636.

Johnny Rockets: If you and your dog are fans of the '50s, you'll feel right at home at the outside tables here. Try the chocolate malted! It's really decadent. 245 Pine Avenue; (310) 983-1332.

Pasta Presto: They've got lots of tables outside for you and your favorite pooch. 200 Pine Avenue; (310) 436-7200.

PLACES TO STAY

Clarion Hotel Edgewater: You can get a marina view or a pool view here. Dogs seem to prefer the pool view. The activity is closer and more animated. Rates are $60 to $70. There's a $50 dog deposit. 6400 East Pacific Coast Highway, Long Beach, CA 90803; (310) 434-8451.

Long Beach Hilton at the World Trade Center: This is a beautiful hotel in a jazzy location. Small dogs only (under 25 pounds), please. Two World Trade Center, Long Beach, CA 90831; (310) 983-3400.

Motel 6: Rates are $34 for one adult, $4 for a second adult. All Motel 6s allow one small dog per room. 5665 East 7th Street, Long Beach, CA 90804; (310) 597-1311.

Ramada Inn: This one's close to Cal State Long Beach. Rates are $65 to $95. A $250 deposit is required for pooches, and they say they like dogs who are "not too big." 5325 East Pacific Coast Highway, Long Beach, CA 90804; (310) 597-1341.

Travelodge-Convention Center: Rates are $49 to $65. 80 Atlantic Avenue, Long Beach, CA 90802; (310) 435-2471 or (800) 522-1555.

LOS ANGELES

Many communities within the city have their own listings. See individual headings if you don't find what you need here.

PARKS, BEACHES & RECREATION AREAS

• **Elysian Park** 🐾 🐾 🐾 1/2

The views of Dodger Stadium and downtown Los Angeles don't get much better than from this 585-acre park. The hills here often rise above the smog, and the Los Angeles skyline actually looks attractive from a couple of high-altitude picnic spots.

Angel's Point is a must-see for leashed dogs and baseball fans. Dogs like the breezes that blow in from the different sections of the city. Ball fans enjoy being able to peer into a little segment of Dodger Stadium. If only we San Francisco Giants fans had known about this during the last game of the 1993 Giants season, we could have saved ourselves $120 in scalper's fees and we wouldn't have been forced to sit among thousands of tomahawking Dodgers fans during the 12-to-1 beating.

The park is conveniently nestled between Interstate 5, US 101 and Highway 110. To get to Angel's Point and the many roads and trails beyond, exit Interstate 5 at Stadium Way and follow the signs to the park. Once you're in the park, take your first left, Elysian Park Drive. If you're on your way to drop off friends at a Dodger game and your dog needs a quick walk, take your first right after you enter the park. It's a very green, tree-laden area that won't take you far off track from your destination. (213) 225-2044. → *See #26 on map pp. 640-641.*

•Ernest E. Debs Park 🐾 🐾 🐾

There's something for almost every dog at this large park. Adventurous leashed dogs can accompany you along the fire roads here, while pooches who prefer to lounge around can stretch out on the manicured grass. And those who prefer to eat with you can do so with gusto at the dozens of picnic tables in the civilized part of the park.

The park is located between the communities of Lincoln Heights and Highland Park. The best way to enjoy any of this difficult-to-access park is to take the entrance just south of Terrill Avenue, off Monterey Road. Be forewarned: The speed bumps will drive you crazy. (213) 485-5054. → *See #27 on map pp. 640-641.*

•Griffith Park 🐾 🐾 🐾 1/2 🐾

If only this 4,017-acre park had an off-leash trail, or at least a few acres for a fenced-in dog exercise spot, it would be a four-paw chunk of dog heaven. But alas, much of the acreage is taken up by such non-dog attractions as the city's zoo, an observatory and planetarium, a bird sanctuary, an outdoor theater, an equestrian center, golf courses, tennis courts, a swimming pool, a transportation museum and a Western heritage museum.

Fortunately, two-thirds of the park is wild and wonderful, straddling the eastern end of the Santa Monica Mountains. You can explore the undeveloped sections of park via more than 57 miles of trails! This is the U.S.A.'s largest municipal park, and it can be a quite an attractive place considering it's in the middle of three major freeways in the city that puts the "m" in metropolis. About 100 tree species thrive here, including oaks, pines and even redwoods. Birds are abundant, which makes sense when you consider their alternatives in the urban realities beyond the park's perimeter.

With all the trails here (few are very developed), you have myriad choices about what kind of hiking you and your dog can do. Here are two suggestions to get you started:

1) Get a map before you arrive, so you'll have time to plan out your trek. Call the ranger headquarters at (213) 665-5188 and they'll send you a free map showing all the trails.

2) Be careful. Because of the remoteness of some of the trail areas, they've become dumping grounds for bodies. And we're not talking bodies of literature, bodies of evidence or even pigeon and squirrel bodies. Even with your dog at your side, you may not want to venture too far by yourself.

One fun hike you can take is the one that winds you as close as is legally possible to the infamous "HOLLYWOOD" sign. From central Hollywood (Franklin Avenue and Beachwood Drive), go north on Beachwood Drive about 1.5 miles. At the street's northernmost end, it will come together with Hollyridge Drive. Park around here, and in about another block of walking, you'll come to a wide trail on your left. It's not marked, but it will take you about 1.5 miles up Mount Lee, where you'll be stopped by an ungracious fence. The fence is there at least in part because of the radio tower at the hilltop. (Maybe they also don't want dogs doing leg lifts on this oft-molested sign.)

One of the most entertaining activities you and your dog can share at Griffith Park is a train ride. (See Diversions, page 670.)

US 101, Interstate 5, and Highway 134 surround the park. A popular entry is off Interstate 5 at Los Feliz Boulevard. (213) 665-5188. ➡ *See #28 on map pp. 640-641.*

• **Hancock Park** 🐾 🐾 👣

Take your dog to a tar pit that once trapped scads of Ice Age animals! What fun! The tar still bubbles up from its pond-like setting, but fear not: It's well-fenced, so even the most ardent water dogs will be safe from the alluring mire. You can see how animals were drawn here thinking it was a place to splash around and guzzle some liquid refreshments. A few replicas of mammoths charging into the tar pit now add a prehistoric air to the park.

The park itself has enough green grass for a pleasant stroll, but it's not big enough for a major exercise experience. There's a snack bar near the tar pit, but hanging around here probably won't give you an appetite: On a hot day, it can smell like roofing tar.

Hancock Park is located alongside the George C. Page Museum, which houses skeletons and recreations of formidable prehistoric animals trapped in the Rancho La Brea Tar Pits during the Ice Age. The Los Angeles County Museum of Art flanks the park's other side, so the park is convenient if you have to drop off a culturally-minded friend.

The park is located between 6th Street and Wilshire Boulevard, and Curson Avenue and Ogden Drive. Your best bet for free parking is along 6th Street. The park is "owned" by one government entity and operated by another, and no one seems to want to take phone calls for it, so the L.A. County Department of Parks and Recreation is the best number we can provide if you need more information: (213) 738-2961. ➡ *See #29 on map pp. 640-641.*

•**Kenneth Hahn State Recreation Area** 🐾🐾🐾 1/2 🐾

Here's a Los Angeles-area park where the birds singing in the trees are actually louder than the drone of the freeways! The hilly section of this large park is a fascinating place to visit. Not only can you and your leashed dog do some intense hiking, you can also experience the world-uniting feel of the Olympics.

In 1932, the area was the site of the 10th Olympiad. Then in 1984, Los Angeles again hosted the Olympics, drawing athletes from 140 nations. To serve as a continual (and growing) reminder of the events, 140 trees have been planted together on the hills where the 1932 events occurred. Each tree represents a nation that took part in the 23rd Olympics.

Watching their young leaves blowing in the breeze is enough to send patriotic shivers up your spine. It's also enough to make most male dogs stretch their leashes to pay their kind of homage to these saplings. But they can't: The trees are fenced in until they are big enough to withstand such assaults.

But there are many other trees to sniff in this large park. Several trails branch out from the parking lot at the Olympic Forest. Most take you up the hill, but you can also hike down by the lake and stream in the adjoining section of park.

Fees are $3 per vehicle on weekends and holidays. Driving north on La Cienega Boulevard in the Ladera Heights neighborhood north of Inglewood, you'll pass an oil drilling site, then come to signs for the park. Although it's a state park, it's operated by Los Angeles County. (213) 298-3660. ➡ *See #30 on map pp. 640-641.*

•**Lincoln Park & Recreation Center** 🐾🐾🐾

There's plenty of shade here, so it's great for leashed dogs in the summer. And there's a really funky Egyptian-themed playground for kids, so the young ones like it year-round. The 46-acre park is centered around a small lake, where neighborhood folks come with their fishing rods and a lunch and spend the day. The park is also home to the fascinating Plaza de la Raza.

Exit Interstate 10 at Soto Street and drive north to Valley Boulevard. Turn left and then go right at the next intersection. There's usually plenty of street parking. (213) 237-1726. ➡️*See #31 on map pp. 640-641.*

• **Pan Pacific Regional Park** 🐾 🐾
   Set next to CBS Television City and the Farmers Market, this park is in a fun, central location. It's a long, narrow park that stretches between Beverly Boulevard and 3rd Street at Curson Avenue, on the former site of the exquisite 1930s Pan Pacific building (which an arsonist burned down in 1989). It's primarily made up of playing fields, but a paved path winds through the other sections of the park. There's not much shade, so it can be relentlessly hot on summer days.
   At the Beverly Boulevard end of the park is a memorial to victims of the Holocaust. If you approach it from the opposite side, it's a very moving, powerful monument. (213) 933-1094. ➡️*See #32 on map pp. 640-641.*

RESTAURANTS

A Votre Sante: This is among our favorite California restaurants. The outdoor area is lovely, they like dogs here, the food is healthful and it's also very delicious. 345 North La Brea Avenue; (213) 857-0412.

Melrose Baking Company: If you want great baked goods at a fun outdoor setting, don't skip this place. 7356 Melrose Avenue; (213) 651-3165.

Nature Club Cafe: We adore this place. The vegetarian food here is out of this world. It's on a lively and lovely part of Melrose, but the atmosphere at the outdoor tables here is mellow. Lots of folks bring their dogs. 7174 Melrose Avenue; (213) 931-8994.

Stir Crazy: They love dogs at this coffee shop. "We don't discriminate against anyone," one of the managers told us. 6917 Melrose Avenue; (213) 934-4656.

PLACES TO STAY

Please see other cities and communities (like Beverly Hills or West Hollywood) for nearby hotels.

Checkers Hotel: This downtown hotel is really special, but dogs don't get to swim in the rooftop lap pool, despite the fact that the hotel was named after Richard Nixon's pooch (who was small, as all dogs who stay here are supposed to be). Rooms are $185 to $205. Suites range up to $1,000. Dogs are charged a one-time $25 fee. 535 South Grand Avenue, Los Angeles, CA 90071; (213) 624-0000.

Hotel Sofitel Ma Maison: Oui, French poodles do feel at home here. This big, attractive hotel is near the best of Beverly Hills. Rates are $190 to $235. There's a $150 to $200 doggy deposit. 8555 Beverly Boulevard, Los Angeles, CA 90048; (310) 278-5444.

Holiday Inn-City Center: Pooches under 30 pounds are okay here. Rates are $90 to $130. 1020 South Figueroa Street, Los Angeles, CA 90017; (213) 748-1291.

Vagabond Inn Figueroa: Rates are $55 to $80. Dogs are $5 extra. 3101 South Figueroa Street, Los Angeles, CA 90007; (213) 746-1531.

DIVERSIONS

Bless your beast: Maybe your dog rummages through rubbish, and maybe he chews your shoes, but you've probably still got a few thousand reasons to be grateful for his companionship. You may bless your dog every day, but why not let a pro do it? Whatever your religious persuasion, you can get your pooch blessed at a couple of ceremonies around town.

The smaller of the celebrations is at the St. Francis of Assisi Church at 1523 Golden Gate Avenue. It's held in early October, around St. Francis Day. The ceremony is inside the church, so you may not want to bring your cows or your non-house-trained dogs. Call (213) 664-1305 for the exact time and date.

The big animal blessing bash is held in February or March, sometime during Holy Week. It's downtown, but outside, so horses and other giant four-footed critters can accompany you and your dog. This blessing is held right across from Our Lady Queen of the Angels Church at 535 North Main Street. Call (213) 629-3101 for more information.

Choo on this: From your seat aboard one of Griffith Park's miniature trains, you and your dog will see goats, horses, llamas, pigs and a little Native American town. Your dog's ears will flap with wonder as the open-air train chugs gently along. The ride lasts only about eight minutes, but the price is right: Dogs go for free. Kids are $1.25 and adults are $1.75. (That's less than one-fourth the price of a movie—and your seat moves!) The train departs dozens of times every day from the section of Griffith Park around Los Feliz Boulevard and Riverside Drive. (213) 664-6788.

You can't be Sirius: But you can look at this bright "dog star" and millions of other heavenly bodies when you attend a Los Angeles Astronomical Society star party. Well-behaved, non-klutzy canines are welcome to join you when you observe the universe with other astronomy buffs a few times a year at the Griffith Observatory hill.

If your dog is an angel, but shares certain characteristics with Gerald Ford and Chevy Chase, don't bring him. Telescopes on tripods can tip over easily, and dogs who go bump in the night don't go over well here. These nice folks who share their expensive equipment with the public deserve the utmost in consideration. If they ask you to bring your pooch home and come back, for any reason, please respect their wishes. Call (818) 303-3873 for information on the Griffith observation schedule.

MALIBU

This mountainous, oceanfront community is L.A.'s final frontier: Too remote for some, too expensive for others, it's one of the more natural and untouched areas in the county. Malibu's combined incorporated and unincorporated areas cover about 45,000 acres, are 27 miles long and up to eight miles wide. Only 27,000 people live here. Compared with the typical Los Angeles ratio of people to acres, this seems like the countryside.

PARKS, BEACHES & RECREATION AREAS

Many of the Santa Monica Mountains National Recreation Area parks are located here. See page 644 for information on these wonderful natural areas you and your leashed dog can explore together. Malibu is also home to the only beaches in L.A. County where pooches are permitted.

• Leo Carrillo State Beach 🐾 🐾 🐾

Leashed dogs are allowed to trot around a portion of this 6,600-foot-long beach that straddles Los Angeles and Ventura counties. Dogs can sniff around the beach north of Lifeguard Tower 1 and south of Lifeguard Tower 4. Ask a ranger about this area's location when you pay your $5 parking fee (plus $1 for the dog).

Dogs may also camp at one of the 136 sites here. Dogs prefer the campsites by the beach, but they go fast, so reserve ahead. Sites are $14 to $16. Dogs are $1 extra. Call MISTIX at (800) 444-PARK for reservations, or (818) 706-1310 for beach info. The beach entrance is on the 36000 block of Pacific Coast Highway, just south of the county border. → *See #33 on map pp. 640-641.*

• Robert H. Meyer Memorial State Beaches 🐾 🐾 🐾 1/2 🐕

This state beach area is divided into three pocket beaches: El Matador State Beach, El Pescador State Beach and La Piedra State Beach. Because the areas are small and remote, leashed dogs are permitted.

El Matador is the most beautiful, and the largest, of the three. Its 18 acres include rocky beaches, hidden coves and bluffs with winding trails. La Piedra, to the north, is nine acres, and has picnic tables on its bluff and a trail leading down to the beach. El Pescador, at 10 acres, is similar to La Piedra, and farther north.

The parking fee is $2 (it just went down from $6, so take advantage). You can also park on the road, but break-ins are not uncommon there. The beaches are located toward the westernmost end of the county, just south of Decker Canyon Road, along the Pacific Coast Highway. You'll see the signs. (310) 457-1324. → *See #34 on map pp. 640-641.*

RESTAURANTS

Johnnie's New York Pizza: Small dogs are preferred here, but if you've got an angelic larger pooch you can bring him to eat with you at the outdoor tables if it's not too crowded and it's okay with your neighbors. 22333 West Pacific Coast Highway; (310) 456-1717.

Scuzzi's Pizzeria: For a great meal with your dog at the outdoor tables, try the stromboli and the organic salad. (Don't pronounce the name of this place wrong or you may decide not to eat here.) 22935 West Pacific Coast Highway; (310) 456-0670.

PLACES TO STAY

Leo Carillo State Beach camping: See page 671.

MANHATTAN BEACH

Dogs and people usually take an automatic liking to this seaside town. It's a friendly place, with people who stop you in the street to talk about how much they like your dog. This is not that common in these parts, so enjoy it. Unfortunately, the friendly attitude doesn't extend to the city's beaches or parks. Only one allows pooches.

PARKS, BEACHES & RECREATION AREAS

•**Manhattan Beach Parkway Park** 🐾 🐾 1/2

This is a jolly green continuation of Hermosa Beach's Hermosa Valley Greenbelt (see page 660). It's skinny and dozens of blocks long, and it's the only public green in town that allows dogs, so enjoy it. Leashes are a must.

The park runs along Ardmore Valley Avenue for much of its length. (310) 545-5621. → *See #35 on map pp. 640-641.*

RESTAURANTS

El Sombrero: They make a mean burrito here. Try one at the sidewalk benches here. 1005 Manhattan Avenue; (310) 374-1366.

PLACES TO STAY

Dockweiler Beach RV Park: Got an RV and an urge to cozy up to the ocean? Stay here for a couple of nights at one of their 118 sites. Pets must be leashed, and they can't officially go to the nearby beach. Rates are $15 to $25. Call MISTIX at (800) 444-PARK.

From Interstate 405 about 12 miles south of Santa Monica, exit at

Imperial West Highway and drive four miles west to Vista del Mar. That's where you'll find the park. Call (310) 322-4951 for more information.

Residence Inn by Marriott: You and your dog can get a roomy apartment-style suite here, and they just may throw in a fireplace for you. Here's a cute dog rule: You may bring up to two pets, totalling under 50 pounds. Rates are $90 to $200. There's a $50 dog deposit. (Is this a per-pound fee?) 1700 North Sepulveda Boulevard, Manhattan Beach, CA 90266; (310) 546-7627.

MARINA DEL REY
RESTAURANTS
The Cow's End: This is a fun coffeehouse where you can sip your stuff under a canopy. 34 Washington Boulevard; (310) 574-1080.

Seaside Grille: It's just a burger stand, but it's got filling food. 14 Washington Boulevard; (310) 827-1791.

PLACES TO STAY
Marina del Rey Marriott: Dogs can stay on the ground floor here, but only if you sign an agreement saying you're liable for any damages. Rates are $139 to $165. 13480 Maxella Avenue, Marina del Rey, CA 90291; (310) 822-8555.

MONTEREY PARK
PARKS, BEACHES & RECREATION AREAS
•**Portero Heights Park** 🐾 🐾 1/2

When this green park is empty, it's a great place to take a dog. With playing fields and picnic tables devoid of people, your leashed dog can frolic to her heart's content. And just in case her leash slips from your hand, you'll feel a little more secure knowing that the park is well-fenced around three sides.

From Highway 60, take the San Gabriel Boulevard exit and drive northwest. When San Gabriel Boulevard veers off to the right, ignore it and continue straight on Del Mar Avenue. The park will be on your left a few blocks after the split. (213) 887-5450. ➔*See #36 on map pp. 640-641.*

NEWHALL
PARKS, BEACHES & RECREATION AREAS
•**William S. Hart Regional Park** 🐾 🐾 🐾 1/2 ⬤

If you and your dog are fans of the Old West, you must amble on down here. Coming to this park is like getting a personal invitation to the house and ranch of the silent Western movie hero, William S. Hart. Unfortunately Hart isn't around anymore to give you a personal tour, but feel free to peruse the property via a couple of trails. If you get a hankering to check out his hacienda, you can leave your dog at the shaded picnic area with your traveling pardner and take a guided tour.

Dogs have to be leashed at the park. Hart, a cowboy himself, might not have liked that rule, but it's a small price to pay to enjoy the hospitality of the ghost of these here hills. Besides, the property houses a little zoo with farm animals and a compost demonstration site—you don't want your pooch meddling with either.

Exit Highway 14 at San Fernando Road and follow the signs west to the park. (805) 259-0855. ➡See #37 on map pp. 640-641.

NORTH HOLLYWOOD
PARKS, BEACHES & RECREATION AREAS
• **North Hollywood Park and Recreation Center** 🐾🐾🐾

Not many parks have giant blue stars on their fences, but after all, this *is* Hollywood's neighbor. The part of the park south of Magnolia Boulevard is the best area for dogs. It's really big—one grand swathe of meadow with a large area shaded by tall old trees. There's even a jogging trail around the park.

The southern section of the park is such a generous size that it would be the perfect place for an off-leash dog exercise area, but alas, dogs must be on leash here. Exit Highway 170 at Magnolia Boulevard. Go east a block, then turn right on Tujunga Avenue. The park is immediately on your right. (818) 763-7651. ➡See #38 on map pp. 640-641.

PACIFIC PALISADES
PARKS, BEACHES & RECREATION AREAS
• **Temescal Canyon Park** 🐾🐾 1/2

This park is nearly a mile long, running from Bowdoin Street to the Pacific Coast Highway. It's narrow at times, and at times it seems to disappear, but the bulk of the park is wide enough so that if you want to pull off the path and picnic in the shade, there's plenty of room.

It's a fun walk. We see people running their dogs from the top of the hill down to the ocean. It's green and tranquil, despite the fact that it's bisected by Temescal Canyon Road. (310) 454-1412. ➡See #39 on map pp. 640-641.

•Will Rogers State Historic Park 🐾 🐾 🐾 🐾

"It's great to be great, but it's greater to be human," said humorist and actor Will Rogers, who made his home here during the 1920s and 1930s. Dogs may not exactly agree with this sentiment, but they do appreciate being able to peruse this 186-acre park.

Leashed dogs may explore along the trails that wind past a polo field, a roping ring and Rogers' ranch house. Dogs can't go into the ranch house, and should stay away from the stables and from the polo fields on weekends, when polo matches are held.

A major warning: Heed the leash law. Rattlesnakes abound in the far reaches of the park, and nosy dogs who are allowed to romp off leash find them fairly frequently. Rangers here say about one dog a month gets bitten in the summer. Half survive it. Half don't. The trail here is wide, and if you stay toward the middle, you'll have no problems.

There's a $5 parking fee, with dogs costing $1 extra. The park is located at 14235 Sunset Boulevard. (310) 454-8212. ➡ *See #40 on map pp. 640-641.*

RESTAURANTS

Palisades Bakery: Choose from a variety of foods here, from burgers to Chinese food to Indian specialties. Eat at umbrella-covered tables with your pooch. 15231 1/2 La Cruz Drive; (310) 459-6160.

Viva la Pasta: They've got 400 variations of pastas and pizzas here, as well as soups and salads. If it's hot, they'll put an umbrella on your table. 15300 Sunset Boulevard; (310) 459-9974.

PALOS VERDES ESTATES

PARKS, BEACHES & RECREATION AREAS

•Malaga Park 🐾

We mention this tiny park only because it's so close to a really lovely European-style part of this luxurious city. You and your leashed dog can catch a refreshing ocean breeze at this park, since it's high on a hill. Dogs like to relax on the small plot of lush grass and contemplate what it would be like if their backyard looked like this. People enjoy sitting on the stone benches and contemplating the same thing. In the spring, a little garden comes alive with color. Make sure your leashed dog doesn't think the park is larger than it is and accidentally wander into the flower beds.

From Palos Verdes Drive going west, go right on Via Corta. Park on the street. The park is immediately on your left. Don't blink or you'll miss it. (310) 378-0383. ➡ *See #41 on map pp. 640-641.*

RESTAURANTS

Palos Verdes Cafe: This cafe is very beautiful and very European. The tables have umbrellas for the hot days and heat lamps for the cool evenings. 425 Via Corta; (310) 373-1688.

Rive Gauche: Elegance is the operative word at this four-star French restaurant. Yet the managers gladly permit pooches to dine with you at the patio tables. Some patrons have been bringing their dogs here for years, much as they would if this restaurant were in France. 320 Tejon Place; (310) 378-0267.

PASADENA

Residents here have been fighting to get a much-needed off-leash park or dog-run area for years. As of this book's press time, one was being considered in Oak Grove Park, but the battle was far from over. If you need an update, call the city's parks department at (818) 405-4306.

PARKS, BEACHES & RECREATION AREAS

• **Brookside Park** 🐾 🐾 🐾 1/2

Brookside Park, home of the Rose Bowl, is a beautiful place, with roses hither and thither. The park has a playground, ball fields, trees and acres of green grass. When there are no major games going on, it's a quiet park. There's even a trail you and your leashed pooch can take to get farther away from the madding crowd, in case you happen to be accompanying someone who has only one Rose Bowl ticket. My alma mater, Northwestern University, last played in a Rose Bowl game 13 years before I was born, so I don't think I'll be heading here for any bowl games in the near future.

Exit Interstate 210 at Seco Street and follow the signs to the Rose Bowl. As you approach the Rose Bowl stadium, look for a big green meadow on your left. It's part of this large park complex. (818) 405-4306. ➔*See #42 on map pp. 640-641.*

• **Central Park** 🐾 🐾 1/2

Visiting Old Town Pasadena? Bring your leashed dog here for a little siesta between your cafe-hopping adventures. The park has several tall old trees that boy dogs are wild about, and plenty of other good dog amenities like big grassy areas, a shaded paved path and lawn bowling. (Okay, they can't bowl, but they enjoy watching for a few seconds.) The park is at Del Mar Boulevard and Fair Oaks Avenue. (818) 405-4306. ➔*See #43 on map pp. 640-641.*

• **Eaton Canyon County Park** 🐾 🐾 🐾 1/2

Sadly, this was one of the worst-hit areas during the 1993 fires.

The enchanting old Nature Center building was leveled. But the 184-acre park is expected to recuperate soon, bringing new life to chaparral, coastal sage scrub and oak woodlands. It could be fascinating to visit periodically to watch how a natural area recovers from devastation. Dogs must be leashed—an especially important rule during the healing process here. (818) 821-3246.
→*See #44 on map pp. 640-641.*

•**Lower Arroyo Park** 😺 😺 😺 1/2
The dirt trails here go and go and go until you and your dog are so pooped you can't go anymore. Wander through the bottom of the canyon, safe from cars, free from the sounds of civilization. The canyon bottom is pretty wide, so you'll have your choice of paths. It's really important to keep your dog leashed here, because the park is home to wild animals, and some dogs have been harassing them out of their homes, according to park watchers.

If landlubbing activities like hiking fatigue you, try perfecting your casting skills at the casting pool located next to the parking lot. Take advantage of this park, because the adjoining Arroyo Seco Park in South Pasadena doesn't even allow a dog to set paw inside it.

Take Interstate 210 to its southernmost end. At its termination point it becomes St. John Avenue. Go two blocks on St. John Avenue and turn right on California Boulevard. In about four blocks, the park will be directly in front of you. Turn right on Arroyo Boulevard and drive a couple of blocks. On your left, you'll find an driveway to the parking lot. (818) 405-4306. →*See #45 on map pp. 640-641.*

RESTAURANTS
The Old Town district of Pasadena is thoroughly charming. It feels more like Portland than metropolitan Los Angeles. It's worth a visit if you're anywhere near it, and one of these restaurants might be just the excuse you need:

Burger Continental: Forget the burgers—this restaurant with dog-friendly outdoor tables has 150 other menu items that promise to please your palate (and your pooch's, should you permit). Middle Eastern food is big here. The shish kebabs are scrumptious. 535 South Lake Avenue; (818) 792-6634.

Jurgenson's Ivy Hare: This is a wonderful, magical restaurant with a large outdoor area. The tables are all shaded, which is excellent when you feel like taking your time eating your pâté, tortes or big sandwich on a warm summer afternoon. 605 South Lake Avenue; (818) 792-3121.

Q Billiard Club: Choose from Italian, Mexican and typical

American food. Dine at the two outdoor tables here. 99 East Colorado Boulevard; (818) 405-9777.

PLACES TO STAY

Holiday Inn: This one's a cut above some of the other Holiday Inns in the county. Rates are $88 to $125. There's a $50 dog deposit. 303 East Cordova Street, Pasadena, CA 91101; (818) 449-4000.

Millard Campground: This tiny five-tent site is the perfect getaway just north of town. Since it's in Angeles National Forest, your dog is welcome. And outside the campground, he can go off leash on the many first-rate trails here. The beauty of this camping area is that you don't have to make a reservation, and it's free.

Exit Interstate 210 at Lake Avenue and drive north to Loma Alta Drive. Go left on Loma Alta Drive. Follow the signs to the campground. (818) 790-1151.

Vagabond Inn: Rates are $45 to $75. There's a $5 fee for dogs. 2863 East Colorado Boulevard, Pasadena, CA 91107; (818) 449-3020.

PICO RIVERA

PARKS, BEACHES & RECREATION AREAS

• Pico Park 🐾 🐾

This is your typical, respectable-sized neighborhood park. It's grassy, with picnic tables, a playground, ball fields and quite a few trees. It's not dog heaven, but it's large enough for leashed dogs to at least stretch their hairy legs.

From Interstate 605, take the Beverly Boulevard exit west across the San Gabriel River. The park will be on your left within a few blocks. (213) 942-2000. → *See #46 on map pp. 640-641.*

POMONA

PARKS, BEACHES & RECREATION AREAS

• Ganesha Park 🐾 🐾 🐾

If you don't feel like paying $6 to get into the nearby Frank G. Bonelli Regional Park (see page 681), try this fee-free park. It's a popular place, but people generally congregate around the swimming pool, tennis courts and playground. Leashed dogs can zip around the rest of the park without much fear of crashing into hordes of people. The grassy, rolling hills and flat meadows are perfect for a good romp.

The park is at White Avenue, just north of Interstate 10 and south of the Los Angeles County Fairplex. (909) 620-2321. → *See #47 on map pp. 640-641.*

PLACES TO STAY

Motel 6: Rates are $30 for one adult, $6 for the second adult. All Motel 6s allow one small dog per room. 2470 South Garey Avenue, Pomona, CA 91766; (909) 591-1871.

Sheraton Suites Fairplex: "The bigger the dog, the better," a staffer here told us. That's the attitude we like to see. If you and your dog are going to be spending some time at the adjacent Fairplex Exhibition Center, this might be the place to stay. It's pretty exotic for this area. Rates are $95 to $105. There's a $75 deposit required for dogs, who also get charged $7 extra. 600 West McKinley Avenue, Pomona, CA 91768; (909) 622-2220.

Shilo Inn Hotel: Rates are $60 to $120. Dogs are $6 extra. They don't want huge ones. 3200 Temple Avenue, Pomona, CA 91768; (909) 598-0073.

RANCHO PALOS VERDES

PARKS, BEACHES & RECREATION AREAS

• **Ladera Linda Community Center** 🐾🐾 1/2

This isn't the biggest park in Rancho Palos Verdes, but since it doesn't get nearly as much use as many others, it's one of the better places to take a dog. It's about 33 acres, much of it devoted to playing fields and open space.

From Palos Verdes Drive in the Portuguese Bend area, go north on Forrestal Drive. The park will be on your left in a few blocks. (310) 541-4566. ➤*See #48 on map pp. 640-641.*

REDONDO BEACH

Even though Joe and I have visited and dined at the city's famed King Harbor boardwalk restaurants, the city's recreation department says ixnay to ogdays—no dogs allowed.

PARKS, BEACHES & RECREATION AREAS

• **Dominguez Park** 🐾🐾🐾 1/2 🐕

Until the summer of 1993, dogs were banned from all city parks, beaches and open space lands. But finally, after two and a half years of negotiating with the city, a group of dog lovers got that rule changed. In fact, the result is a two-and-a-half-acre fenced-in parcel of leash-free living! (That works out to one acre per year of begging and bargaining.)

When we last visited, there were still signs everywhere screaming that no dogs are allowed in the park. But don't be fooled. Look for huge overhead powerlines and you'll find the dog-exercise area. The dog park has no trees, so that means no shade and no targets for leg lifting. But it also means dogs can sprint all-out, and they'll never crash into a wayward willow.

It's not the prettiest dog park in the county, but dogs don't care. There's drinking water and plenty of strange smells for them to enjoy. And humans are so happy to see their dogs racing around with each other that most don't care about the slightly unsightly nature of the park.

Driving north on Highway 1, go right on Beryl Street. In about 10 blocks you'll come to Flagler Lane. Go left and take the second entrance into the park. (310) 318-0610. ➡ *See #49 on map pp. 640-641.*

RESTAURANTS

Fatburger No. 4: The burgers here really are fat, so bring a big appetite or a dog who won't mind helping you finish. The outdoor tables make for really good people watching. 1698 South Pacific Coast Highway; (310) 316-9205.

Surf-Break: Okay, dogs and dog people, you've struck gold here! This family-owned business is so dog-friendly that dogs have been known to run away from home to come here. They supply pooches with water, and will always give a dog a biscuit or two from their bottomless jar of dog treats. Dogs and their people are some of their best customers. Oh, by the way, the home-style food here is really good and the outdoor seating is enjoyable. 1700 South Catalina Avenue; (310) 540-5652.

Tribes: Turkeyburgers are popular here, or just grab a pizza or sandwich and eat at the picnic table with your pooch 1304½ South Pacific Coast Highway; (310) 316-6363.

ROWLAND HEIGHTS

PARKS, BEACHES & RECREATION AREAS

• Schabarum Regional Park 🐾 🐾 🐾 1/2

Your dog will enjoy rolling on the many acres of well-manicured grass here almost as much as he enjoys sniffing the hundreds of trees for the history of dogs who have visited before. You can explore this park via a fitness trail or a winding paved path, or just traipse through the meadows. Dogs need to be leashed. It's a good idea here, because there's a horseback riding school on the premises. While dogs can be awestruck by what they think are the gods of dogs, they can also decide these dog gods look like fun things to chase.

We like driving to the end of the park, near Picnic Area No. 8. When it's a fairly crowded day, this is where you're bound to find the fewest people.

If you get street parking or arrive early enough, you won't have to pay the $3 fee. But don't grumble if you pay—the county needs every penny it can get to maintain these parks. Exit Highway 60 at Azusa Avenue and head south. Turn left on Colima. The park will be immediately on your right. (818) 854-5560. → *See #50 on map pp. 640-641.*

SAN DIMAS

PARKS, BEACHES & RECREATION AREAS

• **Frank G. Bonelli Regional Park** 🐾 🐾 🐾 1/2

The good rating we're giving this park has nothing to do with friendliness. Park officials (the ones in the office, not out and about in the park) were so rude that we almost decided not to include this place in the book. If you can avoid it, don't go to the visitors center. At least, don't go there and let them know you have a dog.

After they let us into the park (for the standard $6 fee), we drove past the entry kiosk and a tree immediately came crashing down. It would have landed right on the car, but I was able to swerve. The dogs ended up squished together in the corner, but at least they weren't squished to the floor by a lumberjack's mistake.

When we were done dealing with the humans here, it became obvious that this really is a great place to take a dog. Some 14 miles of trails can easily make you forget about any churlish people you may have encountered earlier. The trails are rugged and geared toward equestrians, so be sure to keep that leash on your dog. You can hike up grassy hills and scrubby, weedy areas to majestic views of the region. The best spot we found to start one of these hikes was right across from the entrance to the east picnic valley. It's perfect, because after a rigorous hike, you can hang out at a shaded picnic table and enjoy a little wine/water and cheese with your dog.

Puddingstone Reservoir is the centerpiece of the park, and the bass and trout fishing here is rumored to be pretty hot. But dogs aren't allowed to swim in it. Too bad, because it's a whopping 250 acres when full. When we visited, humans weren't even allowed to swim in the lake because of bacteria. But you can still pull a bunch of fish out and eat them for dinner.

The park is right next to Raging Waters, so it's a convenient place to take your dog if you don't feel like going home after you've dropped off the kids at that exhilarating attraction. From Interstate 210, exit at Raging Waters Drive/Via Verde and follow the signs east into the park. (909) 599-8411. → *See #51 on map pp. 640-641.*

SAN PEDRO

The smog here can turn the sky such a grim color that you can't imagine how so many tourists frequent the place. But you and your dog can survive nicely and even enjoy this city, if you stick close to the waterfront. Los Angeles Harbor is a working harbor, where you can see tankers, container vessels, cruise ships and pleasure craft going about their business.

PARKS, BEACHES & RECREATION AREAS

Angel's Gate Park looks huge and green on the map, but don't let cartographers fool you. Except for an area around the Korean Friendship Bell, the place is almost entirely off-limits to hikers, since it's got roads and barracks-like buildings almost everywhere. Your best bet is to try Fermin Park, on the ocean, just below Angel's Gate Park.

• Fermin Park 🐾 🐾 1/2

Lined with palm trees, this long green park would be attractive enough inland, but since it's on the ocean, it's especially appealing. Dogs have to be leashed, which is only appropriate since the park is narrow and close to the road. But they still have a fun time sniffing the sea breezes and rolling on the lush lawns here.

The park is on Paseo del Mar, just west of Gaffey Street. It's a convenient place to visit if you're taking your dog to Ports O' Call (see below) or any of the other Port of Los Angeles attractions. (310) 548-7671. ➡ *See #52 on map pp. 640-641.*

RESTAURANTS

Ports O' Call is an enchanting shopping and eating area modeled after a New England-style seaside village. At one entrance, you and your dog will come muzzle to muzzle with a store called The Cat's Meow, *the* place for cat lovers. Watch your pooch carefully, because if she's anything like Joe, she can smell the place a mile away.

Ports O' Call, directly on the harbor, is full of crafts shops and small boutiques, and some allow perfect pooches to browse with you. But more important, it's home to many restaurants that welcome dogs at their outside tables. For details, call (310) 831-0287.

And in case you end up downtown, here some dog-friendly downtown eateries:

Petit Garden Restaurant: If you're around town on a Sunday morning, don't miss the Sunday champagne brunch. The only problem is that you can't take your dog onto the patio, so you'll have to tie him on the other side as you dine. 302 West 5th Street; (310) 831-3118.

Sacred Grounds: Desserts, pastries and robust coffees are the specialties here. Eat, drink and be merry at the sidewalk tables. 399 West 6th Street; (310) 514-0800.

PLACES TO STAY

Vagabond Inn: Rates are $44 to $70. Dogs are $3 extra. 215 South Gaffey Street, San Pedro, CA 90731; (310) 831-8911.

SANTA CLARITA

PLACES TO STAY

Hampton Inn: Rates are $65 to $79. Small pets only, please, and they're $8 extra. 25259 The Old Road, Santa Clarita, CA 91381; (805) 253-2400.

Hilton Garden Inn: If the kids are going to Magic Mountain, you and the small pooch (no big dogs allowed) may decide to lounge around here for the day. Rates are $80 to $120. You'll have to sign a waiver ensuring that your pooch won't eat the furniture and do other rotten things. 27710 The Old Road, Santa Clarita, CA 91355; (805) 254-8800.

SANTA MONICA

Until January of 1994, no dogs were allowed in any Santa Monica parks. It was enough to make a grown dog grimace. Several citizen groups had been organized to change the archaic law in the last couple of decades, but no one succeeded until a coalition organized by resident Karen Brooks hit City Hall.

Brooks is a longtime Santa Monica dog owner who has always managed to rack up tickets for dog violations. "I couldn't keep my dogs on leash and out of the parks. It's cruel," she says. So almost every day, she and about 30 other local dog people would meet at one of the parks and let their pooches play off leash. "When authorities came around, we'd all scramble and run. Sometimes a few would get caught. They'd call police backups, threaten to impound your dog. It was like living like a criminal."

One day, she tired of her subversive lifestyle and started the Santa Monica Dog Owners Group (Santa Monica DOG). She figured that since Santa Monica has 5,000 registered dogs (and countless unregistered ones), the political clout of their owners alone would turn a few heads at City Hall. Their plans and pleadings didn't initially work, but they kept fighting. They brought in the press and state senators, and eventually they managed to crack through the bureaucracy.

The result is a tough, but infinitely better, set of dog rules:

Anyone can take a leashed dog to any Santa Monica city park. If you don't have a pooper scooper implement showing, you can automatically be fined $75. (Bring extra bags just in case the cop comes after your dog goes.) If your dog poops and you don't scoop, you can be nailed for $200 for the first offense.

Letting your dog off leash also qualifies you for a whopping fine. But if your dog is a registered Santa Monica pooch, and if you go to Marine Park or Joslyn Park, you'll be allowed to let your dog go leashless. Out-of-towners won't have that luxury.

Local dog owners say they're grateful for the chance to be able to let their dogs be dogs. "A lot of people were fighting this, but the dogs finally won," says a victorious Brooks.

For more information on how to join Santa Monica DOG, call (310) 392-3583.

PARKS, BEACHES & RECREATION AREAS

A new law allowing leashed pooches in all parks (but not beaches) was going through a trial period as of press time, as was a new law allowing registered Santa Monica pooches to go leashless at two parks. Call the Santa Monica City Council at (310) 458-2101 to find out the laws' status in case they failed the trial period.

•**Joslyn Park** 🐾 🐾 🐾 1/2 🐕

The park may be small, but it's beautiful. It's set on a grassy hill with a few trees, and has great views of the city. And better yet, it's completely enclosed, so those lucky pooches who get to go leashless are safe from traffic.

Licensed Santa Monica dogs may run leash-free from 6 a.m. to 9 a.m. and 6 p.m. to 10 p.m., and must stay away from the play-ground and recreation area. All other dogs must be leashed. The rules may change at any time, so call (310) 458-2101 before you visit. The park is at 7th Street and Kensington Road. *→See #53 on map pp. 640-641.*

•**Marine Park** 🐾 🐾 🐾 1/2 🐕

If you think this park is huge, you're falling for the same optical illusion many others have. The park is just a few acres, but since it's connected to a large golf course, it looks bigger. What's fun about this park is that you don't see many buildings, so you can pretend you're not even in the city if you feel the need for escapism.

Licensed Santa Monica dogs may run leash-free in the enclosed section west of the tennis courts from 6 a.m. to 9 a.m. and 6 p.m. to 10 p.m. All other pooches have to be leashed. The laws could change at any time, so call (310) 458-2101 before your visit. The park is at Marine and 16th streets. *→See #54 on map pp. 640-641.*

RESTAURANTS

If we listed all, or even most, of the restaurants in the popular eating parts of Santa Monica, we'd run out of pages in the book. So here are just a few:

The Third Street Promenade is located on Third Street between Wilshire and Broadway streets. Some of Santa Monica's most unusual and trendy restaurants reside here, and most have outdoor areas. That doesn't necessarily mean your dog is welcome at all of them, but your chances are better than walking down a row of restaurants in Tahoe in January. You may want to watch your food, though, because a few of the homeless here have been known to sneak up and grab it out from under you. Here are three restaurants that welcome dogs:

Chillers: Besides their icy drinks, they serve mouth-watering salads, chicken and steaks here. Dine with your dog tied up on the other side of the patio railing. 1446 Third Street; (310) 394-1993.

Monkee's Cafe: The Chinese food is really tasty here. Dogs enjoy watching the world go by as you eat outside. 1315 Third Street; (310) 393-8822.

Sunset Bar & Grill: Eat continental cuisine on their happening patio with your happy pooch. 1240 Third Street; (310) 395-7012.

Main Street restaurants are in a quieter setting than the restaurants in the Third Street Promenade. Unfortunately, we've found that most of the more upscale eateries won't allow dogs to dine with you outside. Here's a sampling of the mellower places:

Joe's Diner: Joe likes this one. He thinks the name is in good taste, but thinks the good old-fashioned American cuisine here is even tastier. Eat at one of two outdoor tables. 2917 Main Street; (310) 396-8804.

Sparky's Frozen Yogurt Shop: 3110 Main Street; (310) 399-4531.

Starbuck's Coffee Company: 2671 Main Street; (310) 392-3559.

PLACES TO STAY

Loews Santa Monica Beach Hotel: Rates are $200 to $475 per night. This is a great place for people, but dogs don't take well to steam rooms and health clubs. They don't seem to mind the elegant atmosphere, though. 1700 Ocean Avenue, Santa Monica, CA 90401; (310) 458-6700.

SAUGUS

PARKS, BEACHES & RECREATION AREAS

• **Vasquez Rocks Natural Area Park** 🐾 🐾 🐾 1/2 🐾

This is Los Angeles County? It looks more like another planet.

The slanted, jagged rocks and hidden caves are among the state's most famous geological wonders. They're so unusually beautiful that film crews routinely use them as a backdrop. When you call the park, chances are the answering machine will tell you how to get permission to make movies here. It's probably not the kind of information you and your dog need to know, but that's entertainment.

This smog-free 745-acre park, located in the high desert near Agua Dulce, also features Tataviam Indian archaeological sites. Many trails branch off through chaparral and riparian plant communities. Make sure you bring drinking water, because there is none here and you can work up a mighty thirst.

Dogs must be leashed, but back in the days of the bandit Tiburicio Vasquez, there were no such rules. And if there had been, Vasquez, the park's namesake, would have found a way to break them. In the mid-1800s, Vasquez was sort of Robin Hood character, robbing from the wealthy and giving the money to poor Mexicans. He used the caves and rocks as a hideaway from the sheriff's posses and vigilantes who were always on his trail. When you visit the park, stop at the entry kiosk and read about Vasquez' dramatic final days here. Then take your dog for a hike on the very trails Vasquez may have fled on, and let your imagination take you back to the days of the Wild West.

There's a $3 fee per vehicle on weekends and holidays. Exit Highway 14 at Agua Dulce Canyon Road and follow the signs to the park. (805) 268-0840. →*See #55 on map pp. 640-641.*

SHERMAN OAKS
PARKS, BEACHES & RECREATION AREAS
•Van Nuys-Sherman Oaks Park & Recreation Center 🐾 🐾 1/2

The backdrop is ugly, scattered with little apartment buildings. But the park itself is one huge green, grassy field, with a great fitness course. You'll have no excuse not to exercise here, but dogs have to be leashed.

Take the Van Nuys Boulevard exit from US 101 and drive north to Hartsook Street. The park will be on your right. (818) 783-5121. →*See #56 on map pp. 640-641.*

SOUTH EL MONTE
PARKS, BEACHES & RECREATION AREAS
•Whittier Narrows Regional Park 🐾 🐾 🐾 1/2

Is your pooch picky about parks? This one is bound to please: There's something for almost every dog in this very large chunk of county land. For dogs who like to hang out near lakes, this park is home to the Legg Lakes. These are actually three ponds connected together. The fishing for trout is about as good as it gets in the middle of a major metropolitan area. The section of the park with the lake also has a long path around it for dogs who prefer not to get grass on their paws.

For dogs who like to explore nature, try the self-guiding nature trail at the Whittier Narrows Nature Center. Starting at the visitors center, get a pamphlet explaining the various phenomena you might encounter on the half-mile nature trail. Make sure your leashed dog doesn't disturb this precious little piece of nature. There's a chicken who sometimes runs around the parking lot, so beware in case your dog plans to be self-sufficient for dinner.

And for chow hounds, a very big area east of Santa Anita Boulevard is devoted almost entirely to picnic tables. When it's not crowded, it's a great place to run around with your dog. Although dogs are supposed to be leashed, it's nice to know that two sides of this large section are fenced.

Until recently, there was actually a small segment of the park where dogs were allowed off leash for sport training. At last check, the section is now a petting zoo. Park officials say it might be returned to an off-leash area, but they aren't sure when. Call the park to find out the status.

From Highway 60, exit at Rosemead Boulevard and go south to Durfee Boulevard. Turn left. The Legg Lakes part of the park is in about three-quarters of a mile and the parking lot is on the left. On summer weekends there can be a $3 fee per car, but there's plenty of free street parking if you drive a little farther and go left on Santa Anita Avenue. This is also the place to park if you want to take your dog to the very large picnic section of the park. For the nature trail, continue on Durfee past Santa Anita Avenue and follow the signs to the visitors center. The park also extends north of Highway 60, both to the east and west of Rosemead Boulevard. (818) 444-9305. ➡See #57 on map pp. 640-641.

STUDIO CITY

PARKS, BEACHES & RECREATION AREAS

• **Laurel Canyon Park** 🐾🐾🐾🐾 🐕

Yee haw! Dogs, throw off your leashes and come here to be all the dog you can be! This is the biggest of the off-leash dog runs in Los Angeles County, and many consider it the best. It's nearly 20 acres, and there are sufficient trees and picnic tables to make everyone comfortable.

If you and your dog like to socialize, you couldn't ask for a better place. Canine rush hour (around 5 p.m., depending on the time of year) is a real scene. On a typical dog day afternoon, you'll find more than 100 dogs running like mad, sniffing each other in unmentionable places and pushing their noses to the ground in search of unusual odors. Their owners, meanwhile, chitchat about this and that (often, "this" being their dog and "that" being your dog).

People flock here from all over Los Angeles and the San Fernando Valley. There's plenty of water, plenty of pooper scoopers, plenty of fence and, most importantly, plenty of good dog fun. And for people who like to watch the stars, we hear that celebrities sometimes frequent the place on weekends.

Dogs are allowed during limited hours: from 6 a.m. to 10 a.m., and from 3 p.m. to dusk. Get here early so you can nab a parking space. The park is on Mulholland Drive, about a quarter-mile west of Laurel Canyon Boulevard. From Laurel Canyon Boulevard, go west on Mulholland and take the first left. The road will wind you down a hill and into the parking lot. (818) 989-8188. ➡ *See #58 on map pp. 640-641.*

TORRANCE

PARKS, BEACHES & RECREATION AREAS

• **Columbia Park** 🐾 🐾 1/2

The park may be under many powerlines, but it has the most amusing dog-rule signs we've seen. Joe didn't even try to lift his leg on them. If other cities would approach the pooper scooper issue like this, it would make the task much more pleasant task. Stop by and check them out. When you do, you may as well run around the huge swathes of grass with your leashed dog.

Exit Interstate 405 at Crenshaw Boulevard and drive south about 15 blocks. Go right at 190th Street and right again into the park. (310) 618-2930. ➡ *See #59 on map pp. 640-641.*

• **Miramar Park** 🐾 1/2

Is your dog thirsty? This tiny, grassy park overlooking the ocean provides the best dog-watering hole in the county. Fido Fountain was built in 1990 because dogs were drinking from the human water fountain, and many humans were complaining. "The large dogs jump up as their masters turn on the water for them," wrote one resident. "Very upsetting to me, and others, if they knew they were drinking after dogs. I myself love my dog, but I do not eat or drink after my own dog."

Fortunately, City Hall didn't allow such letters to result in more regulations against dogs. The city just went ahead and built a dog-sized fountain right beside the other drinking fountain. Then the tables were turned: Sand-covered humans started rinsing off their feet in the Fido Fountain. So the city built a miniature headstone reading "Fido Fountain—Dogs only, please." It did the trick. Now human feet and dog lips rarely come together at Miramar Park.

The park is at the northern border of the city, just south of Redondo Beach on Paseo de La Playa. (310) 618-2930. ➡See #60 on map pp. 640-641.

UNIVERSAL CITY

If you go to the exciting Universal Studios tour/theme park here, your pooch will be pleased to know that she can accompany you at least part of the way.

Universal Studios has a kennel, which dogs of visitors get to use for free. Bring a blanket and her favorite toy, and you won't feel terribly guilty knowing she's not with you as you fly the friendly skies with E.T. or get jostled around a bit by King Kong. The climate-controlled kennel is unattended, but locked. You can visit your dog any time, though, by getting a key-bearing information booth employee to accompany you.

To use the kennel, bring your leashed dog to the information booth just before the main entrance. (818) 622-3801.

PARKS, BEACHES & RECREATION AREAS
•**South Weddington Park** 😺 😺 1/2

Golf, anyone? This park is so green and trim that you can't help but think of Arnold Palmer. Joe likes it because of its proximity to Universal Studios—it's right across the street. He enjoys the kennels there (see above for details), because he knows a cat could end up spending the day just down the row from him.

The park is bordered by a couple of small side roads, so it's fairly safe from traffic. But since dogs are supposed to be leashed, that's not something you have to worry about.

Heading south on Lankersheim Boulevard, go right on Bluffside Drive (directly across from the north gate of Universal Studios). (818) 989-8188. ➡See #61 on map pp. 640-641.

VAN NUYS
PARKS, BEACHES & RECREATION AREAS
•**Woodley Park** 😺 😺 😺

If you like your parks big and grassy, check out this one. Dogs really enjoy it here. There's ample shade, plenty of picnic areas and a fitness course to keep you and the pooch in good condition. Unfortunately, there's also an unattractive water reclamation plant on the north side of the park, but they have to put them somewhere.

The park is located between Interstate 405 and US 101. Take the Burbank Boulevard exit from Interstate 405 and drive west into the park. Turn right on Woodley Avenue and drive past signs for the Japanese garden. The meadow area will be on your right. (818) 989-8188. ➡See #62 on map pp. 640-641.

RESTAURANTS
Don's Plum: Feel like American food? How about Mexican? Oh, you want Italian? This restaurant has many different faces and all of them are attractive. Joe prefers the pasta. Dine at any of several outdoor tables with your pooch. 16153 Victory Boulevard; (818) 786-1500.

VENICE
Looking around Venice these days, you can see barely a hint of the dream of Abbot Kinney, the city's founder. In 1900, he began creating a city that was a near-duplicate to Italy's Venice, complete with canals, Italian architecture and imported singing gondoliers. He had hoped to create a cultural renaissance in America.

If he could see the scantily-clad roller skaters, the punkers with earrings in every conceivable body part, the homeless, and the body builders and religious zealots in action, old Mr. Kinney would shudder. But despite the wayward ways of those inhabiting his dream, the place has a wild charm, a playland quality. And what really counts is that dogs think Venice is cool.

There are plenty of dogs here. They're not allowed on the beach, but other than that, leashed dogs can have about as much fun as all the unleashed people running around. And that's saying a lot.

RESTAURANTS
In addition to these restaurants, little eateries abound along Ocean Front Walk (see Diversions, page 691). Just grab a chair and table from the communal sidewalk restaurant furniture and enjoy one of the most scenic and unusual lunches you've ever experienced.

Figtree Cafe: The food here is fantastic and eclectic. You may eat at the patio here as long as you tie your dog to the other side of the rail. She'll still be at your side, but there will be a couple of bars between you. 429 Ocean Front Walk; (310) 392-4937.

Siamese Garden: Eat good Thai food at an umbrella-topped table with your fuzzy-headed beast. 301 Washington Street; (310) 821-0098.

El Tarasco: Your dog may join you outside for tasty Mexican cuisine here. 109 Washington Boulevard; (310) 306-8552.

DIVERSIONS

Stroll to a different drummer: Since Venice's parks are so tiny, most dog owners like to take their dogs for a jaunt along Ocean Front Walk, between Rose Avenue and Venice Boulevard. This is about as close to the beach as dogs are allowed, and for many, it's close enough. This is where you can consult a psychic, have your cards read by a tarot dealer, listen to street musicians, buy incense, T-shirts or sunglasses, and watch skaters skate and lovers love.

It's also where Joe almost met the Big Dog in the Sky. He was trotting merrily along sniffing the air for all the great, cheap places to eat along the walk, when suddenly a hand appeared on the path before him. It wouldn't have been a big deal, except the hand wasn't attached to a body. It was writhing and doing sickening somersaults. He trembled and ran backwards right into a juggler. He stood there wrapped around the juggler's leg until the hand crawled away, back to the pile of motionless rubber hands from which it had strayed. He gave a shudder, unwrapped himself, and marched onward, never glancing back.

All was well until a G.I. Joe-type mechanical doll crawled in front of us, blasting his semiautomatic weapon. Joe (that is, the Joe without the camouflage attire) gave me that "Can we go home now?" look, and we did.

WATTS

PARKS, BEACHES & RECREATION AREAS

•Will Rogers Community Regional Park 🐾 🐾 1/2

Perhaps because it's not in as luxurious a setting as Beverly Hills' Will Rogers Memorial Park, your dog may feel more like he can be himself here. The park sports a couple of large shaded areas, a big green field for romping (on leash), a gazebo and a fenced-in ball field.

The oodles of picnic tables here attract crowds on the weekends, so it might be a good idea to bring your pooch here Monday through Friday, unless you're planning to bring him to a picnic. The park is between Century Boulevard and 103rd Street, at Success Avenue. (213) 566-8284. → *See #63 on map pp. 640-641.*

WEST HOLLYWOOD

RESTAURANTS

Comedy Store: Have a drink on a Friday or Saturday night with your best bud at the comedy palace of Los Angeles. As you sip your screwdriver and eat your little pizzas at the outdoor bar, you and your pooch can watch for your favorite comic. Joe's favorite is Dave "I'm really not Woody Allen" Colton, one of my Washington D.C. editors at *USA Today* who got up on stage here on a break from coordinating riot coverage and discovered he was a bit of a riot himself. If you get here early enough, you can have a drink with your dog, drive her home and come back in time for one of the shows here. 8433 West Sunset Boulevard; (213) 650-6268.

The Greenery: You can enjoy all the good basics at this eatery's outdoor tables. 8945 Santa Monica Boulevard; (310) 275-9518.

Greenwich Village Pizza: Eat delicious New York-style pizza with your pooch at the shaded tables here. 8937 Santa Monica Boulevard; (213) 272-8646.

Le Petit Four: The food here is exquisite and the outdoor setting is very precious. Only the most exemplary dogs may dine with you. Elaine Young, realtor to the stars, claims this is an exciting place to dine if you're single. "It's where I meet most of my men," says Young, 58, who has been married six times. For more on Young and the adventures of her teacup poodles, see page 645-646. 8654 Sunset Boulevard; (310) 652-3863.

Rage: It's all the rage to eat the continental cuisine with your dog at the shaded tables out front. 8911 Santa Monica Boulevard; (310) 652-7055.

Silver Screen Bistro Restaurant & Sports Bar: The outdoor tables are a good place to take a good dog for burgers and other diner food. 8401 West Sunset Boulevard; (213) 656-1234.

Tango Grill: Chicken and steak are the specialties here, and they're pretty tasty, too. Dine outside with the dog of your choice. 8807 Santa Monica Boulevard; (310) 659-3663.

WEST LOS ANGELES

RESTAURANTS

Penguin's Place Frozen Yogurts: 11901 Santa Monica Boulevard (310) 473-3066.

Two Part Coffee House: They get a lot of regular dogs and their people sipping coffee every morning at the outdoor tables. Dogs get their own water here! 11769 Santa Monica Boulevard; (310) 473-6135.

WESTWOOD

This lively University of California community is a fun place to have a dog if for no other reason than it's got great dog dining joints.

PARKS, BEACHES & RECREATION AREAS

•Westwood Park 🐾 🐾 1/2

For a flat, squarish park, this isn't a bad place for a leashed dog. Long dirt paths wind their way through very green grass, past modern sculptures and many shaded picnic tables.

Exit Interstate 405 at the Wilshire exit heading toward Westwood. Take your first right (on Veteran Avenue). The park will be on your right shortly after the federal building. Another section of the park is on Sepulveda Boulevard, just north of Ohio Avenue. (310) 473-3610. ➡See #64 on map pp. 640-641.

RESTAURANTS

Falafel King: Eat mouth-watering Middle Eastern food with your pooch at the outdoor tables here. 1029 Broxton Avenue; (310) 208-4444.

Numero Uno Pizza, Pasta & More: 1077 Broxton Avenue; (310) 208-5070.

Piccolo Mondo: Dogs love to join their people for a luscious Italian lunch at the outdoor tables here. 10917 Lindbrook Drive; (310) 824-0240.

Stan's Corner Donut Shop: Lots of local cops hang out here, so it's got to be good. If you're in the mood for Indian food or a hot dog, Stan's serves them, too. Stan says, "I love dogs. I have a little French blood in me!" And dogs love the outdoor tables on this sunny corner. 10948 Weyburn Avenue; (310) 208-8660.

Subway: 1151 Westwood Boulevard; (310) 208-7774.

PLACES TO STAY

Beverly Hills Ritz: I've been dogless when I've stayed here, and it's a good thing: There's a $500 deposit required when you stay with a pooch. If Joe had visited during his furniture-gnawing days, it would have been like watching 25 huge bags of dog food fly out the window. The place is charming, though, and it's got all the fine touches of an elegant European getaway. Rates are $95 to $295. 10300 Wilshire Boulevard, Westwood, CA 90024; (310) 275-5575.

DIVERSIONS

Walk and clown around: The Friends of Animals' Dog Walk-a-thon is one of the best dog activities in Southern California. You and your pooch can walk a two-mile or five-mile course, and when you return to the starting point, clowns, balloons and free human and doggy treats will be there to greet you. The money raised goes to help the homeless and abandoned animals being cared for by the organization. It's a very good cause. Grab a dog, and walk your "a-thons" off.

The walk and party usually start at the federal building's parking lot, at Wilshire Boulevard and Veteran Avenue. The event is held in mid-October. Call (310) 479-5089 for details.

WHITTIER

PARKS, BEACHES & RECREATION AREAS

Dogs are banned at all but one Whittier city park.

•Hellman Park 🐾 🐾 🐾

We tried to visit a couple of times (before the big fire of '93), but the park was closed due to fire hazards, so we couldn't really get in to take a good look. But from what we could see, dogs would have a fun time frolicking around here. It's hilly and rough, with 200 acres of trees and shrubs and even some grass to roll on.

City park folks tell us the park is usually closed from May to December because of potential fires, so you and your leashed dog are very limited in your walking days here. Remember what Sinatra crooned: "It's a long, long time from May to December." It may even be closed at other times of the year. Be prepared to walk elsewhere.

The park is at the northernmost end of Greenleaf Avenue. Call (310) 945-8238 about its status. ➡ *See #65 on map pp. 640-641.*

WILLOWBROOK

PARKS, BEACHES & RECREATION AREAS

•Willowbrook State Recreation Area 🐾 🐾 🐾

This large, grassy park looks like a huge bedsheet being shaken out by the Jolly Green Giant because the hills are so gently rolling. There's a little lake in the middle, and plenty of picnic tables. The trees here are adolescents, but they provide adequate shade on warm summer days. Leashed dogs like to roam from tree to tree trying to figure out who's been there before them.

You can park anywhere along 120th Street, or in the park's main lot at 120th Street near Wadsworth Avenue. Although it's a state park, it's operated by Los Angeles County. (213) 586-6543. ➡ *See #66 on map pp. 640-641.*

ORANGE COUNTY

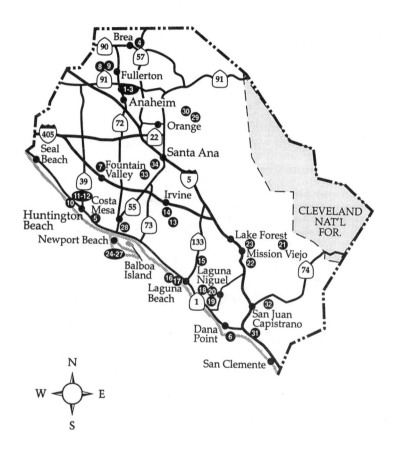

53

ORANGE COUNTY

This is the amusement capital of America, and that's not an amusing thought to dogs. They're banned from such first-rate attractions as Disneyland and Knott's Berry Farm. But the county is also home to some dog-friendly places that just might put a grin on your pooch's rubbery lips and make a stay well worth his time.

There's money here—the land is some of the most expensive in the country. That ends up being a boon for dogs, because the communities can afford to support hundreds of parks.

Dogs are allowed at all county-run parks except wilderness parks. The only beaches that permit pooches are those of Huntington Beach, Newport Beach and Laguna Beach, and dogs are very restricted as far as times they can use the parks or sections they can use. See the headings for these cities for details.

If you and your dog are salty sea dogs, make a beeline to Newport Beach's Balboa Pavilion. You can sail away with any of three different boat companies here. You won't go far—the shortest trip lasts three minutes, while the longest trip goes to Catalina Island in an hour. But you will have a splashingly smashing good time. See Diversions, page 712.

As of this book's press time, there was only one off-leash dog park in the entire county. That could change very soon, with communities like Costa Mesa, Irvine and Seal Beach considering similar dog runs. If anyone feels like rallying behind a canine cause, enlist these crusaders.

NATIONAL FORESTS

See the National Forests/Wilderness Areas chapter starting on page 801 for important information and safety tips for visiting national forests with your dog.

•**Cleveland National Forest** 🐾 🐾 🐾 🐾 🐕
See page 803.

ANAHEIM

Anaheim is the home of Disneyland, and just a few miles from Knott's Berry Farm, Movieland Wax Museum, Medieval Times Dinner Tournament and Wild Bill's Western Dinner Extravaganza.

It's fun and laughs for humans. But these attractions don't

exactly make a dog howl with joy. "Who cares?" say the dogs. If humans were banned, you'd feel the same way.

If someone in your party is sick of Disneyland and has just come along for the ride, he can take the dog around while you play. There are several parks around here that make life a little easier for the canines among us.

Otherwise, if you go to Disneyland and don't have a dogsitter, you can bring your dog to the Disneyland Kennel Club for the day. Rates are $10 per day (no dogs overnight). Bring your dog's favorite toy or blanket. (The Kennel Club supplies food and water, but you can bring your own food if you prefer.) You can take a break from Fantasyland, Tomorrowland or any of the other incredible lands and take your pooch for a leashed walk in the kennel's tiny exercise area whenever you want. For details, call (714) 999-4565 and ask for the kennel.

PARKS, BEACHES & RECREATION AREAS

•Boysen Park 😺 😺 1/2

Not only is this park attractive and green, it's also fairly close to Disneyland. Leashed dogs enjoy romping in the short grass, lounging under a big shade tree and watching the kids ride in the faux-rockets in the creative playground here.

From Harbor Boulevard around Disneyland, go north several blocks and turn right on Vermont Avenue. The park will be on your right in about 1.5 miles. You can park on the street, or turn right on State College Boulevard and make a quick right onto Wagner Avenue, which will take you to the parking lot. (714) 254-5191. ➡ See #1 on map p. 696.

•Pearson Park 😺 😺

This park is a straight shot north from Disneyland. Besides all the recreational facilities, which include tennis courts and a pool, there are plenty of trees and a ducky little pond. Leashed dogs like walking in the green, grassy fields here.

From Disneyland, continue north on Harbor Boulevard for a little more than 1.5 miles. The park will be on your right, at Cypress Street. If it's too crowded here, drive up the street another six blocks and take your dog to La Palma Park, a triangular park with a winding path and palm trees. (714) 254-5191. ➡ See #2 on map p. 696.

•Yorba Regional Park 😺 😺 😺

If you like suburban-style parks, this one's for you. There are tot lots, ball fields and plenty of picnic areas in this 166-acre park. You can also fish at the little lakes and connecting streams, or ride your bike or hike around the trails here.

The park can get very crowded, so try to visit on a weekday. Dogs must be leashed. The parking fee is $2 per car. From Highway 91 in the far east reaches of Anaheim, exit at Weir Canyon Road/ Yorba Linda Boulevard, drive north to La Palma Avenue, and follow the signs to the park. (714) 970-1460. *See #3 on map p. 696.*

PLACES TO STAY

A minuscule percentage of Anaheim's zillion or so hotels permit pooches. A big reason is that folks often leave them behind when they go off for a day at Disneyland or Knott's Berry Farm. Do not do this! If no one is going to be around to hang out with the dog, either leave him at home or find a suitable local kennel. Dogs left unattended in strange places can get scared and anxious. It's not good for them, the hotel room or the housekeeper. Disneyland's kennel is a pretty good deal if you're doing the Disney scene. See page 697 for details.

Anaheim Hilton and Towers: This luxurious hotel takes small pooches only. Rates are $150 to $230. 777 Convention Way, Anaheim, CA 92802; (714) 750-4321.

Anaheim Marriott Hotel: Rates are $160 to $190. They charge a deposit for dogs. 700 West Convention Way, Anaheim, CA 92802; (714) 750-8000.

Canyon RV Park: This is a really attractive park, with 700 acres of wilderness and 117 campsites. But you and your dog can only come to the park if you camp. Observe the leash law here, as they've lost a couple dogs to coyotes in the past. Sites are $10. Dogs are $1 extra. Reservations are required from mid-May through October. From Highway 91 in the eastern part of Anaheim, exit at Gypsum Canyon Road and follow the signs to the park. Since it borders the highway, it's just a couple of minutes until you're there. To reserve a campsite, call (714) 637-0210.

Hampton Inn: Small dogs are preferred here, but if you and your medium-sized pooch bat your big browns at the managers, they might let the two of you spend a night at the inn. Rates are $55 to $85. 300 East Katella Way, Anaheim, CA 92802; (714) 772-8713.

Motel 6: This one's about a block away from Disneyland. Rates are $34 for one adult, $4 for the next. All Motel 6s allow one small pooch per room. 100 West Freedman Way, Anaheim, CA 92801; (714) 520-9696.

Quality Hotel & Conference Center: Rates are $62 to $85. 616 Convention Way, Anaheim, CA 92802; (714) 750-3131.

Raffles Inn & Suites: Although there's a little leeway, generally only *very* small dogs (under 10 pounds—smaller than many cats!) are allowed here. Rates are $55 to $100. Dogs are $10 extra. 2040 South Harbor Boulevard, Anaheim, CA 92802; (714) 750-6100.

BALBOA ISLAND

This small Newport Harbor island is a bayfront wonderland. You can drive here from the mainland, but dogs prefer to take the ferry from Newport Beach (see Diversions, page 712). All that ocean air may lead to a big case of the munchies, but you may have to satisfy them elsewhere since the island is not exactly loaded with dog-friendly eateries.

RESTAURANTS

The Main Squeeze: This juice bar has a bench out front where you and the pooch can share a drink. 211 Marine Avenue; (714) 673-3060.

BREA

PARKS, BEACHES & RECREATION AREAS

•**Carbon Canyon Regional Park** 🐾 🐾 🐾

This 124-acre park is nestled among the rolling foothills of the Chino Hill Range. It has the usual recreational facilities, including tennis courts, ball fields and tot lots. But by far the favorite attraction for dogs and their people is a 10-acre grove of coastal redwoods located near the Carbon Canyon Dam.

Joe thinks I should mention that dogs can also check out the pepper trees, sycamores, eucalyptuses and Canary Island pines. But be careful not to let the trails lead you into the adjacent Chino Hills State Park. Pooches are not permitted in most places there.

Exit Highway 57 at Lambert Road and drive four miles east (Lambert becomes Carbon Canyon Road). The park entrance is one mile east of Valencia Avenue. (714) 996-5252. ➡ *See #4 on map p. 696.*

PLACES TO STAY

Hyland Motel: Small, well-trained dogs are welcome here. Rates are $36 to $40. 727 South Brea Boulevard, Brea, CA 92621; (714) 990-6867.

Best Western Buena Park Inn: Rates are $36 to $52. The managers only want small pets here, and they charge a $50 deposit and $6 extra per pooch. 8580 Stanton Avenue, Buena Park, CA 90620; (714) 828-5211.

COSTA MESA

PARKS, BEACHES & RECREATION AREAS

By the time you read this, Costa Mesa may have its own off-leash dog park, **Tewinkle Park Dog Run**. If all goes as planned, by July of 1994, leashless dogs will be able to enjoy a three-acre, fenced-in section of this 50-acre park, which is loaded with big, beautiful trees. In exchange for giving dog owners a chunk of land, the city might rescind some pooch privileges at other parks. For the time being, leashed dogs are allowed in all city parks. For info on the status of Tewinkle and local leash laws, call (714) 754-5300.

• **Fairview Park** 🐾 🐾 🐾

The pooper scoopers here are handsome, and the city offers them free to all dog owners. But if you need a better reason to visit this park with your pooch, try this one: It's a big, mostly undeveloped park, with dirt trails that wind through grassy, weedy areas. Your dog will have a good time sniffing around. The farther back you go, the less likely you are to run into other people.

Traveling north on Placentia Avenue, the entry road is on your left. (714) 754-5300. → *See #5 on map p. 696.*

PLACES TO STAY

Ana Mesa Suites: Rates are $50 to $77. Dogs are $25 extra and require a $50 deposit. 3597 Harbor Boulevard, Costa Mesa, CA 92626; (714) 662-3500.

La Quinta Motor Inn: Rates are $45 to $50. 1515 South Coast Drive, Costa Mesa, CA 92626; (714) 957-5841.

Vagabond Inn: Rates are $40 to $60. Dogs are $5 extra. 3205 Harbor Boulevard, Costa Mesa, CA 92626; (714) 557-8360.

The Westin South Coast Plaza Hotel: This is a fine place to take a medium-sized well-bred mutt. Rates are $140 to $170. 686 Anton Boulevard, Costa Mesa, CA 92626; (714) 540-2500.

DANA POINT

PARKS, BEACHES & RECREATION AREAS

Dogs are not allowed in any beaches here or at any Dana Point city park. The city's adventure-loving namesake, Richard Henry Dana, Jr., who wrote the high seas novel *Two Years Before the Mast*, probably wouldn't have liked Dana Point's attitude. But he's been dead for more than a century, so there's little he can do about it.

• **Lantern Bay Park** 🐾 🐾 🐾

Since this is a county park, pooches are permitted. It's a beautiful stretch of grass and trees set high above the ocean. Paved walkways meander throughout and there are picnic tables galore. Leashed dogs love to sniff the sea breezes and watch the gulls.

From Highway 1, turn toward the beach on Harbor Drive and make a right onto Lantern Street. (714) 771-6731. ➡*See #6 on map p. 696.*

RESTAURANTS

Beach Street Diner & Bakery: You and the pooch can relive the '50s at the outdoor tables of this diner. 34242 Del Obispo Street; (714) 496-2434.

Yama Teppan: Dine in comfort on Japanese delights. This place will keep you and your pooch warm in the winter and cool in the summer with its heat lamps and umbrellas. 24961 Dana Point Harbor Drive; (714) 240-6610.

PLACES TO STAY

Doheney State Beach: Dogs can't go on the long sandy beach here, but if you camp with them at one of the 122 sites they can hang out on the grassy area of the park. Some campsites border the beach. Rates are $14 to $19. Dogs are $1 extra. From Highway 1, turn toward the beach on Harbor Drive and make a left onto Lantern Street. Call (714) 496-6172 for information, or call MISTIX for reservations at (800) 446-PARK.

FOUNTAIN VALLEY

PARKS, BEACHES & RECREATION AREAS

•**Mile Square Regional Park** 🐾 🐾 🐾

The park has many miles of scenic trails that leashed dogs love to explore. The trails go through 200 acres of grass, trees and picnic areas. If your pooch is a sports enthusiast, take her to the fishing lakes, the soccer fields or the ball fields. She's even permitted to watch from a suitable distance as folks in the large hobby area play with model rockets, remote-control airplanes and model cars.

This is a welcome expanse of green for folks in the dense residential developments that surround the park. The parking fee is $2 per vehicle. The park is at Edinger Avenue and Euclid Street. There are entrances on both sides. (714) 962-5549. ➡*See #7 on map p. 696.*

FULLERTON

PARKS, BEACHES & RECREATION AREAS

Most Fullerton parks don't permit pooches. Here are a couple that do, plus a dog-friendly county park.

• **Brea Dam Recreation Area** 🐾🐾🐾 1/2

A stream winds through this 250-acre park, and dogs love to cool their heels in it. While there are plenty of trails throughout the park, not one runs by the stream for any significant length. But it's fairly open land with only occasional thick brush, so it's not too tough to get around.

For dogs who like trees (and what canine isn't an arborist at heart?), you'll find oaks and California peppers galore. Joe likes to picnic under a shady oak and sleep on his back, all four legs pointed straight up to the sky.

Enter at the Fullerton Tennis Center area, at Harbor Boulevard and Valencia Mesa Drive. (714) 738-6300. ➤*See #8 on map p. 696.*

• **Craig Regional Park** 🐾🐾🐾

This natural haven's undulating tiers of green slopes create an island of tranquillity right next to the bordering Highway 57. A nature trail leads for 2.2 miles through the hills and flats of the park. Pick up a brochure at the ranger kiosk and learn about the multitude of plant and animal life that hides from civilization here.

For the humans in your crew, there are facilities for basketball, softball, volleyball and racquetball. You can picnic with your pooch or have your dog help you watch your kids at the playground.

The parking fee is $2 per car. The entrance is on State College Boulevard, just south of Highway 90. (714) 997-0210. ➤*See #9 on map p. 696.*

PLACES TO STAY

Fullerton Marriott Hotel: If you and your small pooch need to stay near California State, this is the place for you. Rates are $80 to $90. 2701 East Nutwood Avenue, Fullerton, CA 92631; (714) 738-7800.

HUNTINGTON BEACH

Hey, dog dude! This is the surfing capital of the Orange Coast. Dogs are allowed at only a small section of the beach here, and they have to be leashed, but at least they get to get their paws wet (see Dog Beach below).

The downtown/village area is a charming place to take a pooch for a cappuccino. "We're a darned dog-friendly place," a Chamber of Commerce representative told me. "Dogs always look happy here." Joe dog wasn't exactly smiling about the lack of leashless areas, but he concedes that this isn't such a bad place for dogs, considering it's on the oh-so-restrictive Southern California coast.

PARKS, BEACHES & RECREATION AREAS

Dogs are banned from the Huntington State Beach and from

most of the city beach. They're not even permitted on the paved path that parallels the beach. But there are still plenty of places for a pooch to play.

•**Dog Beach** 🐾 🐾 🐾

Wow, a place called Dog Beach right here in Orange County? Don't get excited! Stop panting! This portion of the Huntington City Beach isn't a leashless dog heaven. Dogs must remain fully clothed here, leashes and all.

The beach probably got this somewhat optimistic name from people who were enthusiastic that dogs could even set paw on a beach. After all, if you're coming south from Los Angeles County, where dogs are banned on all beaches, this is the first beach you'll come to where they're permitted.

The section of beach that allows dogs is the area from Golden West Street north to Lifeguard Tower #22. The beach is usually fairly wide, but check your tide tables before a friend drops you off to spend a few hours with your pooch—a very high tide can cover the entire sandy beach area, leaving absolutely no dry space between the breakwater and the ocean. (714) 536-5281. ➡ *See #10 on map p. 696.*

•**Farquhar Park** 🐾 🐾

This is a beautiful park that's just north of the dog-friendly strip of restaurants on Main Street. It's not very big, but the lush green grass and thickets of healthy palm trees create a charming place for even the most discriminating dog to lift a leg.

The park is on Main and 11th streets. (714) 536-5486. ➡ *See #11 on map p. 696.*

•**Huntington Central Park** 🐾 🐾 🐾 1/2

This huge city park has everything a dog could want and more. Unfortunately, the "more" comes in the form of a leash law. Hills, meadows, foresty areas, lakes and trails are everywhere. You can walk on the paths that wind through the park and suddenly you'll come upon an enchanting grassy knoll hidden behind a circle of trees, or you'll find yourself in the middle of an intriguing nature observation area.

Unless you visit the park on a sunny weekend day, it isn't hard to find a peaceful place where you can be away from people and just have a restful picnic with your favorite person, your favorite book and your favorite dog.

The park is divided in half by Golden West Road. It's almost as if there are two separate parks. Each half even has a truly wonderful restaurant chock full of outdoor tables (see Alice's Breakfast in the Park and the Park Bench Cafe, below). You can enter the east half of the park by heading east on the entry road, just across from Rio Vista Drive. The west half is accessible by driving west on Ellis Avenue. (714) 848-0690. ➡️*See #12 on map p. 696.*

RESTAURANTS

Alice's Breakfast in the Park: Many folks bring their dogs to this enchanting restaurant during a Sunday morning stroll. It's located in the western half of Huntington Central Park, and has plenty of outdoor tables. The cinnamon rolls are to die for. 6622 Lakeview Drive; (714) 848-0690.

Breadcrumb Sugar Shack: This place serves breakfast and lunch, and the patio sees its share of canine companions. 215 Main Street; (714) 960-5051.

Midnight Espresso: Find yourself needing energy to keep up with your dog? Stop here and sip strong coffee on the patio. 2110 Main Street; (714) 960-5858.

Park Bench Cafe: Conveniently located at the entrance to the east side of Huntington Central Park, this quaint restaurant has lots of outdoor tables under pretty weeping willows. And adorable though it may be, Justin, a staffer, says, "Please don't put a dog dish on the table to get your dog to eat like a human—other people frown on that." 17732 Golden West; (714) 842-0775.

PLACES TO STAY

We couldn't find any dog-friendly hotels in Huntington Beach. If you're traveling and want to spend the night with your dog here, the following campground is about your only choice.

Bolsa Chica State Beach campsites: Your dog can come mighty close to the beach here if she joins you for a night of camping at one of their 60 sites. Fees are $14. Dogs are $1 extra. The camping area turns into a parking lot by day, so don't be expecting to lounge around.

There's a small paved trail where you and your dog can go for a stroll. Sorry, pooches, no setting a paw on the beach itself. Fortunately, just down the sand a bit is Dog Beach (see page 704).

The state beach is on Highway 1, about three miles north of the main section of Huntington Beach. For information, call (714) 846-3460. For reservations, call MISTIX at (800) 444-CAMP.

IRVINE

PARKS, BEACHES & RECREATION AREAS

• Turtle Rock Park 🐾 🐾

During the week, this 20-acre park gets little use. That's what makes it so comfortable for dogs. Leashed pooches can walk around the hills and the flats of the park with little danger of getting hit by a foul ball.

The park is on Turtle Rock Drive at Sunnyhill, between the suburbs and the San Joaquin Hills. (714) 724-6000. *→See #13 on map p. 696.*

• **William R. Mason Regional Park** 🐾 🐾 🐾 1/2

If you're a local University of California dog and you need to get away from campus for a few hours, tell your owner about this county park. Three miles of hiking and biking trails wind through the park's eastern wilderness. It's a great escape from the urban realities lurking just outside the park's perimeters.

The park has the usual human recreational facilities, as well as one unusual one: a frisbee golf course. It's a good thing dogs have to be leashed, or it would be pure, unbridled, ecstatic mayhem among the retrieving pooches here.

Here's some exciting news: The county has given the city of Irvine the okay to install a fenced-in dog exercise area on about two acres of land here. If the city goes through with its tentative plan to install the dog run, it will be the best thing to happen to Irvine dogs and their families since *US News & World Report* cited the city as one of the 10 best places to live in the United States. If you know any of the decision-makers here, you may want to do a little lobbying.

There's a $2 parking fee, but you don't have to pay a thing if you walk in. The park is at University and Culver drives. (714) 854-2491. *→See #14 on map p. 696.*

PLACES TO STAY

Irvine Marriott Hotel: This fancy hotel permits pups of every poundage. Rates are $90 to $140. 18000 Von Karman Avenue, Irvine, CA 92715; (714) 553-0100.

La Quinta Inn: Some of the rooms here are architecturally fascinating—one of the buildings used to be a lima bean silo! You must see this place for yourself. Rates are $56 to $64. 14972 Sand Canyon Avenue, Irvine, CA 92718; (714) 551-0909.

LAGUNA BEACH

The canyons may still be blackened from the devastating 1993 fire that swept through here, but regardless, this is a beautiful area. Laguna Beach is exclusive but friendly, with an unmistakable Mediterranean feel because of the mild seaside climate and all the fine art galleries and outdoor cafes.

PARKS, BEACHES & RECREATION AREAS

Laguna Beach is home to Bark Park, the only off-leash dog park in all of Orange County. See page 707 for details. Other cities in the county may soon be following the Bark Park example and getting their own off-leash pooch parks. Costa Mesa (see page 700) will probably be next in line.

• Bark Park/Laguna Beach Dog Run 🐾 🐾 🐾 🐾 🐕

People come from many miles around to take their dogs to this fenced-in dog-exercise area in the canyon. During dog rush hour, it's not uncommon to see a couple dozen leashless, grinning dogs running and tumbling around in great joy.

Although there's no shade here, there's plenty of doggy drinking water. Picnic tables add a dimension of comfort for the park's humans.

The park has to close periodically because of the danger of mudslides, so if you're traveling a long way to get here, you may want to call the city first to check on the situation. In addition, we've heard that a few aggressive dogs have stirred up problems for the other pooches here—and potentially for the future of the park. If your dog has a tendency to do battle, please don't bring him here.

From Highway 1, go north on Broadway/Laguna Canyon Road. The park will be on your right in 2.6 miles, just before the GTE building. (714) 497-0706. ➡ *See #15 on map p. 696.*

• Heisler Park 🐾 🐾

The landscaping is lovely and the view is just as good. This small, palm-filled park sits on a bluff just above Picnic Beach. Dogs must be leashed, but they enjoy cruising around here during the times they're restricted from the beaches.

The park runs from Canyon Drive to Broadway/Laguna Canyon Road, just west of Cliff Drive. (714) 497-0706. ➡ *See #16 on map p. 696.*

• Laguna Beach beaches 🐾 🐾 🐾

Leashed dogs can peruse the beaches, but from June 1 to mid-September, their visiting times are limited. During that period, pooches aren't allowed on the beach from 8 a.m. to 6 p.m.

Main Beach is a long, sandy beach that has a playground and basketball courts. A good entry point is just south of the Heisler Park area (see above). If you want to get away from people, you may be better off at any of the pocket beaches that dot the city's coast. There are also several small, rocky pocket beaches you can reach via walkways off Cliff Drive. (714) 497-0706. ➡ *See #17 on map p. 696.*

RESTAURANTS

A la Carte: You and your dog are welcome on the patio of this pink restaurant. With 16 different entrées (not to mention numerous salads and desserts), it's likely that no one will go away hungry. 1915 South Coast Highway; (714) 497-4927.

The Cottage Restaurant: As long as you and the pooch sit on the outer rim of the patio, the folks here will be happy to see you. 308 North Coast Highway; (714) 494-3023.

The Heidelberg Pastry Bistro: Besides tasty pastries, you and your best furry friend can dine on all sorts of traditional European foods amid the trees at the outdoor area. 1100 South Coast Highway; (714) 497-4594.

Subway: There are plenty of benches for you and the hungry pooch. 1350 South Coast Highway; (714) 376-1995.

242 Cafe: Wow, dogs! Check out this dog-friendly cafe. It features a dog station just for you, complete with water bowls and tasty dog bones! The food for humans is good, too, but really now—who cares? 242 North Coast Highway; (714) 494-2444.

PLACES TO STAY

The Carriage House: Only the most well-behaved dogs are welcome here. After all, it's not every day a dog gets to stay in a 1920s bed-and-breakfast that's a historic landmark. Rates are $90 to $150. 1322 Catalina Street, Laguna Beach, CA 92651; (714) 494-8945.

LAGUNA NIGUEL

PARKS, BEACHES & RECREATION AREAS

• **Aliso/Wood Canyons Regional Park** 🐾 🐾 🐾 1/2

Since dogs aren't permitted in county wilderness areas, they're banned from the Wood Canyon section of this 2,500-acre park. But because Aliso Canyon isn't considered wilderness, leashed dogs are welcome. The good news is that about two-thirds of the acreage is in Aliso Canyon.

The "eh" news is that Aliso Canyon is brushy and scrubby, with none of the wonderful trees that grace Wood Canyon. One school of thought behind the contrasting landscapes is that back around 1776, when Father Junipero Serra was building missions, his men may have denuded this canyon to create the San Juan Capistrano Mission. The county is considering reforesting the canyon, but it's an expensive task.

There's an entrance off Alicia Parkway, just west of town. Call (714) 567-6206 for directions to specific parts of the park. → *See #18 on map p. 696.*

• **Crown Valley Community Park** 🐾 🐾 🐾

It's so peaceful here that it's hard to believe you're in a community park. The park is fairly large, with green hills, lots of trees and trails that wind through all this splendor. You and your leashed dog will enjoy the tranquillity here.

The park is on the west side of Crown Valley Parkway, just north of Niguel Road. (714) 362-4300. *➡See #19 on map p. 696.*

• **Laguna Niguel Regional Park** 🐾 🐾 🐾

A big chunk of the accessible land here is devoted to a lake where you and your leashed dog can fish for rainbow trout from shore. It's a fun pastime, but dogs can get bored just watching you cast and reel in all day.

If your dog needs a hiking break, the equestrian trail here isn't a bad place for a walk. Parts of it are too close to La Paz Road for traffic-free ambience, but other sections (especially the trail far west of the lake) are more secluded. You'll be shaded by eucalyptus trees and acacias as you hike up and down the rolling hills.

From Crown Valley Parkway, turn northwest on La Paz Road and follow the signs to the entrance. The fee is $2 per car, but if you walk in, it's free. (714) 831-2791. *➡See #20 on map p. 696.*

MISSION VIEJO

PARKS, BEACHES & RECREATION AREAS

• **O'Neill Regional Park** 🐾 🐾 🐾 1/2

So close to suburbia, and yet so far, this is the paws-down favorite Orange County park for dogs who like wilderness. Dogs are not permitted in the county's true wilderness parks, but for some reason, this 1,700-acre piece of lush land doesn't fall into that category.

Dogs love to hike along the six-and-a-half miles of trails that go past streamside oak and sycamore woodlands. They have to be leashed, which is something the mountain lions here don't appreciate. Besides the woodlands, you can peruse grassy meadows and shrub-covered hillsides. And if you're in a hungry mood, the area near the entryway has plenty of picnic tables. You supply the food and the park will supply the ambience.

Camping is available along the creek and in the higher elevation Mesa Camp area. There are 90 campsites, all first come, first served. Fees are $10. Camping pooches are $1 extra. If you're just here for the day, you'll be charged $2 to park.

Follow El Toro Road (in the city's northernmost reaches) northeast. It eventually turns into Live Oak Canyon Road and veers to the south. About three miles past where the road changes names, you'll come to the park's main entrance. It's just south of the Rama Krishna Monastery, on the right side of the road. (714) 858-9365. →*See #21 on map p. 696.*

• **Oso Viejo Park** 🐾🐾 1/2

It can get mighty crowded here on days when the sports fields are jammed with ballplayers. But you can almost always find an escape by heading to the creek that runs along the northwest side of the park. There, you'll find some trees, shrubs, and enough room for you and your dog to sit down and read a good book. Make sure to keep your dog on leash, because rattlesnakes and mountain lions have been seen here.

The park is on La Paz Road at Oso Viejo, just east of Marguerite Drive. (714) 582-2489. →*See #22 on map p. 696.*

• **Wilderness Glen Park** 🐾🐾🐾

At certain times of year, a creek rushes through this narrow, two-mile-long wooded park and provides a refreshing escape from the surrounding suburbs. This is a hidden, unmarked park that most people just drive past without realizing it's there. It's in a narrow canyon, surrounded by lush foliage. A trail follows the creek, so you and your leashed dog can have a waterside sojourn. You can even dip all your feet in the water to cool off on a warm afternoon.

The park is bordered by Los Alisos Boulevard on the east side. You can enter the park at many points by turning left on any street that runs into the park. Our favorite is Via Noveno. Park around Atomo Drive and walk down the wooden stairs into the park. (714) 582-2489. →*See #23 on map p. 696.*

NEWPORT BEACH

If your dog enjoys the water-dog lifestyle, he's sure to love Newport Beach. Between the beaches, bays and boats (see Diversions, page 712), many watery adventures await any dog who doesn't get seasick while watching you fill the bathtub.

The city encompasses several communities, including Balboa Island, Corona del Mar and Mariners Mile. Balboa Island has its own heading in this chapter (see page 700).

Newport Beach was looking into the possibility of a leash-free dog park as of this book's press time. To check on the status of this great idea, call (714) 633-3151.

PARKS, BEACHES & RECREATION AREAS

• **Balboa Beach** 🐾🐾🐾

Balboa Beach is wide and sandy enough for a dog to forget that it's a dog's life. The only reminders here are the mandatory leash attire and the restricted dog-access hours.

Dogs aren't permitted on the beach at all from June 15 to September 15, and the rest of the year they can only go to the beach before 9 a.m. and after 5 p.m.

The beach runs from around Main Street to the West Jetty area. You can enter the beach at the ends of many of the streets here. (714) 644-3047. →*See #24 on map p. 696.*

•Corona del Mar State Beach 🐾 🐾 🐾

Fear not! Although this is a state beach, dogs are permitted during certain times of year. That's because the city of Newport Beach maintains it and makes most of the rules. Dogs aren't allowed on the beach at all from June 15 to September 15, and the rest of the year they're permitted before 9 a.m. and after 5 p.m.

If you happen to be east of the eastern jetty at the entrance to Newport Harbor, you'll be happy to know that this large and popular beach permits pooches during the off-season. The beach starts at the eastern jetty at the entrance to Newport Harbor. (714) 644-3047. →*See #25 on map p. 696.*

•Newport Beach 🐾 🐾 🐾

This beach starts out quite narrow at the northern border of Newport Beach and widens as it continues south to around Main Street. You'll have fun watching the surfers surf and the sun worshippers worship.

The only problem is that during the times when dogs are allowed, there's not a whole lot of sun to worship. Dogs aren't permitted on the beach at all from June 15 to September 15, and the rest of the year they can only go to the beach before 9 a.m. and after 5 p.m. And they always have to be leashed.

Joe enjoys hanging out by the pier area and grabbing a bite from the nearby restaurants. Your dog will, too. (714) 644-3047. →*See #26 on map p. 696.*

•Peninsula Park 🐾 1/2

What? It's summer, you're near the beach, and your leashed dog needs to go for a walk? If she can't hold it until fall, when the beaches here permit pooches, a visit to this square-block park is a tolerable solution.

The park is west of Ocean Front Avenue, just south of the Balboa Pier. It's flat and grassy, with a bandshell, baseball diamonds, a playground and picnic tables. There's not much shade here, but the ocean breeze usually cools things off enough. (714) 644-3151. →*See #27 on map p. 696.*

• **Upper Newport Bay Regional Park** 🐾 🐾 🐾 1/2

The Upper Newport Bay is surrounded by shopping centers and suburban sprawl. But fortunately, this large park preserves the remaining sanctity of the once-pristine bayside.

The myriad dirt trails in this open, hilly area provide you and your leashed dog with a great way to get around. Dog footprints are embedded in the trails—evidence of happy pooches on muddy days.

The park is made up of tall grasses and twiggy weeds. No trees get in the way of the birdwatching here. Bring your binoculars and try to ignore the tall office buildings in the distance.

You can also do some excellent, up-close birdwatching from Back Bay Road, on the east side of the bay. But it's easier to get to the regional park section, and it's less stress for the birds if you keep your dog far from them. The poor birds have enough on their minds with the onward march of malls and suburban subdivisions.

Traveling north on Irvine Avenue, turn right on University Drive. About the equivalent of a block down the road, turn around and park on the other side of the street (there's no parking on the south side) and walk back across the street and to the park entrance. (714) 644-3151. → *See #28 on map p. 696.*

RESTAURANTS

La Dolce Vita Italian Pastry Shop: Share a pastry with your pooch at the outdoor tables here. 3635 East Coast Highway; (714) 675-5388.

Kelly's Coffee Factory: "We love dogs!" says one Kelly's employee. Besides coffee, you can savor a delightful assortment of homemade candies, cinnamon rolls and muffins at the outdoor section of this cafe. 309 Palm Street; (714) 723-0798.

DIVERSIONS

Pooches make great passengers: The historic Balboa Pavilion/ Balboa Fun Zone is where you and your dog can embark on nautical adventures on any of three separate boat lines! This is one of our favorite places to go with pooches because they're so welcome on these vessels. It's easy for your dog to feel like one of the family here. Best of all, pooches go for free on all three excursions.

The smallest of these boats is the Balboa Island Ferry. It's open-hulled and fits only three cars and a few passengers at a time. The trip to lovely Balboa Island (see page 700) takes only a few minutes, but it's a good way to test if your dog is up for a longer journey on one of the other dog-friendly boat lines here. Fees range from a quarter for a walk-on passenger to 90 cents for a car and passenger.

The ferries run every few minutes during daylight hours.

The next step up is a Showboat Cruise. Your dog can join you for a cruise of Newport Harbor—one of the nation's finest yacht harbors. On one tour, you'll see the homes and yachts of celebrities and learn the history of the area. On another, you'll cruise up to the haunts of the vocal, local sea lions. "The sea lions are fascinated by the dogs, and the dogs are fascinated by the sea lions," says Captain Mike. "It's quite a sight." Each tour is 45 minutes long and costs $6 per adult and $1 per child. Or take a 90-minute tour that combines both of the shorter jaunts. It costs $8 per adult and $1 per child. Call (714) 673-0240.

If you and your dog are sure you have your sea legs, then it's time to try the Catalina Flyer—the largest passenger-carrying catamaran in the United States. This big boat will whisk you to beautiful Catalina Island (see page 651) in about an hour. The roundtrip fare is $28 for adults. Call (714) 673-5245 for schedule information.

Before or after any of these trips, make sure you check out the Balboa Pavilion area. Dogs love to watch the merry-go-round go round and the ferris wheel whirl. It's also a great place for watching the famed Christmas Boat Parade of Lights. The pavilion is located two blocks north of Balboa Boulevard, at the north end of Main Street.

ORANGE

No dogs are permitted in any City of Orange parks.

• **Irvine Regional Park** 🐾 🐾 🐾 1/2

This 447-acre park is home to the Orange County Zoo, but since dogs aren't allowed at the zoo, they don't care much for it. They prefer to hike along the miles of equestrian and nature trails that run through chaparral and forests of huge oaks and sycamores.

There's something for everyone here. You can rent a horse, a pony, a bicycle or a paddleboat. You can walk by the creek, eat lunch at shaded picnic tables, play softball, throw horseshoes, or just do nothing and take a snooze with your dog under a big old tree. Dogs usually opt for the hike or the snooze, or both.

The parking fee is $2 per vehicle. If you walk in, there is no fee. From Highway 55, take the Chapman exit and head east for about five miles to the park entrance. (714) 633-8074. → *See #29 on map p. 696.*

• **Santiago Oaks Regional Park** 🐾 🐾 🐾 1/2

This 350-acre wildlife reserve is dominated by majestic coast live oaks and California sycamores. Santiago Creek, the main tributary of the Santa Ana River in Orange County, runs through much of this park.

Dogs love it here, but they have to be leashed. Boy dogs seem to have a special fondness for the park: It includes thousands of ornamental trees on the north side of the creek.

Bring your binoculars. The wildlife watching is terrific. More than 130 species of birds have been observed here. Coyotes, bobcats and mountain lions have also been known to frequent the park. If you need any extra inspiration to keep your dog leashed, that should do the trick.

It will cost you $2 to park here. From Highway 55, take the Katella Avenue exit east about 4.5 miles to Windes Drive (Katella Avenue eventually becomes Santiago Canyon Road). Turn left on Windes Drive and follow its angular turns as it leads you north to the park entrance. (714) 538-4400. → *See #30 on map p. 696.*

RESTAURANTS
Pickle's: This deli serves great sandwiches and fries at its outdoor tables. 312 South Main Street; (714) 978-6071.

PLACES TO STAY
Doubletree Hotel at the City: Rates are $125 to $155. A $75 pooch deposit is required. 100 The City Drive, Orange, CA 92668; (714) 634-4500.

SAN CLEMENTE
Dogs are not permitted at any of the city's parks or beaches, or at the county beach here. Fortunately for San Clemente dogs, the pooch restrictions may be eased in the not-so-distant future. Call (714) 361-8264 for an update.

RESTAURANTS
Beach Garden Cafe: The views from the outdoor tables are gorgeous, and the breakfast and lunch fare is just as delectable. 618 1/2 Aveneda Victoria; (714) 498-8145.

Cafe Americana: This cafe serves all kinds of mouth-watering, elegant delights at its outdoor seating. 800 Pico Street; (714) 498-2233.

Louise's: You and your dog can share a refreshing snack outside this yogurt/juice bar. 1624 North El Camino Real; (714) 361-1825.

PLACES TO STAY
Holiday Inn San Clemente: If you're lucky, you might get a room with an ocean view here. Rates are $70 to $90. There's a $10 charge for your dog. 111 South Avenida de Estrella, San Clemente, CA 92672; (714) 361-3000.

SAN JUAN CAPISTRANO

The rebuilt version of the mission that was constructed by Father Junipero Serra in 1776 attracts some 300,000 visitors annually. Around March 19 every year, the swallows arrive from Argentina to nest in the valley. They used to flock to the mission, but with recent noisy renovations and hordes of visitors, they've taken to other parts of the valley. "They've gone to the suburbs, just like humans," says one docent.

Dogs aren't allowed on the grounds of the mission, but you can watch this annual migration from just about anywhere in town. It's not as dramatic as Alfred Hitchcock's *The Birds*, but it's still a great way to pass a lazy afternoon in one of the parks here.

PARKS, BEACHES & RECREATION AREAS

• Acu Park 🐾 🐾 1/2

This park is about 11 blocks long, but only a couple of blocks wide. When the park isn't packed with people, you and your leashed pooch can cruise through the soccer fields, play in the open areas or picnic at the many tables here. Trees surround the park, but there's not much shade in the heart of the park.

The park is between Connemara Drive and Camino Las Ramblas, and Kinkerry and Pescador lanes. (714) 493-5911. → *See #31 on map p. 696.*

• C. Russell Cook Park 🐾 🐾 🐾

Big old trees line the perimeter of this park, where you and your leashed dog may choose to amble along the shaded path near the creek bed.

If your dogs likes his paws to hit green grass with every step, you can hang out on the greenbelt area. You'll find ball fields and playgrounds here, but you'll also find some open areas where you can get away from other folks. The park is on Calle Arroyo, and stretches for several blocks between Calle del Campo and Avenida Siega. (714) 493-5911. → *See #32 on map p. 696.*

PLACES TO STAY

Best Western Capistrano Inn: They offer a complimentary breakfast to humans on weekdays. Rates are $60 to $75, and there's a $50 deposit for dogs. 27174 Ortega Highway, San Juan Capistrano, CA 92675; (714) 493-5661.

SANTA ANA

It's refreshing to see that a few farm fields still thrive in the midst of this governmental center of Orange County. The downtown area is a charmer, but there's not much for a dog to do, unless he feels like soaking up history on a walking tour of the renovated district. Call the Orange County Historical Society at (714) 557-7074 for information.

PARKS, BEACHES & RECREATION AREAS

• **Centennial Regional Park** 🐾 🐾 🐾

If you want a real treat, get here early on a cool morning and watch the steam from the park's lake rising up through the surrounding willows. As the sun's rays turn the vapors a golden-orange hue, you'll swear you've never seen such a beautiful sight.

The sign on the lake says "No Swimming," but the ducks just don't listen. You and your leashed dog should stay high and dry, though, no matter how tempting a little wade would be on a hot summer afternoon.

The park has many big green fields, most of which are sports fields. But if you visit during a non-athletic time, you'll just about have the whole place to yourself. Walkways run throughout the park, so you and your dog can cover lots of ground with ease.

The park's main entrance is at Centennial Park and Mohawk drives. (714) 571-4200. ➡ *See #33 on map p. 696.*

• **Prentice Park** 🐾 🐾

While your kids are visiting the adjacent Santa Ana Zoo, you and your leashed dog are free to wander around the attractive parkland surrounding it. Dogs like the grass and picnic tables, but they're often so intoxicated by the ripe animal odors emanating from the zoo that they notice little else.

Exit Interstate 5 at the 1st/4th Avenue exit and follow the signs to the zoo. It's at Chestnut Avenue, a few blocks east of Grand Avenue. (714) 571-4200. ➡ *See #34 on map p. 696.*

RESTAURANTS

Red Robin Burger and Spirits Emporium: This restaurant serves big burgers and lots of other tasty dishes at its sidewalk tables. 1307 Sunflower Avenue; (714) 432-1111.

PLACES TO STAY

Holiday Inn Express: Rates are $55 to $75. A $35 pooch deposit is required. 1600 East First Street, Santa Ana, CA 92701; (714) 835-3051.

Nendels Inn: Very small dogs (under 15 pounds) can stay here. Rates are $38 to $48. Dogettes are $5 extra. 1519 East First Street, Santa Ana, CA 92701; (714) 547-9426.

SAN DIEGO COUNTY

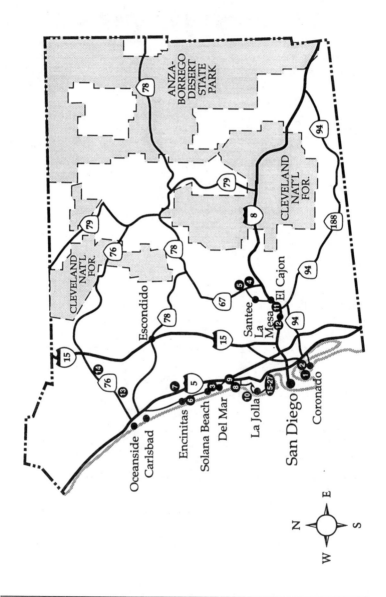

54
SAN DIEGO COUNTY

Look at a map of the county and you'll see green blotches everywhere. But don't be fooled! Most of these verdant expanses are golf courses. Golf is the game of choice here, and since dogs don't play golf very well (their hair gets in their eyes), you can ignore all those areas.

But fear not. San Diego County isn't such a tough place for dogs. Most county-run parks permit them, although they're banned from trails. And there are four parks (not including Cleveland National Forest) where dogs are allowed to run in leash-free ecstasy.

The majority of the eastern half of the county is taken up by Anza-Borrego Desert State Park and Cleveland National Forest. The forest is heavenly for dogs (see page 803). The 600,000-acre desert park, on the other hand, is a doggy drag. Pooches are permitted only in campgrounds and on roads. Granted, there are some dirt roads that aren't used much, but it's just not the same as hiking the trails here. And dogs are banned from walking on the desert itself.

Speaking of deserts, the coastal area from Oceanside all the way down to Cardiff is a virtual desert for dogs: They don't get to go near the water at all because beaches in this stretch ban the beasts.

Fortunately, once you get down to the Del Mar area, little bits of dog heaven pop up fairly frequently. Many adventures await you, and if you get dirty while cavorting, don't worry. San Diego is full of self-service doggy bath-o-mats. One even serves "cappoochino" (see Diversions, page 740).

NATIONAL FORESTS

See the National Forests/Wilderness Areas chapter starting on page 801 for important information and safety tips for visiting national forests with your dog.

• **Cleveland National Forest** 🐾 🐾 🐾 🐾 👣 🐕
   See page 803.

CARLSBAD

Dogs aren't allowed in any city parks or beaches here. Joe thinks we should pronounce this city with the emphasis on the second syllable: Carls*bad*.

RESTAURANTS

La Costa Coffee Roasting Company: As long as they don't go hopping onto the furniture, dogs are fine here. The staff will even give your dog a "glass" of water. And since the patio is in a mall, you could go shopping if you have a pooch-sitter along with you. 6965 El Camino Real; (619) 438-8160.

Spirito's: If you're in the mood for Italian food, this patio is for you (and your dog). They even have handmade raviolis. Joe likes the frozen kind better, but only if they're still frozen when he eats them. 300 Carlsbad Village Drive; (619) 720-1132.

PLACES TO STAY

Inns of America: This place overlooks the freeway, but the price is right. Rates are $30 to $50. 751 Raintree Drive, Carlsbad, CA 92009; (619) 931-1185.

South Carlsbad State Beach: Dogs aren't allowed on the beach here, but they're welcome to camp with you, even at the oceanside campground. There are 224 sites, with nightly fees ranging from $14 to $21. Dogs are $1 extra. For reservations, call MISTIX at (800) 444-PARK. For campground information, call (619) 438-2232.

CORONADO

Folks traveling with dogs aren't allowed to take the ferry to this island-like destination across the San Diego Bay. But a graceful 2.2-mile bridge will get you there just as fast—which is the speed your dog will want to go when she learns she can run off leash at one of the beaches here.

PARKS, BEACHES & RECREATION AREAS

• **Coronado City Beach** 🐾 🐾 🐾 🐾 🐕

The westernmost part of this beach is a nude beach for dogs—they can strip off their leashes and revel in their birthday furs. And since few people know about it, even the shyest dog will feel at home running around flaunting her more natural self.

As long as your dog is under voice control, she can be leash-free at a small segment of this little beach. Your dog has only a few hundred feet of shoreline to run along, but the area between the beach border and the water is fairly wide.

The off-leash section is marked by signs and runs along Ocean Boulevard from around the foot of Sunset Park (on Ocean Drive) to the border of the U.S. Naval Station. From the bridge, continue straight. In a few blocks, turn left on Orange Avenue and drive through town all the way down to the traffic circle. Go around the circle to Loma Avenue and follow it south about a block to Ocean

Boulevard. Drive northwest a few blocks and park on the street around Sunset Park. (619) 522-7380. →*See #1 on map p. 718.*

•**Coronado Tidelands Regional Park** 🐾 🐾 🐾

Located on San Diego Bay just north of the toll plaza, this is the largest of Coronado's parks and it's got a little of everything. From manicured golf course-like lawns to playing fields, walking paths and terrific views of San Diego, the park suits the needs of just about any dog. There's even a small beach here. Dogs must be leashed, though, so there's no swimming back to San Diego!

After crossing the bridge, take your first right onto Glorietta Boulevard. Go right again into the park on Mullinix Drive. (619) 291-3900, extension 222. →*See #2 on map p. 718.*

RESTAURANTS

Bay Books Cafe: Besides coffees, teas and pastries, this place sells books. Make sure you have a pooch sitter along to hang out at the outdoor tables with your dog while you scope out the selections inside. 1029 Orange Avenue; (619) 435-0070.

Cafe 1134: Pooches are welcome to keep you company at these outdoor tables while you dine on sandwiches and coffee. 1134 Orange Avenue; (619) 437-1134.

Cecil's: "I'll give a dog a bone," says a server from Cecil's. We like this guy. Dine at the outdoor tables with your pooch, and keep your paws crossed that you run into this dog-loving waiter. 1031 Orange Avenue; (619) 435-4660.

Dairy Queen: Your pooch will beg you to take him to this DQ—they'll give him a free vanilla soft-serve while you dine at the outdoor tables! 926 Orange Avenue; (619) 437-4183.

Deli by the Bay: Stop and smell the cool ocean breezes with your dog as you eat on the patio. The deli has tasty soups, sandwiches and salads. 1201 First Street; (619) 437-1006.

Fresh-Baked Goodies: Besides the usual cakes and muffins, this place serves cappuccino and other specialty coffee drinks. You and your dog are welcome to partake in these treats at the outdoor seating. 853 Orange Avenue; (619) 435-9272.

Primavera Pastry Cafe: This bakery/cafe serves a mean breakfast and a meaner lunch. Sit outside with your pooch and try their delectable waffles or grilled sandwiches. 956 Orange Avenue; (619) 435-4191.

Viva Nova: The folks at this restaurant love dogs. The vegetarian cuisine includes hot soups and chili, which you can eat at the outdoor tables. There's also a juice bar and a health food store that stocks all-natural pet supplies. 1138 Orange Avenue; (619) 435-2124.

PLACE TO STAY

Loews Coronado Bay Resort: This is quite a resort, but only small dogs are allowed. If you feel like getting some exercise, you can take your leashed dog with you to the jogging area just outside the hotel gate. The bay views are beautiful here. Rates are $180 to $475. 4000 Coronado Bay Road, Coronado, CA 92118; (619) 424-4000.

DEL MAR

This stylish-but-sweet coastal community has wonderful, dog-friendly restaurants and a four-paw beach.

PARKS, BEACHES & RECREATION AREAS

• Del Mar City Beach 🐾 🐾 🐾 🐾 🐕

Okay, dogs, if you're reading this in the summer, don't get your hopes up. You can't be off your leashes anywhere on public land from June through September. But for the rest of the year, the north end of this beach is your kind of place—off leash and rugged.

Here's the breakdown of the rules for the different segments of beach:

The part of the beach most dogs like to know about is the north section. Dogs congregate at the northernmost end, near the bluffs. It's not a long segment, but it's wide and very far from the road. Dogs have so much fun here that they usually collapse in ecstatic exhaustion when they get back to the car.

Leashes are the law from June through September, but the rest of the year, your dog can go leash-free. The entire off-leash area runs from 29th Street north to the Solano border. The best way to access it from Interstate 5 is to exit at Via de la Valle and drive west to Camino del Mar, where you'll go south for just about a block before you should start looking for street parking. It's across from the Del Mar Racetrack.

The middle section of the beach, from 17th Street to 29th Street, prohibits dogs from June though September. During the rest of the year, they can visit with a leash.

Dogs who visit the south portion of the beach, from 6th Street up to 17th Street, can visit year-round, as long as they wear a leash.

Unfortunately, not enough people are cleaning up after their dogs, so the city is considering requiring all dog owners to carry a visible pooper scooper at the beach. If you've used one and a cop comes around, tough luck. You'll still have to have a pooper scooper in plain sight if you don't want a fine. Call (619) 755-1556 for updates. → *See #3 on map p. 718.*

RESTAURANTS

Board & Brew: You and your canine friend can dine on the patio here on award-winning sandwiches, soups and salads. 1212 Camino del Mar; (619) 481-1021.

Cafe Classico: Share a bench and a sandwich with your pooch as you watch the trains go by. The cafe offers a huge selection of coffee drinks, too. 600 West Broadway Street; (619) 234-8838.

Garden Taste: This scenic little sidewalk cafe facing the beach offers fresh, tasty organic vegetarian food. What could be healthier? ("A rare T-bone steak," says Joe. Such sarcasm.) 1555 Camino del Mar; (619) 793-1500.

Poseidon: This restaurant is on the beach in Del Mar. Your pooch can sit right beside you at the outdoor seating as you dine on seafood and steak. In addition, if you're in the mood for breakfast on the beach, you'll get it here. 1670 Coast Boulevard; (619) 755-9345.

DIVERSIONS

Walk with llamas, ponies and birds: Wow, it sounds kind of like a canine dream. Each August for the last few years about 2,000 people have brought animals of every shape, type and model to take part in the Helen Woodward Animal Center's Pacific Classic Walk for Animals. (Well, every kind but cats. They're not banned—they just have smart owners.) It's a fun and relatively calm four-mile walk along the beach. Keep your camera poised for the moment your dog sees his first llama. That shocked, dropped-jaw look is definitely worth a photo.

The money raised by this event goes to the center's programs that help people and pets in need. In addition to a large animal adoption facility, the center has several therapeutic pet encounter programs for injured or ill people.

The center is also the home of Club Pet, a premier boarding facility that gives your dog huge doses of love. The staff even plays soft music all night so your dog pooch gets maximum relaxation. If you need to board your dog, the place comes with high recommendations and the money goes to a good cause. Call (619) 756-4117 for details and event information.

EL CAJON

PARKS, BEACHES & RECREATION AREAS

•**Lake Jennings County Park** 😺 😺 😺

Since this is a county park, dogs aren't allowed to hike on the miles of trails that unfold along the chaparral-covered hills here. But there's plenty of open land, and as long as your dog doesn't set foot on the trails, she's free to enjoy it.

Lake Jennings holds three billion gallons of water for use by local residents. All this water harbors a tantalizing variety of fish, including largemouth bass, rainbow trout and bluegill. Most dogs enjoy the ease of lolling around (on leash) while their angling companions cast around for supper.

There are 76 campsites. Nightly fees range from $10 to $16. It seems dogs like the walk-in sites better than the drive-in sites. It must have something to do with their dogged search to get back to nature. From Interstate 8 about four miles northeast of central El Cajon, exit at Lake Jennings Park Road and drive north one mile to the park entrance. Call (619) 694-3049 for park information, or (619) 565-3600 for camping reservations. *See #4 on map p. 718.*

•**Louis A. Stelzer Regional Park** 🐾 🐾 🐾

You and your favorite leashed pooch can walk in dreamy seclusion on most winter weekdays here. A series of small meadows and a mile-long stretch of riparian woodland begs to be visited. Unfortunately, dogs and their people must stay off the trails here (county park rules), but there's plenty of room elsewhere in this 314-acre park. With a little ingenuity, you can even make it to Stelzer Ridge, where you'll get spectacular views of the surrounding land.

If civilization is more your style, you can picnic under big, shady trees while the kids frolic at the two playgrounds here. Louis A. Stelzer, who donated his ranch to create this park, specified in his will that he wanted the park to be developed for disadvantaged and disabled children. The results are commendable.

From Highway 67, exit at Mapleview Street and drive east about a half mile to Ashwood Street. Turn left and follow it for a couple of miles as it changes its name to Wildcat Canyon Road and leads you into the park. (619) 694-3049. *See #5 on map p. 718.*

PLACES TO STAY

Budget Host Hacienda: Small pooches only, please. Rates are $31 to $36. 588 North Mollison Avenue, El Cajon, CA 92021; (619) 579-1144.

Days Inn: Rates are $35 to $50. Dogs are $6 extra. 1250 El Cajon Boulevard, El Cajon, CA 92020; (619) 588-8808.

Lake Jennings County Park campsites: See above.

ENCINITAS

Although this is the home of Paramahansa Yogananda's gold-domed Self Realization Fellowship Center, and although the city calls itself "the flower capital of the world," not everything is bright and beautiful here: Dogs are banned from the city's municipal beaches (including Swami's Beach!).

The beach that does allow dogs is a state beach in the charming Cardiff-by-the-Sea district of Encinitas. See below.

Fortunately, most of the city's parks allow dogs. We visited the biggest and most beautiful, Quail Botanical Gardens, only to find out that dogs aren't allowed there. But there's still plenty of green space in town.

PARKS, BEACHES & RECREATION AREAS

•Cardiff State Beach 🐾 🐾 🐾

We last visited here during the highest tide of the year. Joe looked at me as if I were crazy for bringing him to a beach that was all ocean and no sand. He slowly shook his head, glared at me and pulled me back to the car.

But normally there really *is* sand here, and quite a bit of it, too. It's a good place to bring a dog—the last beach area that allows dogs for many, many miles as you drive north.

The beach is on Old Highway 101, directly west of the San Elijo Lagoon, in Cardiff-by-the-Sea. (619) 753-5091. →*See #6 on map p. 718.*

•Pacific Scene Recreation Trail 🐾 🐾 🐾

You and your leashed dog can walk almost two miles one-way on this rugged trail. The trail goes through both chaparral land and a lush riparian creekside area. The Escondido Creek runs the entire length of the trail.

Eventually, city officials are hopeful that the trail will be connected with another trail, so the roundtrip won't entail turning around and walking the same path back. You may encounter some horses on the trail, but they're generally not going to be going very fast on this terrain. Enter at Lone Jack Road and Camino del Rancho. (619) 633-2740. →*See #7 on map p. 718.*

RESTAURANTS

Colors Pizza Cafe: You and your pooch can sit outdoors and have some great pizza here. 745 First Street; (619) 944-1447.

Sakura Bana: If you're in the mood for sushi, teriyaki or tempura, this patio is for you. 1031 First Street; (619) 942-6414.

Star of India: You and your best doggy friend can dine together at the outdoor tables on scrumptious Indian cuisine. Lots of people bring dogs here. 927 First Street; (619) 632-1113.

PLACES TO STAY

San Elijo State Beach campgrounds: Dogs aren't permitted on the cobblestone beach here, but they can camp right above it on the bluffs. There are 171 sites, and they cost $14 to $21. Dogs are $1 extra. Reservations are required from Memorial Day to Labor Day. The entrance is on Old Highway 101, north of Chesterfield Drive, in Cardiff-by-the-Sea. For campsite reservations, call MISTIX at (800) 444-PARK. For beach information, call (619) 753-5091.

ESCONDIDO

Dogs are banned from this city's parks. The only exception is an undeveloped service road in a portion of Kit Carson Park, but it's generally just used by very local neighbors. Even the large Dixon Lake Recreation Area bans dogs, since it's operated by Escondido.

But a trip to the beautiful-if-odd land of the Lawrence Welk Resort (see below) is certain to cure any dog of the parkless blues. Be sure to take your dog's picture with the infamous statue of the maestro himself.

RESTAURANTS

The Metaphor: Share pastries and pastas with your pooch at the outdoor benches of this happening coffee shop. 258 East Second Avenue; (619) 489-8890.

PLACE TO STAY

Lawrence Welk Resort: A one-uh or a two-uh of you-uh can bring your favorite dog to the resort built by the king of tiny bubbles. Dogs are allowed at one of the buildings here, and it just happens to overlook the expansive golf course. That means your dog will have plenty of entertainment while you and someone special are eating breakfast in bed.

The resort is on 1,000 acres—much of which is a golf course. But there's still plenty of room to romp with a leashed dog. Rates are $100 to $120. There's a refundable doggy-deposit of $50. 8860 Lawrence Welk Drive, Escondido, CA 92026; (619) 749-3000.

Motel 6: Rates are $25 for the first adult, $4 for the second. All Motel 6s allow one small pooch per room. 509 West Washington Avenue, Escondido, CA 92025; (619) 743-6669.

LA JOLLA

Back in the 1950s, Raymond Chandler wrote that La Jolla is "a nice place...for old people and their parents." He could have added two more categories to his description and it would have been more accurate. Something like: La Jolla is "a nice place for old people, their parents, young people and dogs."

Dogs, young folks, old folks and older folks adore strolling along the seven miles of cliff-lined seacoast here. And they all equally love the impressive restaurant scene.

Unfortunately, your pooch won't be able to visit the parks and beaches of this stunning coastline from 9 a.m. to 6 p.m., but few dogs mind a nighttime stroll above the pounding Pacific. Luckily, cool cafes and elegant eateries abound. Many of them allow dogs to hang out with you as you dine at their outdoor tables.

La Jolla means "the jewel" in Spanish. The name couldn't be more appropriate for this pristine, sparkling village. That's why, although it's actually part of the city of San Diego, it's being given its own listing here. It's kind of like Monaco—a ravishing principality unto itself.

PARKS, BEACHES & RECREATION AREAS

• La Jolla Shores Beach 😺 😺 😺

Just down the road from the famous Scripps Institution of Oceanography, this beach provides some breathtaking views of the La Jolla coast. But if you're visiting in the dark winter months, you might not get to see the views if you're with a dog. Dogs are banned year-round from 9 a.m. to 6 p.m. During their visiting hours, they must wear the mandatory leash.

The beach here is wide and lined with palms. Since you can't come here before 6 p.m. anyway, try to visit at sunset, when the gulls circle the bright gold sky and the orange waves crash on the distant cliffs. It's a stunning sight.

The beach is located just west of Camino del Oro in the northern part of La Jolla. (619) 221-8901. → *See #8 on map p. 718.*

• Mount Soledad Park 😺 🐾

If you've never been to La Jolla, this is the ideal starting place for your visit. Unlike other city parks, this one allows dogs during daylight hours, so get on up here and take a gander. The views of San Diego and the La Jolla coast are phenomenal. Spending a few minutes up here is a great way to get your bearings.

That's about all you can do up here. The park looks quite large on the map, but most of the land is made up of impassable cliffs. The flat, walkable area on the hilltop is actually quite small. Unless you own a teacup poodle, your leashed dog won't feel exercised after a visit to this park. But boy will he know his geography.

From the south part of the La Jolla coast, take Nautilus Street east about two miles to South Street. Turn left and then make a right onto Soledad Road, in a couple of blocks. You'll know you're here when you see the large white cross which is visible from many areas of San Diego. It's a memorial to the war dead, and every

Easter, it's the site of a magical sunrise service. (619) 552-1568.
→*See #9 on map p. 718.*

•**Point La Jolla cliffs and beaches** 🐾 🐾 🐾 🐾

This is another one of those 9-to-6ers famous in the San Diego area. Dogs can visit the cliffs and beaches here only before 9 a.m. or after 6 p.m. Get out those infrared goggles and have a great time with your leashed pooch. Okay, a flashlight would be more appropriate, but the goggles would make a better statement.

What's great about this area is that there's access to the beach, via stairs that take you down the cliffs, and there's also a grassy little park at the top of the cliffs. It's extremely beautiful and dramatic here. During the right tides, tidepooling is magnificent. Just make sure your dog doesn't stick his snout in the tidepools. The critters who call them home need all the peace they can get.

Enter on Coast Boulevard around Girard Avenue, and when you're done go grab a bite to eat in any of the nearby mouth-watering restaurants. (619) 221-8901. →*See #10 on map p. 718.*

RESTAURANTS

Casa La Jolla: Sí or oui? If you and a friend can't agree on what to eat, you might find something to suit you both at this Mexican/French combination restaurant. French poodles, Chihuahuas and all their friends are allowed on the patio. 828 Prospect Street; (619) 454-0859.

Catalina's: Bring your Italian sandwich onto the patio and share it with your drooling pooch. 8008 Girard Avenue; (619) 454-2356.

Il Forno: If you're in the mood for delectable Italian food, your pooch and you will love this place. 909 Prospect Street; (619) 459-5010.

Froglander's Yogurt: The dog-loving owner here will gladly give your canine companion a free yogurt sample. 915 Pearl Street; (619) 459-3764.

Girard Gourmet: Enjoy the beautiful blue skies while Girard's serves you gourmet food at the outdoor tables here. 7837 Girard Avenue; (619) 454-3321.

La Terrazza: Trees and grass surround you and your dog as you dine on fine Italian food on the patio tables here. 8008 Girard Avenue; (619) 459-9750.

The Living Room: Dogs can accompany you at the tables on the sidewalk. Enjoy soups, sandwiches, salads and pastries. 1010 Prospect Street; (619) 459-1187.

Shelby's: Feel a cold coming on? Or just want some warm and cozy soup? This soup restaurant's for you. When the weather is nice, ornate tables are set up on the patio outside where you can sit with your dog. 6737 La Jolla Boulevard; (619) 456-6660.

PLACES TO STAY

La Jolla Palms Inn: This hotel is just a block from the beach. Rates are $61 to $100. Small pooches only, please, and they're $10 extra. 6705 La Jolla Boulevard, La Jolla, CA 92037; (619) 454-7101.

Residence Inn by Marriott: This is a lovely place for humans, but it gets pricey with a dog. Rooms are $85 to $140. Dogs require a deposit of approximately $150 (depending on how big the dog is) and a $50 cleaning fee, and they cost $6 extra nightly. 8901 Gilman Drive, La Jolla, CA 92037; (619) 587-1770.

Scripps Inn: Dogs love the location. It's set on a bluff overlooking the Pacific. Rates are $90 to $170. 555 Coast Boulevard South, La Jolla, CA 92037; (619) 454-3391.

LA MESA

PARKS, BEACHES & RECREATION AREAS

• Harry Griffen Park 🐾 🐾 🐾

This grassy, 53-acre park is home to a pleasant little reservoir and some good fields for a leashed dog's enjoyment. For even better exercise, try the jogging path here. Dogs like it almost as much as they like the shaded picnic area.

The park is in the easternmost portion of the city, on the border of El Cajon. The main entrance is on Milden Street, in back of Grossmont High School. (619) 469-4128. ➡ *See #11 on map p. 718.*

• Lake Murray 🐾 🐾 1/2

If you have a water-loving pooch, think twice about visiting this park: Dogs have to stay at least 50 feet away from the lake's edge. That's tough when you're fishing with your dog. To make things a little easier on the angling front, call (619) 465-3474 for the lake's ever-helpful Fishline.

Fortunately for dogs, paved and dirt paths circle the lake, so there's more for them to do than just sit around and drool at the water. For instance, they can walk around and drool at the water.

The park's setting is not what you'd want to see on a postcard, but scenery isn't everything. The place is kind of barren, with few trees but plenty of grass and dirt areas to exercise a leashed dog.

The park is officially run by San Diego water entities, but most people think it's in La Mesa, so that's why we're listing it here. Exit Interstate 8 at Lake Murray Boulevard and drive northeast for about one mile. Turn left at Kiowa Drive. The street will take you into the park. (619) 668-2050. ➡ *See #12 on map p. 718.*

RESTAURANTS

Caruso's: Dogs often frequent the patio. The place is casual, serving light breakfast and dinner fare. 8201 La Mesa Boulevard; (619) 460-4800.

Por Favor Mexican Restaurant: You and your pooch can enjoy a Mexican meal at the outdoor tables here. 8302 La Mesa Boulevard; (619) 698-5950.

OCEANSIDE

This is the second largest city in the county, but it's a bummer for surf-loving dogs. They're banned from the city's beaches, as well as the Oceanside Pier.

•Buddy Todd Memorial Park 🐾 🐾 🐾

This is a really green, fairly quiet park that's far enough off the beaten path to dissuade most visitors. Dogs should be happy here—they're allowed to have 24 additional inches on their leashes, making for a grand total of eight feet!

There are plenty of pines here, and fun little trails on the hilly part of the park. Kids love it, too, because the playgrounds here have a train theme.

From Interstate 5, exit at Highway 76 and drive east about 1.5 miles to Butler Street. Go right and follow it as it curves, then turn left onto Barnwell, left again on Mesa and then left into the park. (619) 966-4520. ➡*See #13 on map p. 718.*

•Guajome Regional Park 🐾 🐾 🐾

Bring your binoculars and settle in for a day of birdwatching and hiking in one of the richest riparian areas in the county. Spring-fed lakes and a marsh are the centerpieces of this 569-acre park.

It's a little tricky to get around this place with a dog, because while there are miles of hiking trails, dogs aren't allowed on any of them. That's the general rule in San Diego County's parks and it's a doggy drag. But you can fish with your dog or picnic in the grassy hilltops here.

Humans like visiting the historic 22-room adobe ranch house on the park's eastern boundary. About 150 years ago, when this land was part of a vast Mexican land grant and the hub of the area's cultural life, the ranch house was the centerpiece of social activity.

Seventeen campsites are available at $14 per site. From Interstate 5, take Mission Avenue east seven miles to Guajome Lakes Road, then south to the park's entrance. Call (619) 694-3049 for park information or (619) 565-3600 for camping reservations. ➡*See #14 on map p. 718.*

RESTAURANTS

Amedeo's Italian Cafe: Dogs are welcome to join you on the patio at this upscale Italian restaurant. 2780 State Street; (619) 729-8799.

Armenian Cafe: Have a craving for Armenian food? Bring the pooch onto the deck and dig into a delicious meal. 3126 Carlsbad Boulevard; (619) 720-2233.

Beach Break Cafe: You and your dog can enjoy each other's company at the tables outside this daytime cafe. 1902 South Hill Street; (619) 439-6355.

PLACES TO STAY

Guajome Regional Park campsites: See page 730.

Sandman Motel: If the dog who wants to dream here is big, she's out of luck. Rates are $36 to $50. Doggettes cost $5 extra. 1501 Carmelo Drive, Oceanside, CA 92054; (619) 722-7661.

SAN DIEGO

Every dog-owning San Diego resident should be given a pair of infrared scopes when they license their pooches at City Hall. Since so many city parks and beaches have a tough rule banning dogs between 9 a.m. and 6 p.m., sometimes the only time to walk a dog around here is at night. Being able to have those Desert Storm-type glasses that let you see into the night would be a great boon.

San Diego is laid-back and exciting. You and your dog can stroll through the old Gaslamp district, eating up the local history as well as the good food served at a few dog-friendly eateries here. You can visit La Jolla's pristine shores (see page 727) for breathtaking scenery and clean-breathing air. You can even walk on historic land where California actually started (see Presidio Park, page 737). If that's not stimulating enough, you can stroll down action-packed beaches together at sunset (see page 735, Mission Beach/Pacific Beach).

Unfortunately, dogs are banned from beautiful Seaport Village. The restaurants and shops are wonderful, but liability problems prevent the managers of this renovated waterfront area from allowing pooches. Joe secretly suspects it's because of the shop called Whiskers, which touts itself as "the ultimate cat shop," but I think he's being paranoid.

PARKS, BEACHES & RECREATION AREAS

•**Balboa Park** 🐾 🐾 🐾 🐕

This luxurious semi-tropical park is one of California's best urban parks—for humans. I could go on for pages and pages about the attractions here, including the world-renowned San Diego Zoo, the enormous planetarium, several theaters and a few world-class museums.

But dogs aren't allowed at these places, so they're just plain not interested. The lush, green center of this 1,452-acre park makes for a civilized walk, but what dogs really seem to love are the dirt paths that run on the east and west sides of the park.

The east-side trails are in somewhat dry, unshaded Florida Canyon. To get there from Interstate 5, exit at Park Boulevard and head north to the northernmost limits of the park. Turn right at Morley Field Drive. Just after you pass Florida Canyon Drive, you'll make a right and drive to the lower parking lot. Walk south to the canyon, and you'll find numerous trails.

A shadier and more scenic series of bridle paths lie on the west side of the park. From 6th Avenue, which runs along the park's west border, a good access point is via Laurel Street. Head east into the park on Laurel Street and park on Balboa Drive. Find a trail and hike your heart out. The Park Information Center is located just a little farther down Laurel Street, which becomes El Prado as you cross Cabrillo Bridge. Visit or call for more information and maps. (619) 239-0512. ➤*See #15 on map p. 718.*

•**Black Mountain Open Space** 🐾 🐾 🐾 1/2

It's utterly quiet here. So quiet you can here your dog breathe when he's sitting still. So quiet you'll swear you hear his fleas gnashing their teeth. And except when people are shooting bullets through the signs that say "No Liquor" and "No Firearms," it's almost always this silent.

A few miles of trails run through this mountainous, shrubby, completely undeveloped 200-acre park. It's not exactly Mount Whitney, but from the top of Black Mountain (elevation 1,552 feet), you can get some good views of the surrounding hills and peaks.

The trek here looks complicated, but it's not bad. Exit Interstate 15 at Rancho Penasquitos Boulevard/Mountain Road and drive west about two miles to Black Mountain Road. Turn right and drive north about 2.5 miles, where the road will come to an abrupt end. Just before it does, turn right on the dirt road there. Follow the winding road up the mountain and eventually you'll come to a sharp right, where the road becomes paved. The road ends in a small parking lot. From here, you can see the start of the trail. (619) 525-8281. ➤*See #16 on map p. 718.*

•**Dog Beach** 🐾 🐾 🐾 🐾 🐕

See the Ocean Beach/Dog Beach entry on page 737. ➤*See #25 on map p. 718.*

• **Embarcadero Marina Park** 🐾 🐾 🐾

This park is like a big green thumb jutting into the San Diego Bay. It's a terrific place for a little walk with your leashed dog. Dogs and their people enjoy watching the seabirds glide around the fresh air over impressive views of the city and Coronado.

The big bummer here is that dogs are not allowed to visit Seaport Village, a major dining and shopping attraction located right next to the park. Hey, who needs to spend money anyway? Take Kettner Boulevard (it runs parallel to Pacific Highway, one block to the east) to its southernmost end. (619) 291-3900, ext. 222. ➡ *See #17 on map p. 718.*

• **Fiesta Island** 🐾 🐾 🐾 🐾 🐕

Hey, dogs! You're going to find out just why they call this one-and-a-half-mile-long island Fiesta Island! You can have a fabulous fiesta, then take a soothing siesta—and you can do it all off leash.

Yes, pooches, you can meet with friends, swim in the bay, chase your shadow and catch a stick without ever wearing that pesky old leash. As long as you listen to your people and don't cause any problems, this island is all yours! There's no development (as of this printing, anyway, although there's plenty of talk about it)—just dirt and sand and a little grass.

If you aren't very good at listening to your owners, ask them to take you to the far side of the island, where fewer cars cruise by. The perimeter of the island is a beach, and unfortunately, the road runs right behind the beach. It doesn't give water dogs a whole lot of room to run around, but it's enough for most.

If you choose to stay on the beach, you can avoid annoying little jet skiers by staying away from the watercraft recreation sections of water, which are clearly marked. The interior of the island is made up of fields of dirt. Since this is a bigger area, you'll be farther from traffic here.

The views of downtown San Diego and Mission Bay Park are really spectacular from the south side of the island. Cameras come in mighty handy here. (Fiesta Island is actually part of Mission Bay Park, but the rules are so different that I prefer to discuss them separately. See page 735 for Mission Bay Park information.)

From Interstate 5, take the Sea World Drive/Tecolote Road exit southeast to Fiesta Island Road, which is your first right. The road will take you onto the island. (619) 221-8901. ➡ *See #18 on map p. 718.*

• **Kate O. Sessions Park** 🐾 🐾 🐾

This is another of those San Diego parks that looks so much like a golf course that it fools people. In fact, this park even has a sign: "Golf practice prohibited!" The other major rule up here is that dogs must be leashed.

Kate O. Sessions Park is very green, very hilly, very peaceful and very charming. Not that dogs care, but the views of the city are terrific from up here.

The park is located between Pacific Beach and the Muirlands districts of town, on Soledad Road at Park Drive. (619) 581-9924. →*See #19 on map p. 718.*

• **Los Penasquitos Canyon Preserve** 🐾 🐾 🐾 1/2
You may have to say goodbye to this gem any minute now, dogs. This sprawling, 4,100-acre preserve in the Mira Mesa is an intoxicating place for a leashed dog to hike. The trails are long and the preserve is full of fascinating plants and animals.

That's just why county officials are working to ban dogs. They were hoping to ban dogs by the summer of 1994. However, since the park is co-managed by the city, there may be a minor scuffle that could delay or prevent this new dog-unfriendly rule.

The last time we visited, there were three confusing signs. One said that dogs have to be on a six-foot leash. Another said dogs have to be on an eight-foot leash. The third had a picture of a dog with a slash through it, meaning no dogs are allowed at all. The city ranger attributed the sign confusion to city-versus-county rules. As of this book's press time, he said the six-foot law is the one to follow.

The preserve is in the Mira Mesa area. If you're there and you really want to walk your dog, call (619) 484-7504 (the county ranger) or (619) 533-4067 (that's the more dog-friendly city ranger) to check on the status of the anti-dog ruling. If it's still open to dogs, you can get there by exiting Interstate 15 at Mercy Road and driving west. As soon as you pass Black Mountain Road, you'll be in the park. Park in the lot at the end of the road. →*See #20 on map p. 718.*

• **Marian Bear Memorial Park** 🐾 🐾 🐾 1/2
A stream flows through much of the length of this long and narrow park, and it's easy to access from the dirt trail that parallels it. As long as there are no trees and bushes preventing you and your leashed pooch from reaching the stream without getting all scraped up, you can veer between the trail and the stream all afternoon.

Despite this 466-acre park's proximity to Highway 52, dogs seem to like it here. There are all kinds of good smells and sights along the path. But keep your eyes peeled. Your dog may get a few sights he didn't bargain for if you visit here at the wrong time: Signs here warn against "lewd acts." Gosh...and just when Joe was going to lift his leg.

Exit Highway 52 at Regents/Clairemont Mesa Boulevard, drive south very briefly, and the park will be on your right. Once in the park, you can head left or right. Joe recommends going to the right, but that's just one Airedale's opinion. (619) 525-8281. *→See #21 on map p. 718.*

•Mission Bay Park 🐾 🐾 🐾 1/2

Dogs are not allowed here from 9 a.m. to 6 p.m., making for some rather tight daylight hours in the winter. But when it's light enough to see, you can't help but enjoy yourself here. This is one of the nation's largest and most beautiful aquatic parks.

It's so big (4,600 acres, including the bay), with so many more entry points than signs, that you may make the same mistake many others have when seeing the park for the first time: "I thought it was a bloody golf course! Gawd! Okay, Ginger, let's go for a walk," said Henry Miles, a 74-year-old British chap. He was walking Ginger for his sister, who had told him about Mission Bay Park and how to get there. But when he saw the perfect grass, the gently rolling hills and the sand, he figured he'd gotten the directions wrong. "They've got a lot of golf courses here, you know. Gawd, even their parks look like them. Ginger looks relieved, eh?"

I ran into Miles at the section of park near the San Diego Visitor Information Center. That portion is particularly reminiscent of a golf course—in fact, it's just around the bend from a golf course that's a dead ringer for the park.

If you're on Interstate 5 and your pooch wants to exercise while you get tourist information, exit at the Clairemont Drive/Visitor Center turnoff and follow the signs to the visitors center. Keep in mind that the visitor center and the pooch-walking hours rarely coincide, so it helps if you have a friend who can get the necessary tourist information while you walk your dog. You can park in the parking lot for only an hour, so if you're planning on a longer stay, there's street parking a little farther south.

The zillions of other access points are located north of the San Diego River and south of Pacific Beach Drive. The east-west boundaries are East Mission Bay Drive (which parallels Interstate 5) and Mission Boulevard (which runs a block east of the Pacific). For information on dog-friendly Fiesta Island, which is actually part of this park's territory, see page 733. (619) 221-8901. *→See #22 on map p. 718.*

•Mission Beach/Pacific Beach 🐾🐾🐾 1/2

The great thing about strolling down these two contiguous beaches with a dog is that no one seems to care if you don't have bulging biceps or a bikini-perfect body. Having a dog eliminates the need for physical prowess here. And on beaches that have built a worldwide reputation on how dazzling its bathers look, that's a mighty big plus.

On the down side, dogs are allowed to accompany you here only before 9 a.m. and after 6 p.m. The same hours hold for the paved promenade that runs behind the beaches. It's an understandable law during crowded summer days, but it would be a real boon for dogs if that rule could be eliminated during the winter months. Since the poor pooches have to be leashed anyway, what's the harm? (Joe made me write that.)

To make the best of these restricted hours, try a visit to beautiful Belmont Park. The big attraction at this old-style amusement park is a restored 65-year-old roller coaster, the Giant Dipper. In addition, there's a quaint old carousel and a historic indoor swimming pool. Dogs are required to be leashed and remain with all four feet planted firmly on the ground, but they can still have a good time watching the kids have fun. The park area is also home to dozens of shops and restaurants. It's located at West Mission Bay Drive and Mission Boulevard. Its back faces Mission Beach. Call (619) 491-2988 for Belmont Park hours and information.

Pacific Beach is north of Mission Beach. It starts around Tourmaline Street. The beach hooks up with Mission Beach and is one long, never-ending strip all the way down to the Mission Bay Channel. (619) 221-8901. → *See #23 on map p. 718.*

•Mission Trails Regional Park 🐾🐾🐾

This is a really big chunk of green—5,109 acres, to be exact. Actually, it's a good deal greener on a map than it is in reality. Several miles of dirt trails wind through low brush and boulders, all in a rather desolate setting. Because this park is managed by the city (although owned by the county), dogs are permitted on the trails.

They love to bound up and down hill after hill with you tagging along behind them. There's a leash law here, so make sure that if they're bounding, you're bounding, too.

One good destination for your leaps and bounds is the Old Mission Dam Historical Site. Native Americans built it many decades back and it's still in good working order.

Exit Interstate 8 at Mission Gorge Road (one of the exits for the

San Diego-Jack Murphy Stadium) and drive northeast past all the gas stations and fast-food marts. In about four miles, turn left on Father Junipero Serra Trail and you're in the park. Or if you want, you can park on Mission Gorge Road, at the trailhead off Jackson Road, just before you get to Father Junipero Serra Trail. (619) 533-4051.
➡ *See #24 on map p. 718.*

• **Ocean Beach Park/Dog Beach** 🐾 🐾 🐾 🐾 🐕

"Welcome to Dog Beach!" the sign announces at just about the same place that your dog charges out of the car to meet with all his best buddies. Dogs truly do feel welcome here. They're free to run off leash, and to get down to the business of being a dog. As long as they listen when you call and don't get into trouble, they can hang out leashless all day. Many dog people bring a folding chair so they can relax while their dog experiences heaven on earth.

We've seen several folks visit here because, although they don't have a dog, they get great joy out of watching the footloose creatures tearing around. "They have such innocent happiness when they run about and play so gleefully," said dogless dog-lover Maxine Chambers one grey morning. "It makes my day."

There are more dog footprints in the sand than human footprints, and not just because dogs have more feet. People come from many miles around, sometimes bringing their friends' dogs and their neighbors' dogs to participate in the whirlwind of excitement.

Dogs are allowed off leash at the north end of the beach, which is wide enough to be very safe from traffic. It's marked by signs. If you wander onto the other part of the beach, make sure you do so before 9 a.m. or after 6 p.m., and be sure to leash your dog.

Exit Interstate 5 at Interstate 8. Drive west and follow the signs to Sunset Cliffs Boulevard. After several blocks, bear right at Voltaire Street. Follow Voltaire Street to its end and the entrance to Dog Beach. (619) 221-8901. ➡ *See #25 on map p. 718.*

• **Presidio Park** 🐾 🐾 🐾 1/2 🦴

This is where California began. The hill here is known as the "Plymouth Rock of the West." Dogs are stepping on very historic land when they walk here. Back in 1769, Father Junipero Serra dedicated his first of many California missions on this very same hill.

The mission has since moved, but a fascinating museum is a major draw here. But dogs don't have great interest in the Spanish furniture and historic documents in the museum, and they're not permitted inside anyway. They prefer the many wide dirt trails that run around the hill.

The trails are on rolling hills, shaded by plenty of trees. The views from here are incredible. On a clear day, you can see all of the city. Someone marching up here with a telescope said he could check out the beach scene from here, but Joe and I didn't confirm that.

From Highway 8, take the Taylor Street exit west. Go left at Presidio Drive, which will take you up to the park. You can park at the museum and get a map of the park. There's also a lower parking lot that has easy trail access. Call (619) 297-3258 for the history of the area and general park information. ➜*See #26 on map p. 718.*

•**Tecolote Canyon Natural Park** 🐾 🐾 🐾 1/2
There's a brand new, nine-acre nature center just as you enter one end of this huge canyon. Dogs love looking at the whale skeleton that was found here, and they even seem to like listening to rangers chat about the geologic wonders and natural history of the place. But they'd give it all up to go on a hike down this rugged eight-mile canyon.

The trails don't go all the way through the canyon in one neat sweep. If you dare to do the entire hike, you'll have to negotiate a golf course, some fairly rough terrain and a couple of roads. But once you reach the northern Clairemont area of the park, you're in for some real beauty. Tecolote Creek is particularly refreshing here, and the scrub doesn't look as scrubby as it does elsewhere. There are even some shaded little ponds where you still might be able to find some crawdads.

From Interstate 5, take at Seaworld Drive/Tecolote Drive exit (just north of the intersection with Interstate 5) and drive east. You'll be dumped off almost immediately into the recreation center/nature center area. (619) 581-9930.

A word of warning: Rangers here beg folks not to let their dogs off leash. They say there's a real danger that Africanized honey bees could be here soon and the insects can be deadly. In two other U.S. cities, dogs rummaging through bushes have been killed by these bees, which defend a quarter-mile radius much faster than you or your dog can run. The bees won't attack out of the blue, so just hiking and minding your own beeswax probably won't get you in any trouble. It's only when you start poking around their hives that they get upset, rangers say. ➜*See #27 on map p. 718.*

RESTAURANTS
Brewski's: This is a laid-back restaurant/brewery for laid-back dogs. Your dog can come to this Gaslamp district joint to drool

while you dine on burgers or steaks and home-brewed beer, but she has to be tied up to the outer rim of the patio. That's no problem, because if you get a table on the edge of the patio, you'll barely feel separated. 310 Fifth Avenue; (619) 231-7700.

Cheese Shop: "We're one of the cool shops," says one waiter. And he's right—while dining with your dog under umbrella-topped tables outside, the two of you can enjoy mouth-watering cheese samplers and delicious sandwiches. If your dog is a cheese nut (like Joe's good friend Grinny, a.k.a. "Cheesehead"), she'll find it an ecstatic experience just to sit and sniff the Brie. 401 G Street; (619) 232-2303.

Slice 'n Ice: This place has only outdoor seating, so it's perfect for you and your happy pooch. You'll enjoy the deli-style sandwiches and pizza. And since it's right in dog-friendly Belmont Park (see page 736), dogs are especially welcome. 3146 Mission Boulevard; (619) 488-7760.

Trattoria La Strada: Enjoy a delicious meal outside with your pooch at this classy Gaslamp district restaurant. If you like Northern Italian cuisine, or just plain pizza, you'll love it here. 702 Fifth Avenue; (619) 239-3400.

PLACES TO STAY

Beach Haven Inn: Dogs have to be itsy-bitsy angels on their best behavior to stay here—20 pounds is the limit and they have to be "well-behaved and well-trained." The hotel is in the Pacific Beach area. Rates are $60 to $105, and there is a $50 deposit for the dog. 4740 Mission Boulevard, San Diego, CA 92109; (619) 272-3812.

Campland on the Bay: Dogs can stay at one of the 240 sites in a special (less landscaped) section of this 42-acre park on Mission Bay. They probably won't notice the reduced scenic value, though, if you take them to Dog Beach, which is only two miles away (see page 737). Rates run anywhere from $19 to $52, depending on the time of year and how rustic you want your site to be. Dogs cost an additional $2 in winter, and $3 in summer. Reservations are recommended in the summer. 2211 Pacific Beach Drive, San Diego, CA 92109; (619) 581-4260 or (800) 422-9386.

Crown Point View Suite-Hotel: If you can afford a steep dog deposit, this place is worth a stay. It's located a mere five-minute walk from Mission Bay Park (see page 735). Rates at these apartment/motel rooms are $70 to $150, and the pooch deposit is $250. 4088 Crown Point Drive, San Diego, CA 92109; (619) 272-0676.

Holiday Inn on the Bay: As long as you're willing to sign a contract stating you will accept responsibility for any damage you dog may do and you won't leave him alone in your room, you and your dog are welcome here. But don't try to sneak and leave the pooch alone—they'll call the pound folks, who will arrive pretty quickly since they're located just across the street. How convenient. Rates are $70 to $100. 1355 North Harbor Drive, San Diego, CA 92101; (619) 232-3861.

Marriott San Diego Marina: Wow! This is an impressive place, right next to Seaport Village (which bans pooches). Oh well, dogs love the harbor views. Two dogs reside here permanently, so it's definitely a dog-friendly lodging. The hotel can provide you with everything from children's programs to scuba diving instruction. Rates are $150 to $180. 333 West Harbor Drive, San Diego, CA 92101; (619) 234-1500.

San Diego Marriott Mission Valley: This one's just a ball's throw from the San Diego–Jack Murphy Stadium, not that that matters to your dog (who must weigh under 50 pounds to stay here). Rates are $150 to $160, and there is a $200 dog deposit. 8757 Rio San Diego Drive, San Diego, CA 92108; (619) 692-3800.

San Diego Princess Resort: Stay here and you're staying in beautiful Mission Bay Park. Set on the lush Vacation Island, just minutes from the off-leash dog havens of Fiesta Island and Dog Beach (see pages 733 and 737), your medium or small dog will be wagging her tail all day. There's so much to do here that you wouldn't know where to start. Rates for the cabana-style rooms are $120 to $350. There are no deposits for dogs, but you must sign a pet agreement. 1404 West Vacation Road, San Diego, CA 92109; (619) 274-4630.

Vagabond Inn: This one's in the Mission Valley area. Rates are $41 to $67. Dogs are $5 extra. 625 Hotel Circle South, San Diego, CA 92108; (619) 297-1691.

DIVERSIONS

Scrub-a-dub-dog: If you're in San Diego, there's no excuse for having a dirty dog. Self-service dog washes abound.

Our favorite is called Poochies. Not only can you scrub your dog to a smooth shine, for your efforts you can also treat yourself to a cup of espresso and a slice of cheesecake at the outdoor tables. And if your dog was well behaved during his bath, you can go to the pet store section of Poochies and get him a dog's version of cheese-cake—desiccated liver treats do the trick.

When you arrive at Poochies, follow the paw prints on the floor to the dog washing area. For $5.50, you'll get a waist-high tub, warm water, an assortment of shampoos, a rubber apron, a massaging mitt and a basket of fresh towels or a blow dryer. An extra $3 will get your pooch some time in the automated pet dryer.

While you're struggling to get your precious pooch to stay still while you soap him up, you'll be providing live entertainment for the folks in the espresso bar—which is separated from the bathing area by glass. If your dog is modest, you may want to turn him around so he's not being bared to the world.

Poochies is in the Tierrasanta area at 6030 Santo Road, Suite F, just off Highway 52. Call (619) 541-2525.

The Dog Beach Dog Wash is another wonderful place to keep your pooch looking like he just strolled out of a dog-food commercial. If location is everything, this business has it all. It's only two blocks from infamous Dog Beach (see page 737)! The owners say that some folks bring their dogs here almost every time they visit the beach. It's a great way to get rid of all that sand and dog slobber before getting back in your car.

A $5 bill will get your dog the works in any of five waist-high tubs. While the shop doesn't have its own espresso bar, there are coffeehouses just down the block. The Dog Beach Dog Wash is at 4933 Voltaire Street, Suite C. (916) 523-1700.

SOLANA BEACH

Dogs aren't allowed at the city's beaches, but since you're so close to beautiful, off-leash Del Mar City Beach, there's little reason to visit anyway.

RESTAURANTS

Coast Carbo Station: Your dog can join you in carbo-loading here on the big outdoor patio. The food is very healthy—it's all low-fat, low-sodium, high-carbohydrates—but don't let that scare you. It's delicious. And if your pooch looks up at Denise, the owner, with his big brown eyes and blinks a couple of times, he's bound to get his share of the milk bones she keeps behind the counter. 125 North Highway 101; (619) 481-9800.

SOUTH INLAND COUNTIES

INYO COUNTY

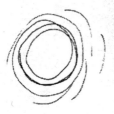

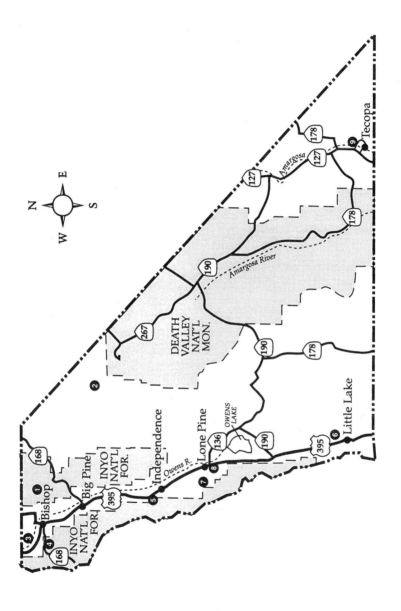

55

INYO COUNTY

The elevation: As low as 282 feet below sea level.

Some of the hot spots to visit: Funeral Mountains. Chloride City. Death Valley. Furnace Creek.

It may sound like pure hell, but a visit to this county during the cooler months of the year actually could be one of the most interesting adventures you and your dog can share in California.

Inyo County has an incredible variety of landscapes. The desert contains the lowest land in the United States, at 282 feet below sea level. The adjacent Sierra Nevadas and the silver, knife-like pinnacles of towering Mount Whitney make a strong contrast. In fact, Mount Whitney, with its peak at 14,494 feet, is the highest point in the contiguous United States. Because its sheer eastern wall rises out of the low desert landscape of the Owens Valley, the effect is especially dramatic.

But Mount Whitney is a place you just want to observe with your dog. First of all, while many areas of Inyo National Forest are enchanting places to take a dog, this climb is very difficult, and no pooch should be asked to perform such feats. But even more importantly, dogs aren't allowed anywhere near the mountain's peak. It happens to be in Sequoia National Park, which pretty much bans dogs. Rangers tell me that a few avid, sicko climbers have left their dogs behind (tied up) at the national forest border when they discovered no dogs were allowed at the peak. Stick with the lower elevations here.

In spring, wildflowers are everywhere. The sight of towering mountains against flowering desert makes dogs sniff the air in heavenly awe.

The canine and human folks who inhabit these areas are every bit as colorful as the desert springtime. During my research, I received a letter from Martha Watkins of the Death Valley Chamber of Commerce. It could have been from Mark Twain.

She wrote, "The only mayors of Shoshone and Tecopa have been dogs. B.J. was the mayor of Tecopa for many years. He was a small wire-haired terrier mix who really had a way with (human) women. I had the dubious distinction of running him over. My name was mud for a long time. No dog since B.J. has reached his stature.

"Shoshone's mayor is a small wiener-and-Doberman mix named Lifter. You can guess where his name came from. He's very macho."

Watkins still occasionally gets the evil eye from women who were seduced by B.J.'s scruffy looks. She told me that the late mayor lived with one of "our very hard-rock miners. Talk about a big wheel. B.J. would get up in the morning and sit by the side of the road until someone gave him a ride into town. He'd hang out at the bar all day. If he saw a girl with bare shoulders sitting in a booth by herself, he'd jump in the adjoining booth and start kissing her shoulders."

B.J.'s charms won him the unofficial vote as mayor of this small Death Valley town. Alas, he met Death Valley face-to-face under Watkins' tire on his bar-hopping rounds one fateful day. But his spirit still lives on in this dog-lovin' land.

Warning: Don't bring your dog to the desert areas of the county in the summer or early fall. Dogs who aren't used to the heat may not survive the average daily temperatures of 116 degrees Fahrenheit, not to mention the perilously hot ground. It's not much fun for most humans, either.

NATIONAL FORESTS

See the National Forests/Wilderness Areas chapter starting on page 801 for important information and safety tips for visiting national forests with your dog.

•Inyo National Forest 🐾 🐾 🐾 🐾 🦴 🐕

Dogs love the 28,000-acre Ancient Bristlecone Pine Forest, part of this national forest northeast of Big Pine. The gnarled pines that look like living driftwood are thought to be the world's oldest living trees—and probably the oldest living things on Earth! Tell your boy dog to be respectful of these aged arbors. Temperatures here are cooler than in much of the surrounding area because of the 10,000-foot elevation.

See page 804 for more information on Inyo National Forest.

NATIONAL MONUMENTS

•Death Valley National Monument 🐾 🐾 🐾 1/2 🦴

What's in a name? When I first thought about taking Joe to Death Valley, I pictured him ending up as a pile of bones in the sand while coyotes bayed and vultures licked their lips. Taking a dog to Death Valley seemed like something Cruella de Vil would do.

But not so! So long as you stay away during the gruelling months before, during and after summer (from April through

September), you and your dog could have some of your best adventures ever. Dogs must be leashed, but it's for their own good. There are some hungry coyotes here, and the heat of the sun can surprise you even during the cooler months. It's best to have your pooch close at hand.

Dogs aren't permitted on trails at this park, but there are so few trails that it won't matter to you. What matters is that they're allowed to hike at your side on the 500 miles of roadway that stretches from one landscape to another within Death Valley. Most of these roads are unpaved and barely get used by vehicles, so chances are you can get plenty of pure desert solitude with pure desert air.

Keep in mind that dogs also aren't supposed to wander far off the road into backcountry. About 100 yards is the limit. Remember that with air as clean and land as flat as this, rangers are omniscient. Watch yourselves, because they are sure to be watching as well.

You'll see some of the most fascinating geologic formations on Earth here. Of course, most of the time it won't look like you're even on Earth, but don't let that bother you. The park's otherworldly nature is one of its charms. Much of the park is below sea level. The lowest point in the United States is here, in Badwater Basin. Within the park are elevations from 282 feet below sea level to 11,049 feet above sea level. Betwixt and between, you'll find vast salt flats, endless sand ridges, huge glimmery rocks and twisting mountainsides.

When you get to the visitors center, pick up brochures on the history and geology of the place and decide which parts of Death Valley you and your dog would enjoy most. The park has nine campgrounds, three of which are open all year. There are over 1,500 campsites available on a first-come, first-served basis. Fees range from $6 to $8.

The entry fee for the park is $5 per carload, good for visits of up to a week. To get to the visitors center from US 395, take either Highway 136 or 190 east. Highway 136 will join up with Highway 190. From US 395, the drive is a little more than 100 miles. Follow Highway 190 through all its confusing turns and you can't miss it. Even in the cooler months of the year, it's a good idea to bring extra stocks of water, just in case you break down and the temperature decides to do one of its soaring routines. (619) 786-2331.

BIG PINE

• Ancient Bristlecone Pine Forest 🐾 🐾 🐾 🐾 🐕

This remarkable area is located in Inyo National Forest, about 25 miles northeast of Big Pine. See page 746 for a description.

Winter usually makes the roads getting here impassable but the forest is accessible from early June to late October. From US 395 in Big Pine, take Highway 168 east about 15 miles to White Mountain Road. Turn left, and in another 10 miles you'll come to the south end of the forest. (619) 873-4207. ➡ *See #1 on map p. 744.*

• Eureka Sand Dunes National Natural Landmark
🐾 🐾 🐾 🐾 🐕

If your dog likes to roll in sand, she'll be overjoyed here. This is a gigantic sandbox, complete with a 700-foot mountain of sand— California's tallest sand dune. The pale sand in this park has mesmerizing, undulating patterns that contrast in artistic perfection with the dark backdrop of the Last Chance Mountains.

Well-behaved dogs are welcome to be off leash. Most pooches love running up and down the dunes with you. Kick off your shoes, try not to get sand down your pants and listen hard. A few of the dunes will sing to you. Astute dogs look around in dazed confusion until they realize it doesn't matter what's making that string bass sound. (But in case they ask, it's the vibration of all that sand falling down the dune.) And don't worry—rangers tell us there's no danger you'll be swallowed by hungry sand pits, à la Lawrence of Arabia.

You can camp here for free. The sites are remote and primitive. In the morning, wake up early and explore the sand. You'll see all sorts of evidence of desert nightlife, from slithering snake trails to mammal footprints. Be sure your dog's paw prints aren't among them—dogs should be kept in your tent or camper at night to keep them out of the clutches of the few predators who hunt here.

From US 395 in Big Pine, take Highway 168 east about 2.5 miles, take the south fork (Death Valley Road). Follow the road for about 40 miles and turn right on Eureka Valley Road. Drive another 10 miles, and you'll be there. Remember: Don't go with your dog during the scorching months of summer and early fall. (619) 375-7125. ➡ *See #2 on map p. 744.*

PLACES TO STAY

Big Pine Motel: Rates are $30 to $38. 370 South Main Street, Big Pine, CA 93513; (619) 938-2282.

Eureka Sand Dunes camping: See above.

BISHOP

Set between the state's two highest mountain ranges, Bishop has become the hub of this recreational wonderland. It's a small, laid-back town with only one thing that peeves pooches: Dogs are banned from the only city park here.

PARKS, BEACHES & RECREATION AREAS

•**Pleasant Valley County Park** 😺 😺 😺

This park has the long, narrow Pleasant Valley Reservoir as its centerpiece. The reservoir is created by the Owens River, and fishing here is pretty hot (thanks in part to planted trout). Leashed dogs are allowed to cheer at your side as you catch supper from shore.

For dogs who aren't fishing fans, try the hiking trail located on the reservoir's east side. The big rocky bluffs here are interesting, but the surrounding mountains topped with snow year-round are really impressive. However, dogs don't seem to care much for the visuals here. Something about this place keeps their flaring nostrils pressed firmly to the ground. Since leashes are the law, you may feel some tugging when your dog decides to try to track one of these enticing smells.

There are 200 campsites, but they're pretty far from the lake. Sites are $6. Reservations are not necessary. Take US 395 about seven miles north of Bishop, then turn north on Pleasant Valley Road and drive about 1.5 miles to the lake. (619) 878-0272. *See #3 on map p. 744.*

•**Izaak Walton County Park** 😺 😺 😺

Do you like clear mountain creeks and wooden footbridges that take you over them? Does your dog like to go for short walks on a leash after a long drive on a highway? Come to this special little park to stretch all your car-cramped legs.

It's a really pretty park with green grass most of the year and plenty of trees for shade. There's a narrow trail cutting through brush to the back of the park, which is brambly, but fenced and safe from traffic.

This park is where I first discovered that Bill likes to "eat" fast-flowing ribbons of water. He stuck his snout in the creek and grabbed mouthful after mouthful of the evasive stuff for 20 minutes, but he stopped and looked downright embarrassed when a stranger said nice and loud, "That your dog? He sure is weird."

From Highway 395 in the middle of town, go west on West Line Street for about 2.5 miles. The park will be on your left. (619) 878-0272. *See #4 on map p. 744.*

RESTAURANTS

Erick Schat's Bakery: This has been the home of the Original Sheepherder Bread since 1938. Stop with your dog in the summertime and break some of this bread at the outdoor tables. 763 North Main Street; (619) 873-7156.

Manor Market: This grocery store is home to some pretty good grub, including hot chicken and soup. There are a few outdoor tables in the warmer months. 3100 West Line Street; (619) 873-4296.

PLACES TO STAY

Rodeway Inn: No huge dogs, please. Rates are $45 to $60. 150 East Elm Street, Bishop, CA 93514; (619) 873-3564.

Bishop Inn: Rates are $47 to $62. The place even has a fish-cleaning station. 805 North Main Street, Bishop, CA 93514; (619) 873-4284.

Millpond Recreation Area: Dogs with human children in the family enjoy spending the night here, because little humans are allowed in the adjacent park. There's a playground, sports fields, tennis courts, a pond and horseshoe pits. The campground itself is comfortable, but not too exciting. There are 60 sites available. Dogs must be leashed.

Fees are $8 to $12. From US 395 about six miles north of town, take Ed Powers Road south. Go the equivalent of about three city blocks, and turn west on Sawmill Road. In about a half mile, you'll be at the park. The campground is open March through November. (619) 873-5342.

Pleasant Valley County Park camping: See page 749.

Sierra Foothills Motel: They prefer small and medium-sized dogs here. Rates are $33 to $47. Dogs require a $10 deposit. 535 South Main Street, Bishop, CA 93514; (619) 872-1386.

Thunderbird Motel: Rates are $40 to $60. There's a $10 doggy deposit. 190 West Pine Street, Bishop, CA 93514; (619) 873-4215.

Vagabond Inn: This one comes with its own fish-cleaning facilities and a freezer. If you and your dog have a successful day angling, this might be the place for you. Rates are $44 to $66. Pooches are $5 extra. 1030 North Main Street, Bishop, CA 93514; (619) 873-6351.

DIVERSIONS

Go together like a dog and carriage: Irv Moore, owner of the Cottonwood Carriage Company, allows anyone to ride in his antique horse-drawn carriage. "We even take mother-in-laws," says Moore. Well-behaved, leashed dogs can sit on your lap or on the floor of this romantic carriage while two stunning draft horses clip-clop their way through town, the desert or even a nearby Indian reservation. Moore offers a variety of landscapes to his riders. One of the more popular rides is called "Champagne under the Stars." What could be more romantic than sipping champagne with your dog drooling at your feet?

Rates start at $35 for a half-hour jaunt through town. Moore may soon be adding less formal hay wagon rides to his repertoire. Call (619) 872-4432 to check on the status of the wagon rides or to reserve time on the carriage. Or write to the Cottonwood Carriage Company, 1521 Lazy-A Drive, Bishop, CA 93514.

INDEPENDENCE

PARKS, BEACHES & RECREATION AREAS

• Dehy Park 🐾 🐾 🐾

A river doesn't run through this park, but a creek sure does. Besides the usual picnic tables and shade trees, the park is home to an attractive old locomotive. But the best feature of this county park is that it's directly off US 395, so weary travelers don't have to go far out of their way. It's at the very north end of Independence, at West Wall Street. (619) 878-0272. → *See #5 on map p. 744.*

LITTLE LAKE

PARKS, BEACHES & RECREATION AREAS

• Fossil Falls 🐾 🐾 🐾 1/2 👞 🦴

Before you read any further, heed this warning: Although dogs may run off leash here, you may want to leash yours when you're anywhere near the park's main feature—the 80-foot deep chasm that was once a waterfall. It's probably a good idea to keep an eye on the kids here, too.

Pick up a brochure and you'll learn all about the intriguing history and geology behind what caused the fossilized falls to form. Dogs don't usually give a hoot for such subjects, but they do seem interested in the bumpy lava covering the ground on your way from the parking lot to the falls. Joe tries to dig at it, but we discourage this behavior. It's not every day a volcano leaves behind such amazing tracks.

From about three miles north of Little Lake on US 395, turn east onto Cinder Cone Road (watch for the cinder cone) and follow to the park. The parking lot is about 1.5 miles from the highway. Your drive will take you through a large volcanic field, which is almost

as interesting as the fossilized falls themselves. (619) 375-7125.
➡ *See #6 on map p. 744.*

LONE PINE

This is a one-stoplight town—the gateway to Mount Whitney. As Marilyn, an enthusiastic native who works at the Chamber of Commerce put it: "We've got a real pretty town, real Western."

And real Westerns are what they've been shooting here for decades. See the Alabama Hills description below for details of the show biz history of this area. This place is a must-visit location for dogs and their people.

PARKS, BEACHES & RECREATION AREAS

• **Alabama Hills** 🐾 🐾 🐾 🐾 ➡ 🐕

Pardner, if you like those Western films and TV shows, you're gonna love this place. For more than 70 years, Hollywood has used the unique scenery here in almost 300 films and countless TV shows.

This is where the Lone Ranger ambush was first filmed, where Roy Rogers found Trigger and *Bonanza* became a bonanza. Giants like Gene Autry, Roy Rogers, Hopalong Cassidy, Humphrey Bogart, Cary Grant, Gregory Peck, Spencer Tracy and Clint Eastwood did their big scenes here. In fact, this is where both Roy Rogers and Robert Mitchum were filmed for their first features.

Put a bandana on your four-legged varmint and have a rip-roaring time exploring the rock formations, canyons and barren flats that are the real stars here. Some photo markers are placed in the area showing which famous scenes were shot where. It's a real education for your and your obedient, leashless dog.

From US 395, take the Whitney Portal Road about 2.5 miles west of Lone Pine and you'll find yourself on Movie Road. That's where your trek through movieland begins. Don't forget to bring a camera. (619) 872-4881. ➡ *See #7 on map p. 744.*

• **Diaz Lake** 🐾 🐾 1/2

This small lake is set under the watchful eye of the Sierra Nevadas and Mount Whitney. It really bustles here in the summer. Leashed dogs can hike around the 86-acre lake with you and hang out while you catch bass, bluegill or trout.

Camping here costs $7. It's a convenient place to spend the night, since it's just off US 395, two miles south of Lone Pine. (619) 878-0272. ➡ *See #8 on map p. 744.*

RESTAURANTS
Frosty Stop: You can have your hamburgers and eat ice cream, too, at the outdoor tables here. 701 South Main Street; (619) 876-5000.

PLACES TO STAY
Diaz Lake camping: See page 752.

Dow Villa Motel: Dogs can stay in smoking rooms only, but the managers like dogs and will make them feel at home. Rates are $52 to $60. 310 South Main Street, Lone Pine, CA 93545; (619) 876-5521.

National 9 Trails Motel: Small pets only, please. Rates are $32 to $49. Dogs are $4 extra. 633 South Main Street, Lone Pine, CA 93545; (619) 876-5555.

FESTIVALS
Git in line, lil' doggie: Leashed dogs are welcome to attend all the outdoor segments of the three-day Lone Pine Film Festival celebrating the myriad Western flicks shot in the nearby Alabama Hills (see page 752). Some of the most famous old cowboys and cowgals gather during this three-day festival each October to talk with fans and even re-enact a scene or two. If your dog is lucky, maybe he'll get to shake paws with one of the greats. Call (619) 876-4314 for information on this year's event.

TECOPA
The population is 300, which is a big number when you get this deep into the desert. The neighboring community of Shoshone has a whopping 30 residents. See page 745 for the tale of the mutty mayors of these tiny towns.

PARKS, BEACHES & RECREATION AREAS
• **Tecopa Hot Springs County Park** 🐾 🐾 🐾 🐾
The Paiute Indians used to bring their lame and sick ancestors to bathe in the hot mineral springs here, and now people from all over the world come for a soak. The 107-degree waters are supposed to help alleviate the pain of arthritis, rheumatism and other bodily woes.

While dogs can't take a dip, they are allowed to roam the 40-acre park with you. Switch off hanging out with the dog with a friend as you take turns rejuvenating yourselves in the baths.

Most of the park is taken up by a large, 300-site campground. Sites are $6.50 to $8 per night and are available on a first-come, first-served basis. The bathing is free!!! Make sure you don't come with your dog in the hot months. It gets to be around 118 degrees

Fahrenheit some summer months, and that's hotter than the mineral baths.

From the Death Valley junction (highways 190 and 127), follow the road about 36 miles to the park. (619) 852-4264. ➤ *See #9 on map p. 744.*

PLACES TO STAY
Tecopa Hot Springs County Park camping: See page 753.

SAN BERNARDINO COUNTY

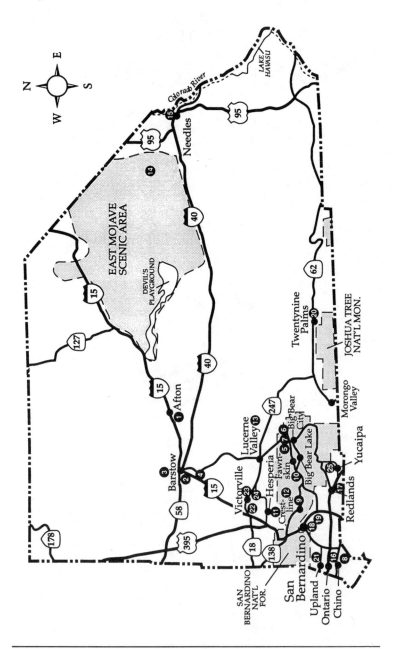

56
SAN BERNARDINO COUNTY

This is the Texas of California. It's just plain big. In fact, it's the biggest county in the nation, weighing in at more than 20,000 square miles.

That means you'll find a lot of variety here. This is where dogs can do just about everything they ever imagined a dog could do. They can ride the rail through a ghost town, herd goats in Chino, take a horse-and-buggy ride in Big Bear, and even visit Santa and his elves in a beautiful place called Skyforest.

Best of all, dogs can experience off-leash ecstasy on millions of amazing acres. Some of these acres are sandy, some are densely forested, but all the off-leash areas are splendid in some way. This more than makes up for places like Fontana which ban dogs from all city parks. Who needs uptight towns with places like San Bernardino National Forest around?

Try to visit the San Bernardino Mountains at sunset, when occasionally they play an optical trick. A few of the mountains will turn purply-pink, while others stay the same sandy brown and forest green. Then everything fades into a surreal orange mist. For people, it's a stunning sight. If dogs really do have black-and-white vision, they're probably not quite so thrilled.

NATIONAL FORESTS

See the National Forests/Wilderness Areas chapter starting on page 801 for important information and safety tips for visiting national forests with your dog.

• **San Bernardino National Forest** 🐾 🐾 🐾 🐾 🐕

Much of the southwest corner of San Bernardino County is San Bernardino National Forest land. So far, dogs are allowed off leash in most parts of the forest, except for several times when they meet up with state parks. (Dogs aren't even allowed there on leash.) Unfortunately, local national forest rangers are facing the question of whether off-leash rules are appropriate in the forest. Complaints about dogs running up to frightened humans or fighting with each other have led to this dilemma. So make absolutely certain your dog is Mr., Mrs. or Ms. Obedience before taking off that leash.

On the way up to Big Bear Lake via Highway 38, you'll find numerous forest trailheads and picnic areas that make great rest stops on a long journey. See the Big Bear Lake entry on page 762 for a description of the forest in that popular resort area. For general information on San Bernardino National Forest, turn to page 807.

NATIONAL MONUMENTS

• **Joshua Tree National Monument** 🐾🐾🐾 1/2 🐾

Although most of this 870-square-mile park is in Riverside County, Twentynine Palms is where you'll find the visitors center and the gateways to some of the most beautiful areas in the park.

This is amazing land, with striking granite formations rising around dramatic desert plants and wildlife. In spring, it becomes a showcase of brilliant wildflowers. The giant Joshua tree plants are in the higher western half and they're definitely worth a visit.

Dogs can be walked on paved and dirt roads, but not on hiking trails. They're permitted to wander on leash up to 300 feet from the road, and there are plenty of small dirt roads where you'll be far from most traffic. Leashes are the law here, but they're also a very good idea because of critters like cougars and bobcats. A bigger danger than those cats is actually the cactus. Dogs sometimes rub up against the prickly plants or try to bite them, and end up with a major problem.

There's a $5 entrance fee, and if you want to camp without water, you can camp for free. Otherwise, sites are $8 to $10. There are 492 sites available on a first-come, first-served basis. However, the 100 sites at Black Rock Canyon require reservations. Always bring lots of water on your hikes here, and make sure your dog gets her fill. It doesn't usually get nearly as hot as in other parts of the desert, but you don't want to take a chance. From Interstate 10, exit at Highway 62 and drive northeast for about 39 miles to the town of Twentynine Palms. The visitors center is on Utah Trail, just south of the highway about a mile east of town. (619) 367-7511.

AFTON

PARKS, BEACHES & RECREATION AREAS

• **Afton Canyon Natural Area** 🐾🐾🐾🐾 🐾 🐕

Wow. Woof. How does 42,000 acres of mostly off-leash land sound to you and your canine companion? If you don't demand lush green meadows to be part of your Elysian ideal, this can be heaven on earth.

Afton Canyon is one of only three places where the Mojave River flows above ground year-round, so not only has it attracted visitors throughout history, it's also a water dog's delight. If you don't expect fine fishing here, no one will be disappointed.

Keep in mind that hundreds of bird, mammal and reptile species call Afton Canyon their home, or at least their migratory hotel. It's a great place for wildlife watching, but unless you can trust your dog to stay at your side, you should keep her leashed when anywhere near these creatures.

Camping here isn't the prettiest, but it's comforting to know you're just a stone's throw from another day of off-leash adventures. Sites are $4, and dogs must be leashed in the campground. There are about a dozen sites available on a first-come, first-served basis.

Afton is about 40 miles east of Barstow. From Interstate 15, exit at Afton Canyon Road and drive three miles south to the park. (619) 256-8313. ➤*See #1 on map p. 756.*

PLACES TO STAY
Afton Canyon Natural Area camping: See above.

BARSTOW

PARKS, BEACHES, & RECREATION AREAS

• **Foglesong Park** 🐾 🐾 1/2

This is a decent-sized city park with plenty of shade for those searing summer days. The kids will like the playground, and the dogs are sure to enjoy the open grassy fields. Enter at Avenue G, just north of Nancy Street. (619) 256-3531. ➤*See #2 on map p. 756.*

• **Rainbow Basin Natural Area** 🐾 🐾 🐾 🐾 ◀ 🐕

If you or your dog like bones, faults, sediment deposits or leash-free walks, don't miss this geological and anthropological wonder. Fossils of ancient animals are everywhere in the colorful sedimentary layers of the canyon walls (once a lake). Mastodons, camels, three-toed horses, rhinos and dog-bears are among the animals whose remains have been discovered here. As you hike around, you'll be able to see insect fossils that are among the best-preserved in the world. You and your dog need to keep your paws off these fossils so they remain undisturbed for others to enjoy them.

The geology of the place is also fascinating. Rainbow Basin's sediment deposits are textbook examples of folds, faults and other disturbances of the earth's crust. If you're studying geology in school, this is the place to visit if you want to get the big picture.

Unfortunately, your dog probably doesn't give a hoot about bones she can't eat and sediment she can't wallow in. She knows what's important—being able to be at your side, off leash, while you peruse the area. The Bureau of Land Management, which operates the park, has some of the most lenient, dog-friendly rules in the state for obedient pooches.

The best place to take an off-leash dog is any flat area where she won't have much chance of disturbing this national natural landmark. There are no developed paths or trails, but since the place is nearly devoid of trees and thick underbrush, it's easy to navigate a course almost anywhere here. Be aware that you may run across desert kit foxes and bobcats. If you can't control your dog with critters like these around, keep her leashed. And make sure she goes nowhere near desert tortoises, the California state reptile (bet your dog didn't know that). Tortoises are easily traumatized, and contact with people or dogs could lead to their death.

For your pet's sake, don't visit in the summer. Our favorite time to hike here is in late autumn, when it's crisp but not freezing. Leashed dogs are allowed to camp with you at the 31-site Owl Canyon Campground. The fee is $4 per vehicle. No reservations are necessary.

From Highway 58 in Barstow, drive 5.5 miles north on Fort Irwin Road and turn left on Fossil Bed Road. It's a rough dirt road, and it will seem like an eternity of bouncing before you reach your destination, but it's actually just three miles. (619) 256-8313. → *See #3 on map p. 756.*

• **Stoddard Valley Open Area** 🐾🐾🐾🐾 🐕
Is your dog tired of those five-acre parks where leashes are a must? Does she long for wide-open desert ranges where she can tear around without a care in the world (except rattlesnakes and their friends)?

This 52,000-acre parcel of land just southeast of Barstow could be the answer to her poochie prayers. Not only are there mountains and endless open areas, there are also plenty of fascinating rock formations for you and your dog to explore.

To enter at the northern end, where there's a campground, exit Interstate 15 at Sidewinder Road and drive the only way the road takes you. The campground has no developed sites, and no reservations or permits are required. The public land here is interspersed with private land, but Bureau of Land Management folks say unless an area is fenced off, posted or developed, it's probably okay for hiking. (619) 256-3591. → *See #4 on map p. 756.*

RESTAURANTS
Foster Freeze: 1580 West Main Street; (629) 256-8842.

PLACES TO STAY

There's no shortage of dog-friendly lodgings in Barstow.

Barstow Inn: Dogs are welcome in the first-floor rooms here. Rates are $25 to $35. 1261 East Main Street, Barstow, CA 92311; (619) 256-7581.

Best Motel: Rates are $24 to $32. 1281 East Main Street, Barstow, CA 92311; (619) 256-6836.

Calico Ghost Town camping: See page 762.

Desert Inn Motel: Rates are $28 to $38. There's a $20 dog deposit. 1100 East Main Street, Barstow, CA 92311; (619) 256-2146.

Econo Lodge: Rates are $24 to $53. A $5 deposit is required for dogs. 1230 East Main Street, Barstow, CA 92311; (619) 256-2133.

Gateway Motel: Rates are $22 to $42. 1630 East Main Street, Barstow, CA 92311; (619) 256-8931.

Hillcrest Motel: Rates are $24 to $30. 1111 East Main Street, Barstow, CA 92311; (619) 256-1063.

Rainbow Basin Natural Area camping: See page 759.

Quality Inn: The folks here really like dogs. But because of guests' allergies, you'll have to stay in a room designated for smokers. Rates are $49 to $64. 1520 East Main Street, Barstow, CA 92311; (619) 256-6891.

Stoddard Valley Open Area camping: See page 760.

Vagabond Inn: Rates are $38 to $65. Pooches are $5 extra. 1243 East Main Street, Barstow, CA 92311; (619) 256-5601.

FESTIVALS

Calico Hullaboo: The main attraction at this Old West event held each Palm Sunday weekend is the tobacco spitting contest. Dogs love to watch the contestants chew, but they really get a kick out of seeing the spit fly. Other events include horseshoe pitching and stew cooking. The admission price of $6 includes entry into the Calico Ghost Town, where the Hullaboo is held (see Diversions, below, for details and directions). Call (619) 254-2122 for more information.

DIVERSIONS

Go west, young pup: How many dogs can say they watched an Old West shootout on a dusty saloon-packed street? How many can tell their buddies they rode aboard a narrow-gauge railroad through a silver mining boomtown/ghost town? And how many can brag that they got to see a piano player striking up old haunting tunes?

Your dog can be that lucky dog, if you take him on a visit to Calico Ghost Town. It's a campy, kitschy, but thoroughly entertaining town-turned-park. Calico thrived during the 1880s silver boom, and you can still roam around the tunnels of silver mines and stroll along the wooden sidewalks of Main Street. If you're a real fan of this era, why not spend the night? Camping costs $9 to $15, and leashed dogs are welcome for an additional $1. There are about 260 campsites available here. Reservations are recommended in the spring and fall.

Admission to Calico Ghost Town Regional Park is $4 for adults, $2 for children. Train rides are $1.95 for humans. Dawgs go free. From Barstow, drive about six miles east on Interstate 15, and exit at Calico Ghost Town/Ghost Town Road. Drive north for three miles. When you see a yellow wagon, you'll know you're there. (619) 254-2122.

BIG BEAR LAKE

This lakeside mountain resort community isn't exactly Lake Tahoe, but that's part of its charm. It's generally more rustic, more natural and far less crowded. The crisp, clean alpine air is a godsend any time of year.

The town's old-fashioned honesty and lack of smooth public relations pros is evident as soon as you approach the old village section. There, you'll see a road sign for skiing, with an arrow pointing to the left. Immediately below that is a sign for the hospital, with an arrow pointing to the right. It's not a joke.

Several dogs we know dream of going along on their owners' annual cross-country ski trip through San Bernardino National Forest. Before Joe can join them, he has to learn that he can walk in the snow, not just roll on top of it.

This is a very dog-friendly community, complete with incomparable off-leash hikes, great restaurants and hotels where dogs are as welcome as their chauffeurs. Check out the old Big Bear Lake village. It gives a new meaning to old-style charm.

PARKS, BEACHES & RECREATION AREAS

Although this book doesn't normally go into detail on specific trails in national forests, we're mentioning a couple here because they're so integral to your pooch having a doggone good time in the Big Bear Lake area.

• Cougar Crest Trail 🐾 🐾 🐾 🐾 🐕

This two-mile trail goes through a mixed conifer section of San Bernardino National Forest. It's full of juniper, Jeffrey pines and pinyons. Obedient dogs are welcome to peruse the area *sans* leash, but keep in mind that this off-leash rule might be reconsidered by the authorities.

We like it best here in late autumn, when a dusting of snow rests on the pine needles and the air is crisp. We've never run into another person on the trail during this time of year. Cougar Crest Trail eventually connects with the Pacific Crest Trail, which traverses 39 miles of the Big Bear area. The scenery here is outstanding.

From the Big Bear Lake village, cross the lake at the Stanfield Cutoff and turn left on Highway 38. As you drive west, the trail is just over a half mile west of the ranger station, on the right side of the road. There's plenty of parking. (909) 866-3437. → *See #5 on map p. 756.*

• **Pedal Path** 🐾🐾🐾 1/2

This is one way to hike the Big Bear Lake area without roughing it too much. This six-mile paved path allows you and your leashed, lake-loving dog to hike along the scenic north shore of Big Bear Lake.

Sometimes bikers think they own the trail (it *is* called Pedal Path, not Four-Paw Path, after all), so make sure your dog is close. The trail starts at the north end of the Stanfield Cutoff. (909) 866-3437. → *See #6 on map p. 756.*

• **Woodland Trail** 🐾🐾🐾🐾 🦴 🐕

This 1.5-mile nature trail in San Bernardino National Forest has 20 stops where you and your well-behaved, leashless dog may learn about the flora and fauna of this mountainous region. It's especially glorious in an early-morning mist.

The trail rarely gets crowded. If you encounter more than a few people, be courteous and keep your dog leashed. Rangers are reconsidering the off-leash rule for the forest, so good pooch public relations are essential.

From the Big Bear Lake village, cross the lake at the Stanfield Cutoff and turn left on Highway 38. Shortly after you turn, the trail will be on your right. (909) 866-3437. → *See #7 on map p. 756.*

RESTAURANTS

Many of the restaurants listed below are in the old-style Alpine village in the heart of Big Bear Lake. Whenever you visit here, you'll feel like it's Christmas.

Belotti's: The pizza here is really tasty, and the fresh-baked goods will send you running to the nearest aerobics class. 41248 Big Bear Boulevard; (909) 866-7686.

Boo Bear's Den: Families and dogs are very welcome here, as long as they don't eat off the restaurant's plates (the dogs, that is). The patio area is quite large, and is graced by grass and trees. 5721 Pine Knot Avenue; (909) 866-2932.

Hansel's Restaurant: This place looks like a huge alpine cottage, with a big wooden deck where dogs may watch their people dine. 40701 Village Drive; (909) 866-9497.

The Log Cabin: You can eat on the deck here, which is three feet above the lawn, where your dog has to be tied. You can tie your dog securely under a shady tree and hover above her as you eat the German-American food here or sip any of the 10 beers they have on tap. 39976 Big Bear Boulevard; (909) 866-3667.

Paoli's Country Kitchen: The Italian food here is really tasty. Your dog gets to hang out with you as you dine on the patio. 40821 Pennsylvania Avenue; (909) 866-2020.

Pine Knot Coffee & Bakery: Mmm. Come here on a cool autumn afternoon and try the hot pot pies or mulligan stew while sitting on the small deck. 535 Pine Knot Avenue; (909) 866-3537.

PLACES TO STAY

Big Bear Lake is one of the best places in the entire state to spend the night with your dog. There are so many lodgings that accept dogs that you'll have a hard time choosing. Here are just a few. For a more complete list, call the Big Bear Chamber of Commerce at (909) 866-7000 and ask for their Lodging Guide. Be sure you request the one that lists whether pets are allowed.

Bear Claw Cabins: These homey cabins are one-quarter mile from the lake and skiing. Rates are $55 to $94, and dogs can stay in all rooms except the ones with Jacuzzis. 586 Main Street, Big Bear Lake, CA 92315; (800) 487-3168.

Big Pine Flat Campground: This is one of the more out-of-the-way campgrounds in the Big Bear area. You and your dog can hike around the area and be fully enveloped by ravishing Mama Nature. Or you can drive a few miles and be in the heart of Big Bear Lakes. Sites are $8. From Fawnskin, follow Rim of the World Drive (its name will change) for seven miles to Big Pine Flat Station. The campground is on your right. (909) 866-3437.

Cozy Hollow Lodge: This lodge deserves its name. Most cottages here have fireplaces. It's a great place to stay after a long day on the slopes. In summer, a stream runs through the woods behind here. Rates are $50 to $130. There's a $50 deposit for dogs and an additional $5 fee for each pooch. 40409 Big Bear Boulevard, Big Bear Lake, CA 92315; (909) 866-8886.

Eagle's Nest Bed & Breakfast: This romantic getaway is furnished with country antiques. The cottages have fireplaces. Dogs love it here. Rates are $75 to $140. There's a $50 deposit for dogs. 41675 Big Bear Boulevard, Big Bear Lake, CA 92315; (909) 866-6465.

Frontier Lodge: There's a big covered wagon in front of these cabins, so dogs who like the Old West feel right at home here. Rates are $65 to $90. Dogs are $10 extra. 40472 Big Bear Boulevard, Big Bear Lake, CA 92315; (800) 457-6401.

Grey Squirrel Resort: These charming cottages are a half block from the lake, on four-and-a-half acres. Several of the cottages have fireplaces. For those achy muscles fraught with post-skiing-stress-disorder, the resort has a heated pool, which is enclosed in the winter (but pooches can't paddle here.). Rates are $60 to $125. There's a $100 deposit for pets and an additional $5 fee per pooch. The cabins are on Highway 18, just west of town. The mailing address is P.O. Box 5404, Big Bear Lake, CA 92315; (909) 866-4335.

Happy Bear Village: All the cottages here have fireplaces. Dogs enjoy the large grassy areas that come complete with picnic tables and barbecues. Rates are $70 to $100. There's a $100 deposit for dogs, and an additional $10 per pooch. 40154 Big Bear Boulevard, Big Bear Lake, CA 92315; (909) 866-2350 or (909) 866-6816.

Quail Cove: The cottages are in a wooded, park-like setting by the water. Rates are $69 to $99. Dogs are $5 extra. 39117 North Shore Drive, Big Bear Lake, CA 92315; (909) 866-5957.

Serrano Campground: It's not cheap to spend the night at this San Bernardino National Forest campground, but if you like rustic campsites and good hot showers, it's worth the $15 to $24 fee. The 132 sites are close to Big Bear Lake and the solar observatory (which is open to the public during certain days in the summer). The campground is on the north side of the lake, about two miles east of Fawnskin. It's very close to the Cougar Crest Trail (see page 762). Call (800) 280-CAMP for reservations. Call (909) 866-3437 for more information. The campground is closed in the winter.

Shore Acres Lodge: This one's on the lake, and has its own boat dock. They prefer small dogs here, but will go for larger ones if they're well behaved. Rates are $65 to $85. Dogs are $5 extra. 40090 Lakeview Drive, Big Bear Lake, CA 92315; (800) 524-6600.

Smoke Tree Lodge: Rates at this charming inn are $59 to $169. Dogs require a $100 deposit, and a fee of $10 extra. 40210 Big Bear Boulevard, Big Bear Lake, CA 92315; (906) 866-6816.

Snuggle Creek Lodge: It's a short walk to the lake from here. Dogs are permitted only in the cottages, not the lodge. No puppies, please. Rates are $79 to $109. 40440 Big Bear Boulevard, Big Bear Lake, CA 92315; (909) 826-2555.

Timberline Lodge: This one is close to the village, but set in a little forest area. Rates are $55 to $75. 39921 Big Bear Boulevard, Big Bear Lake, CA 92315; (800) 457-6401.

DIVERSIONS

Wag in the wagon: So you're in beautiful Big Bear Lake village with your dog. You see a gent with a huge beard, shiny top hat and fancy coat standing beside his English draft horse and antique carriage, waiting for a passenger. "Gee, honey, too bad we have Rex with us," you say to your loved one as Rex gives you the evil eye. "That horse-and-buggy ride sure looks like a good time."

Say no more. As long as owner and driver Michael Homan thinks Rex is cool (and not too huge), you'll all be able to take a spin through town. His horses don't mind well-behaved dogs, but some dogs don't take well to the horses, so make sure you've got your pooch under control before even approaching Homan.

If you catch Homan at his carriage stand, on Village Drive across from Chad's Place, a half-hour tour will run you about $30 per couple (less if more than one couple goes for the ride in his larger carriage, which holds six passengers). Or you can reserve the carriage for about $100 an hour. Homan also runs a hay ride that can take up to 25 people. Dogs really enjoy this back-to-the-farm setup. The carriage rides run year-round. You can find Homan at his stand most weekends and holidays. Call (909) 866-7137 for more information.

Get hitched, with your dog's help: The Hitching Post Wedding Chapel is a dog's kind of marriage sanctuary. It's got a mountain/western theme and no overly frilly froufrous.

Owner Rob Hastings says he's played host to canine ring bearers and canine best men. Once he even helped a dog sign a marriage certificate (not the license, though). "We just put his paw on the ink pad, then stamped the certificate. He was a smart dog, but his penmanship wasn't good enough to sign his name," says Hastings.

Hastings asks that dogs attend only midweek weddings. On busy days like Saturday, he doesn't have enough time to vacuum up dog hairs, and a few people visiting after dogs participated have complained about their allergies flaring up.

The fee for getting hitched here is $75 and includes the chapel and a donation for the minister. Licenses are extra. For more information, call (800) 828-4433 or (909) 866-7821 or write them at P.O. Box 6489, Big Bear Lake, CA 92315.

CHINO

PARKS, BEACHES & RECREATION AREAS

• **Prado Regional Park/Prado Recreation, Inc.** 🐾 🐾 🐾 🐾 🐕
This 2,200-acre park is actually in two sections: There's the

regular old regional park, with lakes, huge manicured fields and playgrounds, and the dog park, with 1,100 acres of land for dogs to go leashless.

The regular old park charges $4 per vehicle, $1 per dog. Dogs must be on leash. A day here makes for a pleasant family outing.

The dog training park will cost you $8 per person or per couple per day (up to two dogs are included in the fee). Camping anywhere on the 1,100 acres costs $5.50. There are 75 campsites available here. Reservations are recommended. But don't get the idea that this place is just a heavenly area where your dog can run like a crazy California canine. This is a dog training area, and we're generally not talking about the old sit-stay stuff. We're talking hunting and herding. We're talking dogs who work for a living.

Prado Recreation is not for vegetarians or anti-hunting folks. Chances are good that you'll see some dead birds here. You'll even see the people shooting and the dogs retrieving what they've shot. As we drove through, we saw labs and springers everywhere obeying hand signals in ponds and fields where there were bound to be birds.

People laughed at poor old Joe Airedale as we cruised through. "Ha ha ha" was all we could hear as they pointed at his dumbfounded, curly head. Somehow they could tell that his retrieval instincts stop where his nose starts. He was embarrassed, but he continued to stick his out the window anyway.

Dogs who herd really can go to town here. On a mist-shrouded field, we saw an elderly gent walking with a long wooden staff. He would quietly whistle or give subtle hand signals to two very intense border collies who were keeping a couple of big goats in line. It was as if we'd been transported across the Atlantic. Aye, rarely have we seen a more lovely dog scene.

The regular section of Prado Regional Park is located about seven miles south of Highway 60, on the left side of Euclid Avenue. Phone (909) 597-4260. To get to the dog section, take the first left after Prado Regional Park. You'll be on a very bumpy dirt road for what may seem like a long time, but eventually you'll come to the park's office. Call (909) 597-6366 for more information. ➡ *See #8 on map p. 756.*

CRESTLINE

PARKS, BEACHES & RECREATION AREAS

• Lake Gregory 🐾 🐾 🐾 1/2

Here's a county park the way we like to see them: Free. It's rare, but it happens. Lake Gregory is an 86-acre lake in a park that has only about 20 acres of dry land. But the land is lush and forested, with ponderosa pines, sugar pines and cedar trees everywhere.

A 2.75-mile path (complete with fitness stops) takes you around the lake, but alas, dogs aren't allowed in the water. They must be leashed at all times.

From Highway 18, take the Crestline exit, which turns into Lake Drive. Follow the road into the park. For the hiking path, start at the south shore. (909) 338-2233. →See #9 on map p. 756.

FAWNSKIN

PARKS, BEACHES & RECREATION AREAS

• **Dana Point Park** 🐾 🐾 🐾

Swimming dogs adore this county park. It's located along the north side of Big Bear Lake's Grout Bay, so it's somewhat off the beaten track. It's a fairly small park, but it has some romping room for leashed dogs, as well as a picnic area for hungry dogs and their people. Birdwatching is one of the big activities here, so be sure to bring your binoculars: From November to March, you might see bald eagles roosting and feeding.

The park is located just off the main part of this charming old village, on the south side of Highway 38. (909) 866-0130. →See #10 on map p. 756.

HESPERIA

PARKS, BEACHES & RECREATION AREAS

• **Hesperia Lake Park** 🐾 🐾 🐾

Most people visit this 200-acre park to nab a trout or catfish out of the seven-acre lake. But since dogs aren't allowed on the lake bank, or in the lake, it's probably not the activity of choice if you're looking for something you can do with your pooch at your side.

The park has plenty of trees for shade and leg lifts, and sports fields and playgrounds for the humans in the family. Look for the small waterfall, which feeds a meandering rock-lined stream that eventually leads to the lake. It's a great spot to stop for a picnic.

While there's no day-use fee here, you'll be charged $5 to fish. Camping is $10, and dogs are $2 extra. The 86 campsites are set near the lake. The campsites are available on a first-come, first-served basis. Although there's a sign for this park from the Bear Valley Cutoff exit of Interstate 15, don't be fooled into thinking it's just off the highway, especially if your dog is getting that glazed look that tells you he can wait no longer. The park is actually several miles southeast of the exit. The route is complicated, but the signage is excellent, so follow the brown signs all the way. (619) 244-5951. → *See #11 on map p. 756.*

• **Silverwood Lake State Recreation Area** 🐾 🐾 🐾 1/2

Water-loving dogs, brace yourselves for bad news: You have to stay high and dry here. You can't go to the beaches at this 1,000-surface-acre lake. In fact, you're not even allowed in the lake in the most remote areas.

While people can swim, fish, waterski and sail on the lake, dogs must be content just to watch. Fortunately for dogs and their landlubbing human companions, this 2,500-acre park has 13 miles of paved hiking/biking trails. You'll go through high chaparral country here, with all the bushes and trees a boy dog could ever dream of claiming for himself. And if that's not enough, you can head over to the national forest land on the lake's east side and hike forever.

Dogs must be leashed at Silverwood Lake. There are coyotes and bobcats and bears, oh my. Camping costs $14 to $16 a night. There are 126 sites available on a first-come, first-served basis. (Reservations are also accepted.) The day-use fee for the park is $6 per vehicle. Dogs are charged $1 extra for day use and camping, so make sure yours brings his allowance. From the Crestline area, 10 miles north of San Bernardino, take Interstate 15 to Highway 138 and drive east about 11 miles on Highway 138 to the park. (619) 389-2281. → *See #12 on map p. 756.*

PLACES TO STAY

Days Inn Suites: Rates are $39 to $69. 14865 Bear Valley Road, Hesperia, CA 92345; (619) 948-0600.

Mojave River Forks Regional Park: Last time we visited, you had to camp here to have access to the park's 1,100 acres. No more day users were allowed, the ranger told us. There are 84 campsites and four group areas available here. Reservations are recommended. Sites are $12 to $18. Dogs are $2 extra. But if you camp here, you can hike here, explore the often-dry Mojave River, and have access to the nearby Pacific Crest Trail. Be sure not to miss the Santa Fe Mormon Trail, complete with ruins. The park is on Highway 173 between Silverwood Lake and Hesperia. (619) 389-2322.

Silverwood Lake State Recreation Area camping: See above.

LUCERNE VALLEY

PARKS, BEACHES & RECREATION AREAS

•**Johnson Valley Open Area** 🐾🐾🐾🐾 🐕

If city life has your dog tied in knots, a visit to the Johnson Valley Open Area is bound to unkink him. There's nothing like 250,000 acres of leashless terrain—including mountains, scrubby desert, dry lakes, sand dunes and rock formations—to take the "d" out of doldrums and put it back in dog.

While you may not run into any other people during your visit, keep in mind that much of this land is okay for off-highway vehicles to cruise. If you hear one of these loud beasts coming, make sure your dog is close by. Some dog owners like to put something bright orange on their dog just in case.

There are many access points to this huge acreage. One good bet is to exit Highway 247 at Bessimer Mine Road and drive north a few miles. Big signs will show you the way. The public land here is interspersed with private land, but Bureau of Land Management folks say unless an area is fenced off, posted or developed, it's probably okay for hiking. (619) 256-3591. ➡ *See #13 on map p. 756.*

NEEDLES

Named for the sharp peaks at the southern end of the valley, this Colorado River town is surrounded by some of the most fascinating desert landscapes in the world.

If all the wide-open territory near Needles makes you and your dog feel like insignificant specks in the universe, try a sidetrip to London Bridge, just down the road a bit in Lake Havasu City, Arizona. This is the same London Bridge that was sinking into the Thames River in 1962, until developers of this town bought it for $2.5 million and shipped it over granite block by block. Your dog can go back home and tell all his buddies that he visited London Bridge, and they'll be impressed (most of them think it's still in London). English springer spaniels get a misty, faraway look when they come here.

PARKS, BEACHES & RECREATION AREAS

•**East Mojave National Scenic Area** 🐾🐾🐾🐾 🐕

The next time your dog gives you one of those sideways glances that says "I gotta get outta the city," you might want to consider spending a few days exploring a desert environment that seems to go on forever. It actually does go on forever, or at least for one-and-a-half million acres to the west and north of Needles, whichever comes first.

Within this gigantic swath of land are volcanic cinder cones, booming sand dunes, old mines, new mines, mysterious petroglyphs and dramatic cliffs. If you're a newcomer to desert life, you'll find the wildflowers, cacti and yucca fascinating.

Dogs are allowed off leash here, although Bureau of Land Management rangers say they've heard that the county once or twice has tried to enforce its own leash law over the BLM's lack of one. The rangers say as long as your dog doesn't make trouble, you should be fine.

Keep in mind that nearly 300 species of animals live here, including coyotes and Mojave green rattlesnakes. Since these rattlers are more aggressive than most other rattlers, and since dogs have been known to be a coyote delicacy, you'll want to make sure your pooch doesn't wander too far.

The Scenic Area has a two-mile trail and an eight-mile trail, but old mining roads and open desert land are also popular hiking habitats for dogs and their people.

Camping is $6, and dogs must be leashed at the campgrounds. There are 65 campsites available on a first-come, first-served basis. It can be entered from Interstate 40, but there are so many access points that you should call the Bureau of Land Management at (619) 326-3896 to find out which would best suit you. ➤*See #14 on map p. 756.*

•Moabi Regional Park/Park Moabi 🐾 🐾 🐾

If your dog likes the water, tell her that the Colorado River runs through this park. If she's a landlubber, let her know that most of the park is lawns and desert land. There's something for most tastes at this 1,025-acre county park.

Unfortunately, it's the most expensive park in the county. With a $6-per-vehicle day-use fee, $1 per dog, and $10 to $18 for camping (the pricier sites are on the river), you're not looking at cheap outdoor fun. There are 45 campsites And it's not always the quietest place in the world. Anglers can become frustrated with all the jetskiers and fast boats that cruise around here. To have the run of the lake, you can try renting a houseboat from the park's marina. It's loads of fun, and all your dog has to do to go for a swim is hop out the back door.

The park is at the intersection of Interstate 40 and Park Moabi Road. (619) 326-3831. ➤*See #15 on map p. 756.*

RESTAURANTS

Burger Hut: Sure, you can get their traditional beef burgers, but vegetarians will be happy to know that they also serve a mean veggie burger here. 701 Broadway; (619) 326-2342.

Jack-in-the-Box: It's so refreshing to find a dog-friendly link in a restaurant chain. This one allows pooches to dine at the 12 outdoor tables, and they will even supply your dog with water if you tell them he's thirsty. 221 J Street; (619) 326-4746.

PLACES TO STAY

Best Motel: Rates are $25 to $30. 1900 West Broadway, Needles, CA 92363; (619) 326-3824.

Best Western Colorado River Inn: As long as you don't bring your dog in the office when you check in or out, you and your pooch are welcome here. Rates are $40 to $90. 2271 West Broadway, Needles, CA 92363; (619) 326-4552.

East Mojave National Scenic Area campsites: See page 770.

Moabi Regional Park campsites: See page 771.

River Valley Motor Lodge: If your dog has short hair, the management here will be much more welcoming than they'd be to a pooch with a long and flowing coat that sheds everywhere. Rates are $21 to $40. 1707 West Broadway, Needles, CA 92363; (619) 326-3839.

ONTARIO

PARKS, BEACHES & RECREATION AREAS

•John Galvin Park 🐾 🐾 1/2

Lazy leashed dogs like this park. The big old trees seem like they were made for shading dogs whose main focus is sleeping. For a perfectly lazy afternoon outing, bring a book, lean against a tree and revel in the sound of your snoring dog. An open field in one section of this municipal park provides just enough room to roam should your mellow dog choose not to snooze.

Exit Interstate 10 at 4th Street and go west a couple of blocks. The park will be on your left. (909) 391-2513. → *See #16 on map p. 756.*

RESTAURANTS

Joey's Pizza: 790 North Archibald Avenue; (909) 944-6701.

Superburgers: Dogs tend to drool here when it comes to the beefy burgers. 1436 Euclid Avenue; (909) 391-1346.

Taco Bell: The managers have a specific rule for dogs here: They're not allowed on the tables. I guess they've had a few bad experiences with table-top terriers. 1885 East 4th Street; (909) 391-6174.

PLACES TO STAY

Country Suites by Carlson: Rates are $62 to $72. Dogs are $25 extra. 231 North Vineyard Avenue, Ontario, CA 91764; (909) 983-8484.

Howard Johnson Lodge-Ontario Airport South: Rates are $40 to $75. Dogs are $5 extra. 2425 South Archibald Avenue, Ontario, CA 91761; (909) 923-2728.

Inn Suites Ontario Airport Hotel: This is the best hotel for dogs who have to stay near the airport. Not only do you get a continental breakfast, but all the rooms are actually suites, complete with kitchenettes. And guess what else? Fire hydrants are pretty prominent outside the hotel. It's a boy dog's dream. People prefer the Jacuzzis that grace half the rooms. Rates are $60 to $80. There's a $50 dog deposit. 3400 Shelby Street, Ontario, CA 91764; (909) 466-9600.

Red Lion Hotel: Rates are $60 to $80. 222 North Vineyard Avenue, Ontario, CA 91764; (909) 983-0909.

REDLANDS

Parts of this lush, resort-like town provide a breath of fresh air from smog-ridden and traffic-filled Southern California.

PARKS, BEACHES & RECREATION AREAS

• **Prospect Park** 🐾 🐾 🐾 1/2 🐾

You'll be surrounded by exquisite views, towering palms, multitudes of orange trees and flowers everywhere at this enchanting, verdant park. This park is out of a fairy tale. It's one big hill, with delicate wooden seats overlooking the surrounding orchards. At the top, you'll find an open-air theater, some peacocks and a resident cat, so be sure to follow the rules and leash your dog.

This one's well worth the short trek from Interstate 10. For the most scenic ride, exit the freeway at Orange Street and drive south, through the quaint downtown area. In about seven blocks, bear right at Cajon Street. The park is on your right in about one mile. Park on Cajon Street just after Highland Avenue (just past the orange grove and before the picnic area on your right). Walk back several feet to the wide paved path and embark on your wondrous journey. (909) 798-7509. ➤ *See #17 on map p. 756.*

RESTAURANTS

Cafe Society: Dogs are welcome to help you dine on good sandwiches and tasty bakery items at the sidewalk and patio tables here. 308 West State Street, #1A; (909) 798-5578.

Rama Garden Thai Restaurant: The big dog rule here is that pooches should not walk in the waterfall. Joe, my water-hating Airedale, doesn't mind this restriction at all. 309 West State Street; (909) 798-7747.

PLACES TO STAY

Motel 6: Rates are $25 for one adult, $6 for the second adult. One small pooch per room, please. 1160 Arizona Street, Redlands, CA 92374; (909) 792-3175.

SAN BERNARDINO

Dogs aren't allowed at the wild and wonderful events held at Court House Square, but they're welcome at many parks in the area. The Renaissance Pleasure Faire permits pooches, but discourages them from attending because of the crowds. If you really want to go with your favorite medieval pooch, call (800) 52-FAIRE for information.

PARKS, BEACHES & RECREATION AREAS

• **Glen Helen Regional Park** 🐾 🐾 🐾 1/2 🐾

This 1,425-acre park features two lakes that are regularly stocked with such goodies as trout and catfish. But if your dog doesn't like to fish, she's sure to enjoy such goodies as an ecology trail and lots of grassy little hills that await your leashed dog's happy feet.

Rangers tell us that some dogs seem to get a kick out of watching kids zoom down the 300-foot, two-part waterslide at the swim complex in the park's southeast corner. Dogs aren't allowed there, but the park has plenty of viewing spots for pooches and their people.

With all these activities, Glen Helen Regional Park is a great place for your dog to take the family. You can even camp here. There are 50 sites available. No reservations are necessary. The fee is $9. Dogs are $1 extra.

The day-use fee here is $4 per vehicle and $1 per dog. Fishing is $4 per person over six years old. Exit Interstate 215 at Devore Road (just south of the Interstate 15/215 junction) and follow the signs about 1.5 miles to the park. (909) 880-2522. → *See #18 on map p. 756.*

• **Perris Hill Park** 🐾 🐾 🐾

This park makes dogs happy. There's dense shade almost everywhere. The trees providing this comfort are generally very big and very old. Although dogs must be leashed, they have smiles on their snouts when they gather during dog rush hour, around 5 p.m. or so. The park is at Highland and Valencia avenues. (909) 384-5233. → *See #19 on map p. 756.*

RESTAURANTS

For a city the size of San Bernardino, it's disappointing to find so few dog-friendly eateries.

Molly's Cafe: Eat cafe food with your favorite dog at the long bench here. 350 North D Street; (909) 888-1778.

La Palapa: 331 East 9th Street; (909) 885-0666.

PLACE TO STAY

Best Western Sands Motel: Rates are $55 to $70. 606 North H Street, San Bernardino, CA 92410; (909) 889-8391.

Glen Helen Regional Park camping: See page 774.

SKYFOREST

DIVERSIONS

He knows if your dog's been bad or good: Your pooch should be good, for goodness sake, when he visits Santa's Village, a Christmas fantasyland located at elevation 5,800 feet in the mountains near Lake Arrowhead. If he's naughty, not nice, that Christmas stocking might end up stuffed with dog toothpaste and gift certificates for worming treatments.

This is a great family outing, where leashed dogs can tag along through the majestic pine forests as the kids visit Santa's house, ride the ferris wheel and get dizzy on a giant spinning Christmas tree. Dogs aren't allowed on most rides, but we have heard of dogs being permitted to ride through the woods in Cinderella's horse-drawn pumpkin coach. Quiet, well-behaved dogs can also get within sniffing distance of the resident reindeer, as well as the petting zoo.

Admission for everyone older than two years old is $9.50. The fee includes unlimited rides. Dogs and babies are free. From Interstate 215, exit at Highway 30 and drive east two miles to Waterman Avenue/Highway 18. Go north on Highway 18 and drive along the winding road to Santa's Village. It's about two miles past the Lake Arrowhead turnoff. Be sure to phone before you visit, because the schedule is very varied (the place is closed March, April and May). (909) 337-2481 or (909) 336-3661.

TWENTYNINE PALMS

This old desert town sure knows how to make people happy. Long ago it was a watering spot for prospectors. Now it's a watering spot of sorts for dog owners.

In the fall of 1993, city residents were disgruntled because dogs were pooping in public parks and their owners often weren't cleaning up after them. It looked as though it was curtains for dogs in the city parks, but then it was suggested that all pooches be relegated to one park. The idea took hold, and the lucky, off-leash dogs who use Knott's Sky Park are majorly mirthful.

PARKS, BEACHES & RECREATION AREAS

• **Joshua Tree National Monument** 🐾🐾🐾 1/2 🐾

This town houses the headquarters and a good-sized swatch of this stunning park. See page 758 for details.

• **Knott's Sky Park** 🐾🐾🐾 1/2 🐕

This is the quietest and quaintest of the city's parks, so dogs are lucky just to be able to hang out here. Not only can they hang out here, they can do it off leash! Bowwow!

The park isn't very big—only about the size of half a ball field—but it's got plenty of picnic tables, and lots of shade from the many trees who call this place home. There's even a dog water fountain. Only some of the area is fenced from traffic, but it's quite safe. It's at El Sol Avenue, just off Twentynine Palms Highway/Highway 62. (619) 367-7562. →*See #20 on map p. 756.*

RESTAURANTS

Foster's Freeze: 73629 2 Mile Road; (619) 367-9303.

UPLAND

PARKS, BEACHES & RECREATION AREAS

• **Upland Memorial Park** 🐾🐾🐾

You feel as if you're in a royal garden at this peaceful city park. The front of the park is almost entirely shaded by large old trees. The back is open land. A colorful rose garden is the centerpiece. Dogs must be leashed, which is a good thing if your dog likes to stop and smell the flowers, then lift his leg on them. The park is located at the junction of the infamous Route 66 (Foothill Boulevard) and 11th Avenue. (909) 931-4280. →*See #21 on map p. 756.*

VICTORVILLE

PARKS, BEACHES & RECREATION AREAS

• **Center Street Park** 🐾🐾 1/2

While it's only a couple of blocks long, this park is Victorville's most attractive municipal park. It's full of trees, so there's plenty of shade and plenty of places for your leashed dog to sniff. And it's usually quiet, except when there's a ball game going on at one of the playing fields here.

Exit Interstate 15 at Mojave Drive and go east a little more than a mile to Hesperia Road. The park is on your right. (619) 955-5257. →*See #22 on map p. 756.*

• **Eva Dell Park** 🐾

This park is literally on the other side of the tracks. Just a couple of blocks from the railroad tracks, it's not in the most desirable part of town. Nor is it the most desirable park. It's got a rough, dusty feel. But if you find yourself in this part of town with a pooch who's got to go, the fenced-in ball fields aren't bad. Keep in mind that dogs are supposed to be leashed.

Eva Dell Park is just above the Mojave River (tough access, though). Take D Street to 6th Street and drive northeast, following the signs to the park. (619) 955-5257. → *See #23 on map p. 756.*

• **Mojave Narrows Regional Park** 😺 😺 😺

This 840-acre park is by far the largest park in the area. It's kind of triangular, bordered on the left by railroad tracks and on the right by the Mojave River. The rangers tell that to people hiking with dogs, lest they get a little lost in their eagerness to get back to nature.

There are plenty of fields here, but the best place for walking around with your leashed dog is the more forested part of the park. If you're an angler with a dog who likes to cheer you on as you cast for supper, you'll be happy to know there's fishing year-round for $4 per day.

Camping costs $9 to $15. Dogs are $1 extra. There are approximately 65 campsites available. Reservations are recommended. The park's day-use fee is $4 per vehicle, $1 per dog. From Interstate 15, take the Bear Valley Cutoff exit and drive east for five miles. When you come to the railroad track overpass, turn left at Ridgecrest Road. Drive three miles north to the park. (619) 245-2226. → *See #24 on map p. 756.*

PLACES TO STAY

Budget Inn: Rates are $20 to $45. Small pets only, please, and there's a small deposit for them. 14153 Kentwood Boulevard, Victorville, CA 92392; (619) 241-8010.

High Desert Travelers Motel: This motel is conveniently close to Mojave Narrows Regional Park. Rates are $45 to $52, and include a continental breakfast. There's a $20 pooch deposit required. 13409 Mariposa Road, Victorville, CA 92392; (619) 241-1577.

Mojave Narrows Regional Park camping: See above.

Travelodge: Rates are $30 to $57. 16868 Stoddard Wells Road, Victorville, CA 92392; (619) 243-7700.

YUCAIPA

PARKS, BEACHES & RECREATION AREAS

• **Yucaipa Regional Park** 😺 😺 😺 1/2

This picturesque park is surrounded by San Bernardino Mountains and Mount San Gorgonio. But dogs who visit here have more important things on their mind than pretty scenery. First of all, they're not relegated to the usual six-foot leash—their leashes can be 10 feet long! Joy of joys. Then there's the size of this park—it's 885 acres, with enough grassy fields to tire even the friskiest hound dog.

Water-loving dogs enjoy accompanying their people to the three trout-stocked lakes, and water-loving kids get a kick out of the 350-foot waterslides at the swim lagoon (no dogs allowed on the slides...they're too hairy). Several campsites are available near the lake, so if you're in the mood for a little camping with your angling, you couldn't ask for a much more convenient location. Sites are $9 to $15. There are about 35 campsites here. Reservations are recommended.

The day-use fee is $4 per vehicle on weekdays, $5 on weekends and holidays from April through October. Dogs are $1 extra. Fishing permits are $4 daily for anyone over five years old.

From Interstate 10, take the Yucaipa exit and follow the brown signs for "Regional Park." It's about five miles from the freeway. (909) 790-3127. ➡See #25 on map p. 756.

RIVERSIDE COUNTY

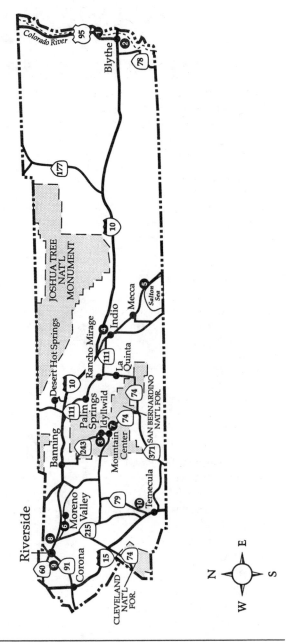

57
RIVERSIDE COUNTY

The most frequently visited cities here ban dogs from their parks. Palm Springs, Riverside and Desert Hot Springs are the bad guys: They force dogs to pace the sidewalks, find a distant county park or go to the desert for their recreation.

Actually, a trip to the desert during the more temperate months isn't a bad idea at all. In fact, dogs think it's a four-paws notion. But if it's hot or even warm outside, please forget it. The sand can be scorching even if the air isn't, and can poach a pooch's paws.

The Bureau of Land Management oversees millions of acres of desert and mountain land out here and dogs applaud the great job the agency does. On almost all the BLM land (except places like nature preserves), pooches are permitted to go leashless.

Our favorite BLM land in Riverside County is the Santa Rosa Mountains National Scenic Area. It's rugged, desolate and utterly pristine. It's also so sweeping that giving general directions here is futile. It spans much of the area of the central county from Interstate 10 south to the north border of the Anza-Borrego State Desert. Call the BLM's Palm Springs district office at (619) 251-0812 for specifics.

County parks welcome leashed dogs, but be forewarned: Most of these parks charge $4 per vehicle plus $2 per pooch. That adds up if you use the parks for your daily dog walks. You can often park on the street outside the entrance and avoid the $4 fee, but you can't get out of the $2 canine charge.

NATIONAL FORESTS

See the National Forests/Wilderness Areas chapter starting on page 801 for important information and safety tips for visiting national forests with your dog.

• **Cleveland National Forest** 🐾🐾🐾🐾 🐾 🐕
See page 803.

• **San Bernardino National Forest** 🐾🐾🐾🐾 🐾 🐕
See page 807.

NATIONAL MONUMENTS

• **Joshua Tree National Monument** 🐾🐾🐾 1/2 🐾
Although the bulk of this huge desert park is in Riverside County, the large visitors center area with easily accessible hikes is

north of the border, in San Bernardino County. Please see page 758 for details.

BLYTHE

If you're traveling from the east on Interstate 10, and vow that you'll stop in the first California town you hit, get ready to brake. Blythe isn't an exciting town, but it's a welcome sight if you've traveled across the country with the Golden State as your goal.

PARKS, BEACHES & RECREATION AREAS

• Mayflower Park 🐾 🐾 🐾

This park is only 24 acres, but because it backs up on the refreshing Colorado River, it seems much bigger. The folks here are pretty laid-back about dogs when it's not crowded. Pooches should be leashed, but you can still let them do a little wading in the water. Just watch out for those pesky boats.

Mayflower Park is an excellent place to stop if you've been driving all day and feel like fishing for stripers or catfish, cooking your catch for dinner and then camping by the river. The day-use parking fee is $4, plus $2 extra for dogs. Camping costs $15, with dogs costing $2 extra. There are 180 sites available. The park is six miles northeast of Blythe, just north of 6th Avenue and Colorado River Road. Call MISTIX at (800) 234-PARK for camping reservations. For park info, call (619) 922-4665. ➤ See #1 on map p. 780.

• Todd Park 🐾 🐾 1/2

This is a really attractive park which is so green that it seems out of place around here. It's full of big old shade trees and oleander bushes. Dogs must be leashed here, but it's still a really refreshing break from being cooped up in the car all afternoon.

Exit Interstate 10 at Lovekin Boulevard and drive south. At 14th Avenue, go east and drive about two more blocks to the next stop sign, Broadway. Turn left on Broadway and drive a few more blocks. The park is on Broadway at Bernard Street, just off Main Street. (619) 922-4266. ➤ See #2 on map p. 780.

PLACES TO STAY

Best Western Sahara Motel: Small dogs only, please. Rates are $49 to $64. 825 West Hobsonway, Blythe, CA 92225; (619) 922-7105.

Comfort Inn: Rates are $38 to $62. Small pooches are preferred. 903 West Hobsonway, Blythe, CA 92225; (619) 922-4146.

Hidden Beaches: This is one of the many camping resorts along the Colorado River. Sites are $17 per day, and pooches cost $1 extra. There are 92 sites available. Reservations are recommended in the summer. 6951 Sixth Avenue, Blythe, CA 92225; (619) 922-7276.

Lost Lake Resort: Campsites are $12 per day. There are 106 sites available. A reservation with payment in advance is required. It's located 31 miles north of Blythe on Highway 395. The mailing address is P.O. Box 6046, Blythe, CA 92225; (619) 664-4413.

Mayflower Park camping: See page 782.

McIntyre Park: Dogs can stay here only in winter, from November through March. The camping fee is $14 per car. There are sites to accommodate approximately 2,000 people. Sites are available on a first-come, first-served basis. 8750 East 26th Avenue, Blythe, CA 92225; (619) 922-8205.

Red Rooster Resort: There are 11 campsites along the river for $5 per human. Reservations are required. The campground is on Highway 95, P.O. Box 2725, Blythe, CA 92225; (619) 922-5567.

IDYLLWILD

PARKS, BEACHES & RECREATION AREAS

• **Idyllwild County Park** 🐾 🐾 🐾 1/2

In the morning, the cool mountain air is delicately scented with fresh pines, and you may find yourself so invigorated that you might actually want to get out of your tent and start the day early. There are six sites available (winter only) on a first-come, first-served basis.

This is an attractive park, with scenic self-guided nature trails for you and your leashed pooch to peruse. Better yet, there's easy access to the wonderful, off-leash trails of San Bernardino National Forest (see page 807). But you must check with a ranger before venturing out, because you could easily find yourself in the middle of Mount San Jacinto State Park—a major no-no for four-legged beasts of the domestic persuasion.

The drive-in day-use fee is $4. Dogs are $2 extra. Campsites cost $10, with dogs being charged the usual $2 county fee. There are 96 campsites available. The camp is open from the first weekend in April to the last weekend in October. The park is one mile north of Idyllwild, at the end of County Park Road. (909) 659-2656. ➡ *See #3 on map p. 780.*

PLACES TO STAY

Idyllwild County Park camping: See above.

INDIO

It may look flat and boring, but this dry old town has the distinction of being the king of the only region in the United States that grows dates. And we're not talking a few trees—we're talking

4,000 acres worth, making a semi-oasis out of an otherwise blah, depressing area.

If you thought you and your dog had absolutely no reason to visit here, think again. One look at the date-oriented diversion described below, and you may decide to come here next weekend.

PARKS, BEACHES & RECREATION AREAS

• Miles Avenue Park 🐾 1/2

If you're dropping someone off at the adjacent Coachella Valley Museum and Cultural Center, your dog might appreciate a little pause at this grassy, meadowy park. It looks like a golf course, but miraculously enough in this golf-inundated land, it's not.

There are some deciduous trees, as well as palms, for the benefit of the boy dogs in the crowd. The park is on Deglet Noor Street and Miles Avenue, about three blocks north of Highway 111. (619) 347-8522. ➡ *See #4 on map p. 780.*

RESTAURANTS

Andy's Restaurant: The outdoor seating area is not huge, but that won't make your dog drool any less over the burgers, pastrami and hot dogs you can eat here. Breakfast is also available. 83-699 Indio Boulevard; (619) 347-1794.

Shield's Date Gardens: See Diversions, below.

PLACES TO STAY

Best Western Date Tree Motor Hotel: Rates are $42 to $78. Pooches require a $50 deposit. 81-909 Indio Boulevard, Indio, CA 92201; (619) 347-3421.

Big America Hotel: Rates are $40 to $78. A $25 deposit is required for your dog. 84-096 Indio Springs Drive, Indio, CA 92201; (619) 342-6344.

Royal Plaza Inn: Rates are $36 to $60. Dogs require a $50 deposit. 82-347 Highway 111, Indio, CA 92201; (619) 347-0911.

DIVERSIONS

Date your dog: Blech! The thought sends shivers up the spine, until you realize that to date your dog in these parts merely means to take him on a date date. You know, inundate him with dates. Still not clear?

Fadi Saab, general manager of Shield's Date Gardens, explains: "You come here, and you and your dog can sit at the outside tables and drink our delicious date shakes and eat our good food near the date trees. You are also free to visit our 30 acres of date trees, so your dog can stretch his tired legs. We love dogs here, almost as much as we love dates."

While you're at Shield's Date Gardens, be sure to step inside (leave your pooch outside in the shade with a friend and take turns dogsitting) and watch the ongoing slide show entitled "The Romance and Sex Life of the Date." The date trees might rate it "X," but humans definitely give it a "G." (That stands for General Audiences or, in this case, Good Gawd!)

Shield's Date Gardens is at 80-225 Route 111; (619) 347-0996.

MECCA

PARKS, BEACHES & RECREATION AREAS

• **Salton Sea State Recreation Area** 🐾 🐾 🐾 1/2 🐾

If you ever wanted to explore the Salton Sea (see the introduction to the Imperial County chapter, page 795, for information on this strange and wonderful body of water), this is a great place to start your observations. The park has 16 miles of shoreline, including five beaches. Dogs must wear the mandatory leash attire, but they manage to have a fabulous time anyway.

Unfortunately, dogs are not allowed on the trails that connect a couple of these areas together, but you can transport your pooch from one area to another by car. You should try to spend at least one night. Three of the beaches are primitive and they have campsites right at the seaside. While dogs must be leashed, they still love dunking their paws in the very buoyant water here.

The day-use fee is $5. Camping costs $7 to $16. There are 149 developed sites available on a first-come, first-served basis. Dogs generally prefer the cheaper, more primitive sites. About half of the park is in Imperial County. If you're approaching the lake from the southeast side, see page 796 for directions. Otherwise, take Highway 111 southeast of Mecca about 10 miles, and you'll find the park headquarters and visitors center on the west side of the highway. (619) 393-3052. →*See #5 on map p. 780.*

PLACES TO STAY

Salton Sea State Recreation Area camping: See above.

MORENO VALLEY

PARKS, BEACHES & RECREATION AREAS

• **Lake Perris State Recreation Area** 🐾 🐾 🐾

When people talk about this park, they generally focus on the lake. Comments I got when I asked friends about the park included the following: "You can catch some world-class fish there." "We had a great time swimming at the beach." And "I like to stand on the edge and watch for birds."

Great. Well, dogs, if you're into any of the above activities, forget it. You can't go near the lake, much less in it or on it. But fortunately, you are allowed to wear a leash and hike the trails here. You'll be in sage scrub countryside, and there's not much shade, so go somewhere else if it's a hot day.

The day-use fee is $6 per vehicle and $1 per pooch. Camping here costs $8 to $16. Dogs are $1 extra. There are 167 sites for tents only and 265 sites for RVs. Reserve through MISTIX at (800) 444-PARK. From Highway 60, exit at Moreno Beach Drive and drive south a little more than three miles to the park. (909) 657-9000.
→*See #6 on map p. 780.*

PLACES TO STAY
Lake Perris State Recreation Area camping: See above.

MOUNTAIN CENTER

While in town, stop by the Living Free animal sanctuary and see just how beautiful and livable an animal rescue facility can be. Living Free occupies 160 acres of scenic mountain country at the edge of the San Bernardino Forest. You and your dog can visit together, and while you are on tour finding out about the many wonderful programs here, your dog will be cared for in a special pen. Your dog is guaranteed tender loving care while you learn about ways to help other animals get the same kind of love. For more information, call (909) 659-4684.

• **Hurkey Creek Park** 🐾 🐾 🐾 1/2

At an elevation of about 4,500 feet, and surrounded by 7,000-foot-high peaks, it's cool at this meadow-like park even in the summer. Hurkey Creek flows through here; it attracts lots of critters, so be sure your dog is leashed.

There are a couple of hiking trails here and dogs love them. They'd really like to be able to sneak into the adjacent San Jacinto Wilderness, but it's one of the few national forest wilderness areas that doesn't permit pooches (because of its intermingling with a state park that bans dogs).

The day-use parking fee is $4. Pooches are $2 extra. Camping is $12, with dogs paying $2 for the privilege. The park is four miles south of Mountain Center off Highway 74. There are 100 campsites available. For camping reservations, call MISTIX at (800) 234-PARK. The park phone number is (909) 659-2656. →*See #7 on map p. 780.*

PLACES TO STAY
Hurkey Creek camping: See above.

PALM SPRINGS

First, the warning, straight from the typewriter of Esther M. W. Petersen, of the Palm Springs Animal Shelter: "Our area can be quite warm (HOT!!!!) all year-round, so please, Please, *please* be sure to warn travelers about the dangers…Our visitors don't seem to realize how hot it is. With our low humidity, it doesn't feel as hot as it really is, and pets can't handle the hot cement sidewalks, hot desert sand and hot asphalt without getting burned pads."

Petersen knows her stuff. She has seen too many dogs whimper their last breaths because of heat stroke and other heat-related horrors. The municipal code forbids dogs to be left unattended in enclosed vehicles, no matter what time of year. The law is a good one. Since it was enacted in 1988, not a single pet has been lost to this disastrous practice.

Believe it or not, the entire posh desert playground city of Palm Springs is a wildlife preserve. You can routinely spot coyotes, bobcats, raccoons, snakes, lizards and migratory birds around town. Occasionally, mountain lions and badgers have been sighted. Make sure your dog is leashed and that you hold the leash securely at all times.

You won't be tempted to stray from the leash law while visiting the city's parks, because dogs aren't allowed to set paw in any of them. Fortunately, there are a few natural areas around town where you can take your pooch for a good walk. And you can also take your dog to some fun, if unnatural, places.

Many restaurants here permit dogs to dine outside with you. Some terrific festivals also allow well-behaved dogs. And many of the shops on Palm Canyon Drive (north and south) permit pets to shop with their people. They don't want to be mentioned for fear of being inundated with leg-lifters. But if someone beckons you and your dog inside while you're window shopping, you'll know which ones we're talking about. Petersen, of the animal shelter, tells me that one store has a resident pot-bellied pig, so if your dog likes his ham rare, beware.

PARKS, BEACHES & RECREATION AREAS

The city bans dogs from its parks, but that doesn't mean you and your pooch have to sneak onto empty lots to get your exercise. Palm Springs is surrounded by land run by the Bureau of Land Management. Call (619) 251-0812 for information on places to hike during the cooler months.

Dog owners in town frequently use the many local "wash" areas (dry stream beds) to run on leash with their dogs. You'll see them on the outskirts of town and beyond.

You can also take your leashed pooch to two nearby hiking areas for fascinating desert hikes. The Carl Lykken Hiking Trail starts at the extreme west end of Ramon Road. Another favorite among dogs is a hike through the beautiful, rugged Indian Canyons. To reach the trail, drive to the far south end of Palm Canyon Drive.

RESTAURANTS

Palm Springs is full of fine restaurants with outdoor areas where dogs are welcome.

Blue Coyote Grill: You and your dog can't exactly eat together here, since she must remain tied up just outside the railing while you sit just inside it. But she'll still be close enough to drool over the Southwestern delights on your dish. 445 North Palm Canyon Drive; (619) 327-1196.

Carlo's Italian Deli & Restaurant: The outdoor area here is well-suited for dogs and their people. 119 South Indian Canyon Drive; (619) 325-5571.

Hula's: Share teriyaki with your pup at the sidewalk seating of this Japanese restaurant. 330 North Palm Canyon Drive; (619) 864-7107.

Harry's Hoffbrau: With so much outdoor seating there's bound to be space here for you and your pooch. This cafeteria-style place serves all kinds of dishes, including sandwiches and stews. 205 South Palm Canyon Drive; (619) 320-2911.

Nate's Deli & Restaurant: Lots of dogs come here to dine under the umbrellas. Maybe they know that the owner's daughter is the secretary of the local bull terrier club and that the folks here love dogs. Corned beef is the specialty, and there's also a full bar. 100 South Indian Canyon Drive; (619) 325-3506.

Peabody's: This restaurant is a real doggy delight. Canine customers get free dog bones! Dog owners who don't like to dine on dog bones themselves can sip on coffee and eat a variety of light lunch items beside their pooch at the patio. 134 South Palm Canyon Drive; (619) 322-1877.

Restaurant Matoi: Try Matoi's chicken teriyaki with tempura. It's fine food for a breezy desert day. The patio dining is perfect for you and your dog friend. 394 North Palm Canyon Drive; (619) 322-0090.

PLACES TO STAY

Palm Springs has plenty of quality canine accommodations. If you're in the mood for a condo, contact Desert Condo Rentals at (619) 320-6007 or (619) 321-4427. The folks there might be able to set up you and your dog in a home away from home.

Casa Cody Country Inn: Dogs love this quaint, quiet historic country inn almost as much as their peace-seeking people do. Past canine visitors have caused some problems because irresponsible owners have left them alone in the room. Don't even think of doing this. Rates are $40 to $160. Dogs are $10 extra. 175 South Cahuilla Road, Palm Springs, CA 92262; (619) 320-9346.

Hyatt Regency Suites Palm Springs: This is a beautiful, roomy place to take a small dog. Rates are $200 to $230. Dogettes cost $25 extra. 285 North Palm Canyon Drive, Palm Springs, CA 92262; (619) 322-9000.

Ingleside Inn: You and your lucky pooch can sleep where the likes of Greta Garbo, Salvador Dali and Howard Hughes have spent the night. This gorgeous mountainside inn feels like your own private estate, from the jasmine-covered veranda to the antique-furnished rooms. Very small dogs (under 10 pounds) are welcome with prior approval.

If your dog is any bigger than the average cat, he won't be able to stay here with you. But don't worry. Ingleside manager Tom Ward wants your pooch to be as happy as possible, so he's made a special arrangement with the exclusive Desert View Pet Resort in Rancho Mirage. The Pet Resort will pick up your pooch in a dog limousine and transport him to a world of canine opulence. See page 790 for details on the Pet Resort. Rates for the Ingleside Inn are $95 to $550. 200 West Ramon Road, Palm Springs, CA 92264; (619) 325-0046.

Musicland Hotel: Smallish dogs only, please. Rates are $39 to $89. The doggy deposit is $25 to $50. 1342 South Palm Canyon Drive, Palm Springs, CA 92264; (619) 325-1326.

Quality Inn: Small dogs enjoy sniffing around the spacious grounds here. Rates are $40 to $169. Pooches are $10 extra. 1269 East Palm Canyon Drive, Palm Springs, CA 92264; (619) 323-2775.

FESTIVALS

Villagefest Street Fair: On Thursday evenings from 6 p.m. to 10 p.m., well-behaved, leashed pooches may accompany you to glamorous Palm Canyon Drive, where an old-fashioned street fair will charm the spots off your dog. Musicians, food, arts and crafts vendors and a certified farmers market make this street even more charming than it normally is. The fair takes place between Tahquitz Canyon Drive and Baristo Road. Parking is best behind the Desert Inn Fashion Plaza. Call (800) 34-SPRINGS for more information.

RANCHO MIRAGE

This exclusive desert community is home to one of dog's best friends, the Desert View Pet Resort. It's a terrific place for your dog to repose while you bask in the glory of the local arid opulence. In addition to good food and lots of love, dogs get at least two off-leash playtimes daily in an enclosed grassy yard.

And if you have special instructions for the care of your dearly beloved, almost anything goes. "We have one dog who only eats waffles, so we make them and he loves them," says employee Jim Prindle. "One woman has a dog who has to have a special day bed, a night bed, and he'll only eat out of his crystal bowl. She also likes his bum to be wiped with baby powder after he does his thing. We get unusual requests, but we understand how important it is for owners to know their pet is happy."

Rates are $17 daily. A "dog limousine" is available. Rates range from $15 to $200, depending on how far your dog needs to travel. The Pet Resort is at 71-075 Highway 111; (619) 341-1166.

PLACES TO STAY

Marriott's Rancho Las Palmas Resort: You and your dog can hang out on several acres of gorgeous land here, or just enjoy the surroundings from your balcony. The staff even gives doggy gifts to repeat doggy guests, to welcome them as "friends of the family." Rates are $75 to $175. 41-000 Bob Hope Drive, Rancho Mirage, CA 92270; (619) 568-2727.

The Westin Mission Hills Resort: You and your medium or small dog (that's all they take here) can pretend you're in Morocco during your stay at this luxurious resort hotel. The Moroccan-style architecture fits in beautifully with the many acres that surround the hotel. Rates are $115 to $385. Dogettes require a variable dog deposit. 71-333 Dinah Shore Drive, Rancho Mirage, CA 92270; (619) 328-5955.

RIVERSIDE

Dogs are banned from all Riverside city parks. Booo!

PARKS, BEACHES & RECREATION AREAS

• **Box Springs Mountain Park** 🐾 🐾 🐾

I'm not sure why this place has its name, but I found that, like a box spring, it's not all that comfortable by itself. You need a little padding to enjoy it. Lots of people bring their horses here, but a dog will do. When you decide to take a break from hiking the many trails, you can lie down and rest against your reposing pooch.

There's little shade here and it's hilly. It may not be an ideal place to take a dog (don't take her if it's hot), but there aren't many options in this city.

Driving east on Highway 60, exit at Pigeon Pass Road (about five miles east of town) and drive north to the park. (909) 275-4310. →*See #8 on map p. 780.*

• **Santa Ana River Regional Park** 🐾🐾🐾 1/2

This huge county park encompasses a few others, including Rancho Jurupa Park and the Hidden Valley Wildlife Area. Stretching east to west for almost 10 miles, it more than makes up for all those smaller city parks than say "no way" to dogs.

Depending on which section you visit, you and your leashed dog can see lots of wildlife, fish for your supper, hike through fields and woods, or relax on the manicured grass of a shaded picnic area. Since our tastes are sometimes dictated by money, we like to go where we can avoid paying the $4 car fee and $2 pooch fee—especially if we just need to stretch our legs. We've found a wonderful spot next to the park's nature center, where many interesting hikes originate.

To reach this fee-free area, exit Highway 60 at Rubidoux Boulevard, drive southwest a few blocks and turn right on Mission Boulevard. In about six blocks, turn left on Riverview Drive/ Limonite Avenue. In just a little more than a half mile, there should be a sign for a county park. That's where Riverview Drive veers to the left (Limonite will continue straight). Follow Riverview for about another 1.5 miles. It will be smaller and more rural than the previous road. The park will be on your left. Park in the lot near the nature center. Look for a trail and have yourselves a great hike.

If camping is your bag, you'll have to go to the fee area at Rancho Jurupa. From Highway 60, exit at Rubidoux Boulevard and drive south to Mission Boulevard. Turn left and drive about a half mile to Crestmore Boulevard. Follow Crestmore as it curves around the north side of the park. In about 1.5 miles, you'll be at the gate. Sites are $14. Dogs are $2 extra. There are approximately 70 sites available here. For camping information, call Rancho Jurupa at (909) 684-7032. For camping reservations, call MISTIX at (800) 234-PARK. For general information on Santa Ana Regional Park, call (909) 781-0143. →*See #9 on map p. 780.*

RESTAURANTS

Aroma Coffee House Roasters: This place is located in the pretty, old mission district of Riverside. You and your four-legged friend can make yourselves at home at the sidewalk cafe as you delight in delectable coffee drinks, sandwiches and salads. 3527 Main Street; (909) 788-5414.

Chester Fried Chicken: The chicken and ribs here taste even better at the patio, where your dog can join you for a drool. 4975 Arlington Avenue; (909) 359-6628.

Simple Simon's: This bakery and cafe in the old mission district is a great place to lunch with your pooch. There's plenty of outdoor seating. 3639 Main Street; (909) 369-6030.

PLACES TO STAY

Dynasty Suites: This lodging is not overly enthusiastic about housing dogs and generally won't give an okay over the phone. But if you arrive and look very polite and responsible, and your small dog gives them one of her "I'll love you forever" looks, you're in. Rates are $40 to $50. Pooches are $5 extra. 3735 Iowa Avenue, Riverside, CA 92507; (909) 369-8200.

Econo Lodge: Huge dogs are not permitted here, but all others are. Rates are $37 to $42. Dogs require a $25 deposit. 9878 Magnolia Avenue, Riverside, CA 92503; (909) 687-3090.

Santa Ana Regional Park camping: See page 791.

TEMECULA

PARKS, BEACHES & RECREATION AREAS

•Lake Skinner County Park 🐾 🐾 🐾 1/2

So what if your dog can't swim in the lake here or even hang out in your boat with you? Of the 6,040 acres of park, the lake makes up only about 1,200 acres. That means several thousand acres of hilly chaparral country is all yours. Leashed pooches are permitted to peruse the trails and run around the open turf areas.

During the rainy season, the trails may be closed. Call before you visit. The day-use fee is $4. It's possible to walk in and avoid the $4 charge, but foot access from the rural roads can be difficult. Campsites are $12 to $17. Dogs are $2 extra. There are approximately 265 campsites available by reservation only. From Interstate 15, take the Rancho California Avenue exit northeast and drive about nine miles to the park. Call MISTIX for camping reservations at (800) 234-PARK. For park information, call (909) 926-1541. ➡ *See #10 on map p. 780.*

PLACES TO STAY

Lake Skinner County Park camping: See above.

Ramada Inn: Rates are $50 to $60. There's a $35 deposit for dogs. 28980 Front Street, Temecula, CA 92592; (909) 676-8770.

IMPERIAL COUNTY

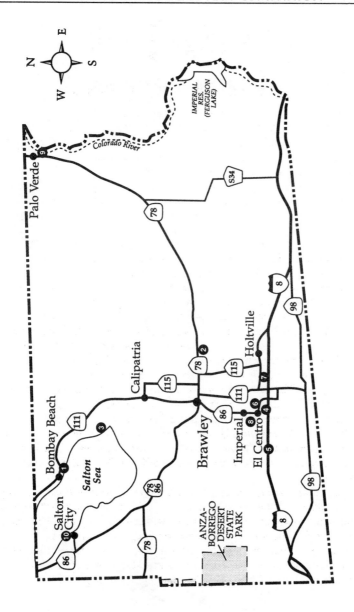

58
IMPERIAL COUNTY

Although this county is home of the Imperial Valley, one of the richest farming areas in the world, it's much more than just an agricultural wonderland. In fact, when you wander into the most dog-friendly areas, you'll wonder how land around here could be used for anything but sandboxes.

Some one-and-a-half million acres of desert here is run by the Bureau of Land Management—those dog-friendly folks who rarely demand a leash. The dune areas are fascinating, and your dog will love racing up and down the sandy expanses.

Nearby is the strange and salty Salton Sea. At 36 miles long and 15 miles wide, it's one of the world's largest inland bodies of saltwater. Although officially considered a lake, it's got most of the qualities of a sea, including the fact that from most of its shoreline, you can look across and see vast, astounding nothingness.

The sea is situated at 234 feet below sea level (the "normal" sea level, that is), directly atop the San Andreas Fault. Millions of years ago, the valley region here was filled with lakes and streams. But the lakes dried up as the mountains to the west grew due to seismic activity and cut off the moist, cool air from the ocean.

Then in 1905, the Colorado River flooded in Mexico and caused a two-year flood through the brand new Imperial Valley irrigation system. It sparked the rebirth of the lake known as the Salton Sea.

Mixed with minerals left by earlier seas, as well as present-day evaporation and fertilizer runoff, the water is 10 percent saltier than an ocean. Dogs like to float around in it, but watch out for their eyes.

And if you smell a really foul stench while you're here, you may be tempted to drive away as fast as your four wheels will take you. The occasionally malodorous air is caused by an algae bloom and resulting fish die-off, and the operative expression here is "Peeuuuw!" But before you zip away, stop for a moment and let your dog take a few good, deep breaths of this wretched stink. She'll be on an olfactory high for the rest of the day.

BOMBAY BEACH

PARKS, BEACHES & RECREATION AREAS

• **Salton Sea State Recreation Area** 🐾 🐾 🐾 1/2

Since most people visit the north end of this 16-mile-long park that sits on the northeast portion of the Salton Sea, you'll find its description in the Riverside County chapter, on page 785. But if you have a hankering to discover the Imperial County portion of the park, take Highway 111 to any of several entrances, including the popular Bombay Beach area. (619) 393-3052. ➡ *See #1 on map p. 794.*

PLACES TO STAY

Salton Sea State Recreation Area camping: See page 785 in the Riverside County Chapter for details.

BRAWLEY

PARKS, BEACHES & RECREATION AREAS

• **Imperial Sand Dunes** 🐾 🐾 🐾 🐾 🖜 🐕

Before going on about how enthralling this enormous, off-leash desert sandbox is, I want to play back something local Bureau of Land Management staffer Roseann Madrigal told me.

"Too often we get calls from someone who starts out crying, and when we ask what's wrong, they say they lost their poor dog in the desert," she said. "We hate those kind of calls. It's so sad. People let their pets wander too far sometimes, and they get disoriented and lost. Out here, there's not a good chance for survival, even when it's not extremely hot. We try to help them find their dog, but this is a big place. You feel so helpless.

"Please tell your readers not to let their dog go far, and always have an eye on him. If they can't, then just keep him leashed," she said.

Got it? This applies to any off-leash area discussed in this book, but out here in the desert, follow Madrigal's words like the gospel. She's fielded many of these distraught phone calls and she knows what she's talking about.

And now the good stuff: The Bureau of Land Management oversees one-and-a-half million acres in Imperial County. Much of the acreage is within this vast dune system, full of wind-sculpted crests and ripples that extend for more than 40 miles. The Imperial Dunes (also known as the Algodones Dunes) rise up to 300 feet, and they're great fun to hike on or around. And your pooch can do it without a leash.

Two-thirds of the dune area north of Highway 78 is closed to vehicles, so it's an ideal place for a dog hike. This is also where you may spot all sorts of desert wildflowers. An added bonus: You can set up your tent just about anywhere in the area, and there's no fee.

The BLM ranger station is a good place to start your adventure. No permit is necessary. From central Brawley, drive east on Highway 78 about 19 miles to Gecko Road. Turn right, and the ranger station is about a mile down the road. (619) 353-1060. →*See #2 on map p. 794.*

PLACES TO STAY
Imperial Sand Dunes camping: See above.

Town House Lodge: All rooms come with a microwave and a refrigerator, so if you and your dog want to eat in, this is a good choice. Rates are $43 to $47. 135 Main Street, Brawley, CA 92227; (619) 344-5120.

CALIPATRIA
PARKS, BEACHES & RECREATION AREAS
• **Red Hill Marina County Park** 🐾🐾🐾

This peninsular park jutting into the southeast corner of the Salton Sea feels more like an island. The terrain is early moonscape and the 240-acre park is pretty much one big hill. You and your dog can see all the way to the Mexican border from here!

Dogs must be leashed, but at least they're allowed. They're banned from the neighboring Salton Sea National Wildlife Refuge.

The day-use fee is $3. Campsites are $7. There are 400 campsites available. No reservations are necessary. From Highway 111 just north of Calipatria, go west on Schrimpf Road, which is a graded dirt road. In about five miles, you'll be at the park. (619) 348-2310. →*See #3 on map p. 794.*

PLACES TO STAY
Red Hill Marina County Park camping: See above.

EL CENTRO
PARKS, BEACHES & RECREATION AREAS
• **Bucklin Park** 🐾🐾 1/2

It's like a golf course here, complete with ultra-green, ultra-short turf, the occasional palm tree and a little pond. It's a lovely place to take a Sunday afternoon stroll with your favorite leashed pooch.

The park is at 8th Street and Ross Avenue. (619) 337-4557. →*See #4 on map p. 794.*

• **Sunbeam Lake County Park** 🐾 🐾 🐾
This county park is filled with big old eucalyptus trees. That's not normally a selling point, but boys who are tired of lifting their legs on desert boulders around this area seem to appreciate any kind of tree.

Sunbeam Lake itself is a fun fishing and swimming hole. Dogs must be leashed, so swimming is a bit restricted. The trails in this 140-acre park provide a fun walk for you and the leashed pooch.

It'll cost you $3 to use this park during the day and $20 to camp here. There are 309 sites for RVs only. Reservations are required. The park is seven miles west of El Centro. Exit Interstate 8 at Drew Road and drive about a half mile north. (619) 339-4384. ➤ *See #5 on map p. 794.*

• **Swarthout Park** 🐾 🐾
The bulk of this park is made up of ball fields, but there's some unclaimed grassy turf here too. Leashed dogs enjoy trotting around with you. If they happen to slip out of your grip for a minute, it could be worse. The park is well fenced, with only a couple of escape hatches.

From Highway 86, go east on Euclid Avenue. The park will be on your left, at Cross Street. Park in the lot. (619) 337-4557. ➤ *See #6 on map p. 794.*

PLACES TO STAY

Brunner's Motel: Rates are $46 to $75. 215 North Imperial Avenue, El Centro, CA 92243; (619) 352-6431.

Del Coronado Crown Motel: Rates are $41. Dogs are $6 extra, and small pooches are preferred. 330 North Imperial Avenue, El Centro, CA 92243; (619) 353-0030.

El Dorado Motel: In the mornings, you get sweet rolls, coffee and juice here. This is a very animal-friendly joint. There's even a special grassy area here just for their relief. "We like dogs, cats, fish and birds," says Virginia, one of the hotel receptionists. "They're always better behaved than certain people." Rates are $30 to $45. 1464 Adams Avenue, El Centro, CA 92243; (619) 352-7333.

Sands Motel: Small pets only, please. Rates are $30 to $44. 611 North Imperial Avenue, El Centro, CA 92243; (619) 352-0715.

Sunbeam Lake County Park camping: See above.

HOLTVILLE

PARKS, BEACHES & RECREATION AREAS

• **Heber Dunes County Park** 🐾 🐾 🐾 1/2
Dunes, native vegetation and former farmland make up this 300-

acre park. Leashed dogs love a good romp down the trails here. The picnic spots are worthy of lunch, but better yet is the camping: Unlike many of the county's other parks, it's free, as is admission to the park. Dogs on a tight budget are sure to appreciate that.

From Highway 111, take Heber Road east about 6.5 miles to the short road that takes you to the park. (619) 339-4384. ➡*See #7 on map p. 794.*

PLACES TO STAY

Barbara Worth Country Club & Hotel: Rates are $48 to $54. 2050 Country Club Drive, Holtville, CA 92250; (619) 356-2806.

Heber Dunes County Park camping: See above.

IMPERIAL

PARKS, BEACHES & RECREATION AREAS

• **Eager Park** 🐾

Stop here if your dog is longing to get out of the car or house and doesn't mind visiting a postage stamp-sized park. There are a few small trees here and a small playground. Maybe the park should be reserved for Chihuahuas and Pekingese pooches, or at least dogs with small expectations. Dogs must be leashed.

From Highway 86, go west on 10th Street and left on H Street. (619) 355-4371. ➡*See #8 on map p. 794.*

PALO VERDE

• **Palo Verde County Park** 🐾🐾 1/2

While this is only a 10 acre park, its location at the border of Arizona directly off Highway 78 makes it a popular stopping point for dogs and their human chauffeurs.

The park is set on a backwater of the Colorado River. It's a refreshing place to spend an hour, a day or a night. Camping and day-use fees are nonexistent and no permits are required. The fishing's pretty decent here too, in case you're hankering to angle.

From Interstate 10 in the Blythe area (Riverside County), exit at Highway 78 and drive south, following the occasional westward jogs in the highway. After about 18 miles, you'll cross into Imperial County. The park is another 2.5 miles down the road, just off the highway. (619) 339-4384. ➡*See #9 on map p. 794.*

PLACES TO STAY

Palo Verde County Park camping: See above.

SALTON CITY

If you happen to have a tape of the *Twilight Zone* theme in your car, pop it in as you approach this land that time forgot.

After you notice the bright blue Salton Sea in the background, you'll become aware of lots and lots of lots. Empty ones. Many miles of curved, suburban-style roads wind in and out of this flat waterfront community, but no one is home. There should be thousands of houses on these paved grids, but there's only a smattering. It's as if Rod Serling went all out and made one of his eerie dollhouse-scale sets lifesize.

What actually happened was an optimistic real estate sellout in the 1950s and '60s. An extensive road system was developed and some 20,000 lots were sold. But the folks who bought them generally just kept their investment without plopping down so much as a mobile home. So the roads here essentially lead to nowhere. When you get lost on them, don't panic. Just remember that Rod Serling isn't around anymore, so this really couldn't be as strange as it seems, and you really couldn't be in the Twilight Zone. Could you?

PARKS, BEACHES & RECREATION AREAS
• **Martin Flora Park** 🐾 1/2

Although the Salton City area is full of empty shoreline, community service folks ask that you stick to the public parks with your dog. This isn't such a bad place to take a leashed pooch. It looks a little like a gravel parking lot, but never mind that. The Salton Sea is right here and so are plenty of picnic tables. The park is an unusual place to stop for lunch.

From Highway 86, turn northeast on North Marina Drive and follow it past all the empty streets. As the road approaches the sea, it will curve to the right. In a few blocks, you'll come to Sea Port Avenue. Go left, and follow it a few more blocks to the park. Make sure you can figure out how to get back to Highway 86 before you leave, because many people have become mighty lost here, and there aren't many homes where you can stop and ask for help. (619) 394-4446. ➡ *See #10 on map p. 794.*

APPENDIX

ABOUT NATIONAL FORESTS

Dogs of California, rejoice! If you really want to stretch those gams, the U.S. Department of Agriculture's Forest Service has a real treat for you. Instead of a walk in your friendly neighborhood park, how does an exhilarating, off-leash hike sound? You'll have your choice of 20 million acres of national forests (an astounding 20 percent of California) spread over a fascinating variety of terrains.

Most dogs call the forests "dog heaven." Those who don't speak English just pant with joy. There's something for every dog's tastes in national forests. Desert dogs are as happy as dogs who like dank redwood forests. National forests have no entry fees, few leash rules, plenty of free camping and some of the most beautiful land in California.

If your dog is obedient enough to come when she's called, and you trust her not to wander off in pursuit of deer or other wildlife, she's more than welcome to be off leash in most of the forest areas. In the descriptions that follow, I mention the exceptions to the off-leash policies that I'm aware of, but there may well be more. And since rules change frequently, you should call before you visit. Be aware that the front-line personnel at the forests might tell you that dogs must be on leash, but they're not always right. Ask for a supervisor or ranger if you have reason to think the leash laws are more lax.

Always carry a leash with you, just in case. Dogs must be leashed in developed campgrounds (which usually charge a small fee) and in developed recreation areas. But most areas of the forests are set up so that you can plop down a tent just about anywhere you please (for free). When you find that perfect, cool stream with a flat, soft area on the bank, your dog doesn't have to be leashed. But it's a bad idea to leave your dog leashless and outside your tent at night. (See the Introduction for more on camping safety, page 11.)

In each entry, I've noted any wilderness areas that fall within the forest I'm describing. Many require permits for hiking and camping. Contact a ranger to find out about the rules in a particular wilderness area. (Sometimes wilderness areas spread out to two or more forests, so don't be baffled if you see the same name more than once. Joe hasn't been pawing around with my computer keyboard again.)

For a free guide to all of California's wilderness areas, write the U.S.D.A. Forest Service, Public Affairs Office, 630 Sansome Street, San Francisco, CA 94111, or call (415) 705-2874. Maps of specific national forests and wilderness areas are available for $3 to $6 each. Call or write for a list.

Now for the obligatory poop paragraph: As far as bathroom etiquette goes, it's not necessary to pack out the poop. If you don't mind it squishing along in your backpack, that's great. But if you bury it, as you should bury your own, that's okay. Leave the forest as you found it. And please don't let your dog go to the bathroom near a stream. It can be a health hazard to anyone drinking the water later.

And dogs, if you come to really love your national forests, tell your people that because of severely reduced budgets, trail maintenance is suffering. Tell them that the trails could sure use a hand. Tell them that rangers would be thrilled to have teams of dog owners working together to help upkeep the trails they use. Your people can contact a ranger to see how they can volunteer.

What follows is a very brief description of each forest. Again, be sure to contact a ranger before setting out so you can check on changed rules, and portions of forests or trails that might be closed.

ANGELES NATIONAL FOREST

This 693,000-acre forest covers about one-quarter of Los Angeles County and most of the San Gabriel Mountains. With more than 620 miles of trails, the forest provides an essential recreational outlet for millions of Southern Californians and their city-weary dogs.

Highlights include waterfalls, out-of-the-way canyons and streams, wildflower-covered slopes and thousands of acres of bighorn sheep territory. (Leash your dog if you go sheep-watching.)

The Cucamonga, San Gabriel and Sheep Mountain wilderness areas are all part of Angeles National Forest.

For more information, contact Forest Headquarters, 701 North Santa Anita Avenue, Arcadia, CA 91006; (818) 574-5200.

CLEVELAND NATIONAL FOREST

Cleveland National Forest takes you and your *perro* within five miles of the Mexican border. This 566,000-acre chaparral and conifer land has 331 miles of trails, including a section of the Pacific Crest Trail that runs between the Anza-Borrego Desert and Mexico.

Because of high fire danger, due in part to strong Santa Ana winds, rangers prefer that campers stay at developed sites.

The Agua Tibia, Hauser and Pine Creek, and San Mateo Canyon wilderness areas are within the forest.

For more information, contact Forest Headquarters, 10845 Rancho Bernardo Road, Rancho Bernardo, CA 92127-2107; (619) 674-2901.

ELDORADO NATIONAL FOREST

You and your dog can hike from gentle oak foothills all the way up to the 10,000-foot crest of the Sierra Nevada (although that's recommended only for the most athletic of pooches) on hundreds of miles of trails here.

Alpine meadows, rivers, streams and glacial lakes are among the refreshing landscapes you'll come across in this forest, which encompasses 884,000 acres. More than 320 species of birds, mammals and reptiles make their home in the forest. Beware: The black bears here are known to enjoy goodies like freeze-dried fettucine alfredo and donuts.

The Desolation and Mokelumne wilderness areas are within the forest. Dogs must be leashed in the Carson Pass area of the Mokelumne Wilderness, as well as in all of Desolation Wilderness Area. "A few people cause the problems by being irresponsible about their dogs, and everyone gets hit with stricter rules," a forest spokesperson said. The official map of the forest also states that dogs must be leashed on trails, but a ranger told me as long as the dog is under voice control, off leash is okay.

For more information, contact Forest Headquarters, 100 Forni Road, Placerville, CA 95667; (916) 622-5061.

INYO NATIONAL FOREST

This 1.8 million-acre forest stretches 165 miles from eerie, salty Mono Lake south past Owens Lake. It borders Mount Whitney, the highest peak in the lower 48 states, and is home to hundreds of waterfalls and glacial lakes.

The Ancient Bristlecone Pine Forest is set within Inyo's borders. The thick, twisted trees of this astounding forest are the oldest living things on earth—some date back to 2000 B.C. Guy dogs should treat them with the reverence such trees deserve.

A whopping 1,200 miles of trails meander through the forest. In addition, Inyo comprises the Ansel Adams, Golden Trout, Hoover, John Muir (584,000 acres!) and South Sierra wilderness areas.

For more information, contact Forest Headquarters, 873 North Main Street, Bishop, CA 93514; (619) 873-5841.

KLAMATH NATIONAL FOREST

Tired of traffic, loud neighbors and people snarling at your dog? Come here! (But don't tell anyone else about it.) This lovely 1.7 million-acre forest is one of the least-used of California's national forests.

With 1,160 miles of trails running through wildflower-filled meadows, you and your dog will have no problem finding an escape route from civilization. Ponderosa pines, incense cedars and dozens of other species of trees help make every inhalation a breath of fresh air.

The fast-moving Klamath River is a terrific place for anglers with dogs. Some of the nearby trails also make it a perfect location for a refreshing riverside hike.

Marble Mountain, Red Buttes, Russian, Siskiyou and Trinity Alps wilderness areas are all part of this forest.

For more information, contact Forest Headquarters, 1312 Fairlane Road, Yreka, CA 96097; (916) 842-6131.

LAKE TAHOE BASIN MANAGEMENT UNIT

The bulk of this 205,000-acre unit of national forest is on the southern half of beautiful Lake Tahoe. Because it gets such heavy use, dogs are required to be leashed at all times.

Pooches and their people enjoy the underground viewing area of the stream profile chamber at the Lake Tahoe Visitor Center. Water dogs also like frolicking around Fallen Leaf Lake and Echo Lake, especially when Lake Tahoe is just too crowded. Both offer excellent trailheads into the Desolation Wilderness.

In addition to the Desolation Wilderness Area, the Mount Rose Wilderness Area is part of this forest. As in the rest of this forest, dogs must be leashed.

For more information, contact Forest Headquarters, 870 Emerald Bay Road, Suite 1, South Lake Tahoe, CA 96150; (916) 573-2600.

LASSEN NATIONAL FOREST

Beautiful Lassen National Forest is full of so many fascinating volcanic features that it more than makes up for Lassen Volcanic National Park's ban on dogs in any interesting areas (unless you consider parking lots intriguing).

This 1.4 million-acre forest completely surrounds that restrictive National Park, so you and your pooch have to be very careful about where you tread. But wherever you tread will be breathtaking. Try a 1,300-foot lava tube, or take an educational one-and-a-half-mile hike among volcanic craters and lava domes on the Spattercone Trail. If that's not enough, you can walk along some 300 miles of trails within the forest.

The Caribou, Ishi and Thousand Lakes wilderness areas are located here.

For more information, contact Forest Headquarters, 55 South Sacramento Street, Susanville, CA 96130; (916) 257-2151.

LOS PADRES NATIONAL FOREST

Ranging in elevations from sea level at Big Sur to nearly 9,000 feet at the crest of Mount Pinos, this spectacular forest is one of the most rugged and beautiful in the West.

It's also the second-largest forest in California, with much of its 1.9 million acres encompassing the Big Sur area. Some of the forest's trails crisscross cool streams, where you can set up a tent and sleep deeply as the sound of the rushing water blocks out those oh-so-appealing sounds of your dog chewing and scratching himself.

The Ventana, Santa Lucia, Machesna Mountain, Dick Smith and San Rafael wilderness areas are all part of the forest. Joe loves hiking in the Ventana Wilderness, on easy trails shaded by coast redwood and the spire-like Santa Lucia fir.

For more information, contact Forest Headquarters, 6144 Calle Real, Goleta, CA 93117; (805) 683-6711.

MENDOCINO NATIONAL FOREST

Many Bay Area residents come to this million-acre forest for quick day or weekend trips. This is the only one of California's national forests which is not crossed by a paved road or highway, so if you're looking to escape the world of wheels, you'll find your peace here.

The forest's 615 miles of trails provide dramatic vistas of forested mountains and rugged river canyons. And if you like wildflowers, you'll be in horticultural heaven here. Blue lupine, orange poppies, bush lilac and red bud are among the wildflowers that add brilliance to the meadows during spring and early summer.

If your dog has a penchant for trees, you'll find huge stands of conifers as well as dogwoods (Joe likes these), beech trees and oaks.

There's some disagreement about the off-leash rules here. Some rangers say dogs should be leash-free only in wilderness areas, others say they can be leash-free anywhere but developed camp-grounds. The rules on the official forest map ask that dogs be "on leash in campgrounds, picnic areas and trails." We tell it like we see it, and we see confusion. It's probably best to ask the ranger when you call with other questions.

For more information, contact Forest Headquarters, 420 East Laurel Street, Willows, CA 95998; (916) 934-3316.

MODOC NATIONAL FOREST

If you and your dog feel like getting away from civilization, this 1.9 million-acre forest in the far northeast reaches of the state will whisk you away from the modern world and into an unusually peaceful setting. This is where the wild horses and the antelope play, unfettered by crowds that can make parts of some other national forests seem more like national parks.

The spartan chaparral- and juniper-covered Modoc Plateau and the surrounding evergreen lands are home to more than 300 species of wildlife. Bald eagles are known to inhabit the area, so if you bring your binoculars, you won't regret the extra baggage. (Let your dog carry them in her doggy backpack.)

The forest lies in an area once occupied by the Modoc, Achomawi and Northern Paiute Indian tribes. Petroglyphs and pictographs from these tribes, which may have started inhabiting the area 10,000 years ago, are common in portions of the forest.

About 120 miles of trails wind throughout the forest. The South Warner Wilderness Area is located here.

For more information, contact Forest Headquarters, 441 North Main Street, Alturas, CA 96101; (916) 233-5811.

PLUMAS NATIONAL FOREST

Canine hikers and other outdoors enthusiasts are attracted year-round to this magical forest's streams, lakes, deep canyons and lush mountain valleys. The forest has more than 1,000 miles of sparkling rivers and streams, along with some 100 lakes.

You and your dog can hike, fish, pan for gold, cross-country ski, swim and relax in the serenity of this 1.2 million-acre forest. A terrific adventure for able-bodied creatures is a two-hour hike through the woods to reach the Feather Falls. This 640-foot water-fall is the sixth highest in the nation, and it's well worth the effort to traverse the sometimes steep terrain leading you there.

Bucks Lake Wilderness Area is within Plumas National Forest.

For more information, contact Forest Headquarters, P.O. Box 11500, 159 Lawrence Street, Quincy, CA 95971; (916) 283-2050.

SAN BERNARDINO NATIONAL FOREST

This forest is home to the famed Big Bear Lake and Lake Arrow-head, popular Southern Californian resorts. It comprises 810,000 acres of land that ranges from thick pine woods to rocky, cactus-filled desert.

A favorite activity here is cross-country skiing. Leashless dogs love to lope beside their skiing people in the winter. About 700 miles of trails are open to hikers and skiers.

Because of recent complaints about dogs, they could soon have to be leashed throughout the forest. Check with a ranger before setting out. And dogs are not permitted in much of the the San Jacinto Wilderness, because it runs into Mount San Jacinto State Park (which bans dogs from its trails and backcountry).

The Cucamonga, San Gorgonio, San Jacinto and Santa Rosa wilderness areas are part of the forest.

For more information, contact Forest Headquarters, 1824 Commercenter Circle, San Bernardino, CA 92408; (909) 383-5588.

SEQUOIA NATIONAL FOREST

Giant sequoias, among the world's largest trees, grow in more than 35 magnificent groves on Sequoia National Forest's lower slopes. The famed Boole Tree, at 90 feet in circumference and 269 feet tall, is the largest tree in any national forest. (Talk about boy dog heaven.)

Portions of the Kern River Canyon are closed to dogs, and it may be just as well if you happen to have a dog who thinks he's Mark Spitz: An average of seven people drown each year in a section of the Kern River that runs through this region. But the water that makes the river flow fast also contributes to an abundance of wildflowers and lush mountain meadows.

The park encompasses 1.1 million acres and has 830 miles of trails. It's home to the Domeland, Golden Trout, Jennie Lakes, Monarch and Southern Sierra wilderness areas.

For more information, contact Forest Headquarters, 900 West Grand Avenue, Porterville, CA 93257; (209) 784-1500.

SHASTA-TRINITY NATIONAL FOREST

The magnificent, massive Mount Shasta is the most striking of many visual highlights within this 2.1 million-acre forest. Dogs can explore the less steep parts of this 17-mile-wide, 14,162-foot-high mountain, but the forest has a whopping 1,500 miles of other, more appropriate trails to try.

This is the largest of the California-based national forests. Anglers and their dogs adore the gigantic Shasta and Trinity lakes. Shasta Lake, when full, has 370 miles of shoreline—more than San Francisco Bay. A trip to Trinity Lake is like a trip to the Swiss Alps, with the magnificent Trinity Alps towering in the background.

Dog-owning cross-country skiers, wildlife watchers and hikers love this land. While the area is spectacular year-round, I find it particularly breathtaking in autumn, when the deep oranges and reds of the quaking aspen stand in stark contrast to the snow-capped peak of Mount Shasta.

Castle Crags, Chanchelulla, Mount Shasta, Trinity Alps and Yolla Bolly-Middle Eel wilderness areas are all part of the forest.

For more information, contact Forest Headquarters, 2400 Washington Avenue, Redding, CA 96001; (916) 246-5222.

SIERRA NATIONAL FOREST

Dogs, go ahead and thumb your snouts at Yosemite National Park to the north. Do the same to Sequoia and Kings Canyon national parks to the south. They may not want you, but this forest is almost as spectacular and it welcomes your kind.

The Sierra National Forest encompasses more than 1.3 million acres with elevations between 900 feet and 13,157 feet. There's abundant fish and wildlife here, with oak-covered foothills, heavily forested slopes, more than 400 lakes, and the stark and stunning alpine landscape of the high Sierra. Explore it via 1,100 miles of trails.

The Ansel Adams, Dinkey Lakes, John Muir, Kaiser and Monarch wilderness areas are located here.

For more information, contact Forest Headquarters, 1600 Tollhouse Road, Clovis, CA 93612; (209) 297-0706.

SIX RIVERS NATIONAL FOREST

Six major rivers (surprise!) are among the 1,500 miles of water in the forest. If you have a water dog who promises not to get in over her head if the water's too fast, these rivers beckon. You'll have your choice of exploring the Eel, Klamath, Mad, Smith, Trinity and Van Duzen rivers.

This long, narrow forest encompasses one million acres of Douglas firs, incense cedars, ponderosa pines and dozens of other types of trees. The wildlife viewing is excellent here. From hummingbirds to black bears, the forest has it all. (Just a reminder: Don't let your dog get near a bear. If you don't trust your dog to come as soon as you call her in any situation, keep her leashed.)

North Fork, Siskiyou, Trinity Alps and Yolla Bolly-Middle Eel wilderness areas are part of this forest.

For more information, contact Forest Headquarters, 1330 Bayshore Way, Eureka, CA 95501; (707) 442-1721.

STANISLAUS NATIONAL FOREST

You and your dog can hike on 660 miles of trails that take you over volcanic ridges, through lush alpine meadows, and under tall pines and cedars. This million-acre forest is an enchanting place to take your dog for a day of cross-country skiing. Lake Alpine is a major attraction, but as with all recreation areas within these forests, dogs must be leashed. The official national forest map of Stanislaus requests that dogs be leashed everywhere, but rangers told me the official rule for most of the forest calls for voice control only. The Carson-Iceberg, Emigrant and Mokelumne wilderness areas are located here.

For more information, contact Forest Headquarters, 19777 Greenley Road, Sonora, CA 95370; (209) 532-3671.

TAHOE NATIONAL FOREST

Lake Tahoe, the blue jewel of the Sierra, makes up this forest's southeast boundary. A hike on even a small portion of the forest's 600 miles of trail will take you and your dog through a vast variety of vegetation, including mountain chaparral, mixed conifers, alpine plants, lodgepole pine and pinyon-juniper. Dogs and their people enjoy a good hike along the North Fork of the American River.

While dogs are not welcome at the many downhill ski resorts within the forest, they like to romp beside their cross-country skiing human companions on the many miles of groomed roads and nordic trails. The Granite Chief Wilderness Area is located at the headwaters of the American River. Dogs are prohibited in the northwest portion of this wilderness from May 15 to July 15 because of deer fawning.

For more information, contact Forest Headquarters, Highway 49 & Coyote Street, Nevada City, CA 95959; (916) 265-4531.

TOIYABE NATIONAL FOREST

Although most of this 3.5 million-acre forest is spread through-out Nevada, a portion of it crosses into California. You and your dog can peruse thundering waterfalls, clear streams, glacial lakes and alpine meadows here. You can also *ooh* and *ahh* and woof at a bunch of 10,000-foot peaks in the portion of the Toiyabe near Lake Tahoe.

This is the largest national forest in the Lower 48, but the section in California is relatively small. Still, it includes hundreds of miles of trails, and the Hoover and Carson-Iceberg wilderness areas.

For more information, contact Forest Headquarters, 1200 Franklin Way, Sparks, NV 89431; (702) 355-5301.

INDEX

About the Los Angeles Society for the Prevention of Cruelty to Animals/Southern California Humane Society

The Los Angeles Society for the Prevention of the Cruelty to Animals/Southern California Humane Society (SPCA/SCHS) supports a wide range of humane programs that benefit both animals and the greater Southern California community. Originally incorporated in 1877 as a protection agency for children and animals, the Los Angeles SPCA/SCHS remains the area's largest and most active nonprofit dealing with prevention of cruelty to animals and providing outreach programs to the public.

The comprehensive programs available include:

• **Investigation and Rescue:** The Investigation and Rescue Department pursues animal cruelty cases, performs search warrants, impounds abused animals, arrests perpetrators and files charges with the district attorney's office. They conduct inspections of pet shops and kennels and are often called in by other agencies throughout California to assist in cruelty cases or to patrol events such as rodeos and fairs.

Their other function is to perform emergency animal rescues. Animals can get themselves into the oddest places and the Rescue Team is available to assist them out of trees, from under houses and between walls, and from most places

they shouldn't be. The department also assists other rescue and emergency agencies during a time of crisis or disaster.

• **Humane Education:** The Humane Education Department teaches respect and compassion for all living things to over 12,000 students each year. The program awakens in students an awareness of the interdependency between humans and nature, and an acceptance of responsibility for their companion animals. Presentations at schools, camps, libraries and various youth groups not only give

Pets visit children in schools, day camps and at career days as part of the Los Angeles SPCA/SCHS Human Education Program.

students a deeper understanding of the animals around them, but also assists teachers in fulfilling the humane education mandate of the California Education Code.

• **Pet-Assisted Therapy:** Volunteers and staff of the Los Angeles SPCA/SCHS visit patients and residents in hospitals and convalescent homes with their well-trained pets. The therapeutic value of these visits is well-known, and the volunteers are greatly rewarded by the smiles, and sometimes tears of joy, that greet them and their animals.

• **Adoptions and Shelter Services:** Animals that are lost, homeless, mistreated or injured are medically treated and cared for at the Society's shelters. The staff of animal health technicians, officers, kennel personnel and volunteers give the pets much-needed tender, loving care. Once the animals are healthy and socialized, they are put into one or more of the Adoption Programs. The Mobile Adoption Program takes shelter animals to various locations throughout the Southland where they are adopted and taken to their new homes. Through the Purina Pets For People Program, the Los Angeles SPCA/SCHS puts seniors together with a suitable companion animal. The Society is also involved with several media adoption programs involving television, cable and newspapers.

• **Volunteers and Foster Parents:** Nearly every department within the agency utilizes volunteers to enhance the work they do for animals. Volunteers from all over Southern California work in nine programs, special projects and special events. One area is special to the volunteer program—foster parenting. Volunteers take home litters of under-age kittens and puppies, hand-feed them, and return them to the shelter when they are old enough and healthy enough to be placed in the Adoption Programs. These youngsters would not survive without this special love and care.

The Caring for Animals Network was created in 1991 in response to animal needs after the Los Angeles riots. Since that time, the C.A.N. program has been activated for the Firestorms of 1993 and the Northridge Earthquake of 1994. Thousand of animals were cared for through the C.A.N. program with free medical care, free food and free kenneling. The Los Angeles SPCA/SCHS C.A.N. program is now connected with the American Red Cross, the Salvation Army and F.E.M.A. to provide assistance to wildlife and families with animals during an emergency or disaster.

For more information about the programs and services provided by the Los Angeles SPCA/SCHS, contact the Advancement Division at (213) 730-5323 or write to:

Los Angeles SPCA/SCHS
Advancement Division
5026 West Jefferson Boulevard
Los Angeles, CA 90016